PLATO, the great philosopher of Athens, son of Ariston, was born in 427 B.C. In early manhood admirer of Socrates, he later founded the famous school of philosophy in the grove Academus. Much else recorded of his life is uncertain; that he left Athens for a time after Socrates' execution is probable; that later he went to Cyrene, Egypt, and Sicily is possible; that he was wealthy is likely; that he was critical of 'advanced' democracy is obvious. He lived to be 80 years old. Linguistic tests including those of computer science still try to establish the order of his extant philosophical dialogues, written in splendid prose and revealing Socrates' mind fused with Plato's thought. In *Laches*, *Charmides*, and *Lysis*, Socrates and others discuss separate ethical conceptions. *Protagoras*, *Io*, and *Meno* discuss whether righteousness can be taught. In *Gorgias*, Socrates is estranged from his city's thought, and his fate is impending. The *Apology* (not a dialogue), *Crito*, *Euthyphro*, and the unforgettable *Phaedo* relate the trial and death of Socrates and propound the immortality of the soul. In the famous *Symposium* and *Phaedrus*, written when Socrates was still alive, we find the origin and meaning of love. *Cratylus* discusses

Continued on back flap

THE LOEB CLASSICAL LIBRARY

FOUNDED BY JAMES LOEB, LL.D.

EDITED BY

G. P. GOOLD, PH.D.

PLATO

I

REPUBLIC

II

PLATO

IN TWELVE VOLUMES

VI

THE REPUBLIC

WITH AN ENGLISH TRANSLATION BY

PAUL SHOREY, Ph.D., LL.D., Litt.D.

LATE PROFESSOR OF GREEK, UNIVERSITY OF CHICAGO

IN TWO VOLUMES

II

BOOKS VI—X

CAMBRIDGE, MASSACHUSETTS
HARVARD UNIVERSITY PRESS
LONDON
WILLIAM HEINEMANN LTD
MCMLXXXVII

American
ISBN 0-674-99304-7

British
ISBN 0 434 99276 3

First printed 1935
Reprinted 1942, 1948, 1956, 1963, 1970, 1980, 1987

Printed in Great Britain by
Thomson Litho Ltd, East Kilbride, Scotland

CONTENTS OF VOLUME II

	PAGE
List of Plato's Works	vii
Introduction	ix
The Text	lxxi
The Translation	lxxii
Book VI.	2
Book VII.	118
Book VIII.	234
Book IX.	334
Book X.	418
I. Index of Names	523
II. Index of Subjects	529

LIST OF PLATO'S WORKS

SHOWING THEIR DIVISION INTO VOLUMES
IN THIS EDITION AND THEIR PLACE IN
THE EDITION OF
H. STEPHANUS (VOLS. I.–III., PARIS, 1578).

VOLUME		PAGES	
I.	Euthyphro	I.	2A–16
	Apology	I.	17A–42
	Crito	I.	43A–54E
	Phaedo	I.	57A–118
	Phaedrus	III.	227A–279C
II.	Laches	II.	178A–201C
	Protagoras	I.	309A–362
	Meno	II.	70A–100B
	Euthydemus	I.	271A–307C
III.	Lysis	II.	203A–223B
	Symposium	III.	172A–223D
	Gorgias	I.	447A–527E
IV.	Cratylus	I.	383A–440E
	Parmenides	III.	126A–166C
	Greater Hippias	III.	281A–304E
	Lesser Hippias	I.	363A–376C
V.	Republic I.: Books I.–V.	II.	327A–480
VI.	Republic II.: Books VI.–X.	II.	484A–621D

LIST OF PLATOS WORK'S

VOLUME		PAGES
VII.	Theaetetus	I. 142A–210D
	Sophist	I. 216A–268B
VIII.	The Statesman	II. 357A–311C
	Philebus	II. 11A–67B
	Ion	I. 530A–542B
IX.	Timaeus	III. 17A–92C
	Critias	III. 106A–121C
	Cleitophon	III. 406A–410E
	Menexenus	II. 234A–249E
	Epistles	III. 309A–363C
X.	The Laws I.: Books I.–VI.	II. 624A–785B
XI.	The Laws II.: Books VII.–XII.	II. 788A–969D
XII.	Charmides	II. 153A–176D
	Alcibiades I. and II.	II. 103A–151C
	Hipparchus	II. 225A–232C
	The Lovers	I. 132A–139
	Theages	I. 121A–131
	Minos	II. 313A–321D
	Epinomis	II. 973A–992E

INTRODUCTION

THERE is a sufficient outline of the *Republic* in the introduction to the first volume. Here it remains to consider more argumentatively certain topics of the last five books which were treated summarily there. They may be listed as (1) the theory of ideas and the idea of good, (2) the higher education and Plato's attitude toward science, (3) some further details of Plato's political theories, (4) the logic and psychology of the main ethical argument of the *Republic*, (5) the banishment of poetry, (6) the concluding myth.

Regarded as metaphysics, Plato's theory of ideas is, technically speaking, the deliberate and conscious hypostatization of all concepts—the affirmation that every abstract general notion of the human mind is also somehow, somewhere, in some sense, an objective entity, a real thing, outside of any mind. Some philologians and some sensitive aesthetic critics object to the use of the words concept and hypostatization in this connexion. They have a right to their personal distaste, but it contributes nothing to the interpretation of Plato. Both words convey definite meanings to students of philosophy and there are no words that can replace them. The Socratic dialogues are in fact largely concerned with the definition of concepts, general or abstract ideas,

The Theory of Ideas.

ix

INTRODUCTION

general terms, *Begriffe*, call them what you will, and some convenient synonym for this meaning is indispensable in any rational discussion of Plato's philosophy. The Platonic word *eidos* may have retained some of the associations of physical form, and the modern psychology of the concept may involve in some cases a more developed logic than Plato possessed. The word *eidos* or *idea* in Herodotus, Thucydides, Democritus, the Hippocratic *corpus* and Isocrates [a] may show the meaning *concept* or *Begriff* imperfectly freed from the association of physical form, but that does not justify the inference that it was never so freed in Plato. The terminology of the transcendental idea is indistinguishable from the terminology of the concept and the definition.[b] It is impossible to say at what point the metaphysical doctrine emerges in the minor dialogues, or—on the, I believe, mistaken hypothesis that the later dialogues abandon it—just when the change took place. The logic of the definition in the minor dialogues implies a practically sufficient notion of the nature of a concept,[c] and it is sophistry

---

[a] *Cf.* Shorey, *De Platonis Idearum Doctrina*, Munich, 1884, p. 1, and review of A. E. Taylor's *Varia Socratica*, in *Class. Phil.* vi., 1911, pp. 361 ff.; Ritter, *Neue Untersuchungen*, Munich, 1910, pp. 228-326; Lewis Campbell, *The Theaetetus of Plato*, 2nd ed., Oxford, 1883, pp. 268-269; C. M. Gillespie, "The Use of *Eidos* and *Idea* in Hippocrates," *Class. Quarterly*, vi., 1912, pp. 178-203; Zeller, ii. 1⁴, pp. 658, n. 2 and 661, n. 1; Wilamowitz, *Platon*, ii. pp. 248 ff.; Friedländer, *Platon*, i. pp. 16 ff.

[b] *Cf. What Plato Said*, p. 75.

[c] It is hard to understand the acceptance by several scholars of Stenzel's view that the concept and consequently the idea is a late discovery in the Platonic dialogues, a result in fact of the analyses of the *Sophist*. He must take concept

to try to suppress so plain a fact by capitalizing the word Form and insisting that Plato always or till his latest works visualized the " Forms " as types. He did for some purposes and for others he did not, and he always knew what he was doing. The ideas, as I have often pointed out, are ideals, types, or hypostatized concepts or simply concepts according to the purpose and the context.[a]

Many interpreters of Plato seem to assume that philosophy is, like mathematics or chemistry, a pro-

in some very esoteric significance. For to common sense nothing can be plainer than that the concept is implied in Socrates' attempts to define ethical terms and that it distinctly emerges together with the terminology at least of the idea in the minor dialogues of Plato and especially in the *Euthyphro*. Stenzel's thought seems to be that the concept involves predication and that predication can be fully understood only after the analysis of sentence structure in the Sophist and the discovery of the meaning of " is." But surely the conscious analysis of sentence structure and the function of the copula is one thing and the correct use of predication, of propositions and the conversion of propositions and their combination in virtual syllogisms is another. All the elements of a sound logic are present in Plato's minor dialogues. They are correctly employed in inductive and deductive reasoning, in the quest for definitions and in the testing of them when found. If Stenzel means that the nature of the concept, of the general idea, of abstractions is not definitively understood in the minor dialogues his postulate proves or demands too much. The ultimate nature of the concept is still debated to-day. But for all practical purposes of common sense any one who consistently endeavours to define abstract and general terms and who applies a sound logic to the testing of the definitions proposed, has a sufficient notion of the concept. And anyone who apprehends the concept may go on to hypostatize it either by an instinctive tendency of human nature and speech, or with conscious metaphysics as Plato did.

[a] *Cf. Unity of Plato's Thought*, pp. 27 ff.

gressive science ; that Plato, though a great artist, was a primitive thinker whose methods and opinions have only an historical interest to-day ; and that his doctrine of ideas is the endeavour of an immature mind to deal with a problem which modern psychology or the common sense of any dissertation-writing philologian can settle in a paragraph. These assumptions close the door to any real understanding of Plato's philosophy. The ultimate nature of general ideas, of abstract and conceptual thought in relation both to the human mind and to the universe is as much a matter of debate to-day as it was in the age of the schoolmen. This plain fact of literary history is not affected by the opinion of a certain number of materialists and behaviourists that the matter is quite simple and that there is or ought to be no problem. They may or may not be right. But the discussion continues, as any bibliography of psychology and philosophy will show. The entire literature of the " meaning of meaning " and of " imageless thought " is a renewal of the controversy in other terms.

A great many thinkers are not satisfied with the simple evasion of Aristotle that the human mind is " such " as to be able to experience this, namely the separation in thought of things inseparable in experience. They cannot find any enlightenment in the modern tautology that a general idea is an image of a particular idea plus a feeling of generality. And they are not convinced that the movements of the body, even if we concede that they run exactly parallel to the movements of the mind, really explain them. And if we turn to the other side of the problem we find that many of the leaders of modern

INTRODUCTION

physics and mathematics are unable to conceive and refuse to admit that there is nothing in the objective universe corresponding to the ideas, the concepts, the laws, the principles by which they get their results.

The Platonic theory of ideas is a convenient shorthand, symbolic expression of the opinions that I have thus summarized. If we disregard the rhetoric and physical imagery of the myths by which Plato exalts the importance of the doctrine or makes it the expression of the ideal for ethics, politics and aesthetics, all that it affirms is, first, that conceptual thought is a distinct and differentiated prerogative of man not sufficiently accounted for by the structure of his body and the sensations which he shares with the animals ; and second, that there must be something in the universe, something in the nature of things, that corresponds to our concepts and our ideals—to the principles, for example, of ethics and mathematics. These affirmations of Plato are primitive animism only in the sense in which the same could be said of the beliefs of some of the greatest mathematicians and physicists of to-day or of Matthew Arnold when he talks of a power not ourselves that makes for righteousness. This is not reading modern philosophies into Plato. It is merely giving him credit for knowing and intending what he in fact says. The opposite interpretation underrates his intelligence and really does read into his writings modern ideas, the notions, namely, of modern anthropologists as to how savages think. Gomperz' comparison of the doctrine of ideas to Iroquois animism (iii. 323 ; cf. iii. 1-2), Ogden and Richards' designation of the ideas as "name-souls" (*The Meaning of Meaning*, p. 45), Jowett's illustration of what he deems hair-splitting refinements in Plato by the " distinction so plentiful in savage languages," Cornford's fancy (*From Religion to Philosophy*, p. 254) that " the idea is a group-soul related to its group as a mystery-demon like Dionysus is related to the group of worshippers, his *thiasos*," and all similar utterances are uncritical, whatever airs of science or pseudo-science they assume. The relevant illustrations of Plato's doctrine of ideas are to be sought in the most subtle debates of the schoolmen, or in modern psychological and epistemological literature about the meaning of meaning.[a]

There were, of course, some other more special considerations that determined Plato's deliberate and defiant hypostatization of all concepts. It accepted a natural tendency of the human, and not merely of the primitive, mind, and rendered it harmless by applying it consistently to everything. If all concepts are hypostatized, the result for practical logic and for everything except metaphysics and ultimate epistemological psychology is to leave concepts where they were, as indispensable instruments of human thinking. The hypostatization of abstractions operated practically as a short answer to the sophisms of crude nominalists who obstructed ordinary reasoning by raising ultimate objections to the validity of all abstractions or general terms. This motive is distinctly apparent in Plato's writings and there is a strong presumption that he was conscious of it.

However that may be, Plato did in fact, partly as a matter of imaginative style, partly as a matter of

[a] See Shorey in *Proceedings of the Sixth International Congress of Philosophy*, pp. 579-583.

metaphysics, speak of concepts as if they were real objects. He did, as his writings conclusively show, hypostatize all concepts, and all attempts to show that he hypostatized only a few of the sublimer or more dignified concepts are *a priori* improbable because they deprive the doctrine of all rational meaning and consistency,[a] and they are also refuted by the incontrovertible evidence of the dialogues themselves. Plato affirms this monstrous paradox, not because he is a naïve thinker unacquainted with the elementary psychology of abstraction and generalization,[b] but because, as we have said, he regards it as the most convenient expression of his rejection of all materialistic and relativistic philosophies[c] and of all crude nominalism.[d] He recognized that the doctrine is a paradox hard to accept but also hard to reject.[e] But he deliberately affirmed it as the most convenient alternative to inacceptable or unworkable philosophies.[f] He perhaps, as we have already suggested, justified this procedure to himself, and we may certainly justify it for him, by the reflection that the theory is no more of a paradox than that involved in every theology and ultimately in all science and philosophy except the crudest dogmatic materialism. And we may find further confirmation of this opinion in the fact that both the metaphysics and the transcendental physics of the past two decades discover

[a] *Cf.* Aristot. *Met.* 1043 b 21 and 991 b 6 ; Ross, i. pp. 192 and 199; and *What Plato Said*, p. 584.

[b] *Cf. Charmides* 158 E, *Phaedo* 96 B, *What Plato Said*, p. 533, *Unity of Plato's Thought*, pp. 47-48.

[c] *Cf. Cratyl.* 440 B-C.

[d] *Cf. What Plato Said*, p. 574.

[e] *Cf. What Plato Said*, p. 586, on *Parmen.* 135 c.

[f] *Cf. What Plato Said*, pp. 39, 268, 574.

more helpful analogies in the Platonic theory of ideas and in Plato's applications of it to the philosophy of nature than they do in any other philosophy of the past.

In disregard of these considerations many critics in every age, and notably Natorp and Stewart in ours, have tried to free Plato from the stigma of paradox or naïveté by trying to show that this uncompromising realism (in the proper medieval sense of the word) is not to be taken seriously, and that it was only a poetic and emphatic form of conceptualism. This, as we have seen, is at the best a half truth. All Platonic ideas are also concepts, but we cannot infer that they were only concepts.[a] For many purposes of logic, ethics and politics Plato practically treats them as concepts. Why not ? No reasonable writer obtrudes his ultimate metaphysics into everything. And Plato is always particularly careful to distinguish metaphysical hypotheses and their imaginative embodiments in myth and allegory from the simple truths of a working logic and a practical ethics which are all that he dogmatically affirms.[b] But he always affirms the metaphysical idea when challenged. To this extent Natorp and those who agree with him are right. But they pay too high a price for their rightness on this point when they insist on deducing all Plato's opinions from his ontology, and obtrude the metaphysical idea into passages where the doctrine at the most lends rhetorical and poetical colouring to the practical affirmation of the necessity of concepts and the value of ideals.

[a] See *Unity of Plato's Thought*, p. 30, *What Plato Said*, p. 585, on *Parmen.* 132 B.

[b] *Cf. Meno* 81 D-E and *What Plato Said*, p. 515, on *Meno* 86 B.

INTRODUCTION

An example will perhaps make these distinctions more plain. Plato in the *Republic* (501) says that his philosophic statesman will contemplate the divine pattern of justice as an artist looks away to his model, and that like the artist he will frequently glance from the copy that he is producing to the model and back again to the copy.[a] This may reasonably be understood as only a heightened way of saying that the true statesman must be guided by definite conceptions and strive for the realization of clearly apprehended ideals. The fact that Plato, the metaphysician, believed the transcendental reality of the idea to be a necessary assumption of ultimate epistemology adds nothing to the practical meaning of this passage. When in the *Phaedrus*, however (247 D, 249 B-C), Plato says that every human soul has beheld the idea of justice in pre-natal vision, since otherwise it would not have the power to reduce the confused multiplicity of sensation to the unities of conceptual thought, he is clothing in mythical garb an epistemological argument for the reality of the transcendental idea, and he is not, as in the *Republic* passage, thinking mainly of the explicit affirmation that the true statesman must have submitted to a higher education in conceptual thinking and have thus framed in his mind ideals to guide his practice. The historian of philosophy who, without calling attention to this distinction, merely cites the two passages together in a footnote, only confuses the uncritical reader.

But again in the *Parmenides* (135 A-C), the *Sophist* (246-247), the *Cratylus* (439 D f.; cf. *What Plato Said*, pp. 266-267), the *Politicus* (283-284, *What Plato Said*, p. 309), the *Timaeus* (51-52 and *What Plato Said*, p.

[a] Cf. *What Plato Said*, p. 458, on *Euthyphro* 6 E.

INTRODUCTION

613 on 28 A-B), there are passages in which, without mythical dress, and with no specific reference to the practical value of concepts and ideals, Plato postulates the transcendental ideas as an epistemological necessity, and the only escape from materialism and the flux of relativity. No legerdemain of interpretation or speculations about the chronology of the evolution of Plato's thought can explain away these passages, and the interpreter who realizes that some virtual equivalent of the Platonic idea is still to-day the alternative to thorough-going and unequivocal materialism will not desire to explain them away.

All that is needed in order to understand Plato and to do justice to him as a rational philosopher is to remember again[a] that, though the doctrine of ideas is always in the background of his mind and would always be reaffirmed on a challenge, he is not always thinking explicitly of it when he is speaking of logic, ethics, or politics, and we need not think of it in order to enjoy his art or apprehend his meaning. The transcendental idea, for example, is not needed in the *Republic* except for the characterization of the philosophic mind and the higher education of the Platonic rulers.[b] It is not indispensable even there. The concept will serve. The philosopher is he who can think and reason consecutively in abstractions.[c]

[a] See *supra*, p. xvi.

[b] *Cf.* Vol. I. pp. xl-xli, and *What Plato Said*, pp. 226-227. It is also used in an intentionally crude form to confirm the banishment of the poets. The poet does not deal in essential truth, he copies the copy of the reality. *Cf. infra*, p. lxii, on 596 A ff. and *What Plato Said*, p. 249. Stenzel's justification of this (*Platon der Erzieher*, p. 175) by the consideration that good joiners' work involves mathematics seems fanciful and is certainly not in Plato's text.

[c] *Supra*, Vol. I. pp. 516 ff.

INTRODUCTION

The curriculum of the higher education is designed to develop this faculty in those naturally fitted to receive it.[a] The thought and the practical conclusions will not be affected if we treat the accompanying symbolic rhetoric as surplusage. Such statements as that the philosopher is concerned with pure being,[b] dwells in a world of light,[c] is devoted to the most blessed part of reality,[d] satisfies and fills the continent part of his soul,[e] undoubtedly suggest the metaphysical background of Plato's thought and the emotional and imaginative connotations of his ideas. But in the context of the *Republic* they are little more than an expression of the intensity of Plato's feeling about his political and educational ideas.

It is obvious that the concept or idea is in many eloquent Platonic passages an ideal, a type, a pattern, to which aesthetic, moral and social experience may approximate but which they never perfectly realize, just as mathematical conceptions are ideals never actually met with in the world of sense.[f] It is possible, though not probable, that in some of the minor dialogues we get glimpses of a stage of Plato's youthful thought in which, though he already uses, in speaking of the concept or the definition, much of the terminology associated with the doctrine of ideas,

[a] Cf. *supra*, Vol. I. pp. 516-517, 520-521, *What Plato Said*, pp. 233-234.

[b] 477 A ff., 479 E, 484 B, 486 A, 500 B.

[c] 517 B, 518 A, 518 C, 520 D.   [d] 526 E.

[e] *Rep.* 586 B, *Gorg.* 493 B.

[f] *Phaedo* 74 A. For the threefold aspect of the Platonic ideas in metaphysics, logic and aesthetics see my *Unity of Plato's Thought*, p. 27, and T. E. Jessup, "The Metaphysics of Plato," *Journ. of Philos. Studies* (1930), pp. 41-42. See *supra*, Vol. I. pp. 504-505.

he has not yet consciously and systematically hypostatized the concept.[a] These and similar qualifications and speculative possibilities do not in the least alter the fact that throughout the main body of his work Plato is ready to affirm the metaphysical theory of the hypostatized idea whenever the issue is raised,[b] and there is not an iota of evidence in his own writings that he ever abandoned or altered the doctrine, however much he varied the metaphors and the terms in which he expressed it. It is quite certain that he did not, except in obviously mythical or poetical passages, say more of the ideas than that they exist and that they are in some sense real.[c] He did not say that they are the thoughts of God.[d] There is no indication in his writings that he said that they are numbers.[e]

[a] See *Unity of Plato's Thought*, p. 31, *What Plato Said*, p. 458.

[b] *Cf. supra*, pp. xvi and xviii.

[c] *Cf. Unity of Plato's Thought*, p. 28 and p. 29, n. 188.

[d] This Neoplatonic doctrine—based on a misinterpretation of such passages as *Rep.* 597 B f.—was adopted by many Christian fathers and mediaeval scholars. *Cf.* Alcinous in Hermann, *Plato*, vi. p. 163 ; Baumgartner, *Philos. des Alanus de Insulis*, p. 54 ; Zeller ii. 1⁴, p. 664, n. 5 ; Taylor, *Mediaeval Mind*, ii. pp. 485-486 ; Webb, *Studies in the Hist. of Nat. Theol.* p. 241 ; Harris, *Duns Scotus*, ii. p. 195 ; C. G. Field, *The Origin and Development of Plato's Theory of Ideas*, pp. 21-22 ; Otto Kluge, *Darstellung u. Beurteilung der Einwendungen des Aristot. gegen die Plat. Ideenlehre*, p. 24.

[e] It is very difficult to argue with those who attribute this doctrine of ideas and numbers to Plato. Sometimes they seem to affirm it only on the authority of Aristotle, which they admit is in most cases hopelessly confused with his statements about Speusippus and Xenocrates and other members of the Academy. Sometimes they seem to admit that the doctrine is not to be found in Plato's extant writings. Sometimes they hint rather than say that certain passages of the *Philebus*

INTRODUCTION

And he never admitted that they are only thoughts in the human mind,[a] though for practical purposes, as we have said, they may usually be treated as such when no metaphysical issue is involved.

It ought not to be necessary to debate these questions further. The only question open to debate is the extent of Plato's consciousness of what some critics think the modern meanings that I have read into him. The question of course is not whether he

and the *Timaeus* suggest that Plato's mind was working in this direction, though they are usually too cautious now to affirm anything positive about *Philebus* 15-16 D, or *Timaeus* 53 B. I have more than once shown that there is no difficulty in treating numerical ideas precisely like other ideas in their relation to concretes. The number five is to five apples as redness is to red apples. It is present with them. I have repeatedly collected and interpreted the Platonic passages that probably misled uncritical students of the Academy (*cf. What Plato Said*, p. 605, and *infra* on 525 D, 526 A). And the distinction that there is only one idea while there are many numbers of the same kind is quite pointless. There is one idea of redness that is metaphysically or teleologically really present entire in many red things and there is one idea of five or fiveness which is similarly present in many groups of five. There is no more difficulty about the fives that are present as factors in ten, fifteen, twenty, and twenty-five than there is about any other ideas that may mingle with or enter into the definition of another idea. The whole theory is a piece of scholastic hair-splitting to which a sound interpretation of what Plato says lends no support. And there is no space and no need to transcribe here the exhaustive collections of Robin (*La Théorie platonicienne des Idées et des Nombres d'après Aristote*) or Ross's repeated summaries of them in his commentary on Aristotle's *Metaphysics*.

If Plato's mind was really working towards such conclusions, why is there no hint of them in his huge work of the *Laws*, or—if we grant them genuine for the sake of the argument—in the *Epistles*?

[a] *Cf. Parmen.* 132 B-C, and *What Plato Said*, p. 585, and *ibid.* p. 594 on *Soph.* 250 B, *Unity of Plato's Thought*, p. 30.

could feel all the associations and connotations of the modern words in which we have to express his meaning, but whether his meaning is on the whole substantially that which I have attributed to him.

The obvious conclusion is that we can infer nothing as to the composition or date of the *Republic* from the fact that the ideas are not mentioned where there is no reason for mentioning them, and that all hypotheses that different stages of the evolution of Plato's thought are indicated by the various aspects in which the ideas are presented when they are mentioned are uncritical.[a] There is no occasion for the metaphysical doctrine of ideas in the first four books. But the general concept, the type, the ideal are referred to in language which could be understood of the ideas. The fact that it does not necessarily have to be so understood is no proof that the doctrine was not present to Plato's mind at the time.

In the fifth, sixth, and seventh books the theory is explicitly enunciated,[b] illustrated by imagery and applied to education. There is even a much disputed but certain anticipation of the later doctrine that while the idea is a unity its relation to things and to other ideas seems to break it up into a plurality.[c]

The uncompromising statement of the subject in the tenth book is sometimes taken to represent an earlier and more naïve form of the doctrine. But the style of the passage is evidently that of a defiant affirmation of the whole length of the paradox, or rather perhaps of an expert explaining the matter to

[a] *Cf. What Plato Said*, p. 560, *Unity of Plato's Thought*, p. 35 and n. 238.
[b] 476 A f. *Cf.* Vol. I. pp. 516-517, 505 A ff., 517 B ff.
[c] *Cf.* 476 A, *Unity of Plato's Thought*, p. 34.

INTRODUCTION

laymen.[a] The fact that the argument of the third
man is distinctly mentioned in the same connexion is
in itself evidence that the passage does not represent
an earlier and more primitive stage of Plato's thought.
For the third man is mentioned in the *Parmenides*.[b]
But there would not be much profit in further discussion of hypotheses that have no basis in the text of
Plato or in the philosophical probabilities of the case.

All that has been said of the ideas in general applies
to the idea of good. It is the hypostatization of the
concept "good." Its significance in the Platonic
system is that of its importance in human thought.
In ethics it is what modern ethical philosophy calls
the sanction. In politics it is the ideal, whatever it
may be, of social welfare. In theology and the philosophy of nature it is the teleological principle, the
design that implies a designing mind in the universe.
The first of these meanings is predominant in the
minor dialogues where all problems and all attempted
definitions point to an unknown good so consistently
and systematically that Plato must have been aware
of the reference.[c] The second meaning is most
prominent in the *Republic*, but there is explicit reference to the first and to the discussions of the minor
dialogues. In any case, ethical and social good are
not sharply separable in Plato.

The idea of good is nowhere defined, but its supreme
importance and all of its meanings are symbolized in
the images of the sun and the cave. Its main mean-

The Idea of Good.

---

[a] Cf. 597 A ὡς γ' ἂν δόξειε τοῖς περὶ τοὺς τοιούσδε λόγους
διατρίβουσιν.

[b] 132 E-133 A. Cf. *infra* on 597 c.

[c] See *What Plato Said*, pp. 71-73, with marginal references
there.

INTRODUCTION

ing for the *Republic* is the ideal of social welfare on which the statesman, as opposed to the opportunist politician, must fix his eye, and which he can apprehend only by a long course of higher education which will enable him to grasp it. Plato rightly feels that no other definition is possible or desirable unless the entire polity of the *Republic* was to be taken as its definition. The *Timaeus* is the poetical embodiment of the third meaning, though single phrases of the *Republic* glance at it.[a] If there is a beneficent creator, his purpose, his idea of good, is the chief cause of the existence of the world and the best key to the understanding of it.

I am not attributing these three meanings of the good to Plato by an imposed symmetry of my own. It is what Plato himself says and the chief problem of my interpretation is not to understand Plato but to account for the failure to recognize his plain meaning.

In view of my repeated expositions of Plato's doctrine of the idea of good there would be little point in attempting here once more to set it forth in a smooth, consecutive, literary statement.[b] It will be more to my purpose to enumerate in the briefest, baldest, most explicit fashion some of my reasons for feeling that I have been misunderstood, and that the definite issues raised by my arguments have never

[a] *Cf. infra*, pp. xxv and 102.
[b] See my paper, " The Idea of Good in Plato's Republic," *University of Chicago Studies in Classical Philology*, vol. i. (1895), pp. 188-239 ; my article, " Summum Bonum," in *Hastings' Encycl. of Relig. and Ethics*, vol. xii. pp. 44-48 ; my review of Jowett and Campbell's *Republic*, *The Nation*, 61, 1895, pp. 83-84 ; *Unity of Plato's Thought*, p. 17 and n. 94 ; *What Plato Said*, pp. 71-72, 230 ff., 534 on *Phaedo* 99 A.

been met. I have never intended to deny that Plato's language about the idea of good is in large part the language of poetry and religion, that he intends to suggest by it the ineffable and infinite unknowable beyond our ken, and that his eloquence has been a source of inspiration to many readers who care little for his dialectics and for the critical interpretation of his specific thought. What I have been trying to say is that the mere repetition of Plato's rhetoric or the attempt to better it in our own paraphrases will not contribute much to the interpretation of the precise meaning of the passages of the *Republic* in question, assuming that in addition to their inspirational value they are intended to convey some definite meaning and are not merely ejaculations thrown out at an infinite object.

In the first place, then, since all Platonic ideas are hypostatized concepts the hypostatization of the idea of good is presumably irrelevant to its main significance for the ethical and political thought of the *Republic*. It does, of course, suggest the metaphysical background of Plato's thought; there are a few sentences in which it involves the goodness which teleologists discover in the structure of the universe and in the designs of its creator, the theme of the *Timaeus*; [a] and since goodness is the chief attribute of God in religious literature from the New Testament to Whittier's hymn, there is a certain plausibility in identifying it with God himself. But the text of Plato, and especially the text of the *Republic*, does not justify any of these extensions of the idea if taken absolutely. The idea of good is undoubtedly the most important of ideas, but it is

[a] *Cf.* on 508 B and 509 B; Zeller ii. 1⁴, pp. 687-688.

not true that it is the most comprehensive in the
sense that all other ideas are deduced from it,[a] as in
some Platonizing pantheistic philosophies they are
deduced from the idea of Being. There is no hint
of such deduction in Plato's writings. It is only
teleological ideas in ethics, politics and cosmogony
that are referred to the idea of good as the common
generalization or idea that includes them all. Even
the ideas are not in Plato's own reasoning deduced
from the idea of good. It is merely said that a
scientific moralist, a true statesman, will be able so
to deduce them, and that the higher education is
designed to give him this ability. In *Republic* 534
B-C, the dialectician is he who is able ἑκάστου . . .
λόγον . . . διδόναι and the idea of good is a special
example of the ἕκαστον. It is not said that the man
who does not know the idea of good does not know
any other idea, but that he does not know ἄλλο
ἀγαθὸν οὐδέν.

It is not even true that Plato's philosophic ethics
is deduced from the idea of good. He only says that
the ethics of the guardians will be so deduced. So
far as Plato himself expounds a scientific ethics it rests
on the preferability of the intellectual life and the
comparative worthlessness of the pleasures of sense.[b]
The idea of good in the dialogues is a regulative not
a substantive concept.

Whatever its religious suggestions it cannot in
any metaphysical or literal sense be identified with
the Deity.[c] The idea of God was taken by Plato

[a] *Cf.* my review of Paul Hinneberg, *Die Kultur der
Gegenwart, Class. Phil.* vi. p. 108.
[b] *Cf. Unity of Plato's Thought*, p. 24, and *infra*, pp. lvi f.
[c] *Cf.* my *Idea of Good*, pp. 188-189, *Unity of Plato's
Thought*, n. 94, *What Plato Said*, p. 231.

INTRODUCTION

from the religion of the Greek people and purified by criticism. The idea of good came to him on an altogether different line of thought. It is the outcome of those Socratic quests for definitions of ethical virtues and social ends which always break down because the interlocutors are never able to discover the sanction which makes the proposed virtue or end a good and desirable thing.[a]

When these misapprehensions are cleared away I trust that I shall not any longer be misunderstood if I say that the chief and essential meaning of the idea of good in the *Republic* is " precisely " that conception of an ultimate sanction for ethics and politics which the minor dialogues sought in vain. Plato does not profess to have discovered it in the *Republic* except so far as it is implied in the entire ethical, social and political ideals of his reformed state. He intentionally and wisely refuses to define it in a formula.[b] He merely affirms that it is something which can be apprehended only by those who have received the training and the discipline of his higher education.

[a] For the idea of good and God *cf.* also V. Brochard, " Les Mythes dans la philos. de Platon," *L'Année Philos.*, 1900, p. 11 ; Pierre Bovet, *Le Dieu de Platon*, Paris, 1902, p. 177 ; Raeder, *Platos philosophische Entwicklung*, pp. 237, 381 f. ; Zeller, *Phil. d. Gr.* ii. 1⁴, p. 718, n. 1, pp. 667, 694, 707 ff. ; *Aristotle and the Earlier Peripatetics* (Eng. tr.), ii. p. 327 ; Gomperz, *Greek Thinkers*, iii. pp. 85 and 211 ; Inge, *The Philosophy of Plotinus*, ii. p. 126 ; Gustave Schneider, *Die plat. Metaphysik*, p. 109 ; Taylor, *Plato*, pp. 85-89 ; Adam, *The Vitality of Platonism*, pp. 22 and 132 ; *The Religious Teachers of Greece*, pp. 442 f., with my review in *Philos. Rev.* vol. 18, pp. 62-63; Apelt, *Beiträge zur Geschichte der griechischen Philos.*, Vorrede, p. vi. ; H. Tietzel, *Die Idee des Guten in Platons Staat und der Gottesbegriff*, Progr. Wetzlar, 1894.

[b] *Cf. infra* on 506 E, p. 95, note *f*.

INTRODUCTION

The consummation of this education is characterized briefly and soberly as a vision, just as in the *Symposium* the long ascent of the scale of beauty culminates in a vision which alone makes life worth living.[a] This language expresses the intensity of Plato's feeling about the intellectual life and his own ethical and social ideals, but it does not make him a visionary or a mystic in the ordinary sense of the words.

If the interpretation here outlined is in itself a rational sequence of thought and makes sense of what Plato says, it surely creates a presumption which cannot be rebutted by evading issues and charging me with insensibility to Plato's deeper religious and mystic meanings. It can be refuted only by giving specific answers to specific arguments and testing them by the texts. The interpretation of the images, symbols, allegories (the synonym does not matter) of the sun, the divided line and the cave, provides the chief test, as the too literal acceptance of them is perhaps the main cause of misunderstanding.

The aptness of the sun as a symbol of Plato's idea of good might be illustrated by many quotations from modern poetry and from the literature of sun-worship.[b] It would be interesting to compare what Plato says of the sun as the primal source of light, heat, life, growth, all things, with the language of modern science. Herbert Spencer, for example, innocently says (*First Principles of a New System of Philos.*, 1865, Amer. ed. p. 454) : " Until I recently

---

[a] *Rep.* 516 B, 517 B-C, *Symp.* 210 B ff.   *Cf. Rep.* 500 B-C.
[b] *Cf. infra*, pp. 100-101, on 508 A.

INTRODUCTION

consulted his *Outlines of Astronomy* on another question I was not aware that so far back as 1833 Sir John Herschel had enunciated the doctrine that ' the sun's rays are the ultimate source of almost every motion which takes place on the surface of the earth.' " Another line of illustration would lead through the Latin poet Manilius and Plotinus to Goethe's " Wär' nicht das Auge sonnenhaft." [a] This thought might be extended to include modern debates on the nice preadjustment of the eye to its function of vision. Does it, or does it not, imply a creator and a design? Lastly, Plato's statement that, as the sun is the source of light, but is not itself light (508 B), so the idea of good is not knowledge or being but the cause of both and something that is beyond and transcends being—this superhuman hyperbole (509 B-C) is the source of all so-called negative theologies and transcendental metaphysics from Philo and Plotinus to the present day.

But our present concern is not with these things but with the direct evidence that the idea of good is essentially for the interpretation of the *Republic* what modern ethical theory calls the sanction. One sentence I admit seems to identify the idea of good with God. The sun, it is said, is that which the Good created in the visible world to be its symbol and analogue. This would seem to identify the idea of good with the Demiurgos of the *Timaeus*, who is both the supreme God and a personification of the idea of good or the principle of teleology in nature. But we have already seen that it is uncritical to press Plato's language about God, a word which he accepts from traditional religion and employs as

[a] *Cf. infra*, p. 101, note *c*, on 508 B.

freely for edification and the rejection of militant
atheism as Matthew Arnold does. Moreover, there
are other sentences in this part of the *Republic* which,
if pressed, are irreconcilable with the identification
of the idea of good with God. In any case, apart from
one or two sentences of vague and disputable meaning,
the acceptance of the idea of good as the sanction more
nearly lends an intelligible and reasonable meaning
to everything that Plato says than does any other
interpretation. On this view, then, I repeat, the
idea of good is simply the hypostatization of what
the idea of good means for common sense in modern
usage. It is the good purpose in some mind able
to execute its purposes. It is what such a mind
conceives to be the supreme end to which all other
ends are subordinated and referred.

The divided line and the cave are also images and
symbols employed to bring out certain other aspects
of the theory of ideas and of the idea of good in
particular. The main object common to both is to
put the thought " Alles vergängliche ist nur ein
Gleichnis " into a proportion. The four terms of such
a proportion may be secured either by invention or by
forcing special meanings on some of the terms. In
the case of the cave, the cave itself, the fettered
prisoners, the fire and the apparatus by which the
shadows of graven images are cast on the wall of the
cave are clearly inventions. There is a real analogy
between the release of the prisoners with their ascent
to the light of day (515 c ff.) and the Socratic *elenchus*
which releases the mind and draws it up from a world
of sense to the world of thought (517 B-C). But it is
obvious that all the details of the imagery cannot be
pressed and that we need not ask too curiously to

what in Plato's serious thought every touch that fills
out the picture corresponds.

On my interpretation critics have likewise erred by
refusing to admit a similar qualification of their too
literal acceptance of the image of the divided line.
The proportion : ideas are to things as things are to
their reflections in mirrors or in water, has only three
terms. The fourth term is found in mathematical
ideas, which in their use in education and in respect
of the method by which the mind deals with them are
in some sort intermediate between ideas and things.
We thus get our proportion. But in the description
of it Plato is careful to distinguish the mathematical
ideas only by the method of their treatment in science,
not in dialectics, and not as entities of another kind.
This raises the presumption that Plato, as usual,
knows what he is doing and does not intend to distinguish objectively mathematical ideas *as ideas* from
other ideas. I support this presumption by pointing
out that in the later and final interpretation of
the line Plato names the objective correlates of the
mental processes corresponding to three divisions
of the line but omits the fourth on the pretext that
it would take too long. (*Cf.* on 534 A.) He names
the mathematical attitude of mind or method but
does not name its objects as something distinct from
ideas or a distinct kind of ideas. I go on to show that
there is no evidence in the Platonic writings for the
doctrine that mathematical ideas differ in themselves
from other concepts, and that the testimony of Aristotle is too confused to prove anything.[a] These
assumptions raise a definite issue which can only be
met by equally definite arguments. Instead of that

[a] *Cf. supra*, pp. xx-xxi, *Unity of Plato's Thought*, pp. 82 f.

critics rebuke me for attributing insincerity to Plato,
or at the best they ask, How could Aristotle be mistaken ?

Plato himself regards all literature except dialectics as a form of play and much that passes for
dialectics as conscious or unconscious jesting. Whenever he himself employs imagery, symbolism and
myth or an eristic dialectic he is careful to warn us
that it is not to be taken too literally or seriously,[a]
and he usually points out just how much of his
apparent conclusions it is necessary to accept for the
carrying on of the argument. Now the particular
synonyms I employ to describe this characteristic
trait of Plato's method and style are obviously irrelevant to my main argument. Yet if in view of
the frequency of the idea and word παίζειν in Plato
I express the thought that the intermediate place of
mathematical ideas in the proportion of the divided
line is not to be taken literally and add that the
ambiguous coinage εἰκασία, or conjecture, is a term
of disparagement playfully thrown in to secure symmetry of subdivision in the two worlds and to suggest
a depth below the lowest depth,[b] I am sternly told
that " It is surely a strange reading of the character
of Plato as a seeker after truth to maintain that in
the very heart of his greatest work and at the very
core of the problem of knowledge he should disturb
and confuse those who are seeking to understand his
doctrine with a little wholly uncalled-for ' playful-
ness,' even though it should be for the sake of
' symmetry.' "[c] Now I am quite willing to sub-

[a] Cf. infra on 539 c, p. 227, note d.
[b] Idea of Good, p. 229.
[c] H. J. Paton, Plato's Theory of EIKASIA, Aristotelian
Society, 1922, p. 69.

stitute some other expression for " playfully thrown in." But my precise expression, I repeat, is not the point. Plato in fact does here, as elsewhere, resort to artificial constructions and inventions in order to express the relation between the ideas and what we call realities by proportion. The εἰκόνες and εἰκασία are in fact introduced here to complete the symmetry of such a proportion and to suggest ironical disparagement of the inferior type of thought. They contribute nothing further to the solution of the " problem of knowledge." To recognize this plain fact is not to impugn the character of Plato, and to rebuke my frivolity with solemn eloquence is no answer to my argument. Plato himself never thinks it incompatible with a serious search for truth to mingle jest with earnest and seriousness with irony.

Similarly of the ἀνυπόθετον (510 B). It obviously suggests to modern interpreters the metaphysical first principle, the Unconditioned, the absolute ground, the *noumenon*, call it what you will. Plato himself may have been willing to let the word convey such overtones, and those who are not interested in his precise meanings may stop there and cry with Rousseau, " O Mighty Being ! " But it is also equally obvious that the ἀνυπόθετον has a definite and less purely emotional meaning in its context. It expresses Plato's distinction between the man of science, who starts from assumptions that he does not allow to be questioned (510 C-D), and the philosopher or Platonic dialectician, who is able and willing to carry the discussion back, not necessarily always to a metaphysical first principle, but at least to a proposition on which both parties to the argument agree and which therefore is not arbitrarily assumed as an hypothesis by the questioner. This meaning could be illustrated by the *Crito*, in which it is said that all discussion is vain without such a starting-point of agreement.[a] It is the essential meaning of the passage in the *Phaedo* (101 D-E), where ἱκανόν, the adequate, the sufficient, is for all practical purposes a virtual synonym of the ἀνυπόθετον, though it does not suggest the possible metaphysical connotations of the word.

Now this distinction between dialectics or philosophy and the sciences is repeatedly borrowed by Aristotle[b] and even retains much of its validity under the changed conditions of modern thought. There will always be these two ways of thinking and these two types of mind. The passage, then, makes good sense so interpreted and lends a rational meaning to the ἀνυπόθετον without denying the mystic overtones which are all that seem to interest some interpreters of Plato.

To return to the political and social idea of good. Plato's conception of ultimate good in this sense must be gathered from his writings as a whole. Neither in the *Republic* nor elsewhere does he commit himself to a defining formula of social welfare. It is enough for his purpose to emphasize the distinction between the statesman and the politician and describe the education and the way of life that will produce the statesman and develop in him the ideals and the unity of purpose that distinguish him. But it would not be difficult to gather Plato's general conception of political and social good from the *Republic* and the *Laws* and certain passages of the *Gorgias* and *Politicus*. The true statesman's chief aim will be not

[a] *Crito* 49 D, *infra*, p. 175, note *c*, on 527 E.
[b] *Cf. infra*, p. 111.

wealth and power and amusements, but the virtue of the citizens.[a] A sober disciplined life is preferable to the unlimited license and expansiveness of an imperialistic and decadent democracy. The statesman's chief instruments for realizing his ideals will be the control of education and what to-day is called eugenics.[b]

Is this plain common sense, then, all that is meant by Plato's idealistic eloquence and the imagery of the sun, the divided line and the cave ? I never meant to say that it is all, but it is the central core of meaning without which Plato's transcendentalism is only a rhapsody of words. If nature is more than mechanism, if there is a God, as Plato himself believes and believes indispensable to morality and social order, his purposes, his idea of good, or, metaphysically or mythologically speaking, the idea of good which he contemplates as a pattern,[c] becomes the first and chief cause of the ordered world, and such understanding of his purposes as is possible for us is a better explanation of things than the material instruments that serve his ends.[d] This is the type of explanation that the Socrates of the *Phaedo* desires but cannot discover and that the *Timaeus* ventures to present only in mythical and poetical form.[e] It has little place in the *Republic*, though we may suppose it to be in the background of Plato's mind and to be suggested by his allegories. The idea of good in

---

[a] *Gorg.* 513 E, 517 B-C, 504 D-E, *Laws* 705 D-E, 693 B-C, 770 D, 962 D, 963 A.
[b] *Polit.* 309-310, *Unity of Plato's Thought*, p. 62, n. 481 ; *Laws* and *Rep. passim.*
[c] *Cf. What Plato Said*, p. 613 on *Tim.* 28 A-B.
[d] *Cf. What Plato Said*, pp. 329, 346-347.
[e] *Cf.* my *Idea of Good*, p. 232.

this sense, like the heat and light of the sun, is both the cause of the things we think " real " and the condition of our apprehension and understanding of them. It is not the substance of things; it is not their " being," but something apart from and transcending " being " in the ordinary sense of the word (509 B). But the allegory and the transcendental language apply equally well to the ethical and political ideas which are the chief theme of the *Republic*, and it is not necessary to look further. The cause of any political or social institution is the purpose or idea of good in some controlling mind, and, as Coleridge said and Mill repeated after him, the best way to understand any human institution or contrivance is to appreciate that purpose. That will throw a flood of light on everything.[a]

I have never meant to deny the mystic and metaphysical suggestions of Plato's language. I have merely tried to bring out the residuum of practical and intelligible meaning for the political and ethical philosophy of the *Republic*. It is a meaning that is still true to-day, and it is the only interpretation that makes intelligible sense of what Plato says. That surely creates a presumption which can be met only by definite arguments.

Whatever the more remote suggestions of the idea of good for general or ethical philosophy, this its simple practical meaning for the *Republic* is clearly indicated by Plato himself. It symbolizes the distinction between the ideal statesman and the politician of decadent Athens and marks the purpose and goal of all the studies of the Platonic higher education. The guardians have already received in a purified

[a] *Cf.* my *Idea of Good*, p. 227.

INTRODUCTION

form the normal Greek education in gymnastics and "music," described in the *Protagoras*, 325 c ff., and virtually repeated in the education prescribed for the entire citizenship in the *Laws*. The product of this Platonic elementary and secondary education would be a band of healthy, wholesome, sunburnt boys and girls, who, in Ruskin's phrase, " have had all the nonsense boxed and raced and spun out of them." They would have dipped into fewer books than our graduates, but they would know a few of the world's greatest books by heart, they would have no theory of art or sentimentality about it, but their taste would have been refined, almost to infallibility, by hearing only the best music and seeing only the best statues. They would have heard of fewer things but would know what they *did* know perfectly. They would have never studied a text-book of civics, ethics, or " sociology," but the essential principles of obedience, patriotism, modesty, order, temperance, good manners, would have been so instilled into them that the possibility of violating them would hardly occur to their minds. They would not only be strong and healthy, but through gymnastics, choral singing and dancing, and military drill, would have acquired the mastery of their bodies and a dignified and graceful bearing.

But already in the age of the sophists Athens had become too sophisticated for her ambitious youth to remain content with this simple old Greek education however reformed and idealized. There was a demand for a higher university education, which was met first by the sophists, and then in the next generation by Plato himself and his great rival, the orator Isocrates, who conducted academies side by

INTRODUCTION

side in Athens for forty years. The content of this higher education is given in every age by the knowledge of that age. What else can it be? These Greek teachers did not offer " electives " in the chemistry of the carbon compounds, or the origin of Shintoism in Japan, or the evolution of the English novel from *Tom Jones* to *Ulysses*, for the simple reason that these interesting branches of study had not yet been developed. The sophists taught a practical theory of politics and business and the new art of rhetoric, promising to make their pupils effective speakers and shrewd men of affairs.[a] The publicist Isocrates taught what he knew, the application of this sophistic doctrine to the composition of more serious political and ethical essays. Plato taught what we should call ethics, sociology and philosophy, but what he called dialectics—the closely reasoned argumentative discussion of problems of ethics, politics, social life, philosophy and religion.

But with wider experience Plato came to feel that the " Socratic method " of plunging mere lads directly into these difficult questions was unwise. It was doubtless stimulating ; but it unsettled their moral faith, confused their minds, and converted them into pert and precocious disputants.[b] Dialectics demanded a preparatory training in some simpler methods of close, consecutive, abstract thinking. This preparation Plato found in the new sciences of arithmetic and geometry and in the sciences which he was among the first to constitute or predict—the sciences of mathematical astronomy,

---

[a] *Cf. Protag.* 318-319, *Gorg.* 452 E, 456-457.
[b] *Cf. infra*, p. 220, note *a*, on 537 D ff.

physics, and acoustics.[a] By these studies the youthful mind could be gradually lifted out of the region
of loose pictorial thinking, habituated to the thin
pure air of abstractions, taught the essential nature
of definitions, axioms, principles, and rules of logic,
and made capable of following with continuous
attention long trains of reasoning. We value
mathematics and the exact sciences largely for their
practical applications.[b] In the *Republic* Plato prized
them as the indispensable preparation for equally
severe abstract thinking about the more complex
and difficult problems of life, morals and society.[c]
In his *Republic* he combines this idea drawn from
the practice of his own school with his fundamental
political and social ideal, the government of mankind
by the really wise, and not by the politicians who
happen to get the votes. We need not stop to ask
whether a Utopia designed for a small Greek city is
applicable to a democracy of 120 millions inhabiting
a territory of three million square miles. We are
concerned with the ideal and its embodiment in a
theory of education.

The Platonic rulers are chosen by a process of
progressive selection through ever higher educational tests applied to young men and women who
have stood most successfully the tests of the lower
education.[d] Through arithmetic, geometry, and astro-

---

[a] *Cf.* notes on Book vii. 521 ff., esp. on 521 c, 523 A, 527 A.
[b] *Cf.* on 525 c.
[c] Herbert Spencer speaks of " Social science . . . the
science standing above all others in subtlety and complexity ;
the science which the highest intelligence alone can master..."
—the science now taught to undergraduates who have not
received the Platonic preparation.
[d] *Cf.* 537 A, B, D.

nomy, mechanics and acoustics, so far as these admit of mathematical treatment, they are led up to the final test in ethics and sociology, which is not speech-making or slumming, or the running of university settlements, but the power of close, exact, consecutive reasoning about complex moral phenomena. It must not be forgotten, however, that this theoretical discipline is supplemented by many years of practical experience in minor offices of administration.[a]

The consummation of it all is described poetically as the " vision of the idea of good " (540 A)—which, however, as we have seen, turns out to mean for all practical purposes the apprehension of some rational unified conception of the social aim and human well-being, and the consistent relating of all particular beliefs and measures to that ideal—a thing which can be achieved only by the most highly disciplined intelligence. For in Plato's time as in ours the opinions of the average man are not so unified and connected, but jostle one another in hopeless confusion in his brain. Plato's conception of the higher education, then, may be summed up in a sentence : " Until a man is able to abstract and define rationally his idea of good, and unless he can run the gauntlet of all objections and is ready to meet them, not by appeals to opinion but to absolute truth, never faltering at any stage of the argument—unless he can do all this he knows neither the idea of good nor any other good. He apprehends only a shadow of opinion, not true and real knowledge." [b]

Starting from the sound psychological principle that the old-fashioned rote recitation of a text-book

<hr>

[a] *Cf.* 539 E-540 A.
[b] See *Rep.* 534 B-C and notes.

INTRODUCTION

is an abomination, that verbal knowledge is no knowledge, that the concrete must precede the abstract,
that we must visualize before we theorize, and
apprehend objects before we analyse relations, we
have in practice abandoned altogether the attempt
to teach young people hard consecutive abstract
thinking. We scorn to drill them in the old-
fashioned studies that developed this power, such
as grammatical analysis, " parsing," puzzling problems in arithmetic, algebra, or mechanics, elementary
logic,—mental science, as it was called,—and the
exact, if incomplete, methods of the orthodox
political economy ; and instead of this we encourage
them to have and express opinions about large and
vague questions of literary criticism, aesthetics,
ethics and social reform. A true apprehension of
Plato's ideal of education would not swing the
pendulum back again to the other extreme, but it
would help us to realize that no multiplication of
entertaining knowledge, and no refinements of the
new psychology, can alter the fact that all instruction
is wasted on a flabby mind, and that true education,
while it will not neglect entertainment, useful knowledge, and the training of the eye and hand, will
always consist largely in the development of firm,
hard, intellectual muscle. The studies best adapted
to this end will always retain a value independent
of practical utility or superficial attractiveness ; for
to change the figure and adapt Plato's own language :
By such studies the eye of the mind, more precious
than a thousand bodily eyes, is purged and quickened
and made more keen for whatever truth higher
education or life or business may present to it
(527 D–E).

INTRODUCTION

Plato's own account of the curriculum of his higher education ought to be a sufficient answer to the charge that in the training of his guardians he manifests an anti-scientific spirit. It is only by wresting phrases from their context and refusing to make allowances for the quality of Plato's rhetoric that the imputation of hostility to modern experimental science can be fastened upon him.[a] As I have shown elsewhere [b] and point out again in the notes, Plato is (1) using scientific studies to develop the faculty of abstract reasoning; (2) incidentally predicting the mathematical astronomy and physics of the future.[c] Both purposes tempt him to hammer his main point with Emersonian emphasis and to surprise attention with Ruskinian *boutades* in order to mark more clearly the distinction between himself and contemporary empiricists. Hence his satire of the substitution of experiment for mathematics in acoustics (531 A-B), and the intentional epigrammatic extravagance of his " leave the stars alone " (530 B). It is uncritical to quote these sentences apart from their entire context and treat them as if they were a deliberate and systematic attack on modern experimental science.

The Four Polities. The description of the four degenerate types of state in the eighth book relieves the strain of dialectics and the tedium of continuous argument by one of the most brilliant pieces of writing in Plato. Macaulay says it is " . . . beyond all criticism. I

---

[a] *Cf.* on 529 A, 530 B.
[b] " Platonism and the History of Science," *Am. Philos. Soc. Proc.* lxvi. pp. 171 f., *What Plato Said*, pp. 235-236.
[c] *Cf.* on 530 B.

INTRODUCTION

remember nothing in Greek philosophy superior to this in profundity, ingenuity and eloquence." It serves further to lead up to the embodiment in the tyrant of the analogical argument that the unhappiness of the worst man matches the misery of the worst state. The objections to the book or to its place in the economy of the *Republic* raised by Aristotle and others are mostly captious irrelevances.[a]

The transition from the ideal state is resumed at the point where it was interrupted at the beginning of the fifth book,[b] and it is pretended that Books V., VI. and VII. are a digression, though they are obviously an indispensable part of the *Republic*.[c] Matter-of-fact critics have argued that an ideal or perfect state would contain within itself no seeds of destruction and could not decay. But as Plato himself said, the philosophic state is a pattern or ideal which retains its value even if imperfectly realized.[d] It is a fundamental Platonic principle that only the divine is eternal and unchangeable.[e] All created and material things are subject to change. The universe itself is only as good as the Demiurgos was able to make it, and the created gods are preserved from destruction only by his sustaining will.[f]

The riddle of the " nuptial " number that deter-

---

[a] *Cf.* Aristot. *Pol.* 1316 a 1 f. ἐν δὲ τῇ Πολιτείᾳ λέγεται μὲν περὶ τῶν μεταβολῶν ὑπὸ τοῦ Σωκράτους, οὐ μέντοι λέγεται καλῶς, which is rather cool after all his borrowings from *Rep.* viii. in the preceding pages. And in 1286 b 15 ff. he seems to accept the development of *Rep.* viii. See also Frutiger, *Mythes de Platon*, p. 42.

[b] *Cf.* Vol. I. on 449 A-B.

[c] *Cf.* Vol. I. p. xvi, *What Plato Said*, p. 225.

[d] *Cf.* on 499 D and *What Plato Said*, p. 564.

[e] *Cf. Symp.* 207-208, *Rep.* vii. on the heavens, 530 B.

[f] *Cf. Tim.* 37 D, 41 C-D, *What Plato Said*, p. 335.

mines the beginning of the decline has never been
solved to the satisfaction of a majority of competent
critics. The solution would contribute something to
our knowledge of early Greek mathematical terminology but nothing to our understanding of Plato's
thought. Emerson's definitive word about it is,
" He (Plato) sometimes throws a little mathematical
dust into our eyes." The " meaning " of the number
is simply Burke's statement (iv. p. 312) in *Regicide
Peace*, p. 2, " I doubt whether the history of mankind is yet complete enough, if ever it can be so, to
furnish grounds for a sure theory on the internal
causes which necessarily affect the fortune of a
state." [a] But though the ultimate causes of de-

---

[a] For Aristotle's opinion *cf. Pol.* 1316 a 5 ff. For discussions of the number *cf.* Zeller, *Phil. d. Gr.* ii. 1⁴, pp.
857-860 ; Jowett's translation of the *Republic* (1888), pp.
cxxx ff. ; Adam, *Republic*, vol. ii. pp. 264-312 ; Ueberweg-
Praechter, *Philos. des Altertums* (1926), 94* ff. ; Paul
Tannery, " Le Nombre Nuptial dans Platon," *Rev. Philos.* i.,
1876, pp. 170-188 ; Georg Albert, *Die platonische Zahl*,
Wien, 1896, and " Der Sinn der plat. Zahl," *Philologus*, vol.
66 (1907), pp. 153-156 ; J. Dupuis, " Le Nombre Géométrique
de Platon," *Annuaire de l'Assoc. des Ét. grecques*, vol. 18,
pp. 218-255 ; Frutiger, *Mythes de Platon*, pp. 47-48. *Cf.*
also Gomperz, *Greek Thinkers*, iii. p. 336, C. Ritter, *Platons
Stellung zu den Aufgaben der Naturwissenschaft*, pp. 91-94 ;
Friedländer, *Platon*, i. p. 108 ; G. Kafka in *Philologus* 73,
pp. 109-121 ; D. B. Monro in *Class. Rev.* vi. (1892) pp.
152-156 ; and Adam, *ibid.* pp. 240-244, and xvi. p. 17-23 ;
Fr. Hultsch in *Phil. Woch.* xii. (1892) pp. 1256-1258. *Cf.*
further Burnet, *Early Greek Philosophy*, p. 25 " It is to
be observed that Plato's ' perfect year ' is also 36,000 solar
years (Adam's *Republic*, vol. ii. p. 302), and that it is probably
connected with the precession of the equinoxes " ; Carl
Vering, *Platons Staat*, p. 167 " Den Biologen wird die
Zahlenmystik Platons an die Mendelschen Vererbungs-
tabellen erinnern, durch welche die geniale Ahnung Platons,
dass es zahlenmässig darstellbare Vererbungsgesetze geben

generation escape our ken, Plato mentions a practical
point that is of considerable significance to-day.
Revolutions are due to the divisions and discords of
the dominant and educated classes.[a] The allegory
of the four metals is kept up. The decline begins
when the rulers no longer breed true and the gold
is mixed with base alloy.[b]

The limitation of the degenerate types of state to
four is conscious and artistic. It should not be used
to prove Plato's impatience of facts. There are endless minor varieties of social and political structure
among the barbarians (544 c-d). Plato leaves it to
Aristotle and the political and social science depart-
ments of the American universities to collect them.[c]
The sequence, timocracy, oligarchy, democracy and
tyranny does not always reproduce the actual history
of cities of Greece, but it anticipates many of the
vicissitudes of modern history more suggestively than
Aristotle's laborious collection of instances.[d] Plato
occasionally forgets himself or lets himself go in contemporary satire or allusion that points to Athens

müsse, nach mehr als 2000 Jahren ihre wissenschaftliche
Rechtfertigung gefunden hat." *Cf.* Baudrillart, *J. Bodin
et son temps*, p. 360 " . . . A tout cela Bodin ajoute des
calculs cabalistiques sur la durée des empires, sur le nombre
nuptial . . ."

[a] *Rep.* 545 D, *Laws* 683 E, 682 D-E, *Class. Phil.* xvii.
pp. 154-155. *Cf.* Aristot. *Pol.* 1305 a 39.

[b] 547 B. *Cf.* 415 A-B.

[c] Aristotle says that there are not only more kinds of
government than these, but there are many sub-species of
each. *Cf.* Aristot. *Pol.* vi., 1288 ff., 1279 b, 1229 a 8, 1289 a 8,
Newman, vol. i. pp. 494 ff., and also *Unity of Plato's Thought*,
pp. 62-63.

[d] The case of the French Revolution and the rise of
Napoleon is one of the most outstanding examples.

rather than to any one of his four or five types.[a] But the consistency of his hypothesis is sufficiently maintained to satisfy any reasonable reader. The individual types corresponding to the four political patterns are the earliest and among the best systematic character-sketches in extant European literature and may be counted among the sources of the *Characters* of Theophrastus and their successors.[b]

The Ethical Argument.

Book IX. sums up and concludes the main ethical argument of the *Republic*. This is not the place for a systematic exposition of the Platonic ethics. Ethical philosophy as distinguished from exhortation and the code can always be stated in the form of a discussion of the validity of the moral law and the motives for obedience to it, in other words, the quest for the sanction.[c] But this mode of statement is especially suited to ages of so-called enlightenment and transition when the very existence of a moral law or its binding force is challenged, whether seriously or as an intellectual game.

Such in Plato's opinion was the age in which he lived. The main drift of the speculations of the pre-Socratic philosophers had been in the direction of materialism if not exactly atheism.[d] The populariza-

[a] *Cf.*, *e.g.*, 549 c and 553 a with Adam's notes, 551 b, 556 e, 562 d, 563 c, 565 b.

[b] *Cf.* also Matthew Arnold's description of the Barbarians and the Philistines in *Culture and Anarchy*.

[c] *Cf.* Mill, *Diss. and Disc.* iii. p. 300 "The question concerning the *summum bonum* or what is the same thing, concerning the foundation of morality," etc.

[d] This has recently been denied. But the essential truth of the generalization is not appreciably affected by a few fragments whose religious, ethical and spiritual purpose is doubtful.

xlvi

tion of these ideas by the so-called sophists and their application to education, morals, politics and criticism of life had further tended to do away with all traditional moral and religious checks upon instinct and individualism. And the embittered class conflicts and the long demoralization of the thirty years' war had completed the work of moral and spiritual disintegration.[a] The Greeks had lost their old standards and had acquired no new, more philosophic, principles to take their place.[b] Plato's ears were dinned, he said, by the negations of materialists, atheists, relativists, and immoralists.[c] How to answer them was the chief problem of his ethical philosophy. To satirize these immoralists or to depict their defeat in argument was one of the main motives of his dramatic art.[d]

The evidence in support of Plato's interpretation of contemporary Greek life and thought has been repeatedly collected from Aristophanes, Euripides, and Thucydides, the fragments of the sophists and the pre-Socratics and Plato's own writings.[e] This conservative view of the Greek " enlightenment " has in turn often been challenged by modern historians of liberal or radical tendencies, a Grote, a

[a] See T. R. Glover, *Democracy in the Ancient World*, pp. 75-77 ; *supra*, Vol. I. p. xxxvi; *What Plato Said*, pp. 6, 141-142.

[b] Cf. *Rep.* 538 c-e.

[c] Cf. *Rep.* 358 c, *Protag.* 333 c, *Euthydem.* 279 b, *Phileb.* 66 e, *Gorg.* 470 d, *Laws* 662 c, 885 d, *Soph.* 265 c, *Phaedo* 92 d.

[d] Cf. *Gorg.* 527 a-b, *Rep.* i., *Unity of Plato's Thought*, p. 25.

[e] Cf. *What Plato Said*, p. 503, on *Gorg.* 461 c, for references, and *ibid.* pp. 137, 145, 215 ff., 392-393, also W. Jaeger, " Die griechische Staatsethik im Zeitalter des Platon," *Die Antike*, Bd. x. Heft 1, esp. p. 8.

INTRODUCTION

Mill, a Gomperz, and their followers.[a] The interpreter of the *Republic* need only note the sincerity and intensity of Plato's conviction and its effect upon the form of his presentation of ethics.

A complete study of the Platonic ethics would incorporate many other ideas drawn from the *Protagoras*, the *Philebus*, the *Laws*, the minor Socratic dialogues, and perhaps from the *Phaedrus* and *Symposium*.[b] But the two chief ethical dialogues, the *Gorgias* and the *Republic*, are cast in the form of an answer to dogmatic and unabashed ethical nihilism. What is to be said to an uncompromising immoralist? Is it possible to convince him, or failing that, to refute or seem to refute him to the edification of the bystander?[c] The serious aim of both *Gorgias* and *Republic* is to convince and refute, but there are parts of the *Gorgias* and of the first book of the *Republic* in which the chief dramatic purpose is the exhibition of Socrates' superiority in argument to the sceptic.

Many commentators ancient and modern object that Plato has not proved his case. They are not necessarily such immoralists as Plato had in mind. Such moralists as Grote, Mill and Leslie Stephen say that all men of goodwill would like to believe in the identity of virtue and happiness, but that the facts of experience are against it.[d] It is at best a general

---

[a] *Cf.*, *e.g.*, *Greek Thinkers*, vol. i. ch. iv., esp. pp. 403-411.

[b] See *International Journal of Ethics*, Jan. 1929, pp. 232-233; *What Plato Said*, pp. 317, and 364; *Unity of Plato's Thought*, pp. 9-27.

[c] *Cf. What Plato Said*, p. 141.

[d] *Cf.*, *e.g.*, *Science of Ethics*, pp. 397-398, 434, and the whole problem of the book of Job. *Cf.* also Sidgwick, *Method of Ethics*, pp. 172-173.

tendency or probability, not an invariable rule. Dryden is not sure that the law can always be verified on individuals, but is half humorously certain that it infallibly applies to nations, because in their case Providence is too deeply engaged.

The problem is too large to be incidentally solved by a commentator on the *Republic*. It is, as Plato himself would admit, partly a question of faith,[a] and partly of the kind of evidence that is admitted as relevant. " Do you ask for sanctions ? " exclaims John Morley. " One whose conscience has been strengthened from youth in this faith can know no greater bitterness than the stain cast by a wrong act . . . and the discords that have become the ruling harmony of his days." [b] That is the kind of evidence to which Plato appeals when he argues that his

---

[a] Cf. *Gorg.* 526 D, *Laws* 728, 904 D-E, *Crito* 54 B-C; and Arnold, *God and the Bible*, chap. iii. p. 136 : " These truths . . . are the matter of an immense experience which is still going forward. . . . But if any man is so entirely without affinity for them . . . for him *Literature and Dogma* was not written."

[b] Cf. also Morley, *Rousseau*, ii. 280, *Voltaire*, p. 293 ; Faguet, *Pour qu'on lise Platon*, pp. 99-101, 138 ; Gomperz, *Greek Thinkers*, iv. 257-258, 293-294 ; Huxley, *Science and Hebrew Tradition*, p. 339, and the entire controversy arising out of his *Evolution and Ethics* ; Arcesilas *apud* Brochard, *Les Sceptiques grecs*, p. 171. *Cf.* George Eliot's novels *passim*, and Mill's " Those whose conscientious feelings are so weak as to allow of their asking this question," which is practically equivalent to Shaftesbury's " If any gentleman asks why he should not wear a dirty shirt I reply that he must be a very dirty gentleman to ask the question." *Cf.* also Cicero, *De officiis*, iii. 29 ; Leslie Stephen, *Science of Ethics, passim*, *e.g.* 426 ff., and the arguments of Hazlitt, Macaulay and others against the Utilitarians. Such passages are a conclusive answer to the objection that Plato has not proved his case.

guardians will find more happiness in duty fulfilled than they would by grasping at what are commonly thought the good things of life.[a] It is an argument that will not appeal to men of stunted moral sensibilities. The issue is, as Plato says, whether they are the best judges.[b] The question has always been debated and always will be debatable, and there is little to add to the considerations on either side which Cicero develops in his perpetual reargument of the Stoic paradox, that virtue alone suffices for a happy life, and that the sage will be happy on the rack. Matthew Arnold, Emerson and George Eliot are as fixed in the faith as Plato. Experience, says Arnold, is perpetually sending the denier who says in his heart, There is no God, back to school to learn his lesson better.[c] The writers most in vogue to-day would agree with Mill and Leslie Stephen, if not with Thrasymachus and Callicles.[d] It is not necessary to determine this controversy in order to justify the *Republic*. To condemn the *Republic* because it is not a demonstration that leaves no room for doubt is to affirm that the question is not worth discussing, or that Plato's treatment of it falls short of what could reasonably be expected. If it is not a proof, has any one come nearer to a demonstration ?[e]

[a] *Rep.* 419-420. *Cf.* Vol. I. pp. 314-315.

[b] *Cf. Rep.* 580 D ff., *Laws* 658-659.

[c] *God and the Bible*, p. xxxv.

[d] Brochard, *La Morale de Platon*, says : "Aucun moraliste moderne n'entreprendrait de défendre la doctrine de Platon, qui apparaît comme une gageure." *Cf.* Westermarck, *Origin and Development of Moral Ideas*, i. pp. 17, 18, 321, and *passim*.

[e] *Cf.* Leslie Stephen, *Science of Ethics*, p. 354 : " Evolution implies that there must be at least an approximate coincidence, and there is no apparent *a priori* reason why the coincidence should not be indefinitely close."

INTRODUCTION

As to the desirability of the attempt, Plato thought that it is not safe to expose young minds to the un-answered propaganda of philosophies of immoralism and relativity. And recent experience of an amoral and irreligious education of the masses has not yet proved him wrong.[a] He believed in his own argu-ments and in the doctrine which he taught. But apart from that he also believed that civilized society would disintegrate if morality were not effectively preached.[b] The charge hinted by Aristotle (*Eth.* x., 1172 a 34-35) and often repeated that this implies the " economy of truth " [c] and the inner or double doc-trine is sufficiently refuted by the depth and intensity of Plato's own " adamantine " moral faith.[d] But however that may be, the question which he asks in his *Laws* still brings heart-searchings to the parent who has inherited a conscience from a generation that had not been swept from its moorings : What *is* a father to tell his son ? [e] But I cannot give more space to these eternal controversies and must turn to the direct summing-up of Plato's argument in the ninth book.

Plato sums up the conclusions of the *Republic* in three formal arguments. The first is the broad

[a] See my article in the June, 1934, number of the *Atlantic Monthly*, pp. 722-723.

[b] Cf. *Laws* 890 D, 907 c, 718 D.

[c] *Laws* 663 c-D (*What Plato Said*, p. 364) may imply " economy " in theology, but not in ethical religion. Cf. also *What Plato Said*, p. 626, and Isoc. *Antid.* 283 καὶ ταῦτα καὶ ταῖς ἀληθείαις οὕτως ἔχει καὶ συμφέρει τὸν τρόπον τοῦτον λέγεσθαι περὶ αὐτῶν. Cf. Harnack, *Hist. of Dogma*, pp. 183-184 : " Gregory of Nazianzus speaks of a necessary and salutary οἰκονομηθῆναι τὴν ἀλήθειαν."

[d] Cf. *Rep.* 618 E, *Laws* 662 B.

[e] Cf. *Laws* 662 D-663 A, *What Plato Said*, p. 364.

INTRODUCTION

analogy between the individual and the state, which runs through the entire work.[a] Plato feels that here he is not only clinching the subject, but finally grappling with the problem debated in the *Gorgias* and to which he returns in the *Laws*. He is gathering up all his forces for a defiant reply to the immoralist and ethical nihilist. The result is an elaboration, an intensity, an insistency, a repetition that are offensive to readers who feel distaste for anything that savours of moral didacticism.

The argumentative force of such an analogy is the cumulative impression of the detail that makes it plausible. Plato points the application of this argument by a psychological portrait of the typical tyrannical man, developed out of the democratic man as the democrat was developed from the oligarch. The literary symmetry strains the logic a little, for while the democratic man is the typical citizen of a democracy, the typical citizen of a tyranny is not the tyrant himself, but any one of those whom he oppresses. But it does not matter. To heighten his effect Plato describes first the soul of the man destined to become a Greek tyrant, and then the intensification of all its defects and miseries by the actual possession and exercise of usurped power.

Latent in all men are lawless instincts and appetites which reason and disciplined emotion hold in check, but which are sometimes revealed in dreams (571 B f.). In the tyrannical soul these lower propensities are unleashed. The censor, to borrow the language of a fashionable modern psychology, is dethroned, all control is abolished and the soul is at the mercy of the instincts of the night. Plato depicts the rake's

[a] *Cf.* Vol. I. p. xxxv.

progress of what again in modern terminology we may call the typical gangster and boss in a lawless democracy. He is the son of a democratic father, but, unlike his father, does not settle down into a tolerable compromise between the caprices of unregulated desire and the principles of tradition (572 D). In him desire grown great, a monstrous Eros, a ruling passion with its attendant train of appetites, usurps the throne and seizes the empty citadel of the mind, vacant of the only true guardians, the precepts of culture and right reason (573 A). He wastes his portion of the family inheritance, encroaches on the portion of his brothers, and if further advances are refused him does not shrink from the last outrage that Greek conservatism attributed to the " younger generation "—and " strikes his father." [a] He becomes the chosen leader of a gang of like-minded roisterers from whom he is distinguished only by a more enterprising spirit and the greater strength of the principle of desire in his soul ; and the gang, if few, terrorize the city with crime (575 A-B), if many, strike the father- and mother-land, overthrow the constitution and establish a tyranny (575 D).

A modern moralist might improve the text that the gangster lives in an atmosphere of greed, suspicion and fear, and is destined finally to be shot by an ambitious rival. Plato, speaking in terms of Greek experience, makes the " tyrannical man " fulfil his nature and perfect his type by becoming an actual tyrant of a Greek city. And he then describes, perhaps in reminiscence of his own observations at the court of Dionysius at Syracuse, and in

[a] 574 c. *Cf.* Aristoph. *Clouds* 1321 ff., 1421 ff.

prophetic anticipation of Caligula and Louis Napoleon, the hell of suspicion, fear and insatiate and unsatisfied desires in which such a tyrant lives.[a] As the city which he misrules is, for all the splendour of the court and the courtiers, as a whole the most miserable of states, so is he, to the eye that can penetrate the dazzling disguise of pomp and power, " the farced title running 'fore the king," the most miserable of men (577-579).

It is obvious that Plato forces the note a little in the interest of his thesis. In actual history the tyrant need not be the sensualist of Plato's description. He may be only a cold-blooded, hard-headed Machiavellian,—in Plato's language a lover of honour and victory, not a lover of the pleasures that money purchases. But these cavils of a meticulous logic are beside the mark. The real argument, as we have said, is the psychological analysis and the facts of Greek experience that lend plausibility to the analogy. It prepares us to receive the more strictly philosophic and scientific arguments that are to follow.

The gist of the second argument is that the intellectual, the philosopher, has necessarily experienced all three kinds of pleasure in his life, while the representatives of the two other types have no experience of the pleasures of pure intelligence (581-582). To this is added the consideration that the organ or instrument of all such judgements, reason and rational

[a] Cf. Tacitus, Ann. vi. 6 " neque frustra praestantissimus sapientiae firmare solitus est, si recludantur tyrannorum mentes, posse aspici laniatus et ictus, quando ut corpora verberibus, ita . saevitia, libidine, malis consultis animus dilaceretur."

INTRODUCTION

speech, is the special possession of the philosopher (582 A). This argument is never mentioned again by Plato and is by many critics, including Leslie Stephen,[a] rejected as a fallacy. But John Stuart Mill accepts and makes use of it.

The issue thus raised is really the old question of a distinction of quality and value in pleasure. No one can judge or prescribe another's pleasure, it is argued ; pleasure *qua* pleasure admits no differences.[b] But is there any such thing as pleasure *qua* pleasure ? Are there not always inseparable accompaniments and consequences ? And though the hog may be sole judge of his own pleasures, is it on the whole as desirable or as pleasurable to be a hog as a man ?[c] There is room for interminable argument, for the entire problem of relativity is involved. If all judgements are relative, Plato elsewhere argues, we are committed to chaos. The dog-faced baboon, and not man or God, is the measure of all things.[d] The very existence of the arts and the sciences presupposes that things are measured against standards and not merely against one another.[e] Thus, though the argument is not repeated by Plato in this form, it suggests and implies most of the fundamental questions of his ethical philosophy.

[a] He calls it " a familiar short cut to the desired conclusion " (*Science of Ethics*, p. 399). *Cf.* also Sidgwick, *Method of Ethics*, p. 148.

[b] *Cf. Gorg.* 494 E (*What Plato Said*, p. 508) and 499 B. See too Leslie Stephen, *Science of Ethics*, p. 400.

[c] *Cf. Phileb.* 67 B, *What Plato Said*, p. 611. There is no space to repeat or quote here the arguments against the utilitarian point of view set forth by Macaulay and others. *Cf.* also Sidgwick, *Method of Ethics*, pp. 93-94, 121.

[d] *Cf. Theaet.* 161 C, *Laws* 716 C.

[e] *Cf. Politicus* 284 B-C, 285 A-B.

INTRODUCTION

The third argument, drawn from the negativity of the pleasure of sense, is the basis of the Platonic ethics, so far as it is an arguable doctrine. It is necessary to dwell upon this point, for it is commonly said that Plato's ethical philosophy is deduced from the idea of good.[a] That is true only from one quite special point of view. The idea of good, as we have seen, is a postulate of the logic of ethics and of the higher education of the philosopher. It is a blank cheque that supports the credit of the system but which is not filled in. No virtue and no particular " good " is adequately defined until it is explicitly related to an idea of good (505 A, 506 A). It may be defined provisionally and sufficiently for a given purpose in terms of psychology or tradition or with a tacit reference to an implied conception of good (504 A-B). But nowhere in Plato's writings are definite controversial arguments or substantive principles of ethical philosophy or rules of practice deduced from the idea of good. It is merely said that an ethical philosophy is not complete until we have decided what is our sanction.

But such principles *are* deduced from the negativity of the " lower " pleasures throughout Plato's writings.[b] This supplies the missing link in the argument of the *Protagoras* that virtue and happiness depend on the correct estimate of pleasures and pains.[c] The doctrine is implied in the *Phaedo* (83-84). It is distinctly suggested in the *Gorgias* (493 ff.). It crowns the

[a] *Cf.* W. H. Fairbrother, " The Relation of Ethics to Metaphysics," *Mind*, xiii., 1904, p. 43 ; Martineau, *Types of Ethical Theory*, 1886, p. xxvi. *Cf. supra*, p. xxvi.

[b] *Cf. supra*, p. xxvi.

[c] *Cf. What Plato Said*, pp. 130-131.

INTRODUCTION

argument of the *Republic* (583 B ff.). It is elaborated in the *Philebus* in order to reach a final settlement of the controversy dramatized in the *Gorgias*. It is tacitly employed in the endeavour of the *Laws* (660 E-663 B) to attach a practicable edifying conclusion to the utilitarian arguments of the *Protagoras*. The statement of the doctrine in the *Republic*, though briefer than that of the *Philebus*, touches on all the essential points, as the notes will show. It cannot be proved to be either a résumé or an imperfect anticipation of the developed theory. It cannot be used to date the ninth book of the *Republic* relatively to the *Philebus.*[a]

I am not here speaking of the absolute truth of the doctrine, but only of its demonstrable relation to Plato's ethical philosophy. As I have elsewhere said,[b] Plato teaches that sensuous pleasures are in their nature impure and illusory. They are preconditioned by, and mixed with, desire, want, pain. " Surgit amari aliquid " is ever true of them. They are the relief of an uneasiness, the scratching of an itch, the filling of a vacuum.[c] To treat them as real, or to make them one's aim (except so far as our human estate requires), is to seek happiness in a pro-

---

[a] Though the *Philebus* is in fact later than the *Republic*, as Mill said long before style statistics were thought of.

[b] *Unity of Plato's Thought*, p. 24.

[c] Already in the *Gorgias*, 493 E, 494 C and the *Phaedrus* 258 E ὧν προλυπηθῆναι δεῖ ἢ μηδὲ ἡσθῆναι, etc. ; *Rep.* 584 A-B. It has even been argued that the *Phaedrus* passage takes for granted the fuller discussion of the *Philebus* (W. H. Thompson, *Phaedrus*, *ad loc.*), and why not? Anything may be argued if the dialogues are supposed to grow out of one another and not out of Plato's mind.

cess rather than a state,[a] in becoming rather than in
being. It is to bind oneself to the wheel of Ixion
and pour water into the bottomless jar of the
Danaids.[b] Far happier, far more pleasurable, is the
life that consistently aims at few and calm pleasures,
to which the sensualist would hardly give the name,
a life which he would regard as torpor or death.[c]

Both the physiology and the psychology of this
doctrine have been impugned. It has been argued
that, up to the point of fatigue, the action of healthy
nerves involves no pain, and must yield a surplus
of positive sensuous pleasure. It is urged that the
present uneasiness of appetite is normally more than
counterbalanced by the anticipation of immediate
satisfaction. Such arguments will carry no weight
with those who accept Plato's main contention, that
the satisfactions of sense and ambition, however
" necessary," have no real worth, and that to seek
our true life in them is to weave and unweave the
futile web of Penelope. Whatever qualifications
modern psychology may attach to the doctrine, it is
the logical basis of Plato's ethics. The unfeigned

---

[a] *Phileb.* 53 c ff., 54 E virtually = *Gorg.* 493 E. *Cf. What
Plato Said*, pp. 322-323. The literal-minded objection of
Aristotle, *Eth. Nic.* 1174 b, and some moderns, that pleasure
is not literally = κίνησις, is beside the point.

[b] *Gorg.* 493 B τετρημένος πίθος, etc., *Phaedo* 84 A ἀν-
ήνυτον ἔργον . . . Πηνελόπης ἱστόν, *Gorg.* 507 E, *Phileb.*
54 E.

[c] *Phaedo* 64 B, *Gorg.* 492 E, *Phileb.* 54 E καί φασι ζῆν οὐκ
ἂν δέξασθαι, etc. In *Laws* 733, 734 B, the hedonistic calculus
of the *Protagoras* is retained, but is applied not directly to
the individual acts, but to types of life. The life of moderate
pleasures is *a priori* the more pleasurable because it necessarily yields a more favourable balance than the life of intense
pleasures.

INTRODUCTION

recognition of the inherent worthlessness of the lower pleasures removes at once the motive and the lures to evil.[a] It is the chief link in the proof that virtue is happiness. It insures the domination of reason over feeling and appetite. It moulds man into that likeness to the divine pattern which is Plato's expression for the ethical ideal,[b] for the divine life knows neither pleasure nor pain.[c] It is the serious argument that explains Plato's repudiation of the hedonistic formulas of the *Protagoras* [d] and justifies the noble anti-hedonistic rhetoric of the *Gorgias*,[e] the *Phaedo*,[f] and the *Philebus* (*in fine*).

Regarded as a logical system, then, and metaphysics apart, the Platonic ethics is not to be deduced from the idea of good. It is best studied and expounded under a few simple heads : (1) illustrations in the minor dialogues of the necessity and the difficulty of defining ethical terms ; (2) the search for arguments that will convince, or at least confute, the ethical nihilism of a war-weary, cynical and over-enlightened generation—for proof, in short, that virtue and happiness coincide ; (3) the attempt to find a compromise between the necessity of acknowledging the truth in a certain sense of hedonistic utilitarianism and our justifiable idealistic distaste for that way of describing the moral life ; (4) as an essential part of the argument of both (2) and (3), the principle of the comparative worthlessness of the

[a] *Phaedo* 66 c, *Rep.* 586 A-B, 588.
[b] *Theaetet.* 176 B ff., *Laws* 716 D, 728 A-B, *Rep.* 352 A-B, 612 E, *Phileb.* 39 E.
[c] *Phileb.* 33 B.
[d] Cf. *What Plato Said*, p. 500.
[e] 512 D-E, *What Plato Said*, p. 149.
[f] 69 A, *What Plato Said*, pp. 171 and 174.

INTRODUCTION

lower or sensual pleasures, which, except so far as necessary, are bought at too high a price, because they are preconditioned by pain.[a]

These categories are not of my invention. They are the topics on which ethical discussion actually turns in the dialogues. The *Republic* supplies ample illustration of all these topics. The first book, like the *Gorgias*, dramatizes Socrates' dialectic superiority to the immoralist. The second book restates the issue in its most fundamental form. The fourth book resumes and for practical purposes provisionally solves the puzzles of the definition of the virtues in the minor Socratic dialogues. The allegory of the idea of good, rightly understood, shows what Plato meant in these minor dialogues by making the failure to define virtue always turn on the inability to discover the " good." The ninth book, as we have seen, sums up the argument and adds a sufficiently explicit exposition of the doctrine of the negativity of pleasure, which, as the *Philebus* shows, is the indispensable basis of the scientific and calculating ethics postulated in the *Protagoras*.

But true virtue is something more than argument, and its mood, as an eloquent passage of the *Phaedo* protests, is not that of the prudential, calculating reason.[b] And so the argument of the ninth book, like that of the fourth, culminates in an appeal through imagery and analogy to the imaginative reason and the soul. There (444-445) it was urged that the health and harmony of the soul must be still more indispens-

[a] See my review of Lodge in *International Journal of Ethics*, xxxix. pp. 232-233, and for the ethical argument of the *Republic* as a whole my " Idea of Justice in Plato's Republic," *The Ethical Record*, January 1890, pp. 185-199.

[b] *Phaedo* 69 A f., *What Plato Said*, p. 500.

able to true happiness than that of the body. And
we saw that the most scientific of modern ethical
philosophies is finally forced back upon the same
analogy.[a] In the conclusion of the ninth book the
motif recurs with still greater elaboration and in a
more eloquent climax. Every animal of the barnyard, Plato says in anticipation of Emerson and Freud,
has found lodgement within this external sheath of
humanity. And the issue for every human soul is
whether it chooses to foster the snake, the lion and
the ape, or the man, the mind, and the god within the
mind.[b] Surely the wiser choice is that which values
all the so-called goods, for which men scramble and
contend, only as they tend to preserve or destroy the
true constitution and health of the soul. This polity
of the sober and righteous soul is the symbol of that
City of God which may exist nowhere on earth but
on which as a pattern laid up in heaven he who will
may fix his eyes and constitute himself its citizen.[c]

A characteristic feature of Plato's art both in great
and little matters is the climax after the apparent
climax.[d] The tenth book of the *Republic*, which is in
a sense an appendix, adds the climax of the originally
disavowed religious sanction of immortality to that of
the appeal to the imaginative reason. The interven-
ing digression in defence of the banishment of the
poets is in effect, if not in Plato's conscious intention,
a relieving interval of calm between the two peaks of
feeling. For the rest, the deeper psychology of the

The Banishment of Poetry.

[a] *Cf.* Vol. I. p. xvi.
[b] *Rep.* 589 D-E. *Cf. Tim.* 90 A-B.
[c] *Cf.* Vol. I. pp. xlii-xliii.
[d] *Cf. supra*, Vol. I. pp. xxi-xxii, *What Plato Said*, pp. 140,
189, 248, *infra*, p. 104.

INTRODUCTION

philosophic books and the theory of ideas expounded there invited a reconsideration of the subject and provided arguments based, not on the content of the Homeric epic, but on the essential nature of poetry and its influence.

The two arguments that have exercised the defenders of poetry from Aristotle to Arnold [a] are that poetry is not truth but imitation, a copy of a copy, and that poetry fosters emotion and so weakens the salutary control of feeling by the reason and the will. In support of the first the theory of ideas is invoked in a form so intentionally simplified that it has given rise to the fantastic hypothesis that this book must represent an earlier period of Plato's philosophy.[b] God made one idea of a couch. The artisan copies it in many material couches. The artist with words or colours copies, not the idea, but the copy. This argument of course could be and has been answered in its own terms by the claim of Browning's *Fra Lippo Lippi* that the genius of the artist does directly apprehend the idea or essence of things and reveal it to those who can see only through his eyes.[c] But the real question whether art deals with truth or appearance is independent of Plato's half-serious formulation of it in the language of the theory of ideas. It is still debated, and it is the business of the interpreters of Plato to understand, not necessarily to pronounce judgement.

The question whether poetry's chief function is to

[a] Sidney's *Defense of Poesy* is probably the most familiar.
[b] Cf. *What Plato Said*, p. 249, *supra*, p. xviii.
[c] For, don't you mark, we're made so that we love
First when we see them painted, things we have passed
Perhaps a hundred times nor cared to see ;
And so they are better, painted—better to us.

stimulate and exercise emotion, or to relieve, purge,[a] refine, purify, sublimate and exalt it, likewise raises an issue which still divides psychologists, educators and critics. Its determination perhaps involves a great and deliberate choice in the acceptance and management of life as a whole. Plato's decision to banish the honeyed Muse from his ideal city represents only one aspect of his many-sided nature. It is obviously not, as is sometimes absurdly said, an expression of his insensibility to Hellenic poetry and art. It was his own sensitiveness that made him fear its power. He himself wrote verse in youth.[b] His imagery, the invention of his myths and the poetic quality of his prose rank him with the world's major poets.[c] He quotes poetry with exquisite and fond aptness throughout his writings.[d] And there are no more wistful words than his reluctant dismissal of the supreme· poet, the author and source of all these beauties of epic and tragedy, the Ionian father of the rest—Homer.[e] However, Plato's ethical convictions gave him the courage of Guyon (*Faery Queene*, II. xii. 83) in dealing with these enchantments :

[a] Aristotle's doctrine of κάθαρσις. *Cf.* my review of Finsler, " Platon und die aristotelische Poetik," *Class. Phil.* iii. pp. 461-462 ; also *The Nation*, xc. (1910) p. 319 ; Sikes, *Greek View of Poetry*, pp. 118-125.

[b] *Cf. What Plato Said*, pp. 17 ff.

[c] *Cf.* Friedländer, *Platon*, i. pp. 196 and 200 ; Sidney, in *English Men of Letters*, p. 150 " Of all the philosophers he is the most poetical ; " Chesterton, *The Resurrection of Rome*, p. 57 " But when we remember that the great poet Plato (as he must be called) banished poets from his *Republic*, we have a glimmer of why the great Greek Emperor banished sculptors from his empire."

[d] *Cf. What Plato Said*, pp. 7-9 ; *Unity of Plato's Thought*, pp. 81-82.

[e] *Rep.* 607 C-D ; *cf. What Plato Said*, p. 250.

> But all those pleasaunt bowres and Pallace brave
> Guyon broke downe with rigour pittilesse;
> Ne ought their goodly workmanship might save
> Them from the tempest of his wrathfulnesse.[a]

TheDoctrine
of Immorta-
lity.

The guerdons of righteousness, worldly or other-worldly, were explicitly excluded in the original formulation of the question whether justice is or is not intrinsically its own reward.[b]   But now, having proved his case independently of these, Plato thinks that no one can fairly object if he points out that in fact honesty is usually the best policy even in this world, and that there is good hope that the legends of a life and judgement to come are in essence true.[c]

There are hints of a life after death earlier in the *Republic*.[d]   And nothing can be inferred from Glaucon's perhaps affected surprise at Socrates' offer to prove it.   The immortality of the soul as an article of faith and hope, a sanction of moral law, an inspiration of poetry, will be treated lightly by no student of humanity.   But there is a certain lack of intellectual seriousness in taking it seriously as a thesis of meta-physical demonstration.[e]   Plato's belief in immortality was a conviction of the psychological and moral impossibility of sheer materialism, and a broad faith in the unseen, the spiritual, the ideal.   The logical obstacles to a positive demonstration of personal immortality were as obvious to him as they are to his critics.[f]   The immortality of the individual soul

---

[a] See also my review of Pater, *Plato and Platonism* in *The Dial*, xiv. (1893) p. 211.

[b] *Cf.* Bk. ii., esp. 367 B-E.

[c] *Cf. What Plato Said*, p. 251.

[d] *Cf.* 330 D-E and Vol. I. p. 16.

[e] *Cf. What Plato Said*, pp. 180, 177, 535.

[f] See my review of Gaye, *The Platonic Conception of Immortality*, in *Philos. Rev.* xiv., 1905, pp. 590-595.

INTRODUCTION

is for Plato a pious hope [a] and an ethical postulate [b]
rather than a demonstrable certainty.[c] He essays
various demonstrations, but nearly always in connexion with a myth, and of all the proofs attempted
but one is repeated.[d] In the *Apology* Socrates,
addressing his judges, affects to leave the question
open.[e] But we cannot infer from this that the
Apology antedates Plato's belief in immortality, and
Socrates' language in *Crito* 54 B is precisely in the
tone of the *Gorgias* and the *Phaedo*.[f]

Immortality was affirmed before Plato by Pythagorean and Orphic mystics, and in the magnificent
poetry of Pindar's *Second Olympian Ode* it is distinctly
associated with a doctrine of future rewards and
punishments. But Plato was the first great writer
to enforce it by philosophical arguments, or impress
it upon the imagination by vivid eschatological myths.
And the Platonic dialogues, as Rohde shows,[g] remained the chief source of the hopes and aspirations
of the educated minority throughout subsequent
antiquity. Plato's name was the symbol and rally-
ing point of the entire religious and philosophic

[a] *Phaedo* 114 D χρὴ τὰ τοιαῦτα ὥσπερ ἐπᾴδειν ἑαυτῷ, *Gorg.*
524 A-B, *Phaedo* 67 B.

[b] *Rep.* 608 c ff., *Laws* 881 A, 967 D-E, 959 A-B ; with τὸν
δὲ ὄντα ἡμῶν ἕκαστον ὄντως ἀθάνατον [εἶναι] ψυχήν cf.
Phaedo 115 D-E, and with the idea, 959 B, that the only
βοήθεια at the bar of Hades is a just life in this world, cf.
Gorg. 522 C-D, 526 E, *Crito* 54 B.

[c] *Phaedo* 85 c τὸ μὲν σαφὲς εἰδέναι ἐν τῷ νῦν βίῳ ἢ
ἀδύνατον εἶναι ἢ παγχάλεπόν τι. Cf. 107 A-B, *Tim.* 72 D,
Meno 86 A-B, *Phaedr.* 265 c.

[d] That based on the theory that the soul is the source of all
motion, *Phaedr.* 245 c ff., *Laws* 893 B ff.

[e] 40 D. Cf. also *Phaedo* 91 B.

[f] *Cratylus* 403 D-E implies the doctrine of *Phaedo* 67, 68.

[g] *Psyche* 5th and 6th ed., vol. ii. p. 265.

opposition to the dogmatic materialism of the Epicureans and of the positive wing of the Peripatetics. Cicero and Plutarch were in this his disciples. The more wistful and religious spirits of Stoicism—a Seneca, a Marcus Aurelius—came more and more to see in Platonism the hopeful " alternative " of the great perhaps. Neo-Platonists and Neo-Pythagoreans never grew weary of expanding and allegorizing the great myths of the *Gorgias*, *Phaedo*, and *Republic*. They were directly or indirectly the chief inspiration of the sixth book of the *Aeneid*, and in the majority of later sepulchral epigrams that express the hope of immortality a Platonic colouring is perceptible. All this was due far more to the spell of Plato's genius than to the force of his arguments. That the soul is the principle of motion (*Phaedr.* 245 c ff., *Laws* 893 b ff.), that it must have pre-existed because its apprehension of the ideas is reminiscence (*Phaedo* 72 e ff.), that it could be destroyed only by its own specific evil, injustice, which does not in fact destroy it (*Rep.* 608-611), that it cannot cease to exist because the idea of life which is essentially present with it will not admit its opposite (*Phaedo* 105 d-e)—these arguments may convince metaphysicians, but they will not stir the " emotion of conviction " that is fostered by the serene confidence of Socrates in the hour of death (*Phaedo* 114-118), by the vivid vision of the scarred and naked soul shivering at the bar of Rhadamanthus (*Gorg.* 524 d-e), by the detailed verisimilitude of the message brought back by the " Angel from there," Er, the son of Armenius (*Rep.* 614 b ff.).

The Epicureans and the more austere Stoics

INTRODUCTION

censured this mythological symbolism as unworthy of a philosopher ; and Emerson contrasts Plato's license of affirmation with the self-restraint of the Author of Christianity, who refused to entertain the populace with that picture. But Plato has anticipated their criticism, saying in substance : No reasonable man will affirm that these things are precisely as I have described them. But since the soul is immortal, something of the kind must be true, and we ought to repeat and croon it over to ourselves in order to keep faith and hope alive (*Phaedo* 114 D). This plea could be rejected only by those who are willing to affirm that Plato's poetical imaginings have been more harmful in the encouragement of superstition than helpful in the maintenance of religious hope and moral faith.[a]

But what of the metaphysical arguments ? Did Plato himself take them seriously ? And are they, therefore, to be taken seriously by the interpreters of his philosophy ? Are they essential links in a system ? Can we find in them clues to the progress and development of his thought and even date the dialogues with their aid ? It is not necessary to answer these questions here. On the validity of the arguments it would be idle to waste words. Some of them, reinforced by the *Theaetetus*, may help to show the inadequacy of a dogmatic materialistic psychology. At the most they prove the eternity of something other than " matter " which may be called " soul." They do not prove the immortality of the individual soul, which is nevertheless plainly taken as proved in the eschatological myths and their ethical applica-

[a] *Cf.* my article in the June, 1934, number of the *Atlantic Monthly*, p. 721.

tions. That the supreme dialectician, Plato, was himself unaware of that which is so readily perceived by every puny whipster who thinks to get his sword is to me unthinkable. A semblance of precedent proof was essential even to the literary effect of the concluding myths. And Plato himself in the *Laws* has warned us that an affirmative answer to some questions is required for the salvation of society and the moral government of mankind.[a]

But the myth itself is the really significant expression of Plato's hope and faith, and of its influence, hardly less than that of some national religions, upon the souls of men. After enumerating the blessings that normally attend the old age of the righteous man in this world, he says, we may fitly allow our imagination to dwell upon the rewards that await him in the world to come.

The enormous literature of the Platonic myths [b] deals partly with their conjectural sources, partly with their place and function in Plato's art and philosophy, and too little with the framework of definite meaning as distinguished from the remoter and more fanciful suggestions with which the ingenuity of commentators has sometimes obscured it. Leaving the translation and the notes to speak for themselves, I need here say only a few words on this last point.

[a] *Cf. supra*, p. li.
[b] *Cf., e.g.*, L. Couturat, *De mythis Platonicis*, Stewart, *The Myths of Plato*, with my review in *Journal of Philos., Psy. and Scientific Method*, 3, pp. 495-498; P. Frutiger, *Les Mythes de Platon*; Karl Reinhardt, *Platons Mythen*, Bonn, 1927; Friedländer, *Platon*, i. pp. 199 ff.; W. Willi, *Versuch einer Grundlegung der platonischen Mythopoiie*; J. Tate, "Socrates and the Myths," *Class. Quarterly*, xxvii. (April 1933) pp. 74-80; V. Brochard, "Les Mythes dans la philosophie de Platon," *L'Année Philos.*, 1900, pp. 1-13.

INTRODUCTION

If I may use without entirely adopting Professor Stewart's distinction between myth and allegory, the distinctive feature of the Platonic myth is that it embodies and reconciles the conflicting excellences of both—the transcendental feeling, the poetic mysticism of the true myth and the, to Professor Stewart, almost offensive lucidity of the allegory. In this it only exalts and intensifies a feature of Plato's style as a whole. He is unique in his power to reconcile formal dialectic and deliberate rhetoric with imagination and sincerity of feeling. He announces the effect that he intends to produce and produces it in defiance of the psychology of Goethe's "Da fühlt man Absicht und man wird verstimmt." He can pour his imagination, his poetry, his mysticism, his exhortation, and his edification into a predetermined logical mould. He modulates from one chord to the other at the precise moment when satiety begins.[a] He starts from a definition, proceeds by analysis and division through firstlies and secondlies to perorations that sweep the emotional reader off his feet and make him forget or deny the dialectic that conducted him to the mount of vision. As Emerson puts it, "He points and quibbles; and by and by comes a sentence that moves the sea and land." [b]

[a] *Cf.*, *e.g.*, *Phaedo* 115 A, 77 E-78 A, *Euthyphro* 6 B-C, 11 B-C, *Gorg.* 507 E. The little sermons scattered through the *Laws* have the same effect. *Cf.* in Goethe's *Faust* the chorus of angels followed by the devil. *Cf.* Carl Vering, *Platons Staat*, p. 7 " Ein Dialog Platons wirkt niemals ermüdend; jedesmal greift der Dichter Platon sofort ein, wenn der Philosoph durch ein schweres Problem dem Leser hart zugesetzt hat." *Cf.* also Sikes, *Greek View of Poetry*, p. 128.

[b] *Cf.*, *e.g.*, *Symp.* 211-212, *Gorgias*, *in fine*, *Phaedo* 114 c, *Rep.*, *in fine*.

INTRODUCTION

The definite thoughts embodied in the myth of Er the son of Armenius belong to Plato's permanent stock of opinions and do not differ appreciably from those of his other myths or the implied conclusions of his arguments.[a] The saving faith in immortality and judgement to come cannot rest on scientific demonstration only. It needs the confirmations of imagination, intuition, vision, revelation. The universe is a wonderful place whose structure is known to us only imperfectly and in part. Symbols are the fit expression of our dim apprehensions of its infinite possibilities. Heaven and hell are symbols of the most vital of all divisions, that which separates the virtuous from the vicious will. Purgatory may mark the distinction between remediable and curable wrong and that which admits of no pardon.[b] They are perhaps states of mind rather than places, but imagination may use what our imperfect science knows or divines of the world beneath our feet or the universe above our heads to give them a local habitation and a name, and our fancy may play in like manner with the ultimate unanswerable questions of philosophy: Whence comes evil[c]? and are our wills free[d]? If the soul is immortal and lives through endless transformations and transmigrations, it may be that the evil which baffles us here had its origin in some defect of will in worlds before the man (*Rep.* 613 A). Perhaps a great choice was offered to us and we chose wrong under the influence of mistaken ideas acquired in a former misspent life (618-619). Whatever the

---

[a] *Cf.* the notes on 614 ff.
[b] *Cf. What Plato Said*, p. 536, on *Phaedo* 113 D and 113 E.
[c] *Cf. What Plato Said*, p. 578, on *Theaet.* 176 A.
[d] *Cf. What Plato Said*, pp. 644-645, on *Laws* 904 C.

measure of truth in these fancies two principles of religion and morals stand fast. God is blameless (617 E), and we must always blame rather ourselves.[a] Our wills are somehow ours to make them his; though we must think of the sins of others as due solely to ignorance.[b] It matters not that the Aristotelians will argue that this is reasoning in a circle.[c] We know and must believe that virtue is free (617 E). And all the divinations of the soul and all the profounder interpretations of experience reiterate the lesson that the way of life that will present us fearless at the bar of eternal justice is the way that will yield the truest happiness here.[d] If we hold to that faith, then both in our earthly pilgrimage and in all the adventures of the soul hereafter, with us it will be well.

THE TEXT

As regards the text I have little to add to what was said in the first volume, except a few qualifications to avoid misunderstanding. I have tried to be a little more careful than I was in the first volume in correcting minor inconsistencies due to the reprinting of the Teubner text of Hermann. But the opportunities which these might afford to captious criticism do not in the least affect the main principle or its applications. That is simply that the variations between the

---

[a] Cf. Laws 727 B, Rep. 619 C, Phaedo 90 D, Cratyl. 411 C, etc.

[b] Cf. Protag. 345 D-E, 358 C-D, Laws 734 B, and What Plato Said, p. 640, on 860 D.

[c] Cf. Aristot. Eth. 1114 b 19.

[d] Rep. 621 C. Cf. Gorg. 526 D-E, Phaedo 114 E.

chief modern editions rarely make any difference for Plato's thought or even for his style, and that the decision between different readings in the case of Plato should usually turn, not on any scientific principle of text criticism, but on knowledge of Plato and knowledge of the Greek language. To put it drastically : for all practical purposes of the student of the Greek language, literature and philosophy, Hermann's text of the *Republic* is quite as good as the more scientific text of Burnet or the text that might be constructed from the critical notes in Wilamowitz' appendix. Hermann's judgement on questions of Greek idiom and Platonic usage was quite as good as theirs. This is not meant as an illiberal disparagement of the great and indispensable special disciplines of text criticism and palaeography. It is merely a commonsense vindication of the intellectual right of those who prefer to do so to approach the study of Plato from another point of view.

THE TRANSLATION

As regards the translation, I impenitently reaffirm the principles that I stated in the preface to the first volume—whatever errors of judgement I may commit in their application. Much of the *Republic* can be made easy reading for any literate reader. But some of the subtler and more metaphysical passages can be translated in that way only at the cost of misrepresentation of the meaning. In order to bring out the real significance of Plato's thought it is sometimes necessary to translate the same phrase in two ways, sometimes to vary a phrase which Plato repeats or

lxxii

INTRODUCTION

repeat a synonym which he prefers to vary. It is often desirable to use two words to suggest the twofold associations of one. To take the simplest example, it is even more misleading to translate *eidos* " Form " than it is to translate it " idea "—" idea or form " (without a capital letter) is less likely to be misunderstood.

Again, Plato did not write in the smooth, even style which Dionysius of Halicarnassus admired in Lysias and Matthew Arnold in Addison, and it is not the business of the translator to clothe him in the garb of that style.

Provided the meaning is plain and the emphasis right, he allows himself unlimited freedom in anacoluthons, short cuts, sharp corners, ellipses and generally in what I have elsewhere called illogical idiom. Anyone who does not like that style should give his days and nights to the study of Isocrates and Lysias. According to his mood and the context Plato's style ranges from Attic simplicity to metaphysical abstraction, from high-flown poetical prose to plain colloquial diction. And his colloquialism, though usually kept within the bounds of Attic urbanity, is not lacking in Aristophanic touches which, if rightly rendered, shock the taste of critics who approach him with a stronger sense of the dignity of philosophy than they have of Greek idiom. In deference to friendly criticism I have generally suppressed or transferred to footnotes my attempts to reproduce this feature of Plato's style. But I am not convinced. As Taine aptly says (*Life and Letters*, p. 53), " M. Cousin's elegant Plato is not at all like the easy . . . but always natural Plato of reality. He would shock us if we saw him as he is."

PLATO
THE REPUBLIC
BOOKS VI—X

ΠΟΛΙΤΕΙΑ

[Η ΠΕΡΙ ΔΙΚΑΙΟΥ, ΠΟΛΙΤΙΚΟΣ]

TA TOY ΔΙΑΛΟΓΟΥ ΠΡΟΣΩΠΑ

ΣΩΚΡΑΤΗΣ, ΓΛΑΥΚΩΝ, ΠΟΛΕΜΑΡΧΟΣ, ΘΡΑΣΥΜΑΧΟΣ,

ΑΔΕΙΜΑΝΤΟΣ, ΚΕΦΑΛΟΣ

ς

I. Οἱ μὲν δὴ φιλόσοφοι, ἦν δ' ἐγώ, ὦ Γλαύκων,
καὶ οἱ μὴ διὰ μακροῦ τινος διεξελθόντος[1] λόγου
μόγις πως ἀνεφάνησαν οἵ εἰσιν ἑκάτεροι. Ἴσως
γάρ, ἔφη, διὰ βραχέος οὐ ῥᾴδιον. Οὐ φαίνεται,
εἶπον· ἐμοὶ γοῦν ἔτι δοκεῖ ἂν βελτιόνως φανῆναι εἰ
περὶ τούτου μόνου ἔδει ῥηθῆναι, καὶ μὴ πολλὰ τὰ
λοιπὰ διελθεῖν μέλλοντι κατόψεσθαι τί διαφέρει
B βίος δίκαιος ἀδίκου. Τί οὖν, ἔφη, τὸ μετὰ τοῦτο
ἡμῖν; Τί δ' ἄλλο, ἦν δ' ἐγώ, ἢ τὸ ἑξῆς; ἐπειδὴ
φιλόσοφοι μὲν οἱ τοῦ ἀεὶ κατὰ ταὐτὰ ὡσαύτως
ἔχοντος δυνάμενοι ἐφάπτεσθαι, οἱ δὲ μὴ ἀλλ' ἐν

[1] διεξελθόντος ADM, διεξελθόντες F.

---

[a] The argument is slightly personified. *Cf.* on 503 A.
[b] It is captious to object that the actual discussion of the
philosopher occupies only a few pages.
[c] This is the main theme of the *Republic*, of which Plato
never loses sight.

2

THE REPUBLIC

[OR ON JUSTICE : POLITICAL]

CHARACTERS

Socrates, Glaucon, Polemarchus, Thrasymachus,
Adeimantus, Cephalus

BOOK VI

I. " So now, Glaucon," I said, " our argument after
winding[a] a long[b] and weary way has at last made clear
to us who are the philosophers or lovers of wisdom
and who are not." " Yes," he said, " a shorter way
is perhaps not feasible." " Apparently not," I said.
" I, at any rate, think that the matter would have
been made still plainer if we had had nothing but this
to speak of, and if there were not so many things left
which our purpose[c] of discerning the difference between the just and the unjust life requires us to
discuss." " What, then," he said, " comes next ? "
" What else," said I, " but the next in order ? Since
the philosophers are those who are capable of appre-
hending that which is eternal and unchanging,[d] while
those who are incapable of this, but lose themselves and

---

[d] For κατὰ ταὐτὰ ὡσαύτως ἔχοντος cf. Phaedo 78 c, Soph.
248 A, Tim. 41 D, 82 B, Epin. 982 B and E.

3

PLATO

484 πολλοῖς καὶ παντοίως ἴσχουσι πλανώμενοι οὐ φιλόσοφοι, ποτέρους δὴ δεῖ πόλεως ἡγεμόνας εἶναι;
Πῶς οὖν λέγοντες ἂν αὐτό, ἔφη, μετρίως λέγοιμεν;
Ὁπότεροι ἄν, ἦν δ' ἐγώ, δυνατοὶ φαίνωνται
φυλάξαι νόμους τε καὶ ἐπιτηδεύματα πόλεων,
C τούτους καθιστάναι φύλακας. Ὀρθῶς, ἔφη. Τόδε
δέ, ἦν δ' ἐγώ, ἆρα δῆλον, εἴτε τυφλὸν εἴτε ὀξὺ
ὁρῶντα χρὴ φύλακα τηρεῖν ὁτιοῦν; Καὶ πῶς,
ἔφη, οὐ δῆλον; Ἦ οὖν δοκοῦσί τι τυφλῶν
διαφέρειν οἱ τῷ ὄντι τοῦ ὄντος ἑκάστου ἐστερημέ-
νοι τῆς γνώσεως, καὶ μηδὲν ἐναργὲς ἐν τῇ ψυχῇ
ἔχοντες παράδειγμα, μηδὲ δυνάμενοι ὥσπερ γραφεῖς
εἰς τὸ ἀληθέστατον ἀποβλέποντες κἀκεῖσε ἀεὶ
ἀναφέροντές τε καὶ θεώμενοι ὡς οἷόν τε ἀκριβέ-
D στατα, οὕτω δὴ καὶ τὰ ἐνθάδε νόμιμα καλῶν τε
πέρι καὶ δικαίων καὶ ἀγαθῶν τίθεσθαί τε, ἐὰν δέῃ
τίθεσθαι, καὶ τὰ κείμενα φυλάττοντες σώζειν; Οὐ
μὰ τὸν Δία, ἦ δ' ὅς, οὐ πολύ τι διαφέρει. Τούτους
οὖν μᾶλλον φύλακας στησόμεθα, ἢ τοὺς ἐγνωκότας
μὲν ἕκαστον τὸ ὄν, ἐμπειρίᾳ δὲ μηδὲν ἐκείνων
ἐλλείποντας μηδ' ἐν ἄλλῳ μηδενὶ μέρει ἀρετῆς
ὑστεροῦντας; Ἄτοπον μέντ' ἄν, ἔφη, εἴη ἄλλους
αἱρεῖσθαι, εἴ γε τἆλλα μὴ ἐλλείποιντο· τούτῳ γὰρ
485 αὐτῷ σχεδόν τι τῷ μεγίστῳ ἂν προέχοιεν. Οὐκοῦν
τοῦτο δὴ λέγωμεν, τίνα τρόπον οἷοί τ' ἔσονται οἱ

---

[a] Cf. p. 89, note h, on 505 c.
[b] Cf. Luke vi. 39, Matt. xv. 14, John xix. 39-41.
[c] Cf. Polit. 277 B, 277 D f., etc., Soph. 226 c, Parmen.
132 D.
[d] ἀποβλέποντες belongs to the terminology of the ideas.
Cf. supra 472 c, Cratyl. 389 A, Gorg. 503 E, Tim. 28 A,
Prot. 354 c, and my What Plato Said, p. 458 on Euthyph. 6 E.

4

wander[a] amid the multiplicities of multifarious things,
are not philosophers, which of the two kinds ought to
be the leaders in a state?" "What, then," he said,
"would be a fair statement of the matter?" "Which-
ever," I said, "appear competent to guard the laws
and pursuits of society, these we should establish as
guardians." "Right," he said. "Is this, then," said
I, "clear, whether the guardian who is to keep watch
over anything ought to be blind or keen of sight?"
"Of course it is clear," he said. "Do you think,
then, that there is any appreciable difference between
the blind[b] and those who are veritably deprived of the
knowledge of the veritable being of things, those who
have no vivid pattern[c] in their souls and so cannot,
as painters look to their models, fix their eyes[d] on
the absolute truth, and always with reference to that
ideal and in the exactest possible contemplation of
it establish in this world also the laws of the beautiful,
the just and the good, when that is needful, or guard
and preserve those that are established?" "No,
by heaven," he said, "there is not much difference."
"Shall we, then, appoint these blind souls as our
guardians, rather than those who have learned to know
the ideal reality of things and who do not fall short
of the others in experience[e] and are not second to
them in any part of virtue?" "It would be strange
indeed," he said, "to choose others than the philosophers, provided they were not deficient in those
other respects, for this very knowledge of the ideal
would perhaps be the greatest of superiorities."
"Then what we have to say is how it would be possible for the same persons to have both qualifications,

[e] *Cf. infra* 539 E, 521 B, *Phileb.* 62. *Cf.* Introd. p. xl;
Apelt, *Republic*, p. 490.

485 αὐτοὶ κἀκεῖνα καὶ ταῦτα ἔχειν; Πάνυ μὲν οὖν. Ὁ
τοίνυν ἀρχόμενοι τούτου τοῦ λόγου ἐλέγομεν, τὴν
φύσιν αὐτῶν πρῶτον δεῖν καταμαθεῖν· καὶ οἶμαι,
ἐὰν ἐκείνην ἱκανῶς ὁμολογήσωμεν, ὁμολογήσειν καὶ
ὅτι οἷοί τε ταῦτα ἔχειν οἱ αὐτοί, ὅτι τε οὐκ ἄλλους
πόλεων ἡγεμόνας δεῖ εἶναι ἢ τούτους. Πῶς;

II. Τοῦτο μὲν δὴ τῶν φιλοσόφων φύσεων πέρι
B ὡμολογήσθω ἡμῖν, ὅτι μαθήματός γε ἀεὶ ἐρῶσιν,
ὃ ἂν αὐτοῖς δηλοῖ ἐκείνης τῆς οὐσίας τῆς ἀεὶ οὔσης
καὶ μὴ·πλανωμένης ὑπὸ γενέσεως καὶ φθορᾶς.
Ὡμολογήσθω. Καὶ μήν, ἦν δ᾽ ἐγώ, καὶ ὅτι πάσης
αὐτῆς, καὶ οὔτε σμικροῦ οὔτε μείζονος οὔτε τιμιω-
τέρου οὔτε ἀτιμοτέρου μέρους ἑκόντες ἀφίενται,
ὥσπερ ἐν τοῖς πρόσθεν περί τε τῶν φιλοτίμων καὶ
ἐρωτικῶν διήλθομεν. Ὀρθῶς, ἔφη, λέγεις. Τόδε
τοίνυν μετὰ τοῦτο σκόπει εἰ ἀνάγκη ἔχειν πρὸς
C τούτῳ ἐν τῇ φύσει, οἳ ἂν μέλλωσι ἔσεσθαι οἵους
ἐλέγομεν. Τὸ ποῖον; Τὴν ἀψεύδειαν καὶ τὸ
ἑκόντας εἶναι μηδαμῇ προσδέχεσθαι τὸ ψεῦδος,
ἀλλὰ μισεῖν, τὴν δ᾽ ἀλήθειαν στέργειν. Εἰκός γ᾽,
ἔφη. Οὐ μόνον γε, ὦ φίλε, εἰκός, ἀλλὰ καὶ πᾶσα
ἀνάγκη τὸν ἐρωτικῶς του φύσει ἔχοντα πᾶν τὸ
ξυγγενές τε καὶ οἰκεῖον τῶν παιδικῶν ἀγαπᾶν.
Ὀρθῶς, ἔφη. Ἦ οὖν οἰκειότερον σοφίᾳ τι ἀληθείας ἂν εὕροις; Καὶ πῶς; ἦ δ᾽ ὅς. Ἦ οὖν
δυνατὸν εἶναι τὴν αὐτὴν φύσιν φιλόσοφόν τε καὶ

---

[a] Lit. " is not made to wander by generation and decay."
Cf. *Crat.* 411 c, *Phaedo* 95 ᴇ, whence Aristotle took his title.
See *Class. Phil.* xvii. (1922) pp. 334-352.

[b] *Supra* 474 c-ᴅ.

[c] For similar expressions cf. 519 ʙ, *Laws* 656 ʙ, 965 c,
Symp. 200 ᴀ.

[d] This and many other passages prove Plato's high regard

is it not ? " " Quite so." " Then, as we were saying at the beginning of this discussion, the first thing to understand is the nature that they must have from birth ; and I think that if we sufficiently agree on this we shall also agree that the combination of qualities that we seek belongs to the same persons, and that we need no others for guardians of states than these." " How so ? "

II. " We must accept as agreed this trait of the philosophical nature, that it is ever enamoured of the kind of knowledge which reveals to them something of that essence which is eternal, and is not wandering between the two poles of generation and decay.[a] " " Let us take that as agreed." " And, further," said I, " that their desire is for the whole of it and that they do not willingly renounce a small or a great, a more precious or a less honoured, part of it. That was the point of our former illustration [b] drawn from lovers and men covetous of honour." " You are right," he said. " Consider, then, next whether the men who are to meet our requirements must not have this further quality in their natures." " What quality ? " " The spirit of truthfulness, reluctance to admit falsehood in any form, the hatred of it and the love of truth." " It is likely," he said. " It is not only likely, my friend, but there is every necessity [c] that he who is by nature enamoured of anything should cherish all that is akin and pertaining to the object of his love." " Right," he said. " Could you find anything more akin to wisdom than truth [d] ? " " Impossible," he said. " Then can the same nature be a lover of

for the truth. *Cf. Laws* 730 c, 861 D, *Crat.* 428 D, *supra* 382 A. In 389 B he only permits falsehood to the rulers as a drastic remedy to be used with care for edification. *Cf.* Vol. I. on 382 c and D.

PLATO

485 D φιλοψευδῆ; Οὐδαμῶς γε. Τὸν ἄρα τῷ ὄντι
φιλομαθῆ πάσης ἀληθείας δεῖ εὐθὺς ἐκ νέου ὅ τι
μάλιστα ὀρέγεσθαι. Παντελῶς γε. Ἀλλὰ μὴν
ὅτῳ γε εἰς ἕν τι αἱ ἐπιθυμίαι σφόδρα ῥέπουσιν,
ἴσμεν που ὅτι εἰς τἆλλα τούτῳ ἀσθενέστεραι,
ὥσπερ ῥεῦμα ἐκεῖσε ἀπωχετευμένον. Τί μήν;
Ὧι δὴ πρὸς τὰ μαθήματα καὶ πᾶν τὸ τοιοῦτον
ἐρρυήκασι, περὶ τὴν τῆς ψυχῆς, οἶμαι, ἡδονὴν αὐτῆς καθ᾽ αὑτὴν εἶεν ἄν, τὰς δὲ διὰ τοῦ σώματος
ἐκλείποιεν, εἰ μὴ πεπλασμένως ἀλλ᾽ ἀληθῶς φιλό-
E σοφός τις εἴη. Μεγάλη ἀνάγκη. Σώφρων μὴν ὅ
γε τοιοῦτος καὶ οὐδαμῇ φιλοχρήματος· ὧν γὰρ
ἕνεκα χρήματα μετὰ πολλῆς δαπάνης σπουδάζεται,
ἄλλῳ τινὶ μᾶλλον ἢ τούτῳ προσήκει σπουδάζειν.
Οὕτως. Καὶ μήν που καὶ τόδε δεῖ σκοπεῖν, ὅταν
486 κρίνειν μέλλῃς φύσιν φιλόσοφόν τε καὶ μή. Τὸ
ποῖον; Μή σε λάθῃ μετέχουσα ἀνελευθερίας·
ἐναντιώτατον γάρ που σμικρολογία ψυχῇ μελλούσῃ
τοῦ ὅλου καὶ παντὸς ἀεὶ ἐπορέξεσθαι θείου τε καὶ
ἀνθρωπίνου. Ἀληθέστατα, ἔφη. Ἧι οὖν ὑπάρχει διανοίᾳ μεγαλοπρέπεια καὶ θεωρία παντὸς μὲν
χρόνου, πάσης δὲ οὐσίας, οἷόν τε οἴει τούτῳ μέγα

---

[a] For this figure cf. Laws 844 A and 736 B, Eurip. Suppl.
1111 παρεκτρέποντες ὀχετόν, Empedocles, Diels[1] 195 λόγου
λόγον ἐξοχετεύων, Lucretius ii. 365 "derivare queunt animum"; and for the idea cf. also Laws 643 C-D.

[b] Cf. my Unity of Plato's Thought, pp. 45-46, esp. n. 330,
followed by Apelt, Republic, pp. 490-491. Cf. also Friedländer, Platon, ii. pp. 579-580, 584.

[c] For πεπλασμένως cf. Soph. 216 c μὴ πλαστῶς ἀλλ᾽ ὄντως
φιλόσοφοι.

[d] Cf. Theaet. 144 D χρημάτων ἐλευθεριότητα.

8

wisdom and of falsehood ? " " By no means."
" Then the true lover of knowledge must, from childhood up, be most of all a striver after truth in every
form." " By all means." " But, again, we surely
are aware that when in a man the desires incline
strongly to any one thing, they are weakened for
other things. It is as if the stream had been diverted
into another channel.ᵃ " " Surely." " So, when a
man's desires have been taught to flow in the channel
of learning and all that sort of thing, they will be concerned, I presume, with the pleasures of the soul in
itself, and will be indifferent to those of which the body
is the instrument,ᵇ if the man is a true and not a sham ᶜ
philosopher." "That is quite necessary." "Such a man
will be temperate and by no means greedy for wealth ;
for the things for the sake of which money and great
expenditure are eagerly sought others may take
seriously, but not he." " It is so." " And there is
this further point to be considered in distinguishing
the philosophical from the unphilosophical nature."
" What point ? " " You must not overlook any
touch of illiberality.ᵈ For nothing can be more contrary than such pettiness to the quality of a soul that
is ever to seek integrity and wholenessᵉ in all things
human and divine." " Most true," he said. " Do you
think that a mind habituated to thoughts of grandeur
and the contemplation of all time and all existence ᶠ

ᵉ Cf. Goethe's " Im Ganzen, Guten, Schönen resolut zu
leben."

ᶠ Cf. Theaet. 174 E, of the philosopher, εἰς ἅπασαν εἰωθὼς
τὴν γῆν βλέπειν, and 173 E, infra 500 B-C. Cf. Marc. Aurel.
vii. 35, Livy xxiv. 34 " Archimedes is erat unicus spectator
caeli siderumque," Mayor, Cic. De nat. deor. ii. p. 128.

For πᾶς χρόνος cf. infra 498 D, 608 C, Phaedo 107 C, Gorg.
525 C, Apol. 40 E, Tim. 36 E, 47 B, 90 D. Cf. Isoc. i. 11,
Pindar, Pyth. i. 46.

PLATO

486 τι δοκεῖν εἶναι τὸν ἀνθρώπινον βίον; Ἀδύνατον,
B ἦ δ' ὅς. Οὐκοῦν καὶ θάνατον οὐ δεινόν τι ἡγήσεται
ὁ τοιοῦτος; Ἥκιστά γε. Δειλῇ δὴ καὶ ἀνελευ-
θέρῳ φύσει φιλοσοφίας ἀληθινῆς, ὡς ἔοικεν, οὐκ
ἂν μετείη. Οὔ μοι δοκεῖ. Τί οὖν; ὁ κόσμιος καὶ
μὴ φιλοχρήματος μηδ' ἀνελεύθερος μηδ' ἀλαζὼν
μηδὲ δειλὸς ἔσθ' ὅπῃ ἂν δυσσύμβολος ἢ ἄδικος
γένοιτο; Οὐκ ἔστιν. Καὶ τοῦτο δὴ ψυχὴν σκοπῶν
φιλόσοφον καὶ μὴ εὐθὺς νέου ὄντος ἐπισκέψει, εἰ
ἄρα δικαία τε καὶ ἥμερος ἢ δυσκοινώνητος καὶ
ἀγρία. Πάνυ μὲν οὖν. Οὐ μὴν οὐδὲ τόδε παρα-
C λείψεις, ὡς ἐγῷμαι. Τὸ ποῖον; Εὐμαθὴς ἢ δυσ-
μαθής. ἢ προσδοκᾷς ποτέ τινά τι ἱκανῶς ἂν
στέρξαι, ὃ πράττων ἂν ἀλγῶν τε πράττοι καὶ μόγις
σμικρὸν ἀνύτων; Οὐκ ἂν γένοιτο. Τί δ'; εἰ
μηδὲν ὧν μάθοι σώζειν δύναιτο, λήθης ὢν πλέως,
ἆρ' ἂν οἷός τ' εἴη ἐπιστήμης μὴ κενὸς εἶναι; Καὶ
πῶς; Ἀνόνητα δὴ πονῶν οὐκ, οἴει, ἀναγκασθήσεται τελευτῶν αὑτόν τε μισεῖν καὶ τὴν τοιαύτην
D πρᾶξιν; Πῶς δ' οὔ; Ἐπιλήσμονα ἄρα ψυχὴν ἐν
ταῖς ἱκανῶς φιλοσόφοις μή ποτε ἐγκρίνωμεν, ἀλλὰ
μνημονικὴν αὐτὴν ζητῶμεν δεῖν εἶναι. Παντάπασι
μὲν οὖν. Ἀλλ' οὐ μὴν τό γε τῆς ἀμούσου τε καὶ
ἀσχήμονος φύσεως ἄλλοσέ ποι ἂν φαῖμεν ἕλκειν ἢ

---

[a] Cf. Aristot. *Eth. Nic.* 1123 b 32, the great-souled man,
ᾧ γ' οὐδὲν μέγα, Diog. Laert. vii. 128 πάντων ὑπεράνω, Cic.
De fin. iii. 8 "infra se omnia humana ducens." *Cf. infra*
on 500 B-C.

For similar pessimistic utterances about human life and
mankind *cf.* 604 B-C, 496 D-E, 500 B-C, 516 D, *Laws* 803 B.
Cf. also *Laws* 708 E-709 B.

[b] *Cf.* Vol. I. pp. 200 f. on 386 B-C; *Laws* 727 D, 828 D,
881 A, *Gorg.* 522 E, *Phaedo* 77 E, *Crito* 43 B, *Apol.* 35 A,

can deem this life of man a thing of great concern[a]?"
"Impossible," said he. "Hence such a man will not
suppose death to be terrible?[b]" "Least of all."
"Then a cowardly and illiberal spirit, it seems, could
have no part in genuine philosophy." "I think not."
"What then? Could a man of orderly spirit, not a
lover of money, not illiberal, nor a braggart nor a
coward, ever prove unjust, or a driver of hard bar-
gains[c]?" "Impossible." "This too, then, is a
point that in your discrimination of the philosophic
and unphilosophic soul you will observe—whether
the man is from youth up just and gentle or unsocial
and savage.[d]" "Assuredly." "Nor will you overlook this, I fancy." "What?" "Whether he is
quick or slow to learn. Or do you suppose that anyone
could properly love a task which he performed pain-
fully[e] and with little result[f] from much toil?" "That
could not be." "And if he could not keep what he
learned, being steeped in oblivion,[g] could he fail to
be void of knowledge?" "How could he?" "And
so, having all his labour for naught, will he not finally
be constrained to loathe himself and that occupation?"
"Of course." "The forgetful soul, then, we must
not list in the roll of competent lovers of wisdom, but
we require a good memory." "By all means."
"But assuredly we should not say that the want of
harmony and seemliness in a nature conduces to
anything else than the want of measure and propor-

---

40 c. *Cf.* Spinoza's "There is nothing of which the free
man thinks so little as death."

[c] *Cf. supra*, Vol. I. on 442 E. [d] *Cf.* 375 B.

[e] *Cf. Laches* 189 A-B ἀηδῶς μανθάνων.

[f] *Cf. Theaet.* 144 B.

[g] *Cf. Theaet.* 144 B λήθης γέμοντες. *Cf.* Cleopatra's "Oh,
my oblivion is a very Antony" (*Ant. and Cleo.* I. iii. 90).

486 εἰς ἀμετρίαν. Τί μήν; Ἀλήθειαν δὲ ἀμετρίᾳ
ἡγεῖ ξυγγενῆ εἶναι ἢ ἐμμετρίᾳ; Ἐμμετρίᾳ. Ἔμ-
μετρον ἄρα καὶ εὔχαριν ζητῶμεν πρὸς τοῖς ἄλλοις
διάνοιαν φύσει, ἣν ἐπὶ τὴν τοῦ ὄντος ἰδέαν ἑκά-
E στου τὸ αὐτοφυὲς εὐάγωγον παρέξει. Πῶς δ' οὔ;
Τί οὖν; μή πῃ δοκοῦμέν σοι οὐκ ἀναγκαῖα
ἕκαστα διεληλυθέναι καὶ ἑπόμενα ἀλλήλοις τῇ
μελλούσῃ τοῦ ὄντος ἱκανῶς τε καὶ τελέως ψυχῇ
487 μεταλήψεσθαι; Ἀναγκαιότατα μὲν οὖν, ἔφη.
Ἔστιν οὖν ὅπῃ μέμψει τοιοῦτον ἐπιτήδευμα, ὃ μή
ποτ' ἄν τις οἷός τε γένοιτο ἱκανῶς ἐπιτηδεῦσαι,
εἰ μὴ φύσει εἴη μνήμων, εὐμαθής, μεγαλοπρεπής,
εὔχαρις, φίλος τε καὶ ξυγγενὴς ἀληθείας, δικαιοσύνης, ἀνδρείας, σωφροσύνης; Οὐδ' ἂν ὁ Μῶμος,
ἔφη, τό γε τοιοῦτον μέμψαιτο. Ἀλλ', ἦν δ' ἐγώ,
τελειωθεῖσι τοῖς τοιούτοις παιδείᾳ τε καὶ ἡλικίᾳ
ἆρα οὐ μόνοις ἂν τὴν πόλιν ἐπιτρέποις;

III. Καὶ ὁ Ἀδείμαντος, Ὦ Σώκρατες, ἔφη,
B πρὸς μὲν ταῦτά σοι οὐδεὶς ἂν οἷός τ' εἴη ἀντειπεῖν·
ἀλλὰ γὰρ τοιόνδε τι πάσχουσιν οἱ ἀκούοντες

---

[a] ἰδέαν is not exactly "idea." *Cf. Cratyl.* 389 B, *What
Plato Said*, p. 458 on *Euthyph.* 6 D, *ibid.* p. 560 on *Rep.*
369 A and p. 585 on *Parmen.* 130 C-D. *Cf. Class. Phil.* xx.
(1925) p. 347.

[b] Lit. "following one upon the other." *Cf. Tim.* 27 c
ἑπομένως, *Laws* 844 E.

[c] μεγαλοπρεπής is frequently ironical in Plato, but not here.
For the list of qualities of the ideal student *cf.* also 503 c,
Theaet. 144 A-B, and Friedländer, *Platon,* ii. p. 418. *Cf. Laws*
709 E on the qualifications of the young tyrant, and Cic.
Tusc. v. 24, with Renaissance literature on education.

[d] The god of censure, who finds fault with the gods in
Lucian's dialogues. *Cf.* Overbeck, *Schriftquellen,* p. 208,

12

tion." "Certainly." "And do you think that truth is akin to measure and proportion or to disproportion?" "To proportion." "Then in addition to our other requirements we look for a mind endowed with measure and grace, whose native disposition will make it easily guided to the aspect of the ideal[a] reality in all things." "Assuredly." "Tell me, then, is there any flaw in the argument? Have we not proved the qualities enumerated to be necessary and compatible[b] with one another for the soul that is to have a sufficient and perfect apprehension of reality?" "Nay, most necessary," he said. "Is there any fault, then, that you can find with a pursuit which a man could not properly practise unless he were by nature of good memory, quick apprehension, magnificent,[c] gracious, friendly and akin to truth, justice, bravery and sobriety?" "Momus[d] himself," he said, "could not find fault with such a combination." "Well, then," said I, "when men of this sort are perfected by education and maturity of age, would you not entrust the state solely to them?"

III. And Adeimantus said, "No one, Socrates, would be able to controvert these statements of yours. But, all the same, those who occasionally hear you[e]

n. 1091, Otto, p. 227, s.v. Momus. *Cf.* Callimachus, fr. 70: and *Anth. Pal.* xvi. 262. 3-4:

αὐτὸς ὁ Μῶμος
φθέγξεται, Ἄκρητος, Ζεῦ πάτερ, ἡ σοφίη,

"Momus himself will cry out 'Father Zeus, this was perfect skill.'" (L.C.L. translation.) Stallbaum refers to Erasmus, *Chiliad*, i. 5. 75 and interpreters on Aristaenet. *Epist.* i. 1, p. 239, ed. Boissonade.

[e] *Cf. Unity of Plato's Thought*, p. 35, n. 236, and *What Plato Said*, p. 468 on *Crito* 46 B. A speaker in Plato may thus refer to any fundamental Platonic doctrine. Wilamowitz' suggested emendation (*Platon*, ii. p. 205) ἃ ἂν λέγῃς is due to a misunderstanding of this.

13

487 ἑκάστοτε ἃ νῦν λέγεις· ἡγοῦνται δι' ἀπειρίαν τοῦ
ἐρωτᾶν καὶ ἀποκρίνεσθαι ὑπὸ τοῦ λόγου παρ'
ἕκαστον·τὸ ἐρώτημα σμικρὸν παραγόμενοι, ἀθροι-
σθέντων τῶν σμικρῶν ἐπὶ τελευτῆς τῶν λόγων
μέγα τὸ σφάλμα καὶ ἐναντίον τοῖς πρώτοις ἀναφαί-
νεσθαι, καὶ ὥσπερ ὑπὸ τῶν πεττεύειν δεινῶν οἱ
μὴ τελευτῶντες ἀποκλείονται καὶ οὐκ ἔχουσιν ὅ
C τι φέρωσιν, οὕτω καὶ σφεῖς τελευτῶντες ἀποκλεί-
εσθαι, καὶ οὐκ ἔχειν ὅ τι λέγωσιν ὑπὸ πεττείας αὖ
ταύτης τινὸς ἑτέρας, οὐκ ἐν ψήφοις ἀλλ' ἐν λόγοις·
ἐπεὶ τό γε ἀληθὲς οὐδέν τι μᾶλλον ταύτῃ ἔχειν.
λέγω δ' εἰς τὸ παρὸν ἀποβλέψας. νῦν γὰρ φαίη
ἄν τίς σοι λόγῳ μὲν οὐκ ἔχειν καθ' ἕκαστον τὸ
ἐρωτώμενον ἐναντιοῦσθαι, ἔργῳ δὲ ὁρᾶν, ὅσοι ἂν

---

[a] A *locus classicus* for Plato's anticipation of objections.
Cf. 475 B, *Theaet.* 166 A-B, *Rep.* 609 c, 438-439, and Apelt,
Republic, p. 492.   Plato does it more tactfully than Isocrates,
e.g. Demon. 44.
[b] *Cf.* Apelt, *Aufsätze*, p. 73, Minto, *Logic, Induction and
Deduction*, pp. 4 ff.; also *Gorg.* 461 D, 462 A, *Soph.* 230 B.
[c] *Cf. Phaedrus* 262 B.
[d] *Cf. supra* 451 A, and *Theaet.* 166 A, 168 A, *infra* 534 c
ἁπτῶτι.
[e] *Cf. Phaedr.* 262 B, *Cleitophon* 410 A, *Gorg.* 495 A, schol.,
τοὺς πρώτους λόγους τοὺς ἑαυτοῦ δηλονότι, *Gorg.* 457 E οἷς τὸ
πρῶτον ἔλεγες, and also Agathon in *Symp.* 201 B.
[f] For this figure *cf. Laws* 739 A, 820 c-D, 903 D, *Eryxias*
395 A-B, *Hipparchus* 229 E, Eurip. *Suppl.* 409.
Aristotle, *Soph. El.* 165 a 10 ff., borrows the metaphor, but
his ψῆφοι are those of book-keeping or reckoning. *Cf.* also
Dem. *De cor.* 227 f.
[g] *Cf. Hipp. Minor* 369 B-c and Grote ii. p. 64 " Though
Hippias admits each successive step he still mistrusts the
conclusion "; also Apelt, p. 492, *supra* 357 A-B and *Laws*
903 A βιάζεσθαι τοῖς λόγοις, and also *Hipparchus* 232 B for

argue thus feel in this way [a] : They think that owing to their inexperience in the game of question and answer [b] they are at every question led astray [c] a little bit by the argument, and when these bits are accumulated at the conclusion of the discussion mighty is their fall [d] and the apparent contradiction of what they at first said [e]; and that just as by expert draught-players [f] the unskilled are finally shut in and cannot make a move, so they are finally blocked and have their mouths stopped by this other game of draughts played not with counters but with words ; yet the truth is not affected by that outcome. [g] I say this with reference to the present case, for in this instance one might say that he is unable in words to contend against you at each question, but that when it comes to facts [h] he sees that of those who turn to philosophy, [i]

the idea that dialectic constrains rather than persuades. In the *Ion*, 533 c, Ion says he cannot ἀντιλέγειν, but the fact remains that he knows Homer but not other poets. *Cf.* also 536 D. The passage virtually anticipates Bacon's *Novum Organum*, App. XIII. "(syllogismus) . . . assensum itaque constringit, non res." *Cf.* Cic. *De fin.* iv. 3, *Tusc.* i. 8. 16, and the proverbial οὐ γὰρ πείσεις, οὐδ' ἢν πείσῃς, Aristoph. *Plutus* 600.

[h] See *Soph.* 234 E for a different application of the same idea. There is no change of opinion. The commonplace Greek contrast of word and deed, theory and fact, is valid against eristic but not against dialectic. See *What Plato Said*, p. 534 on *Phaedo* 99 E, and *supra* on 473 A; also *What Plato Said*, p. 625 on *Laws* 636 A.

A favourite formula of Aristotle runs, "This is true in theory and is confirmed by facts." *Cf. Eth. Nic.* 1099 b 25, 1123 b 22, 1131 a 13, *Pol.* 1323 a 39-b 6, 1326 a 25 and 29, 1334 a 5-6.

[i] Scholars in politics cut a sorry figure. For this popular view of philosophers *cf. Theaet.* 173 c ff., 174 c-D, *Gorg.* 484-486 c, *Phaedo* 64 B. *Cf.* also Isoc. *passim*, *e.g. Antid.* 250, 312.

487 ἐπὶ φιλοσοφίαν ὁρμήσαντες μὴ τοῦ πεπαιδεῦσθαι
D ἕνεκα ἁψάμενοι νέοι ὄντες ἀπαλλάττωνται, ἀλλὰ
μακρότερον ἐνδιατρίψωσι, τοὺς μὲν πλείστους καὶ
πάνυ ἀλλοκότους γιγνομένους, ἵνα μὴ παμπονή-
ρους εἴπωμεν, τοὺς δ᾽ ἐπιεικεστάτους δοκοῦντας
ὅμως τοῦτό γε ὑπὸ τοῦ ἐπιτηδεύματος οὗ σὺ
ἐπαινεῖς πάσχοντας, ἀχρήστους ταῖς πόλεσι γιγνομένους. καὶ ἐγὼ ἀκούσας, Οἴει οὖν, εἶπον, τοὺς
ταῦτα λέγοντας ψεύδεσθαι; Οὐκ οἶδα, ἦ δ᾽ ὅς,
E ἀλλὰ τὸ σοὶ δοκοῦν ἡδέως ἂν ἀκούοιμι. Ἀκούοις
ἄν, ὅτι ἔμοιγε φαίνονται τἀληθῆ λέγειν. Πῶς οὖν,
ἔφη, εὖ ἔχει λέγειν, ὅτι οὐ πρότερον κακῶν παύ-
σονται αἱ πόλεις, πρὶν ἂν ἐν αὐταῖς οἱ φιλόσοφοι
ἄρξωσιν, οὓς ἀχρήστους ὁμολογοῦμεν αὐταῖς εἶναι;
Ἐρωτᾷς, ἦν δ᾽ ἐγώ, ἐρώτημα δεόμενον ἀποκρί-
σεως δι᾽ εἰκόνος λεγομένης. Σὺ δέ γε, ἔφη, οἶμαι,
οὐκ εἴωθας δι᾽ εἰκόνων λέγειν.

IV. Εἶεν, εἶπον· σκώπτεις ἐμβεβληκώς με εἰς
λόγον οὕτω δυσαπόδεικτον; ἄκουε δ᾽ οὖν τῆς
488 εἰκόνος, ἵν᾽ ἔτι μᾶλλον ἴδῃς, ὡς γλίσχρως εἰκάζω.
οὕτω γὰρ χαλεπὸν τὸ πάθος τῶν ἐπιεικεστάτων, ὃ
πρὸς τὰς πόλεις πεπόνθασιν, ὥστε οὐδ᾽ ἔστιν ἐν
οὐδὲν ἄλλο τοιοῦτον πεπονθός, ἀλλὰ δεῖ ἐκ πολλῶν αὐτὸ ξυναγαγεῖν εἰκάζοντα καὶ ἀπολογού-

---

[a] The perfect tense is ironical in *Crat.* 384 B, serious in
Laws 670 A-B. In *Gorg.* 485 A it is replaced by ὅσον παιδείας
χάριν.

[b] Cf. *What Plato Said*, p. 506 on *Gorg.* 484 c.

[c] Cf. *Euthydem.* 306 E, *Protag.* 346 A, and for the idea
without the word, *Soph.* 216 c.

[d] Cf. Eurip. *Medea* 299, and on 489 B.

[e] Cf. *supra* 487 A. In *Euthydem.* 307 B Plato uses both
ἐπιτήδευμα and πρᾶγμα.

not merely touching upon it to complete their education [a] and dropping it while still young, but lingering
too long [b] in the study of it, the majority become
cranks,[c] not to say rascals, and those accounted the
finest spirits among them are still rendered useless [d] to
society by the pursuit [e] which you commend." And I,
on hearing this, said, " Do you think that they are
mistaken in saying so ? " " I don't know," said
he, " but I would gladly hear your opinion." " You
may hear, then, that I think that what they say is
true." " How, then," he replied, " can it be right
to say that our cities will never be freed from their
evils until the philosophers, whom we admit to be
useless to them, become their rulers ? " " Your
question," I said, " requires an answer expressed in
a comparison or parable.[f] " " And you," he said, " of
course, are not accustomed to speak in comparisons ! "

IV. " So," said I, " you are making fun of me after
driving me into such an impasse of argument. But,
all the same, hear my comparison so that you may
still better see how I strain after [g] imagery. For so
cruel is the condition of the better sort in relation to
the state that there is no single thing [h] like it in nature.
But to find a likeness for it and a defence for them
one must bring together many things in such a com-

---

[f] Cf. *Gorg.* 517 D, *Laws* 644 c, *Symp.* 215 A with Bury's
note. *Cf.* the parable of the great beast *infra* 493, and of
the many-headed beast, 588-589.

[g] The word γλίσχρως is untranslatable, and often misunderstood. In 553 c it means " stingily "; in *Cratyl.* 414 c
it is used of a strained etymology, and so in 435 c, usually
misunderstood; in *Crito* 53 E of clinging to life; *cf. Phaedo*
117 A; in Plutarch, *De Is. et Osir.* 28 of a strained allegory
and *ibid.* 75 of a strained resemblance; in Aristoph. *Peace*
482 of a dog. [h] *Cf. Laws* 747 B.

488 μενον ὑπὲρ αὐτῶν, οἷον οἱ γραφεῖς τραγελάφους
καὶ τὰ τοιαῦτα μιγνύντες γράφουσι. νόησον γὰρ
τοιουτονὶ γενόμενον εἴτε πολλῶν νεῶν πέρι εἴτε
μιᾶς· ναύκληρον μεγέθει μὲν καὶ ῥώμῃ ὑπὲρ τοὺς
B ἐν τῇ νηὶ πάντας, ὑπόκωφον δὲ καὶ ὁρῶντα ὡσαύτως βραχύ τι, καὶ γιγνώσκοντα περὶ ναυτικῶν
ἕτερα τοιαῦτα, τοὺς δὲ ναύτας στασιάζοντας πρὸς
ἀλλήλους περὶ τῆς κυβερνήσεως, ἕκαστον οἰόμενον
δεῖν κυβερνᾶν, μήτε μαθόντα πώποτε τὴν τέχνην
μήτε ἔχοντα ἀποδεῖξαι διδάσκαλον ἑαυτοῦ μηδὲ
χρόνον ἐν ᾧ ἐμάνθανε, πρὸς δὲ τούτοις φάσκοντας
μηδὲ διδακτὸν εἶναι, ἀλλὰ καὶ τὸν λέγοντα ὡς
C διδακτὸν ἑτοίμους κατατέμνειν, αὐτοὺς δὲ αὐτῷ
ἀεὶ τῷ ναυκλήρῳ περικεχύσθαι δεομένους καὶ

---

^a Cf. Horace, *Ars Poetica, init.*; *What Plato Said,* p. 550
on *Phaedr.* 229 D-E, and *infra* 588 c f. The expression is
still used, or revived, in Modern Greek newspapers.

^b The syntax of this famous allegory is anacoluthic and
perhaps uncertain; but there need be no doubt about the
meaning. *Cf.* my article in the *Classical Review,* xx. (1906)
p. 247.

Huxley commends the allegory, *Methods and Results,*
p. 313. *Cf.* also Carlyle's famous metaphor of the ship
doubling Cape Horn by ballot. *Cf. Class. Phil.* ix. (1914)
p. 362.

^c The Athenian demos, as portrayed *e.g.* in Aristophanes'
Knights 40 ff. and *passim. Cf.* Aristot. *Rhet.* 1406 b 35 καὶ
ἡ εἰς τὸν δῆμον, ὅτι ὅμοιος ναυκλήρῳ ἰσχυρῷ μὲν ὑποκώφῳ δέ,
Polyb. vi. 44 ἀεὶ γάρ ποτε τὸν τῶν Ἀθηναίων δῆμον παραπλήσιον
εἶναι τοῖς ἀδεσπότοις σκάφεσι, etc. *Cf.* the old sailor in Joseph
Conrad's *Chance,* ch. i. "No ship navigated . . . in the
happy-go-lucky manner . . . would ever arrive into port."

For the figure of the ship of state *cf. Polit.* 302 A ff.,
299 B, *Euthydem.* 291 D, Aesch. *Seven against Thebes* 2-3,
Theognis 670-685, Horace, *Odes* i. 15 with my note, Urwick,

bination as painters mix when they portray goat-stags [a] and similar creatures. [b] Conceive this sort of thing happening either on many ships or on one : Picture a shipmaster [c] in height and strength surpassing all others on the ship, but who is slightly deaf [d] and of similarly impaired vision, and whose knowledge of navigation is on a par with [e] his sight and hearing. Conceive the sailors to be wrangling with one another for control of the helm, each claiming that it is his right to steer though he has never learned the art and cannot point out his teacher [f] or any time when he studied it. And what is more, they affirm that it cannot be taught at all, [g] but they are ready to make mincemeat of anyone [h] who says that it can be taught, and meanwhile they are always clustered about [i] the shipmaster importuning him and sticking

The Message of Plato, pp. 110-111, Ruskin, Time and Tide, xiii: "That the governing authority should be in the hands of a true and trained pilot is as clear and as constant. In none of these conditions is there any difference between a nation and a boat's company." Cf. Longfellow's The Building of the Ship, in fine. Cf. Laws 758 A, 945 C.

For the criticism of democracy by a figure cf. also Polit. 297 E ff.

[d] Cf. Aristoph. Knights 42-44.

[e] Cf. 390 C, 426 D, 498 B, Theaetet. 167 B, and Milton's "unknown and like esteemed," Comus 630.

[f] For this and similar checks on pretenders to knowledge cf. Laches 185 E, 186 A and C, Alc. I. 109 D and Gorg. 514 B-C.

[g] Plato of course believed that virtue or the political art can be taught in a reformed state, but practically was not taught at Athens. Cf. Unity of Plato's Thought, p. 14, infra on 518 D, What Plato Said, pp. 70 and 511, Newman, Introd. Aristot. Pol. p. 397, Thompson on Meno 70 A.

[h] A hint of the fate of Socrates. Cf. infra 517 A, 494 E, and Euthyphro 3 E.

[i] The participle περικεχυμένους occurs in Polit. 268 C, but is avoided here by anacoluthon.

488 πάντα ποιοῦντας, ὅπως ἂν σφίσι τὸ πηδάλιον
ἐπιτρέψῃ, ἐνίοτε δ' ἂν μὴ πείθωσιν ἀλλὰ ἄλλοι
μᾶλλον, τοὺς μὲν ἄλλους ἢ ἀποκτεινύντας ἢ ἐκβάλλοντας ἐκ τῆς νεώς, τὸν δὲ γενναῖον ναύκληρον
μανδραγόρᾳ ἢ μέθῃ ἤ τινι ἄλλῳ ξυμποδίσαντας
τῆς νεὼς ἄρχειν χρωμένους τοῖς ἐνοῦσι, καὶ πίνον-
τάς τε καὶ εὐωχουμένους πλεῖν ὡς τὸ εἰκὸς τοὺς
τοιούτους, πρὸς δὲ τούτοις ἐπαινοῦντας ναυτικὸν
D μὲν καλοῦντας καὶ κυβερνητικὸν καὶ ἐπιστάμενον
τὰ κατὰ ναῦν, ὃς ἂν ξυλλαμβάνειν δεινὸς ᾖ, ὅπως
ἄρξουσιν ἢ πείθοντες ἢ βιαζόμενοι τὸν ναύκληρον,
τὸν δὲ μὴ τοιοῦτον ψέγοντας ὡς ἄχρηστον, τοῦ δὲ
ἀληθινοῦ κυβερνήτου πέρι μηδ' ἐπαΐοντας,[1] ὅτι
ἀνάγκη αὐτῷ τὴν ἐπιμέλειαν ποιεῖσθαι ἐνιαυτοῦ

---

[1] ἐπαΐοντας q, ἐπαΐοντες AFDM.

[a] For the idiom πάντα ποιεῖν cf. Euthyph. 8 c, infra 504 D-E,
571 c, 575 E, 494 E, Gorg. 479 c, Phaedr. 252 E, Apol. 39 A,
and, slightly varied, Eurip. Heracleidae 841.

[b] The word ἐκβάλλοντας helps the obvious allegory, for it
also means banish.

[c] Here figurative. Cf. Gorg. 482 E, Theaet. 165 E. Infra
615 E it is used literally.

[d] Cf. Polit. 297 E. The expression is slightly ironical.
Such is frequently the tone of γενναῖος in Plato. Cf. Rep.
454 A, 363 A, 544 c, 348 c, Hipp. Min. 370 D, Soph. 231 B,
Hipp. Maj. 290 E, Polit. 274 E.

[e] Cf. Polit. 302 A, Laws 906 E, Jebb on Soph. Antig.
189-190.

[f] Cf. 407 D with Thucyd. iv. 26, vi. 69, vii. 25.

[g] Cf. 427 E, Laws 905 c, Eryx. 396 E, Aristoph. Knights 229.

[h] Neither here nor in D-E can ὅπως with the future mean
"in what way," and all interpretations based on that
assumption are plainly wrong. The expression in both cases
refers to getting control. Cf. 338 E, Laws 757 D, 714 c,
962 D-E, Xen. Rep. Lac. 14. 5. Cf. Class. Phil. ix. (1914)
pp. 358 and 362.

[i] For τὸν δὲ μὴ τοιοῦτον cf. Alc. II. 145 c.

20

at nothing [a] to induce him to turn over the helm to them. And sometimes, if they fail and others get his ear, they put the others to death or cast them out [b] from the ship, and then, after binding [c] and stupefying the worthy shipmaster [d] with mandragora or intoxication or otherwise, they take command of the ship, consume its stores and, drinking and feasting, make such a voyage [e] of it as is to be expected [f] from such, and as if that were not enough, they praise and celebrate as a navigator, a pilot, a master of shipcraft, the man who is most cunning to lend a hand [g] in persuading or constraining the shipmaster to let them rule,[h] while the man who lacks this craft [i] they censure as useless. They have no suspicion [j] that the true pilot must give his attention [k] to the time of the year,

[j] The ppl. must refer to the sailors; hence the acc. (see crit. note).

Whatever the text and the amount of probable anacoluthon in this sentence, the meaning is that the unruly sailors (the mob) have no true conception of the state of mind of the real pilot (the philosophic statesman), and that it is he (adopting Sidgwick's οἰομένῳ for the MS. οἰόμενοι in E) who does not believe that the trick of getting possession of the helm is an art, or that, if it were, he could afford time to practise it. Those who read οἰόμενοι attribute the idea of the incompatibility of the two things to the sailors. But that overlooks the points I have already made about ὅπως, and τέχνη and is in any case improbable, because the sentence as a whole is concerned with the attitude of the true pilot (statesman), which may be represented by the words of Burke to his constituents, " I could hardly serve you as I have done and court you too."

Cf. Sidgwick, "On a Passage in Plato's Republic," Journal of Philology, v. pp. 274-276, and my notes in A.J.P. xiii. p. 364 and xvi. p. 234.

[k] For the force of the article cf. Thucyd. ii. 65 τὸ ἐπίφθονον λαμβάνει, and my article in T.A.P.A. 1893, p. 81, n. 6. Cf. also Charm. 156 E and Rep. 496 E.

PLATO

488 καὶ ὡρῶν καὶ οὐρανοῦ καὶ ἄστρων καὶ πνευμάτων
καὶ πάντων τῶν τῇ τέχνῃ προσηκόντων, εἰ μέλλει
τῷ ὄντι νεὼς ἀρχικὸς ἔσεσθαι, ὅπως δὲ κυβερνήσει
Ε ἐάν τέ τινες βούλωνται ἐάν τε μή, μήτε τέχνην τούτου μήτε μελέτην οἰομένῳ¹ δυνατὸν εἶναι λαβεῖν
ἅμα καὶ τὴν κυβερνητικήν. τοιούτων δὴ περὶ τὰς
ναῦς γιγνομένων τὸν ὡς ἀληθῶς κυβερνητικὸν οὐχ
ἡγεῖ ἂν τῷ ὄντι μετεωροσκόπον τε καὶ ἀδολέσχην
489 καὶ ἄχρηστόν σφισι καλεῖσθαι ὑπὸ τῶν ἐν ταῖς
οὕτω κατεσκευασμέναις ναυσὶ πλωτήρων; Καὶ
μάλα, ἔφη ὁ Ἀδείμαντος. Οὐ δή, ἦν δ' ἐγώ, οἶμαι
δεῖσθαί σε ἐξεταζομένην τὴν εἰκόνα ἰδεῖν, ὅτι ταῖς
πόλεσι πρὸς τοὺς ἀληθινοὺς φιλοσόφους τὴν διά-
θεσιν ἔοικεν, ἀλλὰ μανθάνειν ὃ λέγω. Καὶ μάλα,
ἔφη. Πρῶτον μὲν τοίνυν ἐκεῖνον τὸν θαυμάζοντα,
ὅτι οἱ φιλόσοφοι οὐ τιμῶνται ἐν ταῖς πόλεσι,
δίδασκέ τε τὴν εἰκόνα καὶ πειρῶ πείθειν, ὅτι πολὺ
Β ἂν θαυμαστότερον ἦν, εἰ ἐτιμῶντο. Ἀλλὰ διδάξω,

¹ οἰομένῳ Sidgwick : οἰόμενοι mss.

ᵃ ὅπως ... κυβερνήσει. Cf. p. 20, note h.
ᵇ The translation gives the right meaning. Cf. infra
518 D, and the examples collected in my emendation of
Gorgias 503 D in Class. Phil. x. (1915) 325-326. The contrast
between subjects which do and those which do not admit of
constitution as an art and science is ever present to Plato's
mind, as appears from the Sophist, Politicus, Gorgias, and
Phaedrus. And he would normally express the idea by a
genitive with τέχνη. Cf. Protag. 357 A, Phaedrus 260 E,
22

the seasons, the sky, the winds, the stars, and all that pertains to his art if he is to be a true ruler of a ship, and that he does not believe that there is any art or science of seizing the helm [a] with or without the consent of others, or any possibility of mastering this alleged art [b] and the practice of it at the same time with the science of navigation. With such goings-on aboard ship do you not think that the real pilot would in very deed [c] be called a star-gazer, an idle babbler, a useless fellow, by the sailors in ships managed after this fashion ? " " Quite so," said Adeimantus. " You take my meaning, I presume, and do not require us to put the comparison to the proof [d] and show that the condition [e] we have described is the exact counterpart of the relation of the state to the true philosophers." " It is indeed," he said. " To begin with, then, teach this parable [f] to the man who is surprised that philosophers are not honoured in our cities, and try to convince him that it would be far more surprising if they were honoured." " I

also Class. Rev. xx. (1906) p. 247. See too Cic. *De or.* i. 4 " neque aliquod praeceptum artis esse arbitrarentur," and *infra* 518 D.

[c] τῷ ὄντι verifies the allusion to the charge that Socrates was a babbler and a star-gazer or weather-prophet. *Cf.* *Soph.* 225 D, *Polit.* 299 B, and *What Plato Said*, p. 527 on *Phaedo* 70 c; Blaydes on Aristoph. *Clouds* 1480.

[d] Plato like some modern writers is conscious of his own imagery and frequently interprets his own symbols. *Cf.* 517 A-B, 531 B, 588 B, *Gorg.* 493 D, 517 D, *Phaedo* 87 B, *Laws* 644 C, *Meno* 72 A-B, *Tim.* 19 B, *Polit.* 297 E. *Cf.* also the cases where he says he cannot tell what it is but only what it is like, *e.g. Rep.* 506 E, *Phaedr.* 246 A, *Symp.* 215 A 5.

[e] διάθεσις and ἕξις are not discriminated by Plato as by Aristotle.

[f] *Cf.* 476 D-E.

489 ἔφη. Καὶ ὅτι τοίνυν τἀληθῆ λέγει, ὡς ἄχρηστοι
τοῖς πολλοῖς οἱ ἐπιεικέστατοι τῶν ἐν φιλοσοφίᾳ·
τῆς μέντοι ἀχρηστίας τοὺς μὴ χρωμένους κέλευε
αἰτιᾶσθαι, ἀλλὰ μὴ τοὺς ἐπιεικεῖς. οὐ γὰρ ἔχει
φύσιν κυβερνήτην ναυτῶν δεῖσθαι ἄρχεσθαι ὑφ᾽
αὑτοῦ, οὐδὲ τοὺς σοφοὺς ἐπὶ τὰς τῶν πλουσίων
θύρας ἰέναι, ἀλλ᾽ ὁ τοῦτο κομψευσάμενος ἐψεύσατο,
τὸ δὲ ἀληθὲς πέφυκεν, ἐάν τε πλούσιος ἐάν τε
πένης κάμνῃ, ἀναγκαῖον εἶναι ἐπὶ ἰατρῶν θύρας
C ἰέναι καὶ πάντα τὸν ἄρχεσθαι δεόμενον ἐπὶ τὰς τοῦ
ἄρχειν δυναμένου, οὐ τὸν ἄρχοντα δεῖσθαι τῶν ἀρχο-
μένων ἄρχεσθαι, οὗ ἂν τῇ ἀληθείᾳ τι ὄφελος ᾖ.
ἀλλὰ τοὺς νῦν πολιτικοὺς ἄρχοντας ἀπεικάζων οἷς
ἄρτι ἐλέγομεν ναύταις οὐχ ἁμαρτήσει, καὶ τοὺς ὑπὸ
τούτων ἀχρήστους λεγομένους καὶ μετεωρολέσχας

ᵃ This passage illustrates one of the most interesting
characteristics of Plato's style, namely the representation of
thought as adventure or action. This procedure is, or was,
familiar to modern readers in Matthew Arnold's account in
God and the Bible of his quest for the meaning of God, which
in turn is imitated in Mr. Updegraff's *New Word*. It lends
vivacity and interest to Pascal's *Provinciales* and many
other examples of it can be found in modern literature. The
classical instance of it in Plato is Socrates' narrative in the
Phaedo of his search for a satisfactory explanation of natural
phenomena, 96 A ff. In the *Sophist* the argument is represented as an effort to track and capture the sophist. And
the figure of the hunt is common in the dialogues (*cf. supra*
Vol. I. p. 365). *Cf.* also *Rep.* 455 A-B, 474 B, 588 C-D,
612 C, *Euthyd.* 291 A-B, 293 A, *Phileb.* 24 A ff., 43 A, 44 D,
45 A, *Laws* 892 D-E, *Theaet.* 169 D, 180 E, 196 D, *Polit.*
265 B, etc.
ᵇ *Cf.* 487 D. *Cf.* Arnold, *Culture and Anarchy*, p. 3

24

will teach him,"[a] he said. "And say to him further: You are right in affirming that the finest spirits among the philosophers are of no service to the multitude. But bid him blame for this uselessness,[b] not the finer spirits, but those who do not know how to make use of them. For it is not the natural[c] course of things that the pilot should beg the sailors to be ruled by him or that wise men should go to the doors of the rich.[d] The author of that epigram[e] was a liar. But the true nature of things is that whether the sick man be rich or poor he must needs go to the door of the physician, and everyone who needs to be governed[f] to the door of the man who knows how to govern, not that the ruler should implore his natural subjects to let themselves be ruled, if he is really good for anything.[g] But you will make no mistake in likening our present political rulers to the sort of sailors we were just describing, and those whom these call useless

---

"I am not sure that I do not think this the fault of our community rather than of the men of culture."

[c] For the idiom φύσιν ἔχει cf. 473 A, Herod. ii. 45, Dem. ii. 26. Similarly ἔχει λόγον, Rep. 378 E, 491 D, 564 A, 610 A, Phaedo 62 B and D, Gorg. 501 A, etc.

[d] This saying was attributed to Simonides. Cf. schol. Hermann, Plato, vol. vi. p. 346, Joel, Der echte und der xenophontische Sokrates, ii.[1] p. 81, Aristot. Rhet. 1391 a 8. Cf. Phaedr. 245 A ἐπὶ ποιητικὰς θύρας, Thompson on Phaedr. 233 E, supra 364 B ἐπὶ πλουσίων θύρας, Laws 953 D ἐπὶ τὰς τῶν πλουσίων καὶ σοφῶν θύρας, and for the idea cf. also infra 568 A and Theaet. 170 A, Timon of Athens IV. iii. 17 "The learned pate ducks to the golden fool."

[e] For Plato's attitude toward the epigrams of the Pre-Socratics cf. Unity of Plato's Thought, pp. 68-69.

[f] Cf. Theaet. 170 B and infra 590 C-D.

[g] For the idiom with ὄφελος cf. 530 C, 567 B, Euthyphro 4 E, Apol. 36 C, Crito 46 A, Euthydem. 289 A, Soph. O.C. 259, where it is varied.

25

489 τοῖς ὡς ἀληθῶς κυβερνήταις. Ὀρθότατα, ἔφη.
Ἔκ τε τοίνυν τούτων καὶ ἐν τούτοις οὐ ῥᾴδιον
εὐδοκιμεῖν τὸ βέλτιστον ἐπιτήδευμα ὑπὸ τῶν
D τἀναντία ἐπιτηδευόντων, πολὺ δὲ μεγίστη καὶ
ἰσχυροτάτη διαβολὴ γίγνεται φιλοσοφίᾳ διὰ τοὺς
τὰ τοιαῦτα φάσκοντας ἐπιτηδεύειν, οὓς δὴ σὺ φῇς
τὸν ἐγκαλοῦντα τῇ φιλοσοφίᾳ λέγειν ὡς παμπόνηροι
οἱ πλεῖστοι τῶν ἰόντων ἐπ᾽ αὐτήν, οἱ δὲ ἐπιεικέστατοι ἄχρηστοι, καὶ ἐγὼ συνεχώρησα ἀληθῆ
σε λέγειν. ἦ γάρ; Ναί.

V. Οὐκοῦν τῆς μὲν τῶν ἐπιεικῶν ἀχρηστίας τὴν
αἰτίαν διεληλύθαμεν; Καὶ μάλα. Τῆς δὲ τῶν
πολλῶν πονηρίας τὴν ἀνάγκην βούλει τὸ μετὰ
τοῦτο διέλθωμεν, καὶ ὅτι οὐδὲ τούτου φιλοσοφία
E αἰτία, ἂν δυνώμεθα, πειραθῶμεν δεῖξαι; Πάνυ
μὲν οὖν. Ἀκούωμεν δὴ καὶ λέγωμεν ἐκεῖθεν
ἀναμνησθέντες, ὅθεν διῆμεν τὴν φύσιν, οἷον ἀνάγ-
490 κη φῦναι τὸν καλόν τε κἀγαθὸν ἐσόμενον. ἡγεῖτο
δ᾽ αὐτῷ, εἰ νῷ ἔχεις, πρῶτον μὲν ἀλήθεια, ἣν
διώκειν αὐτὸν πάντως καὶ πάντῃ ἔδει ἢ ἀλαζόνι
ὄντι μηδαμῇ μετεῖναι φιλοσοφίας ἀληθινῆς. Ἦν
γὰρ οὕτω λεγόμενον. Οὐκοῦν ἐν μὲν τοῦτο
σφόδρα οὕτω παρὰ δόξαν τοῖς νῦν δοκουμένοις
περὶ αὐτοῦ; Καὶ μάλα, ἔφη. Ἆρ᾽ οὖν δὴ οὐ
μετρίως ἀπολογησόμεθα, ὅτι πρὸς τὸ ὂν πεφυκὼς

---

[a] Cf. *Theaet.* 173 c, why speak of unworthy philosophers?
and *infra* 495 c ff.

[b] Possibly "wooers." *Cf.* 347 c, 521 B. Plato frequently
employs the language of physical love in speaking of
philosophy. *Cf. infra* 495-496, 490 B, *Theaet.* 148 E ff.,
Phaedo 66 E, *Meno* 70 B, *Phaedr.* 266 B, etc.

[c] *Cf. Theaet.* 169 D.

and star-gazing ideologists to the true pilots."
" Just so," he said. " Hence, and under these conditions, we cannot expect that the noblest pursuit
should be highly esteemed by those whose way of
life is quite the contrary. But far the greatest and
chief disparagement of philosophy is brought upon
it by the pretenders *a* to that way of life, those whom
you had in mind when you affirmed that the accuser
of philosophy says that the majority of her followers *b*
are rascals and the better sort useless, while I admitted *c* that what you said was true. Is not that so ? "
" Yes."

V. " Have we not, then, explained the cause of
the uselessness of the better sort ? " " We have."
" Shall we next set forth the inevitableness of the
degeneracy of the majority, and try to show if we
can that philosophy is not to be blamed for this
either ? " " By all means." " Let us begin, then,
what we have to say and hear by recalling the starting-point of our description of the nature which he
who is to be a scholar and gentleman *d* must have from
birth. The leader of the choir for him, if you recollect, was truth. *That* he was to seek always and
altogether, on pain of *e* being an impostor without part
or lot in true philosophy." " Yes, that was said."
" Is not this one point quite contrary to the prevailing
opinion about him ? " " It is indeed," he said. " Will
it not be a fair plea in his defence to say that it was
the nature of the real lover of knowledge to strive

---

d The quality of the καλὸς κἀγαθός gave rise to the abstrac-
tion καλοκἀγαθία used for the moral ideal in the Eudemian
Ethics. *Cf.* Isoc. *Demon.* 6, 13, and 51, Stewart on *Eth.
Nic.* 1124 a 4 (p. 339) and 1179 b 10 (p. 460).

e For ἤ = " or else " *cf. Prot.* 323 A and c, *Phaedr.* 237 c,
239 A, 245 D, *Gorg.* 494 A, *Crat.* 426 B, etc.

490 εἴη ἁμιλλᾶσθαι ὅ γε ὄντως φιλομαθής, καὶ οὐκ
B ἐπιμένοι ἐπὶ τοῖς δοξαζομένοις εἶναι πολλοῖς ἑκάστοις, ἀλλ' ἴοι καὶ οὐκ ἀμβλύνοιτο οὐδ' ἀπολήγοι
τοῦ ἔρωτος, πρὶν αὐτοῦ ὃ ἔστιν ἑκάστου τῆς
φύσεως ἅψασθαι ᾧ προσήκει ψυχῆς ἐφάπτεσθαι
τοῦ τοιούτου· προσήκει δὲ ξυγγενεῖ· ᾧ πλησιάσας
καὶ μιγεὶς τῷ ὄντι ὄντως, γεννήσας νοῦν καὶ ἀλήθειαν, γνοίη τε καὶ ἀληθῶς ζῴη καὶ τρέφοιτο καὶ
οὕτω λήγοι ὠδῖνος, πρὶν δ' οὔ. 'Ως οἷόν τ', ἔφη,
μετριώτατα. Τί οὖν; τούτῳ τι μετέσται ψεῦδος
C ἀγαπᾶν ἢ πᾶν τοὐναντίον μισεῖν; Μισεῖν, ἔφη.
'Ηγουμένης δὴ ἀληθείας οὐκ ἄν ποτε, οἶμαι,
φαῖμεν αὐτῇ χορὸν κακῶν ἀκολουθῆσαι. Πῶς
γάρ; 'Αλλ' ὑγιές τε καὶ δίκαιον ἦθος, ᾧ καὶ
σωφροσύνην ἔπεσθαι. 'Ορθῶς, ἔφη. Καὶ δὴ τὸν
ἄλλον τῆς φιλοσόφου φύσεως χορὸν τί δεῖ πάλιν
ἐξ ἀρχῆς ἀναγκάζοντα τάττειν; μέμνησαι γάρ
που, ὅτι ξυνέβη προσῆκον τούτοις ἀνδρεία, μεγαλοπρέπεια, εὐμάθεια, μνήμη· καὶ σοῦ ἐπιλα-
D βομένου, ὅτι πᾶς μὲν ἀναγκασθήσεται ὁμολογεῖν
οἷς λέγομεν, ἐάσας δὲ τοὺς λόγους, εἰς αὐτοὺς
ἀποβλέψας περὶ ὧν ὁ λόγος, φαίη ὁρᾶν αὐτῶν
τοὺς μὲν ἀχρήστους, τοὺς δὲ πολλοὺς κακοὺς
πᾶσαν κακίαν, τῆς διαβολῆς τὴν αἰτίαν ἐπισκο-

---

[a] Similar metaphors for contact, approach and intercourse
with the truth are frequent in Aristotle and the Neoplatonists.
For Plato cf. Campbell on Theaet. 150 B and 186 A. Cf. also
supra on 489 D.

[b] Cf. Phaedo 65 E f., Symp. 211 E-212 A.

[c] Lit. "be nourished." Cf. Protag. 313 C-D, Soph. 223 E,
Phaedr. 248 B.

[d] A Platonic and Neoplatonic metaphor. Cf. Theaet.
148 E ff., 151 A, and passim, Symp. 206 E, Epist. ii. 313 A,
Epictet. Diss. i. 22. 17.

emulously for true being and that he would not linger over the many particulars that are opined to be real, but would hold on his way, and the edge of his passion would not be blunted.nor would his desire fail till he came into touch with[a] the nature of each thing in itself by that part of his soul to which it belongs [b] to lay hold on that kind of reality—the part akin to it, namely—and through that approaching it, and consorting with reality really, he would beget intelligence and truth, attain to knowledge and truly live and grow,[c] and so find surcease from his travail[d] of soul, but not before?" "No plea could be fairer." "Well, then, will such a man love falsehood, or, quite the contrary, hate it?" "Hate it," he said. "When truth led the way, no choir[e] of evils, we, I fancy, would say, could ever follow in its train." "How could it?" "But rather a sound and just character, which is accompanied by temperance." "Right," he said. "What need, then, of repeating from the beginning our proof of the necessary order of the choir that attends on the philosophical nature? You surely remember that we found pertaining to such a nature courage, grandeur of soul, aptness to learn, memory.[f] And when you interposed the objection that though everybody will be compelled to admit our statements,[g] yet, if we abandoned mere words and fixed our eyes on the persons to whom the words referred, everyone would say that he actually saw some of them to be useless and most of them base with all baseness, it was in our search for the

---

[e] For the figurative use of the word χορός cf. 560 E, 580 B, *Euthydem.* 279 C, *Theaet.* 173 B.

[f] For the list of virtues cf. *supra* on 487 A.

[g] *Cf.* for the use of the dative *Polit.*.258 A συγχωρεῖς οὖν οἷς λέγει, *Phaedo* 100 C τῇ τοιᾷδε αἰτίᾳ συγχωρεῖς, Horace, *Sat.* ii. 3. 305 "stultum me fateor, liceat concedere veris."

490 ποῦντες ἐπὶ τούτῳ νῦν γεγόναμεν, τί ποθ' οἱ πολλοὶ
κακοί, καὶ τούτου δὴ ἔνεκα πάλιν ἀνειλήφαμεν τὴν
τῶν ἀληθῶς φιλοσόφων φύσιν καὶ ἐξ ἀνάγκης
E ὡρισάμεθα. Ἔστιν, ἔφη, ταῦτα.

VI. Ταύτης δή, ἦν δ' ἐγώ, τῆς φύσεως δεῖ
θεάσασθαι τὰς φθοράς, ὡς διόλλυται ἐν πολλοῖς,
σμικρὸν δέ τι ἐκφεύγει, οὓς δὴ καὶ οὐ πονηρούς,
ἀχρήστους δὲ καλοῦσι· καὶ μετὰ τοῦτο αὖ τὰς
491 μιμουμένας ταύτην καὶ εἰς τὸ ἐπιτήδευμα καθιστα-
μένας αὐτῆς, οἷαι οὖσαι φύσεις ψυχῶν εἰς ἀνάξιον
καὶ μεῖζον ἑαυτῶν ἀφικνούμεναι ἐπιτήδευμα, πολλαχῇ πλημμελοῦσαι, πανταχῇ καὶ ἐπὶ πάντας
δόξαν οἵαν λέγεις φιλοσοφίᾳ προσῆψαν. Τίνας δέ,
ἔφη, τὰς διαφθορὰς λέγεις; Ἐγώ σοι, εἶπον, ἂν
οἷός τε γένωμαι, πειράσομαι διελθεῖν. τόδε μὲν
οὖν, οἶμαι, πᾶς ἡμῖν ὁμολογήσει, τοιαύτην φύσιν
καὶ πάντα ἔχουσαν, ὅσα προσετάξαμεν νῦν δή,
B εἰ τελέως μέλλοι φιλόσοφος γενέσθαι, ὀλιγάκις
ἐν ἀνθρώποις φύεσθαι καὶ ὀλίγας· ἢ οὐκ οἴει;
Σφόδρα γε. Τούτων δὴ τῶν ὀλίγων σκόπει ὡς
πολλοὶ ὄλεθροι καὶ μεγάλοι. Τίνες δή; Ὁ μὲν
πάντων θαυμαστότατον ἀκοῦσαι, ὅτι ἓν ἕκαστον
ὧν ἐπῃνέσαμεν τῆς φύσεως ἀπόλλυσι τὴν ἔχουσαν
ψυχὴν καὶ ἀποσπᾷ φιλοσοφίας· λέγω δὲ ἀνδρείαν,
σωφροσύνην, καὶ πάντα ἃ διήλθομεν. Ἄτοπον,
C ἔφη, ἀκοῦσαι. Ἔτι τοίνυν, ἦν δ' ἐγώ, πρὸς

---

[a] Le petit nombre des élus. *Cf. infra* 496 A-B and *Phaedo*
69 C-D, *Matt.* xx. 16, xxii. 14.

[b] For the Greek double use of ἄξιος and ἀνάξιος *cf. Laws*
943 E, Aesch. *Ag.* 1527. *Cf.* " How worthily he died who
died unworthily " and Wyatt's line " Disdain me not without desert."

cause of this ill-repute that we came to the present
question: Why is it that the majority are bad?
And, for the sake of this, we took up again the nature
of the true philosophers and defined what it must
necessarily be?" "That is so," he said.

VI. "We have, then," I said, "to contemplate the
causes of the corruption of this nature in the majority,
while a small part escapes,[a] even those whom men
call not bad but useless; and after that in turn we are
to observe those who imitate this nature and usurp
its pursuits and see what types of souls they are that
thus entering upon a way of life which is too high [b] for
them and exceeds their powers, by the many discords and disharmonies of their conduct everywhere
and among all men bring upon philosophy the repute
of which you speak." "Of what corruptions are you
speaking?" "I will try," I said, "to explain them
to you if I can. I think everyone will grant us this
point, that a nature such as we just now postulated
for the perfect philosopher is a rare growth among
men and is found in only a few. Don't you think so?"
"Most emphatically." "Observe, then, the number
and magnitude of the things that operate to destroy
these few." "What are they?" "The most surprising fact of all is that each of the gifts of nature
which we praise tends to corrupt the soul of its possessor and divert it from philosophy. I am speaking
of bravery, sobriety, and the entire list.[c]" "That does
sound like a paradox," said he. "Furthermore," said I,

[c] Cf. Burton, *Anatomy*, i. 1 "This St. Austin acknow-
ledgeth of himself in his humble confessions, promptness of
wit, memory, eloquence, they were God's good gifts, but he
did not use them to his glory."

Cf. *Meno* 88 A-c, and Seneca, *Ep.* v. 7 "multa bona
nostra nobis nocent."

PLATO

491 τούτοις τὰ λεγόμενα ἀγαθὰ πάντα φθείρει καὶ ἀποσπᾷ, κάλλος καὶ πλοῦτος καὶ ἰσχὺς σώματος καὶ
ξυγγένεια ἐρρωμένη ἐν πόλει καὶ πάντα τὰ τούτων οἰκεῖα· ἔχεις γὰρ τὸν τύπον ὧν λέγω. Ἔχω,
ἔφη· καὶ ἡδέως γ' ἂν ἀκριβέστερον ἃ λέγεις πυθοί-
μην. Λαβοῦ τοίνυν, ἦν δ' ἐγώ, ὅλου αὐτοῦ ὀρθῶς,
καί σοι εὔδηλόν τε φανεῖται καὶ οὐκ ἄτοπα δόξει
τὰ προειρημένα περὶ αὐτῶν. Πῶς οὖν, ἔφη,
D κελεύεις; Παντός, ἦν δ' ἐγώ, σπέρματος πέρι ἢ
φυτοῦ, εἴτε ἐγγείων εἴτε τῶν ζῴων, ἴσμεν, ὅτι τὸ
μὴ τυχὸν τροφῆς ἧς προσήκει ἑκάστῳ μηδ' ὥρας
μηδὲ τόπου, ὅσῳ ἂν ἐρρωμενέστερον ᾖ, τοσούτῳ
πλειόνων ἐνδεῖ τῶν πρεπόντων· ἀγαθῷ γάρ που
κακὸν ἐναντιώτερον ἢ τῷ μὴ ἀγαθῷ. Πῶς δ' οὔ;
Ἔχει δή, οἶμαι, λόγον, τὴν ἀρίστην φύσιν ἐν
ἀλλοτριωτέρᾳ οὖσαν τροφῇ κάκιον ἀπαλλάττειν τῆς
φαύλης. Ἔχει. Οὐκοῦν, ἦν δ' ἐγώ, ὦ Ἀδεί-
E μαντε, καὶ τὰς ψυχὰς οὕτω φῶμεν τὰς εὐφυε-
στάτας κακῆς παιδαγωγίας τυχούσας διαφερόντως
κακὰς γίγνεσθαι; ἢ οἴει τὰ μεγάλα ἀδικήματα
καὶ τὴν ἄκρατον πονηρίαν ἐκ φαύλης, ἀλλ' οὐκ
ἐκ νεανικῆς φύσεως τροφῇ διολομένης γίγνεσθαι,

---

[a] Cf. *What Plato Said*, p. 479 on *Charm.* 158 A. For
" goods " *cf. ibid.* p. 629 on *Laws* 697 B. The minor or
earlier dialogues constantly lead up to the point that goods
are no good divorced from wisdom, or the art to use them
rightly, or the political or royal art, or the art that will make
us happy. *Cf. What Plato Said*, p. 71.

[b] This is for Plato's purpose a sufficiently clear statement
of the distinction between contradictory and contrary opposition. Plato never drew out an Aristotelian or modern
logician's table of the opposition of propositions. But it is
a misunderstanding of Greek idiom or of his style to say
that he never got clear on the matter. He always understood

" all the so-called goods [a] corrupt and divert, beauty and wealth and strength of body and powerful family connexions in the city and all things akin to them—you get my general meaning?" " I do," he said, " and I would gladly hear a more precise statement of it." "Well," said I, "grasp it rightly as a general proposition and the matter will be clear and the preceding statement will not seem to you so strange." " How do you bid me proceed ? " he said. " We know it to be universally true of every seed and growth, whether vegetable or animal, that the more vigorous it is the more it falls short of its proper perfection when deprived of the food, the season, the place that suits it. For evil is more opposed to the good than to the not-good. [b] " "Of course." " So it is, I take it, natural that the best nature should fare worse [c] than the inferior under conditions of nurture unsuited to it." " It is." " Then," said I, " Adeimantus, shall we not similarly affirm that the best endowed souls become worse than the others under a bad education ? Or do you suppose that great crimes and unmixed wickedness spring from a slight nature [d] and not from a vigorous one corrupted by its

it. *Cf. Symp.* 202 a-b, and *supra* on 437 a-b, *What Plato Said*, p. 595 on *Soph.* 257 b, and *ibid.* p. 563 on *Rep.* 436 b ff.

[c] "Corruptio optimi pessima." *Cf.* 495 a-b, Xen. *Mem.* i. 2. 24, iv. 1. 3-4, Dante, *Inferno*, vi. 106 :

> Ed egli a me: Ritorna a tua scienza
> Che vuol, quanto la cosa è più perfetta,
> Più senta il bene e così la doglienza.

Cf. Livy xxxviii. 17 " generosius in sua quidquid sede gignitur : insitum alienae terrae in id quo alitur, natura vertente se, degenerat," Pausanias vii. 17. 3.

[d] *Cf.* 495 b ; La Rochefoucauld, *Max.* 130 " la faiblesse est le seul défaut qu'on ne saurait corriger " and 467 " la faiblesse est plus opposée à la vertu que le vice."

PLATO

491 ἀσθενῆ δὲ φύσιν μεγάλων οὔτε ἀγαθῶν οὔτε κακῶν
αἰτίαν ποτὲ ἔσεσθαι; Οὔκ, ἀλλά, ἦ δ' ὅς, οὕτως.
492 Ἦν τοίνυν ἔθεμεν τοῦ φιλοσόφου φύσιν, ἂν μέν,
οἶμαι, μαθήσεως προσηκούσης τύχῃ, εἰς πᾶσαν
ἀρετὴν ἀνάγκη αὐξανομένην ἀφικνεῖσθαι, ἐὰν δὲ
μὴ ἐν προσηκούσῃ σπαρεῖσά τε καὶ φυτευθεῖσα
τρέφηται, εἰς πάντα τἀναντία αὖ, ἐὰν μή τις αὐτῇ
βοηθήσας θεῶν τύχῃ. ἢ καὶ σὺ ἡγεῖ, ὥσπερ οἱ
πολλοί, διαφθειρομένους τινὰς εἶναι ὑπὸ σοφιστῶν
νέους, διαφθείροντας δέ τινας σοφιστὰς ἰδιωτικούς,
ὅ τι καὶ ἄξιον λόγου, ἀλλ' οὐκ αὐτοὺς τοὺς ταῦτα
B λέγοντας μεγίστους μὲν εἶναι σοφιστάς, παιδεύειν
δὲ τελεώτατα καὶ ἀπεργάζεσθαι οἵους βούλονται
εἶναι καὶ νέους καὶ πρεσβυτέρους καὶ ἄνδρας καὶ
γυναῖκας; Πότε δή; ἦ δ' ὅς. Ὅταν, εἶπον,
ξυγκαθεζόμενοι ἀθρόοι οἱ πολλοί[1] εἰς ἐκκλησίας
ἢ εἰς δικαστήρια ἢ θέατρα ἢ στρατόπεδα ἤ τινα
ἄλλον κοινὸν πλήθους ξύλλογον ξὺν πολλῷ θορύβῳ

---

[1] οἱ πολλοί Hermann : πολλοί mss., οἱ secl. Cobet.

---

[a] Cf. infra 497 B, Tim. 42 D.

[b] This is the θεία μοῖρα of 493 A and Meno 99 E. Cf. What
Plato Said, p. 517.

[c] See What Plato Said, pp. 12 ff. and on Meno 93-94. Plato
again anticipates many of his modern critics. Cf. Grote's
defence of the sophists passim, and Mill, Utility of Religion
(Three Essays on Religion, pp. 78, 84 ff.).

[d] ἰδιωτικούς refers to individual sophists as opposed to the
great sophist of public opinion. Cf. 492 D, 493 A, 494 A.

[e] For καὶ ἄξιον λόγου cf. Euthydem. 279 c, Laches 192 A,
Laws 908 B, supra 445 c, Thucyd. ii. 54. 5, Aristot. Pol.
1272 b 32, 1302 a 13, De part. an. 654 a 13, Demosth. v. 16,
Isoc. vi. 56.

[f] Cf. Gorg. 490 B, Emerson, Self-Reliance: " It is easy
. . . to brook the rage of the cultivated classes. . . .
But . . . when the unintelligent brute force that lies at the

nurture, while a weak nature will never be the cause
of anything great, either for good or evil ? " " No,"
he said, " that is the case." " Then the nature
which we assumed in the philosopher, if it receives
the proper teaching, must needs grow and attain to
consummate excellence, but, if it be sown [a] and planted
and grown in the wrong environment, the outcome
will be quite the contrary unless some god comes to
the rescue.[b] Or are you too one of the multitude who
believe that there are young men who are corrupted
by the sophists,[c] and that there are sophists in private
life [d] who corrupt to any extent worth mentioning,[e]
and that it is not rather the very men who talk in this
strain who are the chief sophists and educate most
effectively and mould to their own heart's desire
young and old, men and women ? " " When ? " said
he. " Why, when," I said, " the multitude are seated
together [f] in assemblies or in court-rooms or theatres
or camps or any other public gathering of a crowd,

bottom of society is made to growl and mow, it needs the
habit of magnanimity and religion to treat it godlike as a
trifle of no concernment," Carlyle, *French Revolution*:
" Great is the combined voice of men. . . . He who can
resist that has his footing somewhere beyond time."

For the public as the great sophist *cf.* Brimley, *Essays*,
p. 224 (The Angel in the House): " The miserable view of
life and its purposes which society instils into its youth of
both sexes, being still, as in Plato's time, the sophist *par
excellence* of which all individual talking and writing sophists
are but feeble copies." *Cf.* Zeller, *Ph. d. Gr.*[4] II. 1. 601 " Die
sophistische Ethik ist seiner Ansicht nach die einfache Kon-
sequenz der Gewöhnlichen." This is denied by some recent
critics. The question is a logomachy. Of course there is
more than one sophistic ethics. *Cf.* Mill, *Dissertations and
Discussions*, iv. pp. 247 ff., 263 ff., 275.

For Plato's attitude toward the sophists see also *Polit.*
303 c, *Phaedr.* 260 c, *What Plato Said*, pp. 14-15, 158.

PLATO

492 τὰ μὲν ψέγωσι τῶν λεγομένων ἢ πραττομένων, τὰ
δὲ ἐπαινῶσιν, ὑπερβαλλόντως ἑκάτερα, καὶ ἐκ-
C βοῶντες καὶ κροτοῦντες, πρὸς δ' αὐτοῖς αἵ τε
πέτραι καὶ ὁ τόπος ἐν ᾧ ἂν ὦσιν ἐπηχοῦντες
διπλάσιον θόρυβον παρέχωσι τοῦ ψόγου καὶ
ἐπαίνου. ἐν δὴ τῷ τοιούτῳ τὸν νέον, τὸ λεγόμενον,
τίνα οἴει καρδίαν ἴσχειν; ἢ ποίαν ἂν αὐτῷ παιδείαν ἰδιωτικὴν ἀνθέξειν, ἣν οὐ κατακλυσθεῖσαν
ὑπὸ τοῦ τοιούτου ψόγου ἢ ἐπαίνου οἰχήσεσθαι
φερομένην κατὰ ῥοῦν, ᾗ ἂν οὗτος φέρῃ, καὶ
φήσειν τε τὰ αὐτὰ τούτοις καλὰ καὶ αἰσχρὰ εἶναι,
D καὶ ἐπιτηδεύσειν ἅπερ ἂν οὗτοι, καὶ ἔσεσθαι
τοιοῦτον; Πολλή, ἦ δ' ὅς, ὦ Σώκρατες, ἀνάγκη.

VII. Καὶ μήν, ἦν δ' ἐγώ, οὔπω τὴν μεγίστην
ἀνάγκην εἰρήκαμεν. Ποίαν; ἔφη. Ἣν ἔργῳ προσ-
τιθέασι, λόγῳ μὴ πείθοντες, οὗτοι οἱ παιδευταί
τε καὶ σοφισταί. ἢ οὐκ οἶσθα, ὅτι τὸν μὴ πειθόμενον ἀτιμίαις τε καὶ χρήμασι καὶ θανάτοις
κολάζουσιν; Καὶ μάλα, ἔφη, σφόδρα. Τίνα οὖν
ἄλλον σοφιστὴν οἴει ἢ ποίους ἰδιωτικοὺς λόγους
E ἐναντία τούτοις τείνοντας κρατήσειν; Οἶμαι μὲν
οὐδένα, ἦ δ' ὅς. Οὐ γάρ, ἦν δ' ἐγώ, ἀλλὰ καὶ τὸ
ἐπιχειρεῖν πολλὴ ἄνοια. οὔτε γὰρ γίγνεται οὔτε
γέγονεν οὐδὲ οὖν μὴ γένηται [ἄλλο ἢ][1] ἀλλοῖον
ἦθος πρὸς ἀρετὴν παρὰ τὴν τούτων παιδείαν

---

[1] ἄλλο ἢ was added by Hermann, unnecessarily.

---

[a] Cf. Eurip. Orest. 901, they shouted ὡς καλῶς λέγοι,
also Euthydem. 303 B οἱ κίονες, 276 B and D, Shorey on
Horace, Odes i. 20. 7 "datus in theatro cum tibi plausus,"
and also the account of the moulding process in Protag. 323-326.

[b] What would be his plight, his state of mind; how would
he feel? Cf. Shorey in Class. Phil. v. (1910) pp. 220-221,
Iliad xxiv. 367, Theognis 748 καὶ τίνα θυμὸν ἔχων; Symp.

36

and with loud uproar censure some of the things that are said and done and approve others, both in excess, with full-throated clamour and clapping of hands, and thereto the rocks and the region round about re-echoing redouble the din of the censure and the praise.[a] In such case how do you think the young man's heart, as the saying is, is moved within him?[b] What private teaching do you think will hold out and not rather be swept away by the torrent of censure and applause, and borne off on its current, so that he will affirm[c] the same things that they do to be honourable and base, and will do as they do, and be even such as they?" "That is quite inevitable, Socrates," he said.

VII. "And, moreover," I said, "we have not yet mentioned the chief necessity and compulsion." "What is it?" said he. "That which these 'educators' and sophists impose by action when their words fail to convince. Don't you know that they chastise the recalcitrant with loss of civic rights and fines and death?" "They most emphatically do," he said. "What other sophist, then, or what private teaching do you think will prevail in opposition to these?" "None, I fancy," said he. "No," said I, "the very attempt[d] is the height of folly. For there is not, never has been and never will be,[e] a divergent type of character and virtue created by an education running

219 D 3 τίνα οἴεσθέ με διάνοιαν ἔχειν; Eurip. I.A. 1173 τίν' ἐν δόμοις με καρδίαν ἕξειν δοκεῖς;

[c] Adam translates as if it were καὶ φήσει. Cf. my "Platonism and the History of Science," Amer. Philos. Soc. Proc. lxvi. p. 174 n. See Stallbaum ad loc.

[d] Cf. Protag. 317 A-B, Soph. 239 c, Laws 818 D.

[e] Cf. Od. xvi. 437. See Friedländer, Platon, ii. 386 n. who says ἀλλοῖον γίγνεσθαι can only = ἀλλοιοῦσθαι, "be made different."

492 πεπαιδευμένον, ἀνθρώπειον, ὦ ἑταῖρε· θεῖον μέντοι
κατὰ τὴν παροιμίαν ἐξαιρῶμεν λόγου· εὖ γὰρ
χρὴ εἰδέναι, ὅ τί περ ἂν σωθῇ τε καὶ γένηται οἷον
493 δεῖ ἐν τοιαύτῃ καταστάσει πολιτειῶν, θεοῦ μοῖραν
αὐτὸ σῶσαι λέγων οὐ κακῶς ἐρεῖς. Οὐδ' ἐμοὶ
ἄλλως, ἔφη, δοκεῖ. Ἔτι τοίνυν σοι, ἦν δ' ἐγώ,
πρὸς τούτοις καὶ τόδε δοξάτω. Τὸ ποῖον; Ἕκαστος τῶν μισθαρνούντων ἰδιωτῶν, οὓς δὴ οὗτοι
σοφιστὰς καλοῦσι καὶ ἀντιτέχνους ἡγοῦνται, μὴ
ἄλλα παιδεύειν ἢ ταῦτα τὰ τῶν πολλῶν δόγματα,
ἃ δοξάζουσιν ὅταν ἀθροισθῶσι, καὶ σοφίαν ταύτην
καλεῖν· οἷόνπερ ἂν εἰ θρέμματος μεγάλου καὶ
ἰσχυροῦ τρεφομένου τὰς ὀργάς τις καὶ ἐπιθυμίας
B κατεμάνθανεν, ὅπῃ τε προσελθεῖν χρὴ καὶ ὅπῃ
ἅψασθαι αὐτοῦ, καὶ ὁπότε χαλεπώτατον ἢ πρᾳό-
τατον καὶ ἐκ τίνων γίγνεται, καὶ φωνὰς δὴ ἐφ'
οἷς ἑκάστας εἴωθε φθέγγεσθαι, καὶ οἵας αὖ ἄλλου
φθεγγομένου ἡμεροῦταί τε καὶ ἀγριαίνει, κατα-
μαθὼν δὲ ταῦτα πάντα ξυνουσίᾳ τε καὶ χρόνου
τριβῇ σοφίαν τε καλέσειεν καὶ ὡς τέχνην συστησά-

---

[a] Cf. 529 c for the idiom, and Laws 696 A οὐ γὰρ μή ποτε
γένηται παῖς καὶ ἀνὴρ καὶ γέρων ἐκ ταύτης τῆς τροφῆς διαφέρων
πρὸς ἀρετήν.

[b] Cf. Symp. 176 c (of Socrates), Phaedr. 242 B, Theaet.
162 D-E.

[c] Cf. supra on 492 A, Apol. 33 c, Phaedo 58 E, Protag.
328 E, Meno 99 E, Phaedr. 244 c, Laws 642 c, 875 c, Ion 534 c.

[d] Cf. Arnold, Preface to Essays in Criticism; Phaedo
60 D, Laws 817 B, On Virtue 376 D.

[e] Cf. Epist. v. 321 D ἔστιν γὰρ δή τις φωνὴ τῶν πολιτειῶν
ἑκάστης καθάπερεί τινων ζῴων, "each form of government has
a sort of voice, as if it were a kind of animal" (tr. L.A. Post).
Hackforth says this is a clumsy imitation of the Republic
which proves the letter spurious. Cf. Thomas Browne,
Religio Medici, ii. 1 "If there be any among those common

counter to theirs[a]—humanly speaking, I mean, my friend; for the divine, as the proverb says, all rules fail.[b] And you may be sure that, if anything is saved and turns out well in the present condition of society and government, in saying that the providence of God[c] preserves it you will not be speaking ill." "Neither do I think otherwise," he said. "Then," said I, "think this also in addition." "What?" "Each of these private teachers who work for pay, whom the politicians call sophists and regard as their rivals,[d] inculcates nothing else than these opinions of the multitude which they opine when they are assembled and calls this knowledge wisdom. It is as if a man were acquiring the knowledge of the humours and desires of a great strong beast[e] which he had in his keeping, how it is to be approached and touched, and when and by what things it is made most savage or gentle, yes, and the several sounds it is wont to utter on the occasion of each, and again what sounds uttered by another make it tame or fierce, and after mastering this knowledge by living with the creature and by lapse of time should call it wisdom, and should construct

objects of hatred I do contemn and laugh at, it is that great enemy of reason, virtue, and religion, the multitude . . . one great beast and a monstrosity more prodigious than Hydra," Horace, *Epist.* i. 1. 76 "belua multorum es capitum." Also Hamilton's "Sir, your people is a great beast," Sidney, *Arcadia*, bk. ii. "Many-headed multitude," Wallas, *Human Nature in Politics*, p. 172 ". . . like Plato's sophist is learning what the public is and is beginning to understand 'the passions and desires' of that 'huge and powerful brute,'" Shakes. *Coriolanus* iv. i. 2 "The beast with many heads Butts me away," *ibid.* ii. iii. 18 "The many-headed multitude." For the idea *cf.* also *Gorg.* 501 B-C ff., *Phaedr.* 260 c δόξας δὲ πλήθους μεμελετηκώς, "having studied the opinions of the multitude," Isoc. ii. 49-50.

493 μενος ἐπὶ διδασκαλίαν τρέποιτο, μηδὲν εἰδὼς τῇ
ἀληθείᾳ τούτων τῶν δογμάτων τε καὶ ἐπιθυμιῶν,
ὅ τι καλὸν ἢ αἰσχρὸν ἢ ἀγαθὸν ἢ κακὸν ἢ δίκαιον
C ἢ ἄδικον, ὀνομάζοι δὲ πάντα ταῦτα ἐπὶ ταῖς τοῦ
μεγάλου ζῴου δόξαις, οἷς μὲν χαίροι ἐκεῖνο ἀγαθὰ
καλῶν, οἷς δὲ ἄχθοιτο κακά, ἄλλον δὲ μηδένα ἔχοι
λόγον περὶ αὐτῶν, ἀλλὰ τἀναγκαῖα δίκαια καλοῖ
καὶ καλά, τὴν δὲ τοῦ ἀναγκαίου καὶ ἀγαθοῦ φύσιν,
ὅσον διαφέρει τῷ ὄντι, μήτε ἑωρακὼς εἴη μήτε
ἄλλῳ δυνατὸς δεῖξαι. τοιοῦτος δὴ ὢν πρὸς Διὸς
οὐκ ἄτοπος ἄν σοι δοκεῖ εἶναι παιδευτής; Ἔμοιγ᾽,
ἔφη. Ἦ οὖν τι τούτου δοκεῖ διαφέρειν ὁ τὴν τῶν
D πολλῶν καὶ παντοδαπῶν ξυνιόντων ὀργὴν καὶ
ἡδονὰς κατανενοηκέναι σοφίαν ἡγούμενος, εἴτ᾽ ἐν
γραφικῇ εἴτ᾽ ἐν μουσικῇ εἴτε δὴ ἐν πολιτικῇ; ὅτι
μὲν γάρ, ἐάν τις τούτοις ὁμιλῇ ἐπιδεικνύμενος ἢ
ποίησιν ἤ τινα ἄλλην δημιουργίαν ἢ πόλει δια-
κονίαν, κυρίους αὐτοῦ ποιῶν τοὺς πολλοὺς πέρα
τῶν ἀναγκαίων, ἡ Διομήδεια λεγομένη ἀνάγκη
ποιεῖν αὐτῷ ταῦτα ἃ ἂν οὗτοι ἐπαινῶσιν· ὡς δὲ
καὶ ἀγαθὰ καὶ καλὰ ταῦτα τῇ ἀληθείᾳ, ἤδη

---

[a] Cf. Class. Phil. ix. (1914) p. 353, n. 1, ibid. xxiii. (1928)
p. 361 (Tim. 75 D), What Plato Said, p. 616 on Tim. 47 E,
Aristot. Eth. 1120 b 1 οὐχ ὡς καλὸν ἀλλ᾽ ὡς ἀναγκαῖον, Emerson, Circles, " Accept the actual for the necessary," Eurip.
I.A. 724 καλῶς ἀναγκαίως τε. Mill iv. 299 and Grote iv. 221
miss the meaning. Cf. supra Bk. I. on 347 c, Newman,
Aristot. Pol. i. pp. 113-114, Iamblichus, Protrept. Teubner
148 K. ἀγνοοῦντος . . . ὅσον διέστηκεν ἐξ ἀρχῆς τὰ ἀγαθὰ καὶ τὰ
ἀναγκαῖα, " not knowing how divergent have always been the
good and the necessary."

thereof a system and art and turn to the teaching of it, knowing nothing in reality about which of these opinions and desires is honourable or base, good or evil, just or unjust, but should apply all these terms to the judgements of the great beast, calling the things that pleased it good, and the things that vexed it bad, having no other account to render of them, but should call what is necessary just and honourable,[a] never having observed how great is the real difference between the necessary and the good, and being incapable of explaining it to another. Do you not think, by heaven, that such a one would be a strange educator ? " " I do," he said. " Do you suppose that there is any difference between such a one and the man who thinks that it is wisdom to have learned to know the moods and the pleasures of the motley multitude in their assembly, whether about painting or music or, for that matter, politics ? For if a man associates with these and offers and exhibits to them his poetry [b] or any other product of his craft or any political service,[c] and grants the mob authority over himself more than is unavoidable,[d] the proverbial necessity of Diomede [e] will compel him to give the public what it likes, but that what it likes is really good and honourable, have you ever heard an

---

[b] Cf. Laws 659 B, 701 A, Gorg. 502 B.

[c] Cf. 371 C, Gorg. 517 B, 518 B.

[d] Plato likes to qualify sweeping statements and allow something to necessity and the weakness of human nature. Cf. Phaedo 64 E καθ' ὅσον μὴ πολλὴ ἀνάγκη, infra 558 D-E, 500 D, 383 C.

[e] The scholiast derives this expression from Diomedes' binding Odysseus and driving him back to camp after the latter had attempted to kill him. The schol. on Aristoph. Eccl. 1029 gives a more ingenious explanation. See Frazer, Pausanias, ii. p. 264.

493 πώποτέ του ἤκουσας αὐτῶν λόγον διδόντος οὐ
E καταγέλαστον; Οἶμαι δέ γε, ἦ δ' ὅς, οὐδ'
ἀκούσομαι.

VIII. Ταῦτα τοίνυν πάντα ἐννοήσας ἐκεῖνο
ἀναμνήσθητι· αὐτὸ τὸ καλόν, ἀλλὰ μὴ τὰ πολλὰ
καλά, ἢ αὐτό τι ἕκαστον καὶ μὴ τὰ πολλὰ ἕκαστα,
ἔσθ' ὅπως πλῆθος ἀνέξεται ἢ ἡγήσεται εἶναι;
"Ηκιστά γ', ἔφη. Φιλόσοφον μὲν ἄρα, ἦν δ' ἐγώ,
494 πλῆθος ἀδύνατον εἶναι. 'Αδύνατον. Καὶ τοὺς
φιλοσοφοῦντας ἄρα ἀνάγκη ψέγεσθαι ὑπ' αὐτῶν.
'Ανάγκη. Καὶ ὑπὸ τούτων δὴ τῶν ἰδιωτῶν, ὅσοι
προσομιλοῦντες ὄχλῳ ἀρέσκειν αὐτῷ ἐπιθυμοῦσιν.
Δῆλον. 'Εκ δὴ τούτων τίνα ὁρᾷς σωτηρίαν
φιλοσόφῳ φύσει, ὥστ' ἐν τῷ ἐπιτηδεύματι μεί-
νασαν πρὸς τέλος ἐλθεῖν; ἐννόει δ' ἐκ τῶν ἔμ-
B προσθεν. ὡμολόγηται γὰρ δὴ ἡμῖν εὐμάθεια καὶ
μνήμη καὶ ἀνδρεία καὶ μεγαλοπρέπεια ταύτης εἶναι
τῆς φύσεως. Ναί. Οὐκοῦν εὐθὺς ἐν παισὶν ὁ
τοιοῦτος πρῶτος ἔσται ἐν ἅπασιν, ἄλλως τε καὶ
ἐὰν τὸ σῶμα φυῇ προσφερὴς τῇ ψυχῇ; Τί δ' οὐ
μέλλει; ἔφη. Βουλήσονται δή, οἶμαι, αὐτῷ χρη-

ᵃ καταγέλαστον is a strong word. "Make the very jack-
asses laugh" would give the tone. *Cf.* Carlyle, *Past and
Present*, iv. "Impartial persons have to say with a sigh
that . . . they have heard no argument advanced for it but
such as might make the angels and almost the very jack-
asses weep."

Cf. also Isoc. *Panegyr.* 14, *Phil.* 84, 101, *Antid.* 247,
Peace 36, and καταγέλαστος in Plato *passim*, *e.g. Symp.* 189 B.

ᵇ A commonplace of Plato and all intellectual idealists.
Cf. 503 B, *Polit.* 292 E, 297 B, 300 E.

Novotny, *Plato's Epistles*, p. 87, uses this to support his
view that Plato had a secret doctrine. Adam quotes *Gorg.*
474 A τοῖς δὲ πολλοῖς οὐδὲ διαλέγομαι, which is not quite

attempted proof of this that is not simply ridiculous [a]?"
"No," he said, "and I fancy I never shall hear it
either."

VIII. "Bearing all this in mind, recall our former
question. Can the multitude possibly tolerate or
believe in the reality of the beautiful in itself as
opposed to the multiplicity of beautiful things, or
can they believe in anything conceived in its essence
as opposed to the many particulars?" "Not in the
least," he said. "Philosophy, then, the love of
wisdom, is impossible for the multitude.[b]" "Impossible." "It is inevitable,[c] then, that those who
philosophize should be censured by them." "Inevitable." "And so likewise by those laymen who,
associating with the mob, desire to curry favour [d] with
it." "Obviously." "From this point of view do
you see any salvation that will suffer the born philosopher to abide in the pursuit and persevere to the
end? Consider it in the light of what we said before.
We agreed [e] that quickness in learning, memory,
courage and magnificence were the traits of this
nature." "Yes." "Then even as a boy [f] among boys
such a one will take the lead in all things, especially
if the nature of his body matches the soul." "How
could he fail to do so?" he said. "His kinsmen and

relevant. *Cf.* Renan, *Études d'histoire relig.* p. 403 "La
philosophie sera toujours le fait d'une imperceptible
minorité," etc.

[c] It is psychologically necessary. *Cf. supra*, Vol. I. on
473 E. *Cf.* 527 A, *Laws* 655 E, 658 E, 681 C, 687 C, *Phaedr.*
239 C, 271 B, *Crito* 49 D.

[d] *Cf. Gorg.* 481 E, 510 D, 513 B.

[e] In 487 A.

[f] *Cf.* 386 A. In what follows Plato is probably thinking of
Alcibiades. *Alc. I.* 103 A ff. imitates the passage. *Cf.* Xen.
Mem. i. 2. 24.

494 σθαι, ἐπειδὰν πρεσβύτερος γίγνηται, ἐπὶ τὰ αὑτῶν
πράγματα οἵ τε οἰκεῖοι καὶ οἱ πολῖται. Πῶς δ᾽
C οὔ; Ὑποκείσονται ἆρα δεόμενοι καὶ τιμῶντες,
προκαταλαμβάνοντες καὶ προκολακεύοντες τὴν
μέλλουσαν αὐτοῦ δύναμιν. Φιλεῖ γοῦν, ἔφη, οὕτω
γίγνεσθαι. Τί οὖν οἴει, ἦν δ᾽ ἐγώ, τὸν τοιοῦτον
ἐν τοῖς τοιούτοις ποιήσειν, ἄλλως τε καὶ ἐὰν τύχῃ
μεγάλης πόλεως ὢν καὶ ἐν ταύτῃ πλούσιός τε καὶ
γενναῖος, καὶ ἔτι εὐειδὴς καὶ μέγας; ἆρ᾽ οὐ
πληρωθήσεσθαι ἀμηχάνου ἐλπίδος, ἡγούμενον καὶ
τὰ τῶν Ἑλλήνων καὶ τὰ τῶν βαρβάρων ἱκανὸν
D ἔσεσθαι πράττειν, καὶ ἐπὶ τούτοις ὑψηλὸν ἐξαρεῖν
αὑτόν, σχηματισμοῦ καὶ φρονήματος κενοῦ ἄνευ
νοῦ ἐμπιπλάμενον; Καὶ μάλ᾽, ἔφη. Τῷ δὴ οὕτω
διατιθεμένῳ ἐάν τις ἠρέμα προσελθὼν τἀληθῆ
λέγῃ, ὅτι νοῦς οὐκ ἔνεστιν αὐτῷ, δεῖται δέ, τὸ δὲ
οὐ κτητὸν μὴ δουλεύσαντι τῇ κτήσει αὐτοῦ, ἆρ᾽
εὐπετὲς οἴει εἶναι εἰσακοῦσαι διὰ τοσούτων κακῶν;
Πολλοῦ γε δεῖ, ἦ δ᾽ ὅς. Ἐὰν δ᾽ οὖν, ἦν δ᾽ ἐγώ,
διὰ τὸ εὖ πεφυκέναι καὶ τὸ ξυγγενὲς τῶν λόγων
E εἷς αἰσθάνηταί τέ πῃ καὶ κάμπτηται καὶ ἕλκηται
πρὸς φιλοσοφίαν, τί οἰόμεθα δράσειν ἐκείνους τοὺς
ἡγουμένους ἀπολλύναι αὐτοῦ τὴν χρείαν τε καὶ

---

[a] For ὑποκείσονται cf. Gorg. 510 c, infra 576 A ὑποπεσόντες,
Eurip. Orest. 670 ὑποτρέχειν, Theaet. 173 A ὑπελθεῖν.

[b] i.e. endeavouring to secure the advantage of it for themselves by winning his favour when he is still young and
impressionable.

[c] Cf. Alc. I. 104 B-c ff.

[d] Cf. Alc. I. 105 B-c.

[e] ὑψηλὸν ἐξαρεῖν, etc., seems to be a latent poetic quotation.

fellow-citizens, then, will desire, I presume, to make use of him when he is older for their own affairs." "Of course." "Then they will fawn upon[a] him with petitions and honours, anticipating[b] and flattering the power that will be his." "That certainly is the usual way." "How, then, do you think such a youth will behave in such conditions, especially if it happen that he belongs to a great city and is rich and well-born therein, and thereto handsome and tall? Will his soul not be filled with unbounded ambitious hopes,[c] and will he not think himself capable of managing the affairs of both Greeks and barbarians,[d] and thereupon exalt himself, haughty of mien and stuffed with empty pride and void of sense[e]?" "He surely will," he said. "And if to a man in this state of mind[f] someone gently[g] comes and tells him what is the truth, that he has no sense and sorely needs it, and that the only way to get it is to work like a slave[h] to win it, do you think it will be easy for him to lend an ear[i] to the quiet voice in the midst of and in spite of these evil surroundings[j]?" "Far from it," said he. "And even supposing," said I, "that owing to a fortunate disposition and his affinity for the words of admonition one such youth apprehends something and is moved and drawn towards philosophy, what do we suppose will be the conduct of those who think that they are

[f] Or perhaps "subject to these influences." Adam says it is while he is sinking into this condition.
[g] Cf. *supra* Vol. I. on 476 E. Cf. 533 D, *Protag.* 333 E, *Phaedo* 83 A, *Crat.* 413 A, *Theaet.* 154 E.
[h] Cf. *Phaedo* 66 D, *Symp.* 184 C, *Euthydem.* 282 B.
[i] Cf. *Epin.* 990 A, *Epist.* vii. 330 A-B.
[j] Cf. *Alc. I.* 135 E.

PLATO

494 ἑταιρείαν; οὐ πᾶν μὲν ἔργον, πᾶν δ' ἔπος λέ-
γοντάς τε καὶ πράττοντας καὶ περὶ αὐτόν, ὅπως
ἂν μὴ πεισθῇ, καὶ περὶ τὸν πείθοντα, ὅπως ἂν μὴ
οἷός τ' ᾖ, καὶ ἰδίᾳ ἐπιβουλεύοντας καὶ δημοσίᾳ εἰς
495 ἀγῶνας καθιστάντας; Πολλή, ἦ δ' ὅς, ἀνάγκη.
Ἔστιν οὖν ὅπως ὁ τοιοῦτος φιλοσοφήσει; Οὐ
πάνυ.

IX. Ὁρᾷς οὖν, ἦν δ' ἐγώ, ὅτι οὐ κακῶς ἐλέγομεν ὡς ἄρα καὶ αὐτὰ τὰ τῆς φιλοσόφου φύσεως
μέρη, ὅταν ἐν κακῇ τροφῇ γένηται, αἴτια τρόπον
τινὰ τοῦ ἐκπεσεῖν ἐκ τοῦ ἐπιτηδεύματος, καὶ τὰ
λεγόμενα ἀγαθά, πλοῦτοί τε καὶ πᾶσα ἡ τοιαύτη
παρασκευή; Οὐ γάρ, ἀλλ' ὀρθῶς, ἔφη, ἐλέχθη.
Οὗτος δή, εἶπον, ὦ θαυμάσιε, ὄλεθρός τε καὶ
B διαφθορὰ τοσαύτη τε καὶ τοιαύτη τῆς βελτίστης
φύσεως εἰς τὸ ἄριστον ἐπιτήδευμα, ὀλίγης καὶ
ἄλλως γιγνομένης, ὡς ἡμεῖς φαμεν. καὶ ἐκ τούτων δὴ τῶν ἀνδρῶν καὶ οἱ τὰ μέγιστα κακὰ ἐργα-
ζόμενοι τὰς πόλεις γίγνονται καὶ τοὺς ἰδιώτας, καὶ
οἱ τἀγαθά, οἳ ἂν ταύτῃ τύχωσι ῥυέντες· σμικρὰ
δὲ φύσις οὐδὲν μέγα οὐδέποτε οὐδένα οὔτε ἰδιώτην
οὔτε πόλιν δρᾷ. Ἀληθέστατα, ἦ δ' ὅς. Οὗτοι
C μὲν δὴ οὕτως ἐκπίπτοντες, οἷς μάλιστα προσήκει,
ἔρημον καὶ ἀτελῆ φιλοσοφίαν λείποντες αὐτοί τε
βίον οὐ προσήκοντα οὐδ' ἀληθῆ ζῶσι, τὴν δὲ

---

[a] For πᾶν ἔργον cf. Sophocles, El. 615.
[b] Cf. 517 A.

losing his service and fellowship ? Is there any word or deed that they will stick at [a] to keep him from being persuaded and to incapacitate anyone who attempts it,[b] both by private intrigue and public prosecution in the court ? " " That is inevitable," he said. " Is there any possibility of such a one continuing to philosophize ? " " None at all," he said.

IX. " Do you see, then," said I, " that we were not wrong in saying that the very qualities that make up the philosophical nature do, in fact, become, when the environment and nurture are bad, in some sort the cause of its backsliding,[c] and so do the so-called goods—[d] riches and all such instrumentalities [e] ? " " No," he replied, " it was rightly said." " Such, my good friend, and so great as regards the noblest pursuit, is the destruction and corruption [f] of the most excellent nature, which is rare enough in any case,[g] as we affirm. And it is from men of this type that those spring who do the greatest harm to communities and individuals, and the greatest good when the stream chances to be turned into that channel,[h] but a small nature [i] never does anything great to a man or a city." " Most true," said he. " Those, then, to whom she properly belongs, thus falling away and leaving philosophy forlorn and unwedded, themselves live an unreal and alien life, while other unworthy wooers [j] rush in and

---

[c] For ἐκπεσεῖν cf. 496 c.

[d] Cf. supra on 491 c, p. 32, note a.

[e] Cf. Lysis 220 A; Arnold's "machinery," Aristotle's χορηγία.

[f] Cf. 491 B-E, Laws 951 B. ἀδιάφθαρτος, Xen. Mem. i. 2. 24.

[g] For καὶ ἄλλως cf. Il. ix. 699.

[h] Cf. on 485 D ὥσπερ ῥεῦμα.

[i] Cf. on 491 E, p. 33, note d.

[j] Cf. on 489 D, and Theaet. 173 c.

PLATO

495 ὥσπερ ὀρφανὴν ξυγγενῶν ἄλλοι ἐπεισελθόντες
ἀνάξιοι ᾔσχυνάν τε καὶ ὀνείδη περιῆψαν, οἷα καὶ
σὺ φῂς ὀνειδίζειν τοὺς ὀνειδίζοντας, ὡς οἱ ξυνόντες
αὐτῇ οἱ μὲν οὐδενός, οἱ δὲ πολλοὶ πολλῶν κακῶν
ἄξιοί εἰσιν. Καὶ γὰρ οὖν, ἔφη, τά γε λεγόμενα
ταῦτα. Εἰκότως γε, ἦν δ' ἐγώ, λεγόμενα. καθ-
ορῶντες γὰρ ἄλλοι ἀνθρωπίσκοι κενὴν τὴν χώραν
ταύτην γιγνομένην, καλῶν δὲ ὀνομάτων καὶ προ-
D σχημάτων μεστήν, ὥσπερ οἱ ἐκ τῶν εἰργμῶν εἰς
τὰ ἱερὰ ἀποδιδράσκοντες ἄσμενοι καὶ οὗτοι ἐκ
τῶν τεχνῶν ἐκπηδῶσιν εἰς τὴν φιλοσοφίαν, οἳ ἂν
κομψότατοι ὄντες τυγχάνωσι περὶ τὸ αὑτῶν τεχνίον. ὅμως γὰρ δὴ πρός γε τὰς ἄλλας τέχνας
καίπερ οὕτω πραττούσης φιλοσοφίας τὸ ἀξίωμα
μεγαλοπρεπέστερον λείπεται· οὗ δὴ ἐφιέμενοι
πολλοὶ ἀτελεῖς μὲν τὰς φύσεις, ὑπὸ δὲ τῶν τεχνῶν
τε καὶ δημιουργιῶν, ὥσπερ τὰ σώματα λελώβηνται,
E οὕτω καὶ τὰς ψυχὰς ξυγκεκλασμένοι τε καὶ ἀπο-
τεθρυμμένοι διὰ τὰς βαναυσίας τυγχάνουσιν. ἢ οὐκ
ἀνάγκη; Καὶ μάλα, ἔφη. Δοκεῖς οὖν τι, ἦν δ'

---

[a] *Cf.* Taine, à Sainte-Beuve, Aug. 14, 1865 : "Comme
Claude Bernard, il dépasse sa spécialité et c'est chez des
spécialistes comme ceux-là que la malheureuse philosophie
livrée aux mains gantées et parfumées d'eau bénite va
trouver des maris capables de lui faire encore des enfants."
Cf. Epictet. iii. 21. 21. The passage is imitated by Lucian
3. 2. 287, 294, 298.

For the shame that has befallen philosophy *cf. Euthydem.*
304 ff., *Epist.* vii. 328 E, Isoc. *Busiris* 48, Plutarch 1091 E,
Boethius, *Cons.* i. 3. There is no probability that this is
aimed at Isocrates, who certainly had not deserted the
mechanical arts for what he called philosophy. Rohde,
Kleine Schriften, i. 319, thinks Antisthenes is meant. But

48

THE REPUBLIC, BOOK VI

defile. her as an orphan bereft of her kin,[a] and attach
to her such reproaches as you say her revilers taunt
her with, declaring that some of her consorts are of
no account and the many accountable for many
evils." "Why, yes," he replied, "that is what they
do say." "And plausibly," said I; "for other
mannikins, observing that the place is unoccupied
and full of fine terms and pretensions, just as men
escape from prison to take sanctuary in temples, so
these gentlemen joyously bound away from the
mechanical arts [b] to philosophy, those that are most
cunning in their little craft.[c] For in comparison with
the other arts the prestige of philosophy even in her
present low estate retains a superior dignity ; and this
is the ambition and aspiration of that multitude of
pretenders unfit by nature, whose souls are bowed
and mutilated [d] by their vulgar occupations [e] even as
their bodies are marred by their arts and crafts. Is
not that inevitable ? " "Quite so," he said. "Is

Plato as usual is generalizing. See *What Plato Said*, p. 593
on *Soph.* 242 c.

[b] *Cf.* the different use of the idea in *Protag.* 318 E.

[c] τεχνίον is a contemptuous diminutive, such as are common
in Epictetus and Marcus Aurelius. *Cf.* also ἀνθρωπίσκοι
in c, and ψυχάριον in 519 A.

[d] *Cf. infra* 611 C-D, *Theaet.* 173 A-B.

[e] For the idea that trade is ungentlemanly and incompatible with philosophy *cf. infra* 522 B and 590 C, *Laws* 919 C ff.,
and *What Plato Said*, p. 663 on *Rivals* 137 B. *Cf.* Richard
of Bury, *Philobiblon*, Prologue, "Fitted for the liberal arts,
and equally disposed to the contemplation of Scripture, but
destitute of the needful aid, they revert, as it were, by a
sort of apostasy, to mechanical arts." *Cf.* also Xen. *Mem.*
iv. 2. 3, and *Ecclesiasticus* xxxviii. 25 f. "How can he get
wisdom that holdeth the plough and glorieth in the goad
. . . and whose talk is of bullocks? . . . so every carpenter
and workmaster . . . the smith . . . the potter . . ."

PLATO

495 ἐγώ, διαφέρειν αὐτοὺς ἰδεῖν ἀργύριον κτησαμένου
χαλκέως φαλακροῦ καὶ σμικροῦ, νεωστὶ μὲν ἐκ
δεσμῶν λελυμένου, ἐν βαλανείῳ δὲ λελουμένου,
νεουργὸν ἱμάτιον ἔχοντος, ὡς νυμφίου παρεσκευα-
σμένου, διὰ πενίαν καὶ ἐρημίαν τοῦ δεσπότου
496 τὴν θυγατέρα μέλλοντος γαμεῖν; Οὐ πάνυ, ἔφη,
διαφέρει. Ποῖ' ἄττα οὖν εἰκὸς γεννᾶν τοὺς τοιούτους; οὐ νόθα καὶ φαῦλα; Πολλὴ ἀνάγκη. Τί
δαί; τοὺς ἀναξίους παιδεύσεως, ὅταν αὐτῇ πλησιά-
ζοντες ὁμιλῶσι μὴ κατ' ἀξίαν, ποῖ' ἄττα φῶμεν
γεννᾶν διανοήματά τε καὶ δόξας; ἆρ' οὐχ ὡς
ἀληθῶς προσήκοντα ἀκοῦσαι σοφίσματα, καὶ οὐδὲν γνήσιον οὐδὲ φρονήσεως ἀληθινῆς¹ ἐχόμενον;
Παντελῶς μὲν οὖν, ἔφη.

X. Πάνσμικρον δή τι, ἦν δ' ἐγώ, ὦ Ἀδείμαντε,
B λείπεται τῶν κατ' ἀξίαν ὁμιλούντων φιλοσοφίᾳ, ἤ
που ὑπὸ φυγῆς καταληφθὲν γενναῖον καὶ εὖ τεθραμμένον ἦθος, ἀπορίᾳ τῶν διαφθερούντων κατὰ
φύσιν μεῖναν ἐπ' αὐτῇ, ἢ ἐν σμικρᾷ πόλει ὅταν
μεγάλη ψυχὴ φυῇ καὶ ἀτιμάσασα τὰ τῆς πόλεως
ὑπερίδῃ· βραχὺ δέ πού τι καὶ ἀπ' ἄλλης τέχνης
δικαίως ἀτιμάσαν εὐφυὲς ἐπ' αὐτὴν ἂν ἔλθοι. εἴη
δ' ἂν καὶ ὁ τοῦ ἡμετέρου ἑταίρου Θεάγους χαλινὸς

---

¹ ἄξιον secl. Ast: ἄξιον ἀληθινῆς AM, ἄξιον ὡς ἀληθινῆς D,
ἀληθινῆς ὡς ἄξιον F: ἀξίως conj. Campbell.

ᵃ For a similar short vivid description *cf. Erastae* 134 B,
Euthyphro 2 B. Such are common in Plautus, *e.g. Mer-
cator* 639.

ᵇ It is probably fanciful to see in this an allusion to the
half-Thracian Antisthenes. *Cf.* also *Theaet.* 150 C, and *Symp.*
212 A.

ᶜ *Cf. Euthydem.* 306 D.

ᵈ *Cf. Phaedrus* 250 A ὀλίγαι δὴ λείπονται, and *supra* 494 A
and on 490 E.

not the picture which they present," I said, " precisely that of a little bald-headed tinker [a] who has made money and just been freed from bonds and had a bath and is wearing a new garment and has got himself up like a bridegroom and is about to marry his master's daughter who has fallen into poverty and abandonment ? " " There is no difference at all," he said. " Of what sort will probably be the offspring of such parents ? Will they not be bastard [b] and base ? " " Inevitably." " And so when men unfit for culture approach philosophy and consort with her unworthily, what sort of ideas and opinions shall we say they beget ? Will they not produce what may in very deed be fairly called sophisms, and nothing that is genuine or that partakes of true intelligence [c] ? " " Quite so," he said.

X. " There is a very small remnant,[d] then, Adeimantus," I said, " of those who consort worthily with philosophy, some well-born and well-bred nature, it may be, held in check [e] by exile,[f] and so in the absence of corrupters remaining true to philosophy, as its quality bids, or it may happen that a great soul born in a little town scorns [g] and disregards its parochial affairs ; and a small group perhaps might by natural affinity be drawn to it from other arts which they justly disdain ; and the bridle of our companion Theages [h] also might operate as a restraint. For in the

[e] Perhaps "overtaken." *Cf.* Goodwin on Dem. *De cor.* § 107.

[f] It is possible but unnecessary to conjecture that Plato may be thinking of Anaxagoras or Xenophon or himself or Dion. [g] *Cf. Theaet.* 173 B, *infra* 540 D.

[h] This bridle has become proverbial. *Cf.* Plut. *De san. tuenda* 126 B, Aelian, *Var. Hist.* iv. 15. For Theages *cf.* also *Apol.* 33 E and the spurious dialogue bearing his name.

PLATO

496 οἷος κατασχεῖν· καὶ γὰρ Θεάγει τὰ μὲν ἄλλα πάντα
C παρεσκεύασται πρὸς τὸ ἐκπεσεῖν φιλοσοφίας, ἡ δὲ
τοῦ σώματος νοσοτροφία ἀπείργουσα αὐτὸν τῶν
πολιτικῶν κατέχει. τὸ δ' ἡμέτερον οὐκ ἄξιον
λέγειν, τὸ δαιμόνιον σημεῖον· ἢ γάρ πού τινι ἄλλῳ
ἢ οὐδενὶ τῶν ἔμπροσθεν γέγονε. καὶ τούτων δὴ
τῶν ὀλίγων οἱ γενόμενοι καὶ γευσάμενοι ὡς ἡδὺ
καὶ μακάριον τὸ κτῆμα, καὶ τῶν πολλῶν αὖ ἱκανῶς
ἰδόντες τὴν μανίαν, καὶ ὅτι οὐδεὶς οὐδὲν ὑγιὲς ὡς
ἔπος εἰπεῖν περὶ τὰ τῶν πόλεων πράττει, οὐδ' ἔστι
D ξύμμαχος, μεθ' ὅτου τις ἰὼν ἐπὶ τὴν τῶν δικαίων
βοήθειαν σώζοιτ' ἄν, ἀλλ' ὥσπερ εἰς θηρία ἄνθρωπος ἐμπεσών, οὔτε ξυναδικεῖν ἐθέλων οὔτε
ἱκανὸς ὢν εἷς πᾶσιν ἀγρίοις ἀντέχειν, πρίν τι τὴν

---

^a The enormous fanciful literature on the daimonion does
not concern the interpretation of Plato, who consistently
treats it as a kind of spiritual tact checking Socrates from
any act opposed to his true moral and intellectual interests.
Cf. What Plato Said, pp. 456-457, on *Euthyphro* 3 в, Jowett
and Campbell, p. 285.

^b For τούτων . . . γενόμενοι *cf.* Aristoph. *Clouds* 107 τούτων
γενοῦ μοι.

^c The irremediable degeneracy of existing governments is
the starting-point of Plato's political and social speculations. *Cf. infra* 497 в, *Laws* 832 c f., *Epist.* vii. 326 ᴀ;
Byron, *apud* Arnold, *Essays in Crit.* ii. p. 195 " I have
simplified my politics into an utter detestation of all existing
governments."

This passage, *Apol.* 31 ᴇ ff. and *Gorg.* 521-522 may be con-
sidered Plato's apology for not engaging in politics. *Cf.*
J. V. Novak, *Platon u. d. Rhetorik*, p. 495 (Schleiermacher,
Einl. z. Gorg. pp. 15 f.), Wilamowitz, *Platon*, i. 441-442
" Wer kann hier die Klage über das eigene Los überhören ? "

There is no probability that, as an eminent scholar has
maintained, the *Republic* itself was intended as a programme
of practical politics for Athens, and that its failure to win
popular opinion is the chief cause of the disappointed tone

case of Theages all other conditions were at hand
for his backsliding from philosophy, but his sickly
habit of body keeping him out of politics holds him
back. ' My own case, the divine sign,[a] is hardly
worth mentioning—for I suppose it has happened to
few or none before me. And those who have been
of this little company [b] and have tasted the sweetness
and blessedness of this possession and who have also
come to understand the madness of the multitude
sufficiently and have seen that there is nothing, if I
may say so, sound or right in any present politics,[c] and
that there is no ally with whose aid the champion
of justice [d] could escape destruction, but that he
would be as a man who has fallen among wild beasts,[e]
unwilling to share their misdeeds [f] and unable to hold
out singly against the savagery of all, and that he
would thus, before he could in any way benefit his

of Plato's later writings. *Cf.* Erwin Wolff in Jaeger's *Neue
Phil. Untersuchungen*, Heft 6, *Platos Apologie*, pp. 31-33,
who argues that abstinence from politics is proclaimed in the
Apology before the *Gorgias* and that the same doctrine in
the seventh *Epistle* absolutely proves that the *Apology* is
Plato's own.

Cf. also *Theaet.* 173. c ff., *Hipp. Maj.* 281 c, *Euthydem.*
306 B, Xen. *Mem.* i. 6. 15.

[d] *Cf. supra* 368 B, *Apol.* 32 E εἰ . . . ἐβοήθουν τοῖς δικαίοις
and 32 A μαχούμενον ὑπὲρ τοῦ δικαίου.

[e] *Cf.* Pindar, *Ol.* i. 64. For the antithetic juxtaposition
cf. also εἰς πᾶσιν below; see too 520 B, 374 A, *Menex.* 241 B,
Phaedr. 243 c, *Laws* 906 D, etc.

More in the *Utopia* (Morley, *Ideal Commonwealths*, p. 84)
paraphrases loosely from memory what he calls " no ill simile
by which Plato set forth the unreasonableness of a philosopher's meddling with government."

[f] *Cf.* Democrates fr. 38, Diels ii.³ p. 73 καλὸν μὲν τὸν
ἀδικέοντα κωλύειν· εἰ δὲ μή, μὴ ξυναδικεῖν, " it is well to prevent
anyone from doing wrong, or else not to join in wrong-
doing."

496 πόλιν ἢ φίλους ὀνῆσαι προαπολόμενος ἀνωφελὴς
αὑτῷ τε καὶ τοῖς ἄλλοις ἂν γένοιτο—ταῦτα πάντα
λογισμῷ λαβὼν ἡσυχίαν ἔχων καὶ τὰ αὑτοῦ πράττων, οἷον ἐν χειμῶνι κονιορτοῦ καὶ ζάλης ὑπὸ
πνεύματος φερομένου ὑπὸ τειχίον ἀποστάς, ὁρῶν
τοὺς ἄλλους καταπιμπλαμένους ἀνομίας ἀγαπᾷ, εἴ
Ε πῃ αὐτὸς καθαρὸς ἀδικίας τε καὶ ἀνοσίων ἔργων
τόν τε ἐνθάδε βίον βιώσεται καὶ τὴν ἀπαλλαγὴν
αὐτοῦ μετὰ καλῆς ἐλπίδος ἵλεώς τε καὶ εὐμενὴς
ἀπαλλάξεται. Ἀλλά τοι, ἦ δ᾽ ὅς, οὐ τὰ ἐλάχιστα
497 ἂν διαπραξάμενος ἀπαλλάττοιτο. Οὐδέ γε, εἶπον,
τὰ μέγιστα, μὴ τυχὼν πολιτείας προσηκούσης· ἐν
γὰρ προσηκούσῃ αὐτός τε μᾶλλον αὐξήσεται καὶ
μετὰ τῶν ἰδίων τὰ κοινὰ σώσει.

XI. Τὸ μὲν οὖν τῆς φιλοσοφίας, ὧν ἕνεκα διαβολὴν εἴληφε καὶ ὅτι οὐ δικαίως, ἐμοὶ μὲν δοκεῖ
μετρίως εἰρῆσθαι, εἰ μὴ ἔτ᾽ ἄλλο λέγεις τι σύ.
Ἀλλ᾽ οὐδέν, ἦ δ᾽ ὅς, ἔτι λέγω περὶ τούτου· ἀλλὰ
τὴν προσήκουσαν αὐτῇ τίνα τῶν νῦν λέγεις πολι-
Β τειῶν; Οὐδ᾽ ἡντινοῦν, εἶπον, ἀλλὰ τοῦτο καὶ

ᵃ Maximus of Tyre 21. 20 comments, "Show me a safe
wall." See Stallbaum *ad loc.* for references to this passage
in later antiquity. *Cf.* Heracleit. fr. 44, Diels³ i. 67, J.
Stenzel, *Platon der Erzieher*, p. 114, Bryce, *Studies in
History and Jurisprudence*, p. 33, Renan, *Souvenirs*, xviii.,
P. E. More, *Shelburne Essays*, iii. pp. 280-281. *Cf.* also
Epist. vii. 331 D, Eurip. *Ion* 598-601.

ᵇ *Cf. supra* Vol. I. on 331 A, *infra* 621 C-D, Marc.
Aurel. xii. 36 and vi. 30 *in fine*. See my article "Hope" in
Hastings's *Encyclopaedia of Religion and Ethics*.

ᶜ *Cf.* Aristot. *Eth. Nic.* 1094 b 9 μεῖζόν γε καὶ τελεώτερον
τὸ τῆς πόλεως φαίνεται καὶ λαβεῖν καὶ σῴζειν, "yet the good of

54

friends or the state come to an untimely end without doing any good to himself or others,—for all these reasons I say the philosopher remains quiet, minds his own affair, and, as it were, standing aside under shelter of a wall[a] in a storm and blast of dust and sleet and seeing others filled full of lawlessness, is content if in any way he may keep himself free from iniquity and unholy deeds through this life and take his departure with fair hope,[b] serene and well content when the end comes." " Well," he said, " that is no very slight thing to have achieved before taking his departure." " He would not have accomplished any very great thing either,[c]" I replied, "if it were not his fortune to live in a state adapted to his nature. In such a state only will he himself rather attain his full stature[d] and together with his own preserve the common weal.

XI. " The causes and the injustice of the calumniation of philosophy, I think, have been fairly set forth, unless you have something to add.[e] " " No," he said, " I have nothing further to offer on that point. But which of our present governments do you think is suitable for philosophy ? " " None whatever," I said; " but the very ground of my complaint is that no the state seems a grander and more perfect thing both to attain and to secure " (tr. F. H. Peters).

[d] For αὐξήσεται cf. Thea-et. 163 c ἵνα καὶ αὐξάνῃ, and Newman, Aristot. Pol. i. p. 68 " As the Christian is said to be complete in Christ so the individual is said by Aristotle to be complete in the πόλις," Spencer, Data of Ethics, xv. " Hence it is manifest that we must consider the ideal man as existing in the ideal social state." Cf. also infra 592 A-B, 520 A-c and Introd. Vol. I. p. xxvii.

[e] An instance of Socrates' Attic courtesy. Cf. 430 B, Cratyl. 427 D, Theaet. 183 c, Gorg. 513 c, Phaedr. 235 A. But in Gorg. 462 c it is ironical and perhaps in Hipp. Maj. 291 A.

PLATO

497 ἐπαιτιῶμαι, μηδεμίαν ἀξίαν εἶναι τῶν νῦν κατάστασιν πόλεως φιλοσόφου φύσεως· διὸ καὶ στρέ-
φεσθαί τε καὶ ἀλλοιοῦσθαι αὐτήν, ὥσπερ ξενικὸν
σπέρμα ἐν γῇ ἄλλῃ σπειρόμενον ἐξίτηλον εἰς τὸ
ἐπιχώριον φιλεῖ κρατούμενον ἰέναι, οὕτω καὶ
τοῦτο τὸ γένος νῦν μὲν οὐκ ἴσχειν τὴν αὑτοῦ
δύναμιν, ἀλλ' εἰς ἀλλότριον ἦθος ἐκπίπτειν· εἰ δὲ
C λήψεται τὴν ἀρίστην πολιτείαν, ὥσπερ καὶ αὐτὸ
ἄριστόν ἐστι, τότε δηλώσει, ὅτι τοῦτο μὲν τῷ ὄντι
θεῖον ἦν, τὰ δὲ ἄλλα ἀνθρώπινα, τά τε τῶν φύσεων
καὶ τῶν ἐπιτηδευμάτων. δῆλος δὴ οὖν εἶ ὅτι μετὰ
τοῦτο ἐρήσει τίς αὕτη ἡ πολιτεία. Οὐκ ἔγνως,
ἔφη· οὐ γὰρ τοῦτο ἔμελλον, ἀλλ' εἰ αὕτη, ἣν ἡμεῖς
διεληλύθαμεν οἰκίζοντες τὴν πόλιν ἢ ἄλλη. Τὰ
μὲν ἄλλα, ἦν δ' ἐγώ, αὕτη· τοῦτο δὲ αὐτὸ ἐρρήθη
μὲν καὶ τότε, ὅτι δεήσοι τι ἀεὶ ἐνεῖναι ἐν τῇ πόλει
D λόγον ἔχον τῆς πολιτείας τὸν αὐτὸν ὅνπερ καὶ
σὺ ὁ νομοθέτης ἔχων τοὺς νόμους ἐτίθεις. Ἐρρήθη γάρ, ἔφη. Ἀλλ' οὐχ ἱκανῶς, εἶπον, ἐδηλώθη,
φόβῳ ὧν ὑμεῖς ἀντιλαμβανόμενοι δεδηλώκατε
μακρὰν καὶ χαλεπὴν αὐτοῦ τὴν ἀπόδειξιν· ἐπεὶ καὶ
τὸ λοιπὸν οὐ πάντως¹ ῥᾷστον διελθεῖν. Τὸ ποῖον;
Τίνα τρόπον μεταχειριζομένη πόλις φιλοσοφίαν οὐ
διολεῖται. τὰ γὰρ δὴ μεγάλα πάντα ἐπισφαλῆ, καὶ

¹ πάντως AFDM : πάντων conj. Bekker.

ᵃ κατάστασις = constitution in both senses. Cf. 414 A, 425 D,
464 A, 493 A, 426 C, 547 B. So also in the Laws. The word
is rare elsewhere in Plato.

ᵇ For ἐξίτηλον cf. Critias 121 A.

ᶜ This need not be a botanical error. In any case the
meaning is plain. Cf. Tim. 57 B with my emendation.

ᵈ For the idiom cf. αὐτὸ δείξει Phileb. 20 C, with Stallbaum's
note, Theaet. 200 E, Hipp. Maj. 288 B, Aristoph. Wasps

56

polity [a] of to-day is worthy of the philosophic nature. This is just the cause of its perversion and alteration ; as a foreign seed sown in an alien soil is wont to be overcome and die out [b] into the native growth,[c] so this kind does not preserve its own quality but falls away and degenerates into an alien type. But if ever it finds the best polity as it itself is the best, then will it be apparent [d] that this was in truth divine and all the others human in their natures and practices. Obviously then you are next going to ask what is this best form of government." " Wrong," he said [e] ; " I was going to ask not that but whether it is this one that we have described in our establishment of a state or another." " In other respects it is this one," said I ; " but there is one special further point that we mentioned even then, namely that there would always have to be resident in such a state an element having the same conception of its constitution that you the lawgiver had in framing its laws.[f] " " That was said," he replied. " But it was not sufficiently explained," I said, " from fear of those objections on your part which have shown that the demonstration of it is long and difficult. And apart from that the remainder of the exposition is by no means easy.[g] " " Just what do you mean ? " " The manner in which a state that occupies itself with philosophy can escape destruction. For all great things are precarious and, as the proverb truly

---

994, *Frogs* 1261, etc., Pearson on *Soph.* fr. 388. *Cf. αὐτὸ σημανεῖ,* Eurip. *Bacch.* 476, etc.

[e] Plato similarly plays in dramatic fashion with the order of the dialogue in 523 B, 528 A, 451 B-C, 458 B.

[f] *Cf. supra* on 412 A and *What Plato Said,* p. 647 on *Laws* 962 ; *infra* 502 D.

[g] *Cf. Soph.* 244 c. See critical note.

497 τὸ λεγόμενον τὰ καλὰ τῷ ὄντι χαλεπά. Ἀλλ᾽
E ὅμως, ἔφη, λαβέτω τέλος ἡ ἀπόδειξις τούτου
φανεροῦ γενομένου. Οὐ τὸ μὴ βούλεσθαι, ἦν δ᾽
ἐγώ, ἀλλ᾽ εἴπερ, τὸ μὴ δύνασθαι διακωλύσει·
παρὼν δὲ τήν γ᾽ ἐμὴν προθυμίαν εἴσει. σκόπει δὲ
καὶ νῦν, ὡς προθύμως καὶ παρακινδυνευτικῶς
μέλλω λέγειν, ὅτι τοὐναντίον ἢ νῦν δεῖ τοῦ ἐπιτηδεύματος τούτου πόλιν ἅπτεσθαι. Πῶς; Νῦν μέν,
498 ἦν δ᾽ ἐγώ, οἱ καὶ ἁπτόμενοι μειράκια ὄντα ἄρτι ἐκ
παίδων τὸ μεταξὺ οἰκονομίας καὶ χρηματισμοῦ
πλησιάσαντες αὐτοῦ τῷ χαλεπωτάτῳ ἀπαλλάτ-
τονται, οἱ φιλοσοφώτατοι ποιούμενοι· λέγω δὲ
χαλεπώτατον τὸ περὶ τοὺς λόγους· ἐν δὲ τῷ ἔπειτα,
ἐὰν καὶ ἄλλων τοῦτο πραττόντων παρακαλούμενοι
ἐθέλωσιν ἀκροαταὶ γίγνεσθαι, μεγάλα ἡγοῦνται,
πάρεργον οἰόμενοι αὐτὸ δεῖν πράττειν· πρὸς δὲ τὸ
γῆρας ἐκτὸς δή τινων ὀλίγων ἀποσβέννυνται πολὺ
B μᾶλλον τοῦ Ἡρακλειτείου ἡλίου, ὅσον αὖθις οὐκ
ἐξάπτονται. Δεῖ δὲ πῶς; ἔφη. Πᾶν τοὐναντίον·
μειράκια μὲν ὄντα καὶ παῖδας μειρακιώδη παιδείαν

ᵃ So Adam. Others take τῷ ὄντι with χαλεπά as part of
the proverb. *Cf.* 435 c, *Crat.* 384 ᴀ-ʙ with schol.

ᵇ For the idiomatic ἀλλ᾽ εἴπερ *cf. Parmen.* 150 ʙ, *Euthydem.*
296 ʙ, Thompson on *Meno*, Excursus 2, pp. 258-264, Aristot.
An. Post. 91 b 33, *Eth. Nic.* 1101 a 12, 1136 b 25, 1155 b 30,
1168 a 12, 1174 a 27, 1180 b 27, *Met.* 1028 a 24, 1044 a 11,
Rhet. 1371 a 16.

ᶜ What Plato here deprecates Callicles in the *Gorgias*
recommends, 484 ᴄ-ᴅ. For the danger of premature study
of dialectic *cf.* 537 ᴅ-ᴇ ff. *Cf.* my *Idea of Education in
Plato's Republic*, p. 11. Milton develops the thought with
characteristic exuberance, *Of Education*: "They present
their young unmatriculated novices at first coming with the
most intellective abstractions of logic and metaphysics . . .

says, fine things are hard.[a]" "All the same," he said,
"our exposition must be completed by making this
plain." "It will be no lack of will," I said, "but if
anything,[b] a lack of ability, that would prevent that.
But you shall observe for yourself my zeal. And note
again how zealously and recklessly I am prepared to
say that the state ought to take up this pursuit in
just the reverse of our present fashion.[c]" "In what
way?" "At present," said I, "those who do take
it up are youths, just out of boyhood,[d] who in the
interval[e] before they engage in business and money-
making approach the most difficult part of it, and
then drop it—and these are regarded forsooth as
the best exemplars of philosophy. By the most
difficult part I mean discussion. In later life they
think they have done much if, when invited, they
deign to listen[f] to the philosophic discussions of others.
That sort of thing they think should be by-work.
And towards old age,[g] with few exceptions, their light
is quenched more completely than the sun of Heracleitus,[h] inasmuch as it is never rekindled." "And
what should they do?" he said. "Just the reverse.
While they are lads and boys they should occupy

to be tossed and turmoiled with their unballasted wits in
fathomless and unquiet deeps of controversy," etc.

[d] Cf. 386 A, 395 C, 413 C, 485 D, 519 A, Demosth. xxi. 154,
Xen. *Ages.* 10. 4, Aristot. *Eth. Nic.* 1103 b 24, 1104 b 11, Isoc.
xv. 289.   [e] Cf. 450 c.

[f] Cf. 475 D, Isoc. xii. 270 ἀλλ' οὐδ' ἄλλου δεικνύοντος καὶ
πονήσαντος ἠθέλησεν ἀκροατὴς γενέσθαι, "would not even be
willing to listen to one worked out and submitted by another"
(tr. Norlin in L.C.L.).

[g] Cf. Antiphon's devotion to horsemanship in the *Parmenides*, 126 c. For πρὸς τὸ γῆρας cf. 552 D, *Laws* 653 A.

[h] Diels i.³ p. 78, fr. 6. Cf. Aristot. *Meteor.* ii. 2. 9,
Lucretius v. 662.

498 καὶ φιλοσοφίαν μεταχειρίζεσθαι, τῶν τε σωμάτων,
ἐν ᾧ βλαστάνει τε καὶ ἀνδροῦται, εὖ μάλα ἐπιμελεῖσθαι, ὑπηρεσίαν φιλοσοφίᾳ κτωμένους· προ-
ϊούσης δὲ τῆς ἡλικίας, ἐν ᾗ ἡ ψυχὴ τελειοῦσθαι
ἄρχεται, ἐπιτείνειν τὰ ἐκείνης γυμνάσια· ὅταν δὲ
C λήγῃ μὲν ἡ ῥώμη, πολιτικῶν δὲ καὶ στρατειῶν
ἐκτὸς γίγνηται, τότε ἤδη ἀφέτους νέμεσθαι καὶ
μηδὲν ἄλλο πράττειν, ὅ τι μὴ πάρεργον, τοὺς
μέλλοντας εὐδαιμόνως βιώσεσθαι καὶ τελευτή-
σαντας τῷ βίῳ τῷ βεβιωμένῳ τὴν ἐκεῖ μοῖραν
ἐπιστήσειν πρέπουσαν.

XII. Ὡς ἀληθῶς μοι δοκεῖς, ἔφη, λέγειν γε
προθύμως, ὦ Σώκρατες· οἶμαι μέντοι τοὺς πολλοὺς
τῶν ἀκουόντων προθυμότερον ἔτι ἀντιτείνειν οὐδ᾿
ὁπωστιοῦν πεισομένους, ἀπὸ Θρασυμάχου ἀρξαμένους. Μὴ διάβαλλε, ἦν δ᾿ ἐγώ, ἐμὲ καὶ
D Θρασύμαχον ἄρτι φίλους γεγονότας, οὐδὲ πρὸ τοῦ
ἐχθροὺς ὄντας. πείρας γὰρ οὐδὲν ἀνήσομεν, ἕως
ἂν ἢ πείσωμεν καὶ τοῦτον καὶ τοὺς ἄλλους, ἢ
προὔργου τι ποιήσωμεν εἰς ἐκεῖνον τὸν βίον, ὅταν
αὖθις γενόμενοι τοῖς τοιούτοις ἐντύχωσι λόγοις.

---

[a] Cf. 410 c and What Plato Said, p. 496 on Protag.
326 B-C.

[b] Like cattle destined for the sacrifice. A favourite figure
with Plato. Cf. Laws 635 A, Protag. 320 A. It is used literally
in Critias 119 D.

[c] Cf. infra 540 A-B, Newman, Aristot. Pol. i. pp. 329-330.
Wilamowitz, Platon, ii. 207-208, fancies that 498 c to 502 A
is a digression expressing Plato's personal desire to be the
philosopher in Athenian politics.

[d] A half-playful anticipation of the doctrine of immortality
reserved for Bk. x. 608 D ff. It involves no contradiction
and justifies no inferences as to the date and composition of
the Republic. Cf. Gomperz iii. 335.

themselves with an education and a culture suitable to youth, and while their bodies are growing to manhood take right good care of them, thus securing a basis and a support [a] for the intellectual life. But with the advance of age, when the soul begins to attain its maturity, they should make its exercises more severe, and when the bodily strength declines and they are past the age of political and military service, then at last they should be given free range of the pasture [b] and do nothing but philosophize,[c] except incidentally, if they are to live happily, and, when the end has come, crown the life they have lived with a consonant destiny in that other world."

XII. " You really seem to be very much in earnest, Socrates," he said ; " yet I think most of your hearers are even more earnest in their opposition and will not be in the least convinced, beginning with Thrasymachus." " Do not try to breed a quarrel between me and Thrasymachus, who have just become friends and were not enemies before either. For we will spare no effort until we either convince him and the rest or achieve something that will profit them when they come to that life in which they will be born again [d] and meet with such discussions as these." " A

Cf. Emerson, *Experience, in fine,* " which in his passage into new worlds he will carry with him." Bayard Taylor (*American Men of Letters,* p. 113), who began to study Greek late in life, remarked, " Oh, but I expect to use it in the other world." Even the sober positivist Mill says (*Theism,* pp. 249-250) " The truth that life is short and art is long is from of old one of the most discouraging facts of our condition : this hope admits the possibility that the art employed in improving and beautifying the soul itself may avail for good in some other life even when seemingly useless in this."

PLATO

498 Εἰς σμικρόν γ', ἔφη, χρόνον εἴρηκας. Εἰς οὐδὲν
μὲν οὖν, ἔφην, ὥς γε πρὸς τὸν ἅπαντα. τὸ
μέντοι μὴ πείθεσθαι τοῖς λεγομένοις τοὺς πολλοὺς
θαῦμα οὐδέν· οὐ γὰρ πώποτε εἶδον γενόμενον τὸ
E νῦν λεγόμενον, ἀλλὰ πολὺ μᾶλλον τοιαῦτ' ἄττα
ῥήματα ἐξεπίτηδες ἀλλήλοις ὡμοιωμένα, ἀλλ'
οὐκ ἀπὸ τοῦ αὐτομάτου ὥσπερ νῦν ξυμπεσόντα·
ἄνδρα δὲ ἀρετῇ παρισωμένον καὶ ὡμοιωμένον
μέχρι τοῦ δυνατοῦ τελέως ἔργῳ τε καὶ λόγῳ,
δυναστεύοντα ἐν πόλει ἑτέρᾳ τοιαύτῃ, οὐ πώποτε
499 ἑωράκασιν οὔτε ἕνα οὔτε πλείους· ἢ οἴει; Οὐδαμῶς γε. Οὐδέ γε αὖ λόγων, ὦ μακάριε, καλῶν τε
καὶ ἐλευθέρων ἱκανῶς ἐπήκοοι γεγόνασιν, οἵων
ζητεῖν μὲν τὸ ἀληθὲς ξυντεταμένως ἐκ παντὸς
τρόπου τοῦ γνῶναι χάριν, τὰ δὲ κομψά τε καὶ
ἐριστικὰ καὶ μηδαμόσε ἄλλοσε τείνοντα ἢ πρὸς
δόξαν καὶ ἔριν καὶ ἐν δίκαις καὶ ἐν ἰδίαις συνουσίαις πόρρωθεν ἀσπαζομένων. Οὐδὲ τούτων, ἔφη.
B Τούτων τοι χάριν, ἦν δ' ἐγώ, καὶ ταῦτα προορώ-
μενοι ἡμεῖς τότε καὶ δεδιότες ὅμως ἐλέγομεν, ὑπὸ

---

[a] For εἰς here cf. Blaydes on *Clouds* 1180, Herod. vii. 46,
Eurip. *Heracleidae* 270.

[b] Cf. *supra* on 486 A. See too Plut. *Cons. Apol.* 17. 111 c
"a thousand, yes, ten thousand years are only an ἀόριστος
point, nay, the smallest part of a point, as Simonides says."
Cf. also *Lyra Graeca* (L.C.L.), ii. p. 338, *Anth. Pal.* x. 78.

[c] γενόμενον . . . λεγόμενον. It is not translating to make no
attempt to reproduce Plato's parody of "polyphonic prose."
The allusion here is to Isocrates and the Gorgian figure of
παρίσωσις and παρομοίωσις is unmistakable. The subtlety of
Plato's style treats the "accidental" occurrence of a Gorgian
figure in his own writing as a symbol of the difference
between the artificial style and insincerity of the sophists and
the serious truth of his own ideals.

brief time [a] your forecast contemplates," he said.
" Nay, nothing at all," I replied, " as compared with
eternity.[b] However, the unwillingness of the multitude to believe what you say is nothing surprising.
For of the thing here spoken they have never
beheld a token,[c] but only the forced and artificial
chiming of word and phrase, not spontaneous and
accidental as has happened here. But the figure of
a man ' equilibrated ' and ' assimilated ' to virtue's self
perfectly, so far as may be, in word and deed, and
holding rule in a city of like quality, that is a thing
they have never seen in one case or in many. Do you
think they have ? " " By no means." " Neither,
my dear fellow, have they ever seriously inclined to
hearken to fair and free discussions whose sole endeavour was to search out the truth [d] at any cost for
knowledge's sake, and which dwell apart and salute
from afar [e] all the subtleties and cavils that lead to
naught but opinion [f] and strife in court-room and in
private talk." " They have not," he said. " For
this cause and foreseeing this, we then despite our
fears [g] declared under compulsion of the truth [h] that

Cf. Isoc. x. 18 λεγόμενος . . . γενόμενος, *What Plato Said*,
p. 544 on *Symp.* 185 c, F. Reinhardt, *De Isocratis aemulis*,
p. 39, Lucilius, bk. v. init. " hoc ' nolueris et debueris ' te
si minu' delectat, quod τεχνίον Isocrateium est," etc.

[d] As the Platonic dialectic does (*Phileb.* 58 c-d, *cf. What
Plato Said*, p. 611) in contrast with the rhetorician, the
lawyer (*Theaet.* 172 d-e) and the eristic (*Euthydem.* 272 b,
Hipp. Maj. 288 d).

[e] *Cf.* Eurip. *Hippol.* 102, *Psalm* cxxxviii. 6 " the proud
he knoweth afar off."

[f] *Cf. Phaedrus* 253 d with *Theaetet.* 187 c, and *Unity
of Plato's Thought*, p. 48.

[g] *Cf.* on 489 a.

[h] *Cf.* Aristot. *Met.* 984 b 10, 984 a 19.

PLATO

499 τἀληθοῦς ἠναγκασμένοι, ὅτι οὔτε πόλις οὔτε πολι
τεία οὐδέ γ' ἀνὴρ ὁμοίως μή ποτε γένηται τέλεος,
πρὶν ἂν τοῖς φιλοσόφοις τούτοις τοῖς ὀλίγοις καὶ
οὐ πονηροῖς, ἀχρήστοις δὲ νῦν κεκλημένοις, ἀνάγκη
τις ἐκ τύχης περιβάλῃ, εἴτε βούλονται εἴτε μὴ πό
λεως ἐπιμεληθῆναι, καὶ τῇ πόλει κατήκοοι γενέσθαι,
ἢ τῶν νῦν ἐν δυναστείαις ἢ βασιλείαις ὄντων
C υἱέσιν ἢ αὐτοῖς ἔκ τινος θείας ἐπιπνοίας ἀληθινῆς
φιλοσοφίας ἀληθινὸς ἔρως ἐμπέσῃ. τούτων δὲ
πότερα γενέσθαι ἢ ἀμφότερα ὡς ἄρα ἐστὶν ἀδύνα
τον, ἐγὼ μὲν οὐδένα φημὶ ἔχειν λόγον. οὕτω γὰρ
ἂν ἡμεῖς δικαίως καταγελώμεθα, ὡς ἄλλως εὐχαῖς
ὅμοια λέγοντες. ἢ οὐχ οὕτως; Οὕτως. Εἰ τοίνυν
ἄκροις εἰς φιλοσοφίαν πόλεώς τις ἀνάγκη ἐπι
μεληθῆναι ἢ γέγονεν ἐν τῷ ἀπείρῳ τῷ παρελη
λυθότι χρόνῳ ἢ καὶ νῦν ἔστιν ἔν τινι βαρβαρικῷ
D τόπῳ, πόρρω που ἐκτὸς ὄντι τῆς ἡμετέρας ἐπ
όψεως, ἢ καὶ ἔπειτα γενήσεται, περὶ τούτου
ἕτοιμοι τῷ λόγῳ διαμάχεσθαι, ὡς γέγονεν ἡ
εἰρημένη πολιτεία καὶ ἔστι καὶ γενήσεταί γε, ὅταν
αὕτη ἡ μοῦσα πόλεως ἐγκρατὴς γένηται. οὐ γὰρ
ἀδύνατος γενέσθαι, οὐδ' ἡμεῖς ἀδύνατα λέγομεν·
χαλεπὰ δὲ καὶ παρ' ἡμῶν ὁμολογεῖται. Καὶ ἐμοί,
ἔφη, οὕτω δοκεῖ. Τοῖς δὲ πολλοῖς, ἦν δ' ἐγώ,

---

[a] Cf. *Laws* 747 E. But we must not attribute personal superstition to Plato. See *What Plato Said*, index, s.v. Superstition.

[b] Cf. *Laws* 711 D, Thuc. vi. 24. 3; so iv. 4. 1 ὁρμὴ ἐπέπεσε.

[c] We might say, "talking like vain Utopians or idle idealists." The scholiast says, p. 348, τοῦτο καὶ κενὴν φασὶ μακαρίαν. Cf. *supra*, Vol. I. on 458 A, and for εὐχαί on 450 D, and Novotny on *Epist.* vii. 331 D.

[d] Cf. *Laws* 782 A, 678 A-B, and *What Plato Said*, p. 627 on

neither city nor polity nor man either will ever be
perfected until some chance compels this uncorrupted
remnant of philosophers, who now bear the stigma of
uselessness, to take charge of the state whether they
wish it or not, and constrains the citizens to obey them,
or else until by some divine inspiration [a] a genuine
passion for true philosophy takes possession [b] either
of the sons of the men now in power and sovereignty
or of themselves. To affirm that either or both of
these things cannot possibly come to pass is, I say, quite
unreasonable. Only in that case could we be justly
ridiculed as uttering things as futile as day-dreams are. [c]
Is not that so?" "It is." "If, then, the best philosophical natures have ever been constrained to take charge
of the state in infinite time past, [d] or now are in some
barbaric region [e] far beyond our ken, or shall hereafter
be, we are prepared to maintain our contention [f] that
the constitution we have described has been, is, or
will be [g] realized [h] when this philosophic Muse has
taken control of the state. [i] It is not a thing impossible
to happen, nor are we speaking of impossibilities.
That it is difficult we too admit." "I also think so,"
he said. "But the multitude—are you going to say?—

Laws 676 A-B; also Isoc. *Panath.* 204-205, seven hundred
years seemed a short time. [e] Cf. *Phaedo* 78 A.
 [f] For the ellipsis of the first person of the verb cf. *Parmen.*
137 c, *Laches* 180 A. The omission of the third person is
very frequent.
 [g] Cf. 492 E, *Laws* 711 E, 739 c, 888 E.
 [h] Cf. Vol. I. Introd. p. xxxii, and *ibid.* on 472 B, and *What
Plato Said*, p. 564, also *infra* 540 D, Newman, Aristot. *Pol.*
i. p. 377.
 [i] This is what I have called the ABA style. Cf. 599 E,
Apol. 20 c, *Phaedo* 57 B, *Laches* 185 A, *Protag.* 344 c, *Theaet.*
185 A, 190 B, etc. It is nearly what Riddell calls binary
structure, *Apology*, pp. 204-217.

499 ὅτι οὐκ αὖ δοκεῖ, ἐρεῖς; Ἴσως, ἔφη. Ὦ μακάριε,
E ἦν δ' ἐγώ, μὴ πάνυ οὕτω τῶν πολλῶν κατηγόρει,
ἀλλοίαν[1] τοι δόξαν ἕξουσιν, ἐὰν αὐτοῖς μὴ φιλο-
νεικῶν ἀλλὰ παραμυθούμενος καὶ ἀπολυόμενος τὴν
τῆς φιλομαθίας διαβολὴν ἐνδεικνύῃ οὓς λέγεις τοὺς
φιλοσόφους, καὶ διορίζῃ ὥσπερ ἄρτι τήν τε φύσιν
500 αὐτῶν καὶ τὴν ἐπιτήδευσιν, ἵνα μὴ ἡγῶνταί σε
λέγειν οὓς αὐτοὶ οἴονται. ἢ καὶ ἐὰν οὕτω θεῶνται,
ἀλλοίαν τ' οὐ[2] φήσεις αὐτοὺς δόξαν λήψεσθαι καὶ
ἄλλα ἀποκρινεῖσθαι; ἢ οἴει τινὰ χαλεπαίνειν τῷ μὴ
χαλεπῷ ἢ φθονεῖν τῷ μὴ φθονερῷ, ἄφθονόν τε καὶ
πρᾶον ὄντα; ἐγὼ μὲν γὰρ σὲ προφθάσας λέγω,
ὅτι ἐν ὀλίγοις τισὶν ἡγοῦμαι ἀλλ' οὐκ ἐν τῷ πλήθει
χαλεπὴν οὕτω φύσιν γίγνεσθαι. Καὶ ἐγὼ ἀμέλει,
B ἔφη, ξυνοίομαι. Οὐκοῦν καὶ αὐτὸ τοῦτο ξυνοίει,
τοῦ χαλεπῶς πρὸς φιλοσοφίαν τοὺς πολλοὺς δια-
κεῖσθαι ἐκείνους αἰτίους εἶναι τοὺς ἔξωθεν οὐ
προσῆκον ἐπεισκεκωμακότας, λοιδορουμένους τε
αὐτοῖς[3] καὶ φιλαπεχθημόνως ἔχοντας καὶ ἀεὶ περὶ

---

[1] ἀλλοίαν AD, ἀλλ' οἴαν F, ἀλλ' οἴαν M.
[2] τ' οὐ Baiter: τοι mss. Burnet brackets the sentence.
[3] αὐτοῖς Burnet and Adam, αὑτοῖς Ast, Stallbaum, Jowett, and Campbell.

---

[a] It is uncritical to find "contradictions" in variations of
mood, emphasis, and expression that are broadly human and
that no writer can avoid. Any thinker may at one moment
and for one purpose defy popular opinion and for another
conciliate it; at one time affirm that it doesn't matter what
the ignorant people think or say, and at another urge that
prudence bids us be discreet. So St. Paul who says (Gal. i.
10) "Do I seek to please men? for if I yet pleased men I
should not be the servant of Christ," says also (Rom. xiv. 16)
"Let not then your good be evil spoken of." Cf. also What
Plato Said, p. 646 on Laws 950 B.
[b] A recurrence to etymological meaning. Cf. ἄθυμον

does not think so," said I. "That may be," he said. "My dear fellow," said I, "do not thus absolutely condemn the multitude.[a] They will surely be of another mind if in no spirit of contention but soothingly and endeavouring to do away with the dispraise of learning you point out to them whom you mean by philosophers, and define as we recently did their nature and their pursuits so that the people may not suppose you to mean those of whom they are thinking. Or even if they do look at them in that way, are you still going to deny that they will change their opinion and answer differently? Or do you think that anyone is ungentle to the gentle or grudging to the ungrudging if he himself is ungrudging[b] and mild? I will anticipate you and reply that I think that only in some few and not in the mass of mankind is so ungentle or harsh a temper to be found." "And I, you may be assured," he said, "concur." "And do you not also concur[c] in this very point that the blame for this harsh attitude of the many towards philosophy falls on that riotous crew who have burst in[d] where they do not belong, wrangling with one another,[e] filled with spite[f]

411 B, Laws 888 A, εὐψυχίας Laws 791 c, Thompson on Meno 78 E, Aristot. Topics 112 a 32-38, Eurip. Heracleidae 730 ἀσφαλῶς, Shakes. Rich. III. v. v. 37 "Reduce these bloody days again."

[c] For a similar teasing or playful repetition of a word cf. 517 c, 394 B, 449 c, 470 B-C.

[d] For the figure of the κῶμος or revel rout cf. Theaet. 184 A, Aesch. Ag. 1189, Eurip. Ion 1197, and, with a variation of the image, Virgil, Aen. i. 148 and Tennyson, "Lucretius":

> As crowds that in an hour
> Of civic tumult jam the doors.

[e] Cf. Adam ad loc. and Wilamowitz, Platon, ii. 121.

[f] Isoc. Antid. 260 seems to take this term to himself; cf. Panath. 249, Peace 65, Lysias xxiv. 24 πολυπράγμων εἰμὶ καὶ θρασὺς καὶ φιλαπεχθήμων, Demosth. xxiv. 6.

500 ἀνθρώπων τοὺς λόγους ποιουμένους, ἥκιστα φιλοσοφίᾳ πρέπον ποιοῦντας; Πολύ γ', ἔφη.

XIII. Οὐδὲ γάρ που, ὦ Ἀδείμαντε, σχολὴ τῷ
γε ὡς ἀληθῶς πρὸς τοῖς οὖσι τὴν διάνοιαν ἔχοντι
C κάτω βλέπειν εἰς ἀνθρώπων πραγματείας, καὶ
μαχόμενον αὐτοῖς φθόνου τε καὶ δυσμενείας ἐμ-
πίπλασθαι, ἀλλ' εἰς τεταγμένα ἄττα καὶ κατὰ
ταὐτὰ ἀεὶ ἔχοντα ὁρῶντας καὶ θεωμένους οὔτ'
ἀδικοῦντα οὔτ' ἀδικούμενα ὑπ' ἀλλήλων, κόσμῳ δὲ
πάντα καὶ κατὰ λόγον ἔχοντα, ταῦτα μιμεῖσθαί
τε καὶ ὅ τι μάλιστα ἀφομοιοῦσθαι. ἢ οἴει τινὰ
μηχανὴν εἶναι, ὅτῳ τις ὁμιλεῖ ἀγάμενος, μὴ
μιμεῖσθαι ἐκεῖνο; Ἀδύνατον, ἔφη. Θείῳ δὴ καὶ
D κοσμίῳ ὅ γε φιλόσοφος ὁμιλῶν κόσμιός τε καὶ
θεῖος εἰς τὸ δυνατὸν ἀνθρώπῳ γίγνεται· διαβολὴ δ'
ἐν πᾶσι πολλή. Παντάπασι μὲν οὖν. Ἂν οὖν τις,

───────────

^a *i.e.* gossip. *Cf.* Aristot. *Eth. Nic.* 1125 a 5 οὐδ' ἀνθρωπο-
λόγος, Epictetus iii. 16. 4. *Cf.* also *Phileb.* 59 B, *Theaet.*
173 D, 174 c.

^b *Cf. supra* on 486 A, also *Phileb.* 58 D, 59 A, *Tim.* 90 D,
and perhaps *Tim.* 47 A and *Phaedo* 79.

This passage is often supposed to refer to the ideas, and
ἐκεῖ in 500 D shows that Plato is in fact there thinking of
them, though in *Rep.* 529 A-B ff. he protests against this
identification. And strictly speaking κατὰ ταὐτὰ ἀεὶ ἔχοντα
in c would on Platonic principles be true only of the ideas.
Nevertheless poets and imitators have rightly felt that the
dominating thought of the passage is the effect on the philosopher's mind of the contemplation of the heavens. This
confusion or assimilation is, of course, still more natural
to Aristotle, who thought the stars unchanging. *Cf. Met.*
1063 a 16 ταὐτὰ δ' αἰεὶ καὶ μεταβολῆς οὐδεμιᾶς κοινωνοῦντα. *Cf.*
also Sophocles, *Ajax* 669 ff., and Shorey in Sneath, *Evolution
of Ethics*, pp. 261-263, Dio Chrys. xl. (Teubner ii. p. 199),

and always talking about persons,[a] a thing least befitting philosophy ? " " Least of all, indeed," he said.

XIII. " For surely, Adeimantus, the man whose mind is truly fixed on eternal realities [b] has no leisure to turn his eyes downward upon the petty affairs of men, and so engaging in strife with them to be filled with envy and hate, but he fixes his gaze upon the things of the eternal and unchanging order, and seeing that they neither wrong nor are wronged by one another, but all abide in harmony as reason bids, he will endeavour to imitate them and, as far as may be, to fashion himself in their likeness and assimilate[c] himself to them. Or do you think it possible not to imitate the things to which anyone attaches himself with admiration ? " " Impossible," he said. " Then the lover of wisdom associating with the divine order will himself become orderly and divine in the measure permitted to man.[d] But calumny [e] is plentiful everywhere." " Yes, truly." " If, then," I said, " some

Boethius, *Cons.* iii. 8 "respicite caeli spatium . . . et aliquando desinite vilia mirari," Dante, *Purg.* 14:

> The heavens call you and o'er your heads revolving
> Reveal the lamps of beauty ever burning;
> Your eyes are fixed on earth and goods dissolving,
> Wherefore He smites you, He, the all-discerning.

Cf. Arnold, " A Summer Night," *in fine*:

> . . . you remain
> A world above man's head to let him see
> How boundless might his soul's horizons be, etc.

[a] ἀφομοιοῦσθαι suggests the ὁμοίωσις θεῷ *Theaet.* 176 ε.   *Cf. What Plato Said*, p. 578.

[d] *Cf.* on 493 D, and for the idea 383 c.

[e] *Cf. Hamlet* iii. i. 141 "thou shalt not escape calumny," Bacchylides 12 (13). 202-203 βροτῶν δὲ μῶμος πάντεσσι μέν ἐστιν ἐπ' ἔργοις.

PLATO

500 εἶπον, αὐτῷ ἀνάγκη γένηται ἃ ἐκεῖ ὁρᾷ μελετῆσαι
εἰς ἀνθρώπων ἤθη καὶ ἰδίᾳ καὶ δημοσίᾳ τιθέναι, καὶ
μὴ μόνον ἑαυτὸν πλάττειν, ἆρα κακὸν δημιουργὸν
αὐτὸν οἴει γενήσεσθαι σωφροσύνης τε καὶ δικαιοσύνης καὶ ξυμπάσης τῆς δημοτικῆς ἀρετῆς;
Ἥκιστά γε, ἦ δ' ὅς. Ἀλλ' ἐὰν δὴ αἴσθωνται οἱ
E πολλοί, ὅτι ἀληθῆ περὶ αὐτοῦ λέγομεν, χαλε-
πανοῦσι δὴ τοῖς φιλοσόφοις καὶ ἀπιστήσουσιν ἡμῖν
λέγουσιν, ὡς οὐκ ἄν ποτε ἄλλως εὐδαιμονήσειε
πόλις, εἰ μὴ αὐτὴν διαγράψειαν οἱ τῷ θείῳ παραδείγματι χρώμενοι ζωγράφοι; Οὐ χαλεπανοῦσιν,
501 ἦ δ' ὅς, ἐάνπερ αἴσθωνται. ἀλλὰ δὴ τίνα λέγεις
τρόπον τῆς διαγραφῆς; Λαβόντες, ἦν δ' ἐγώ,
ὥσπερ πίνακα πόλιν τε καὶ ἤθη ἀνθρώπων, πρῶτον μὲν καθαρὰν ποιήσειαν ἄν· ὃ οὐ πάνυ ῥᾴδιον·
ἀλλ' οὖν οἶσθ' ὅτι τούτῳ ἂν εὐθὺς τῶν ἄλλων

ᵃ The philosopher unwillingly holds office. Cf. on 345 E.
ᵇ ἐκεῖ is frequently used in Plato of the world of ideas. Cf.
Phaedrus 250 ᴀ, Phaedo 109 ᴇ.
ᶜ For the word πλάττειν used of the lawgiver cf. 377 c,
Laws 671 c, 712 ʙ, 746 ᴀ, 800 ʙ, Rep. 374 ᴀ, 377 c, 420 c,
466 ᴀ, 588 c, etc.
For the idea that the ruler shapes the state according to
the pattern cf. infra 540 ᴀ-ʙ.
Plato applies the language of the theory of ideas to the
"social tissue" here exactly as he applies it to the making
of a tool in the Cratylus 389 c. In both cases there is a
workman, the ideal pattern and the material in which it is
more or less perfectly embodied. Such passages are the
source of Aristotle's doctrine of matter and form. Cf. Met.
1044 a 25, De part. an. 639 b 25-27, 640 b 24 f., 642 a 10 ff.,
De an. 403 b 3, Zeller, Aristot. (Eng.) i. p. 357. Cf. also Gorg.
503 ᴅ-ᴇ, Polit. 306 c, 309 ᴅ and Unity of Plato's Thought,
pp. 31-32. Cf. Alcinous, Εἰσαγωγή ii. (Teubner vi. p. 153)
ἃ κατὰ τὸν θεωρητικὸν βίον ὁρᾶται, μελετῆσαι εἰς ἀνθρώπων ἤθη.
ᵈ Cf. Aristot. Pol. 1329 a 21 ἀρετῆς δημιουργόν. Cf. also

70

compulsion [a] is laid upon him to practise stamping on the plastic matter of human nature in public and private the patterns that he visions there,[b] and not merely to mould [c] and fashion himself, do you think he will prove a poor craftsman [d] of sobriety and justice and all forms of ordinary civic virtue [e]?" "By no means," he said. "But if the multitude become aware that what we are saying of the philosopher is true, will they still be harsh with philosophers, and will they distrust our statement that no city could ever be blessed unless its lineaments were traced [f] by artists who used the heavenly model?" "They will not be harsh," he said, "if they perceive that. But tell me, what is the manner of that sketch you have in mind?" "They will take the city and the characters of men, as they might a tablet, and first wipe it clean—[g] no easy task. But at any rate you know that this would be their first point of difference from ordinary

1275 b 29 with Newman, Introd. Aristot. *Pol.* p. 229. *Cf.* 395 c δημιουργοὺς ἐλευθερίας, *Theages* 125 A δημιουργὸν . . . τῆς σοφίας.

[e] *Cf.* Laws 968 A πρὸς ταῖς δημοσίαις ἀρεταῖς, *Phaedo* 82 A and *supra*, Vol. I. on 430 c. Brochard, "La Morale de Platon," *L'Année Philosophique*, xvi. (1905) p. 12 "La justice est appelée une vertu populaire." This is a little misleading if he means that justice itself is "une vertu populaire."

[f] For διαγράψειαν *cf.* 387 B and *Laws* 778 A. See also Stallbaum *ad loc.*

[g] *Cf.* Vol. I. on 426 D. This is one of the passages that may be used or misused to class Plato with the radicals. *Cf.* 541 A, *Laws* 736 A-B, *Polit.* 293 D, *Euthyphro* 2 D-3 A. H. W. Schneider, *The Puritan Mind*, p. 36, says, "Plato claimed that before his Republic could be established the adult population must be killed off."

Cf. however Vol. I. Introd. p. xxxix, *What Plato Said*, p. 83, and *infra*, p. 76, note a on 502 B.

501 διενέγκοιεν, τῷ μήτε ἰδιώτου μήτε πόλεως ἐθε-
λῆσαι ἂν ἅψασθαι μηδὲ γράφειν νόμους, πρὶν ἢ
παραλαβεῖν καθαρὰν ἢ αὐτοὶ ποιῆσαι. Καὶ ὀρθῶς
γ', ἔφη. Οὐκοῦν μετὰ ταῦτα οἴει ὑπογράψασθαι
ἂν τὸ σχῆμα τῆς πολιτείας; Τί μήν; Ἔπειτα,
B οἶμαι, ἀπεργαζόμενοι πυκνὰ ἂν ἑκατέρωσ' ἀπο-
βλέποιεν, πρός τε τὸ φύσει δίκαιον καὶ καλὸν καὶ
σῶφρον καὶ πάντα τὰ τοιαῦτα καὶ πρὸς ἐκεῖνο αὖ
τὸ ἐν τοῖς ἀνθρώποις ἐμποιοῖεν, ξυμμιγνύντες τε
καὶ κεραννύντες ἐκ τῶν ἐπιτηδευμάτων τὸ ἀνδρείκελον, ἀπ' ἐκείνου τεκμαιρόμενοι, ὃ δὴ καὶ
Ὅμηρος ἐκάλεσεν ἐν τοῖς ἀνθρώποις ἐγγιγνόμενον
θεοειδές τε καὶ θεοείκελον. Ὀρθῶς, ἔφη. Καὶ τὸ
μὲν ἂν, οἶμαι, ἐξαλείφοιεν, τὸ δὲ πάλιν ἐγγρά-
C φοιεν, ἕως ὅ τι μάλιστα ἀνθρώπεια ἤθη εἰς ὅσον
ἐνδέχεται θεοφιλῆ ποιήσειαν. Καλλίστη γοῦν ἂν,
ἔφη, ἡ γραφὴ γένοιτο. Ἆρ' οὖν, ἦν δ' ἐγώ,
πείθομέν πη ἐκείνους, οὓς διατεταμένους ἐφ' ἡμᾶς
ἔφησθα ἰέναι, ὡς τοιοῦτός ἐστι πολιτειῶν ζωγράφος, ὃν τότ' ἐπηνοῦμεν πρὸς αὐτούς, δι' ὃν ἐκεῖνοι
ἐχαλέπαινον, ὅτι τὰς πόλεις αὐτῷ παρεδίδομεν, καί
τι μᾶλλον αὐτὸ νῦν ἀκούοντες πραΰνονται; Καὶ

---

[a] The theory of ideas frequently employs this image of
the artist looking off to his model and back again to his
work. *Cf.* on 484 c, and *What Plato Said*, p. 458, *Unity of
Plato's Thought*, p. 37.

[b] *i.e.* the idea of justice. For φύσις and the theory of ideas
cf. infra 597 c, *Phaedo* 103 B, *Parmen.* 132 D, *Cratyl.* 389 c-D,
390 E.

[c] For ἀνδρείκελον *cf. Cratyl.* 424 E.

[d] *Il.* i. 131, *Od.* iii. 416. *Cf.* 589 D, 500 c-D, *Laws* 818
B-c, and *What Plato Said*, p. 578 on *Theaet.* 176 B, Cic. *Tusc.*

reformers, that they would refuse to take in hand either individual or state or to legislate before they either received a clean slate or themselves made it clean." "And they would be right," he said. "And thereafter, do you not think that they would sketch the figure of the constitution?" "Surely." "And then, I take it, in the course of the work they would glance [a] frequently in either direction, at justice, beauty, sobriety and the like as they are in the nature of things,[b] and alternately at that which they were trying to reproduce in mankind, mingling and blending from various pursuits that hue of the flesh, so to speak, deriving their judgement from that likeness of humanity [c] which Homer too called when it appeared in men the image and likeness of God.[d]" "Right," he said. "And they would erase one touch or stroke and paint in another until in the measure of the possible [e] they had made the characters of men pleasing and dear to God as may be." "That at any rate [f] would be the fairest painting." "Are we then making any impression on those who you said [g] were advancing to attack us with might and main? Can we convince them that such a political artist of character and such a painter exists as the one we then were praising when our proposal to entrust the state to him angered them, and are they now in a gentler mood when they hear what we are now saying?" "Much gentler," he said,

i. 26. 65 "divina mallem ad nos." *Cf.* also *Tim.* 90 A, *Phaedr.* 249 c.

The modern reader may think of Tennyson, *In Mem.* cviii. "What find I in the highest place But mine own phantom chanting hymns?" *Cf.* also Adam *ad loc.*

[e] *Cf.* 500 D and on 493 D.

[f] For γοῦν *cf. supra*, Vol. I. on 334 A.   [g] *Cf.* 474 A.

501 D πολύ γε, ἦ δ' ὅς, εἰ σωφρονοῦσιν. Πῇ γὰρ δὴ
ἕξουσιν ἀμφισβητῆσαι; πότερον μὴ τοῦ ὄντος τε
καὶ ἀληθείας ἐραστὰς εἶναι τοὺς φιλοσόφους;
Ἄτοπον μέντ' ἄν, ἔφη, εἴη. Ἀλλὰ μὴ τὴν φύσιν
αὐτῶν οἰκείαν εἶναι τοῦ ἀρίστου, ἣν ἡμεῖς διήλθομεν; Οὐδὲ τοῦτο. Τί δέ; τὴν τοιαύτην τυχοῦ-
σαν τῶν προσηκόντων ἐπιτηδευμάτων οὐκ ἀγαθὴν
τελέως ἔσεσθαι καὶ φιλόσοφον εἴπερ τινὰ ἄλλην;
ἢ ἐκείνους φήσειν[1] μᾶλλον, οὓς ἡμεῖς ἀφωρίσαμεν;
E Οὐ δήπου. Ἔτι οὖν ἀγριανοῦσι λεγόντων ἡμῶν,
ὅτι, πρὶν ἂν πόλεως τὸ φιλόσοφον γένος ἐγκρατὲς
γένηται, οὔτε πόλει οὔτε πολίταις κακῶν παῦλα
ἔσται, οὐδὲ ἡ πολιτεία, ἣν μυθολογοῦμεν λόγῳ,
ἔργῳ τέλος λήψεται; Ἴσως, ἔφη, ἧττον. Βούλει
οὖν, ἦν δ' ἐγώ, μὴ ἧττον φῶμεν αὐτοὺς ἀλλὰ
παντάπασι πράους γεγονέναι καὶ πεπεῖσθαι, ἵνα,
502 εἰ μή τι, ἀλλὰ αἰσχυνθέντες ὁμολογήσωσιν; Πάνυ
μὲν οὖν, ἔφη.

XIV. Οὗτοι μὲν τοίνυν, ἦν δ' ἐγώ, τοῦτο
πεπεισμένοι ἔστων· τοῦδε δὲ πέρι τις ἀμφισβητήσει, ὡς οὐκ ἂν τύχοιεν γενόμενοι βασιλέων
ἔκγονοι ἢ δυναστῶν τὰς φύσεις φιλόσοφοι; Οὐδ' ἂν
εἷς, ἔφη. Τοιούτους δὲ γενομένους ὡς πολλὴ ἀνάγκη
διαφθαρῆναι, ἔχει τις λέγειν; ὡς μὲν γὰρ χαλεπὸν
σωθῆναι, καὶ ἡμεῖς ξυγχωροῦμεν· ὡς δὲ ἐν παντὶ
B τῷ χρόνῳ τῶν πάντων οὐδέποτ' οὐδ' ἂν εἷς σω-
θείη, ἔσθ' ὅστις ἀμφισβητήσει; Καὶ πῶς; Ἀλλὰ
μήν, ἦν δ' ἐγώ, εἷς ἱκανὸς γενόμενος, πόλιν ἔχων

---

[1] φήσειν ADM : Adam reads φήσει; see his r᷄ e ad loc.

[a] Cf. 591 a. This affirmation of the impossibility of denial
or controversy is a motif frequent in the Attic orators. Cf.
Lysias xxx. 26, xxxi. 24, xiii. 49, vi. 46, etc.

" if they are reasonable." " How *can* they controvert it[a]? Will they deny that the lovers of wisdom are lovers of reality and truth ? " " That would be monstrous," he said. " Or that their nature as we have portrayed it is akin to the highest and best ? " " Not that either." " Well, then, can they deny that such a nature bred in the pursuits that befit it will be perfectly good and philosophic so far as that can be said of anyone ? Or will they rather say it of those whom we have excluded ? " " Surely not." " Will they, then, any longer be fierce with us when we declare that, until the philosophic class wins control, there will be no surcease of trouble for city or citizens nor will the polity which we fable[b] in words be brought to pass in deed ? " " They will perhaps be less so," he said. " Instead of less so, may we not say that they have been altogether tamed and convinced, so that for very shame, if for no other reason, they may assent ? " " Certainly," said he.

XIV. " Let us assume, then," said I, " that they are won over to this view. Will anyone contend that there is no chance that the offspring of kings and rulers should be born with the philosophic nature ? " " Not one," he said. " And can anyone prove that if so born they must necessarily be corrupted ? The difficulty[c] of their salvation we too concede ; but that in all the course of time not one of all could be saved,[d] will anyone maintain that ? " " How could he ? " " But surely," said I, " the occurrence of one such is

[b] *Cf.* 376 D, *Laws* 632 E, 841 C, *Phaedr.* 276 E. Frutiger, *Les Mythes de Platon*, p. 13, says Plato uses the word μῦθος only once of his own myths, *Polit.* 268 E.

[c] *Cf. Laws* 711 D τὸ χαλεπόν, and 495 A-B.

[d] *Cf.* 494 A.

502 πειθομένην, πάντ' ἐπιτελέσαι τὰ νῦν ἀπιστούμενα.
Ἱκανὸς γάρ, ἔφη. Ἄρχοντος γάρ που, ἦν δ' ἐγώ,
τιθέντος τοὺς νόμους καὶ τὰ ἐπιτηδεύματα, ἃ
διεληλύθαμεν, οὐ δήπου ἀδύνατον ἐθέλειν ποιεῖν
τοὺς πολίτας. Οὐδ' ὁπωστιοῦν. Ἀλλὰ δή, ἅπερ
ἡμῖν δοκεῖ, δόξαι καὶ ἄλλοις θαυμαστόν τι καὶ
C ἀδύνατον; Οὐκ οἶμαι ἔγωγε, ἦ δ' ὅς. Καὶ μὴν
ὅτι γε βέλτιστα, εἴπερ δυνατά, ἱκανῶς ἐν τοῖς
ἔμπροσθεν, ὡς ἐγῷμαι, διήλθομεν. Ἱκανῶς γάρ.
Νῦν δή, ὡς ἔοικε, ξυμβαίνει ἡμῖν περὶ τῆς νομο-
θεσίας ἄριστα μὲν εἶναι ἃ λέγομεν, εἰ γένοιτο,
χαλεπὰ δὲ γενέσθαι, οὐ μέντοι ἀδύνατά γε. Ξυμβαίνει γάρ, ἔφη.

XV. Οὐκοῦν ἐπειδὴ τοῦτο μόγις τέλος ἔσχε, τὰ
D ἐπίλοιπα δὴ μετὰ τοῦτο λεκτέον, τίνα τρόπον ἡμῖν
καὶ ἐκ τίνων μαθημάτων τε καὶ ἐπιτηδευμάτων οἱ
σωτῆρες ἐνέσονται τῆς πολιτείας, καὶ κατὰ ποίας
ἡλικίας ἕκαστοι ἑκάστων ἁπτόμενοι; Λεκτέον
μέντοι, ἔφη. Οὐδέν, ἦν δ' ἐγώ, τὸ σοφόν μοι
ἐγένετο τήν τε τῶν γυναικῶν τῆς κτήσεως δυσχέ-
ρειαν ἐν τῷ πρόσθεν παραλιπόντι καὶ παιδογονίαν
καὶ τὴν τῶν ἀρχόντων κατάστασιν, εἰδότι ὡς
ἐπίφθονός τε καὶ χαλεπὴ γίγνεσθαι ἡ παντελῶς
E ἀληθής· νῦν γὰρ οὐδὲν ἧττον ἦλθε τὸ δεῖν αὐτὰ

---

[a] Cf. *Epist.* vii. 328 c and Novotny, *Plato's Epistles*, p. 170.
Plato's apparent radicalism again. *Cf.* on 501 A. *Cf.* also
Laws 709 E, but note the qualification in 875 c, 713 E-714 A,
691 c-D. Wilamowitz, *Platon*, ii. pp. 381-383 seems to say
that the εἰς ἱκανός is the philosopher—Plato.

[b] Note the different tone of 565 E λαβὼν σφόδρα πειθόμενον
ὄχλον. *Cf. Phaedr.* 260 c λαβὼν πόλιν ὡσαύτως ἔχουσαν
πείθῃ.

[c] *Cf.* on 499 D, and Frutiger, *Mythes de Platon*, p. 43.

enough,*a* if he has a state which obeys him,*b* to realize *c* all that now seems so incredible." " Yes, one is enough," he said. " For if such a ruler," I said, " ordains the laws and institutions that we have described it is surely not impossible that the citizens should be content to carry them out." " By no means." " Would it, then, be at all strange or impossible for others to come to the opinion to which we have come *d* ? " " I think not," said he. " And further that these things are best, if possible, has already, I take it, been sufficiently shown." " Yes, sufficiently." " Our present opinion, then, about this legislation is that our plan would be best if it could be realized and that this realization is difficult *e* yet not impossible." " That is the conclusion," he said.

XV. " This difficulty disposed of, we have next to speak of what remains, in what way, namely, and as a result of what studies and pursuits, these preservers *f* of the constitution will form a part of our state, and at what ages they will severally take up each study." " Yes, we have to speak of that," he said. " I gained nothing," I said, "by my cunning *g* in omitting heretofore *h* the distasteful topic of the possession of women and procreation of children and the appointment of rulers, because I knew that the absolutely true and right way would provoke censure and is difficult of realization; for now I am none the less compelled

d Cf. *Epist.* vii. 327 B-c, viii. 357 B ff.

e Cf. 502 A, Campbell's note on *Theaet.* 144 A, and Wilamowitz, *Platon,* ii. p. 208.

f Cf. on 412 A-B and 497 C-D, *Laws* 960 B. 463 B is not quite relevant.

g For τὸ σοφόν cf. *Euthydem.* 293 D, 297 D, *Gorg.* 483 A, Herod. v. 18 τοῦτο οὐδὲν εἶναι σοφόν, *Symp.* 214 A τὸ σόφισμα, *Laches* 183 D.

h Cf. 423 E.

PLATO

502 διελθεῖν. καὶ τὰ μὲν δὴ τῶν γυναικῶν τε καὶ
παίδων πεπέρανται, τὸ δὲ τῶν ἀρχόντων ὥσπερ ἐξ
ἀρχῆς μετελθεῖν δεῖ. ἐλέγομεν δ᾽, εἰ μνημονεύεις,
503 δεῖν αὐτοὺς φιλοπόλιδάς τε φαίνεσθαι, βασανι-
ζομένους ἐν ἡδοναῖς τε καὶ λύπαις, καὶ τὸ δόγμα
τοῦτο μήτ᾽ ἐν πόνοις μήτ᾽ ἐν φόβοις μήτ᾽ ἐν ἄλλῃ
μηδεμιᾷ μεταβολῇ φαίνεσθαι ἐκβάλλοντας, ἢ τὸν
ἀδυνατοῦντα ἀποκριτέον, τὸν δὲ πανταχοῦ ἀκή-
ρατον ἐκβαίνοντα, ὥσπερ χρυσὸν ἐν πυρὶ βασανιζό-
μενον, στατέον ἄρχοντα καὶ γέρα δοτέον καὶ ζῶντι
καὶ τελευτήσαντι καὶ ἆθλα. τοιαῦτ᾽ ἄττα ἦν τὰ
λεγόμενα, παρεξιόντος καὶ παρακαλυπτομένου τοῦ
B λόγου, πεφοβημένου κινεῖν τὸ νῦν παρόν. Ἀληθέστατα, ἔφη, λέγεις· μέμνημαι γάρ. Ὄκνος γάρ,
ἔφην, ὦ φίλε, ἐγώ, εἰπεῖν τὰ νῦν ἀποτετολμημένα·
νῦν δὲ τοῦτο μὲν τετολμήσθω εἰπεῖν, ὅτι τοὺς
ἀκριβεστάτους φύλακας φιλοσόφους δεῖ καθιστάναι.
Εἰρήσθω γάρ, ἔφη. Νόησον δή, ὡς εἰκότως ὀλίγοι
ἔσονταί σοι. ἣν γὰρ διήλθομεν φύσιν δεῖν ὑπάρχειν αὐτοῖς, εἰς ταὐτὸ ξυμφύεσθαι αὐτῆς τὰ μέρη

---

^a In Bk. V.

^b *Cf.* 412 D-E, 413 C-414 A, 430 A-B, 537, 540 A, *Laws* 751 C.

^c *Cf.* on 412 E, 413 C, *Soph.* 230 B.

^d τὸ δόγμα τοῦτο is an illogical idiom. The antecedent is only implied. *Cf.* 373 C, 598 C. See my article in *Transactions of the American Phil. Assoc.* xlvii. (1916) pp. 205-236.

^e *Cf.* Theognis 417-418 παρατρίβομαι ὥστε μολίβδῳ χρυσός, *ibid.* 447-452, 1105-1106, Herod. vii. 10, Eurip. fr. 955 (N.). *Cf. Zechariah* xiii. 9 "I . . . will try them as gold is tried," *Job* xxiii. 10 " When he hath tried me I shall come forth as gold." *Cf.* also 1 *Peter* i. 7, *Psalm* xii. 6, lxvi. 10, *Isaiah* xlviii. 10.

^f The translation preserves the intentional order of the Greek. For the idea *cf.* 414 A and 465 D-E and for ἆθλα *cf.* 460 B. Cobet rejects καὶ ἆθλα, but emendations are needless.

to discuss them. The matter of the women and children has been disposed of,[a] but the education of the rulers has to be examined again, I may say, from the starting-point. We were saying, if you recollect, that they must approve themselves lovers of the state when tested[b] in pleasures and pains, and make it apparent that they do not abandon[c] this fixed faith[d] under stress of labours or fears or any other vicissitude, and that anyone who could not keep that faith must be rejected, while he who always issued from the test pure and intact, like gold tried in the fire,[e] is to be established as ruler and to receive honours in life and after death and prizes as well.[f] Something of this sort we said while the argument slipped by with veiled face[g] in fear[h] of starting[i] our present debate." "Most true," he said; "I remember." "We shrank, my friend," I said, "from uttering the audacities which have now been hazarded. But now let us find courage for the definitive pronouncement that as the most perfect[j] guardians we must establish philosophers." "Yes, assume it to have been said," said he. "Note, then, that they will naturally be few,[k] for the different components of the nature which we said their education presupposed rarely consent to

---

[g] Cf. *Phaedr.* 237 A, *Epist.* vii. 340 A. For the personification of the λόγος cf. *What Plato Said*, p. 500 on *Protag.* 361 A-B. So too Cic. *Tusc.* i. 45. 108 "sed ita tetra sunt quaedam, ut ea fugiat et reformidet oratio."

[h] Cf. 387 B.

[i] Cf. the proverbial μὴ κινεῖν τὰ ἀκίνητα, do not move the immovable, "let sleeping dogs lie," in *Laws* 684 D-E, 913 B. Cf. also *Phileb.* 16 c, and the American idiom "start something."

[j] Cf. 503 D, 341 B, 340 E, 342 D.

[k] Cf. on 494 A

503 ὀλιγάκις ἐθέλει, τὰ πολλὰ δὲ διεσπασμένη φύεται.

C Πῶς, ἔφη, λέγεις; Εὐμαθεῖς καὶ μνήμονες καὶ
ἀγχίνοι καὶ ὀξεῖς καὶ ὅσα ἄλλα τούτοις ἕπεται
οἶσθ' ὅτι οὐκ ἐθέλουσιν ἅμα φύεσθαι καὶ νεανικοί[1] τε
καὶ μεγαλοπρεπεῖς τὰς διανοίας, οἷοι κοσμίως
μετὰ ἡσυχίας καὶ βεβαιότητος ἐθέλειν ζῆν, ἀλλ'
οἱ τοιοῦτοι ὑπὸ ὀξύτητος φέρονται ὅπη ἂν τύχωσι,
καὶ τὸ βέβαιον ἅπαν αὐτῶν ἐξοίχεται. Ἀληθῆ,
ἔφη, λέγεις. Οὐκοῦν τὰ βέβαια αὖ ταῦτα ἤθη καὶ
οὐκ εὐμετάβολα, οἷς ἄν τις μᾶλλον ὡς πιστοῖς

D χρήσαιτο, καὶ ἐν τῷ πολέμῳ πρὸς τοὺς φόβους
δυσκίνητα ὄντα, πρὸς τὰς μαθήσεις αὖ ποιεῖ ταὐ-
τον· δυσκινήτως ἔχει καὶ δυσμαθῶς ὥσπερ ἀπο-
νεναρκωμένα, καὶ ὕπνου τε καὶ χάσμης ἐμπίπλανται,
ὅταν τι δέῃ τοιοῦτον διαπονεῖν. Ἔστι ταῦτα, ἔφη.
Ἡμεῖς δέ γ' ἔφαμεν ἀμφοτέρων δεῖν εὖ τε καὶ
καλῶς μετέχειν, ἢ μήτε παιδείας τῆς ἀκριβεστάτης
δεῖν αὐτῷ μεταδιδόναι μήτε τιμῆς μήτε ἀρχῆς.
Ὀρθῶς, ἦ δ' ὅς. Οὐκοῦν σπάνιον αὐτὸ οἴει

E ἔσεσθαι; Πῶς δ' οὔ; Βασανιστέον δὴ ἔν τε οἷς
τότε ἐλέγομεν πόνοις τε καὶ φόβοις καὶ ἡδοναῖς,
καὶ ἔτι δὴ ὃ τότε παρεῖμεν νῦν λέγομεν, ὅτι καὶ ἐν

---

[1] On the text see end of note a below.

---

a The translation is correct. In the Greek the anacoluthon
is for right emphasis, and the separation of νεανικοί τε καὶ
μεγαλοπρεπεῖς from the other members of the list is also an
intentional feature of Plato's style to avoid the monotony of
too long an enumeration. The two things that rarely combine are Plato's two temperaments. The description of the
orderly temperament begins with οἷοι and οἱ τοιοῦτοι refers to
the preceding description of the active temperament. The
MSS. have καί before νεανικοί ; Heindorf, followed by Wilamowitz, and Adam's minor edition, put it before οἷοι. Burnet
follows the MSS. Adam's larger edition puts καὶ νεανικοί τε

grow in one ; but for the most part these qualities are found apart." "What do you mean ? " he said. "Facility in learning, memory, sagacity, quickness of apprehension and their accompaniments, and youthful spirit and magnificence in soul are qualities, you know, that are rarely combined in human nature with a disposition to live orderly, quiet, and stable lives ; [a] but such men, by reason of their quickness, [b] are driven about just as chance directs, and all steadfastness is gone out of them." "You speak truly," he said. "And on the other hand, the steadfast and stable temperaments, whom one could rather trust in use, and who in war are not easily moved and aroused to fear, are apt to act in the same way [c] when confronted with studies. They are not easily aroused, learn with difficulty, as if benumbed, [d] and are filled with sleep and yawning when an intellectual task is set them." "It is so," he said. "But we affirmed that a man must partake of both temperaments in due and fair combination or else participate in neither the highest [e] education nor in honours nor in rule." "And rightly," he said. "Do you not think, then, that such a blend will be a rare thing ? " "Of course." "They must, then, be tested in the toils and fears and pleasures of which we then spoke, [f] and we have also now to speak of a

after ἕπεται. The right meaning can be got from any of the texts in a good *viva voce* reading.

Plato's contrast of the two temperaments disregards the possible objection of a psychologist that the adventurous temperament is not necessarily intellectual. *Cf. supra* on 375 c, and *What Plato Said*, p. 573 on *Theaet.* 144 A-B, Cic. *Tusc.* v. 24.   [b] *Cf. Theaet.* 144 A ff.

[c] A touch of humour in a teacher.

[d] For the figure *cf. Meno* 80 A, 84 B and c.

[e] Lit. "most precise." *Cf. Laws* 965 B ἀκριβεστέραν παιδείαν.

[f] In 412 c ff.

503 μαθήμασι πολλοῖς γυμνάζειν δεῖ, σκοποῦντας εἰ
καὶ τὰ μέγιστα μαθήματα δυνατὴ ἔσται ἐνεγκεῖν,
504 εἴτε καὶ ἀποδειλιάσει, ὥσπερ οἱ ἐν τοῖς ἄθλοις¹
ἀποδειλιῶντες. Πρέπει γε τοι δή, ἔφη, οὕτω
σκοπεῖν· ἀλλὰ ποῖα δὴ λέγεις μαθήματα μέγιστα;

XVI. Μνημονεύεις μέν που, ἦν δ' ἐγώ, ὅτι
τριττὰ εἴδη ψυχῆς διαστησάμενοι ξυνεβιβάζομεν
δικαιοσύνης τε πέρι καὶ σωφροσύνης καὶ ἀνδρείας
καὶ σοφίας ὃ ἕκαστον εἴη. Μὴ γὰρ μνημονεύων,
ἔφη, τὰ λοιπὰ ἂν εἴην δίκαιος μὴ ἀκούειν. Ἦ καὶ
B τὸ προρρηθὲν αὐτῶν; Τὸ ποῖον δή; Ἐλέγομέν
που, ὅτι, ὡς μὲν δυνατὸν ἦν κάλλιστα αὐτὰ κατιδεῖν, ἄλλη μακροτέρα εἴη περίοδος, ἣν περι-
ελθόντι καταφανῆ γίγνοιτο, τῶν μέντοι ἔμπροσθεν
προειρημένων ἑπομένας ἀποδείξεις οἷόν τ' εἴη
προσάψαι. καὶ ὑμεῖς ἐξαρκεῖν ἔφατε, καὶ οὕτω
δὴ ἐρρήθη τὰ τότε τῆς μὲν ἀκριβείας, ὡς ἐμοὶ
ἐφαίνετο, ἐλλιπῆ, εἰ δὲ ὑμῖν ἀρεσκόντως, ὑμεῖς ἂν
τοῦτο εἴποιτε. Ἀλλ' ἔμοιγε, ἔφη, μετρίως· ἐφαί-
C νετο μὴν καὶ τοῖς ἄλλοις. Ἀλλ', ὦ φίλε, ἦν δ'

---

¹ ἄθλοις Orelli: ἄλλοις MSS.

ᵃ Cf. infra 535 B, Protag. 326 c.
ᵇ For the tripartite soul cf. Vol. I. on 435 A and 436 B,
Unity of Plato's Thought, p. 42, What Plato Said, p. 526 on
Phaedo 68 c, p. 552 on Phaedr. 246 B, and p. 563 on Rep.
435 B-c.
ᶜ Cf. Vol. I. on 435 D, Phaedr. 274 A, Friedländer, Platon,
ii. pp. 376-377, Jowett and Campbell, p. 300, Frutiger,
Mythes de Platon, pp. 81 ff., and my Idea of Good in
Plato's Republic (Univ. of Chicago Studies in Class. Phil.
vol. i. p. 190). There is no mysticism and no obscurity. The
longer way is the higher education, which will enable the
philosopher not only like ordinary citizens to do the right
from habit and training, but to understand the reasons for it.

point we then passed by, that we must exercise them in many studies, watching them to see whether their nature is capable of enduring the greatest and most difficult studies or whether it will faint and flinch ^a as men flinch in the trials and contests of the body."
" That is certainly the right way of looking at it," he said. " But what do you understand by the greatest studies ? "

XVI. " You remember, I presume," said I, " that after distinguishing three kinds ^b in the soul, we established definitions of justice, sobriety, bravery and wisdom severally." " If I did not remember," he said, " I should not deserve to hear the rest." " Do you also remember what was said before this ? " " What ? " ' " We were saying, I believe, that for the most perfect discernment of these things another longer way ^c was requisite which would make them plain to one who took it, but that it was possible to add proofs on a par with the preceding discussion. And you said that that was sufficient, and it was on this understanding that what we then said was said, falling short of ultimate precision as it appeared to me, but if it contented you it is for you to say." " Well," he said, " it was measurably satisfactory to me, and apparently to the rest of the company."

The outcome of such an education is described as the vision of the idea of good, which for ethics and politics means a restatement of the provisional psychological definition of the cardinal virtues in terms of the ultimate elements of human welfare. For metaphysics and cosmogony the vision of the idea of good may mean a teleological interpretation of the universe and the interpretation of all things in terms of benevolent design. That is reserved for poetical and mythical treatment in the *Timaeus*. The *Republic* merely glances at the thought from time to time and returns to its own theme. *Cf.* also Introd., p. xxxv.

PLATO

504 ἐγώ, μέτρον τῶν τοιούτων ἀπολεῖπον καὶ ὁτιοῦν
τοῦ ὄντος οὐ πάνυ μετρίως γίγνεται· ἀτελὲς γὰρ
οὐδὲν οὐδενὸς μέτρον· δοκεῖ δ' ἐνίοτέ τισιν ἱκανῶς
ἤδη ἔχειν καὶ οὐδὲν δεῖν περαιτέρω ζητεῖν. Καὶ
μάλ', ἔφη, συχνοὶ πάσχουσιν αὐτὸ διὰ ῥᾳθυμίαν.
Τούτου δέ γε, ἦν δ' ἐγώ, τοῦ παθήματος ἥκιστα
προσδεῖ φύλακι πόλεώς τε καὶ νόμων. Εἰκός, ἦ
δ' ὅς. Τὴν μακροτέραν τοίνυν, ὦ ἑταῖρε, ἔφην,
D περιτέον τῷ τοιούτῳ, καὶ οὐχ ἧττον μανθάνοντι
πονητέον ἢ γυμναζομένῳ· ἤ, ὃ νῦν δὴ ἐλέγομεν,
τοῦ μεγίστου τε καὶ μάλιστα προσήκοντος μαθήματος ἐπὶ τέλος οὔποτε ἥξει. Οὐ γὰρ ταῦτα, ἔφη,
μέγιστα, ἀλλ' ἔτι τι μεῖζον δικαιοσύνης τε καὶ ὧν
διήλθομεν; Καὶ μεῖζον, ἦν δ' ἐγώ, καὶ αὐτῶν
τούτων οὐχ ὑπογραφὴν δεῖ ὥσπερ νῦν θεάσασθαι,
ἀλλὰ τὴν τελεωτάτην ἀπεργασίαν μὴ παριέναι·
ἢ οὐ γελοῖον, ἐπὶ μὲν ἄλλοις σμικροῦ ἀξίοις πᾶν
E ποιεῖν συντεινομένους ὅπως ὅ τι ἀκριβέστατα καὶ
καθαρώτατα ἕξει, τῶν δὲ μεγίστων μὴ μεγίστας

ᵃ Cf. Cic. De fin. i. 1 " nec modus est ullus investigandi
veri nisi inveneris."
  Note not only the edifying tone and the unction of the
style but the definite suggestion of Plato's distaste for
relativity and imperfection which finds expression in the
criticism of the *homo mensura* in the *Theaetetus*, in the statement of the *Laws* 716 c, that God is the measure of all things
(*What Plato Said*, p. 631), and in the contrast in the *Politicus*
283-284 between measuring things against one another and
measuring them by an idea. *Cf. infra* 531 ᴀ.

" Nay, my friend," said I, " a measure of such things that in the least degree falls short of reality proves no measure at all. For nothing that is imperfect is the measure of anything,[a] though some people sometimes think that they have already done enough[b] and that there is no need of further inquiry." " Yes, indeed," he said, " many experience this because of their sloth." " An experience," said I, " that least of all befits the guardians of a state and of its laws." " That seems likely," he said. " Then," said I, " such a one must go around[c] the longer way and must labour no less in studies than in the exercises of the body ; or else, as we were just saying, he will never come to the end of the greatest study and that which most properly belongs to him." " Why, are not these things the greatest ? " said he ; " but is there still something greater than justice and the other virtues we described ? " " There is not only something greater," I said, " but of these very things we need not merely to contemplate an outline[d] as now, but we must omit nothing of their most exact elaboration. Or would it not be absurd to strain every nerve[e] to attain to the utmost precision and clarity of knowledge about other things of trifling moment and not to demand the greatest precision for the

---

[b] Cf. *Menex.* 234 A, *Charm.* 158 c, *Symp.* 204 A, *Epist.* vii. 341 A.

From here to the end of this Book the notes are to be used in connexion with the Introduction, pp. xxiii-xxxvi, where the idea of good and the divided line are discussed.

[c] Cf. *Phaedr.* 274 A.

[d] *i.e.* sketch, adumbration. The ὑπογραφή is the account of the cardinal virtues in Bk. iv. 428-433.

[e] For πᾶν ποιεῖν cf. on 488 c, for συντεινομένους *Euthydem.* 288 D.

504 ἀξιοῦν εἶναι καὶ τὰς ἀκριβείας; Καὶ μάλα, ἔφη,
[ἄξιον τὸ διανόημα][1]· ὃ μέντοι μέγιστον μάθημα καὶ
περὶ ὅ τι αὐτὸ λέγεις, οἴει τιν' ἄν σε, ἔφη, ἀφεῖναι
μὴ ἐρωτήσαντα τί ἐστιν; Οὐ πάνυ, ἦν δ' ἐγώ,
ἀλλὰ καὶ σὺ ἐρώτα. πάντως αὐτὸ οὐκ ὀλιγάκις
ἀκήκοας· νῦν δὲ ἢ οὐκ ἐννοεῖς ἢ αὖ διανοεῖ ἐμοὶ
505 πράγματα παρέχειν ἀντιλαμβανόμενος. οἶμαι δὲ
τοῦτο μᾶλλον· ἐπεὶ ὅτι γε ἡ τοῦ ἀγαθοῦ ἰδέα
μέγιστον μάθημα, πολλάκις ἀκήκοας, ᾗ δὴ δίκαια
καὶ τἆλλα προσχρησάμενα χρήσιμα καὶ ὠφέλιμα
γίγνεται. καὶ νῦν σχεδὸν οἶσθ' ὅτι μέλλω τοῦτο
λέγειν, καὶ πρὸς τούτῳ ὅτι αὐτὴν οὐχ ἱκανῶς
ἴσμεν· εἰ δὲ μὴ ἴσμεν, ἄνευ δὲ ταύτης, εἰ ὅ τι
μάλιστα τἆλλα ἐπισταίμεθα, οἶσθ' ὅτι οὐδὲν ἡμῖν
B ὄφελος, ὥσπερ οὐδ' εἰ κεκτήμεθά τι ἄνευ τοῦ
ἀγαθοῦ. ἢ οἴει τι πλέον εἶναι πᾶσαν κτῆσιν ἐκτῆ-
σθαι, μὴ μέντοι ἀγαθήν; ἢ πάντα τἆλλα φρονεῖν

[1] Bracketed by Scheiermacher, whom the Oxford text
follows. Cf. also Adam ad loc. Stallbaum ad loc. defends.

---

[a] Such juxtaposition of different forms of the same word is
one of the most common features of Plato's style. Cf. 453 B
ἕνα ἕν, 466 D πάντα πάντῃ, 467 D πολλὰ πολλοῖς, 496 C οὐδεὶς
οὐδέν, Laws 835 C μόνῳ μόνος, 958 B ἑκόντα ἑκών. Cf. also
Protag. 327 B, Gorg. 523 B, Symp. 217 B, Tim. 92 B, Phaedo
109 B, Apol. 32 C, and Laws passim.

[b] The answer is to the sense. Cf. 346 E, Crito 47 c, and D,
Laches 195 D, Gorg. 467 E. See critical note.

[c] Plato assumed that the reader will understand that the
unavailing quest for "the good" in the earlier dialogues is
an anticipation of the idea of good. Cf. supra Vol. I. on
476 A and What Plato Said, p. 71. Wilamowitz, Platon, i.
p. 567, does not understand.

[d] Cf. 508 E, 517 c, Cratyl. 418 E. Cf. Phileb. 64 E and
What Plato Said, p. 534, on Phaedo 99 A.

greatest [a] matters ? "   " It would indeed,[b] " he said ;
" but do you suppose that anyone will let you go
without asking what is the greatest study and with
what you think it is concerned ? "   " By no means,"
said I ; " but do you ask the question. You certainly have heard it often, but now you either do not
apprehend or again you are minded to make trouble
for me by attacking the argument. I suspect it is
rather the latter. For you have often heard[c] that the
greatest thing to learn is the idea of good[d] by reference
to which[e] just things[f] and all the rest become useful and
beneficial. And now I am almost sure you know that
this is what I am going to speak of and to say further
that we have no adequate knowledge of it. And if we
do not know it, then, even if without the knowledge of
this we should know all other things never so well,
you are aware that it would avail us nothing, just as
no possession either is of any avail[g] without the possession of the good. Or do you think there is any profit[h]
in possessing everything except that which is good,
or in understanding all things else apart from the

Plato is unwilling to confine his idea of good to a formula
and so seems to speak of it as a mystery. It was so regarded
throughout antiquity (cf. Diog. Laert. iii. 27), and by a
majority of modern scholars. Cf. my Idea of Good in Plato's
Republic, pp. 188-189, What Plato Said, pp. 72, 230-231,
Introd. Vol. I. pp. xl-xli, and Vol. II. pp. xxvii, xxxiv.

[e] Lit. "the use of which," i.e. a theory of the cardinal
virtues is scientific only if deduced from an ultimate sanction
or ideal.

[f] The omission of the article merely gives a vaguely
generalizing colour. It makes no difference.

[g] For the idiom οὐδὲν ὄφελος cf. Euthyph. 4 E, Lysis 208 E,
supra 365 B, Charm. 155 E, etc.

[h] Cf. 427 A, Phaedr. 275 c, Cratyl. 387 A, Euthyd. 288 E,
Laws 751 B, 944 D, etc.

PLATO

505 ἄνευ τοῦ ἀγαθοῦ, καλὸν δὲ καὶ ἀγαθὸν μηδὲν
φρονεῖν; Μὰ Δί᾿ οὐκ ἔγωγ᾿, ἔφη.

XVII. Ἀλλὰ μὴν καὶ τόδε γε οἶσθα, ὅτι τοῖς
μὲν πολλοῖς ἡδονὴ δοκεῖ εἶναι τὸ ἀγαθόν, τοῖς δὲ
κομψοτέροις φρόνησις. Πῶς δ᾿ οὔ; Καὶ ὅτι γε,
ὦ φίλε, οἱ τοῦτο ἡγούμενοι οὐκ ἔχουσι δεῖξαι ἥτις
φρόνησις, ἀλλ᾿ ἀναγκάζονται τελευτῶντες τὴν τοῦ
ἀγαθοῦ φάναι. Καὶ μάλα, ἔφη, γελοίως. Πῶς
C γὰρ οὐχί, ἦν δ᾿ ἐγώ, εἰ ὀνειδίζοντές γε ὅτι οὐκ
ἴσμεν τὸ ἀγαθόν, λέγουσι πάλιν ὡς εἰδόσι; φρόνησιν γὰρ αὐτό φασιν εἶναι ἀγαθοῦ, ὡς αὖ ξυν-
ιέντων ἡμῶν ὅ τι λέγουσιν, ἐπειδὰν τὸ τοῦ ἀγαθοῦ
φθέγξωνται ὄνομα. Ἀληθέστατα, ἔφη. Τί δαί;
οἱ τὴν ἡδονὴν ἀγαθὸν ὁριζόμενοι μῶν μή τι ἐλάτ-
τονος πλάνης ἔμπλεω τῶν ἑτέρων; ἢ οὐ καὶ οὗτοι
ἀναγκάζονται ὁμολογεῖν ἡδονὰς εἶναι κακάς;

ᵃ καλὸν δὲ καὶ ἀγαθόν suggests but does not mean καλοκἀγαθόν
in its half-technical sense. The two words fill out the rhythm
with Platonic fulness and are virtual synonyms. Cf. Phileb.
65 ᴀ and Symp. 210-211 where because of the subject the
καλόν is substituted for the ἀγαθόν.

ᵇ So Polus and Callicles in the Gorgias and later the
Epicureans and Cyrenaics. Cf. also What Plato Said, p. 131 ;
Eurip. Hippol. 382 οἱ δ᾿ ἡδονὴν προθέντες ἀντὶ τοῦ καλοῦ, and
supra on 329 ᴀ-ʙ.
There is no contradiction here with the Philebus. Plato
does not himself say that either pleasure or knowledge is the
good.

ᶜ κομψοτέροις is very slightly if at all ironical here. Cf.
the American "sophisticated" in recent use. See too Theaet.
156 ᴀ, Aristot. Eth. Nic. 1905 a 18 οἱ χαρίεντες.

ᵈ Plato does not distinguish synonyms in the style of
Prodicus (cf. Protag. 337 ᴀ ff.) and Aristotle (cf. Eth. Nic.
1140-1141) when the distinction is irrelevant to his purpose.
Cf. Euthyd. 281 ᴅ, Theaet. 176 ʙ with 176 c.

ᵉ Cf. 428 ʙ-ᴄ, Euthydem. 288 ᴅ f., Laws 961 ᴇ ὁ περὶ τί

good while understanding and knowing nothing that is fair and good *a* ? " " No, by Zeus, I do not," he said.

XVII. " But, furthermore, you know this too, that the multitude believe pleasure *b* to be the good, and the finer *c* spirits intelligence or knowledge.*d*" " Certainly." " And you are also aware, my friend, that those who hold this latter view are not able to point out what knowledge *e* it is but are finally compelled to say that it is the knowledge of the good." " Most absurdly," he said. " Is it *not* absurd," said I, " if while taunting us with our ignorance of the good they turn about and talk to us as if we knew it ? For they say it is the knowledge of the good,*f* as if we understood their meaning when they utter *g* the word ' good.' " " Most true," he said. " Well, are those who define the good as pleasure infected with any less confusion *h* of thought than the others ? Or are not they in like manner *i* compelled to admit that there

---

νοῦς. See *Unity of Plato's Thought*, n. 650. The demand for specification is frequent in the dialogues. *Cf. Euthyph.* 13 D, *Laches* 192 E, *Gorg.* 451 A, *Charm.* 165 C-E, *Alc. I.* 124 E ff.

f There is no " the " in the Greek. Emendations are idle. Plato is supremely indifferent to logical precision when it makes no difference for a reasonably intelligent reader. *Cf.* my note on *Phileb.* 11 B-C in *Class. Phil.* vol. iii. (1908) pp. 343-345.

g φθέγξωνται logically of mere physical utterance (*cf. Theaet.* 157 B), not, I think, as Adam says, of high-sounding oracular utterance.

h Lit. " wandering," the mark of error. *Cf.* 484 B, *Lysis* 213 E, *Phaedo* 79 C, *Soph.* 230 B, *Phaedr.* 263 B, *Parmen.* 135 E, *Laws* 962 D.

i καὶ οὗτοι is an illogical idiom of over-particularization. The sentence begins generally and ends specifically. Plato does not care, since the meaning is clear. *Cf. Protag.* 336 C, *Gorg.* 456 C-D, *Phaedo* 62 A.

PLATO

505 Σφόδρα γε. Συμβαίνει δὴ αὐτοῖς, οἶμαι, ὁμο-
D λογεῖν ἀγαθὰ εἶναι καὶ κακὰ ταῦτά. ἦ γάρ; Τί
μήν; Οὐκοῦν ὅτι μὲν μεγάλαι καὶ πολλαὶ ἀμφισβητήσεις περὶ αὐτοῦ, φανερόν; Πῶς γὰρ οὔ;
Τί δέ; τόδε οὐ φανερόν, ὡς δίκαια μὲν καὶ καλὰ
πολλοὶ ἂν ἕλοιντο τὰ δοκοῦντα, κἂν μὴ ᾖ, ὅμως
ταῦτα πράττειν καὶ κεκτῆσθαι καὶ δοκεῖν, ἀγαθὰ
δὲ οὐδενὶ ἔτι ἀρκεῖ τὰ δοκοῦντα κτᾶσθαι, ἀλλὰ τὰ
ὄντα ζητοῦσι, τὴν δὲ δόξαν ἐνταῦθα ἤδη πᾶς
E ἀτιμάζει; Καὶ μάλα, ἔφη. Ὃ δὴ διώκει μὲν
ἅπασα ψυχὴ καὶ τούτου ἕνεκα πάντα πράττει,
ἀπομαντευομένη τι εἶναι, ἀποροῦσα δὲ καὶ οὐκ
ἔχουσα λαβεῖν ἱκανῶς τί ποτ' ἐστὶν οὐδὲ πίστει
χρήσασθαι μονίμῳ οἵᾳ καὶ περὶ τἆλλα, διὰ τοῦτο
δὲ ἀποτυγχάνει καὶ τῶν ἄλλων εἴ τι ὄφελος ἦν,
506 περὶ δὴ τὸ τοιοῦτον καὶ τοσοῦτον οὕτω φῶμεν δεῖν
ἐσκοτῶσθαι καὶ ἐκείνους τοὺς βελτίστους ἐν τῇ

---

[a] A distinct reference to Callicles' admission in *Gorgias*
499 B τὰς μὲν βελτίους ἡδονάς, τὰς δὲ χείρους, *cf.* 499 c,
Rep. 561 c, and *Phileb.* 13 c πάσας ὁμοίας εἶναι. Stenzel's
notion (*Studien zur Entw. d. Plat. Dialektik*, p. 98) that in
the *Philebus* Plato "ist von dem Standpunkt des Staates
503 c weit entfernt" is uncritical. The *Republic* merely
refers to the *Gorgias* to show that the question is disputed
and the disputants contradict themselves.

[b] ἀμφισβητήσεις is slightly disparaging, *cf. Theaet.* 163 c,
158 c, 198 c, *Sophist* 233 B, 225 B, but less so than ἐρίζειν
in *Protag.* 337 A.

[c] Men may deny the reality of the conventional virtues
but not of the ultimate sanction, whatever it is. *Cf. Theaet.*
167 c, 172 A-B, and Shorey in *Class. Phil.* xvi. (1921)
pp. 164-168.

[d] *Cf. Gorg.* 468 B τὸ ἀγαθὸν ἄρα διώκοντες, *supra* 505 A-B,
Phileb. 20 D, *Symp.* 206 A, *Euthyd.* 278 E, Aristot. *Eth. Nic.*

90

are bad pleasures [a] ? " " Most assuredly." " The outcome is, I take it, that they are admitting the same things to be both good and bad, are they not ? " " Certainly." " Then is it not apparent that there are many and violent disputes [b] about it ? " " Of course." " And again, is it not apparent that while in the case of the just and the honourable many would prefer the semblance [c] without the reality in action, possession, and opinion, yet when it comes to the good nobody is content with the possession of the appearance but all men seek the reality, and the semblance satisfies nobody here ? " " Quite so," he said. " That, then, which every soul pursues [d] and for its sake does all that it does, with an intuition [e] of its reality, but yet baffled [f] and unable to apprehend its nature adequately, or to attain to any stable belief about it as about other things,[g] and for that reason failing of any possible benefit from other things,—in a matter of this quality and moment, can we, I ask you, allow a like blindness and obscurity in those best citizens [h]

1173 a, 1094 a οὖ πάντα ἐφίεται, Zeller, *Aristot.* i. pp. 344-345, 379, Boethius iii. 10, Dante, *Purg.* xvii. 127-129.

[e] Cf. *Phileb.* 64 A μαντευτέον. Cf. Arnold's phrase, *God and the Bible*, chap. i. p. 23 "approximate language thrown out as it were at certain great objects which the human mind augurs and feels after."

[f] As throughout the minor dialogues. *Cf. What Plato Said*, p. 71.

[g] Because, in the language of Platonic metaphysics, it is the παρουσία τοῦ ἀγαθοῦ that makes them good; but for the practical purpose of ethical theory, because they need the sanction. *Cf.* Introd. p. xxvii, and Montaigne i. 24 "Toute aultre science est dommageable à celuy qui n'a la science de la bonté."

[h] As in the "longer way" Plato is careful not to commit himself to a definition of the ideal or the sanction, but postulates it for his guardians.

91

PLATO

506 πόλει, οἷς πάντα ἐγχειριοῦμεν; Ἥκιστά γ᾽, ἔφη.
Οἶμαι γοῦν, εἶπον, δίκαιά τε καὶ καλὰ ἀγνοού-
μενα ὅπῃ ποτὲ ἀγαθά ἐστιν, οὐ πολλοῦ τινὸς ἄξιον
φύλακα κεκτῆσθαι ἂν ἑαυτῶν τὸν τοῦτο ἀγνοοῦντα,
μαντεύομαι δὲ μηδένα αὐτὰ πρότερον γνώσεσθαι
ἱκανῶς. Καλῶς γάρ, ἔφη, μαντεύει. Οὐκοῦν ἡμῖν
B ἡ πολιτεία τελέως κεκοσμήσεται, ἐὰν ὁ τοιοῦτος
αὐτὴν ἐπισκοπῇ φύλαξ, ὁ τούτων ἐπιστήμων;

XVIII. Ἀνάγκη, ἔφη. ἀλλὰ σὺ δή, ὦ Σώκρατες, πότερον ἐπιστήμην τὸ ἀγαθὸν φῂς εἶναι ἢ
ἡδονήν; ἢ ἄλλο τι παρὰ ταῦτα; Οὗτος, ἦν δ᾽ ἐγώ,
ἀνήρ, καλῶς ἦσθα καὶ πάλαι καταφανὴς ὅτι σοι
οὐκ ἀποχρήσοι τὸ τοῖς ἄλλοις δοκοῦν περὶ αὐτῶν.
Οὐδὲ γὰρ δίκαιόν μοι, ἔφη, ὦ Σώκρατες, φαίνεται
τὰ τῶν ἄλλων μὲν ἔχειν εἰπεῖν δόγματα, τὸ δ᾽
αὑτοῦ μή, τοσοῦτον χρόνον περὶ ταῦτα πραγματευό-
C μενον. Τί δαί; ἦν δ᾽ ἐγώ· δοκεῖ σοι δίκαιον εἶναι
περὶ ὧν τις μὴ οἶδε λέγειν ὡς εἰδότα; Οὐδαμῶς
γ᾽, ἔφη, ὡς εἰδότα, ὡς μέντοι οἰόμενον ταῦθ᾽ ἃ
οἴεται ἐθέλειν λέγειν. Τί δέ; εἶπον· οὐκ ᾔσθησαι
τὰς ἄνευ ἐπιστήμης δόξας, ὡς πᾶσαι αἰσχραί;
ὧν αἱ βέλτισται τυφλαί· ἢ δοκοῦσί τί σοι τυφλῶν

---

[a] The personal or *ab urbe condita* construction. *Cf.*
Theaet. 169 E.
[b] The guardians must be able to give a reason, which they
can do only by reference to the sanction. For the idea that
the statesman must know better than other men *cf. Laws*
968 A, 964 C, 858 D-E, 817 C, Xen. *Mem.* iii. 6. 8.
[c] For the effect of the future perfect *cf.* 457 B λελέξεται,
465 A προστετάξεται, Eurip. *Heracleidae* 980 πεπράξεται.

to whose hands we are to entrust all things ? "
" Least of all," he said. " I fancy, at any rate," said
I, " that the just and the honourable, if their relation
and reference to the good is not known,*a* will not have
secured a guardian *b* of much worth in the man thus
ignorant, and my surmise is that no one will understand them adequately before he knows this." "You
surmise well," he said. " Then our constitution will
have its perfect and definitive organization *c* only when
such a guardian, who knows these things, oversees it."

XVIII. " Necessarily," he said. " But you yourself, Socrates, do you think that knowledge is the
good or pleasure or something else and different ? "
" What a man it is," said I ; " you made it very plain *d*
long ago that you would not be satisfied with what
others think about it." " Why, it does not seem
right to me either, Socrates," he said, " to be ready to
state the opinions of others but not one's own when
one has occupied himself with the matter so long.*e* "
" But then," said I, " do you think it right to speak
as having knowledge about things one does not
know ? " " By no means," he said, " as having
knowledge, but one ought to be willing to tell as his
opinion what he opines." " Nay," said I, " have
you not observed that opinions divorced from knowledge *f* are ugly things ? The best of them are
blind.*g* Or do you think that those who hold some

d For the personal construction *cf.* 348 E, Isoc. *To Nic.* 1.
καταφανής is a variation in this idiom for δῆλος. *Cf.* also
Theaet. 189 c, *Symp.* 221 B, *Charm.* 162 c, etc.

e *Cf.* 367 D-E.

f This is not a contradiction of *Meno* 97 B, *Theaet.* 201 B-C,
and *Phileb.* 62 A-B, but simply a different context and
emphasis. *Cf. Unity of Plato's Thought*, p. 47, nn. 338
and 339.

g *Cf.* on 484 c, *Phaedr.* 270 E.

506 διαφέρειν ὁδὸν ὀρθῶς πορευομένων οἱ ἄνευ νοῦ
ἀληθές τι δοξάζοντες; Οὐδέν, ἔφη. Βούλει οὖν
D αἰσχρὰ θεάσασθαι τυφλά τε καὶ σκολιά, ἐξὸν παρ'
ἄλλων ἀκούειν φανά τε καὶ καλά; Μὴ πρὸς Διός,
ᾖ δ' ὅς, ὦ Σώκρατες, ὁ Γλαύκων, ὥσπερ ἐπὶ τέλει
ὢν ἀποστῇς. ἀρκέσει γὰρ ἡμῖν, κἂν ὥσπερ
δικαιοσύνης πέρι καὶ σωφροσύνης καὶ τῶν ἄλλων
διῆλθες, οὕτω καὶ περὶ τοῦ ἀγαθοῦ διέλθῃς. Καὶ
γὰρ ἐμοί, ἦν δ' ἐγώ, ὦ ἑταῖρε, καὶ μάλα ἀρκέσει·
ἀλλ' ὅπως μὴ οὐχ οἷός τ' ἔσομαι, προθυμούμενος
δὲ ἀσχημονῶν γέλωτα ὀφλήσω. ἀλλ', ὦ μακάριοι,
E αὐτὸ μὲν τί ποτ' ἐστὶ τἀγαθὸν ἐάσωμεν τὸ νῦν
εἶναι· πλέον γάρ μοι φαίνεται ἢ κατὰ τὴν παρ-
οῦσαν ὁρμὴν ἐφικέσθαι τοῦ γε δοκοῦντος ἐμοὶ τὰ
νῦν· ὃς δὲ ἔκγονός τε τοῦ ἀγαθοῦ φαίνεται καὶ
ὁμοιότατος ἐκείνῳ, λέγειν ἐθέλω, εἰ καὶ ὑμῖν
φίλον, εἰ δὲ μή, ἐᾶν. Ἀλλ', ἔφη, λέγε· εἰσαῦθις
γὰρ τοῦ πατρὸς ἀποτίσεις τὴν διήγησιν. Βου-
507 λοίμην ἄν, εἶπον, ἐμέ τε δύνασθαι αὐτὴν ἀποδοῦναι

ᵃ Probably an allusion to the revelation of the mysteries.
Cf. Phaedr. 250 c, Phileb. 16 c, Rep. 518 c, 478 c, 479 D,
518 A. It is fantastic to see in it a reference to what Cicero
calls the lumina orationis of Isocratean style. The rhetoric
and synonyms of this passage are not to be pressed.

ᵇ Cf. Phileb. 64 c ἐπὶ μὲν τοῖς τοῦ ἀγαθοῦ ἤδη προθύροις,
"we are now in the vestibule of the good."

ᶜ καὶ μάλα, "jolly well," humorous emphasis on the point
that it is much easier to "define" the conventional virtues
than to explain the "sanction." Cf. Symp. 189 A, Euthydem.
298 D-E, Herod. viii. 66. It is frequent in the Republic.
Ritter gives forty-seven cases. I have fifty-four! But the
point that matters is the humorous tone. Cf. e.g. 610 E.

ᵈ Excess of zeal, προθυμία, seemed laughable to the Greeks.

true opinion without intelligence differ appreciably from blind men who go the right way ? " " They do not differ at all," he said. " Is it, then, ugly things that you prefer to contemplate, things blind and crooked, when you might hear from others what is luminous [a] and fair ? " " Nay, in heaven's name, Socrates," said Glaucon, " do not draw back, as it were, at the very goal.[b] For it will content us if you explain the good even as you set forth the nature of justice, sobriety, and the other virtues." " It will right well [c] content me, my dear fellow," I said, " but I fear that my powers may fail and that in my eagerness I may cut a sorry figure and become a laughing-stock.[d] Nay, my beloved, let us dismiss for the time being the nature of the good in itself ; [e] for to attain to my present surmise of that seems a pitch above the impulse that wings my flight to-day.[f] But of what seems to be the offspring of the good and most nearly made in its likeness [g] I am willing to speak if you too wish it, and otherwise to let the matter drop." " Well, speak on," he said, " for you will duly pay me the tale of the parent another time." " I could wish," I said, " that I were able to make

Cf. my interpretation of *Iliad* i. *in fine*, *Class. Phil.* xxii. (1927) pp. 222-223.

[e] *Cf.* More, *Principia Ethica*, p. 17 "Good, then, is indefinable ; and yet, so far as I know, there is only one ethical writer, Professor Henry Sidgwick, who has clearly recognized and stated this fact."

[f] This is not superstitious mysticism but a deliberate refusal to confine in a formula what requires either a volume or a symbol. See Introd. p. xxvii, and my *Idea of Good in Plato's Republic*, p. 212. τὰ νῦν repeats τὸ νῦν εἶναι (*cf. Tim.* 48 c), as the evasive phrase εἰσαῦθις below sometimes lays the topic on the table, never to be taken up again. *Cf.* 347 E and 430 C.

[g] *Cf. Laws* 897 D-E, *Phaedr.* 246 A.

507 καὶ ὑμᾶς κομίσασθαι, ἀλλὰ μὴ ὥσπερ νῦν τοὺς
τόκους μόνον. τοῦτον δὲ δὴ οὖν τὸν τόκον τε καὶ
ἔκγονον αὐτοῦ τοῦ ἀγαθοῦ κομίσασθε. εὐλαβεῖσθε
μέντοι μή πῃ ἐξαπατήσω ὑμᾶς ἄκων, κίβδηλον
ἀποδιδοὺς τὸν λόγον τοῦ τόκου. Εὐλαβησόμεθα,
ἔφη, κατὰ δύναμιν· ἀλλὰ μόνον λέγε. Διομολο-
γησάμενός γ᾽, ἔφην ἐγώ, καὶ ἀναμνήσας ὑμᾶς τά
τ᾽ ἐν τοῖς ἔμπροσθεν ῥηθέντα καὶ ἄλλοτε ἤδη
B πολλάκις εἰρημένα. Τὰ ποῖα; ἦ δ᾽ ὅς. Πολλὰ
καλά, ἦν δ᾽ ἐγώ, καὶ πολλὰ ἀγαθὰ καὶ ἕκαστα
οὕτως εἶναί φαμέν τε καὶ διορίζομεν τῷ λόγῳ.
Φαμὲν γάρ. Καὶ αὐτὸ δὴ καλὸν καὶ αὐτὸ ἀγαθὸν
καὶ οὕτω περὶ πάντων, ἃ τότε ὡς πολλὰ ἐτίθεμεν,
πάλιν αὖ κατ᾽ ἰδέαν μίαν ἑκάστου ὡς μιᾶς οὔσης
τιθέντες ὃ ἔστιν ἕκαστον προσαγορεύομεν. Ἔστι
ταῦτα. Καὶ τὰ μὲν δὴ ὁρᾶσθαι φαμεν, νοεῖσθαι
C δ᾽ οὔ, τὰς δ᾽ αὖ ἰδέας νοεῖσθαι μέν, ὁρᾶσθαι δ᾽ οὔ.
Παντάπασι μὲν οὖν. Τῷ οὖν ὁρῶμεν ἡμῶν αὐτῶν
τὰ ὁρώμενα; Τῇ ὄψει, ἔφη. Οὐκοῦν, ἦν δ᾽ ἐγώ,
καὶ ἀκοῇ τὰ ἀκουόμενα, καὶ ταῖς ἄλλαις αἰσθήσεσι
πάντα τὰ αἰσθητά; Τί μήν; Ἆρ᾽ οὖν, ἦν δ᾽ ἐγώ,
ἐννενόηκας τὸν τῶν αἰσθήσεων δημιουργὸν ὅσῳ

---

a This playful interlude relieves the monotony of argument
and is a transition to the symbolism. τόκος means both
interest and offspring. *Cf.* 555 E, *Polit.* 267 A, Aristoph.
Clouds 34, *Thesm.* 845, Pindar, *Ol.* x. 12. The equivocation,
which in other languages became a metaphor, has played a
great part in the history of opinion about usury. *Cf.* the
article " Usury " in Hastings's *Encyclopaedia of Relig. and
Ethics*, and Antonio's

. . . when did friendship take
A breed for barren metal of his friend?

and you to receive the payment and not merely as now the interest. But at any rate receive this interest [a] and the offspring of the good. Have a care, however, lest I deceive you unintentionally with a false reckoning of the interest." "We will do our best," he said, " to be on our guard. Only speak on." " Yes," I said, "after first coming to an understanding with you and reminding you of what has been said here before and often on other occasions.[b]" "What?" said he. "We predicate ' to be ' [c] of many beautiful things and many good things, saying of them severally that they *are*, and so define them in our speech." "We do." " And again, we speak of a self-beautiful and of a good that is only and merely good, and so, in the case of all the things that we then posited as many, we turn about and posit each as a single idea or aspect, assuming it to be a unity and call it that which each really is.[d]" " It is so." " And the one class of things we say can be seen but not thought, while the ideas can be thought but not seen." " By all means." " With which of the parts of ourselves, with which of our faculties, then, do we see visible things ? " "With sight," he said. "And do we not," I said, " hear audibles with hearing, and perceive all sensibles with the other senses ? " " Surely." " Have you ever observed," said I, " how much the

---

[b] *Cf.* 475 E f. Plato as often begins by a restatement of the theory of ideas, *i.e.* practically of the distinction between the concept and the objects of sense. *Cf. Rep.* 596 A ff., *Phaedo* 108 B ff.

[c] The modern reader will never understand Plato from translations that talk about " Being." *Cf. What Plato Said*, p. 605.

[d] ὃ ἔστιν is technical for the reality of the ideas. *Cf. Phaedo* 75 B, D, 78 D, *Parmen.* 129 B, *Symp.* 211 C, *Rep.* 490 B, 532 A, 597 A.

507 πολυτελεστάτην τὴν τοῦ ὁρᾶν τε καὶ ὁρᾶσθαι
δύναμιν ἐδημιούργησεν; Οὐ πάνυ, ἔφη. Ἀλλ'
ὧδε σκόπει. ἔστιν ὅ τι προσδεῖ ἀκοῇ καὶ φωνῇ
γένους ἄλλου εἰς τὸ τὴν μὲν ἀκούειν, τὴν δὲ ἀκούε-
D σθαι, ὃ ἐὰν μὴ παραγένηται τρίτον, ἡ μὲν οὐκ
ἀκούσεται, ἡ δὲ οὐκ ἀκουσθήσεται; Οὐδενός, ἔφη.
Οἶμαι δέ γε, ἦν δ' ἐγώ, οὐδ' ἄλλαις πολλαῖς, ἵνα
μὴ εἴπω ὅτι οὐδεμιᾷ, τοιούτου προσδεῖ οὐδενός. ἢ
σύ τινα ἔχεις εἰπεῖν; Οὐκ ἔγωγε, ἦ δ' ὅς. Τὴν
δὲ τῆς ὄψεως καὶ τοῦ ὁρατοῦ οὐκ ἐννοεῖς ὅτι
προσδεῖται; Πῶς; Ἐνούσης που ἐν ὄμμασιν
ὄψεως καὶ ἐπιχειροῦντος τοῦ ἔχοντος χρῆσθαι
αὐτῇ, παρούσης δὲ χρόας ἐν αὐτοῖς, ἐὰν μὴ
E παραγένηται γένος τρίτον ἰδίᾳ ἐπ' αὐτὸ τοῦτο
πεφυκός, οἶσθα, ὅτι ἥ τε ὄψις οὐδὲν ὄψεται τά τε
χρώματα ἔσται ἀόρατα. Τίνος δὴ λέγεις, ἔφη,
τούτου; Ὁ δὴ σὺ καλεῖς, ἦν δ' ἐγώ, φῶς.
Ἀληθῆ, ἔφη, λέγεις. Οὐ σμικρᾷ ἄρα ἰδέᾳ ἡ τοῦ
508 ὁρᾶν αἴσθησις καὶ ἡ τοῦ ὁρᾶσθαι δύναμις τῶν
ἄλλων ξυζεύξεων τιμιωτέρῳ ζυγῷ ἐζύγησαν, εἴπερ
μὴ ἄτιμον τὸ φῶς. Ἀλλὰ μήν, ἔφη, πολλοῦ γε
δεῖ ἄτιμον εἶναι.

ᵃ Creator, δημιουργός, God, the gods, and nature, are all
virtual synonyms in such passages.
ᵇ Cf. Phaedr. 250 D, Tim. 45 B.
ᶜ This is literature, not science. Plato knew that sound
required a medium, Tim. 67 B. But the statement here is
true enough to illustrate the thought.
ᵈ Lit. "kind of thing," γένος. Cf. 507 C-D.
ᵉ Cf. Troland, The Mystery of Mind, p. 82: "In order that
there should be vision, it is not sufficient that a physical
object should exist before the eyes. There must also be a
source of so-called 'light.'" Cf. Sir John Davies' poem on
the Soul:

greatest expenditure the creator [a] of the senses has lavished on the faculty of seeing and being seen ? [b] " " Why, no, I have not," he said. " Well, look at it thus. Do hearing and voice stand in need of another medium [c] so that the one may hear and the other be heard, in the absence of which third element the one will not hear and the other not be heard ? " " They need nothing," he said. " Neither, I fancy," said I, " do many others, not to say that none require anything of the sort. Or do you know of any ? " " Not I," he said. " But do you not observe that vision and the visible do have this further need ? " " How ? " " Though vision may be in the eyes and its possessor may try to use it, and though colour be present, yet without the presence of a third thing [d] specifically and naturally adapted to this purpose, you are aware that vision will see nothing and the colours will remain invisible. [e] " " What [f] is this thing of which you speak ? " he said. " The thing," I said, " that you call light." " You say truly," he replied. " The bond, then, that yokes together visibility and the faculty of sight is more precious by no slight form [g] than that which unites the other pairs, if light is not without honour." " It surely is far from being so," he said.

> But as the sharpest eye discerneth nought
> Except the sunbeams in the air do shine ;
> So the best soul with her reflecting thought
> Sees not herself without some light divine.

[f] Plato would not have tried to explain this loose colloquial genitive, and we need not.

[g] The loose Herodotean-Thucydidean-Isocratean use of ἰδέα. *Cf. Laws* 689 D καὶ τὸ σμικρότατον εἶδος. " Form " over-translates ἰδέᾳ here, which is little more than a synonym for γένος above. *Cf.* Wilamowitz, *Platon*, ii. p. 250.

PLATO

508 XIX. Τίνα οὖν ἔχεις αἰτιάσασθαι τῶν ἐν οὐρανῷ
θεῶν τούτου κύριον, οὗ ἡμῖν τὸ φῶς ὄψιν τε ποιεῖ
ὁρᾶν ὅ τι κάλλιστα καὶ τὰ ὁρώμενα ὁρᾶσθαι;
Ὅνπερ καὶ σύ, ἔφη, καὶ οἱ ἄλλοι· τὸν ἥλιον γὰρ
δῆλον ὅτι ἐρωτᾷς. Ἆρ' οὖν ὧδε πέφυκεν ὄψις
πρὸς τοῦτον τὸν θεόν;ᵃ Πῶς; Οὐκ ἔστιν ἥλιος ἡ
ὄψις οὔτε αὐτὴ οὔτε ἐν ᾧ ἐγγίγνεται, ὃ δὴ κα-
B λοῦμεν ὄμμα. Οὐ γὰρ οὖν. Ἀλλ' ἡλιοειδέστατόν
γε οἶμαι τῶν περὶ τὰς αἰσθήσεις ὀργάνων. Πολύ
γε. Οὐκοῦν καὶ τὴν δύναμιν, ἣν ἔχει, ἐκ τούτου
ταμιευομένην ὥσπερ ἐπίρρυτον κέκτηται; Πάνυ
μὲν οὖν. Ἆρ' οὖν οὐ καὶ ὁ ἥλιος ὄψις μὲν οὐκ
ἔστιν, αἴτιος δ' ὢν αὐτῆς ὁρᾶται ὑπ' αὐτῆς ταύτης;ᵇ

ᵃ Plato was willing to call the stars gods as the barbarians
did (*Cratyl.* 397 D, Aristoph. *Peace* 406 ff., Herod. iv. 188).
Cf. Laws 821 B, 899 B, 950 D, *Apol.* 26 D, *Epinomis* 985 B,
988 B.

ᵇ *Cf.* my *Idea of Good in Plato's Republic*, pp. 223-225,
Reinhardt, *Kosmos und Sympathie*, pp. 374-384, Arnold,
" Mycerinus " :

> Yet, surely, O my people, did I deem
> Man's justice from the all-just Gods was given ;
> A light that from some upper fount did beam,
> Some better archetype, whose seat was heaven ;
> A light that, shining from the blest abodes,
> Did shadow somewhat of the life of Gods.

Complete Poems of Henry More, p. 77 :

> Lift myself up in the Theologie
> Of heavenly Plato.   There I 'll contemplate
> The Archetype of this sunne, that bright Idee
> Of steddie Good, that doth his beams dilate
> Through all the worlds, all lives and beings
>   propagate . . .
>   . . . a fair delineament
> Of that which Good in Plato's school is hight,
> His T'agathon with beauteous rayes bedight.

XIX. " Which one can you name of the divinities in heaven [a] as the author and cause of this, whose light makes our vision see best and visible things to be seen?" "Why, the one that you too and other people mean," he said; " for your question evidently refers to the sun.[b]" "Is not this, then, the relation of vision to that divinity?" "What?" "Neither vision itself nor its vehicle, which we call the eye, is identical with the sun." "Why, no." "But it is, I think, the most sunlike [c] of all the instruments of sense." " By far the most." " And does it not receive the power which it possesses as an influx, as it were, dispensed from the sun?" "Certainly." " Is it not also true that the sun is not vision, yet as being the cause [d] thereof

---

Mediaeval writers have much to say of Plato's mysterious Tagathon. Aristotle, who rejects the idea of good, uses τἀγαθόν in much the same way.

It is naïve to take the language of Platonic unction too literally. *Cf. What Plato Said*, pp. 394 ff.

[c] *Cf.* 509 A, Plotinus, *Enn.* i. 6. 9 οὐ γὰρ ἂν πώποτε εἶδεν ὀφθαλμὸς ἥλιον ἡλιοειδὴς μὴ γεγενημένος and vi. 7. 19, Cic. *Tusc.* i. 25. 63 *in fine* " quod si in hoc mundo fieri sine deo non potest, ne in sphaera quidem eosdem motus Archimedes sine divino ingenio potuisset imitare," Manilius ii. 115:

> quis caelum posset nisi caeli munere nosse,
> et reperire deum nisi qui pars ipse deorum?

Goethe's

> Wär' nicht das Auge sonnenhaft,
> Die Sonne könnt es nie erblicken,

and Goethe to Eckermann, Feb. 26, 1824: " Hätte ich nicht die Welt durch Anticipation bereits in mir getragen, ich wäre mit sehenden Augen blind geblieben."

[d] *Cf. Complete Poems of Henry More*, p. 113:

> Behold a fit resemblance of this truth,
> The Sun begetteth both colours and sight . . ., etc.

508 Οὕτως, ἦ δ' ὅς. Τοῦτον τοίνυν, ἦν δ' ἐγώ, φάναι
με λέγειν τὸν τοῦ ἀγαθοῦ ἔκγονον, ὃν τἀγαθὸν
C ἐγέννησεν ἀνάλογον ἑαυτῷ, ὅ τι περ αὐτὸ ἐν τῷ
νοητῷ τόπῳ πρός τε νοῦν καὶ τὰ νοούμενα, τοῦτο
τοῦτον ἐν τῷ ὁρατῷ πρός τε ὄψιν καὶ τὰ ὁρώμενα.
Πῶς; ἔφη· ἔτι διελθέ μοι. 'Οφθαλμοί, ἦν δ'
ἐγώ, οἶσθ' ὅτι, ὅταν μηκέτι ἐπ' ἐκεῖνά τις αὐτοὺς
τρέπῃ ὧν ἂν τὰς χρόας τὸ ἡμερινὸν φῶς ἐπέχῃ,
ἀλλὰ ὧν νυκτερινὰ φέγγη, ἀμβλυώττουσί τε καὶ
ἐγγὺς φαίνονται τυφλῶν, ὥσπερ οὐκ ἐνούσης
καθαρᾶς ὄψεως; Καὶ μάλα, ἔφη. Ὅταν δέ γ',
D οἶμαι, ὧν ὁ ἥλιος καταλάμπει, σαφῶς ὁρῶσι, καὶ
τοῖς αὐτοῖς τούτοις ὄμμασιν ἐνοῦσα φαίνεται. Τί
μήν; Οὕτω τοίνυν καὶ τὸ τῆς ψυχῆς ὧδε νόει·
ὅταν μέν, οὗ καταλάμπει ἀλήθειά τε καὶ τὸ ὄν, εἰς
τοῦτο ἀπερείσηται, ἐνόησέ τε καὶ ἔγνω αὐτὸ καὶ
νοῦν ἔχειν φαίνεται· ὅταν δὲ εἰς τὸ τῷ σκότῳ
κεκραμένον, τὸ γιγνόμενόν τε καὶ ἀπολλύμενον,
δοξάζει τε καὶ ἀμβλυώττει ἄνω καὶ κάτω τὰς
δόξας μεταβάλλον καὶ ἔοικεν αὖ νοῦν οὐκ ἔχοντι.
E Ἔοικε γάρ. Τοῦτο τοίνυν τὸ τὴν ἀλήθειαν παρέχον
τοῖς γιγνωσκομένοις καὶ τῷ γιγνώσκοντι τὴν

ᵃ *i.e.* creation was the work of benevolent design. This is
one of the few passages in the *Republic* where the idea of
good is considered in relation to the universe, a thesis reserved for poetical or mythical development in the *Timaeus*.
It is idle to construct a systematic metaphysical theology for
Plato by identification of τἀγαθόν here either with God or

is beheld by vision itself ? " " That is so," he said. " This, then, you must understand that I meant by the offspring of the good *a* which the good begot to stand in a proportion *b* with itself : as the good is in the intelligible region to reason and the objects of reason, so is this in the visible world to vision and the objects of vision." " How is that ? " he said ; " explain further." " You are aware," I said, " that when the eyes are no longer turned upon objects upon whose colours the light of day falls but that of the dim luminaries of night, their edge is blunted and they appear almost blind, as if pure vision did not dwell in them." " Yes, indeed," he said. " But when, I take it, they are directed upon objects illumined by the sun, they see clearly, and vision appears to reside in these same eyes." " Certainly." " Apply this comparison to the soul also in this way. When it is firmly fixed on the domain where truth and reality shine resplendent *c* it apprehends and knows them and appears to possess reason ; but when it inclines to that region which is mingled with darkness, the world of becoming and passing away, it opines only and its edge is blunted, and it shifts its opinions hither and thither, and again seems as if it lacked reason." " Yes, it does." " This reality, then, that gives their truth to the objects of knowledge and the power of knowing

with the ideas as a whole. *Cf. Unity of Plato's Thought*, p. 512.

b Cf. *Gorg.* 465 B-C, *infra* 510 A-B, 511 E, 530 D, 534 A, 576 C, *Phaedo* 111 A-B, *Tim.* 29 C, 32 A-B. For ἀνάλογον in this sense *cf.* 511 E, 534 A, *Phaedo* 110 D.

c Plato's rhetoric is not to be pressed. Truth, being, the good, are virtual synonyms. Still, for Plato's ethical and political philosophy the light that makes things intelligible is the idea of good, *i.e.* the "sanction," and not, as some commentators insist, the truth.

PLATO

508 δύναμιν ἀποδιδὸν τὴν τοῦ ἀγαθοῦ ἰδέαν φάθι εἶναι,
αἰτίαν δ' ἐπιστήμης οὖσαν καὶ ἀληθείας ὡς
γιγνωσκομένης μὲν διανοοῦ, οὕτω δὲ καλῶν
ἀμφοτέρων ὄντων, γνώσεώς τε καὶ ἀληθείας, ἄλλο
καὶ κάλλιον ἔτι τούτων ἡγούμενος αὐτὸ ὀρθῶς
ἡγήσει· ἐπιστήμην δὲ καὶ ἀλήθειαν, ὥσπερ ἐκεῖ
509 φῶς τε καὶ ὄψιν ἡλιοειδῆ μὲν νομίζειν ὀρθόν, ἥλιον
δὲ ἡγεῖσθαι οὐκ ὀρθῶς ἔχει, οὕτω καὶ ἐνταῦθα
ἀγαθοειδῆ μὲν νομίζειν ταῦτ' ἀμφότερα ὀρθόν,
ἀγαθὸν δὲ ἡγεῖσθαι ὁπότερον αὐτῶν οὐκ ὀρθόν,
ἀλλ' ἔτι μειζόνως τιμητέον τὴν τοῦ ἀγαθοῦ ἕξιν.
Ἀμήχανον κάλλος, ἔφη, λέγεις, εἰ ἐπιστήμην
μὲν καὶ ἀλήθειαν παρέχει, αὐτὸ δ' ὑπὲρ ταῦτα
κάλλει ἐστίν· οὐ γὰρ δήπου σύ γε ἡδονὴν αὐτὸ

ᵃ No absolute distinction can be drawn between εἶδος and ἰδέα in Plato. But ἰδέα may be used to carry the notion of "apprehended aspect" which I think is more pertinent here than the metaphysical entity of the idea, though of course Plato would affirm that. *Cf.* 369 A, *Unity of Plato's Thought*, p. 35, *What Plato Said*, p. 585, *Class. Phil.* xx. (1925) p. 347.

ᵇ The meaning is clear. We really understand and know anything only when we apprehend its purpose, the aspect of the good that it reveals. *Cf.* Introd. pp. xxxv-xxxvi. The position and case of γιγνωσκομένης are difficult. But no change proposed is any improvement.

ᶜ Plato likes to cap a superlative by a further degree of completeness, a climax beyond the climax. *Cf.* 405 B αἴσχιστον . . . αἴσχιον, 578 B, *Symp.* 180 A-B and Bury *ad loc.* The same characteristic can be observed in his method, *e.g.* in the *Symposium* where Agathon's speech, which seems the climax, is surpassed by that of Socrates; similarly in the *Gorgias* and the tenth book of the *Republic*. *Cf.* Friedländer, *Platon*, i. p. 174, *supra* Introd. p. lxi.

This and the next half page belong, I think, to rhetoric rather than to systematic metaphysics. Plato the idealist uses transcendental language of his ideal, and is never willing

104

THE REPUBLIC, BOOK VI

to the knower, you must say is the idea [a] of good, and you must conceive it as being the cause of knowledge, and of truth in so far as known.[b] Yet fair as they both are, knowledge and truth, in supposing it to be something fairer still [c] than these you will think rightly of it. But as for knowledge and truth, even as in our illustration it is right to deem light and vision sunlike, but never to think that they are the sun, so here it is right to consider these two their counterparts, as being like the good or boniform,[d] but to think that either of them is the good [e] is not right. Still higher honour belongs to the possession and habit [f] of the good." "An inconceivable beauty you speak of," he said, " if it is the source of knowledge and truth, and yet itself surpasses them in beauty. For you surely [g] cannot mean that it is pleasure." " Hush,"

to admit that expression has done justice to it. But Plato the rationalist distinctly draws the line between his religious language thrown out at an object and his definite logical and practical conclusions. *Cf. e.g. Meno* 81 D-E.

[d] ἀγαθοειδῆ occurs only here in classical Greek literature. Plato quite probably coined it for his purpose.

[e] There is no article in the Greek. Plato is not scrupulous to distinguish good and the good here. *Cf.* on 505 c, p. 89, note *f*.

[f] ἕξις is not yet in Plato quite the technical Aristotelian " habit." However *Protag.* 344 c approaches it. *Cf.* also *Phileb.* 11 D, 41 c, Ritter-Preller, p. 285.

Plato used many words in periphrasis with the genitive, *e.g.* ἕξις *Laws* 625 c, γένεσις· *Laws* 691 B, *Tim.* 73 B, 76 E, μοῖρα *Phaedr.* 255 B, 274 E, *Menex.* 249 B, φύσις *Phaedo* 109 E, *Symp.* 186 B, *Laws* 729 c, 845 D, 944 D, etc. He may have chosen ἕξις here to suggest the ethical aspect of the good as a habit or possession of the soul. The introduction of ἡδονή below supports this view. Some interpreters think it = τὸ ἀγαθὸν ὡς ἔχει, which is possible but rather pointless.

[g] For οὐ γὰρ δήπου *cf. Apol.* 20 c, *Gorg.* 455 A, *Euthyph.* 13 A.

509 λέγεις. Εὐφήμει, ἦν δ' ἐγώ· ἀλλ' ὧδε μᾶλλον
B τὴν εἰκόνα αὐτοῦ ἔτι ἐπισκόπει. Πῶς; Τὸν
ἥλιον τοῖς ὁρωμένοις οὐ μόνον, οἶμαι, τὴν τοῦ
ὁρᾶσθαι δύναμιν παρέχειν φήσεις, ἀλλὰ καὶ τὴν
γένεσιν καὶ αὔξην καὶ τροφήν, οὐ γένεσιν αὐτὸν
ὄντα. Πῶς γάρ; Καὶ τοῖς γιγνωσκομένοις τοίνυν
μὴ μόνον τὸ γιγνώσκεσθαι φάναι ὑπὸ τοῦ ἀγαθοῦ
παρεῖναι, ἀλλὰ καὶ τὸ εἶναί τε καὶ τὴν οὐσίαν ὑπ'
ἐκείνου αὐτοῖς προσεῖναι, οὐκ οὐσίας ὄντος τοῦ
ἀγαθοῦ, ἀλλ' ἔτι ἐπέκεινα τῆς οὐσίας πρεσβείᾳ
καὶ δυνάμει ὑπερέχοντος.
C XX. Καὶ ὁ Γλαύκων μάλα γελοίως, Ἄπολλον,
ἔφη, δαιμονίας ὑπερβολῆς! Σὺ γάρ, ἦν δ' ἐγώ,
αἴτιος, ἀναγκάζων τὰ ἐμοὶ δοκοῦντα περὶ αὐτοῦ
λέγειν. Καὶ μηδαμῶς γ', ἔφη, παύσῃ, εἰ μή τι
ἀλλὰ τὴν περὶ τὸν ἥλιον ὁμοιότητα αὖ διεξιών, εἴ
πῃ ἀπολείπεις. Ἀλλὰ μήν, εἶπον, συχνά γε ἀπο-

ᵃ i.e. not only do we understand a thing when we know
its purpose, but a purpose in some mind is the chief cause of
its existence, God's mind for the universe, man's mind for
political institutions. This, being the only interpretation
that makes sense of the passage, is presumably more or less
consciously Plato's meaning. *Cf.* Introd. pp. xxxv-xxxvi.

Quite irrelevant are Plato's supposed identification of the
ἀγαθόν with the ἕν, one, and Aristotle's statement, *Met.*
988 a, that the ideas are the cause of other things and the
one is the cause of the ideas.

The remainder of the paragraph belongs to transcendental
rhetoric. It has been endlessly quoted and plays a great
part in Neoplatonism, in all philosophies of the unknowable
and in all negative and mystic theologies.

ᵇ It is an error to oppose Plato here to the Alexandrians
who sometimes said ἐπέκεινα τοῦ ὄντος. Plato's sentence
would have made ὄντος very inconvenient here. But εἶναι
shows that οὐσίας is not distinguished from τοῦ ὄντος here.
ἐπέκεινα became technical and a symbol for the transcendental

THE REPUBLIC, BOOK VI

said I, " but examine the similitude of it still further in this way.[a]" "How?" "The sun, I presume you will say, not only furnishes to visibles the power of visibility but it also provides for their generation and growth and nurture though it is not itself generation." "Of course not." "In like manner, then, you are to say that the objects of knowledge not only receive from the presence of the good their being known, but their very existence and essence is derived to them from it, though the good itself is not essence but still transcends essence [b] in dignity and surpassing power."

XX. And Glaucon very ludicrously [c] said, "Heaven save us, hyperbole [d] can no further go." "The fault is yours," I said, "for compelling me to utter my thoughts about it." "And don't desist," he said, "but at least [e] expound the similitude of the sun, if there is anything that you are omitting." "Why, certainly," I said, "I am omitting a great deal." "Well,

---

in Neoplatonism and all similar philosophies. *Cf.* Plotinus xvii. 1, Dionysius Areop. *De divinis nominibus*, ii. 2, Friedländer, *Platon*, i. p. 87.

[c] He is amused at Socrates' emphasis. Fanciful is Wilamowitz' notion (*Platon*, i. p. 209) that the laughable thing is Glaucon's losing control of himself, for which he compares Aristoph. *Birds* 61. *Cf.* the extraordinary comment of Proclus, p. 265.

The dramatic humour of Glaucon's surprise is Plato's way of smiling at himself, as he frequently does in the dialogues. *Cf.* 536 B, 540 B, *Lysis* 223 B, *Protag.* 340 E, *Charm.* 175 E, *Cratyl.* 426 B, *Theaet.* 200 B, 197 D, etc. *Cf.* Friedländer, *Platon*, i. p. 172 on the *Phaedo*.

[d] "What a *comble!*" would be nearer the tone of the Greek. There is no good English equivalent for ὑπερβολῆς. *Cf.* Sir Thomas Browne's remark that "nothing can be said hyperbolically of God." The banter here relieves the strain, as is Plato's manner.

[e] *Cf.* 502 A, *Symp.* 222 E, *Meno* 86 E.

509 λείπω. Μηδὲ σμικρὸν τοίνυν, ἔφη, παραλίπῃς.
Οἶμαι μέν, ἦν δ' ἐγώ, καὶ πολύ· ὅμως δέ, ὅσα γ'
ἐν τῷ παρόντι δυνατόν, ἑκὼν οὐκ ἀπολείψω. Μὴ
D γάρ, ἔφη. Νόησον τοίνυν, ἦν δ' ἐγώ, ὥσπερ
λέγομεν, δύω αὐτὼ εἶναι, καὶ βασιλεύειν τὸ μὲν
νοητοῦ γένους τε καὶ τόπου, τὸ δ' αὖ ὁρατοῦ, ἵνα
μὴ οὐρανοῦ εἰπὼν δόξω σοι σοφίζεσθαι περὶ τὸ
ὄνομα. ἀλλ' οὖν ἔχεις ταῦτα διττὰ εἴδη, ὁρατόν,
νοητόν; Ἔχω. Ὥσπερ τοίνυν γραμμὴν δίχα
τετμημένην λαβὼν ἄνισα[1] τμήματα, πάλιν τέμνε
ἑκάτερον τμῆμα ἀνὰ τὸν αὐτὸν λόγον, τό τε τοῦ
ὁρωμένου γένους καὶ τὸ τοῦ νοουμένου, καί σοι
ἔσται σαφηνείᾳ καὶ ἀσαφείᾳ πρὸς ἄλληλα ἐν μὲν
E τῷ ὁρωμένῳ τὸ μὲν ἕτερον τμῆμα εἰκόνες. λέγω
510 δὲ τὰς εἰκόνας πρῶτον μὲν τὰς σκιάς, ἔπειτα τὰ
ἐν τοῖς ὕδασι φαντάσματα καὶ ἐν τοῖς ὅσα πυκνά
τε καὶ λεῖα καὶ φανὰ ξυνέστηκε, καὶ πᾶν τὸ
τοιοῦτον, εἰ κατανοεῖς. Ἀλλὰ κατανοῶ. Τὸ τοίνυν ἕτερον τίθει ᾧ τοῦτο ἔοικε, τά τε περὶ ἡμᾶς
ζῶα καὶ πᾶν τὸ φυτευτὸν καὶ τὸ σκευαστὸν ὅλον
γένος. Τίθημι, ἔφη. Ἦ καὶ ἐθέλοις ἂν αὐτὸ
φάναι, ἦν δ' ἐγώ, διῃρῆσθαι ἀληθείᾳ τε καὶ μή,
ὡς τὸ δοξαστὸν πρὸς τὸ γνωστόν, οὕτω τὸ ὁμοιωθὲν
B πρὸς τὸ ᾧ ὡμοιώθη; Ἔγωγ', ἔφη, καὶ μάλα.
Σκόπει δὴ αὖ καὶ τὴν τοῦ νοητοῦ τομὴν ᾗ τμητέον.

[1] ἄνισα ADM Proclus, ἄν, ἴσα F, ἀν' ἴσα Stallbaum.

---

[a] *Cf.* the similar etymological pun in *Cratyl.* 396 B-C.
Here, as often, the translator must choose between over-
translating for some tastes, or not translating at all.

[b] The meaning is given in the text. Too many com-
mentators lose the meaning in their study of the imagery.
Cf. the notes of Adam, Jowett, Campbell, and Apelt. See
Introd. p. xxxi for my interpretation of the passage.

[c] Some modern and ancient critics prefer ἀν' ἴσα. It is a

don't omit the least bit," he said. " I fancy," I said, " that I shall have to pass over much, but nevertheless so far as it is at present practicable I shall not willingly leave anything out." " Do not," he said. " Conceive then," said I, " as we were saying, that there are these two entities, and that one of them is sovereign over the intelligible order and region and the other over the world of the eye-ball, not to say the sky-ball,[a] but let that pass. You surely apprehend the two types, the visible and the intelligible." " I do." " Represent them then, as it were, by a line divided[b] into two unequal[c] sections and cut each section again in the same ratio (the section, that is, of the visible and that of the intelligible order), and then as an expression of the ratio of their comparative clearness and obscurity you will have, as one of the sections of the visible world, images. By images[d] I mean, first, shadows, and then reflections in water and on surfaces of dense, smooth and bright texture, and everything of that kind, if you apprehend." " I do." " As the second section assume that of which this is a likeness or an image, that is, the animals about us and all plants and the whole class of objects made by man." " I so assume it," he said. " Would you be willing to say," said I, " that the division in respect of reality and truth or the opposite is expressed by the proportion:[e] as is the opinable to the knowable so is the likeness to that of which it is a likeness ? " " I certainly would." " Consider then again the way in which we are to make the division of the intelligible section." " In what way? "

little more plausible to make the sections unequal. But again there is doubt which shall be longer, the higher as the more honourable or the lower as the more multitudinous. *Cf.* Plut. *Plat. Quest.* 3. [d] *Cf. supra* 402 B, *Soph.* 266 B-C.
  [e] *Cf. supra* on 508 c, p. 103, note *b*.

510 Πῇ; Ἦι τὸ μὲν αὐτοῦ τοῖς τότε τμηθεῖσιν[1] ὡς
εἰκόσι χρωμένη ψυχὴ ζητεῖν ἀναγκάζεται ἐξ ὑποθέσεων, οὐκ ἐπ᾽ ἀρχὴν πορευομένη, ἀλλ᾽ ἐπὶ τελευ-
τήν, τὸ δ᾽ αὖ ἕτερον ἐπ[2] ἀρχὴν ἀνυπόθετον ἐξ
ὑποθέσεως ἰοῦσα καὶ ἄνευ ὧνπερ ἐκεῖνο εἰκόνων
αὐτοῖς εἴδεσι δι᾽ αὐτῶν τὴν μέθοδον ποιουμένη.
Ταῦτ᾽, ἔφη, ἃ λέγεις, οὐχ ἱκανῶς ἔμαθον. Ἀλλ᾽
C αὖθις, ἦν δ᾽ ἐγώ· ῥᾷον γὰρ τούτων προειρημένων
μαθήσει. οἶμαι γάρ σε εἰδέναι, ὅτι οἱ περὶ τὰς
γεωμετρίας τε καὶ λογισμοὺς καὶ τὰ τοιαῦτα
πραγματευόμενοι, ὑποθέμενοι τό τε περιττὸν καὶ
τὸ ἄρτιον καὶ τὰ σχήματα καὶ γωνιῶν τριττὰ εἴδη
καὶ ἄλλα τούτων ἀδελφὰ καθ᾽ ἑκάστην μέθοδον,
ταῦτα μὲν ὡς εἰδότες, ποιησάμενοι ὑποθέσεις αὐτά,
οὐδένα λόγον οὔτε αὑτοῖς οὔτε ἄλλοις ἔτι ἀξιοῦσι
περὶ αὐτῶν διδόναι ὡς παντὶ φανερῶν, ἐκ τούτων
D δ᾽ ἀρχόμενοι τὰ λοιπὰ ἤδη διεξιόντες τελευτῶσιν
ὁμολογουμένως ἐπὶ τοῦτο, οὗ ἂν ἐπὶ σκέψιν ὁρμή-
σωσιν. Πάνυ μὲν οὖν, ἔφη, τοῦτό γε οἶδα. Οὐκ-

---

[1] τμηθεῖσιν DM, μιμηθεῖσιν A Proclus, τιμηθεῖσιν F.
[2] [τὸ] ἐπ᾽ Ast.

---

[a] Cf. my Idea of Good in Plato's Republic, pp. 230-234, for
the ἀνυπόθετον. Ultimately, the ἀνυπόθετον is the Idea of
Good so far as we assume that idea to be attainable either
in ethics or in physics. But it is the Idea of Good, not as a
transcendental ontological mystery, but in the ethical sense
already explained. The ideal dialectician is the man who
can, if challenged, run his reasons for any given proposition
back, not to some assumed axioma medium, but to its
relation to ultimate Good. To call the ἀνυπόθετον the Unconditioned or the Absolute introduces metaphysical associations
foreign to the passage. Cf. also Introd. pp. xxxiii-xxxiv.

[b] The practical meaning of this is independent of the
disputed metaphysics. Cf. Introd. pp. xvi-xviii.

" By the distinction that there is one section of it which the soul is compelled to investigate by treating as images the things imitated in the former division, and by means of assumptions from which it proceeds not up to a first principle but down to a conclusion, while there is another section in which it advances from its assumption to a beginning or principle that transcends assumption,[a] and in which it makes no use of the images employed by the other section, relying on ideas [b] only and progressing systematically through ideas." " I don't fully understand [c] what you mean by this," he said. " Well, I will try again," said I, " for you will better understand after this preamble. For I think you are aware that students of geometry and reckoning and such subjects first postulate the odd and the even and the various figures and three kinds of angles and other things akin to these in each branch of science, regard them as known, and, treating them as absolute assumptions, do not deign to render any further account of them [d] to themselves or others, taking it for granted that they are obvious to everybody. They take their start from these, and pursuing the inquiry from this point on consistently, conclude with that for the investigation of which they set out." " Certainly," he said, " I know that."

[c] Cf. Vol. I. p. 79, note c on 347 A and p. 47, note f on 338 D ; What Plato Said, p. 503 on Gorg. 463 D.

[d] Aristot. Top. 100 b 2-3 οὐ δεῖ γὰρ ἐν ταῖς ἐπιστημονικαῖς ἀρχαῖς ἐπιζητεῖσθαι τὸ διὰ τί, exactly expresses Plato's thought and the truth, though Aristotle may have meant it mainly for the principle of non-contradiction and other first principles of logic. Cf. the mediaeval " contra principium negantem non est disputandum." A teacher of geometry will refuse to discuss the psychology of the idea of space, a teacher of chemistry will not permit the class to ask whether matter is " real."

PLATO

510 οὖν καὶ ὅτι τοῖς ὁρωμένοις εἴδεσι προσχρῶνται καὶ
τοὺς λόγους περὶ αὐτῶν ποιοῦνται, οὐ περὶ τούτων
διανοούμενοι, ἀλλ' ἐκείνων πέρι, οἷς ταῦτα ἔοικε,
τοῦ τετραγώνου αὐτοῦ ἕνεκα τοὺς λόγους ποιούμενοι καὶ διαμέτρου αὐτῆς, ἀλλ' οὐ ταύτης ἣν
E γράφουσι, καὶ τἆλλα οὕτως, αὐτὰ μὲν ταῦτα, ἃ
πλάττουσί τε καὶ γράφουσιν, ὧν καὶ σκιαὶ καὶ ἐν
ὕδασιν εἰκόνες εἰσί, τούτοις μὲν ὡς εἰκόσιν αὖ
χρώμενοι, ζητοῦντες δὲ αὐτὰ ἐκεῖνα ἰδεῖν, ἃ οὐκ
511 ἂν ἄλλως ἴδοι τις ἢ τῇ διανοίᾳ. Ἀληθῆ, ἔφη,
λέγεις.

XXI. Τοῦτο τοίνυν νοητὸν μὲν τὸ εἶδος ἔλεγον,
ὑποθέσεσι δ' ἀναγκαζομένην ψυχὴν χρῆσθαι περὶ
τὴν ζήτησιν αὐτοῦ, οὐκ ἐπ' ἀρχὴν ἰοῦσαν, ὡς οὐ
δυναμένην τῶν ὑποθέσεων ἀνωτέρω ἐκβαίνειν,
εἰκόσι δὲ χρωμένην αὐτοῖς τοῖς ὑπὸ τῶν κάτω
ἀπεικασθεῖσι καὶ ἐκείνοις πρὸς ἐκεῖνα ὡς ἐναργέσι
δεδοξασμένοις τε καὶ τετιμημένοις. Μανθάνω,
B ἔφη, ὅτι τὸ ὑπὸ ταῖς γεωμετρίαις τε καὶ ταῖς
ταύτης ἀδελφαῖς τέχναις λέγεις. Τὸ τοίνυν ἕτερον
μάνθανε τμῆμα τοῦ νοητοῦ λέγοντά με τοῦτο, οὗ
αὐτὸς ὁ λόγος ἅπτεται τῇ τοῦ διαλέγεσθαι δυνάμει,

---

[a] *Cf.* 527 A-B. This explanation of mathematical reasoning
does not differ at all from that of Aristotle and Berkeley and
the moderns who praise Aristotle, except that the metaphysical doctrine of ideas is in the background to be asserted
if challenged.

[b] *i.e.* a bronze sphere would be the original of its imitative
reflection in water, but it is in turn only the imperfect
imitation of the mathematical idea of a sphere.

[c] Stenzel, *Handbuch*, 118 " das er nur mit dem Verstande
(διανοίᾳ) sieht " is mistaken.   διανοίᾳ is used not in its special
sense (" understanding." See p. 116, note c), but generally
for the mind as opposed to the senses.   *Cf.* 511 c.

[d] For the concessive μέν *cf.* 546 E, 529 D, *Soph.* 225 c.

"And do you not also know that they further make use of the visible forms and talk about them, though they are not thinking of them but of those things of which they are a likeness, pursuing their inquiry for the sake of the square as such and the diagonal as such, and not for the sake of the image of it which they draw[a]? And so in all cases. The very things which they mould and draw, which have shadows and images of themselves in water, these things they treat in their turn[b] as only images, but what they really seek is to get sight of those realities which can be seen only by the mind.[c]" "True," he said.

XXI. "This then is the class that I described as intelligible, it is true,[d] but with the reservation first that the soul is compelled to employ assumptions in the investigation of it, not proceeding to a first principle because of its inability to extricate itself from and rise above its assumptions, and second, that it uses as images or likenesses the very objects that are themselves copied and adumbrated by the class below them, and that in comparison with these latter[e] are esteemed as clear and held in honour.[f]" "I understand," said he, "that you are speaking of what falls under geometry and the kindred arts." "Understand then," said I, "that by the other section of the intelligible I mean that which the reason[g] itself lays hold of by the power of dialectics,[h] treating its

---

[e] The loosely appended dative ἐκείνοις is virtually a dative absolute. *Cf. Phaedo* 105 A. Wilamowitz' emendation (*Platon*, ii. p. 384) to πρὸς ἐκεῖνα, καὶ ἐκείνοις rests on a misunderstanding of the passage.

[f] The translation of this sentence is correct. But *cf.* Adam *ad loc.*

[g] λόγος here suggests both the objective personified argument and the subjective faculty.

[h] *Cf.* 533 A. *Phileb.* 57 E.

113

511 τὰς ὑποθέσεις ποιούμενος οὐκ ἀρχάς, ἀλλὰ τῷ
ὄντι ὑποθέσεις, οἷον ἐπιβάσεις τε καὶ ὁρμάς, ἵνα
μέχρι τοῦ ἀνυποθέτου ἐπὶ τὴν τοῦ παντὸς ἀρχὴν
ἰών, ἁψάμενος αὐτῆς, πάλιν αὖ ἐχόμενος τῶν
ἐκείνης ἐχομένων, οὕτως ἐπὶ τελευτὴν καταβαίνῃ,
C αἰσθητῷ παντάπασιν οὐδενὶ προσχρώμενος, ἀλλ᾽
εἴδεσιν αὐτοῖς δι᾽ αὐτῶν εἰς αὐτά, καὶ τελευτᾷ εἰς
εἴδη. Μανθάνω, ἔφη, ἱκανῶς μὲν οὔ—δοκεῖς γάρ
μοι συχνὸν ἔργον λέγειν—ὅτι μέντοι βούλει δι-
ορίζειν σαφέστερον εἶναι τὸ ὑπὸ τῆς τοῦ διαλέγεσθαι
ἐπιστήμης τοῦ ὄντος τε καὶ νοητοῦ θεωρούμενον
ἢ τὸ ὑπὸ τῶν τεχνῶν καλουμένων, αἷς αἱ ὑποθέσεις ἀρχαὶ καὶ διανοίᾳ μὲν ἀναγκάζονται ἀλλὰ μὴ
D αἰσθήσεσιν αὐτὰ θεᾶσθαι οἱ θεώμενοι, διὰ δὲ τὸ
μὴ ἐπ᾽ ἀρχὴν ἀνελθόντες σκοπεῖν, ἀλλ᾽ ἐξ ὑποθέσεων, νοῦν οὐκ ἴσχειν περὶ αὐτὰ δοκοῦσί σοι,

---

[a] τῷ ὄντι emphasizes the etymological meaning of the word.
Similarly ὡς ἀληθῶς in 551 E, *Phaedo* 80 D, *Phileb.* 64 E. For
hypotheses *cf.* Burnet, *Greek Philosophy*, p. 229, Thompson
on *Meno* 86 E. But the thing to note is that the word according to the context may emphasize the arbitrariness of an
assumption or the fact that it is the starting-point—ἀρχή
—of the inquiry.

[b] *Cf. Symp.* 211 c ὥσπερ ἐπαναβάσμοις, "like steps of a
stair."

[c] παντὸς ἀρχήν taken literally lends support to the view
that Plato is thinking of an absolute first principle. But in
spite of the metaphysical suggestions for practical purposes
the παντὸς ἀρχή may be the virtual equivalent of the ἱκανόν
of the *Phaedo*. It is the ἀρχή on which all in the particular
case depends and is reached by dialectical agreement, not by
arbitrary assumption. *Cf.* on 510 B, p. 110, note *a*.

assumptions not as absolute beginnings but literally as hypotheses,[a] underpinnings, footings,[b] and spring-boards so to speak, to enable it to rise to that which requires no assumption and is the starting-point of all,[c] and after attaining to that again taking hold of the first dependencies from it, so to proceed down-ward to the conclusion, making no use whatever of any object of sense [d] but only of pure ideas moving on through ideas to ideas and ending with ideas.[e] " " I understand," he said ; " not fully, for it is no slight task that you appear to have in mind, but I do understand that you mean to distinguish the aspect of reality and the intelligible, which is contemplated by the power of dialectic, as something truer and more exact than the object of the so-called arts and sciences whose assumptions are arbitrary starting-points. And though it is true that those who con-template them are compelled to use their understand-ing [f] and not their senses, yet because they do not go back to the beginning in the study of them but start from assumptions you do not think they possess true

[d] This is one of the passages that are misused to attribute to Plato disdain for experience and the perceptions of the senses. *Cf.* on 530 B, p. 187, note *c.* The dialectician is able to reason purely in concepts and words without recurring to images. Plato is not here considering how much or little of his knowledge is ultimately derived from experience.

[e] The description undoubtedly applies to a metaphysical philosophy that deduces all things from a transcendent first principle. I have never denied that. The point of my interpretation is that it also describes the method which distinguishes the dialectician as such from the man of science, and that this distinction is for practical and educational purposes the chief result of the discussion, as Plato virtually says in the next few lines. *Cf. What Plato Said,* pp. 233-234.

[f] διανοίᾳ here as in 511 A is general and not technical.

511 καίτοι νοητῶν ὄντων μετὰ ἀρχῆς. διάνοιαν δὲ
καλεῖν μοι δοκεῖς τὴν τῶν γεωμετρικῶν τε καὶ
τὴν τῶν τοιούτων ἕξιν ἀλλ' οὐ νοῦν, ὡς μεταξύ τι
δόξης τε καὶ νοῦ τὴν διάνοιαν οὖσαν. Ἱκανώτατα,
ἦν δ' ἐγώ, ἀπεδέξω. καί μοι ἐπὶ τοῖς τέτταρσι
τμήμασι τέτταρα ταῦτα παθήματα ἐν τῇ ψυχῇ
γιγνόμενα λαβέ, νόησιν μὲν ἐπὶ τῷ ἀνωτάτω,
Ε διάνοιαν δὲ ἐπὶ τῷ δευτέρῳ, τῷ τρίτῳ δὲ πίστιν
ἀπόδος καὶ τῷ τελευταίῳ εἰκασίαν, καὶ τάξον
αὐτὰ ἀνὰ λόγον, ὥσπερ ἐφ' οἷς ἔστιν ἀληθείας
μετέχειν, οὕτω ταῦτα σαφηνείας ἡγησάμενος μετέχειν. Μανθάνω, ἔφη, καὶ ξυγχωρῶ καὶ τάττω ὡς
λέγεις.

ᵃ νοῦν οὐκ ἴσχειν is perhaps intentionally ambiguous.
Colloquially the phrase means "have no sense." For its
higher meaning cf. Meno 99 c, Laws 962 A.

ᵇ Unnecessary difficulties have been raised about καίτοι
and μετά here. Wilamowitz, Platon, ii. p. 345 mistakenly
resorts to emendation. The meaning is plain. Mathematical
ideas are ideas or concepts like other ideas; but the mathematician does not deal with them quite as the dialectician
deals with ideas and therefore does not possess νοῦς or reason
in the highest sense.

ᶜ Here the word διάνοια is given a technical meaning as a

intelligence ^{a} about them although ^{b} the things themselves are intelligibles when apprehended in conjunction with a first principle. And I think you call
the mental habit of geometers and their like mind or
understanding ^{c} and not reason because you regard
understanding as something intermediate between
opinion and reason." " Your interpretation is quite
sufficient," I said; " and now, answering to ^{d} these
four sections, assume these four affections occurring
in the soul : intellection or reason for the highest,
understanding for the second ; assign belief ^{e} to the
third, and to the last picture-thinking or conjecture, ^{f}
and arrange them in a proportion, ^{g} considering that
they participate in clearness and precision in the same
degree as their objects partake of truth and reality."
" I understand," he said; " I concur and arrange them
as you bid."

faculty inferior to νοῦς, but, as Plato says, the terminology
does not matter. The question has been much and often
idly discussed.

^{d} For ἐπί cf. Polit. 280 A, Gorg. 463 B.

^{e} πίστις is of course not " faith " in Plato, but Neoplatonists, Christians, and commentators have confused the two
ideas hopelessly.

^{f} εἰκασία undoubtedly had this connotation for Plato.

^{g} Cf. on 508 c, p. 103, note b.

Z

514 Ι. Μετὰ ταῦτα δή, εἶπον, ἀπείκασον τοιούτῳ
πάθει τὴν ἡμετέραν φύσιν παιδείας τε πέρι καὶ
ἀπαιδευσίας. ἰδὲ γὰρ ἀνθρώπους οἷον ἐν κατα-
γείῳ οἰκήσει σπηλαιώδει, ἀναπεπταμένην πρὸς τὸ
φῶς τὴν εἴσοδον ἐχούσῃ μακρὰν παρ᾽ ἅπαν τὸ
σπήλαιον, ἐν ταύτῃ ἐκ παίδων ὄντας ἐν δεσμοῖς

ᵃ The image of the cave illustrates by another proportion
the contrast between the world of sense-perception and
the world of thought. Instead of going above the plane of
ordinary experience for the other two members of the proportion, Plato here goes below and invents a fire and shadows
cast from it on the walls of a cave to correspond to the sun
and the "real" objects of sense. In such a proportion our
"real" world becomes the symbol of Plato's ideal world.

Modern fancy may read what meanings it pleases into the
Platonic antithesis of the "real" and the "ideal." It has
even been treated as an anticipation of the fourth dimension.
But Plato never leaves an attentive and critical reader in
doubt as to his own intended meaning. There may be at
the most a little uncertainty as to which precise traits are
intended to carry the symbolism and which are merely
indispensable parts of the picture.

The source and first suggestion of Plato's imagery is an
interesting speculation, but it is of no significance for the
interpretation of the thought. Cf. John Henry Wright,
"The Origin of Plato's Cave" in Harvard Studies in Class.
Phil. xvii. (1906) pp. 130-142. Burnet, Early Greek Philosophy, pp. 89-90, thinks the allegory Orphic. Cf. also
Wright, loc. cit. pp. 134-135. Empedocles likens our world

BOOK VII

I. " Next," said I, " compare our nature in respect of education and its lack to such an experience as this. Picture men dwelling in a sort of subterranean cavern ^{a} with a long entrance open ^{b} to the light on its entire width. Conceive them as having their legs and necks fettered ^{c} from childhood, so that they

to a cave, Diels i.³ 269. *Cf.* Wright, *loc. cit.* Wright refers it to the Cave of Vari in Attica, pp. 140-142. Others have supposed that Plato had in mind rather the puppet and marionette shows to which he refers. *Cf.* Diès in *Bulletin Budé*, No. 14 (1927) pp. 8 f.

The suggestiveness of the image has been endless. The most eloquent and frequently quoted passage of Aristotle's early writings is derived from it, Cic. *De nat. deor.* ii. 37. It is the source of Bacon's " idols of the den." Sir Thomas Browne writes in *Urn Burial* : " We yet discourse in Plato's den and are but embryo philosophers." Huxley's allegory of " Jack and the Beanstalk " in *Evolution and Ethics*, pp. 47 ff. is a variation on it. Berkeley recurs to it, *Siris*, § 263. The Freudians would have still more fantastic interpretations. *Cf.* Jung, *Analytic Psych.* p. 232. Eddington perhaps glances at it when he attributes to the new physics the frank realization that physical science is concerned with a world of shadows. *Cf.* also *Complete Poems of Henry More* (ed. Grossart), p. 44 :

> Like men new made contriv'd into a cave
> That ne'er saw light, but in that shadowy pit
> Some uncouth might them hoodwink hither drave, etc.

^{b} *Cf. Phaedo* 111 c ἀναπεπταμένους.
^{c} *Cf. Phaedo* 67 D.

514 καὶ τὰ σκέλη καὶ τοὺς αὐχένας, ὥστε μένειν τε
B αὐτοῦ¹ εἴς τε τὸ πρόσθεν μόνον ὁρᾶν, κύκλῳ δὲ
τὰς κεφαλὰς ὑπὸ τοῦ δεσμοῦ ἀδυνάτους περιάγειν,
φῶς δὲ αὐτοῖς πυρὸς ἄνωθεν καὶ πόρρωθεν καό-
μενον ὄπισθεν αὐτῶν, μεταξὺ δὲ τοῦ πυρὸς καὶ
τῶν δεσμωτῶν ἐπάνω ὁδόν, παρ' ἣν ἰδὲ τειχίον
παρῳκοδομημένον, ὥσπερ τοῖς θαυματοποιοῖς πρὸ
τῶν ἀνθρώπων πρόκειται τὰ παραφράγματα, ὑπὲρ
ὧν τὰ θαύματα δεικνύασιν. Ὁρῶ, ἔφη. Ὅρα
τοίνυν παρὰ τοῦτο τὸ τειχίον φέροντας ἀνθρώπους
σκεύη τε παντοδαπὰ ὑπερέχοντα τοῦ τειχίου καὶ
515 ἀνδριάντας καὶ ἄλλα ζῷα λίθινά τε καὶ ξύλινα καὶ
παντοῖα εἰργασμένα, οἷον εἰκὸς τοὺς μὲν φθεγ-
γομένους, τοὺς δὲ σιγῶντας τῶν παραφερόντων.
Ἄτοπον, ἔφη, λέγεις εἰκόνα καὶ δεσμώτας ἀτό-
πους. Ὁμοίους ἡμῖν, ἦν δ' ἐγώ· τοὺς γὰρ τοιούτους πρῶτον μὲν ἑαυτῶν τε καὶ ἀλλήλων οἴει ἄν τι
ἑωρακέναι ἄλλο πλὴν τὰς σκιὰς τὰς ὑπὸ τοῦ πυρὸς
εἰς τὸ καταντικρὺ αὐτῶν τοῦ σπηλαίου προσ-
πιπτούσας; Πῶς γάρ, ἔφη, εἰ ἀκινήτους γε τὰς
B κεφαλὰς ἔχειν ἠναγκασμένοι εἶεν διὰ βίου; Τί δὲ
τῶν παραφερομένων; οὐ ταὐτὸν τοῦτο. Τί μήν;
Εἰ οὖν διαλέγεσθαι οἷοί τ' εἶεν πρὸς ἀλλήλους, οὐ
ταῦτα² ἡγεῖ ἂν τὰ παριόντα³ αὐτοὺς νομίζειν ὀνομά-

---

¹ αὐτοῦ Hischig : αὐτούς.
² οὐ ταῦτα D, οὐ ταὐτὰ AFM, οὐκ αὐτὰ ci. Vermehren.
³ παριόντα scr. recc., παρόντα AFDM, ὄντα Iamblichus.

remain in the same spot, able to look forward only,
and prevented by the fetters from turning their heads.
Picture further the light from a fire burning higher
up and at a distance behind them, and between the
fire and the prisoners and above them a road along
which a low wall has been built, as the exhibitors of
puppet-shows [a] have partitions before the men themselves, above which they show the puppets." "All
that I see," he said. "See also, then, men carrying [b]
past the wall implements of all kinds that rise above
the wall, and human images and shapes of animals
as well, wrought in stone and wood and every material,
some of these bearers presumably speaking and
others silent." "A strange image you speak of," he
said, "and strange prisoners." "Like to us," I said ;
"for, to begin with, tell me do you think that these
men would have seen anything of themselves or of
one another except the shadows cast from the fire
on the wall of the cave that fronted them ?" "How
could they," he said, "if they were compelled to
hold their heads unmoved through life ?" "And
again, would not the same be true of the objects
carried past them ?" "Surely." "If then they
were able to talk to one another, do you not think
that they would suppose that in naming the things

[a] H. Rackham, *Class. Rev.* xxix. pp. 77-78, suggests that
the τοῖς θαυματοποιοῖς should be translated "at the marion-
ettes" and be classed with καινοῖς τραγῳδοῖς (Pseph. *ap.*
Dem. xviii. 116). For the dative he refers to Kuehner-Gerth,
II. i. p. 445.

[b] The men are merely a part of the necessary machinery
of the image. Their shadows are not cast on the wall. The
artificial objects correspond to the things of sense and opinion
in the divided line, and the shadows to the world of reflections, εἰκόνες.

PLATO

515 ζειν ἅπερ ὁρῶεν; Ἀνάγκη. Τί δ'; εἰ καὶ ἠχὼ
τὸ δεσμωτήριον ἐκ τοῦ καταντικρὺ ἔχοι, ὁπότε τις
τῶν παριόντων φθέγξαιτο, οἴει ἂν ἄλλο τι αὐτοὺς
ἡγεῖσθαι τὸ φθεγγόμενον ἢ τὴν παριοῦσαν σκιάν;
Μὰ Δί' οὐκ ἔγωγ', ἔφη. Παντάπασι δή, ἦν δ' ἐγώ,
C οἱ τοιοῦτοι οὐκ ἂν ἄλλο τι νομίζοιεν τὸ ἀληθὲς ἢ
τὰς τῶν σκευαστῶν σκιάς. Πολλὴ ἀνάγκη, ἔφη.
Σκόπει δή, ἦν δ' ἐγώ, αὐτῶν λύσιν τε καὶ ἴασιν
τῶν δεσμῶν καὶ τῆς ἀφροσύνης, οἷα τις ἂν εἴη, εἰ
φύσει τοιάδε ξυμβαίνοι αὐτοῖς· ὁπότε τις λυθείη
καὶ ἀναγκάζοιτο ἐξαίφνης ἀνίστασθαί τε καὶ περιάγειν τὸν αὐχένα καὶ βαδίζειν καὶ πρὸς τὸ φῶς
ἀναβλέπειν, πάντα δὲ ταῦτα ποιῶν ἀλγοῖ τε καὶ
διὰ τὰς μαρμαρυγὰς ἀδυνατοῖ καθορᾶν ἐκεῖνα, ὧν
D τότε τὰς σκιὰς ἑώρα, τί ἂν οἴει αὐτὸν εἰπεῖν, εἴ
τις αὐτῷ λέγοι, ὅτι τότε μὲν ἑώρα φλυαρίας, νῦν
δὲ μᾶλλόν τι ἐγγυτέρω τοῦ ὄντος καὶ πρὸς μᾶλλον

ᵃ Cf. *Parmen.* 130 D, *Tim.* 51 B, 52 A, and my *De
Platonis Idearum doctrina*, pp. 24-25; also E. Hoffmann
in *Wochenschrift f. klass. Phil.* xxxvi. (1919) pp. 196-197.
As we use the word tree of the trees we see, though the
reality (αὐτὸ δ ἔστι) is the idea of a tree, so they would speak
of the shadows as the world, though the real reference unknown to them would be to the objects that cause the
shadows, and back of the objects to the things of the " real "
world of which they are copies. The general meaning,
which is quite certain, is that they would suppose the
shadows to be the realities. The text and the precise turn
of expression are doubtful. See crit. note. παριόντα is
intentionally ambiguous in its application to the shadows
or to the objects which cast them. They suppose that the
names refer to the passing shadows, but (as we know) they

that they saw[a] they were naming the passing objects?"
"Necessarily." "And if their prison had an echo[b]
from the wall opposite them, when one of the passers-
by uttered a sound, do you think that they would
suppose anything else than the passing shadow to
be the speaker?" "By Zeus, I do not," said he.
"Then in every way such prisoners would deem
reality to be nothing else than the shadows of the
artificial objects." "Quite inevitably," he said.
"Consider, then, what would be the manner of the
release[c] and healing from these bonds and this folly
if in the course of nature[d] something of this sort
should happen to them : When one was freed from
his fetters and compelled to stand up suddenly and
turn his head around and walk and to lift up his eyes
to the light, and in doing all this felt pain and, because
of the dazzle and glitter of the light, was unable to
discern the objects whose shadows he formerly saw,
what do you suppose would be his answer if someone
told him that what he had seen before was all a cheat
and an illusion, but that now, being nearer to reality

really apply to the objects. Ideas and particulars are hom-
onymous. Assuming a slight illogicality we can get somewhat the same meaning from the text ταὐτά. "Do you
not think that they would identify the passing objects
(which strictly speaking they do not know) with what they
saw?"

Cf. also P. Corssen, *Philologische Wochenschrift*, 1913,
p. 286. He prefers οὐκ αὐτά and renders: "Sie würden in
dem, was sie sähen, das Vorübergehende selbst zu benennen
glauben."

[b] The echo and the voices (515 A) merely complete the
picture.

[c] *Cf. Phaedo* 67 D λύειν, and 82 D λύσει τε καὶ καθαρμῷ.
λύσις became technical in Neoplatonism.

[d] Lit. "by nature." φύσις in Plato often suggests reality
and truth.

515 ὄντα τετραμμένος ὀρθότερα βλέποι, καὶ δὴ καὶ
ἕκαστον τῶν παριόντων δεικνὺς αὐτῷ ἀναγκάζοι
ἐρωτῶν ἀποκρίνεσθαι ὅ τι ἔστιν; οὐκ οἴει αὐτὸν
ἀπορεῖν τε ἂν καὶ ἡγεῖσθαι τὰ τότε ὁρώμενα
ἀληθέστερα ἢ τὰ νῦν δεικνύμενα; Πολύ γ᾽, ἔφη.

II. Οὐκοῦν κἂν εἰ πρὸς αὐτὸ τὸ φῶς ἀναγκάζοι
E αὐτὸν βλέπειν, ἀλγεῖν τε ἂν τὰ ὄμματα καὶ
φεύγειν ἀποστρεφόμενον πρὸς ἐκεῖνα ἃ δύναται
καθορᾶν, καὶ νομίζειν ταῦτα τῷ ὄντι σαφέστερα
τῶν δεικνυμένων; Οὕτως, ἔφη. Εἰ δέ, ἦν δ᾽
ἐγώ, ἐντεῦθεν ἕλκοι τις αὐτὸν βίᾳ διὰ τραχείας
τῆς ἀναβάσεως καὶ ἀνάντους καὶ μὴ ἀνείη πρὶν
ἐξελκύσειεν εἰς τὸ τοῦ ἡλίου φῶς, ἆρα οὐχὶ
ὀδυνᾶσθαί τε ἂν καὶ ἀγανακτεῖν ἑλκόμενον, καὶ
516 ἐπειδὴ πρὸς τὸ φῶς ἔλθοι, αὐγῆς ἂν ἔχοντα τὰ
ὄμματα μεστὰ ὁρᾶν οὐδ᾽ ἂν ἓν δύνασθαι τῶν νῦν
λεγομένων ἀληθῶν; Οὐ γὰρ ἄν, ἔφη, ἐξαίφνης γε.
Συνηθείας δή, οἶμαι, δέοιτ᾽ ἄν, εἰ μέλλοι τὰ ἄνω
ὄψεσθαι· καὶ πρῶτον μὲν τὰς σκιὰς ἂν ῥᾷστα καθ-
ορῷ, καὶ μετὰ τοῦτο ἐν τοῖς ὕδασι τά τε τῶν
ἀνθρώπων καὶ τὰ τῶν ἄλλων εἴδωλα, ὕστερον δὲ
αὐτά· ἐκ δὲ τούτων τὰ ἐν τῷ οὐρανῷ καὶ αὐτὸν τὸν
οὐρανὸν νύκτωρ ἂν ῥᾷον θεάσαιτο, προσβλέπων τὸ
B τῶν ἄστρων τε καὶ σελήνης φῶς, ἢ μεθ᾽ ἡμέραν

---

[a] The entire passage is an obvious allegory of the painful
experience of one whose false conceit of knowledge is tested
by the Socratic *elenchus*. *Cf. Soph.* 230 B-D, and for ἀπορεῖν
Meno 80 A, 84 B-C, *Theaet.* 149 A, *Apol.* 23 D. *Cf.* also
What Plato Said, p. 513 on *Meno* 80 A, Eurip. *Hippol.*
247 τὸ γὰρ ὀρθοῦσθαι γνώμαν ὀδυνᾷ, "it is painful to have
one's opinions set right," and *infra* 517 A, *supra* 494 D.

[b] *Cf. Theaet.* 175 B, Boethius, *Cons.* iii. 12 "quicunque
in superum diem mentem ducere quaeritis"; *infra* 529 A,
521 C, and the Neoplatonists' use of ἀνάγειν and their

and turned toward more real things, he saw more truly? And if also one should point out to him each of the passing objects and constrain him by questions to say what it is, do you not think that he would be at a loss [a] and that he would regard what he formerly saw as more real than the things now pointed out to him?" "Far more real," he said.

II. "And if he were compelled to look at the light itself, would not that pain his eyes, and would he not turn away and flee to those things which he is able to discern and regard them as in very deed more clear and exact than the objects pointed out?" "It is so," he said. "And if," said I, "someone should drag him thence by force up the ascent [b] which is rough and steep, and not let him go before he had drawn him out into the light of the sun, do you not think that he would find it painful to be so haled along, and would chafe at it, and when he came out into the light, that his eyes would be filled with its beams so that he would not be able to see [c] even one of the things that we call real?" "Why, no, not immediately," he said. "Then there would be need of habituation, I take it, to enable him to see the things higher up. And at first he would most easily discern the shadows and, after that, the likenesses or reflections in water [d] of men and other things, and later, the things themselves, and from these he would go on to contemplate the appearances in the heavens and heaven itself, more easily by night, looking at the light of the stars and the moon, than by day

"anagogical" virtue and interpretation. *Cf.* Leibniz, ed. Gerhardt, vii. 270.

[c] *Cf. Laws* 897 D, *Phaedo* 99 D.

[d] *Cf. Phaedo* 99 D. Stallbaum says this was imitated by Themistius, *Orat.* iv. p. 51 B.

516 τὸν ἥλιόν τε καὶ τὸ τοῦ ἡλίου. Πῶς δ' οὔ;
Τελευταῖον δή, οἶμαι, τὸν ἥλιον, οὐκ ἐν ὕδασιν
οὐδ' ἐν ἀλλοτρίᾳ ἕδρᾳ φαντάσματα αὐτοῦ, ἀλλ'
αὐτὸν καθ' αὑτὸν ἐν τῇ αὑτοῦ χώρᾳ δύναιτ' ἂν
κατιδεῖν καὶ θεάσασθαι οἷός ἐστιν. Ἀναγκαῖον,
ἔφη. Καὶ μετὰ ταῦτ' ἂν ἤδη συλλογίζοιτο περὶ
αὐτοῦ ὅτι οὗτος ὁ τάς τε ὥρας παρέχων καὶ
ἐνιαυτοὺς καὶ πάντα ἐπιτροπεύων τὰ ἐν τῷ
C ὁρωμένῳ τόπῳ, καὶ ἐκείνων, ὧν σφεῖς ἑώρων,
τρόπον τινὰ πάντων αἴτιος. Δῆλον, ἔφη, ὅτι ἐπὶ
ταῦτα ἂν μετ' ἐκεῖνα ἔλθοι. Τί οὖν; ἀναμιμνη-
σκόμενον αὐτὸν τῆς πρώτης οἰκήσεως καὶ τῆς ἐκεῖ
σοφίας καὶ τῶν τότε ξυνδεσμωτῶν οὐκ ἂν οἴει αὐτὸν
μὲν εὐδαιμονίζειν τῆς μεταβολῆς, τοὺς δὲ ἐλεεῖν;
Καὶ μάλα. Τιμαὶ δὲ καὶ ἔπαινοι εἴ τινες αὐτοῖς
ἦσαν τότε παρ' ἀλλήλων καὶ γέρα τῷ ὀξύτατα καθ-
ορῶντι τὰ παριόντα, καὶ μνημονεύοντι μάλιστα
D ὅσα τε πρότερα αὐτῶν καὶ ὕστερα εἰώθει καὶ ἅμα
πορεύεσθαι, καὶ ἐκ τούτων δὴ δυνατώτατα ἀπο-
μαντευομένῳ τὸ μέλλον ἥξειν, δοκεῖς ἂν αὐτὸν
ἐπιθυμητικῶς αὐτῶν ἔχειν καὶ ζηλοῦν τοὺς παρ'
ἐκείνοις τιμωμένους τε καὶ ἐνδυναστεύοντας, ἢ τὸ
τοῦ Ὁμήρου ἂν πεπονθέναι καὶ σφόδρα βούλεσθαι

---

[a] It is probably a mistake to look for a definite symbolism
in all the details of this description. There are more stages
of progress than the proportion of four things calls for. All
that Plato's thought requires is the general contrast between
an unreal and a real world, and the goal of the rise from one
to the other in the contemplation of the sun, or the idea of
good. Cf. 517 B-c.   [b] i.e. a foreign medium.
[c] Cf. 508 B, and for the idea of good as the cause of all
things cf. on 509 B, and Introd. pp. xxxv-xxxvi.
    P. Corssen, Philol. Wochenschrift, 1913, pp. 287-288, un-
necessarily proposes to emend ὧν σφεῖς ἑώρων to ὧν σκιὰς ἑ. or

the sun and the sun's light.[a] " " Of course." " And
so, finally, I suppose, he would be able to look upon
the sun itself and see its true nature, not by reflections
in water or phantasms of it in an alien setting,[b] but in
and by itself in its own place." " Necessarily," he
said. " And at this point he would infer and conclude that this it is that provides the seasons and the
courses of the year and presides over all things in the
visible region, and is in some sort the cause [c] of all these
things that they had seen." " Obviously," he said,
" that would be the next step." " Well then, if he
recalled to mind his first habitation and what passed
for wisdom there, and his fellow-bondsmen, do you
not think that he would count himself happy in the
change and pity them [d] ? " " He would indeed." " And
if there had been honours and commendations among
them which they bestowed on one another and prizes
for the man who is quickest to make out the shadows as
they pass and best able to remember their customary
precedences, sequences and co-existences,[e] and so most
successful in guessing at what was to come, do you
think he would be very keen about such rewards, and
that he would envy and emulate those who were
honoured by these prisoners and lorded it among
them, or that he would feel with Homer [f] and greatly

ὧν σφεῖς σκιὰς ἑ., " ne sol umbrarum, quas videbant, auctor
fuisse dicatur, cum potius earum rerum, quarum umbras videbant, fuerit auctor."   [d] Cf. on 486 A, p. 10, note a.
  [e] Another of Plato's anticipations of modern thought. This
is precisely the Humian, Comtian, positivist, pragmatist view
of causation.   Cf. Gorg. 501 A τριβῇ καὶ ἐμπειρίᾳ μνήμην
μόνον σωζομένη τοῦ εἰωθότος γίγνεσθαι, " relying on routine and
habitude for merely preserving a memory of what is wont to
result."   (Loeb tr.)
  [f] Odyss. xi. 489. The quotation is almost as apt as that
at the beginning of the Crito.

516 ἐπάρουρον ἐόντα θητευέμεν ἄλλῳ ἀνδρὶ παρ'
ἀκλήρῳ καὶ ὁτιοῦν ἂν πεπονθέναι μᾶλλον ἢ 'κεῖνά
Ε τε δοξάζειν καὶ ἐκείνως ζῆν; Οὕτως, ἔφη, ἔγωγε
οἶμαι, πᾶν μᾶλλον πεπονθέναι ἂν δέξασθαι ἢ ζῆν
ἐκείνως. Καὶ τόδε δὴ ἐννόησον, ἦν δ' ἐγώ. εἰ
πάλιν ὁ τοιοῦτος καταβὰς εἰς τὸν αὐτὸν θᾶκον
καθίζοιτο, ἆρ' οὐ σκότους ἂν πλέως[1] σχοίη τοὺς
ὀφθαλμούς, ἐξαίφνης ἥκων ἐκ τοῦ ἡλίου; Καὶ
μάλα γ', ἔφη. Τὰς δὲ δὴ σκιὰς ἐκείνας πάλιν εἰ
δέοι αὐτὸν γνωματεύοντα διαμιλλᾶσθαι τοῖς ἀεὶ
517 δεσμώταις ἐκείνοις, ἐν ᾧ ἀμβλυώττει, πρὶν κατα-
στῆναι τὰ ὄμματα, οὗτος δ' ὁ χρόνος μὴ πάνυ ὀλίγος
εἴη τῆς συνηθείας, ἆρ' οὐ γέλωτ' ἂν παράσχοι, καὶ
λέγοιτο ἂν περὶ αὐτοῦ, ὡς ἀναβὰς ἄνω διεφθαρμένος
ἥκει τὰ ὄμματα, καὶ ὅτι οὐκ ἄξιον οὐδὲ πειρᾶσθαι
ἄνω ἰέναι· καὶ τὸν ἐπιχειροῦντα λύειν τε καὶ ἀνάγειν, εἴ πως ἐν ταῖς χερσὶ δύναιντο λαβεῖν καὶ ἀποκτείνειν, ἀποκτεινύναι ἄν[2]; Σφόδρα γ', ἔφη.

III. Ταύτην τοίνυν, ἦν δ' ἐγώ, τὴν εἰκόνα, ὦ
φίλε Γλαύκων, προσαπτέον ἅπασαν τοῖς ἔμπροσθεν
Β λεγομένοις, τὴν μὲν δι' ὄψεως φαινομένην ἕδραν τῇ
τοῦ δεσμωτηρίου οἰκήσει ἀφομοιοῦντα, τὸ δὲ τοῦ
πυρὸς ἐν αὐτῇ φῶς τῇ τοῦ ἡλίου δυνάμει· τὴν δὲ
ἄνω ἀνάβασιν καὶ θέαν τῶν ἄνω τὴν εἰς τὸν νοητὸν

---

[1] ἂν πλέως Stallb., ἀνάπλεως mss., ἂν ἀνάπλεως Baiter. See
Adam ad loc. on the text.

[2] ἀποκτείνειν, ἀποκτεινύναι ἄν F: ἀποκτείνειν, ἀποκτιννύναι ἄν
AD Iamblichus: ἀποκτείνειν, ἀποκτιννύναι αὖ M, ἀποκτείνειαν
ἄν ci. Baiter.

---

[a] On the metaphor of darkness and light cf. also Soph. 254 A.
[b] Like the philosopher in the court-room. Cf. Theaet.
172 c, 173 c ff., Gorg. 484 D-E. Cf. also supra on 487 C-D.
515 D, infra 517 D, Soph. 216 D, Laches 196 B, Phaedr. 249 D.

prefer while living on earth to be serf of another, a landless man, and endure anything rather than opine with them and live that life? " "Yes," he said, " I think that he would choose to endure anything rather than such a life." "And consider this also," said I, " if such a one should go down again and take his old place would he not get his eyes full *a* of darkness, thus suddenly coming out of the sunlight? " " He would indeed." " Now if he should be required to contend with these perpetual prisoners in ' evaluating ' these shadows while his vision was still dim and before his eyes were accustomed to the dark—and this time required for habituation would not be very short—would he not provoke laughter,*b* and would it not be said of him that he had returned from his journey aloft with his eyes ruined and that it was not worth while even to attempt the ascent? And if it were possible to lay hands on and to kill the man who tried to release them and lead them up, would they not kill him *c*? " " They certainly would," he said.

III. " This image then, dear Glaucon, we must apply as a whole to all that has been said, likening the region revealed through sight to the habitation of the prison, and the light of the fire in it to the power of the sun. And if you assume that the ascent and the contemplation of the things above is the soul's

---

c An obvious allusion to the fate of Socrates. For other stinging allusions to this *cf. Gorg.* 486 B, 521 C, *Meno* 100 B-C. *Cf.* Hamlet's "Wormwood, wormwood" (III. ii. 191). The text is disputed. See crit. note. A. Drachmann, "Zu Platons Staat," *Hermes*, 1926, p. 110, thinks that an οἴει or something like it must be understood as having preceded, at least in Plato's thought, and that ἀποκτείνειν can be taken as a gloss or variant of ἀποκτεινύναι and the correct reading must be λαβεῖν, καὶ ἀποκτεινύναι ἄν. See also Adam *ad loc.*

517 τόπον τῆς ψυχῆς ἄνοδον τιθεὶς οὐχ ἁμαρτήσει τῆς
γ' ἐμῆς ἐλπίδος, ἐπειδὴ ταύτης ἐπιθυμεῖς ἀκούειν·
θεὸς δέ που οἶδεν, εἰ ἀληθὴς οὖσα τυγχάνει. τὰ
δ' οὖν ἐμοὶ φαινόμενα οὕτω φαίνεται, ἐν τῷ
γνωστῷ τελευταία ἡ τοῦ ἀγαθοῦ ἰδέα καὶ μόγις
C ὁρᾶσθαι, ὀφθεῖσα δὲ συλλογιστέα εἶναι ὡς ἄρα
πᾶσι πάντων αὕτη ὀρθῶν τε καὶ καλῶν αἰτία, ἔν
τε ὁρατῷ φῶς καὶ τὸν τούτου κύριον τεκοῦσα, ἔν
τε νοητῷ αὐτὴ κυρία ἀλήθειαν καὶ νοῦν παρα-
σχομένη, καὶ ὅτι δεῖ ταύτην ἰδεῖν τὸν μέλλοντα
ἐμφρόνως πράξειν ἢ ἰδίᾳ ἢ δημοσίᾳ. Συνοίομαι,
ἔφη, καὶ ἐγώ, ὅν γε δὴ τρόπον δύναμαι. Ἴθι
τοίνυν, ἦν δ' ἐγώ, καὶ τόδε ξυννοήθητι καὶ μὴ
θαυμάσῃς ὅτι οἱ ἐνταῦθα ἐλθόντες οὐκ ἐθέλουσι
τὰ τῶν ἀνθρώπων πράττειν, ἀλλ' ἄνω ἀεὶ ἐπείγον-
D ται αὐτῶν αἱ ψυχαὶ διατρίβειν· εἰκὸς γάρ που οὕτως,
εἴπερ αὖ κατὰ τὴν προειρημένην εἰκόνα τοῦτ' ἔχει.
Εἰκὸς μέντοι, ἔφη. Τί δέ; τόδε οἴει τι θαυμαστόν,
εἰ ἀπὸ θείων, ἦν δ' ἐγώ, θεωριῶν ἐπὶ τὰ ἀνθρώπειά
τις ἐλθὼν κακὰ ἀσχημονεῖ τε καὶ φαίνεται σφόδρα
γελοῖος ἔτι ἀμβλυώττων καὶ πρὶν ἱκανῶς συνήθης

---

[a] Cf. 508 B-C, where Arnou (Le Désir de dieu dans la
philos. de Plotin, p. 48) and Robin (La Théorie plat. de
l'amour, pp. 83-84) make τόπος νοητός refer to le ciel astro-
nomique as opposed to the ὑπερουράνιος τόπος of the Phaedrus
247 A-E, 248 B, 248 D-249 A. The phrase νοητὸς κόσμος, often
attributed to Plato, does not occur in his writings.

[b] Plato was much less prodigal of affirmation about metaphysical ultimates than interpreters who take his myths
literally have supposed. Cf. What Plato Said, p. 515, on
Meno 86 B.

ascension to the intelligible region,[a] you will not miss my surmise, since that is what you desire to hear. But God knows[b] whether it is true. But, at any rate, my dream as it appears to me is that in the region of the known the last thing to be seen and hardly seen is the idea of good, and that when seen it must needs point us to the conclusion that this is indeed the cause for all things of all that is right and beautiful, giving birth[c] in the visible world to light, and the author of light and itself in the intelligible world being the authentic source of truth and reason, and that anyone who is to act wisely[d] in private or public must have caught sight of this." "I concur," he said, "so far as I am able." "Come then," I said, "and join me in this further thought, and do not be surprised that those who have attained to this height are not willing[e] to occupy themselves with the affairs of men, but their souls ever feel the upward urge and the yearning for that sojourn above. For this, I take it, is likely if in this point too the likeness of our image holds." "Yes, it is likely." "And again, do you think it at all strange," said I, "if a man returning from divine contemplations to the petty miseries[f] of men cuts a sorry figure[g] and appears most ridiculous, if, while still blinking through the gloom, and before he has become sufficiently accustomed

---

[c] Cf. 506 E.

[d] This is the main point for the *Republic*. The significance of the idea of good for cosmogony is just glanced at and reserved for the *Timaeus*. Cf. on 508 B, p. 102, note *a* and pp. 505-506. For the practical application cf. *Meno* 81 D-E. See also Introd. pp. xxxv-xxxvi.

[e] Cf. 521 A, 345 E, and Vol. I. on 347 D, p. 81, note *d*.

[f] Cf. 346 E.

[g] Cf. *Theaet.* 174 C ἀσχημοσύνη.

517 γενέσθαι τῷ παρόντι σκότῳ ἀναγκαζόμενος ἐν
δικαστηρίοις ἢ ἄλλοθί που ἀγωνίζεσθαι περὶ τῶν
τοῦ δικαίου σκιῶν ἢ ἀγαλμάτων ὧν αἱ σκιαί, καὶ
E διαμιλλᾶσθαι περὶ τούτου, ὅπῃ ποτὲ ὑπολαμβάνεται
ταῦτα ὑπὸ τῶν αὐτὴν δικαιοσύνην μὴ πώποτε
ἰδόντων; Οὐδ' ὁπωστιοῦν θαυμαστόν, ἔφη. Ἀλλ'
518 εἰ νοῦν γε ἔχοι τις, ἦν δ' ἐγώ, μεμνῇτ' ἄν, ὅτι
διτταὶ καὶ ἀπὸ διττῶν γίγνονται ἐπιταράξεις ὄμμασιν, ἔκ τε φωτὸς εἰς σκότος μεθισταμένων καὶ
ἐκ σκότους εἰς φῶς· ταὐτὰ δὲ ταῦτα νομίσας
γίγνεσθαι καὶ περὶ ψυχήν, ὁπότε ἴδοι θορυβου-
μένην τινὰ καὶ ἀδυνατοῦσάν τι καθορᾶν, οὐκ ἂν
ἀλογίστως γελῷ, ἀλλ' ἐπισκοποῖ ἂν πότερον ἐκ
φανοτέρου βίου ἥκουσα ὑπὸ ἀηθείας ἐσκότωται ἢ
B ἐξ ἀμαθίας πλείονος εἰς φανότερον ἰοῦσα ὑπὸ λαμ-
προτέρου μαρμαρυγῆς ἐμπέπλησται, καὶ οὕτω δὴ
τὴν μὲν εὐδαιμονίσειεν ἂν τοῦ πάθους τε καὶ βίου,
τὴν δὲ ἐλεήσειεν, καὶ εἰ γελᾶν ἐπ' αὐτῇ βούλοιτο,
ἧττον ἂν καταγέλαστος ὁ γέλως αὐτῷ εἴη ἢ ὁ ἐπὶ
τῇ ἄνωθεν ἐκ φωτὸς ἡκούσῃ. Καὶ μάλα, ἔφη,
μετρίως λέγεις.

IV. Δεῖ δή, εἶπον, ἡμᾶς τοιόνδε νομίσαι περὶ
αὐτῶν, εἰ ταῦτ' ἀληθῆ, τὴν παιδείαν οὐχ οἵαν τινὲς
ἐπαγγελλόμενοί φασιν εἶναι τοιαύτην καὶ εἶναι.

ᵃ For the contrast between the philosophical and the
pettifogging soul *cf.* *Theaet.* 173 c-175 ε. *Cf.* also on
517 λ, p. 128, note *b*.
ᵇ For ἀγαλμάτων *cf.* my *Idea of Good in Plato's Republic*,
p. 237, *Soph.* 234 c, *Polit.* 303 c.

to the environing darkness, he is compelled in court-rooms [a] or elsewhere to contend about the shadows of justice or the images [b] that cast the shadows and to wrangle in debate about the notions of these things in the minds of those who have never seen justice itself?" "It would be by no means strange," he said. "But a sensible man," I said, "would remember that there are two distinct disturbances of the eyes arising from two causes, according as the shift is from light to darkness or from darkness to light,[c] and, believing that the same thing happens to the soul too, whenever he saw a soul perturbed and unable to discern something, he would not laugh[d] unthinkingly, but would observe whether coming from a brighter life its vision was obscured by the unfamiliar darkness, or whether the passage from the deeper dark of ignorance into a more luminous world and the greater brightness had dazzled its vision.[e] And so[f] he would deem the one happy in its experience and way of life and pity the other, and if it pleased him to laugh at it, his laughter would be less laughable than that at the expense of the soul that had come down from the light above." "That is a very fair statement," he said.

IV. "Then, if this is true, our view of these matters must be this, that education is not in reality what some people proclaim it to be in their profes-

---

[c] Aristotle, *De an.* 422 a 20 f. says the over-bright is ἀόρατον but otherwise than the dark.

[d] *Cf. Theaet.* 175 D-E.

[e] Lit. "or whether coming from a deeper ignorance into a more luminous world, it is dazzled by the brilliance of a greater light."

[f] *i.e.* only after that. For οὕτω δή in this sense *cf.* 484 D, 429 D, 443 E, *Charm.* 171 E.

518 C φασὶ δέ που οὐκ ἐνούσης ἐν τῇ ψυχῇ ἐπιστήμης
σφεῖς ἐντιθέναι, οἷον τυφλοῖς ὀφθαλμοῖς ὄψιν
ἐντιθέντες. Φασὶ γὰρ οὖν, ἔφη. Ὁ δέ γε νῦν
λόγος, ἦν δ' ἐγώ, σημαίνει, ταύτην τὴν ἐνοῦσαν
ἑκάστου δύναμιν ἐν τῇ ψυχῇ καὶ τὸ ὄργανον, ᾧ
καταμανθάνει ἕκαστος, οἷον εἰ ὄμμα μὴ δυνατὸν
ἦν ἄλλως ἢ ξὺν ὅλῳ τῷ σώματι στρέφειν πρὸς τὸ
φανὸν ἐκ τοῦ σκοτώδους, οὕτω ξὺν ὅλῃ τῇ ψυχῇ
ἐκ τοῦ γιγνομένου περιακτέον εἶναι, ἕως ἂν εἰς τὸ
ὂν καὶ τοῦ ὄντος τὸ φανότατον δυνατὴ γένηται
D ἀνασχέσθαι θεωμένη· τοῦτο δ' εἶναί φαμεν τἀγα-
θόν· ἦ γάρ; Ναί. Τούτου τοίνυν, ἦν δ' ἐγώ,
αὐτοῦ τέχνη ἂν εἴη τῆς περιαγωγῆς, τίνα τρόπον
ὡς ῥᾷστά τε καὶ ἀνυσιμώτατα μεταστραφήσεται,
οὐ τοῦ ἐμποιῆσαι αὐτῷ τὸ ὁρᾶν, ἀλλ' ὡς ἔχοντι μὲν
αὐτό, οὐκ ὀρθῶς δὲ τετραμμένῳ οὐδὲ βλέποντι οἷ
ἔδει, τοῦτο διαμηχανήσασθαι. Ἔοικε γάρ, ἔφη.

---

[a] ἐπαγγελλόμενοι connotes the boastfulness of their claims.
Cf. Protag. 319 A, Gorg. 447 c, Laches 186 c, Euthyd. 273 E,
Isoc. Soph. 1, 5, 9, 10, Antid. 193, Xen. Mem. iii. 1. 1,
i. 2. 8, Aristot. Rhet. 1402 a 25.
[b] Cf. Theognis 429 ff. Stallbaum compares Eurip. Hippol.
917 f. Similarly Anon. Theaet. Comm. (Berlin, 1905), p. 32,
48. 4 καὶ δεῖν αὐτῇ οὐκ ἐνθέσεως μαθημάτων, ἀλλὰ ἀναμνήσεως.
Cf. also St. Augustine: " Nolite putare quemquam hominem
aliquid discere ab homine. Admonere possumus per stre-
pitum vocis nostrae; " and Emerson's " Strictly speaking, it
is not instruction but provocation that I can receive from
another soul."
[c] περιακτέον is probably a reference to the περίακτοι or tri-
angular prisms on each side of the stage. They revolved
on an axis and had different scenes painted on their three faces.
Many scholars are of the opinion that they were not known
in the classical period, as they are mentioned only by late

sions.[a] What they aver is that they can put true knowledge into a soul that does not possess it, as if they were inserting[b] vision into blind eyes." "They do indeed," he said. "But our present argument indicates," said I, "that the true analogy for this indwelling power in the soul and the instrument whereby each of us apprehends is that of an eye that could not be converted to the light from the darkness except by turning the whole body. Even so this organ of knowledge must be turned around from the world of becoming together with the entire soul, like the scene-shifting periact[c] in the theatre, until the soul is able to endure the contemplation of essence and the brightest region of being. And this, we say, is the good,[d] do we not?" "Yes." "Of this very thing, then," I said, "there might be an art,[e] an art of the speediest and most effective shifting or conversion of the soul, not an art of producing vision in it, but on the assumption that it possesses vision but does not rightly direct it and does not look where it should, an art of bringing this about." "Yes, that seems likely," he said. "Then

writers; but others do not consider this conclusive evidence, as a number of classical plays seem to have required something of the sort. *Cf.* O. Navarre in Daremberg-Saglio *s.v.* Machine, p. 1469.

[d] Hard-headed distaste for the unction or seeming mysticism of Plato's language should not blind us to the plain meaning. Unlike Schopenhauer, who affirms the moral will to be unchangeable, Plato says that men may be preached and drilled into ordinary morality, but that the degree of their intelligence is an unalterable endowment of nature. Some teachers will concur.

[e] Plato often distinguishes the things that do or do not admit of reduction to an art or science. *Cf.* on 488 E, p. 22, note *b*. Adam is mistaken in taking it "Education (ἡ παιδεία) would be an art," etc.

PLATO

518 Αἱ μὲν τοίνυν ἄλλαι ἀρεταὶ καλούμεναι ψυχῆς κινδυνεύουσιν ἐγγύς τι εἶναι τῶν τοῦ σώματος·

E τῷ ὄντι γὰρ οὐκ ἐνοῦσαι πρότερον ὕστερον ἐμποιεῖσθαι ἔθεσί τε καὶ ἀσκήσεσιν· ἡ δὲ τοῦ φρονῆσαι παντὸς μᾶλλον θειοτέρου τινὸς τυγχάνει, ὡς ἔοικεν, οὖσα, ὃ τὴν μὲν δύναμιν οὐδέποτε ἀπόλλυσιν, ὑπὸ δὲ τῆς περιαγωγῆς χρήσιμόν τε καὶ

519 ὠφέλιμον καὶ ἄχρηστον αὖ καὶ βλαβερὸν γίγνεται. ἢ οὔπω ἐννενόηκας, τῶν λεγομένων πονηρῶν μέν, σοφῶν δέ, ὡς δριμὺ μὲν βλέπει τὸ ψυχάριον καὶ ὀξέως διορᾷ ταῦτα ἐφ᾽ ἃ τέτραπται, ὡς οὐ φαύλην ἔχον τὴν ὄψιν, κακίᾳ δ᾽ ἠναγκασμένον ὑπηρετεῖν, ὥστε ὅσῳ ἂν ὀξύτερον βλέπῃ, τοσούτῳ πλείω κακὰ ἐργαζόμενον; Πάνυ μὲν οὖν, ἔφη. Τοῦτο μέντοι, ἦν δ᾽ ἐγώ, τὸ τῆς τοιαύτης φύσεως εἰ ἐκ παιδὸς εὐθὺς κοπτόμενον περιεκόπη τὰς τῆς

B γενέσεως ξυγγενεῖς ὥσπερ μολυβδίδας, αἳ δὴ

---

[a] This then is Plato's answer (intended from the first) to the question whether virtue can be taught, debated in the *Protagoras* and *Meno*. The intellectual virtues (to use Aristotle's term), broadly speaking, cannot be taught; they are a gift. And the highest moral virtue is inseparable from rightly directed intellectual virtue. Ordinary moral virtue is not rightly taught in democratic Athens, but comes by the grace of God. In a reformed state it could be systematically inculcated and "taught." *Cf. What Plato Said*, pp. 511-512 on *Meno* 70 A. But we need not infer that Plato did not believe in mental discipline. *Cf.* Charles Fox, *Educational Psychology*, p. 164 "The conception of mental discipline is at least as old as Plato, as may be seen from the seventh book of the *Republic* . . ."

[b] *Cf.* Aristot. *Eth. Nic.* 1103 a 14-17 ἡ δὲ ἠθικὴ ἐξ ἔθους. Plato does not explicitly name "ethical" and "intellectual" virtues. *Cf.* Fox, *op. cit.* p. 104 "Plato correctly believed

136

the other so-called virtues [a] of the soul do seem akin to those of the body. For it is true that where they do not pre-exist, they are afterwards created by habit [b] and practice. But the excellence of thought,[c] it seems, is certainly of a more divine quality, a thing that never loses its potency, but, according to the direction of its conversion, becomes useful and beneficent, or, again, useless and harmful. Have you never observed in those who are popularly spoken of as bad, but smart men,[d] how keen is the vision of the little soul,[e] how quick it is to discern the things that interest it,[f] a proof that it is not a poor vision which it has, but one forcibly enlisted in the service of evil, so that the sharper its sight the more mischief it accomplishes?" "I certainly have," he said. "Observe then," said I, "that this part of such a soul, if it had been hammered from childhood, and had thus been struck free [g] of the leaden weights, so that all virtues except wisdom could be acquired habitually . . ."

[c] Plato uses such synonyms as φρόνησις, σοφία, νοῦς, διάνοια, etc., as suits his purpose and context. He makes no attempt to define and discriminate them with impracticable Aristotelian meticulousness.

[d] Cf. Theaet. 176 D, Laws 689 C-D, Cic. De offic. i. 19, and also Laws 819 A.

[e] Cf. Theaet. 195 A, ibid. 173 A σμικροὶ . . . τὰς ψυχάς, Marcus Aurelius' ψυχάριον εἶ βαστάζων νεκρόν, Swinburne's "A little soul for a little bears up this corpse which is man " ("Hymn to Proserpine," in fine), Tennyson's "If half the little soul is dirt."

[f] Lit. "Toward which it is turned."

[g] The meaning is plain, the precise nature of the image that carries it is doubtful. Jowett's "circumcision" was suggested by Stallbaum's "purgata ac circumcisa," but carries alien associations. The whole may be compared with the incrustation of the soul, infra 611 C-D, and with Phaedo 81 B f.

519 ἐδωδαῖς τε καὶ τοιούτων ἡδοναῖς τε καὶ λιχνείαις
προσφυεῖς γιγνόμεναι κάτω¹ στρέφουσι τὴν τῆς
ψυχῆς ὄψιν· ὧν εἰ ἀπαλλαγὲν περιεστρέφετο εἰς
τἀληθῆ, καὶ ἐκεῖνα ἂν τὸ αὐτὸ τοῦτο τῶν αὐτῶν
ἀνθρώπων ὀξύτατα ἑώρα, ὥσπερ καὶ ἐφ' ἃ νῦν
τέτραπται. Εἰκός γε, ἔφη. Τί δαί; τόδε οὐκ
εἰκός, ἦν δ' ἐγώ, καὶ ἀνάγκη ἐκ τῶν προειρημένων,
μήτε τοὺς ἀπαιδεύτους καὶ ἀληθείας ἀπείρους
C ἱκανῶς ἄν ποτε πόλιν ἐπιτροπεῦσαι, μήτε τοὺς ἐν
παιδείᾳ ἐωμένους διατρίβειν διὰ τέλους, τοὺς μὲν
ὅτι σκοπὸν ἐν τῷ βίῳ οὐκ ἔχουσιν ἕνα, οὗ στοχαζο-
μένους δεῖ ἅπαντα πράττειν ἃ ἂν πράττωσιν ἰδίᾳ
τε καὶ δημοσίᾳ, τοὺς δὲ ὅτι ἑκόντες εἶναι οὐ
πράξουσιν, ἡγούμενοι ἐν μακάρων νήσοις ζῶντες
ἔτι ἀπῳκίσθαι; Ἀληθῆ, ἔφη. Ἡμέτερον δὴ
ἔργον, ἦν δ' ἐγώ, τῶν οἰκιστῶν τάς τε βελτίστας
φύσεις ἀναγκάσαι ἀφικέσθαι πρὸς τὸ μάθημα ὃ
ἐν τῷ πρόσθεν ἔφαμεν εἶναι μέγιστον, ἰδεῖν τε τὸ
D ἀγαθὸν καὶ ἀναβῆναι ἐκείνην τὴν ἀνάβασιν, καὶ
ἐπειδὰν ἀναβάντες ἱκανῶς ἴδωσι, μὴ ἐπιτρέπειν
αὐτοῖς ὃ νῦν ἐπιτρέπεται. Τὸ ποῖον δή; Τὸ
αὐτοῦ, ἦν δ' ἐγώ, καταμένειν καὶ μὴ ἐθέλειν πάλιν

---

¹ κάτω Hermann: περὶ κάτω MSS.: περὶ τὰ κάτω Iamblichus.

ᵃ Or "eye of the mind." *Cf.* 533 D, *Sym.* 219 A, *Soph.*
254 A, Aristot. *Eth.* 1144 a 30, and the parallels and imitations collected by Gomperz, *Apol. der Heilkunst*, 166-167.
Cf. also *What Plato Said*, p. 534, on *Phaedo* 99 E, Ovid,
Met. xv. 64 :

. . . quae natura negabat
visibus humanis, oculis ea pectoris hausit.

Cf. Friedländer, *Platon*, i. pp. 12-13, 15, and perhaps *Odyssey*,
i. 115, Marc. Aurel. iv. 29 καταμένειν τῷ νοερῷ ὄμματι.
ᵇ For likely and necessary *cf.* on 485 c, p. 6, note c.

to speak, of our birth and becoming, which attaching themselves to it by food and similar pleasures and gluttonies turn downwards the vision of the soul [a] —if, I say, freed from these, it had suffered a conversion towards the things that are real and true, that same faculty of the same men would have been most keen in its vision of the higher things, just as it is for the things toward which it is now turned." " It is likely," he said. " Well, then," said I, " is not this also likely [b] and a necessary consequence of what has been said, that neither could men who are uneducated and inexperienced in truth ever adequately preside over a state, nor could those who had been permitted to linger on to the end in the pursuit of culture—the one because they have no single aim [c] and purpose in life to which all their actions, public and private, must be directed, and the others, because they will not voluntarily engage in action, believing that while still living they have been transported to the Islands of the Blest.[d] " " True," he said. " It is the duty of us, the founders, then," said I, " to compel the best natures to attain the knowledge which we pronounced the greatest, and to win to the vision of the good, to scale that ascent, and when they have reached the heights and taken an adequate view, we must not allow what is now permitted." " What is that ? " "That they should linger there," I said, " and refuse

[c] σκοπόν : this is what distinguishes the philosophic statesman from the opportunist politician. Cf. 452 E, Laws 962 A-B, D, Unity of Plato's Thought, p. 18, n. 102.
[d] Cf. 540 B, Gorg. 526 C, infra 520 D ἐν τῷ καθαρῷ and Phaedo 114 C, 109 B. Because they will still suppose that they are " building Jerusalem in England's green and pleasant land " (Blake).

PLATO

519 καταβαίνειν παρ' ἐκείνους τοὺς δεσμώτας μηδὲ
μετέχειν τῶν παρ' ἐκείνοις πόνων τε καὶ τιμῶν,
εἴτε φαυλότεραι εἴτε σπουδαιότεραι. Ἔπειτ', ἔφη,
ἀδικήσομεν αὐτούς, καὶ ποιήσομεν χεῖρον ζῆν,
δυνατὸν αὐτοῖς ὂν ἄμεινον;

E   V. Ἐπελάθου, ἦν δ' ἐγώ, πάλιν, ὦ φίλε, ὅτι
νόμῳ οὐ τοῦτο μέλει, ὅπως ἕν τι γένος ἐν πόλει
διαφερόντως εὖ πράξει, ἀλλ' ἐν ὅλῃ τῇ πόλει τοῦτο
μηχανᾶται ἐγγενέσθαι, ξυναρμόττων τοὺς πολίτας
πειθοῖ τε καὶ ἀνάγκῃ, ποιῶν μεταδιδόναι ἀλλήλοις
520 τῆς ὠφελείας, ἣν ἂν ἕκαστοι τὸ κοινὸν δυνατοὶ
ὦσιν ὠφελεῖν, καὶ αὐτὸς ἐμποιῶν τοιούτους ἄνδρας
ἐν τῇ πόλει, οὐχ ἵνα ἀφίῃ τρέπεσθαι ὅπῃ ἕκαστος
βούλεται, ἀλλ' ἵνα καταχρῆται αὐτὸς αὐτοῖς ἐπὶ
τὸν ξύνδεσμον τῆς πόλεως. Ἀληθῆ, ἔφη. ἐπ-
ελαθόμην γάρ. Σκέψαι τοίνυν, εἶπον, ὦ Γλαύκων,
ὅτι οὐδ' ἀδικήσομεν τοὺς παρ' ἡμῖν φιλοσόφους
γιγνομένους, ἀλλὰ δίκαια πρὸς αὐτοὺς ἐροῦμεν,
προσαναγκάζοντες τῶν ἄλλων ἐπιμελεῖσθαί τε καὶ
B φυλάττειν. ἐροῦμεν γάρ, ὅτι οἱ μὲν ἐν ταῖς ἄλλαις
πόλεσι τοιοῦτοι γιγνόμενοι εἰκότως οὐ μετέχουσι
τῶν ἐν αὐταῖς πόνων· αὐτόματοι γὰρ ἐμφύονται
ἀκούσης τῆς ἐν ἑκάστῃ πολιτείας, δίκην δ' ἔχει τό
γε αὐτοφυές, μηδενὶ τροφὴν ὀφεῖλον, μηδ' ἐκτίνειν

ᵃ Cf. *infra* 539 E and *Laws* 803 B-C, and on 520 C, Huxley,
Evolution and Ethics, p. 53 " the hero of our story descended
the bean-stalk and came back to the common world," etc.

ᵇ Cf. Vol. I. pp. 314-315 on 419.

ᶜ *i.e.* happiness, not of course exceptional happiness.

ᵈ Persuasion and compulsion are often bracketed or contrasted. Cf. also *Laws* 661 C, 722 B, 711 C, *Rep.* 548 B.

ᵉ Cf. 369 C ff. The reference there however is only to the
economic division of labour. For the idea that laws should

to go down again[a] among those bondsmen and share their labours and honours, whether they are of less or of greater worth." "Do you mean to say that we must do them this wrong, and compel them to live an inferior life when the better is in their power ?"

V. "You have again forgotten,[b] my friend," said I, " that the law is not concerned with the special happiness of any class in the state, but is trying to produce this condition[c] in the city as a whole, harmonizing and adapting the citizens to one another by persuasion and compulsion,[d] and requiring them to impart to one another any benefit[e] which they are severally able to bestow upon the community, and that it itself creates such men in the state, not that it may allow each to take what course pleases him, but with a view to using them for the binding together of the commonwealth." "True," he said, " I did forget it." "Observe, then, Glaucon," said I, " that we shall not be wronging, either, the philosophers who arise among us, but that we can justify our action when we constrain them to take charge of the other citizens and be their guardians.[f] For we will say to them that it is natural that men of similar quality who spring up in other cities should not share in the labours there. For they grow up spontaneously[g] from no volition of the government in the several states, and it is justice that the self-grown, indebted to none for its breeding, should not be zealous either to pay

be for the good of the whole state *cf.* 420 B ff., 466 A, 341-342, *Laws* 715 B, 757 D, 875 A.
   [f] *Noblesse oblige.* This idea is now a commonplace of communist orations.
   [g] αὐτόματοι : *cf. Protag.* 320 A, *Euthyd.* 282 C. For the thought that there are a few men naturally good in any state *cf.* also *Laws* 951 B, 642 C-D.

PLATO

520 τῷ προθυμεῖσθαι τὰ τροφεῖα· ὑμᾶς δ' ἡμεῖς ὑμῖν
τε αὑτοῖς τῇ τε ἄλλῃ πόλει ὥσπερ ἐν σμήνεσιν
ἡγεμόνας τε καὶ βασιλέας ἐγεννήσαμεν, ἄμεινόν τε
C καὶ τελεώτερον ἐκείνων πεπαιδευμένους καὶ μᾶλλον
δυνατοὺς ἀμφοτέρων μετέχειν. καταβατέον οὖν
ἐν μέρει ἑκάστῳ εἰς τὴν τῶν ἄλλων ξυνοίκησιν καὶ
ξυνεθιστέον τὰ σκοτεινὰ θεάσασθαι· ξυνεθιζόμενοι
γὰρ μυρίῳ βέλτιον ὄψεσθε τῶν ἐκεῖ, καὶ γνώσεσθε
ἕκαστα τὰ εἴδωλα ἄττα ἐστὶ καὶ ὧν, διὰ τὸ τἀληθῆ
ἑωρακέναι καλῶν τε καὶ δικαίων καὶ ἀγαθῶν πέρι·
καὶ οὕτω ὕπαρ ἡμῖν καὶ ὑμῖν ἡ πόλις οἰκήσεται,
ἀλλ' οὐκ ὄναρ, ὡς νῦν αἱ πολλαὶ ὑπὸ σκιαμαχούν-
D των τε πρὸς ἀλλήλους καὶ στασιαζόντων περὶ τοῦ
ἄρχειν οἰκοῦνται, ὡς μεγάλου τινὸς ἀγαθοῦ ὄντος.
τὸ δέ που ἀληθὲς ὧδ' ἔχει· ἐν πόλει ᾗ ἥκιστα
πρόθυμοι ἄρχειν οἱ μέλλοντες ἄρξειν, ταύτην
ἄριστα καὶ ἀστασιαστότατα ἀνάγκη οἰκεῖσθαι, τὴν
δ' ἐναντίους ἄρχοντας σχοῦσαν ἐναντίως. Πάνυ

---

[a] Cf. Isoc. Archidamus 108 ἀποδῶμεν τὰ τροφεῖα τῇ πατρίδι.
Stallbaum refers also to Phoenissae 44. For the country as
τροφός see Vol. I. p. 303, note e on 414 E.

[b] Cf. Polit. 301 D-E, Xen. Cyr. v. 1. 24, Oecon. 7. 32-33.

[c] For τελεώτερον . . . πεπαιδευμένους cf. Prot. 342 E τελέως
πεπαιδευμένου.

[d] They must descend into the cave again. Cf. infra 539 E
and Laws 803 B-C. Cf. Burnet, Early Greek Philos. pp. 89-
90: "It was he alone, so far as we know, that insisted on
philosophers descending by turns into the cave from which
they had been released and coming to the help of their
former fellow-prisoners." He agrees with Stewart (Myths
of Plato, p. 252, n. 2) that Plato had in mind the Orphic
κατάβασις εἰς Ἅιδου to "rescue the spirits in prison." Cf.
Wright,-Harvard Studies, xvii. p. 139 and Complete Poems
of Henry More, pp. xix-xx "All which is agreeable to that
opinion of Plato: That some descend hither to declare the
Being and Nature of the Gods; and for the greater Health,

THE REPUBLIC, BOOK VII

to anyone the price of its nurture.[a] But you we have engendered for yourselves and the rest of the city to be, as it were, king-bees[b] and leaders in the hive. You have received a better and more complete education[c] than the others, and you are more capable of sharing both ways of life. Down you must go[d] then, each in his turn, to the habitation of the others and accustom yourselves to the observation of the obscure things there. For once habituated you will discern them infinitely[e] better than the dwellers there, and you will know what each of the 'idols'[f] is and whereof it is a semblance, because you have seen the reality of the beautiful, the just and the good. So our city will be governed by us and you with waking minds, and not, as most cities now which are inhabited and ruled darkly as in a dream[g] by men who fight one another for shadows[h] and wrangle for office as if that were a great good, when the truth is that the city in which those who are to rule are least eager to hold office[i] must needs be best administered and most free from dissension, and the state that gets the contrary type of ruler will be the opposite of this."

Purity and Perfection of this Lower World." This is taking Plato somewhat too literally and confusing him with Plotinus.

[e] For μυρίῳ cf. Eurip. *Androm.* 701.

[f] *i.e.* images, Bacon's "idols of the den."

[g] Plato is fond of the contrast, ὕπαρ . . . ὄναρ. Cf. 476 c, *Phaedr.* 277 D, *Phileb.* 36 E, 65 E, *Polit.* 277 D, 278 E, *Theaet.* 158 B, *Rep.* 574 D, 576 B, *Tim.* 71 E, *Laws* 969 B, also 533 B-C.

[h] Cf. on 586 c, p. 393; Shelley, *Adonais* st. 39 "keep with phantoms an unprofitable strife"; Arnold, "Dover Beach":

> . . . a darkling plain . . .
> Where ignorant armies clash by night.

[i] Cf. on 517 c, p. 131, note e.

520 μὲν οὖν, ἔφη. Ἀπειθήσουσιν οὖν ἡμῖν, οἴει, οἱ
τρόφιμοι ταῦτ' ἀκούοντες, καὶ οὐκ ἐθελήσουσι
ξυμπονεῖν ἐν τῇ πόλει ἕκαστοι ἐν μέρει, τὸν δὲ
πολὺν χρόνον μετ' ἀλλήλων οἰκεῖν ἐν τῷ καθαρῷ;
E Ἀδύνατον, ἔφη· δίκαια γὰρ δὴ δικαίοις ἐπι-
τάξομεν. παντὸς μὴν μᾶλλον ὡς ἐπ' ἀναγκαῖον
αὐτῶν ἕκαστος εἶσι τὸ ἄρχειν, τοὐναντίον τῶν νῦν
ἐν ἑκάστῃ πόλει ἀρχόντων. Οὕτω γὰρ ἔχει, ἦν δ'
ἐγώ, ὦ ἑταῖρε· εἰ μὲν βίον ἐξευρήσεις ἀμείνω τοῦ
521 ἄρχειν τοῖς μέλλουσιν ἄρξειν, ἔστι σοι δυνατὴ
γενέσθαι πόλις εὖ οἰκουμένη· ἐν μόνῃ γὰρ αὐτῇ
ἄρξουσιν οἱ τῷ ὄντι πλούσιοι, οὐ χρυσίου, ἀλλ'
οὗ δεῖ τὸν εὐδαίμονα πλουτεῖν, ζωῆς ἀγαθῆς τε καὶ
ἔμφρονος. εἰ δὲ πτωχοὶ καὶ πεινῶντες ἀγαθῶν
ἰδίων ἐπὶ τὰ δημόσια ἴασιν, ἐντεῦθεν οἰόμενοι
τἀγαθὸν δεῖν ἁρπάζειν, οὐκ ἔστι· περιμάχητον
γὰρ τὸ ἄρχειν γιγνόμενον, οἰκεῖος ὢν καὶ ἔνδον ὁ
τοιοῦτος πόλεμος αὐτούς τε ἀπόλλυσι καὶ τὴν
B ἄλλην πόλιν. Ἀληθέστατα, ἔφη. Ἔχεις οὖν, ἦν
δ' ἐγώ, βίον ἄλλον τινὰ πολιτικῶν ἀρχῶν κατα-
φρονοῦντα ἢ τὸν τῆς ἀληθινῆς φιλοσοφίας; Οὐ μὰ
τὸν Δία, ἦ δ' ὅς. Ἀλλὰ μέντοι δεῖ γε μὴ ἐραστὰς
τοῦ ἄρχειν ἰέναι ἐπ' αὐτό· εἰ δὲ μή, οἵ γε ἀντ-
ερασταὶ μαχοῦνται. Πῶς δ' οὔ; Τίνας οὖν ἄλλους
ἀναγκάσεις ἰέναι ἐπὶ φυλακὴν τῆς πόλεως, ἢ οἱ

---

[a] The world of ideas, the upper world as opposed to that
of the cave. *Cf.* Stallbaum *ad loc.*

[b] *Cf. supra* Vol. I. p. 80, note *b* on 347 c.

[c] *Cf. Phaedrus in fine, supra* 416 E-417 A, *infra* 547 B.

[d] Stallbaum refers to Xen. *Cyr.* viii. 3. 39 οἶμαι σε καὶ διὰ
τοῦτο ἥδιον πλουτεῖν, ὅτι πεινήσας χρημάτων πεπλούτηκας, "for you
must enjoy your riches much more, I think, for the very reason
that it was only after being hungry for wealth that you became
rich." (Loeb tr.) *Cf.* also *infra* 577 E-578 A, and Adam *ad loc.*

144

"By all means," he said. "Will our alumni, then, disobey us when we tell them this, and will they refuse to share in the labours of state each in his turn while permitted to dwell the most of the time with one another in that purer world [a] ?" "Impossible," he said : "for we shall be imposing just commands on men who are just. Yet they will assuredly approach office as an unavoidable necessity,[b] and in the opposite temper from that of the present rulers in our cities." "For the fact is, dear friend," said I, "if you can discover a better way of life than office-holding for your future rulers, a well-governed city becomes. a possibility. For only in such a state will those rule who are really rich,[c] not in gold, but in the wealth that makes happiness—a good and wise life. But if, being beggars and starvelings [d] from lack of goods of their own, they turn to affairs of state thinking that it is thence that they should grasp their own good, then it is impossible. For when office and rule become the prizes of contention,[e] such a civil and internecine strife [f] destroys the office-seekers themselves and the city as well." "Most true," he said. "Can you name any other type or ideal of life that looks with scorn on political office except the life of true philosophers [g] ?" I asked. "No, by Zeus," he said. "But what we require," I said, "is that those who take office [h] should not be lovers of rule. Otherwise there will be a contest with rival lovers." "Surely." "What others, then, will you compel to undertake the guardianship of the city

---

[e] Cf. supra 347 D, Laws 715 A, also 586 C and What Plato Said, p. 627, on Laws 678 E, Isoc. Areop. 24, Pan. 145 and 146.
[f] Cf. Eurip. Heracleidae 415 οἰκεῖος ἤδη πόλεμος ἐξαρτύεται.
[g] Cf. infra 580 D ff., pp. 370 ff.
[h] ἰέναι ἐπί in erotic language means "to woo." Cf. on 489 D, p. 26, note b, also 347 C, 588 B, 475 C.

521 περὶ τούτων τε φρονιμώτατοι, δι᾽ ὧν ἄριστα πόλις
οἰκεῖται, ἔχουσί τε τιμὰς ἄλλας καὶ βίον ἀμείνω
τοῦ πολιτικοῦ; Οὐδένας ἄλλους, ἔφη.

C VI. Βούλει οὖν τοῦτ᾽ ἤδη σκοπῶμεν, τίνα τρόπον
οἱ τοιοῦτοι ἐγγενήσονται καὶ πῶς τις ἀνάξει αὐτοὺς
εἰς φῶς, ὥσπερ ἐξ Ἅιδου λέγονται δή τινες εἰς
θεοὺς ἀνελθεῖν; Πῶς γὰρ οὐ βούλομαι; ἔφη.
Τοῦτο δή, ὡς ἔοικεν, οὐκ ὀστράκου ἂν εἴη περι-
στροφὴ ἀλλὰ ψυχῆς περιαγωγὴ ἐκ νυκτερινῆς τινος
ἡμέρας εἰς ἀληθινήν, τοῦ ὄντος οὖσα ἐπάνοδος,[1] ἣν
δὴ φιλοσοφίαν ἀληθῆ φήσομεν εἶναι. Πάνυ μὲν
οὖν. Οὐκοῦν δεῖ σκοπεῖσθαι τί τῶν μαθημάτων

D ἔχει τοιαύτην δύναμιν; Πῶς γὰρ οὔ; Τί ἂν οὖν
εἴη, ὦ Γλαύκων, μάθημα ψυχῆς ὁλκὸν ἀπὸ τοῦ
γιγνομένου ἐπὶ τὸ ὄν; τόδε δ᾽ ἐννοῶ λέγων ἅμα·
οὐκ ἀθλητὰς μέντοι πολέμου ἔφαμεν τούτους

---

[1] οὖσα ἐπάνοδος Hermann : οὖσαν ἐπάνοδον AFDM, ἰούσης
ἐπάνοδον scr. recc. : οὐσίαν ἐπάνοδος ci. Cobet.

---

[a] Cf. on 515 E, p. 124, note b.

[b] This has been much debated. Cf. Adam ad loc. Professor Linforth argues from Pausanias i. 34 that Amphiaraus
is meant.

[c] Cf. Phaedr. 241 B; also the description of the game in
Plato Comicus, fr. 153, apud Norwood, Greek Comedy,
p. 167. The players were divided into two groups. A shell
or potsherd, black on one side and white on the other, was
thrown, and according to the face on which it fell one group
fled and the other pursued. Cf. also commentators on
Aristoph. Knights 855.

[d] Much quoted by Neoplatonists and Christian Fathers.
Cf. Stallbaum ad loc. Again we need to remember that
Plato's main and explicitly reiterated purpose is to describe
a course of study that will develop the power of consecutive
consistent abstract thinking. All metaphysical and mystical
suggestions of the imagery which conveys this idea are

than those who have most intelligence of the principles that are the means of good government and who possess distinctions of another kind and a life that is preferable to the political life ? " " No others," he said.

VI. " Would you, then, have us proceed to consider how such men may be produced in a state and how they may be led upward *a* to the light even as some *b* are fabled to have ascended from Hades to the gods?" " Of course I would." "So this, it seems, would not be the whirling of the shell *c* in the children's game, but a conversion and turning about of the soul from a day whose light is darkness to the veritable day— that ascension *d* to reality of our parable which we will affirm to be true philosophy." " By all means." " Must we not, then, consider what studies have the power to effect this ? " " Of course." " What, then, Glaucon, would be the study that would draw the soul away from the world of becoming to the world of being ? A thought strikes me while I speak *e* : Did we not say that these men in youth must be athletes

secondary and subordinate. So, *e.g.* Urwick, *The Message of Plato*, pp. 66-67, is mistaken when he says ". . . Plato expressly tells us that his education is designed simply and solely to awaken the spiritual faculty which every soul contains, by ' wheeling the soul round and turning it away from the world of change and decay.' He is not concerned with any of those ' excellences of mind ' which may be produced by training and discipline, his only aim is to open the eye of the soul . . ." The general meaning of the sentence is plain but the text is disputed. See crit. note.

e A frequent pretence in Plato. *Cf.* 370 A, 525 C, *Euthyphro* 9 C, *Laws* 686 C, 702 B, *Phaedr.* 262 C with Friedländer, *Platon*, ii. p. 498, *Laws* 888 D with Tayler Lewis, *Plato against the Atheists*, pp. 118-119. *Cf.* also Vol. I. on 394 D-E, and Isoc. *Antid.* 159 ἐνθυμοῦμαι δὲ μεταξὺ λέγων, *Panath.* 127.

521 ἀναγκαῖον εἶναι νέους ὄντας; Ἔφαμεν γάρ. Δεῖ
ἄρα καὶ τοῦτο προσέχειν τὸ μάθημα ὃ ζητοῦμεν,
πρὸς ἐκείνῳ. Τὸ ποῖον; Μὴ ἄχρηστον πολεμι-
κοῖς ἀνδράσιν εἶναι. Δεῖ μέντοι, ἔφη, εἴπερ οἶόν
Ε τε. Γυμναστικὴ μὴν καὶ μουσικῇ ἔν γε τῷ πρόσθεν
ἐπαιδεύοντο ἡμῖν. Ἦν ταῦτα, ἔφη. Καὶ γυμναστικὴ μέν που περὶ γιγνόμενον καὶ ἀπολλύμενον
τετεύτακε¹· σώματος γὰρ αὔξης καὶ φθίσεως
ἐπιστατεῖ. Φαίνεται. Τοῦτο μὲν δὴ οὐκ ἂν εἴη
522 ὃ ζητοῦμεν μάθημα. Οὐ γάρ. Ἀλλ' ἆρα μουσική,
ὅσην τὸ πρότερον διήλθομεν; Ἀλλ' ἦν ἐκείνη γ',
ἔφη, ἀντίστροφος τῆς γυμναστικῆς, εἰ μέμνησαι,
ἔθεσι παιδεύουσα τοὺς φύλακας, κατά τε ἁρμονίαν
εὐαρμοστίαν τινά, οὐκ ἐπιστήμην, παραδιδοῦσα,
καὶ κατὰ ῥυθμὸν εὐρυθμίαν, ἔν τε τοῖς λόγοις
ἕτερα τούτων ἀδελφὰ ἔθη² ἄττα ἔχουσα, καὶ ὅσοι
μυθώδεις τῶν λόγων καὶ ὅσοι ἀληθινώτεροι ἦσαν·
μάθημα δὲ πρὸς τοιοῦτόν τι ἀγαθόν,³ οἶον σὺ νῦν
Β ζητεῖς, οὐδὲν ἦν ἐν αὐτῇ. Ἀκριβέστατα, ἦν δ'
ἐγώ, ἀναμιμνήσκεις με· τῷ γὰρ ὄντι τοιοῦτον
οὐδὲν εἶχεν. ἀλλ', ὦ δαιμόνιε Γλαύκων, τί ἂν εἴη
τοιοῦτον; αἵ τε γὰρ τέχναι βάναυσοί που ἅπασαι
ἔδοξαν εἶναι. Πῶς δ' οὔ; καὶ μὴν τί ἔτ' ἄλλο

---

¹ τετεύτακε(ν) ADM Euseb., τεύτακε F, τέτευχε d vulg.
² ἔθη F Euseb., ἔφη ADM.
³ ἀγαθὸν ADM, ἄγον Euseb. et γρ D, αγ (sic) F.

ᵃ Cf. 416 D, 422 B, 404 A, and Vol. I. p. 266, note a, on
403 E.
ᵇ προσέχειν is here used in its etymological sense. Cf.
pp. 66-67 on 500 A.
ᶜ This further prerequisite of the higher education follows
naturally from the plan of the Republic; but it does not

of war [a] ? " " We did." " Then the study for which
we are seeking must have this additional [b] qualification." " What one ? " " That it be not useless to
soldiers.[c] " " Why, yes, it must," he said, " if that is
possible." " But in our previous account they were
educated in gymnastics and music.[d] " " They were,"
he said. " And gymnastics, I take it, is devoted [e] to
that which grows and perishes ; for it presides over
the growth and decay of the body.[f] " " Obviously."
"Then this cannot be the study that we seek." " No."
" Is it, then, music, so far as we have already described it ?[g] " " Nay, that," he said, " was the counterpart of gymnastics, if you remember. It educated
the guardians through habits, imparting by the
melody a certain harmony of spirit that is not science,[h]
and by the rhythm measure and grace, and also
qualities akin to these in the words of tales that are
fables and those that are more nearly true. But it
included no study that tended to any such good as
you are now seeking." " Your recollection is most
exact," I said ; " for in fact it had nothing of the
kind. But in heaven's name, Glaucon, what study
could there be of that kind ? For all the arts were
in our opinion base and mechanical.[i] " " Surely ;

interest Plato much and is, after one or two repetitions,
dropped.

[d] *Cf. supra* 376 E ff.

[e] For τετεύτακε *cf. Tim.* 90 B τετευτακότι.

[f] *Cf.* 376 E. This is of course no contradiction of 410 c.

[g] The ordinary study of music may cultivate and refine
feeling. Only the mathematics of music would develop the
power of abstract thought.

[h] Knowledge in the true sense, as contrasted with opinion
or habit.

[i] *Cf. supra,* p. 49, note *e*, on 495 E. This idea is the
source of much modern prejudice against Plato.

522 λείπεται μάθημα, μουσικῆς καὶ γυμναστικῆς καὶ
τῶν τεχνῶν κεχωρισμένον; Φέρε, ἦν δ' ἐγώ, εἰ
μηδὲν ἔτι ἐκτὸς τούτων ἔχομεν λαβεῖν, τῶν ἐπὶ
C πάντα τεινόντων τι λάβωμεν. Τὸ ποῖον; Οἷον
τοῦτο τὸ κοινόν, ᾧ πᾶσαι προσχρῶνται τέχναι τε
καὶ διάνοιαι καὶ ἐπιστῆμαι, ὃ καὶ παντὶ ἐν πρώτοις ἀνάγκη μανθάνειν. Ποῖον; ἔφη. Τὸ φαῦλον
τοῦτο, ἦν δ' ἐγώ, τὸ ἕν τε καὶ τὰ δύο καὶ τὰ τρία
διαγιγνώσκειν· λέγω δὲ αὐτὸ ἐν κεφαλαίῳ ἀριθμόν
τε καὶ λογισμόν. ἢ οὐχ οὕτω περὶ τούτων ἔχει,
ὡς πᾶσα τέχνη τε καὶ ἐπιστήμη ἀναγκάζεται
αὐτῶν μέτοχος γίγνεσθαι; Καὶ μάλα, ἔφη. Οὐκοῦν, ἦν δ' ἐγώ, καὶ ἡ πολεμική; Πολλή,
D ἔφη, ἀνάγκη. Παγγέλοιον γοῦν, ἔφην, στρατηγὸν
Ἀγαμέμνονα ἐν ταῖς τραγῳδίαις Παλαμήδης
ἑκάστοτε ἀποφαίνει. ἢ οὐκ ἐννενόηκας ὅτι φησὶν
ἀριθμὸν εὑρὼν τάς τε τάξεις τῷ στρατοπέδῳ
καταστῆσαι ἐν Ἰλίῳ καὶ ἐξαριθμῆσαι ναῦς τε καὶ
τἆλλα πάντα, ὡς πρὸ τοῦ ἀναριθμήτων ὄντων καὶ
τοῦ Ἀγαμέμνονος, ὡς ἔοικεν, οὐδ' ὅσους πόδας
εἶχεν εἰδότος, εἴπερ ἀριθμεῖν μὴ ἠπίστατο; καίτοι
ποῖόν τιν' αὐτὸν οἴει στρατηγὸν εἶναι; Ἄτοπόν
τιν', ἔφη, ἔγωγε, εἰ ἦν τοῦτ' ἀληθές.
E VII. Ἄλλο τι οὖν, ἦν δ' ἐγώ, μάθημα ἀναγκαῖον
πολεμικῷ ἀνδρὶ θήσομεν καὶ λογίζεσθαί τε καὶ

---

[a] Cf. *Symp.* 186 B ἐπὶ πᾶν τείνει.

[b] διάνοιαι is not to be pressed in the special sense of
511 D-E.

[c] A playful introduction to Plato's serious treatment of the
psychology of number and the value of the study of
mathematics.

and yet what other study is left apart from music, gymnastics and the arts?" "Come," said I, "if we are unable to discover anything outside of these, let us take something that applies to all alike.[a]" "What?" "Why, for example, this common thing that all arts and forms of thought [b] and all sciences employ, and which is among the first things that everybody must learn." "What?" he said. "This trifling matter,[c]" I said, "of distinguishing one and two and three. I mean, in sum, number and calculation. Is it not true of them that every art and science must necessarily partake of them?" "Indeed it is," he said. "The art of war too?" said I. "Most necessarily," he said. "Certainly, then," said I, "Palamedes[d] in the play is always making Agamemnon appear a most ridiculous [e] general. Have you not noticed that he affirms that by the invention of number he marshalled the troops in the army at Troy in ranks and companies and enumerated the ships and everything else as if before that they had not been counted, and Agamemnon apparently did not know how many feet he had if he couldn't count? And yet what sort of a general do you think he would be in that case?" "A very queer one in my opinion," he said, "if that was true."

VII. "Shall we not, then," I said, "set down as a study requisite for a soldier the ability to reckon and

---

[d] Palamedes, like Prometheus, is a "culture hero," who personifies in Greek tragedy the inventions and discoveries that produced civilization. *Cf.* the speech of Prometheus in Aesch. *Prom.* 459 ff. and *Harvard Studies*, xii. p. 208, n. 2.

[e] Quoted by later writers in praise of mathematics. *Cf.* Theo Smyrn. p. 7 ed. Gelder. For the necessity of mathematics *cf. Laws* 818 c.

522 ἀριθμεῖν δύνασθαι; Πάντων γ', ἔφη, μάλιστα, εἰ
καὶ ὁτιοῦν μέλλει τάξεων ἐπαΐειν, μᾶλλον δ' εἰ καὶ
ἄνθρωπος ἔσεσθαι. Ἐννοεῖς οὖν, εἶπον, περὶ
τοῦτο τὸ μάθημα ὅπερ ἐγώ; Τὸ ποῖον; Κινδυ-
523 νεύει τῶν πρὸς τὴν νόησιν ἀγόντων φύσει εἶναι
ὧν ζητοῦμεν, χρῆσθαι δ' οὐδεὶς αὐτῷ ὀρθῶς, ἑλκτι-
κῷ ὄντι παντάπασι πρὸς οὐσίαν. Πῶς, ἔφη,
λέγεις; Ἐγὼ πειράσομαι, ἦν δ' ἐγώ, τό γ' ἐμοὶ
δοκοῦν δηλῶσαι. ἃ γὰρ διαιροῦμαι παρ' ἐμαυτῷ
ἀγωγά τε εἶναι οἳ λέγομεν καὶ μή, ξυνθεατὴς
γενόμενος ξύμφαθι ἢ ἄπειπε, ἵνα καὶ τοῦτο σαφέστερον ἴδωμεν εἰ ἔστιν οἷον μαντεύομαι. Δείκνυ,
ἔφη. Δείκνυμι δή, εἶπον, εἰ καθορᾷς, τὰ μὲν ἐν
B ταῖς αἰσθήσεσιν οὐ παρακαλοῦντα τὴν νόησιν εἰς
ἐπίσκεψιν, ὡς ἱκανῶς ὑπὸ τῆς αἰσθήσεως κρινόμενα, τὰ δὲ παντάπασι διακελευόμενα ἐκείνην
ἐπισκέψασθαι, ὡς τῆς αἰσθήσεως οὐδὲν ὑγιὲς
ποιούσης. Τὰ πόρρωθεν, ἔφη, φαινόμενα δῆλον
ὅτι λέγεις καὶ τὰ ἐσκιαγραφημένα. Οὐ πάνυ, ἦν
δ' ἐγώ, ἔτυχες οὗ λέγω. Ποῖα μήν, ἔφη, λέγεις;
Τὰ μὲν οὐ παρακαλοῦντα, ἦν δ' ἐγώ, ὅσα μὴ

---

[a] Cf. Laws 819 D.

[b] Plato's point of view here, as he will explain, is precisely
the opposite of that of modern educators who would teach
mathematics concretely and not puzzle the children with
abstract logic. But in the Laws where he is speaking of
primary and secondary education for the entire population
he anticipates the modern kindergarten ideas (819 B-C).

[c] For σαφέστερον cf. 523 c. Cf. Vol. I. p. 47, note f, on
338 D, and What Plato Said, p. 503, on Gorg. 463 D.

[d] Cf. Phileb. 38 c, Unity of Plato's Thought, n. 337.

number ? " " Most certainly, if he is to know anything whatever of the ordering of his troops—or
rather if he is to be a man at all.[a]" " Do you observe
then," said I, " in this study what I do ? " " What ? "
" It seems likely that it is one of those studies which
we are seeking that naturally conduce to the awaken-
ing of thought, but that no one makes the right use [b] of
it, though it really does tend to draw the mind to
essence and reality." " What do you mean ? " he
said. " I will try," I said, " to show you at least my
opinion. Do you keep watch and observe the things
I distinguish in my mind as being or not being con-
ducive to our purpose, and either concur or dissent,
in order that here too we may see more clearly [c]
whether my surmise is right." " Point them out,"
he said. " I do point them out," I said, " if you can
discern that some reports of our perceptions do not
provoke thought to reconsideration because the
judgement [d] of them by sensation seems adequate,[e]
while others always invite the intellect to reflection
because the sensation yields nothing that can be
trusted.[f] " " You obviously mean distant [g] appearances," he said, " and shadow-painting.[h]" " You
have quite missed my meaning,[i]" said I. " What do
you mean ? " he said. " The experiences that do not
provoke thought are those that do not at the same

[e] ἱκανῶς is not to be pressed here.
[f] For οὐδὲν ὑγιές cf. 496 c, 584 A, 589 c, Phaedo 69 B, 89 E,
90 E, Gorg. 524 E, Laws 776 E, Theaet. 173 B, Eurip. Phoen.
201, Bacch. 262, Hel. 746, etc.
[g] The most obvious cause of errors of judgement. Cf. Laws
663 B.
[h] Cf. Vol. I. p. 137 on 365 c.
[i] The dramatic misapprehension by the interlocutor is one
of Plato's methods for enforcing his meaning. Cf. on 529 A,
p. 180, note a, Laws 792 B-C.

523 C ἐκβαίνει εἰς ἐναντίαν αἴσθησιν ἅμα· τὰ δ' ἐκβαίνοντα ὡς παρακαλοῦντα τίθημι, ἐπειδὰν ἡ αἴσθησις
μηδὲν μᾶλλον τοῦτο ἢ τὸ ἐναντίον δηλοῖ, εἴτ'
ἐγγύθεν προσπίπτουσα εἴτε πόρρωθεν. ὧδε δὲ ἃ
λέγω σαφέστερον εἴσει. οὗτοι, φαμέν, τρεῖς ἂν
εἶεν δάκτυλοι, ὅ τε σμικρότατος καὶ ὁ δεύτερος
καὶ ὁ μέσος. Πάνυ γ', ἔφη. Ὡς ἐγγύθεν τοίνυν
ὁρωμένους λέγοντός μου διανοοῦ. ἀλλά μοι περὶ
αὐτῶν τόδε σκόπει. Τὸ ποῖον; Δάκτυλος μὲν
D αὐτῶν φαίνεται ὁμοίως ἕκαστος, καὶ ταύτῃ γε
οὐδὲν διαφέρει, ἐάν τε ἐν μέσῳ ὁρᾶται ἐάν τ' ἐν
ἐσχάτῳ, ἐάν τε λευκὸς ἐάν τε μέλας, ἐάν τε παχὺς
ἐάν τε λεπτός, καὶ πᾶν ὅ τι τοιοῦτον. ἐν πᾶσι γὰρ
τούτοις οὐκ ἀναγκάζεται τῶν πολλῶν ἡ ψυχὴ τὴν
νόησιν ἐπερέσθαι τί ποτ' ἐστὶ δάκτυλος· οὐδαμοῦ
γὰρ ἡ ὄψις αὐτῇ ἅμα ἐσήμηνε τὸν δάκτυλον του-
ναντίον ἢ δάκτυλον εἶναι. Οὐ γὰρ οὖν, ἔφη. Οὐκοῦν, ἦν δ' ἐγώ, εἰκότως τό γε τοιοῦτον νοήσεως
E οὐκ ἂν παρακλητικὸν οὐδ' ἐγερτικὸν εἴη. Εἰκότως.
Τί δὲ δή; τὸ μέγεθος αὐτῶν καὶ τὴν σμικρότητα
ἡ ὄψις ἆρα ἱκανῶς ὁρᾷ, καὶ οὐδὲν αὐτῇ διαφέρει ἐν
μέσῳ τινὰ αὐτῶν κεῖσθαι ἢ ἐπ' ἐσχάτῳ; καὶ

---

[a] Cf. Jacks, *Alchemy of Thought*, p. 29 : "The purpose of
the world, then, being to attain consciousness of itself as a
rational or consistent whole, is it not a little strange that the
first step, so to speak, taken by the world for the attainment
of this end is that of presenting itself in the form of contradictory experience?" αἴσθησις is not to be pressed. Adam's
condescending apology for the primitive character of Plato's
psychology here is as uncalled-for as all such apologies.
Plato varies the expression, but his meaning is clear. *Cf.*
524 D. No modern psychologists are able to use " sensation," " perception," " judgement," and similar terms with
perfect consistency.

[b] For προσπίπτουσα *cf. Tim.* 33 A. 44 A, 66 A, *Rep.* 515 A,

154

time issue in a contradictory perception.[a] Those that do have that effect I set down as provocatives, when the perception no more manifests one thing than its contrary, alike whether its impact [b] comes from nearby or afar. An illustration will make my meaning plain. Here, we say, are three fingers, the little finger, the second and the middle." "Quite so," he said. "Assume that I speak of them as seen near at hand. But this is the point that you are to consider." "What?" "Each one of them appears to be equally a finger,[c] and in this respect it makes no difference whether it is observed as intermediate or at either extreme, whether it is white or black, thick or thin, or of any other quality of this kind. For in none of these cases is the soul of most men impelled to question the reason and to ask what in the world is a finger, since the faculty of sight never signifies to it at the same time that the finger is the opposite of a finger." "Why, no, it does not," he said. "Then," said I, "it is to be expected that such a perception will not provoke or awaken [d] reflection and thought." "It is." "But now, what about the bigness and the smallness of these objects? Is our vision's view of them adequate, and does it make no difference to it whether one of them is situated [e] outside or in the middle; and similarly of the relation of

561 c, *Laws* 791 c, 632 A, 637 A, *Phileb.* 21 c; also *accidere* in Lucretius, *e.g.* iv. 882, ii. 1024-1025, iv. 236 and iii. 841, and Goethe's " Das Blenden der Erscheinung, die sich an unsere Sinne drängt."

[c] This anticipates Aristotle's doctrine that " substances " do not, as qualities do, admit of more or less.

[d] We should never press synonyms which Plato employs for ποικιλία of style or to avoid falling into a rut of terminology.

[e] κεῖσθαι perhaps anticipates the Aristotelian category.

523 ὡσαύτως πάχος καὶ λεπτότητα ἢ μαλακότητα καὶ
σκληρότητα ἡ ἁφή; καὶ αἱ ἄλλαι αἰσθήσεις ἀρ'
οὐκ ἐνδεῶς τὰ τοιαῦτα δηλοῦσιν; ἢ ὧδε ποιεῖ
524 ἑκάστη αὐτῶν· πρῶτον μὲν ἡ ἐπὶ τῷ σκληρῷ τε-
ταγμένη αἴσθησις ἠνάγκασται καὶ ἐπὶ τῷ μαλακῷ
τετάχθαι, καὶ παραγγέλλει τῇ ψυχῇ ὡς ταὐτὸν
σκληρόν τε καὶ μαλακὸν αἰσθανομένη; Οὕτως,
ἔφη. Οὐκοῦν, ἦν δ' ἐγώ, ἀναγκαῖον ἐν τοῖς τοιούτοις αὖ τὴν ψυχὴν ἀπορεῖν, τί ποτε σημαίνει αὐτῇ
ἡ αἴσθησις τὸ σκληρόν, εἴπερ τὸ αὐτὸ καὶ μαλακὸν
λέγει, καὶ ἡ τοῦ κούφου καὶ ἡ τοῦ βαρέος, τί τὸ
κοῦφον καὶ βαρύ, εἰ τό τε βαρὺ κοῦφον καὶ τὸ
B κοῦφον βαρὺ σημαίνει; Καὶ γάρ, ἔφη, αὗταί γε
ἄτοποι τῇ ψυχῇ αἱ ἑρμηνεῖαι καὶ ἐπισκέψεως
δεόμεναι. Εἰκότως ἄρα, ἦν δ' ἐγώ, ἐν τοῖς τοιούτοις πρῶτον μὲν πειρᾶται λογισμόν τε καὶ νόησιν
ψυχὴ παρακαλοῦσα ἐπισκοπεῖν, εἴτε ἓν εἴτε δύο
ἐστὶν ἕκαστα τῶν εἰσαγγελλομένων. Πῶς δ' οὔ;
Οὐκοῦν ἐὰν δύο φαίνηται, ἕτερόν τε καὶ ἓν ἑκά-

---

[a] Cf. *Theaet.* 186 ff., *Tim.* 62 B, Taylor, *Timaeus*, p. 233
on 63 D-E, *Unity of Plato's Thought*, nn. 222 and 225,
Diels, *Dialex.* 5 (ii.³ p. 341). *Protag.* 331 D anticipates this
thought, but Protagoras cannot follow it out. *Cf.* also
Phileb. 13 A-B. Stallbaum also compares *Phileb.* 57 D and
56 c f.

[b] Plato gives a very modern psychological explanation.
Thought is provoked by the contradictions in perceptions
that suggest problems. The very notion of unity is contradictory of uninterpreted experience. This use of ἀπορεῖν (*cf.*
supra 515 D) anticipates much modern psychology supposed
to be new. *Cf. e.g.* Herbert Spencer *passim*, and Dewey,
How We Think, p. 12 " We may recapitulate by saying that
the origin of thinking is some perplexity, confusion, or
doubt "; also *ibid.* p. 72. Meyerson, *Déduction relativiste*,

touch, to thickness and thinness, softness and hardness ? And are not the other senses also defective in their reports of such things ? Or is the operation of each of them as follows ? In the first place, the sensation that is set over the hard is of necessity related also to the soft,[a] and it reports to the soul that the same thing is both hard and soft to its perception." " It is so," he said. " Then," said I, " is not this again a case where the soul must be at a loss[b] as to what significance for it the sensation of hardness has, if the sense reports the same thing as also soft ? And, similarly, as to what the sensation of light and heavy means by light and heavy, if it reports the heavy as light, and the light as heavy ? " " Yes, indeed," he said, " these communications[c] to the soul are strange and invite reconsideration." " Naturally, then," said I, " it is in such cases as these that the soul first summons to its aid the calculating reason[d] and tries to consider whether each of the things reported to it is one or two.[e] " " Of course." " And if it appears to be two, each of the two is a distinct unit.[f] "

p. 142, says " Mais Platon . . . n'avait-il pas dit qu'il était impossible de raisonner si ce n'est en partant d'une perception ? " citing *Rep.* 523-524, and Rodier, Aristot. *De anima,* i. p. 197. But that is not Plato's point here. Zeller, *Aristot.* i. p. 166 (Eng.), also misses the point when he says " Even as to the passage from the former to the latter he had only the negative doctrine that the contradictions of opinion and fancy ought to lead us to go further and to pass to the pure treatment of ideas."

[c] For ἑρμηνεῖαι cf. *Theaet.* 209 A.

[d] Cf. *Parmen.* 130 A τοῖς λογισμῷ λαμβανομένοις.

[e] Cf. *Theaet.* 185 B, *Laws* 963 C, *Sophist* 254 D, *Hipp. Major* 301 D-E, and, for the dialectic here, *Parmen.* 143 D.

[f] Or, as the Greek puts it, " both ' one ' and ' other.' " Cf. Vol. I. p. 516, note f on 476 A. For ἕτερον cf. *What Plato Said,* pp. 522, 580, 587-588.

524 τερον φαίνεται; Ναί. Εἰ ἄρα ἓν ἑκάτερον, ἀμφότερα δὲ δύο, τά γε δύο κεχωρισμένα νοήσει· οὐ
C γὰρ ἂν ἀχώριστά γε δύο ἐνόει, ἀλλ' ἕν. Ὀρθῶς.
Μέγα μὴν καὶ ὄψις καὶ σμικρὸν ἑώρα, φαμέν,
ἀλλ' οὐ κεχωρισμένον ἀλλὰ συγκεχυμένον τι. ἦ
γάρ; Ναί. Διὰ δὲ τὴν τούτου σαφήνειαν μέγα αὖ
καὶ σμικρὸν ἡ νόησις ἠναγκάσθη ἰδεῖν, οὐ συγ-
κεχυμένα ἀλλὰ διωρισμένα, τοὐναντίον ἢ 'κείνη.
Ἀληθῆ. Οὐκοῦν ἐντεῦθέν ποθεν πρῶτον ἐπέρ-
χεται ἐρέσθαι ἡμῖν, τί οὖν ποτ' ἐστὶ τὸ μέγα αὖ
καὶ τὸ σμικρόν; Παντάπασι μὲν οὖν. Καὶ οὕτω
δὴ τὸ μὲν νοητόν, τὸ δ' ὁρατὸν ἐκαλέσαμεν.
D Ὀρθότατ', ἔφη.

VIII. Ταῦτα τοίνυν καὶ ἄρτι ἐπεχείρουν λέγειν,
ὡς τὰ μὲν παρακλητικὰ τῆς διανοίας ἐστί, τὰ δ'
οὔ, ἃ μὲν εἰς τὴν αἴσθησιν ἅμα τοῖς ἐναντίοις
ἑαυτοῖς ἐμπίπτει, παρακλητικὰ ὁριζόμενος, ὅσα
δὲ μή, οὐκ ἐγερτικὰ τῆς νοήσεως. Μανθάνω
τοίνυν ἤδη, ἔφη, καὶ δοκεῖ μοι οὕτως. Τί οὖν;

---

[a] γε vi termini. Cf. 379 B, 576 C, Parmen. 145 A, Protag.
358 c.

[b] κεχωρισμένα and ἀχώριστα suggest the terminology of
Aristotle in dealing with the problem of abstraction.

[c] Plato's aim is the opposite of that of the modern theorists
who say that teaching should deal integrally with the total
experience and not with the artificial division of abstraction.

[d] The final use of διά became more frequent in later Greek.
Cf. Aristot. Met. 982 b 20, Eth. Nic. 1110 a 4, Gen. an.
717 a 6, Poetics 1450 b 3, 1451 b 37. Cf. Lysis 218 D, Epin.
975 A, Olympiodorus, Life of Plato, Teubner vi. 191, ibid.
p. 218, and schol. passim, Apsines, Spengel i. 361, line 18.

[e] Plato merely means that this is the psychological origin

" Yes." " If, then, each is one and both two, the very meaning ^{a} of 'two' is that the soul will conceive them as distinct.^{b} For if they were not separable, it would not have been thinking of two, but of one." "Right." "Sight too saw the great and the small, we say, not separated but confounded.^{c} Is not that so?" "Yes." "And for ^{d} the clarification of this, the intelligence is compelled to contemplate the great and small,^{e} not thus confounded but as distinct entities, in the opposite way from sensation." "True." "And is it not in some such experience as this that the question first occurs to us, what in the world, then, is the great and the small?" "By all means." "And this is the origin of the designation *intelligible* for the one, and *visible* for the other." "Just so," he said.

VIII. "This, then, is just what I was trying to explain a little while ago when I said that some things are provocative of thought and some are not, defining as provocative things that impinge upon the senses together with their opposites, while those that do not I said do not tend to awaken reflection." "Well, now I understand," he said, "and agree."

---

of our attempt to form abstract and general ideas. My suggestion that this passage is the probable source of the notion which still infests the history of philosophy, that the great-and-the-small was a metaphysical entity or principle in Plato's later philosophy, to be identified with the indeterminate dyad, has been disregarded. *Cf. Unity of Plato's Thought*, p. 84. But it is the only plausible explanation that has ever been proposed of the attribution of that "clotted nonsense" to Plato himself. For it is fallacious to identify μᾶλλον καὶ ἧττον in *Philebus* 24 c, 25 c, 27 ε, and elsewhere with the μέγα καὶ σμικρόν. But there is no limit to the misapprehension of texts by hasty or fanciful readers in any age.

524 ἀριθμός τε καὶ τὸ ἓν ποτέρων δοκεῖ εἶναι; Οὐ
ξυννοῶ, ἔφη. Ἀλλ' ἐκ τῶν προειρημένων, ἔφην,
ἀναλογίζου. εἰ μὲν γὰρ ἱκανῶς αὐτὸ καθ' αὑτὸ
Ε ὁρᾶται ἢ ἄλλῃ τινὶ αἰσθήσει λαμβάνεται τὸ ἕν,
οὐκ ἂν ὁλκὸν εἴη ἐπὶ τὴν οὐσίαν, ὥσπερ ἐπὶ τοῦ
δακτύλου ἐλέγομεν· εἰ δ' ἀεί τι αὐτῷ ἅμα ὁρᾶται
ἐναντίωμα, ὥστε μηδὲν μᾶλλον ἓν ἢ καὶ τοὐναντίον
φαίνεσθαι, τοῦ ἐπικρινοῦντος δὴ δέοι ἂν ἤδη καὶ
ἀναγκάζοιτ' ἂν ἐν αὐτῷ ψυχὴ ἀπορεῖν καὶ ζητεῖν,
κινοῦσα ἐν ἑαυτῇ τὴν ἔννοιαν, καὶ ἀνερωτᾶν, τί
525 ποτ' ἐστὶν αὐτὸ τὸ ἕν, καὶ οὕτω τῶν ἀγωγῶν ἂν
εἴη καὶ μεταστρεπτικῶν ἐπὶ τὴν τοῦ ὄντος θέαν ἡ
περὶ τὸ ἓν μάθησις. Ἀλλὰ μέντοι, ἔφη, τοῦτό γ'
ἔχει οὐχ ἥκιστα ἡ περὶ αὐτὸ¹ ὄψις· ἅμα γὰρ
ταὐτὸν ὡς ἕν τε ὁρῶμεν καὶ ὡς ἄπειρα τὸ πλῆθος.
Οὐκοῦν εἴπερ τὸ ἕν, ἦν δ' ἐγώ, καὶ ξύμπας ἀριθμὸς
ταὐτὸν πέπονθε τούτῳ; Πῶς δ' οὔ; Ἀλλὰ μὴν
λογιστική τε καὶ ἀριθμητικὴ περὶ ἀριθμὸν πᾶσα.
Β Καὶ μάλα. Ταῦτα δέ γε φαίνεται ἀγωγὰ πρὸς
ἀλήθειαν. Ὑπερφυῶς μὲν οὖν. Ὧν ζητοῦμεν ἄρα,
ὡς ἔοικε, μαθημάτων ἂν εἴη· πολεμικῷ μὲν γὰρ
διὰ τὰς τάξεις ἀναγκαῖον μαθεῖν ταῦτα, φιλο-

---

¹ αὐτὸ F Iamblichus, τὸ αὐτὸ AD.

ᵃ To waive metaphysics, unity is, as modern mathematicians say, a concept of the mind which experience breaks up. The thought is familiar to Plato from the *Meno* to the *Parmenides.* But it is not true that Plato derived the very notion of the concept from the problem of the one and the many. Unity is a typical concept, but the consciousness of the concept was developed by the Socratic quest for the definition.

ᵇ *Cf.* 523 ʙ. The meaning must be gathered from the context.

ᶜ See crit. note and Adam *ad loc.*

"To which class, then, do you think number and the one belong [a] ?" "I cannot conceive," he said. "Well, reason it out from what has already been said. For, if unity is adequately [b] seen by itself or apprehended by some other sensation, it would not tend to draw the mind to the apprehension of essence, as we were explaining in the case of the finger. But if some contradiction is always seen coincidentally with it, so that it no more appears to be one than the opposite, there would forthwith be need of something to judge between them, and it would compel the soul to be at a loss and to inquire, by arousing thought in itself, and to ask, whatever then is the one as such, and thus the study of unity will be one of the studies that guide and convert the soul to the contemplation of true being." "But surely," he said, "the visual perception of it [c] does especially involve this. For we see the same thing at once as one and as an indefinite plurality.[d]" "Then if this is true of the one," I said, "the same holds of all number, does it not?" "Of course." "But, further, reckoning and the science of arithmetic [e] are wholly concerned with number." "They are, indeed." "And the qualities of number appear to lead to the apprehension of truth." "Beyond anything," he said. "Then, as it seems, these would be among the studies that we are seeking. For a soldier must learn them in order to marshal his troops, and a philosopher, because he must rise out of

[d] This is the problem of the one and the many with which Plato often plays, which he exhaustively and consciously illustrates in the *Parmenides*, and which the introduction to the *Philebus* treats as a metaphysical nuisance to be disregarded in practical logic. We have not yet got rid of it, but have merely transferred it to psychology.

[e] Cf. *Gorg.* 450 D, 451 B-C.

PLATO

525 σόφῳ δὲ διὰ τὸ τῆς οὐσίας ἁπτέον εἶναι γενέσεως
ἐξαναδύντι, ἢ μηδέποτε λογιστικῷ γενέσθαι. Ἔστι
ταῦτ', ἔφη. Ὁ δέ γε ἡμέτερος φύλαξ πολεμικός
τε καὶ φιλόσοφος τυγχάνει ὤν. Τί μήν; Προσῆκον δὴ τὸ μάθημα ἂν εἴη, ὦ Γλαύκων, νομοθε-
τῆσαι καὶ πείθειν τοὺς μέλλοντας ἐν τῇ πόλει τῶν
C μεγίστων μεθέξειν ἐπὶ λογιστικὴν ἰέναι καὶ ἀνθ-
άπτεσθαι αὐτῆς μὴ ἰδιωτικῶς, ἀλλ' ἕως ἂν ἐπὶ
θέαν τῆς τῶν ἀριθμῶν φύσεως ἀφίκωνται τῇ
νοήσει αὐτῇ, οὐκ ὠνῆς οὐδὲ πράσεως χάριν ὡς
ἐμπόρους ἢ καπήλους μελετῶντας, ἀλλ' ἕνεκα
πολέμου τε καὶ αὐτῆς τῆς ψυχῆς ῥᾳστώνης
μεταστροφῆς ἀπὸ γενέσεως ἐπ' ἀλήθειάν τε καὶ
οὐσίαν. Κάλλιστ', ἔφη, λέγεις. Καὶ μήν, ἦν δ'
ἐγώ, νῦν καὶ ἐννοῶ ῥηθέντος τοῦ περὶ τοὺς λογισ-
D μοὺς μαθήματος, ὡς κομψόν ἐστι καὶ πολλαχῇ
χρήσιμον ἡμῖν πρὸς ὃ βουλόμεθα, ἐὰν τοῦ γνωρίζειν
ἕνεκά τις αὐτὸ ἐπιτηδεύῃ, ἀλλὰ μὴ τοῦ καπηλεύειν.

---

[a] Cf. my review of Jowett, A.J.P. xiii. p. 365. My view
there is adopted by Adam ad loc., and Apelt translates in
the same way.

[b] It is not true as Adam says that " the nature of numbers
cannot be fully seen except in their connexion with the
Good." Plato never says that and never really meant it,
though he might possibly have affirmed it on a challenge.
Numbers are typical abstractions and educate the mind for
the apprehension of abstractions if studied in their nature,
in themselves, and not in the concrete form of five apples.
There is no common sense nor natural connexion between
numbers and the good, except the point made in the *Timaeus*
53 B, and which is not relevant here, that God used numbers
and forms to make a cosmos out of a chaos.

[c] Instead of remarking on Plato's scorn for the realities
of experience we should note that he is marking the distinctive quality of the mind of the Greeks in contrast with
the Egyptians and orientals from whom they learned and

the region of generation and lay hold on essence or he can never become a true reckoner.[a] " It is so," he said. " And our guardian is soldier and philosopher in one." " Of course." " It is befitting, then, Glaucon, that this branch of learning should be prescribed by our law and that we should induce those who are to share the highest functions of state to enter upon that study of calculation and take hold of it, not as amateurs, but to follow it up until they attain to the contemplation of the nature of number,[b] by pure thought, not for the purpose of buying and selling,[c] as if they were preparing to be merchants or hucksters, but for the uses of war and for facilitating the conversion of the soul itself from the world of generation to essence and truth." " Excellently said," he replied. " And, further," I said, " it occurs to me,[d] now that the study of reckoning has been mentioned, that there is something fine in it, and that it is useful for our purpose in many ways, provided it is pursued for the sake of knowledge[e] and not for

the Romans whom they taught. *Cf. infra* 525 D καπηλεύειν, and Horace, *Ars Poetica* 323-332, Cic. *Tusc.* i. 2. 5. *Per contra* Xen. *Mem.* iv. 7, and Libby, *Introduction to History of Science*, p. 49 : " In this the writer did not aim at the mental discipline of the students, but sought to confine himself to what is easiest and most useful in calculation, ' such as men constantly require in cases of inheritance, legacies, partition, law-suits, and trade, and in all their dealings with one another, or where the measuring of lands, the digging of canals, geometrical computation, and other objects of various sorts and kinds are concerned.'"

[d] *Cf.* on 521 D, p. 147, note *e*.

[e] *Cf.* Aristot. *Met.* 982 a 15 τοῦ εἰδέναι χάριν, and *Laws* 747 c. Montesquieu *apud* Arnold, *Culture and Anarchy*, p. 6 : " The first motive which ought to impel us to study is the desire to augment the excellence of our nature and to render an intelligent being more intelligent."

525 Πῇ δή; ἔφη. Τοῦτό γε, ὃ νῦν δὴ ἐλέγομεν, ὡς
σφόδρα ἄνω ποι ἄγει τὴν ψυχὴν καὶ περὶ αὐτῶν
τῶν ἀριθμῶν ἀναγκάζει διαλέγεσθαι, οὐδαμῇ ἀπο-
δεχόμενον ἐάν τις αὐτῇ ὁρατὰ ἢ ἁπτὰ σώματα
ἔχοντας ἀριθμοὺς προτεινόμενος διαλέγηται. οἶσθα
E γάρ που τοὺς περὶ ταῦτα δεινοὺς ὡς, ἐάν τις
αὐτὸ τὸ ἓν ἐπιχειρῇ τῷ λόγῳ τέμνειν, καταγελῶσί
τε καὶ οὐκ ἀποδέχονται, ἀλλ' ἐὰν σὺ κερματίζῃς
αὐτό, ἐκεῖνοι πολλαπλασιοῦσιν, εὐλαβούμενοι μή
ποτε φανῇ τὸ ἓν μὴ ἓν ἀλλὰ πολλὰ μόρια. Ἀληθέ-
526 στατα, ἔφη, λέγεις. Τί οὖν οἴει, ὦ Γλαύκων, εἴ
τις ἔροιτο αὐτούς, ὦ θαυμάσιοι, περὶ ποίων ἀριθμῶν διαλέγεσθε, ἐν οἷς τὸ ἓν οἷον ὑμεῖς ἀξιοῦτέ
ἐστιν, ἴσον τε ἕκαστον πᾶν παντὶ καὶ οὐδὲ σμικρὸν
διαφέρον, μόριόν τε ἔχον ἐν ἑαυτῷ οὐδέν; τί ἂν
οἴει αὐτοὺς ἀποκρίνασθαι; Τοῦτο ἔγωγε, ὅτι περὶ
τούτων λέγουσιν, ὧν διανοηθῆναι μόνον ἐγχωρεῖ,

---

a Lit. " numbers (in) themselves," *i.e.* ideal numbers or the
ideas of numbers. For this and the following as one of the
sources of the silly notion that mathematical numbers are
intermediate between ideal and concrete numbers, *cf.* my
De Platonis Idearum Doctrina, p. 33, *Unity of Plato's Thought*,
pp. 83-84, *Class. Phil.* xxii. (1927) pp. 213-218.

b Cf. *Meno* 79 c κατακερματίζῃς, Aristot. *Met.* 1041 a 19
ἀδιαίρετον πρὸς αὐτὸ ἕκαστον· τοῦτο δ' ἦν τὸ ἑνὶ εἶναι, *Met.*
1052 b 1 ff., 15 ff. and 1053 a 1 τὴν γὰρ μονάδα τιθέασι πάντῃ
ἀδιαίρετον. κερματίζειν is also the word used of breaking
money into small change.

c Numbers are the aptest illustration of the principle of
the *Philebus* and the *Parmenides* that thought has to
postulate unities which sensation (sense perception) and also
dialectics are constantly disintegrating into pluralities. *Cf.*
my *Idea of Good in Plato's Republic*, p. 222. Stenzel,
Dialektik, p. 32, says this dismisses the problem of the one
and the many " das ihn (Plato) später so lebhaft beschäftigen

huckstering." " In what respect ? " he said. "Why, in respect of the very point of which we were speaking, that it strongly directs the soul upward and compels it to discourse about pure numbers,[a] never acquiescing if anyone proffers to it in the discussion numbers attached to visible and tangible bodies. For you are doubtless aware that experts in this study, if anyone attempts to cut up the ' one ' in argument, laugh at him and refuse to allow it; but if *you* mince it up,[b] *they* multiply, always on guard lest the one should appear to be not one but a multiplicity of parts.[c] " " Most true," he replied. " Suppose now, Glaucon, someone were to ask them, ' My good friends, what numbers [d] are these you are talking about, in which the one is such as you postulate, each unity equal to every other without the slightest difference and admitting no division into parts ? ' What do you think would be their answer ? " " This, I think—that they are speaking of units which can only be conceived by thought, and which it is not possible to deal with in

sollte." But that is refuted by *Parmen.* 159 c οὐδὲ μὴν μόριά γε ἔχειν φαμὲν τὸ ὡς ἀληθῶς ἕν. The "problem" was always in Plato's mind. He played with it when it suited his purpose and dismissed it when he wished to go on to something else. *Cf.* on 525 A, *Phaedr.* 266 B, *Meno* 72 c, *Laws* 964 A, *Soph.* 251.

[d] This is one of the chief sources of the fancy that numbers are intermediate entities between ideas and things. *Cf.* Alexander, *Space, Time, and Deity,* i. p. 219 : "Mathematical particulars are therefore not as Plato thought intermediate between sensible figures and universals. Sensible figures are only less simple mathematical ones." *Cf.* on 525 D. Plato here and elsewhere simply means that the educator may distinguish two kinds of numbers,—five apples, and the number five as an abstract idea. *Cf. Theaet.* 195 E : We couldn't err about eleven which we only think, *i.e.* the abstract number eleven. *Cf.* also Berkeley, *Siris,* § 288.

526 ἄλλως δ' οὐδαμῶς μεταχειρίζεσθαι δυνατόν. Ὁρᾷς
οὖν, ἦν δ' ἐγώ, ὦ φίλε, ὅτι τῷ ὄντι ἀναγκαῖον ἡμῖν
B κινδυνεύει εἶναι τὸ μάθημα, ἐπειδὴ φαίνεταί γε
προσαναγκάζον αὐτῇ τῇ νοήσει χρῆσθαι τὴν ψυχὴν
ἐπ' αὐτὴν τὴν ἀλήθειαν; Καὶ μὲν δή, ἔφη, σφόδρα
γε ποιεῖ αὐτό. Τί δαί; τόδε ἤδη ἐπεσκέψω, ὡς
οἵ τε φύσει λογιστικοὶ εἰς πάντα τὰ μαθήματα ὡς
ἔπος εἰπεῖν ὀξεῖς φύονται, οἵ τε βραδεῖς, ἂν ἐν
τούτῳ παιδευθῶσι καὶ γυμνάσωνται, κἂν μηδὲν
ἄλλο ὠφεληθῶσιν, ὅμως εἴς γε τὸ ὀξύτεροι αὐτοὶ
αὑτῶν γίγνεσθαι πάντες ἐπιδιδόασιν; Ἔστιν, ἔφη,
C οὕτως. Καὶ μήν, ὡς ἐγῷμαι, ἅ γε μείζω πόνον
παρέχει μανθάνοντι καὶ μελετῶντι, οὐκ ἂν ῥᾳδίως
οὐδὲ πολλὰ ἂν εὕροις ὡς τοῦτο. Οὐ γὰρ οὖν.
Πάντων δὴ ἕνεκα τούτων οὐκ ἀφετέον τὸ μάθημα,
ἀλλ' οἱ ἄριστοι τὰς φύσεις παιδευτέοι ἐν αὐτῷ.
Ξύμφημι, ἦ δ' ὅς.

IX. Τοῦτο μὲν τοίνυν, εἶπον, ἓν ἡμῖν κείσθω·
δεύτερον δὲ τὸ ἐχόμενον τούτου σκεψώμεθα ἆρά τι
προσήκει ἡμῖν. Τὸ ποῖον; ἢ γεωμετρίαν, ἔφη,
λέγεις; Αὐτὸ τοῦτο, ἦν δ' ἐγώ. Ὅσον μέν, ἔφη,
D πρὸς τὰ πολεμικὰ αὐτοῦ τείνει, δῆλον ὅτι προσήκει·
πρὸς γὰρ τὰς στρατοπεδεύσεις καὶ καταλήψεις

―――――――――――――――――――――――

ᵃ Cf. Isoc. Antid. 267 αὐτοὶ δ' αὑτῶν εὐμαθέστεροι. For
the idiom αὐτοὶ αὑτῶν cf. also 411 c, 421 D, 571 D, Prot.
350 A and D, Laws 671 B, Parmen. 141 A, Laches 182 c.
Plato of course believed in mental discipline or "spread."
"Educators" have actually cited him as authority for the
opposite view. On the effect of mathematical studies cf.
also Laws 747 B, 809 C-D, 819 c, Isoc. Antid. 265. Cf. Max.
Tyr. 37 § 7 ἀλλὰ τοῦτο μὲν εἴη ἂν τι τῶν ἐν γεωμετρίᾳ τὸ
φαυλότατον. Mill on Hamilton ii. 311 "If the practice of
mathematical reasoning gives nothing else it gives wariness
of mind." Ibid. 312.

any other way." "You see, then, my friend," said I, "that this branch of study really seems to be indispensable for us, since it plainly compels the soul to employ pure thought with a view to truth itself." "It most emphatically does." "Again, have you ever noticed this, that natural reckoners are by nature quick in virtually all their studies? And the slow, if they are trained and drilled in this, even if no other benefit results, all improve and become quicker than they were[a]?" "It is so," he said. "And, further, as I believe, studies that demand more toil in the learning and practice than this we shall not discover easily nor find many of them.[b]" "You will not, in fact." "Then, for all these reasons, we must not neglect this study, but must use it in the education of the best endowed natures." "I agree," he said.

IX. "Assuming this one point to be established," I said, "let us in the second place consider whether the study that comes next[c] is suited to our purpose." "What is that? Do you mean geometry," he said. "Precisely that," said I. "So much of it," he said, "as applies to the conduct of war[d] is obviously suitable. For in dealing with encampments and the occupation

---

[b] The translation is, I think, right. *Cf. A.J.P.* xiii. p. 365, and Adam *ad loc.*

[c] *Cf.* Burnet, *Early Greek Philosophy*, p. 111: "Even Plato puts arithmetic before geometry in the *Republic* in deference to tradition." For the three branches of higher learning, arithmetic, geometry, and astronomy, *cf. Laws* 817 E-818 A, Isoc. *Antid.* 261-267, *Panath.* 26, *Bus.* 226; Max. Tyr. 37 § 7.

[d] *Cf. Basilicon Doron* (Morley, *A Miscellany*, p. 144): "I graunt it is meete yee have some entrance, specially in the Mathematickes, for the knowledge of the art militarie, in situation of Campes, ordering of battels, making fortifications, placing of batteries, or such like."

526 χωρίων καὶ συναγωγὰς καὶ ἐκτάσεις στρατιᾶς, καὶ
ὅσα δὴ ἄλλα σχηματίζουσι τὰ στρατόπεδα ἐν αὐταῖς τε ταῖς μάχαις καὶ πορείαις, διαφέροι ἂν
αὐτὸς αὑτοῦ γεωμετρικὸς καὶ μὴ ὤν. Ἀλλ' οὖν
δή, εἶπον, πρὸς μὲν τὰ τοιαῦτα βραχύ τι ἂν ἐξαρκοῖ
γεωμετρίας τε καὶ λογισμῶν μόριον· τὸ δὲ πολὺ
E αὐτῆς καὶ πορρωτέρω προϊὸν σκοπεῖσθαι δεῖ, εἴ
τι πρὸς ἐκεῖνο τείνει, πρὸς τὸ ποιεῖν κατιδεῖν ῥᾷον
τὴν τοῦ ἀγαθοῦ ἰδέαν. τείνει δέ, φαμέν, πάντα αὐ-
τόσε, ὅσα ἀναγκάζει ψυχὴν εἰς ἐκεῖνον τὸν τόπον
μεταστρέφεσθαι, ἐν ᾧ ἐστὶ τὸ εὐδαιμονέστατον τοῦ
ὄντος, ὃ δεῖ αὐτὴν παντὶ τρόπῳ ἰδεῖν. Ὀρθῶς, ἔφη,
λέγεις. Οὐκοῦν εἰ μὲν οὐσίαν ἀναγκάζει θεάσασθαι,
προσήκει, εἰ δὲ γένεσιν, οὐ προσήκει. Φαμέν γε
527 δή. Οὐ τοίνυν τοῦτό γε, ἦν δ' ἐγώ, ἀμφισβητή-
σουσιν ἡμῖν, ὅσοι καὶ σμικρὰ γεωμετρίας ἔμπειροι,
ὅτι αὕτη ἡ ἐπιστήμη πᾶν τοὐναντίον ἔχει τοῖς ἐν
αὐτῇ λόγοις λεγομένοις ὑπὸ τῶν μεταχειριζομένων.

---

[a] This was Xenophon's view, *Mem.* vi. 7. 2. Whether it
was Socrates' nobody knows. *Cf. supra* pp. 162-163 on 525 c,
Epin. 977 E, Aristoph. *Clouds* 202.

[b] Because it develops the power of abstract thought. Not
because numbers are deduced from the idea of good. *Cf.*
on 525, p. 162, note b.

[c] *Cf.* 518 c. Once more we should remember that for the
practical and educational application of Plato's main thought
this and all similar expressions are rhetorical surplusage or
"unction," which should not be pressed, nor used *e.g.* to
identify the idea of good with God. *Cf.* Introd. p. xxv.

[d] Or "becoming." *Cf.* 485 B, 525 B.

[e] γε δή is frequent in confirming answers. *Cf.* 557 B, 517 C,
Symp. 172 C, 173 E, *Gorg.* 449 B, etc.

of strong places and the bringing of troops into column and line and all the other formations of an army in actual battle and on the march, an officer who had studied geometry would be a very different person from what he would be if he had not." "But still," I said, "for such purposes a slight modicum *a* of geometry and calculation would suffice. What we have to consider is whether the greater and more advanced part of it tends to facilitate the apprehension of the idea of good.*b* That tendency, we affirm, is to be found in all studies that force the soul to turn its vision round to the region where dwells the most blessed part of reality,*c* which it is imperative that it should behold." "You are right," he said. "Then if it compels the soul to contemplate essence, it is suitable; if genesis,*d* it is not." "So we affirm.*e*" "This at least," said I, "will not be disputed by those who have even a slight acquaintance with geometry, that this science is in direct contradiction with the language employed in it by its adepts.*f*" "How so?"

f Geometry (and mathematics) is inevitably less abstract than dialectics. But the special purpose of the Platonic education values mathematics chiefly as a discipline in abstraction. *Cf.* on 523 A, p. 152, note *b*; and Titchener, *A Beginner's Psychology*, pp. 265-266: "There are probably a good many of us whose abstract idea of 'triangle' is simply a mental picture of the little equilateral triangle that stands for the word in text-books of geometry." There have been some attempts to prove (that of Mr. F. M. Cornford in *Mind*, April 1932, is the most recent) that Plato, if he could not anticipate in detail the modern reduction of mathematics to logic, did postulate something like it as an ideal, the realization of which would abolish his own sharp distinction between mathematics and dialectic. The argument rests on a remote and strained interpretation of two or three texts of the *Republic* (*cf. e.g.* 511 and 533 B-D) which, naturally interpreted, merely affirm the general inferiority of the

527 Πῶς; ἔφη. Λέγουσι μέν που μάλα γελοίως τε καὶ ἀναγκαίως· ὡς γὰρ πράττοντές τε καὶ πράξεως ἕνεκα πάντας τοὺς λόγους ποιούμενοι λέγουσι τετραγωνίζειν τε καὶ παρατείνειν καὶ προστιθέναι καὶ πάντα οὕτω φθεγγόμενοι· τὸ δ᾽ Β ἔστι που πᾶν τὸ μάθημα γνώσεως ἕνεκα ἐπιτηδευόμενον. Παντάπασι μὲν οὖν, ἔφη. Οὐκοῦν τοῦτο ἔτι διομολογητέον; Τὸ ποῖον; Ὡς τοῦ ἀεὶ ὄντος γνώσεως, ἀλλ᾽ οὐ τοῦ ποτέ τι γιγνομένου καὶ ἀπολλυμένου. Εὐομολόγητον, ἔφη· τοῦ γὰρ ἀεὶ ὄντος ἡ γεωμετρικὴ γνῶσίς ἐστιν. Ὁλκὸν ἄρα, ὦ γενναῖε, ψυχῆς πρὸς ἀλήθειαν εἴη ἂν καὶ

mathematical method and the intermediate position for education of mathematics as a propaedeutic to dialectics. Plato's purpose throughout is not to exhort mathematicians as such to question their initiatory postulates, but to mark definitely the boundaries between the mathematical and other sciences and pure dialectics or philosophy. The distinction is a true and useful one to-day. Aristotle often refers to it with no hint that it could not be abolished by a new and different kind of mathematics. And it is uncritical to read that intention into Plato's words. He may have contributed, and doubtless did contribute, in other ways to the improvement and precision of mathematical logic. But he had no idea of doing away with the fundamental difference that made dialectics and not mathematics the coping-stone of the higher education—science as such does not question its first principles and dialectic does. Cf. 533 B-534 E.

ᵃ The very etymology of "geometry" implies the absurd practical conception of the science. Cf. Epin. 990 c γελοῖον ὄνομα.

ᵇ Cf. Polit. 302 E, Laws 757 E, 818 B, Phileb. 62 B, Tim. 69 D, and also on 494 A. The word ἀναγκαίως has been variously misunderstood and mistranslated. It simply means that geometers are compelled to use the language he said. "Their language is most ludicrous,[a] though they cannot help it,[b] for they speak as if they were doing something[c] and as if all their words were directed towards action. For all their talk[d] is of squaring and applying[e] and adding and the like,[f] whereas in fact the real object of the entire study is pure knowledge.[g]" "That is absolutely true," he said. "And must we not agree on a further point?" "What?" "That it is the knowledge of that which always is,[h] and not of a something which at some time comes into being and passes away." "That is readily admitted," he said, "for geometry is the knowledge of the eternally existent." "Then, my good friend, it would tend to draw the soul to truth, and would be

of sense perception though they are thinking of abstractions (ideas) of which sense images are only approximations.

[c] Cf. Aristot. *Met.* 1051 a 22 εὑρίσκεται δὲ καὶ τὰ διαγράμματα ἐνεργείᾳ· διαιροῦντες γὰρ εὑρίσκουσιν, "geometrical constructions, too, are discovered by an actualization, because it is by dividing that we discover them." (Loeb tr.)

[d] For φθεγγόμενοι cf. on 505 c, p. 89, note g.

[e] Cf. Thompson on *Meno* 87 A.

[f] E. Hoffmann, *Der gegenwärtige Stand der Platonforschung*, p. 1097 (Anhang, Zeller, *Plato*, 5th ed.), misunderstands the passage when he says: "Die Abneigung Platons, dem Ideellen irgendwie einen dynamischen Charakter zuzuschreiben, zeigt sich sogar in terminologischen Andeutungen; so verbietet er *Republ.* 527 A für die Mathematik jede Anwendung dynamischer Termini wie τετραγωνίζειν, παρατείνειν, προστιθέναι." Plato does not forbid the use of such terms but merely recognizes their inadequacy to express the true nature and purpose of geometry.

[g] Cf. Meyerson, *De l'explication dans les sciences*, p. 33: "En effet, Platon déjà fait ressortir que la géométrie, en dépit de l'apparence, ne poursuit aucun but pratique et n'a tout entière d'autre objet que la connaissance."

[h] *i.e.* mathematical ideas are (Platonic) ideas like other concepts. *Cf.* on 525 D, p. 164, note a.

527 ἀπεργαστικὸν φιλοσόφου διανοίας πρὸς τὸ ἄνω
σχεῖν ἃ νῦν κάτω οὐ δέον ἔχομεν. Ὡς οἷόν τε
C μάλιστα, ἔφη. Ὡς οἷόν τ' ἄρα, ἦν δ' ἐγώ, μάλιστα προστακτέον ὅπως οἱ ἐν τῇ καλλιπόλει σοι
μηδενὶ τρόπῳ γεωμετρίας ἀφέξονται. καὶ γὰρ τὰ
πάρεργα αὐτοῦ οὐ σμικρά. Ποῖα; ἦ δ' ὅς. Ἅ
τε δὴ σὺ εἶπες, ἦν δ' ἐγώ, τὰ περὶ τὸν πόλεμον,
καὶ δὴ καὶ πρὸς πάσας μαθήσεις, ὥστε κάλλιον
ἀποδέχεσθαι, ἴσμεν που ὅτι τῷ ὅλῳ καὶ παντὶ
διοίσει ἡμμένος τε γεωμετρίας καὶ μή. Τῷ παντὶ
μέντοι νὴ Δί', ἔφη. Δεύτερον δὴ τοῦτο τιθῶμεν
μάθημα τοῖς νέοις; Τιθῶμεν, ἔφη.

D X. Τί δαί; τρίτον θῶμεν ἀστρονομίαν; ἢ οὐ
δοκεῖ; Ἔμοιγ' οὖν, ἔφη· τὸ γὰρ περὶ ὥρας εὐ-
αισθητοτέρως ἔχειν καὶ μηνῶν καὶ ἐνιαυτῶν οὐ
μόνον γεωργίᾳ οὐδὲ ναυτιλίᾳ προσήκει, ἀλλὰ καὶ
στρατηγίᾳ οὐχ ἧττον. Ἡδὺς εἶ, ἦν δ' ἐγώ, ὅτι
ἔοικας δεδιότι τοὺς πολλούς, μὴ δοκῇς ἄχρηστα
μαθήματα προστάττειν. τὸ δ' ἔστιν οὐ πάνυ
φαῦλον ἀλλὰ χαλεπὸν πιστεῦσαι, ὅτι ἐν τούτοις
τοῖς μαθήμασιν ἑκάστου ὄργανόν τι ψυχῆς ἐκκαθ-

ᵃ καλλιπόλει: Plato smiles at his own Utopia. There were
cities named Callipolis, *e.g.* in the Thracian Chersonese and
in Calabria on the Gulf of Tarentum. *Cf.* also Herod. vii. 154.
Fanciful is the attempt of some scholars to distinguish the
Callipolis as a separate section of the *Republic*, or to take it
as the title of the *Republic*.

ᵇ Plato briefly anticipates much modern literature on the
value of the study of mathematics. *Cf.* on 526 в, p. 166, note
а. Olympiodorus says that when geometry deigns to enter
into matter she creates mechanics which is highly esteemed.

productive of a philosophic attitude of mind, directing upward the faculties that now wrongly are turned earthward." "Nothing is surer," he said. "Then nothing is surer," said I, "than that we must require that the men of your Fair City *a* shall never neglect geometry, for even the by-products of such study are not slight." "What are they?" said he. "What you mentioned," said I, "its uses in war, and also we are aware that for the better reception of all studies *b* there will be an immeasurable *c* difference between the student who has been imbued with geometry and the one who has not." "Immense indeed, by Zeus," he said. "Shall we, then, lay this down as a second branch of study for our lads?" "Let us do so," he said.

X. "Shall we set down astronomy as a third, or do you dissent?" "I certainly agree," he said; "for quickness of perception about the seasons and the courses of the months and the years is serviceable,*d* not only to agriculture and navigation, but still more to the military art." "I am amused,*e*" said I, "at your apparent fear lest the multitude *f* may suppose you to be recommending useless studies.*g* It is indeed no trifling task, but very difficult to realize that there is in every soul an organ or instrument of knowledge that is purified *h* and kindled afresh by such studies

c For ὅλῳ καὶ παντί cf. 469 c, *Laws* 779 b, 734 e, *Phaedo* 79 e, *Crat.* 434 a.

d Xen. *Mem.* iv. 7. 3 ff. attributes to Socrates a similar purely utilitarian view of science.

e For ἡδὺς εἶ cf. 337 d, *Euthydem.* 300 a, *Gorg.* 491 e ἥδιστε, *Rep.* 348 c γλυκὺς εἶ, *Hipp. Maj.* 288 b.

f Cf. on 499 d-e, p. 66, note *a*.

g Again Plato anticipates much modern controversy.

h Cf. Xen. *Symp.* 1. 4 ἐκκεκαθαρμένοις τὰς ψυχάς, and *Phaedo* 67 b-c.

527 E αἴρεταί τε καὶ ἀναζωπυρεῖται ἀπολλύμενον καὶ τυ-
φλούμενον ὑπὸ τῶν ἄλλων ἐπιτηδευμάτων, κρεῖττον
ὂν σωθῆναι μυρίων ὀμμάτων· μόνῳ γὰρ αὐτῷ
ἀλήθεια ὁρᾶται. οἷς μὲν οὖν ταῦτα ξυνδοκεῖ,
ἀμηχάνως ὡς εὖ δόξεις λέγειν· ὅσοι δὲ τούτου μηδαμῇ ἠσθημένοι εἰσίν, εἰκότως ἡγήσονταί σε λέγειν
οὐδέν· ἄλλην γὰρ ἀπ' αὐτῶν οὐχ ὁρῶσιν ἀξίαν
λόγου ὠφέλειαν. σκόπει οὖν αὐτόθεν, πρὸς ποτέ-
528 ρους διαλέγει, ἢ οὐ πρὸς οὐδετέρους, ἀλλὰ σαυτοῦ
ἕνεκα τὸ μέγιστον ποιεῖ τοὺς λόγους, φθονοῖς μὴν
οὐδ' ἂν ἄλλῳ, εἴ τίς τι δύναιτο ἀπ' αὐτῶν ὄνασθαι.
Οὕτως, ἔφη, αἱροῦμαι, ἐμαυτοῦ ἕνεκα τὸ πλεῖστον
λέγειν τε καὶ ἐρωτᾶν καὶ ἀποκρίνεσθαι. Ἄναγε
τοίνυν, ἦν δ' ἐγώ, εἰς τοὐπίσω· νῦν δὴ γὰρ οὐκ
ὀρθῶς τὸ ἑξῆς ἐλάβομεν τῇ γεωμετρίᾳ. Πῶς
λαβόντες; ἔφη. Μετὰ ἐπίπεδον, ἦν δ' ἐγώ, ἐν
περιφορᾷ ὂν ἤδη στερεὸν λαβόντες, πρὶν αὐτὸ καθ'
B αὐτὸ λαβεῖν· ὀρθῶς δὲ ἔχει ἑξῆς μετὰ δευτέραν
αὔξην τρίτην λαμβάνειν. ἔστι δέ που τοῦτο περὶ
τὴν τῶν κύβων αὔξην καὶ τὸ βάθους μετέχον.
Ἔστι γάρ, ἔφη· ἀλλὰ ταῦτά γε, ὦ Σώκρατες,

---

[a] Another instance of Plato's "unction." *Cf. Tim.* 47 A-B,
Eurip. *Orest.* 806 μυρίων κρείσσων, and Stallbaum *ad loc.*
for imitations of this passage in antiquity.

[b] For ἀμηχάνως ὡς cf. *Charm.* 155 D ἀμήχανόν τι οἷον.
Cf. 588 A, *Phaedo* 80 C, 95 C, *Laws* 782 A, also *Rep.* 331 A
θαυμαστῶς ὡς, *Hipp. Maj.* 282 C, *Epin.* 982 C-D, Aristoph.
Birds 427, *Lysist.* 198, 1148.

[c] This is the thought more technically expressed in the
"earlier" work, *Crito* 49 D. Despite his faith in dialectics

when it has been destroyed and blinded by our ordinary pursuits, a faculty whose preservation outweighs ten thousand eyes[a]; for by it only is reality beheld. Those who share this faith will think your words superlatively[b] true. But those who have and have had no inkling of it will naturally think them all moonshine.[c] For they can see no other benefit from such pursuits worth mentioning. Decide, then, on the spot, to which party you address yourself. Or are you speaking to neither, but chiefly carrying on the discussion for your own sake,[d] without however grudging any other who may be able to profit by it?" "This is the alternative I choose," he said, "that it is for my own sake chiefly that I speak and ask questions and reply." "Fall back[e] a little, then," said I; "for we just now did not rightly select the study that comes next[f] after geometry." "What was our mistake?" he said. "After plane surfaces," said I, "we went on to solids in revolution before studying them in themselves. The right way is next in order after the second dimension[g] to take the third. This, I suppose, is the dimension of cubes and of everything that has depth." "Why, yes, it is," he said; "but this subject, Socrates, does not appear to have been investi-

Plato recognizes that the primary assumptions on which argument necessarily proceeds are irreducible choices of personality. *Cf. What Plato Said*, p. 468, *Class. Phil.* ix. (1914) p. 352.

[d] *Cf. Charm.* 166 D, *Phaedo* 64 C, *Soph.* 265 A, *Apol.* 33 A.

[e] ἀναγε is a military term. *Cf.* Aristoph. *Birds* 383, Xen. *Cyr.* vii. 1. 45, iii. 3. 69.

[f] ἐξῆς: *cf. Laches* 182 B.

[g] Lit. "increase." *Cf.* Pearson, *The Grammar of Science*, p. 411: "He proceeds from curves of frequency to surfaces of frequency, and then requiring to go beyond these he finds his problem lands him in space of many dimensions."

528 δοκεῖ οὔπω εὑρῆσθαι. Διττὰ γάρ, ἦν δ' ἐγώ, τὰ
αἴτια· ὅτι τε οὐδεμία πόλις ἐντίμως αὐτὰ ἔχει,
ἀσθενῶς ζητεῖται χαλεπὰ ὄντα, ἐπιστάτου τε
δέονται οἱ ζητοῦντες, ἄνευ οὗ οὐκ ἂν εὕροιεν,
ὃν πρῶτον μὲν γενέσθαι χαλεπόν, ἔπειτα καὶ γενομένου, ὡς νῦν ἔχει, οὐκ ἂν πείθοιντο οἱ περὶ ταῦτα
C ζητητικοὶ μεγαλοφρονούμενοι. εἰ δὲ πόλις ὅλη
ξυνεπιστατοῖ ἐντίμως ἄγουσα αὐτά, οὗτοί τε ἂν
πείθοιντο καὶ ξυνεχῶς τε ἂν καὶ ἐντόνως ζητούμενα
ἐκφανῆ γένοιτο ὅπῃ ἔχει· ἐπεὶ καὶ νῦν ὑπὸ τῶν
πολλῶν ἀτιμαζόμενα καὶ κολουόμενα[1] ὑπὸ[2] τῶν
ζητούντων, λόγον οὐκ ἐχόντων καθ' ὅ τι χρήσιμα,
ὅμως πρὸς ἅπαντα ταῦτα βίᾳ ὑπὸ χάριτος αὐξά-

[1] κολουόμενα AD, κωλυόμενα F.
[2] ὑπὸ Madvig : ὑπὸ δὲ mss.

---

[a] This is not to be pressed. Plato means only that the
progress of solid geometry is unsatisfactory. *Cf.* 528 D.
There may or may not be a reference here to the "Delian
problem" of the duplication of the cube (*cf.* Wilamowitz,
Platon, i. p. 503 for the story) and other specific problems which
the historians of mathematics discuss in connexion with this
passage. *Cf.* Adam *ad loc.* To understand Plato we need
only remember that the extension of geometry to solids was
being worked out in his day, perhaps partly at his suggestion, *e.g.* by Theaetetus for whom a Platonic dialogue is
named, and that Plato makes use of the discovery of the five
regular solids in his theory of the elements in the *Timaeus*.
Cf. also *Laws* 819 E ff. For those who wish to know more of
the ancient traditions and modern conjectures I add references: Eva Sachs, *De Theaeteto Ath. Mathematico*, Diss.
Berlin, 1914, and *Die fünf platonischen Körper* (Philolog.
Untersuch. Heft 24), Berlin, 1917; E. Hoppe, *Mathematik
und Astronomie im klass. Altertum*, pp. 133 ff.; Rudolf
Ebeling, *Mathematik und Philosophie bei Plato*, Münden,
1909, with my review in *Class. Phil.* v. (1910) p. 115; Seth

gated yet.[a] " "There are two causes of that," said I :
" first, inasmuch as no city holds them in honour,
these inquiries are languidly pursued owing to their
difficulty. And secondly, the investigators need a
director,[b] who is indispensable for success and who, to
begin with, is not easy to find, and then, if he could
be found, as things are now, seekers in this field
would be too arrogant[c] to submit to his guidance. But
if the state as a whole should join in superintending
these studies and honour them, these specialists
would accept advice, and continuous and strenuous
investigation would bring out the truth. Since even
now, lightly esteemed as they are by the multitude
and hampered by the ignorance of their students[d] as
to the true reasons for pursuing them,[e] they nevertheless in the face of all these obstacles force their way
by their inherent charm[f] and it would not surprise us

Demel, *Platons Verhältnis zur Mathematik*, Leipzig, with
my review, *Class. Phil.* xxiv. (1929) pp. 312-313; and, for
further bibliography on Plato and mathematics, Budé, *Rep.*
Introd. pp. lxx-lxxi.

[b] Plato is perhaps speaking from personal experience as
director of the Academy. *Cf.* the hint in *Euthydem.* 290 c.

[c] *i.e.* the mathematicians already feel themselves to be independent specialists.

[d] This interpretation is, I think, correct. For the construction of this sentence *cf.* Isoc. xv. 84. The text is
disputed ; see crit. note.

[e] Lit. "in what respect they are useful." Plato is
fond of the half legal καθ' ὅ τι. *Cf. Lysis* 210 c, *Polit.*
298 c.

[f] An eminent modern psychologist innocently writes: " The
problem of why geometry gives pleasure is therefore a deeper
problem than the mere assertion of the fact. Furthermore,
there are many known cases where the study of geometry
does not give pleasure to the student." Adam seems to
think it may refer to the personality of Eudoxus.

528 D νεται, καὶ οὐδὲν θαυμαστὸν αὐτὰ φανῆναι. Καὶ μὲν δή, ἔφη, τό γε ἐπίχαρι καὶ διαφερόντως ἔχει. ἀλλά μοι σαφέστερον εἰπὲ ἃ νῦν δὴ ἔλεγες. τὴν μὲν γάρ που τοῦ ἐπιπέδου πραγματείαν[a] γεωμετρίαν ἐτίθεις. Ναί, ἦν δ' ἐγώ. Εἶτά γ', ἔφη, τὸ μὲν πρῶτον ἀστρονομίαν μετὰ ταύτην, ὕστερον δ' ἀνεχώρησας. Σπεύδων γάρ, ἔφην, ταχὺ πάντα διεξελθεῖν μᾶλλον βραδύνω·[b] ἑξῆς γὰρ οὖσαν τὴν βάθους αὔξης μέθοδον, ὅτι τῇ ζητήσει γελοίως ἔχει, ὑπερβὰς αὐτὴν μετὰ γεωμετρίαν ἀστρονομίαν
E ἔλεγον, φορὰν οὖσαν βάθους. Ὀρθῶς, ἔφη, λέγεις. Τέταρτον τοίνυν, ἦν δ' ἐγώ, τιθῶμεν μάθημα ἀστρονομίαν, ὡς ὑπαρχούσης τῆς νῦν παραλειπομένης, ἐὰν αὐτὴν πόλις μετίῃ. Εἰκός, ᾗ δ' ὅς· καὶ ὅ γε νῦν δή μοι, ὦ Σώκρατες, ἐπέπληξας περὶ ἀστρονομίας ὡς φορτικῶς ἐπαινοῦντι, νῦν ᾗ σὺ
529 μετέρχει ἐπαινῶ. παντὶ γάρ μοι δοκεῖ δῆλον, ὅτι

---

[a] πραγματείαν: interesting is the development of this word from its use in *Phaedo* 63 A (" interest," " zeal," " inquiring spirit." *Cf.* 64 E, 67 B) to the later meaning, " treatise." *Cf.* Aristot. *Top.* 100 a 18, *Eth. Nic.* 1103 b 26, Polyb. i. 1. 4, etc.

[b] An obvious allusion to the proverb found in many forms in many languages. *Cf.* also *Polit.* 277 A-B, 264 B, Soph. *Antig.* 231 σχολῇ ταχύς, Theognis 335, 401 μηδὲν ἄγαν σπεύδειν, Suetonius, *Augustus* 25, Aulus Gellius x. 11. 5, Macrob. *Sat.* vi. 8. 9, " festina lente," " hâtez-vous lentement" (Boileau, *Art poétique*, i. 171), " Chi va piano va sano e va lontano" (Goldoni, *I volponi*, i. ii.), " Eile mit Weile" and similar expressions; Franklin's " Great haste makes great waste," etc.

if the truth about them were made apparent." "It is true," he said, "that they do possess an extraordinary attractiveness and charm. But explain more clearly what you were just speaking of. The investigation *a* of plane surfaces, I presume, you took to be geometry?" "Yes," said I. "And then," he said, "at first you took astronomy next and then you drew back." "Yes," I said, "for in my haste to be done I was making less speed.*b* For, while the next thing in order is the study *c* of the third dimension or solids, I passed it over because of our absurd neglect *d* to investigate it, and mentioned next after geometry astronomy,*e* which deals with the movements of solids." "That is right," he said. "Then, as our fourth study," said I, "let us set down astronomy, assuming that this science, the discussion of which has been passed over, is available,*f* provided, that is, that the state pursues it." "That is likely," said he; "and instead of the vulgar utilitarian *g* commendation of astronomy, for which you just now rebuked me, Socrates, I now will praise it on your principles. For it is obvious to everybody,

---

c μέθοδον: this word, like πραγματεία, came to mean "treatise."

d This is the meaning. Neither Stallbaum's explanation, "quia ita est comparata, ut de ea quaerere ridiculum sit," nor that accepted by Adam, "quia ridicule tractatur," is correct, and 529 E and 527 A are not in point. *Cf.* 528 B, p. 176, note *a*.

e *Cf. Laws* 822 A ff.

f *i.e.* "assuming this to exist," "vorhanden sein," which is the usual meaning of ὑπάρχειν in classical Greek. The science, of course, is solid geometry, which is still undeveloped, but in Plato's state will be constituted as a regular science through endowed research.

g *Cf.* Vol. I. p. 410, note *c*, on 442 E, *Gorg.* 482 E, *Rep.* 367 A, 581 D, *Cratyl.* 400 A, *Apol.* 32 A, Aristot. *Pol.* 1333 b 9.

529 αὕτη γε ἀναγκάζει ψυχὴν εἰς τὸ ἄνω ὁρᾶν καὶ ἀπὸ
τῶν ἐνθένδε ἐκεῖσε ἄγει. Ἴσως, ἦν δ' ἐγώ, παντὶ
δῆλον πλὴν ἐμοί· ἐμοὶ γὰρ οὐ δοκεῖ οὕτως. Ἀλλὰ
πῶς; ἔφη. Ὡς μὲν νῦν αὐτὴν μεταχειρίζονται
οἱ εἰς φιλοσοφίαν ἀνάγοντες, πάνυ ποιεῖν κάτω
βλέπειν. Πῶς, ἔφη, λέγεις; Οὐκ ἀγεννῶς μοι
δοκεῖς, ἦν δ' ἐγώ, τὴν περὶ τὰ ἄνω μάθησιν λαμ-
B βάνειν παρὰ σαυτῷ ἥ ἐστι· κινδυνεύεις γάρ, καὶ
εἴ τις ἐν ὀροφῇ ποικίλματα θεώμενος ἀνακύπτων
καταμανθάνοι τι, ἡγεῖσθαι ἂν αὐτὸν νοήσει ἀλλ'
οὐκ ὄμμασι θεωρεῖν. ἴσως οὖν καλῶς ἡγεῖ, ἐγὼ
δ' εὐηθικῶς. ἐγὼ γὰρ αὖ οὐ δύναμαι ἄλλο τι
νομίσαι ἄνω ποιοῦν ψυχὴν βλέπειν μάθημα ἢ
ἐκεῖνο ὃ ἂν περὶ τὸ ὄν τε ᾖ καὶ τὸ ἀόρατον· ἐὰν

---

[a] *Cf.* my review of Warburg, *Class. Phil.* xxiv. (1929) p.
319. The dramatic misunderstanding forestalls a possible
understanding by the reader. *Cf. supra* on 523 B. The
misapprehension is typical of modern misunderstandings.
Glaucon is here the prototype of all sentimental Platonists
or anti-Platonists. The meaning of "higher" things in
Plato's allegory is obvious. But Glaucon takes it literally.
Similarly, modern critics, taking Plato's imagery literally
and pressing single expressions apart from the total context,
have inferred that Plato would be hostile to all the applications of modern science to experience. They refuse to make
allowance for his special and avowed educational purpose,
and overlook the fact that he is prophesying the mathematical astronomy and science of the future. The half-serious
exaggeration of his rhetoric can easily be matched by similar
utterances of modern thinkers of the most various schools,
from Rousseau's "écarter tous les faits" to Judd's "Once
we acquire the power to neglect all the concrete facts . . .
we are free from the incumbrances that come through attention to the concrete facts." *Cf.* also on 529 B, 530 B and
534 A.

[b] ἀνάγοντες is tinged with the suggestions of *supra* 517 A, but

I think, that this study certainly compels the soul to look upward [a] and leads it away from things here to those higher things." " It may be obvious to everybody except me," said I, " for I do not think so." " What do you think ? " he said. " As it is now handled by those who are trying to lead us up to philosophy,[b] I think that it turns the soul's gaze very much downward." " What do you mean ? " he said. " You seem to me in your thought to put a most liberal [c] interpretation on the ' study of higher things,' " I said, " for apparently if anyone with back-thrown head should learn something by staring at decorations on a ceiling, you would regard him as contemplating them with the higher reason and not with the eyes.[d] Perhaps you are right and I am a simpleton. For I, for my part, am unable to suppose that any other study turns the soul's gaze upward [e] than that which deals with being

the meaning here is those who use astronomy as a part of the higher education. φιλοσοφία is used in the looser sense of Isocrates. Cf. A.J.P. xvi. p. 237.

[c] For οὐκ ἀγεννῶς cf. Gorg. 462 D, where it is ironical, as here, Phaedr. 264 B, Euthyph. 2 c, Theaet. 184 c. In Charm. 158 c it is not ironical.

[d] The humorous exaggeration of the language reflects Plato's exasperation at the sentimentalists who prefer stargazing to mathematical science. Cf. Tim. 91 D on the evolution of birds from innocents who supposed that sight furnished the surest proof in such matters. Cf. Walt Whitman:

> When I heard the learned astronomer . . .
> Rising and gliding out I wander'd off by myself
> In the mystical moist night air, and from time to time
> Look'd up in perfect silence at the stars.

Yet such is the irony of misinterpretation that this and the following pages are the chief support of the charge that Plato is hostile to science. Cf. on 530 B, p. 187, note c.

[e] Cf. Theaet. 174 A ἄνω βλέποντα.

529 δέ τις ἄνω κεχηνὼς ἢ κάτω συμμεμυκὼς τῶν
αἰσθητῶν ἐπιχειρῇ τι μανθάνειν, οὔτε μαθεῖν ἄν
ποτέ φημι αὐτόν — ἐπιστήμην γὰρ οὐδὲν ἔχειν
τῶν τοιούτων — οὔτε ἄνω ἀλλὰ κάτω αὐτοῦ
C βλέπειν τὴν ψυχήν, κἂν ἐξ ὑπτίας νέων ἐν γῇ ἢ
ἐν θαλάττῃ μανθάνῃ.

XI. Δίκην, ἔφη, ἔχω· ὀρθῶς γάρ μοι ἐπέπληξας.
ἀλλὰ πῶς δὴ ἔλεγες δεῖν ἀστρονομίαν μανθάνειν
παρὰ ἃ νῦν μανθάνουσιν, εἰ μέλλοιεν ὠφελίμως
πρὸς ἃ λέγομεν μαθήσεσθαι; Ὧδε, ἦν δ' ἐγώ.
ταῦτα μὲν τὰ ἐν τῷ οὐρανῷ ποικίλματα, ἐπείπερ
ἐν ὁρατῷ πεποίκιλται, κάλλιστα μὲν ἡγεῖσθαι καὶ
D ἀκριβέστατα τῶν τοιούτων ἔχειν, τῶν δὲ ἀληθινῶν
πολὺ ἐνδεῖν, ἃς τὸ ὂν τάχος καὶ ἡ οὖσα βραδυτὴς

ᵃ Cf. Aristoph. Clouds 172.
ᵇ συμμύω probably refers to the eyes. But cf. Adam ad loc.
ᶜ Cf. Phaedr. 264 ᴀ, and Adam in Class. Rev. xiii. p. 11.
ᵈ Or rather, "serves me right," or, in the American
language, "I've got what's coming to me." The expression is colloquial. Cf. Epist. iii. 319 ᴇ, Antiphon cxxiv. 45.
But δίκην ἔχει in 520 ʙ = " it is just."
ᵉ Cf. Tim. 40 ᴀ κόσμον ἀληθινὸν αὐτῷ πεποικιλμένον, Eurip.
Hel. 1096 ἀστέρων ποικίλματα, Critias, Sisyphus, Diels ii.³ p.
321, lines 33-34 :

τό τ' ἀστερωπὸν οὐρανοῦ δέμας
χρόνου καλὸν ποίκιλμα τέκτονος σοφοῦ.

Cf. also Gorg. 508 ᴀ, Lucretius v. 1205 "stellis micanti-
bus aethera fixum," ii. 1031 ff., Aeneid iv. 482 "stellis
ardentibus aptum," vi. 797, xi. 202, Ennius, Ann. 372,
Shakes. Hamlet ɪɪ. ii. 313 "This majestical roof fretted with
golden fire," Arthur Hugh Clough, Uranus:

Then Plato in me said,
'Tis but the figured ceiling overhead
With cunning diagrams bestarred . . .
Mind not the stars, mind thou thy mind and God

and the invisible. But if anyone tries to learn about the things of sense, whether gaping up[a] or blinking down,[b] I would never say that he really learns—for nothing of the kind admits of true knowledge—nor would I say that his soul looks up, but down, even though he study floating on his back[c] on sea or land."

XI. "A fair retort,[d]" he said; "your rebuke is deserved. But how, then, did you mean that astronomy ought to be taught contrary to the present fashion if it is to be learned in a way to conduce to our purpose?"

"Thus," said I: " these sparks that paint the sky,[e] since they are decorations on a visible surface, we must regard, to be sure, as the fairest and most exact of material things; but we must recognize that they fall far short of the truth,[f] the movements, namely, of

---

The word ποικίλματα may further suggest here the complication of the movements in the heavens.

[f] The meaning of this sentence is certain, but the expression will no more bear a matter-of-fact logical analysis than that of *Phaedo* 69 A-B, or *Rep.* 365 c, or many other subtle passages in Plato. No material object perfectly embodies the ideal and abstract mathematical relation. These mathematical ideas are designated as the true, ἀληθινῶν, and the real, ὄν. As in the *Timaeus* (38 c, 40 A-B, 36 D-E) the abstract and ideal has the primacy and by a reversal of the ordinary point of view is said to contain or convey the concrete. The visible stars are in and are carried by their invisible mathematical orbits. By this way of speaking Plato, it is true, disregards the apparent difficulty that the movement of the visible stars then ought to be mathematically perfect. But this interpretation is, I think, more probable for Plato than Adam's attempt to secure rigid consistency by taking τὸ ὂν τάχος etc., to represent invisible and ideal planets, and τὰ ἐνόντα to be the perfect mathematical realities, which are in them. ἐνόντα would hardly retain the metaphysical meaning of ὄντα. For the interpretation of 529 D *cf.* also my "Platonism and the History of Science," *Am. Philos. Soc. Proc.* lxvi. p. 172.

529 ἐν τῷ ἀληθινῷ ἀριθμῷ καὶ πᾶσι τοῖς ἀληθέσι σχή-
μασι φορᾶς τε πρὸς ἄλληλα φέρεται καὶ τὰ ἐνόντα
φέρει· ἃ δὴ λόγῳ μὲν καὶ διανοίᾳ ληπτά, ὄψει δ᾽
οὔ· ἢ σὺ οἴει; Οὐδαμῶς, ἔφη. Οὐκοῦν, εἶπον, τῇ
περὶ τὸν οὐρανὸν ποικιλίᾳ παραδείγμασι χρηστέον
τῆς πρὸς ἐκεῖνα μαθήσεως ἕνεκα, ὁμοίως ὥσπερ
Ε ἂν εἴ τις ἐντύχοι ὑπὸ Δαιδάλου ἤ τινος ἄλλου
δημιουργοῦ ἢ γραφέως διαφερόντως γεγραμμένοις
καὶ ἐκπεπονημένοις διαγράμμασιν. ἡγήσαιτο γὰρ
ἂν πού τις ἔμπειρος γεωμετρίας, ἰδὼν τὰ τοιαῦτα,
κάλλιστα μὲν ἔχειν ἀπεργασίᾳ, γελοῖον μὴν ἐπισκοπεῖν αὐτὰ σπουδῇ, ὡς τὴν ἀλήθειαν ἐν αὐτοῖς
530 ληψόμενον ἴσων ἢ διπλασίων ἢ ἄλλης τινὸς
συμμετρίας. Τί δ᾽ οὐ μέλλει γελοῖον εἶναι; ἔφη.
Τῷ ὄντι δὴ ἀστρονομικόν, ἦν δ᾽ ἐγώ, ὄντα οὐκ
οἴει ταὐτὸν πείσεσθαι εἰς τὰς τῶν ἄστρων φορὰς
ἀποβλέποντα; νομιεῖν μέν, ὡς οἷόν τε κάλλιστα
τὰ τοιαῦτα ἔργα συστήσασθαι, οὕτω ξυνεστάναι
τῷ τοῦ οὐρανοῦ δημιουργῷ[a] αὐτόν τε καὶ τὰ ἐν
αὐτῷ· τὴν δὲ νυκτὸς πρὸς ἡμέραν ξυμμετρίαν καὶ
τούτων πρὸς μῆνα καὶ μηνὸς πρὸς ἐνιαυτὸν καὶ
Β τῶν ἄλλων ἄστρων πρός τε ταῦτα καὶ πρὸς
ἄλληλα, οὐκ ἄτοπον, οἴει, ἡγήσεται τὸν νομίζοντα
γίγνεσθαί τε ταῦτα ἀεὶ ὡσαύτως καὶ οὐδαμῇ οὐδὲν
παραλλάττειν, σῶμά τε ἔχοντα καὶ ὁρώμενα, καὶ

---

[a] δημιουργῷ: an anticipation of the *Timaeus*.

[b] *Cf.* Bruno *apud* Höffding, *History of Modern Philosophy*,
i. 125 and 128, and Galileo, *ibid.* i. 178; also Lucretius v.
302-305.

[c] Plato was right against the view that Aristotle imposed
on the world for centuries. We should not therefore say
with Adam that he would have attached little significance
to the perturbations of Neptune and the consequent discovery

real speed and real slowness in true number and in all true figures both in relation to one another and as vehicles of the things they carry and contain. These can be apprehended only by reason and thought, but not by sight ; or do you think otherwise ? " " By no means," he said. " Then," said I, " we must use the blazonry of the heavens as patterns to aid in the study of those realities, just as one would do who chanced upon diagrams drawn with special care and elaboration by Daedalus or some other craftsman or painter. For anyone acquainted with geometry who saw such designs would admit the beauty of the workmanship, but would think it absurd to examine them seriously in the expectation of finding in them the absolute truth with regard to equals or doubles or any other ratio." " How could it be otherwise than absurd ? " he said. " Do you not think," said I, " that one who was an astronomer in very truth would feel in the same way when he turned his eyes upon the movements of the stars ? He will be willing to concede that the artisan [a] of heaven fashioned it and all that it contains in the best possible manner for such a fabric ; but when it comes to the proportions of day and night, and of their relation to the month, and that of the month to the year, and of the other stars to these and one another, do you not suppose that he will regard as a very strange fellow the man who believes that these things go on for ever without change [b] or the least deviation [c]—though they possess

of Uranus. It is to Plato that tradition attributes the problem of accounting by the simplest hypothesis for the movement of the heavenly bodies and " saving the phenomena."

The alleged contradiction between this and *Laws* 821 B ff. and *Tim.* 47 A is due to a misapprehension. That the stars in their movements do not perfectly express the exactness of mathe-

530 ζητεῖν παντὶ τρόπῳ τὴν ἀλήθειαν αὐτῶν λαβεῖν;
Ἐμοὶ γοῦν δοκεῖ, ἔφη, σοῦ νῦν ἀκούοντι. Προ-
βλήμασιν ἄρα, ἦν δ᾽ ἐγώ, χρώμενοι ὥσπερ
γεωμετρίαν οὕτω καὶ ἀστρονομίαν μέτιμεν· τὰ
C δ᾽ ἐν τῷ οὐρανῷ ἐάσομεν, εἰ μέλλομεν ὄντως

matical conceptions is no more than modern astronomers say. In the *Laws* passage Plato protests against the idea that there is no law and order governing the movement of the planets, but that they are " wandering stars," as irregular in their movements as they seem. In the *Timaeus* he is saying that astronomy or science took its beginning from the sight and observation of the heavenly bodies and the changing seasons. In the *Republic* Plato's purpose is to predict and encourage a purely mathematical astronomy and to indicate its place in the type of education which he wishes to give his guardians. There is not the slightest contradiction or change of opinion in the three passages if interpreted rightly in their entire context.

ᵃ The meaning is not appreciably affected by a slight doubt as to the construction of ζητεῖν. It is usually taken with ἄτοπον (regarded as neuter), the meaning being that the philosophic astronomer will think it strange to look for the absolute truth in these things. This double use of ἄτοπον is strained and it either makes παντὶ τρόπῳ awkward or attributes to Plato the intention of decrying the concrete study of astronomy. I think ζητεῖν etc. are added by a trailing anacoluthon such as occurs elsewhere in the *Republic*. Their subject is the real astronomer who, using the stars only as " diagrams " or patterns (529 D), seeks to learn a higher exacter mathematical truth than mere observation could yield. Madvig's ζητήσει implies a like view of the meaning but smooths out the construction. But my interpretation of the passage as a whole does not depend on this construction. If we make ζητεῖν depend on ἄτοπον (neuter) ἡγήσεται, the meaning will be that he thinks it absurd to expect to get that higher truth from mere observation. At all events Plato is not here objecting to observation as a suggestion for mathematical studies but to its substitution for them, as the next sentence shows.

ᵇ That is just what the mathematical astronomy of to-day

bodies and are visible objects—and that his unremitting quest [a] is the realities of these things ? " " I at least do think so," he said, " now that I hear it from you." " It is by means of problems,[b] then," said I, " as in the study of geometry, that we will pursue astronomy too, and we will let be the things in the heavens,[c] if we are to have a part in the true science of

does, and it is a πολλαπλάσιον ἔργον compared with the merely observational astronomy of Plato's day. *Cf.* the interesting remarks of Sir James Jeans, *apud* S. J. Woolf, *Drawn from Life*, p. 74 : "The day is gone when the astronomer's work is carried on only at the eyepiece of a telescope. Naturally, observations must be made, but these must be recorded by men who are trained for that purpose, and I am not one of them," etc.

Adam's quotation of Browning's " Abt Vogler " in connexion with this passage will only confirm the opinion of those who regard Plato as a sentimental enemy of science.

[c] *Cf.* also *Phileb.* 59 A, Aristot. *Met.* 997 b 35 οὐδὲ περὶ τὸν οὐρανὸν ἡ ἀστρολογία τόνδε.

This intentional Ruskinian *boutade* has given great scandal. The Platonist, we are told *ad nauseam*, deduces the world from his inner consciousness. This is of course not true (*cf. Unity of Plato's Thought*, p. 45). But Plato, like some lesser writers, loves to emphasize his thought by paradox and surprise, and his postulation and prediction of a mathematical astronomy required emphasis. *Cf.* my *Platonism and the History of Science*, pp. 171-174.

This and similar passages cannot be used to prove that Plato was unscientific, as many hostile or thoughtless critics have attempted to do. *Cf. e.g.* the severe strictures of Arthur Platt, *Nine Essays*, Cambridge Univ. Press, 1927, pp. 12-16, especially p. 16 : " Plato being first and foremost a metaphysician with a sort of religious system would not have us study anything but metaphysics and a kind of mystic religion." Woodbridge Riley, *From Myth to Reason*, p. 47 : " . . . Plato . . . was largely responsible for turning back the clock of scientific progress. To explain the wonders of the world he preferred imagination to observation." *Cf.* also Benn, *Greek Philosophers*, vol. i. pp. 173 and 327, Herrick,

530 ἀστρονομίας μεταλαμβάνοντες χρήσιμον τὸ φύσει
φρόνιμον ἐν τῇ ψυχῇ ἐξ ἀχρήστου ποιήσειν. Ἡ
πολλαπλάσιον, ἔφη, τὸ ἔργον ἢ ὡς νῦν ἀστρονο-
μεῖται προστάττεις. Οἶμαι δέ γε, εἶπον, καὶ
τἆλλα κατὰ τὸν αὐτὸν τρόπον προστάξειν ἡμᾶς,
ἐάν τι ἡμῶν ὡς νομοθετῶν ὄφελος ᾖ.

XII. Ἀλλὰ γὰρ τί ἔχεις ὑπομνῆσαι τῶν προσηκόντων μαθημάτων; Οὐκ ἔχω, ἔφη, νῦν γ᾽
οὑτωσί. Οὐ μὴν ἕν, ἀλλὰ πλείω, ἦν δ᾽ ἐγώ, εἴδη
D παρέχεται ἡ φορά, ὡς ἐγῷμαι. τὰ μὲν οὖν πάντα
ἴσως ὅστις σοφὸς ἕξει εἰπεῖν· ἃ δὲ καὶ ἡμῖν
προφανῆ, δύο. Ποῖα δή; Πρὸς ταύτῳ, ἦν δ᾽
ἐγώ, ἀντίστροφον αὐτοῦ. Τὸ ποῖον; Κινδυνεύει,
ἔφην, ὡς πρὸς ἀστρονομίαν ὄμματα πέπηγεν, ὡς
πρὸς ἐναρμόνιον φορὰν ὦτα παγῆναι, καὶ αὗται
ἀλλήλων ἀδελφαί τινες αἱ ἐπιστῆμαι εἶναι, ὡς οἵ
τε Πυθαγόρειοί φασι καὶ ἡμεῖς, ὦ Γλαύκων,

The Thinking Machine, p. 335, F. C. S. Schiller, *Plato and
his Predecessors*, p. 81: ". . . that Plato's anti-empirical
bias renders him profoundly anti-scientific, and that his
influence has always, openly or subtly, counteracted and
thwarted the scientific impulse, or at least diverted it into
unprofitable channels." Dampier-Whetham, *A History of
Science*, pp. 27-28: " Plato was a great philosopher but in
the history of experimental science he must be counted a
disaster."

Such statements disregard the entire context of the
Platonic passages they exploit, and take no account of
Plato's purpose or of other passages which counteract his
seemingly unscientific remarks.

Equally unfair is the practice of comparing Plato unfavourably with Aristotle in this respect, as Grote *e.g.*
frequently does (*cf. Aristotle*, p. 233). Plato was an artist
and Aristotle an encyclopaedist; but Plato as a whole is far
nearer the point of view of recent science than Aristotle.
Cf. my *Platonism and the History of Science*, p. 163; also
532 A and on 529 A, p. 180, note *a*, and *What Plato Said*, p. 236.

astronomy and so convert to right use from uselessness that natural indwelling intelligence of the soul."
"You enjoin a task," he said, "that will multiply the labour [a] of our present study of astronomy many times." "And I fancy," I said, "that our other injunctions will be of the same kind if we are of any use as lawgivers.

XII. "However, what suitable studies have you to suggest?" "Nothing," he said, "thus off-hand." "Yet, surely." said I, "motion [b] in general provides not one but many forms or species, according to my opinion. To enumerate them all will perhaps be the task of a wise man, [c] but even to us two of them are apparent." "What are they?" "In addition to astronomy, its counterpart," I replied. "What is that?" "We may venture to suppose," I said, "that as the eyes are framed for astronomy so the ears are framed [d] for the movements of harmony; and these are in some sort kindred sciences, [e] as the Pythagoreans [f] affirm and we admit, [g] do we not,

---

[a] Cf. Phaedr. 272 в καίτοι οὐ σμικρόν γε φαίνεται ἔργον.
[b] Plato here generalizes motion as a subject of science.
[c] The modesty is in the tone of the Timaeus.
[d] For πέπηγεν cf. 605 a.
[e] The similar statement attributed to Archytas, Diels i.³ p. 331, is probably an imitation of this.
[f] Pythagoras is a great name, but little is known of him. "Pythagoreans" in later usage sometimes means mystics, sometimes mathematical physicists, sometimes both. Plato makes use of both traditions but is dominated by neither. For Erich Frank's recent book, Plato und die sogenannten Pythagoreer, cf. my article in Class. Phil. vol. xxiii. (1928) pp. 347 ff. The student of Plato will do well to turn the page when he meets the name Pythagoras in a commentator.
[g] For this turn of phrase cf. Vol. I. p. 333, 424 c, Protag. 316 a, Symp. 186 e.

530 ξυγχωροῦμεν. ἢ πῶς ποιοῦμεν; Οὕτως, ἔφη.
Ε Οὐκοῦν, ἦν δ' ἐγώ, ἐπειδὴ πολὺ τὸ ἔργον, ἐκείνων πευσόμεθα, πῶς λέγουσι περὶ αὐτῶν καὶ εἴ
τι ἄλλο πρὸς τούτοις; ἡμεῖς δὲ παρὰ πάντα
ταῦτα φυλάξομεν τὸ ἡμέτερον. Ποῖον; Μή ποτ'
αὐτῶν τι ἀτελὲς ἐπιχειρῶσιν ἡμῖν μανθάνειν οὓς
θρέψομεν, καὶ οὐκ ἐξῆκον ἐκεῖσε ἀεί, οἷ πάντα δεῖ
ἀφήκειν, οἷον ἄρτι περὶ τῆς ἀστρονομίας ἐλέγομεν.
531 ἢ οὐκ οἶσθ' ὅτι καὶ περὶ ἁρμονίας ἕτερον τοιοῦτον
ποιοῦσι; τὰς γὰρ ἀκουομένας αὖ συμφωνίας καὶ
φθόγγους ἀλλήλοις ἀναμετροῦντες ἀνήνυτα ὥσπερ
οἱ ἀστρονόμοι πονοῦσιν. Νὴ τοὺς θεούς, ἔφη, καὶ
γελοίως γε, πυκνώματ' ἄττα ὀνομάζοντες καὶ
παραβάλλοντες τὰ ὦτα, οἷον ἐκ γειτόνων φωνὴν
θηρευόμενοι, οἱ μέν φασιν ἔτι κατακούειν ἐν μέσῳ
τινὰ ἠχὴν καὶ σμικρότατον εἶναι τοῦτο διάστημα,

---

[a] For the reference to experts cf. supra 400 B, 424 C. Cf. also What Plato Said, p. 484, on Laches 184 D-E.

[b] παρά of course here means "throughout" and not "contrary."

[c] I take the word ἀτελές etymologically (cf. pp. 66-67, note b, on 500 A), with reference to the end in view. Others take it in the ordinary Greek sense, "imperfect," "incomplete."

[d] This passage is often taken as another example of Plato's hostility to science and the experimental method. It is of course not that, but the precise interpretation is difficult. Glaucon at first misapprehends (cf. p. 180, note a, on 529 A) and gives an amusing description of the mere empiricist in music. But Socrates says he does not mean these, but those who try to apply mathematics to the perception of sound instead of developing a (Kantian) a priori science of harmony to match the mathematical science of astronomy. Cf. also p. 193, note g, on 531 B, W. Whewell, Transactions of the Cambridge Philos. Soc. vol. ix. p. 589, and for music A. Rivaud, "Platon et la musique," Rev. d'Histoire de la Philos. 1929.

Glaucon?" "We do," he said. "Then," said I, "since the task is so great, shall we not inquire of them [a] what their opinion is and whether they have anything to add? And we in all this [b] will be on the watch for what concerns us." "What is that?" "To prevent our fosterlings from attempting to learn anything that does not conduce to the end [c] we have in view, and does not always come out at what we said ought to be the goal of everything, as we were just now saying about astronomy. Or do you not know that they repeat the same procedure in the case of harmonies [d]? They transfer it to hearing and measure audible concords and sounds against one another,[e] expending much useless labour just as the astronomers do." "Yes, by heaven," he said, "and most absurdly too. They talk of something they call minims [f] and, laying their ears alongside, as if trying to catch a voice from next door,[g] some affirm that they can hear a note between and that this is the least interval and the unit of measurement, while

pp. 1-30; also Stallbaum *ad loc.*, and E. Frank, *Platon u. d. sog. Pyth.*, Anhang, on the history of Greek music. He expresses surprise (p. 139) that Glaucon knows nothing of Pythagorean theories of music. Others use this to prove Socrates' ignorance of music.

[e] This hints at the distinction developed in the *Politicus* between relative measurement of one thing against another and measurement by a standard. *Cf. Polit.* 283 ε, 284 β-c, *Theat.* 186 A.

[f] πυκνώματα (condensed notes). The word is technical. *Cf.* Adam *ad loc.* But, as ἄττα shows, Plato is using it loosely to distinguish a measure of sense perception from a mathematically determined interval.

[g] *Cf.* Pater, *Renaissance*, p. 157. The phrase, ἐκ γειτόνων, is colloquial and, despite the protest of those who insist that it only means in the neighbourhood, suggests overhearing what goes on next door—as often in the New Comedy.

531 ᾧ μετρητέον, οἱ δὲ ἀμφισβητοῦντες ὡς ὅμοιον ἤδη
B φθεγγομένων, ἀμφότεροι ὦτα τοῦ νοῦ προστησά-
μενοι. Σὺ μέν, ἦν δ' ἐγώ, τοὺς χρηστοὺς λέγεις
τοὺς ταῖς χορδαῖς πράγματα παρέχοντας καὶ
βασανίζοντας, ἐπὶ τῶν κολλόπων στρεβλοῦντας·
ἵνα δὲ μὴ μακροτέρα ἡ εἰκὼν γίγνηται, πλήκτρῳ
τε πληγῶν γιγνομένων καὶ κατηγορίας πέρι καὶ
ἐξαρνήσεως καὶ ἀλαζονείας χορδῶν, παύομαι τῆς
εἰκόνος καὶ οὔ φημι τούτους λέγειν, ἀλλ' ἐκείνους
οὓς ἔφαμεν νῦν δὴ περὶ ἁρμονίας ἐρήσεσθαι.
C ταὐτὸν γὰρ ποιοῦσι τοῖς ἐν τῇ ἀστρονομίᾳ· τοὺς
γὰρ ἐν ταύταις ταῖς συμφωνίαις ταῖς ἀκουομέναις
ἀριθμοὺς ζητοῦσιν, ἀλλ' οὐκ εἰς προβλήματα
ἀνίασιν ἐπισκοπεῖν, τίνες ξύμφωνοι ἀριθμοὶ καὶ
τίνες οὔ, καὶ διὰ τί ἑκάτεροι. Δαιμόνιον γάρ, ἔφη,
πρᾶγμα λέγεις. Χρήσιμον μὲν οὖν, ἦν δ' ἐγώ, πρὸς

---

[a] Cf. Aldous Huxley, *Jesting Pilate*, p. 152 : "Much is
enthusiastically taught about the use of quarter tones in
Indian music. I listened attentively at Lucknow in the
hope of hearing some new and extraordinary kind of melody
based on these celebrated fractions. But I listened in vain."
Gomperz, *Greek Thinkers*, iii. pp. 334-335, n. 85, thinks
that Plato " shrugs his shoulders at experiments." He refers
to Plutarch, *Life of Marcellus*, xiv. 5, and *Quaest. Conv.*
viii. 2. 1, 7, where Plato is represented as " having been
angry with Eudoxus and Archytas because they employed
instruments and apparatus for the solution of a problem,
instead of relying solely on reasoning."

[b] So Malebranche, *Entretiens sur la métaphysique*, 3, x. :
" Je pense que vous vous moquez de moi. C'est la raison
et non les sens qu'il faut consulter."

[c] For χρηστός in this ironical sense *cf.* also 479 A, *Symp.*
177 B.

[d] The language of the imagery confounds the torture of
slaves giving evidence on the rack with the strings and pegs
of a musical instrument. For the latter *cf.* Horace, *A. P.* 348,

192

THE REPUBLIC, BOOK VII

others insist that the strings now render identical sounds,[a] both preferring their ears to their minds.[b]" "You," said I, "are speaking of the worthies[c] who vex and torture the strings and rack them[d] on the pegs; but—not to draw out the comparison with strokes of the plectrum and the musician's complaints of too responsive and too reluctant strings[e]—I drop the figure,[f] and tell you that I do not mean these people, but those others[g] whom we just now said we would interrogate about harmony. Their method exactly corresponds to that of the astronomer; for the numbers they seek are those found in these heard concords, but they do not ascend[h] to generalized problems and the consideration which numbers are inherently concordant and which not and why in each case." "A superhuman task," he said. "Say, rather, useful,[i]" said I, "for the investigation of the

nam neque chorda sonum reddit quem vult manus et mens poscentique gravem persaepe remittit acutum.

Stallbaum says that Plato here was imitated by Aristaenetus, *Epist.* xiv. libr. 1 τί πράγματα παρέχετε χορδαῖς;

[e] This also may suggest a reluctant and a too willing witness.

[f] *Cf.* on 489 A, p. 23, note *d*.

[g] He distinguishes from the pure empirics just satirized those who apply their mathematics only to the data of observation. This is perhaps one of Plato's rare errors. For though there may be in some sense a Kantian *a priori* mechanics of astronomy, there can hardly be a purely *a priori* mathematics of acoustics. What numbers are consonantly harmonious must always remain a fact of direct experience. *Cf.* my *Platonism and the History of Science,* p. 176.

[h] *Cf.* Friedländer, *Platon,* i. p. 108, n. 1.

[i] *Cf. Tim.* 47 C-D. Plato always keeps to his point—*cf.* 349 B-C, 564 A-B—or returns to it after a digression. *Cf.* on 572 B, p. 339, note *e*.

531 τὴν τοῦ καλοῦ τε καὶ ἀγαθοῦ ζήτησιν, ἄλλως δὲ
μεταδιωκόμενον ἄχρηστον. Εἰκός· γ᾽, ἔφη.

XIII. Οἶμαι δέ γε, ἦν δ᾽ ἐγώ, καὶ ἡ τούτων
D πάντων ὧν διεληλύθαμεν μέθοδος ἐὰν μὲν ἐπὶ
τὴν ἀλλήλων κοινωνίαν ἀφίκηται καὶ ξυγγένειαν,
καὶ ξυλλογισθῇ ταῦτα ᾗ ἔστιν ἀλλήλοις οἰκεῖα,
φέρειν τι αὐτῶν εἰς ἃ βουλόμεθα τὴν πραγματείαν
καὶ οὐκ ἀνόνητα πονεῖσθαι, εἰ δὲ μή, ἀνόνητα.
Καὶ ἐγώ, ἔφη, οὕτω μαντεύομαι· ἀλλὰ πάμπολυ
ἔργον λέγεις, ὦ Σώκρατες. Τοῦ προοιμίου, ἦν δ᾽
ἐγώ, ἢ τίνος λέγεις; ἢ οὐκ ἴσμεν ὅτι πάντα
ταῦτα προοίμιά ἐστιν αὐτοῦ τοῦ νόμου ὃν δεῖ
μαθεῖν; οὐ γάρ που δοκοῦσί γέ σοι οἱ ταῦτα
E δεινοὶ διαλεκτικοὶ εἶναι. Οὐ μὰ τὸν Δί᾽, ἔφη, εἰ
μὴ μάλα γέ τινες ὀλίγοι ὧν ἐγὼ ἐντετύχηκα.
Ἀλλ᾽ ἤδη,¹ εἶπον, μὴ δυνατοί τινες ὄντες² δοῦναί τε
καὶ ἀποδέξασθαι λόγον εἴσεσθαι ποτέ τι ὧν φαμὲν

¹ ἀλλὰ ἤδη ADM, ἀλλὰ δὴ F.
² μὴ δυνατοί τινες ὄντες A²FDM, οἱ μὴ δυνατοί τινες ὄντες A :
μὴ δυνατοὶ οἵτινες Burnet.

ᵃ Cf. on 505 B, p. 88, note a.
ᵇ μέθοδος, like πραγματείαν in D, is used almost in the
later technical sense of "treatise" or "branch of study."
Cf. on 528 D, p. 178, note a.
ᶜ Cf. on 537 C, Epin. 991 E.
ᵈ Plato is fond of this image. It suggests here also the
preamble of a law, as the translation more explicitly indicates. Cf. 532 D, anticipated in 457 C, and Laws 722 D-E,
723 A-B and E, 720 D-E, 772 E, 870 D, 854 A, 932 A and passim.
ᵉ Cf. Theaet. 146 B, and perhaps Euthyd. 290 C. Though
mathematics quicken the mind of the student, it is, apart
from metaphysics, a matter of common experience that
mathematicians are not necessarily good reasoners on other
subjects. Jowett's wicked jest, "I have hardly ever known
a mathematician who could reason," misled an eminent

beautiful and the good,[a] but if otherwise pursued, useless." "That is likely," he said.

XIII. "And what is more," I said, "I take it that if the investigation[b] of all these studies goes far enough to bring out their community and kinship[c] with one another, and to infer their affinities, then to busy ourselves with them contributes to our desired end, and the labour taken is not lost; but otherwise it is vain." "I too so surmise," said he; "but it is a huge task of which you speak, Socrates." "Are you talking about the prelude,[d]" I said, "or what? Or do we not know that all this is but the preamble of the law itself, the prelude of the strain that we have to apprehend? For you surely do not suppose that experts in these matters are reasoners and dialecticians[e]?" "No, by Zeus," he said, "except a very few whom I have met." "But have you ever supposed," I said, "that men who could not render and exact an account[f] of opinions in discussion would ever know anything of the things

professor of education who infers that Plato disbelieved in "mental discipline" (*Yale Review*, July 1917). *Cf.* also Taylor, Note in Reply to Mr. A. W. Benn, *Mind*, xii. (1903) p. 511; Charles Fox, *Educational Psychology*, pp. 187-188: ". . . a training in the mathematics may produce exactness of thought . . . provided that the training is of such a kind as to inculcate an ideal which the pupil values and strives to attain. Failing this, Glaucon's observation that he had 'hardly ever known a mathematician who was capable of reasoning' is likely to be repeated." On the text *cf.* Wilamowitz, *Platon*, ii. pp. 384-385, and Adam *ad loc.*

[f] λόγον . . . δοῦναι. A commonplace Platonic plea for dialectics. *Cf.* 534 B, *Prot.* 336 A, *Polit.* 286 A, *Theaet.* 202 C, 175 C, 183 D, *Soph.* 230 A, *Phaedo* 78 C-D, 95 D, *Charm.* 165 B, Xen. *Oecon.* 11. 22. *Cf.* also λόγον λαβεῖν *Rep.* 402 A, 534 B, *Soph.* 246 C, *Theaet.* 208 D, and Thompson on *Meno* 75 D.

532 δεῖν εἰδέναι; Οὐδ' αὖ, ἔφη, τοῦτό γε. Οὐκοῦν, εἶπον, ὦ Γλαύκων, οὗτος ἤδη αὐτός ἐστιν ὁ νόμος ὃν τὸ διαλέγεσθαι περαίνει; ὃν καὶ ὄντα νοητὸν μιμοῖτ' ἂν ἡ τῆς ὄψεως δύναμις, ἣν ἐλέγομεν πρὸς αὐτὰ ἤδη τὰ ζῷα ἐπιχειρεῖν ἀποβλέπειν καὶ πρὸς αὐτὰ ἄστρα τε καὶ τελευταῖον δὴ πρὸς αὐτὸν τὸν ἥλιον. οὕτω καὶ ὅταν τις τῷ διαλέγεσθαι ἐπιχειρῇ ἄνευ πασῶν τῶν αἰσθήσεων διὰ τοῦ λόγου ἐπ' αὐτὸ ὃ ἔστιν ἕκαστον ὁρμᾶν,[1] καὶ μὴ ἀποστῇ,

B πρὶν ἂν αὐτὸ ὃ ἔστιν ἀγαθὸν αὐτῇ νοήσει λάβῃ, ἐπ' αὐτῷ γίγνεται τῷ τοῦ νοητοῦ τέλει, ὥσπερ ἐκεῖνος τότε ἐπὶ τῷ τοῦ ὁρατοῦ. Παντάπασι μὲν οὖν, ἔφη. Τί οὖν; οὐ διαλεκτικὴν ταύτην τὴν πορείαν καλεῖς; Τί μήν; Ἡ δέ γε, ἦν δ' ἐγώ, λύσις τε ἀπὸ τῶν δεσμῶν καὶ μεταστροφὴ ἀπὸ τῶν σκιῶν ἐπὶ τὰ εἴδωλα καὶ τὸ φῶς καὶ ἐκ τοῦ καταγείου εἰς τὸν ἥλιον ἐπάνοδος, καὶ ἐκεῖ πρὸς μὲν τὰ ζῷά τε

[1] ὁρμᾶν Clemens: ὁρμᾷ AFDM.

---

[a] Cf. Phileb. 58 D, Meno 75 C-D, Charm. 155 A, Cratyl. 390 c, and on 533 B, pp. 200 f., note f.

[b] This is not a literal rendering, but gives the meaning.

[c] Cf. 516 A-B. Plato interprets his imagery again here and in B infra.

[d] Cf. supra p. 180, note a, and p. 187, note c. Cf. also 537 D, and on 476 A ff. Cf. Bergson, Introduction to Metaphysics, p. 9: " Metaphysics, then, is the science which claims to dispense with symbols "; E. S. Robinson, Readings in General Psych. p. 295: " A habit of suppressing mental imagery must therefore characterize men who deal much with abstract ideas; and as the power of dealing easily and firmly with these ideas is the surest criterion of a high order of intellect . . ."; Pear, Remembering and Forgetting, p. 57: " He (Napoleon) is reported to have said that ' there are some who, from some physical or moral peculiarity of character, form a picture (tableau) of everything. No matter what knowledge, intellect, courage, or good qualities they may have, these men

we say must be known?" "*No* is surely the answer to that too." "This, then, at last, Glaucon," I said, "is the very law which dialectics [a] recites, the strain which it executes, of which, though it belongs to the intelligible, we may see an imitation in the progress [b] of the faculty of vision, as we described [c] its endeavour to look at living things themselves and the stars themselves and finally at the very sun. In like manner, when anyone by dialectics attempts through discourse of reason and apart from all perceptions of sense [d] to find his way to the very essence of each thing and does not desist till he apprehends by thought itself the nature of the good in itself, he arrives at the limit of the intelligible, as the other in our parable came to the goal of the visible." "By all means," he said. "What, then, will you not call this progress of thought dialectic?" "Surely." "And the release from bonds," I said, "and the conversion from the shadows to the images [e] that cast them and to the light and the ascent [f] from the subterranean cavern to the world above, [g] and there the persisting

are unfit to command"; A. Bain, *Mind*, 1880, p. 570: "Mr. Galton is naturally startled at finding eminent scientific men, by their own account, so very low in the visualizing power. His explanation, I have no doubt, hits the mark; the deficiency is due to the natural antagonism of pictorial aptitude and abstract thought"; Judd, *Psychology of High School Subjects*, p. 321: "It did not appear on superficial examination of the standings of students that those who can draw best are the best students from the point of view of the teacher of science."

[e] εἴδωλα: *cf.* my *Idea of Good in Plato's Republic*, p. 238; also 516 A, *Theaet.* 150 c, *Soph.* 240 A, 241 E, 234 c, 266 B with 267 c, and *Rep.* 517 D ἀγαλμάτων.

[f] ἐπάνοδος became almost technical in Neoplatonism. *Cf.* also 515 A, 529 A, and p. 124, note *b*.

[g] Lit. "sun," *i.e.* the world illumined by the sun, not by the fire in the cave.

532 καὶ φυτὰ καὶ τὸ τοῦ ἡλίου φῶς ἔτι ἀδυναμία[1]
C βλέπειν, πρὸς δὲ τὰ ἐν ὕδασι φαντάσματα θεῖα[2] καὶ
σκιὰς τῶν ὄντων, ἀλλ' οὐκ εἰδώλων σκιὰς δι'
ἑτέρου τοιούτου φωτὸς ὡς πρὸς ἥλιον κρίνειν
ἀποσκιαζομένας, πᾶσα αὕτη ἡ πραγματεία τῶν
τεχνῶν, ἃς διήλθομεν, ταύτην ἔχει τὴν δύναμιν καὶ
ἐπαναγωγὴν τοῦ βελτίστου ἐν ψυχῇ πρὸς τὴν τοῦ
ἀρίστου ἐν τοῖς οὖσι θέαν, ὥσπερ τότε τοῦ σα-
φεστάτου ἐν σώματι πρὸς τὴν τοῦ φανοτάτου ἐν
D τῷ σωματοειδεῖ τε καὶ ὁρατῷ τόπῳ. Ἐγὼ μέν,
ἔφη, ἀποδέχομαι οὕτω. καίτοι παντάπασί γέ μοι
δοκεῖ χαλεπὰ μὲν ἀποδέχεσθαι εἶναι, ἄλλον δ' αὖ
τρόπον χαλεπὰ μὴ ἀποδέχεσθαι. ὅμως δέ—οὐ γὰρ
ἐν τῷ νῦν παρόντι μόνον ἀκουστέα, ἀλλὰ καὶ αὖθις
πολλάκις ἐπανιτέον—ταῦτα θέντες ἔχειν ὡς νῦν
λέγεται, ἐπ' αὐτὸν δὴ τὸν νόμον ἴωμεν, καὶ
διέλθωμεν οὕτως ὥσπερ τὸ προοίμιον διήλθομεν.
λέγε οὖν, τίς ὁ τρόπος τῆς τοῦ διαλέγεσθαι δυνά-
E μεως, καὶ κατὰ ποῖα δὴ εἴδη διέστηκε, καὶ τίνες
αὖ ὁδοί. αὗται γὰρ ἂν ἤδη, ὡς ἔοικεν, αἱ πρὸς
αὐτὸ ἄγουσαι εἶεν, οἳ ἀφικομένῳ ὥσπερ ὁδοῦ
ἀνάπαυλα ἂν εἴη καὶ τέλος τῆς πορείας. Οὐκέτ',

---

[1] ἔτι ἀδυναμία Iamblichus: ἐπ' ἀδυναμίᾳ ADM, ἀδυναμία F.
[2] θεῖα mss., bracketed by Stallbaum: θέα Ast and Apelt.
Adam once proposed ⟨καὶ ἐν τοῖς ὄσα πυκνά τε καὶ λ⟩εῖα.

---

[a] See crit. note. The text of Iamblichus is the only reasonable one. The reading of the manuscripts is impossible.
For the adverb modifying a noun cf. 558 B οὐδ' ὁπωστιοῦν
σμικρολογία, Laws 638 B σφόδρα γυναικῶν, with England's
note, Theaet. 183 E πάνυ πρεσβύτης, Laws 791 C παντελῶς
παίδων, 698 C σφόδρα φιλία, Rep. 564 A ἄγαν δουλείαν, with
Stallbaum's note.

inability [a] to look directly at animals and plants and the light of the sun, but the ability to see the phantasms created by God [b] in water and shadows of objects that are real and not merely, as before, the shadows of images cast through a light which, compared with the sun, is as unreal as they—all this procedure of the arts and sciences that we have described indicates their power to lead the best part of the soul up to the contemplation of what is best among realities, as in our parable the clearest organ in the body was turned to the contemplation of what is brightest in the corporeal and visible region." " I accept this," he said, " as the truth; and yet it appears to me very hard to accept, and again, from another point of view, hard to reject. [c] Nevertheless, since we have not to hear it at this time only, but are to repeat it often hereafter, let us assume that these things are as now has been said, and proceed to the melody itself, and go through with it as we have gone through the prelude. Tell me, then, what is the nature of this faculty of dialectic ? Into what divisions does it fall ? And what are its ways ? For it is these, it seems, that would bring us to the place where we may, so to speak, rest on the road and then come to the end of our journey-

---

[b] θεῖα because produced by God or nature and not by man with a mirror or a paint-brush. See crit. note and *Class. Review*, iv. p. 480. I quoted *Sophist* 266 B-D, and Adam with rare candour withdrew his emendation in his Appendix XIII. to this book. Apelt still misunderstands and emends, p. 296 and note.

[c] This sentence is fundamental for the understanding of Plato's metaphysical philosophy generally. *Cf. Unity of Plato's Thought*, p. 30, n. 192, *What Plato Said*, p. 268 and p. 586 on *Parmen.* 135 c. So Tennyson says it is hard to believe in God and hard not to believe.

533 ἦν δ᾽ ἐγώ, ὦ φίλε Γλαύκων, οἷός τ᾽ ἔσει ἀκολουθεῖν·
ἐπεὶ τό γ᾽ ἐμὸν οὐδὲν ἂν προθυμίας ἀπολίποι· οὐδ᾽
εἰκόνα ἂν ἔτι οὗ λέγομεν ἴδοις, ἀλλ᾽ αὐτὸ τὸ
ἀληθές, ὅ γε δή μοι φαίνεται—εἰ δ᾽ ὄντως ἢ μὴ
οὐκέτ᾽ ἄξιον τοῦτο διισχυρίζεσθαι· ἀλλ᾽ ὅτι μὲν
δὴ τοιοῦτόν τι ἰδεῖν, ἰσχυριστέον. ἦ γάρ; Τί μήν;
Οὐκοῦν καὶ ὅτι ἡ τοῦ διαλέγεσθαι δύναμις μόνη ἂν
φήνειεν ἐμπείρῳ ὄντι ὧν νῦν δὴ διήλθομεν, ἄλλῃ
δὲ οὐδαμῇ δυνατόν; Καὶ τοῦτ᾽, ἔφη, ἄξιον δι-
ισχυρίζεσθαι. Τόδε γοῦν, ἦν δ᾽ ἐγώ, οὐδεὶς ἡμῖν
B ἀμφισβητήσει λέγουσιν, ὡς αὐτοῦ γε ἑκάστου

---

[a] This is not mysticism or secret doctrine. It is, in fact,
the avoidance of dogmatism. But that is not all. Plato
could not be expected to insert a treatise on dialectical
method here, or risk an absolute definition which would
only expose him to misinterpretation. The principles and
methods of such reasoning, and the ultimate metaphysical
conclusions to which they may lead, cannot be expounded
in a page or a chapter. They can only be suggested to the
intelligent, whose own experience will help them to understand. As the *Republic* and *Laws* entire explain Plato's
idea of social good, so all the arguments in the dialogues
illustrate his conception of fair and unfair argument. *Cf.
What Plato Said*, Index *s.v.* Dialectics, and note *f* below.

[b] For the idiom οὐδὲν προθυμίας ἀπολίποι *cf. Symp.* 210 A,
Meno 77 A, *Laws* 961 c, Aesch. *Prom.* 343, Thucyd. viii.
22. 1, Eurip. *Hippol.* 285.

[c] On Plato's freedom from the dogmatism often attributed
to him *cf. What Plato Said*, p. 515 on *Meno* 86 B.

[d] The mystical implications of φήνειεν are not to be pressed.
It is followed, as usual in Plato, by a matter-of-fact statement of the essential practical conclusion (γοῦν) that no man
can be trusted to think straight in large matters who has
not been educated to reason and argue straight.

[e] Plato anticipates the criticism that he neglects experience.

[f] *i.e.* dispute our statement and maintain. The meaning
is plain. It is a case of what I have called illogical idiom.

THE REPUBLIC, BOOK VII

ing." "You will not be able, dear Glaucon, to follow me further,[a] though on my part there will be no lack of goodwill.[b] And, if I could, I would show you, no longer an image and symbol of my meaning, but the very truth, as it appears to me—though whether rightly or not I may not properly affirm.[c] But that something like this is what we have to see, I must affirm.[c] Is not that so?" "Surely." "And may we not also declare that nothing less than the power of dialectics could reveal[d] this, and that only to one experienced[e] in the studies we have described, and that the thing is in no other wise possible?" "That, too," he said, "we may properly affirm." "This, at any rate," said I, "no one will maintain in dispute against us[f]: that there is any other way of inquiry[g] that attempts

---

Cf. *T.A.P.A.* vol. xlvii. pp. 205-234. The meaning is that of *Philebus* 58 ᴇ, 59 ᴀ. Other "science" may be more interesting or useful, but sound dialectics alone fosters the disinterested pursuit of truth for its own sake. *Cf. Soph.* 235 c, *Phaedr.* 265-266. Aristotle, *Topics* i. 2. 6, practically comes back to the Platonic conception of dialectics.

The full meaning of dialectics in Plato would demand a treatise. It is almost the opposite of what Hegelians call by that name, which is represented in Plato by the second part of the *Parmenides.* The characteristic Platonic dialectic is the checking of the stream of thought by the necessity of securing the understanding and assent of an intelligent interlocutor at every step, and the habit of noting all relevant distinctions, divisions, and ambiguities, in ideas and terms. When the interlocutor is used merely to relieve the strain on the leader's voice or the reader's attention, as in some of the later dialogues, dialectic becomes merely a literary form.

[g] Cicero's "via et ratione." περὶ παντός is virtually identical with αὐτοῦ γε ἑκάστου πέρι.

It is true that the scientific specialist confines himself to his specialty. The dialectician, like his base counterfeit the sophist (*Soph.* 231 ᴀ), is prepared to argue about anything, *Soph.* 232 c f., *Euthyd.* 272 ᴀ-ʙ.

533 πέρι, ὃ ἔστιν ἕκαστον, ἄλλη τις ἐπιχειρεῖ μέθοδος
ὁδῷ περὶ παντὸς λαμβάνειν. ἀλλ᾽ αἱ μὲν ἄλλαι
πᾶσαι τέχναι ἢ πρὸς δόξας ἀνθρώπων καὶ ἐπιθυμίας εἰσὶν ἢ πρὸς γενέσεις τε καὶ συνθέσεις ἢ
πρὸς θεραπείαν τῶν φυομένων τε καὶ συντιθεμένων
ἅπασαι τετράφαται· αἱ δὲ λοιπαί, ἃς τοῦ ὄντος τι
ἔφαμεν ἐπιλαμβάνεσθαι, γεωμετρίας τε καὶ τὰς
C ταύτῃ ἑπομένας, ὁρῶμεν ὡς ὀνειρώττουσι μὲν
περὶ τὸ ὄν, ὕπαρ δὲ ἀδύνατον αὐταῖς ἰδεῖν, ἕως ἂν
ὑποθέσεσι χρώμεναι ταύτας ἀκινήτους ἐῶσι, μὴ
δυνάμεναι λόγον διδόναι αὐτῶν. ᾧ γὰρ ἀρχὴ μὲν
ὃ μὴ οἶδε, τελευτὴ δὲ καὶ τὰ μεταξὺ ἐξ οὗ μὴ οἶδε
συμπέπλεκται, τίς μηχανὴ τὴν τοιαύτην ὁμολογίαν
ποτὲ ἐπιστήμην γενέσθαι; Οὐδεμία, ἦ δ᾽ ὅς.

XIV. Οὐκοῦν, ἦν δ᾽ ἐγώ, ἡ διαλεκτικὴ μέθοδος
μόνη ταύτῃ πορεύεται, τὰς ὑποθέσεις ἀναιροῦσα,
ἐπ᾽ αὐτὴν τὴν ἀρχήν, ἵνα βεβαιώσηται, καὶ τῷ
D ὄντι ἐν βορβόρῳ βαρβαρικῷ τινὶ τὸ τῆς ψυχῆς ὄμμα

---

[a] Cf. supra 525 C, 527 B.

[b] The interpreters of Plato must allow for his Emersonian
habit of hitting each nail in turn as hard as he can. There
is no real contradiction between praising mathematics in
comparison with mere loose popular thinking, and disparaging it in comparison with dialectics. There is no evidence
and no probability that Plato is here proposing a reform of
mathematics in the direction of modern mathematical logic,
as has been suggested. Cf. on 527 A. It is the nature of
mathematics to fall short of dialectics.

[c] Cf. Phileb. 20 B and on 520 C, p. 143, note g.

[d] Cf. supra on 531 E.

[e] The touch of humour in the expression may be illustrated
by Lucian, Hermotimus 74, where it is used to justify Lucian's
scepticism even of mathematics, and by Hazlitt's remark on
Coleridge, "Excellent talker if you allow him to start from
no premises and come to no conclusion."

[f] Or "admission." Plato thinks of even geometrical

systematically and in all cases to determine what each thing really is. But all the other arts have for their object the opinions and desires of men or are wholly concerned with generation and composition or with the service and tendance of the things that grow and are put together, while the remnant which we said *a* did in some sort lay hold on reality—geometry and the studies that accompany it—are, as we see, dreaming *b* about being, but the clear waking vision *c* of it is impossible for them as long as they leave the assumptions which they employ undisturbed and cannot give any account *d* of them. For where the starting-point is something that the reasoner does not know, and the conclusion and all that intervenes is a tissue of things not really known,*e* what possibility is there that assent *f* in such cases can ever be converted into true knowledge or science ? " " None," said he.

XIV. " Then," said I, " is not dialectics the only process of inquiry that advances in this manner, doing away with hypotheses, up to the first principle itself in order to find confirmation there ? And it is literally true that when the eye of the soul *g* is sunk in

reasoning as a Socratic dialogue. *Cf.* the exaggeration of this idea by the Epicureans in Cic. *De fin.* i. 21 " quae et a falsis initiis profecta, vera esse non possunt: et si essent vera nihil afferunt quo iucundius, id est, quo melius viveremus."

Dialectic proceeds διὰ συγχωρήσεων, the admission of the interlocutor. *Cf. Laws* 957 D, *Phaedr.* 237 C-D, *Gorg.* 487 E, *Lysis* 219 C, *Prot.* 350 E, *Phileb.* 12 A, *Theaet.* 162 A, 169 D-E, 164 C, *Rep.* 340 B. But such admissions are not valid unless when challenged they are carried back to something satisfactory—ἱκανόν—(not necessarily in any given case to the idea of good). But the mathematician as such peremptorily demands the admission of his postulates and definitions. *Cf.* 510 B-D, 511 B.

g Cf. supra on 519 B, p. 138, note *a*.

533 κατορωρυγμένον ἠρέμα ἕλκει καὶ ἀνάγει ἄνω,
συνερίθοις καὶ συμπεριαγωγοῖς χρωμένη αἷς διήλθομεν τέχναις· ἃς ἐπιστήμας μὲν πολλάκις προσ-
είπομεν διὰ τὸ ἔθος, δέονται δὲ ὀνόματος ἄλλου,
ἐναργεστέρου μὲν ἢ δόξης, ἀμυδροτέρου δὲ ἢ
ἐπιστήμης. διάνοιαν δὲ αὐτὴν ἔν γε τῷ πρόσθεν
που ὡρισάμεθα· ἔστι δ', ὡς ἐμοὶ δοκεῖ, οὐ περὶ
E ὀνόματος ἀμφισβήτησις, οἷς τοσούτων πέρι σκέψις
ὅσων ἡμῖν πρόκειται. Οὐ γὰρ οὖν, ἔφη. [ἀλλ' ὃ
ἂν μόνον δηλοῖ πρὸς τὴν ἔξω σαφήνειαν, ἃ λέγει
ἐν ψυχῇ, ἀρκέσει.][1] Ἀρέσκει γοῦν,[2] ἦν δ' ἐγώ,
ὥσπερ τὸ πρότερον, τὴν μὲν πρώτην μοῖραν
534 ἐπιστήμην καλεῖν, δευτέραν δὲ διάνοιαν, τρίτην δὲ
πίστιν καὶ εἰκασίαν τετάρτην· καὶ ξυναμφότερα μὲν
ταῦτα δόξαν, ξυναμφότερα δ' ἐκεῖνα νόησιν· καὶ
δόξαν μὲν περὶ γένεσιν, νόησιν δὲ περὶ οὐσίαν·
καὶ ὅ τι οὐσία πρὸς γένεσιν, νόησιν πρὸς δόξαν,
καὶ ὅ τι νόησις πρὸς δόξαν, ἐπιστήμην πρὸς πίστιν
καὶ διάνοιαν πρὸς εἰκασίαν· τὴν δ' ἐφ' οἷς ταῦτα

---

[1] The text as printed is that of Hermann, brackets by Adam.
ἀλλ' ὃ AM, ἄλλο FD : ἔξιν σαφηνείᾳ AFDM, ἔξω σαφηνείαν
Herm., πως τὴν ἔξιν, σαφηνείᾳ Burnet, τὴν ἔξιν πῶς ἔχει σαφηνείας
Bywater : ἃ addidit et σαφηνείαν emendavit Herm.; λέγει AD,
λέγειν FM, λέγεις A[2]: ἀρκέσει mss. See also Adam, Appendix.
[2] ἀρέσκει mss., καὶ ἀρκέσει Burnet ; γοῦν AM, οὖν FD, Burnet.

---

[a] Orphism pictured the impious souls as buried in mud in
the world below ; cf. 363 D. Again we should not press Plato's
rhetoric and imagery either as sentimental Platonists or hostile
critics. See Newman, Introd. Aristot. Pol. p. 463, n. 3.

[b] All writers and philosophers are compelled to "speak
with the vulgar." Cf. e.g. Meyerson, De l'explication dans
les sciences, i. p. 329 : "Tout en sachant que la couleur n'est
pas réellement une qualité de l'objet, à se servir cependant,
dans la vie de tous les jours, d'une locution qui l'affirme."

the barbaric slough[a] of the Orphic myth, dialectic gently draws it forth and leads it up, employing as helpers and co-operators in this conversion the studies and sciences which we enumerated, which we called sciences often from habit,[b] though they really need some other designation, connoting more clearness than opinion and more obscurity than science. 'Understanding,'[c] I believe, was the term we employed. But I presume we shall not dispute about the name[d] when things of such moment lie before us for consideration." "No, indeed," he said.[e] * * * "Are you satisfied, then," said I, "as before,[f] to call the first division science, the second understanding, the third belief, and the fourth conjecture or picture-thought—and the last two collectively opinion, and the first two intellection, opinion dealing with generation, and intellection with essence, and this relation being expressed in the proportion[h]: as essence is to generation, so is intellection to opinion; and as intellection is to opinion, so is science to belief, and understanding to image-thinking or surmise? But the relation between their objective correlates[i] and the division into two

[c] Cf. on 511 D, pp. 116-117, note c.

[d] This unwillingness to dispute about names when they do not concern the argument is characteristic of Plato. Cf. What Plato Said, p. 516 on Meno 78 B-C for numerous instances. Stallbaum refers to Max. Tyr. Diss. xxvii. p. 40 ἐγὼ γάρ τοι τά τε ἄλλα, καὶ ἐν τῇ τῶν ὀνομάτων ἐλευθερίᾳ πείθομαι Πλάτωνι.

[e] The next sentence is hopelessly corrupt and is often considered an interpolation. The translation omits it. See Adam, Appendix XVI. to Bk. VII., Bywater, Journal of Phil. (Eng.) v. pp. 122-124.   [f] Supra 511 D-E.

[g] Always avoid "faith" in translating Plato.

[h] Cf. on 508 c, p. 103, note b.

[i] That is the meaning, though some critics will object to the phrase. Lit. "the things over which these (mental states) are set, or to which they apply."

534 ἀναλογίαν καὶ διαίρεσιν διχῇ ἑκατέρου, δοξαστοῦ
τε καὶ νοητοῦ, ἐῶμεν, ὦ Γλαύκων, ἵνα μὴ ἡμᾶς
πολλαπλασίων λόγων ἐμπλήσῃ ἢ ὅσων οἱ παρ-
B εληλυθότες. Ἀλλὰ μὴν ἔμοιγ᾽, ἔφη, τά γε ἄλλα,
καθ᾽ ὅσον δύναμαι ἕπεσθαι, ξυνδοκεῖ. Ἦ καὶ
διαλεκτικὸν καλεῖς τὸν λόγον ἑκάστου λαμβάνοντα
τῆς οὐσίας; καὶ τὸν μὴ ἔχοντα, καθ᾽ ὅσον ἂν μὴ
ἔχῃ λόγον αὑτῷ τε καὶ ἄλλῳ διδόναι, κατὰ
τοσοῦτον νοῦν περὶ τούτου οὐ φήσεις ἔχειν; Πῶς
γὰρ ἄν, ἦ δ᾽ ὅς, φαίην; Οὐκοῦν καὶ περὶ τοῦ
ἀγαθοῦ ὡσαύτως· ὃς ἂν μὴ ἔχῃ διορίσασθαι τῷ
λόγῳ ἀπὸ τῶν ἄλλων πάντων ἀφελὼν τὴν τοῦ
C ἀγαθοῦ ἰδέαν, καὶ ὥσπερ ἐν μάχῃ διὰ πάντων
ἐλέγχων διεξιών, μὴ κατὰ δόξαν ἀλλὰ κατ᾽ οὐσίαν
προθυμούμενος ἐλέγχειν, ἐν πᾶσι τούτοις ἀπτῶτι
τῷ λόγῳ διαπορεύηται, οὔτε αὐτὸ τὸ ἀγαθὸν
φήσεις εἰδέναι τὸν οὕτως ἔχοντα οὔτε ἄλλο ἀγαθὸν
οὐδέν, ἀλλ᾽ εἴ πῃ εἰδώλου τινὸς ἐφάπτεται, δόξῃ,

---

[a] There are two probable reasons for this: (1) The objective
classification is nothing to Plato's present purpose; (2) The
second member of the proportion is lacking in the objective
correlates. Numbers are distinguished from ideas not in
themselves but only by the difference of method in dialectics
and in mathematics. Cf. supra on 525 D, 526 A, Unity of
Plato's Thought, pp. 83-84, and Class. Phil. xxii. (1927)
pp. 213-218. The explicit qualifications of my arguments
there have been neglected and the arguments misquoted but
not answered. They can be answered only by assuming the
point at issue and affirming that Plato did assign an intermediate place to mathematical conceptions, for which there
is no evidence in Plato's own writings.

[b] Cf. supra on 531 E, p. 195, note f.

[c] Cf. on 511 D, p. 116, note a.

[d] This would be superfluous on the interpretation that the
ἱκανόν must always be the idea of good. What follows distinguishes the dialectician from the eristic sophist. For the

parts of each of these, the opinable, namely, and the intelligible, let us dismiss,[a] Glaucon, lest it involve us in discussion many times as long as the preceding." "Well," he said, "I agree with you about the rest of it, so far as I am able to follow." "And do you not also give the name dialectician to the man who is able to exact an account[b] of the essence of each thing? And will you not say that the one who is unable to do this, in so far as he is incapable of rendering an account to himself and others, does not possess full reason and intelligence[c] about the matter?" "How could I say that he does?" he replied. "And is not this true of the good likewise[d]—that the man who is unable to define in his discourse and distinguish and abstract from all other things the aspect or idea of the good, and who cannot, as it were in battle, running the gauntlet[e] of all tests, and striving to examine everything by essential reality and not by opinion, hold on his way through all this without tripping[f] in his reasoning—the man who lacks this power, you will say, does not really know the good itself or any particular good; but if he apprehends

short cut, καὶ ... ὡσαύτως, cf. 523 E, 580 D, 585 D, 346 A, etc.

[e] It imports little whether the objections are in his own mind or made by others. Thought is a discussion of the soul with itself (cf. Theaet. 189 E, Phileb. 38 E, Soph. 263 E), and when the interlocutor refuses to proceed Socrates sometimes continues the argument himself by supplying both question and answer, e.g. Gorg. 506 c ff. Cf. further Phaedrus 278 c, Parmen. 136 D-E, Unity of Plato's Thought, p. 17.

[f] Cf. Theaet. 160 D, Phileb. 45 A. The practical outcome = Laws 966 A-B, Phaedr. 278 c, Soph. 259 B-c. Cf. Mill, Diss. and Disc. iv. p. 283: "There is no knowledge and no assurance of right belief but with him who can both confute the opposite opinion and successfully defend his own against confutation."

534 οὐκ ἐπιστήμῃ ἐφάπτεσθαι, καὶ τὸν νῦν βίον
ὀνειροπολοῦντα καὶ ὑπνώττοντα, πρὶν ἐνθάδ' ἐξ-
D εγρέσθαι, εἰς Ἅιδου πρότερον ἀφικόμενον τελέως
ἐπικαταδαρθάνειν; Νὴ τὸν Δία, ἦ δ' ὅς, σφόδρα
γε πάντα ταῦτα φήσω. Ἀλλὰ μὴν τούς γε σαυτοῦ
παῖδας, οὓς τῷ λόγῳ τρέφεις τε καὶ παιδεύεις, εἴ
ποτε ἔργῳ τρέφοις, οὐκ ἂν ἐάσαις, ὡς ἐγᾦμαι,
ἀλόγους ὄντας ὥσπερ γραμμὰς ἄρχοντας ἐν τῇ
πόλει κυρίους τῶν μεγίστων εἶναι. Οὐ γὰρ οὖν,
ἔφη. Νομοθετήσεις δὴ αὐτοῖς ταύτης μάλιστα
τῆς παιδείας ἀντιλαμβάνεσθαι, ἐξ ἧς ἐρωτᾶν τε
καὶ ἀποκρίνεσθαι ἐπιστημονέστατα οἷοί τ' ἔσονται;
E Νομοθετήσω, ἔφη, μετά γε σοῦ. Ἀρ' οὖν δοκεῖ
σοι, ἔφην ἐγώ, ὥσπερ θριγκὸς τοῖς μαθήμασιν ἡ
διαλεκτικὴ ἡμῖν ἐπάνω κεῖσθαι, καὶ οὐκέτ' ἄλλο
τούτου μάθημα ἀνωτέρω ὀρθῶς ἂν ἐπιτίθεσθαι,
535 ἀλλ' ἔχειν ἤδη τέλος τὰ τῶν μαθημάτων; Ἔμοιγ',
ἔφη.

XV. Διανομὴ τοίνυν, ἦν δ' ἐγώ, τὸ λοιπόν σοι,
τίσι ταῦτα τὰ μαθήματα δώσομεν καὶ τίνα τρόπον.
Δῆλον, ἔφη. Μέμνησαι οὖν τὴν προτέραν ἐκλογὴν
τῶν ἀρχόντων, οἵους ἐξελέξαμεν; Πῶς γάρ, ἦ δ'
ὅς, οὔ; Τὰ μὲν ἄλλα τοίνυν, ἦν δ' ἐγώ, ἐκείνας

---

[a] For εἰδώλου cf. on 532 B, p. 197, note e. This may be one
of the sources of Epist. vii. 342 B.

[b] For Platonic intellectualism the life of the ordinary man
is something between sleep and waking. Cf. Apol. 31 A.
Note the touch of humour in τελέως ἐπικἀταδαρθάνειν. Cf.
Bridges, Psychology, p. 382: "There is really no clear-cut
distinction between what is usually called sleeping and
waking. In sleep we are less awake than in the waking
hours, and in waking life we are less asleep than in sleep."

[c] Plato likes to affirm his ideal only of the philosophic
rulers.

any adumbration [a] of it, his contact with it is by opinion, not by knowledge ; and dreaming and dozing through his present life, before he awakens here he will arrive at the house of Hades and fall asleep for ever ? [b] " "Yes, by Zeus," said he, "all this I will stoutly affirm." "But, surely," said I, "if you should ever nurture in fact your children [c] whom you are now nurturing and educating in word,[d] you would not suffer them, I presume, to hold rule in the state, and determine the greatest matters, being themselves as irrational [e] as the lines so called in geometry." "Why, no," he said. "Then you will provide by law that they shall give special heed to the discipline that will enable them to ask and answer [f] questions in the most scientific manner ? " "I will so legislate," he said, "in conjunction with you." "Do you agree, then," said I, "that we have set dialectics above all other studies to be as it were the coping-stone [g]—and that no other higher kind of study could rightly be placed above it, but that our discussion of studies is now complete [h] ? " "I do," he said.

XV. "The distribution, then, remains," said I, "to whom we are to assign these studies and in what way." "Clearly," he said. "Do you remember, then, the kind of man we chose in our former selection [i] of rulers ? " "Of course," he said. "In most respects, then," said I, "you must suppose that we

---

[d] Cf. 376 D, 369 C, 472 E, Critias 106 A.

[e] A slight touch of humour. Cf. the schoolgirl who said, "These equations are inconsiderate and will not be solved."

[f] A frequent periphrasis for dialectics. Cf. τὸ ἐρωτώμενον ἀποκρίνεσθαι, Gorg. 461 E, Charm. 166 D, Prot. 338 D, Alc. I. 106 B.

[g] For ὥσπερ θριγκός cf. Eur. Herc. Fur. 1280, Aesch. Ag. 1283 ; and Phileb. 58 C-D ff.

[h] Cf. 541 B.   [i] Cf. 412 D-E, 485-487, 503 A, C-E.

535 τὰς φύσεις οἵου δεῖν ἐκλεκτέας εἶναι· τούς τε γὰρ
βεβαιοτάτους καὶ τοὺς ἀνδρειοτάτους προαιρετέον,
καὶ κατὰ δύναμιν τοὺς εὐειδεστάτους· πρὸς δὲ
B τούτοις ζητητέον μὴ μόνον γενναίους τε καὶ
βλοσυροὺς τὰ ἤθη, ἀλλὰ καὶ ἃ τῇδε τῇ παιδείᾳ
τῆς φύσεως πρόσφορα ἑκτέον αὐτοῖς. Ποῖα δὴ
διαστέλλει; Δριμύτητα, ὦ μακάριε, ἔφην, δεῖ αὐτοῖς πρὸς τὰ μαθήματα ὑπάρχειν, καὶ μὴ χαλεπῶς μανθάνειν· πολὺ γάρ τοι μᾶλλον ἀποδειλιῶσι
ψυχαὶ ἐν ἰσχυροῖς μαθήμασιν ἢ ἐν γυμνασίοις·
οἰκειότερος γὰρ αὐταῖς ὁ πόνος, ἴδιος ἀλλ' οὐ
κοινὸς ὢν μετὰ τοῦ σώματος. Ἀληθῆ, ἔφη. Καὶ
C μνήμονα δὴ καὶ ἄρρατον καὶ πάντῃ φιλόπονον
ζητητέον. ἢ τινι τρόπῳ οἴει τά τε τοῦ σώματος
ἐθελήσειν τινὰ διαπονεῖν καὶ τοσαύτην μάθησίν τε
καὶ μελέτην ἐπιτελεῖν; Οὐδένα, ἦ δ' ὅς, ἐὰν
μὴ παντάπασί γ' ᾖ εὐφυής. Τὸ γοῦν νῦν ἁμάρτημα, ἦν δ' ἐγώ, καὶ ἡ ἀτιμία φιλοσοφίᾳ διὰ
ταῦτα προσπέπτωκεν, ὃ καὶ πρότερον εἶπον, ὅτι
οὐ κατ' ἀξίαν αὐτῆς ἅπτονται· οὐ γὰρ νόθους ἔδει
ἅπτεσθαι, ἀλλὰ γνησίους. Πῶς; ἔφη. Πρῶτον
D μέν, εἶπον, φιλοπονίᾳ οὐ χωλὸν δεῖ εἶναι τὸν
ἁψόμενον, τὰ μὲν ἡμίσεα φιλόπονον, τὰ δ' ἡμίσεα
ἄπονον· ἔστι δὲ τοῦτο, ὅταν τις φιλογυμναστὴς μὲν
καὶ φιλόθηρος ᾖ καὶ· πάντα τὰ διὰ τοῦ σώματος
φιλοπονῇ, φιλομαθὴς δὲ μή, μηδὲ φιλήκοος μηδὲ

---

[a] Intellectually as well as physically. *Cf.* 357 A, *Prot.*
350 B f.

[b] *Cf. Symp.* 209 B-C, *Phaedr.* 252 E and Vol. I. p. 261 on
402 D. Ascham, *The Schoolmaster*, Bk. I. also approves of
this qualification.   [c] For βλοσυροὺς *cf. Theaet.* 149 A.

[d] *Cf.* 504 A, 374 E, *Gorg.* 480 C, *Protag.* 326 C, *Euthyphro*
15 C.

have to choose those same natures. The most stable, the most brave and enterprising [a] are to be preferred, and, so far as practicable, the most comely.[b] But in addition we must now require that they not only be virile and vigorous [c] in temper, but that they possess also the gifts of nature suitable to this type of education." "What qualities are you distinguishing?" "They must have, my friend, to begin with, a certain keenness for study, and must not learn with difficulty. For souls are much more likely to flinch and faint [d] in severe studies than in gymnastics, because the toil touches them more nearly, being peculiar to them and not shared with the body." "True," he said. "And we must demand a good memory and doggedness and industry [e] in every sense of the word. Otherwise how do you suppose anyone will consent both to undergo all the toils of the body and to complete so great a course of study and discipline?" "No one could," he said, "unless most happily endowed." "Our present mistake," said I, "and the disesteem that has in consequence fallen upon philosophy are, as I said before,[f] caused by the unfitness of her associates and wooers. They should not have been bastards [g] but true scions." "What do you mean?" he said. "In the first place," I said, "the aspirant to philosophy must not limp [h] in his industry, in the one half of him loving, in the other shunning, toil. This happens when anyone is a lover of gymnastics and hunting and all the labours of the body, yet is not fond of learning or

---

[e] The qualities of the ideal student again. *Cf.* on 487 A.
[f] *Cf. supra* 495 c ff., pp. 49-51.
[g] Montaigne, i. 24 (vol. i. p. 73), "les âmes boiteuses, les bastardes et vulgaires, sont indignes de la philosophie."
[h] *Cf. Laws* 634 A, *Tim.* 44 c.

535 ζητητικός, ἀλλ᾽ ἐν πᾶσι τούτοις μισοπονῇ· χωλὸς
δὲ καὶ ὁ τἀναντία τούτου μεταβεβληκὼς τὴν
φιλοπονίαν. Ἀληθέστατα, ἔφη, λέγεις. Οὐκοῦν
καὶ πρὸς ἀλήθειαν, ἦν δ᾽ ἐγώ, ταὐτὸν τοῦτο ἀνά-
Ε πηρον ψυχὴν θήσομεν, ἢ ἂν τὸ μὲν ἑκούσιον
ψεῦδος μισῇ καὶ χαλεπῶς φέρῃ αὐτή τε καὶ ἑτέρων
ψευδομένων ὑπεραγανακτῇ, τὸ δ᾽ ἀκούσιον εὐκόλως
προσδέχηται καὶ ἀμαθαίνουσά που ἁλισκομένη μὴ
ἀγανακτῇ, ἀλλ᾽ εὐχερῶς ὥσπερ θηρίον ὕειον ἐν
536 ἀμαθίᾳ μολύνηται; Παντάπασι μὲν οὖν, ἔφη.
Καὶ πρὸς σωφροσύνην, ἦν δ᾽ ἐγώ, καὶ ἀνδρείαν
καὶ μεγαλοπρέπειαν καὶ πάντα τὰ τῆς ἀρετῆς
μέρη οὐχ ἥκιστα δεῖ φυλάττειν τὸν νόθον τε καὶ
τὸν γνήσιον, ὅταν γάρ τις μὴ ἐπίστηται τὰ τοιαῦτα
σκοπεῖν καὶ ἰδιώτης καὶ πόλις, λανθάνουσι χωλοῖς
τε καὶ νόθοις χρώμενοι, πρὸς ὅ τι ἂν τύχωσι τούτων, οἱ μὲν φίλοις, οἱ δὲ ἄρχουσι. Καὶ μάλα, ἔφη,
οὕτως ἔχει. Ἡμῖν δή, ἦν δ᾽ ἐγώ, πάντα τὰ τοιαῦτα
Β διευλαβητέον, ὡς ἐὰν μὲν ἀρτιμελεῖς τε καὶ ἀρτί-
φρονας ἐπὶ τοσαύτην μάθησιν καὶ τοσαύτην
ἄσκησιν κομίσαντες παιδεύωμεν, ἥ τε δίκη ἡμῖν
οὐ μέμψεται αὐτή, τήν τε πόλιν καὶ πολιτείαν
σώσομεν, ἀλλοίους δὲ ἄγοντες ἐπὶ ταῦτα τἀναντία

---

[a] Cf. 548 E, Lysis 206 c, Euthyd. 274 c, 304 c, and Vol. I.
p. 515, on 475 D.

[b] Cf. supra 382 A-B-C.

[c] Cf. Laws 819 D, Rep. 372 D, Politicus 266 c, and my note
in Class. Phil. xii. (1917) pp. 308-310. Cf. too the proverbial
ὗς γνοίη, Laches 196 D and Rivals 134 A; and Apelt's
emendation of Cratyl. 393 c, Progr. Jena, 1905, p. 19.

[d] Cf. 487 A and Vol. I. p. 261, note c on 402 c. The
cardinal virtues are not rigidly fixed in Plato. Cf. on 427 E,
Vol. I. p. 346.

of listening[a] or inquiring, but in all such matters hates work. And he too is lame whose industry is one-sided in the reverse way." " Most true," he said. " Likewise in respect of truth," I said, " we shall regard as maimed in precisely the same way the soul that hates the voluntary lie and is troubled by it in its own self and greatly angered by it in others, but cheerfully accepts the involuntary falsehood[b] and is not distressed when convicted of lack of knowledge, but wallows in the mud of ignorance as insensitively as a pig.[c]" " By all means," he said. " And with reference to sobriety," said I, " and bravery and loftiness of soul[d] and all the parts of virtue,[e] we must especially be on our guard to distinguish the base-born from the true-born. For when the knowledge necessary to make such discriminations is lacking in individual or state, they unawares employ at random[f] for any of these purposes the crippled and base-born natures, as their friends or rulers." " It is so indeed," he said. " But we," I said, " must be on our guard in all such cases, since, if we bring men sound of limb and mind to so great a study and so severe a training, justice herself will have no fault to find[g] with us, and we shall preserve the state and our polity. But, if we introduce into it the other sort,

---

[e] Plato is using ordinary language and not troubling himself with the problem of *Protag.* 329 D (*What Plato Said*, p. 497) and *Laws* 633 A (*What Plato Said*, p. 624). *Cf.* also on 533 D.

[f] πρὸς ὅ τι ἂν τύχωσι: lit. " for whatsoever they happen to of these (services)." *Cf. Symp.* 181 B, *Prot.* 353 A, *Crito* 44 D and 45 D, *Gorg.* 522 c, *Laws* 656 c, *Rep.* 332 B, 561 D, Dem. iv. 46, Isoc. *Panath.* 25, 74, 239, Aristot. *Met.* 1013 a 6.

[g] *Cf. supra* 487 A. For δίκη *cf.* Hirzel, *Dike, Themis und Verwandtes*, p. 116.

536 πάντα καὶ πράξομεν καὶ φιλοσοφίας ἔτι πλείω
γέλωτα κατανλήσομεν.[a] Αἰσχρὸν μέντ᾽ ἂν εἴη,
ἦ δ᾽ ὅς. Πάνυ μὲν οὖν, εἶπον· γελοῖον δ᾽ ἔγωγε
καὶ ἐν τῷ παρόντι ἔοικα παθεῖν. Τὸ ποῖον; ἔφη.

C ᾿Επελαθόμην,[b] ἦν δ᾽ ἐγώ, ὅτι ἐπαίζομεν, καὶ μᾶλλον
ἐντεινάμενος εἶπον. λέγων γὰρ ἅμα ἔβλεψα πρὸς
φιλοσοφίαν, καὶ ἰδὼν προπεπηλακισμένην ἀναξίως
ἀγανακτήσας μοι δοκῶ καὶ ὥσπερ θυμωθεὶς τοῖς
αἰτίοις σπουδαιότερον εἰπεῖν ἃ εἶπον. Οὐ μὰ τὸν
Δί᾽, ἔφη, οὔκουν ὥς γ᾽ ἐμοὶ ἀκροατῇ. ᾿Αλλ᾽ ὡς
ἐμοί, ἦν δ᾽ ἐγώ, ῥήτορι. τόδε δὲ μὴ ἐπιλανθανώ-
μεθα, ὅτι ἐν μὲν τῇ προτέρᾳ ἐκλογῇ πρεσβύτας
ἐξελέγομεν, ἐν δὲ ταύτῃ οὐκ ἐγχωρήσει· Σόλωνι

D γὰρ οὐ πειστέον, ὡς γηράσκων τις πολλὰ δυνατὸς
μανθάνειν, ἀλλ᾽ ἧττον ἢ τρέχειν, νέων δὲ πάντες
οἱ μεγάλοι καὶ οἱ πολλοὶ πόνοι. ᾿Ανάγκη, ἔφη.

XVI. Τὰ μὲν τοίνυν λογισμῶν τε καὶ γεω-
μετριῶν καὶ πάσης τῆς προπαιδείας, ἣν τῆς διαλεκτικῆς δεῖ προπαιδευθῆναι, παισὶν οὖσι χρὴ
προβάλλειν, οὐχ ὡς ἐπάναγκες μαθεῖν τὸ σχῆμα
τῆς διδαχῆς ποιουμένους. Τί δή; ῞Οτι, ἦν δ᾽ ἐγώ,

E οὐδὲν μάθημα μετὰ δουλείας τὸν ἐλεύθερον χρὴ

---

[a] κατανλήσομεν: cf. 344 D.

[b] Jest and earnest are never far apart in Plato. Fabling
about justice is an old man's game, *Laws* 685 A, 769 A. Life
itself is best treated as play, *Laws* 803 c. Science in *Tim.*
59 D is παιδιά, like literature in the *Phaedrus* 276 D-E, *ibid.*
278 B. *Cf.* Friedländer, *Platon*, i. pp. 38 and 160, and *What
Plato Said*, pp. 553 and 601.

[c] For similar self-checks *cf. Laws* 804 B, 832 B, 907 B-C,
Phaedr. 260 D, 269 B. For ἐντεινάμενος *cf.* Blaydes on Aristoph.
Clouds 969.

the outcome will be just the opposite, and we shall pour a still greater flood[a] of ridicule upon philosophy." "That would indeed be shameful," he said. "Most certainly," said I; "but here again I am making myself a little ridiculous." "In what way?" "I forgot," said I, "that we were jesting,[b] and I spoke with too great intensity.[c] For, while speaking, I turned my eyes upon philosophy,[d] and when I saw how she is undeservedly reviled, I was revolted, and, as if in anger, spoke too earnestly to those who are in fault." "No, by Zeus, not too earnestly for me[e] as a hearer." "But too much so for me as a speaker," I said. "But this we must not forget, that in our former selection we chose old men, but in this one that will not do. For we must not take Solon's[f] word for it that growing old a man is able to learn many things. He is less able to do that than to run a race. To the young[g] belong all heavy and frequent labours." "Necessarily," he said.

XVI. "Now, all this study of reckoning and geometry and all the preliminary studies that are indispensable preparation for dialectics must be presented to them while still young, not in the form of compulsory instruction.[h]" "Why so?" "Because," said I, "a free soul ought not to pursue any study slavishly; for

---

[a] Cf. Isoc. Busiris 49. Whatever the difficulties of the chronology it is hard to believe that this is not one of Isocrates' many endeavours to imitate Platonic effects.

[e] Cf. Soph. 226 c, Sophocles, Ajax 397.

[f] γηράσκω δ' ἀεὶ πολλὰ διδασκόμενος, "I grow old ever learning many things." Cf. Laches 188 A-B; Otto, p. 317.

[g] Cf. Theaet. 146 B. This has been misquoted to the effect that Plato said the young are the best philosophers.

[h] This and παίζοντας below (537 A) anticipate much modern kindergarten rhetoric.

536 μανθάνειν. οἱ μὲν γὰρ τοῦ σώματος πόνοι βίᾳ
πονούμενοι χεῖρον οὐδὲν τὸ σῶμα ἀπεργάζονται,
ψυχῇ δὲ βίαιον οὐδὲν ἔμμονον μάθημα. Ἀληθῆ,
ἔφη. Μὴ τοίνυν βίᾳ, εἶπον, ὦ ἄριστε, τοὺς παῖδας
537 ἐν τοῖς μαθήμασιν ἀλλὰ παίζοντας τρέφε, ἵνα καὶ
μᾶλλον οἶός τ' ἦς καθορᾶν ἐφ' ὃ ἕκαστος πέφυκεν.
Ἔχει ὃ λέγεις, ἔφη, λόγον. Οὐκοῦν μνημονεύεις,
ἦν δ' ἐγώ, ὅτι καὶ εἰς τὸν πόλεμον ἔφαμεν τοὺς
παῖδας εἶναι ἀκτέον ἐπὶ τῶν ἵππων θεωρούς, καὶ
ἐάν που ἀσφαλὲς ᾖ, προσακτέον ἐγγὺς καὶ γευ-
στέον αἵματος, ὥσπερ τοὺς σκύλακας; Μέμνημαι,
ἔφη. Ἐν πᾶσι δὴ τούτοις, ἦν δ' ἐγώ, τοῖς τε
πόνοις καὶ μαθήμασι καὶ φόβοις, ὃς ἂν ἐντρεχέ-
στατος ἀεὶ φαίνηται, εἰς ἀριθμόν τινα ἐγκριτέον.
Β Ἐν τίνι, ἔφη, ἡλικίᾳ; Ἡνίκα, ἦν δ' ἐγώ, τῶν
ἀναγκαίων γυμνασίων μεθίενται. οὗτος γὰρ ὁ
χρόνος, ἐάν τε δύο ἐάν τε τρία ἔτη γίγνηται,
ἀδύνατός τι ἄλλο πρᾶξαι. κόποι γὰρ καὶ ὕπνοι
μαθήμασι πολέμιοι· καὶ ἅμα μία καὶ αὕτη τῶν
βασάνων οὐκ ἐλαχίστη, τίς ἕκαστος ἐν τοῖς γυμνασίοις φανεῖται. Πῶς γὰρ οὔκ; ἔφη. Μετὰ
δὴ τοῦτον τὸν χρόνον, ἦν δ' ἐγώ, ἐκ τῶν εἰκοσι-

ᵃ Newman, Introd. Aristot. *Pol.* 358, says Aristotle rejects
this distinction, *Pol.* 1338 b 40 μέχρι μὲν γὰρ ἥβης κουφότερα
γυμνάσια προσοιστέον, τὴν βίαιον τροφὴν καὶ τοὺς πρὸς ἀνάγκην
πόνους ἀπείργοντας, ἵνα μηδὲν ἐμπόδιον ᾖ πρὸς τὴν αὔξησιν.

ᵇ Cf. 424 E-425 A, *Laws* 819 B-C, 643 B-D, 797 A-B, *Polit.*
308 D.

Cf. the naïve statement in Colvin and Bagley, *Human*

while bodily labours *a* performed under constraint do not harm the body, nothing that is learned under compulsion stays with the mind." "True," he said. "Do not, then, my friend, keep children to their studies by compulsion but by play.*b* That will also better enable you to discern the natural capacities of each." "There is reason in that," he said. "And do you not remember," I said, "that we also declared *c* that we must conduct the children to war on horseback to be spectators, and wherever it may be safe, bring them to the front and give them a taste of blood as we do with whelps?" "I do remember." "And those who as time goes on show the most facility in all these toils and studies and alarms are to be selected and enrolled on a list.*d*" "At what age?" he said. "When they are released from their prescribed gymnastics. For that period, whether it be two or three years, incapacitates them for other occupations.*e* For great fatigue and much sleep are the foes of study, and moreover one of our tests of them, and not the least, will be their behaviour in their physical exercises.*f*" "Surely it is," he said. "After this period," I said, "those who are given preference from the twenty-year class

Behaviour, p. 41 : "The discovery [*sic !*] by Karl Groos that play was actually a preparation for the business of later life was almost revolutionary from the standpoint of educational theory and practice."

c *Cf. supra* 467, Vol. I. pp. 485-487.

d ἐγκριτέον: *cf.* 413 D, 377 C, 486 D, *Laws* 802 B, 820 D, 936 A, 952 A.

e *Cf.* Aristot. *Pol.* 1339 a 7 f. ἅμα γὰρ τῇ τε διανοίᾳ καὶ τῷ σώματι διαπονεῖν οὐ δεῖ, etc.; Plut. *De Ed. Puer.* 11, *De Tuenda San.* c. 25, quoted by Newman, Aristot. *Pol.* i. p. 359, are irrelevant to this passage, but could be referred to the balancing of music and gymnastics in 410-412.

f *Cf. Laws* 829 B-C.

537 ἐτῶν οἱ προκριθέντες τιμάς τε μείζους τῶν ἄλλων
C οἴσονται, τά τε χύδην μαθήματα παισὶν ἐν τῇ
παιδείᾳ γενόμενα τούτοις συνακτέον εἰς σύνοψιν
οἰκειότητος ἀλλήλων τῶν μαθημάτων καὶ τῆς τοῦ
ὄντος φύσεως. Μόνη γοῦν, εἶπεν, ἡ τοιαύτη
μάθησις βέβαιος ἐν οἷς ἂν ἐγγένηται. Καὶ μεγίστη
γε, ἦν δ' ἐγώ, πεῖρα διαλεκτικῆς φύσεως καὶ μή·
ὁ μὲν γὰρ συνοπτικὸς διαλεκτικός, ὁ δὲ μὴ οὔ.
Ξυννοίομαι, ἦ δ' ὅς. Ταῦτα τοίνυν, ἦν δ' ἐγώ,
D δεήσει σε ἐπισκοποῦντα, οἳ ἂν μάλιστα τοιοῦτοι
ἐν αὐτοῖς ὦσι καὶ μόνιμοι μὲν ἐν μαθήμασι, μόνιμοι δ' ἐν πολέμῳ καὶ τοῖς ἄλλοις νομίμοις,
τούτους αὖ, ἐπειδὰν τὰ τριάκοντα ἔτη ἐκβαίνωσιν,
ἐκ τῶν προκρίτων προκρινάμενον εἰς μείζους τε
τιμὰς καθιστάναι καὶ σκοπεῖν, τῇ τοῦ διαλέγεσθαι
δυνάμει βασανίζοντα, τίς ὀμμάτων καὶ τῆς ἄλλης
αἰσθήσεως δυνατὸς μεθιέμενος ἐπ' αὐτὸ τὸ ὂν μετ'
ἀληθείας ἰέναι. καὶ ἐνταῦθα δὴ πολλῆς φυλακῆς

---

[a] σύνοψιν: cf. 531 D. This thought is endlessly repeated
by modern writers on education. Cf. Mill, Diss. and Disc.
iv. 336 ; Bagley, The Educative Process, p. 180 : " The theory
of concentration proposed by Ziller . . . seeks to organize
all the subject matter of instruction into a unified system,
the various units of which shall be consciously related to one
another in the minds of the pupils " ; Haldane, The Philosophy of Humanism, p. 94 : " There was a conference attended
by representatives of various German Universities . . . which
took place at Hanstein, not far from Göttingen in May 1921.
. . . The purpose of the movement is nominally the establishment of a Humanistic Faculty. But in this connexion
'faculty' does not mean a separate faculty of humanistic
studies. . . . The real object is to bring these subjects into
organic relation to one another."

will receive greater honours than the others, and they will be required to gather the studies which they disconnectedly pursued as children in their former education into a comprehensive survey [a] of their affinities with one another and with the nature of things." " That, at any rate," he said, " is the only instruction that abides with those who receive it." " And it is also," said I, " the chief test of the dialectical nature and its opposite. For he who can view things in their connexion is a dialectician; he who cannot, is not." " I concur," he said. " With these qualities in mind," I said, " it will be your task to make a selection of those who manifest them best from the group who are steadfast in their studies and in war and in all lawful requirements, and when they have passed the thirtieth year to promote them, by a second selection from those preferred in the first,[b] to still greater honours, and to prove and test them by the power of dialectic [c] to see which of them is able to disregard the eyes and other senses [d] and go on to being itself in company with truth. And at this point, my friend, the greatest

Cf. Alexander, *Space, Time, and Deity*, vol. i. p. 4 " So true is it that, as Plato puts it, the metaphysician is a ' synoptical ' man." *Cf.* also Aristot. *Soph. El.* 167 a 38 διὰ τὸ μὴ δύνασθαι συνορᾶν τὸ ταὐτὸν καὶ τὸ ἕτερον. Stenzel, *Dialektik*, p. 8, misuses the passage to support the view that Plato's dialectic still looks for unity and not for divisions and distinctions, as in the *Sophist*. *Cf.* also *ibid.* p. 72.

[b] For the technical meaning of the word προκρίτων *cf.* *Laws* 753 B-D.

[c] For this periphrasis *cf.* *Phaedr.* 246 D, *Tim.* 85 E. *Cf.* also on 509 A.

[d] The reader of Plato ought not to misunderstand this now. *Cf. supra* on 532 A, pp. 196 f., note *d*, and 530 B, p. 187, note *c*.

537 ἔργον, ὦ ἑταῖρε. Τί μάλιστα; ἦ δ' ὅς. Οὐκ ἐν-
E νοεῖς, ἦν δ' ἐγώ, τὸ νῦν περὶ τὸ διαλέγεσθαι κακὸν
γιγνόμενον ὅσον γίγνεται; Τὸ ποῖον; ἔφη. Παρα-
νομίας που, ἔφην ἐγώ, ἐμπίπλανται. Καὶ μάλα,
ἔφη. Θαυμαστὸν οὖν τι οἴει, εἶπον, πάσχειν αὐτούς, καὶ οὐ ξυγγιγνώσκεις; Πῇ μάλιστα; ἔφη.
Οἷον, ἦν δ' ἐγώ, εἴ τις ὑποβολιμαῖος τραφείη ἐν
πολλοῖς μὲν χρήμασι, πολλῷ δὲ καὶ μεγάλῳ γένει
538 καὶ κόλαξι πολλοῖς, ἀνὴρ δὲ γενόμενος αἴσθοιτο,
ὅτι οὐ τούτων ἐστὶ τῶν φασκόντων γονέων, τοὺς
δὲ τῷ ὄντι γεννήσαντας μὴ εὕροι, τοῦτον ἔχεις
μαντεύσασθαι, πῶς ἂν διατεθείη πρός τε τοὺς κόλακας καὶ πρὸς τοὺς ὑποβαλομένους ἐν ἐκείνῳ τε
τῷ χρόνῳ, ᾧ οὐκ ᾔδει τὰ περὶ τῆς ὑποβολῆς, καὶ
ἐν ᾧ αὖ ᾔδει; ἢ βούλει ἐμοῦ μαντευομένου ἀκοῦσαι;
Βούλομαι, ἔφη.

XVII. Μαντεύομαι τοίνυν, εἶπον, μᾶλλον αὐτὸν
B τιμᾶν ἂν τὸν πατέρα καὶ τὴν μητέρα καὶ τοὺς
ἄλλους οἰκείους δοκοῦντας ἢ τοὺς κολακεύοντας,
καὶ ἧττον μὲν ἂν περιιδεῖν ἐνδεεῖς τινός, ἧττον δὲ

---

a Plato returns to an idea suggested in 498 A, and warns
against the mental confusion and moral unsettlement that
result from premature criticism of life by undisciplined minds.
In the terminology of modern education, he would not
encourage students to discuss the validity of the Ten Com-
mandments and the Constitution of the United States before
they could spell, construe, cipher, and had learned to distinguish an undistributed middle term from a *petitio
principii.* *Cf. Phaedo* 89 D-E.

We need not suppose with Grote and others that this
involves any "reaction" or violent change of the opinion he
held when he wrote the minor dialogues that portray such
discussions. In fact, the still later *Sophist,* 230 B-C-D, is more
friendly to youthful dialectics.

Whatever the effect of the practice of Socrates or the

care [a] is requisite." "How so?" he said. "Do you not note," said I, "how great is the harm caused by our present treatment of dialectics?" "What is that?" he said. "Its practitioners are infected with lawlessness.[b]" "They are indeed." "Do you suppose," I said, "that there is anything surprising in this state of mind, and do you not think it pardonable [c]?" "In what way, pray?" he said. "Their case," said I, "resembles that of a suppositious son reared in abundant wealth and a great and numerous family amid many flatterers, who on arriving at manhood should become aware that he is not the child of those who call themselves his parents, and should not be able to find his true father and mother. Can you divine what would be his feelings towards the flatterers and his supposed parents in the time when he did not know the truth about his adoption, and, again, when he knew it? Or would you like to hear my surmise?" "I would."

XVII. "Well, then, my surmise is," I said, "that he would be more likely to honour his reputed father and mother and other kin than the flatterers, and that there would be less likelihood of his allowing them to lack for anything, and that he would be less

Sophists, Plato himself anticipates Grote's criticism in the *Republic* by representing Socrates as discoursing with ingenuous youth in a more simple and edifying style. *Cf. Lysis* 207 D ff., *Euthydem.* 278 E-282 c, 288 D-290 D. Yet again the *Charmides* might be thought an exception.

[b] *Cf.* also Zeller, *Phil. d. Griechen*, ii. 1, p. 912, who seems to consider the *Sophist* earlier than the *Republic*.

[b] *i.e.* they call all restrictions on impulses and instincts tyrannical conventions. *Cf. Gorg.* 483-484, Aristoph. *Clouds, passim,* and on nature and law *cf.* Vol. I. p. 116, note *a*, on 359 c.

[c] *Cf.* on 494 A, p. 43, note *c*.

538 παράνομόν τι δρᾶσαι ἢ εἰπεῖν εἰς αὐτούς, ἧττον δὲ
ἀπειθεῖν τὰ μεγάλα ἐκείνοις ἢ τοῖς κόλαξιν, ἐν ᾧ
χρόνῳ τὸ ἀληθὲς μὴ εἰδείη. Εἰκός, ἔφη. Αἰσθό-
μενον τοίνυν τὸ ὂν μαντεύομαι αὖ περὶ μὲν τούτους
ἀνεῖναι ἂν τὸ τιμᾶν τε καὶ σπουδάζειν, περὶ δὲ
τοὺς κόλακας ἐπιτεῖναι, καὶ πείθεσθαί τε αὐτοῖς
C διαφερόντως ἢ πρότερον καὶ ζῆν ἂν ἤδη κατ'
ἐκείνους, ξυνόντα αὐτοῖς ἀπαρακαλύπτως, πατρὸς
δὲ ἐκείνου καὶ τῶν ἄλλων ποιουμένων οἰκείων, εἰ
μὴ πάνυ εἴη φύσει ἐπιεικής, μέλειν τὸ μηδέν.
Πάντ', ἔφη, λέγεις οἷά περ ἂν γένοιτο. ἀλλὰ πῇ
πρὸς τοὺς ἁπτομένους τῶν λόγων αὕτη φέρει ἡ
εἰκών; Τῇδε. ἔστι που ἡμῖν δόγματα ἐκ παίδων
περὶ δικαίων καὶ καλῶν, ἐν οἷς ἐκτεθράμμεθα
ὥσπερ ὑπὸ γονεῦσι, πειθαρχοῦντές τε καὶ τιμῶντες
D αὐτά. Ἔστι γάρ. Οὐκοῦν καὶ ἄλλα ἐναντία
τούτων ἐπιτηδεύματα ἡδονὰς ἔχοντα, ἃ κολακεύει
μὲν ἡμῶν τὴν ψυχὴν καὶ ἕλκει ἐφ' αὑτά, πείθει δ'
οὔ τοὺς καὶ ὁπηοῦν μετρίους· ἀλλ' ἐκεῖνα τιμῶσι
τὰ πάτρια καὶ ἐκείνοις πειθαρχοῦσιν. Ἔστι ταῦτα.

---

[a] διαφερόντως ἢ πρότερον : cf. *Phaedo* 85 B.

[b] οἷά περ ἂν γένοιτο is the phrase Aristotle uses to distinguish
the truth of poetry from the facts of history.

[c] That is the meaning. Lit. "those who lay hold on
discourse."

[d] Plato's warning applies to our day no less than to his
own. Like the proponents of ethical nihilism in Plato's
Athens, much of our present-day literature and teaching
questions all standards of morality and aesthetics, and confuses justice and injustice, beauty and ugliness. Its gospel
is expressed in Mr. Oppenheim's lines :

inclined to do or say to them anything unlawful, and less liable to disobey them in great matters than to disobey the flatterers—during the time when he did not know the truth." "It is probable," he said. "But when he found out the truth, I surmise that he would grow more remiss in honour and devotion to them and pay more regard to the flatterers, whom he would heed more than before [a] and would henceforth live by their rule, associating with them openly, while for that former father and his adoptive kin he would not care at all, unless he was naturally of a very good disposition." "All that you say," he replied, "would be likely to happen.[b] But what is the pertinency of this comparison to the novices of dialectic [c]?" "It is this. We have, I take it, certain convictions [d] from childhood about the just and the honourable, in which, in obedience and honour to them, we have been bred as children under their parents." "Yes, we have." "And are there not other practices going counter to these, that have pleasures attached to them and that flatter and solicit our souls, but do not win over men of any decency; but they continue to hold in honour the teachings of their fathers and obey them?" "It is

> Let nothing bind you.
> If it is duty, away with it.
> If it is law, disobey it.
> If it is opinion, go against it.
> There is only one divinity, yourself,
> Only one god, you.

For the unsettling effects of dialectic *cf. Phaedo* 90 B; also Chesterton, *George Bernard Shaw*, p. 249: "There may have been ages so sluggish . . . that anything that woke them up at all was a good thing. . . . No one . . . does any good to our age merely by asking questions unless he can answer the question." *Cf.* also on 537 D, p. 220, note *a*.

538 Τί οὖν; ἦν δ' ἐγώ· ὅταν τὸν οὕτως ἔχοντα ἐλθὸν
ἐρώτημα ἔρηται, τί ἐστι τὸ καλόν, καὶ ἀποκρινα-
μένου, ὃ τοῦ νομοθέτου ἤκουεν, ἐξελέγχῃ ὁ λόγος,
καὶ πολλάκις καὶ πολλαχῇ ἐλέγχων εἰς δόξαν
E καταβάλῃ, ὡς τοῦτο οὐδὲν μᾶλλον καλὸν ἢ
αἰσχρόν, καὶ περὶ δικαίου ὡσαύτως καὶ ἀγαθοῦ
καὶ ἃ μάλιστα ἦγεν ἐν τιμῇ, μετὰ τοῦτο τί οἴει
ποιήσειν αὐτὸν πρὸς αὐτὰ τιμῆς τε πέρι καὶ
πειθαρχίας; Ἀνάγκη, ἔφη, μήτε τιμᾶν ἔτι ὁμοίως
μήτε πείθεσθαι. Ὅταν οὖν, ἦν δ' ἐγώ, μήτε ταῦτα
ἡγῆται τίμια καὶ οἰκεῖα, ὥσπερ πρὸ τοῦ, τά τε
539 ἀληθῆ μὴ εὑρίσκῃ, ἔστι πρὸς ὁποῖον βίον ἄλλον ἢ
τὸν κολακεύοντα εἰκότως προσχωρήσεται; Οὐκ
ἔστιν, ἔφη. Παράνομος δή, οἶμαι, δόξει γεγονέναι ἐκ νομίμου. Ἀνάγκη. Οὐκοῦν, ἔφην, εἰκὸς
τὸ πάθος τῶν οὕτω λόγων ἁπτομένων καί, ὃ ἄρτι
ἔλεγον, πολλῆς συγγνώμης ἄξιον; Καὶ ἐλέου γ',
ἔφη. Οὐκοῦν ἵνα μὴ γίγνηται ὁ ἔλεος οὗτος περὶ
τοὺς τριακοντούτας σοι, εὐλαβουμένῳ παντὶ τρόπῳ
τῶν λόγων ἁπτέον; Καὶ μάλ', ἦ δ' ὅς. Ἆρ' οὖν
B οὐ μία μὲν εὐλάβεια αὕτη συχνή, τὸ μὴ νέους

---

[a] The question is here personified, as the λόγος so often is,
e.g. 503 A. *Cf. What Plato Said* on *Protag.* 361 A-B.

[b] A possible allusion to the καταβάλλοντες λόγοι of the
sophists. *Cf. Euthydem.* 277 D, 288 A, *Phaedo* 88 C, *Phileb.*
15 E and *What Plato Said*, p. 518, on *Crito* 272 B.

[c] This is the moral counterpart of the intellectual scepti-

THE REPUBLIC, BOOK VII

so." "Well, then," said I, "when a man of this kind is met by the question,[a] ' What is the honourable ? ' and on his giving the answer which he learned from the lawgiver, the argument confutes him, and by many and various refutations upsets[b] his faith and makes him believe that this thing is no more honourable than it is base,[c] and when he has had the same experience about the just and the good and everything that he chiefly held in esteem, how do you suppose that he will conduct himself thereafter in the matter of respect and obedience to this traditional morality ? " "It is inevitable," he said, " that he will not continue to honour and obey as before." "And then," said I, " when he ceases to honour these principles and to think that they are binding on him,[d] and cannot discover the true principles, will he be likely to adopt any other way of life than that which flatters his desires[e] ? " "He will not," he said. "He will, then, seem to have become a rebel to law and convention instead of the conformer that he was." "Necessarily." "And is not this experience of those who take up dialectics in this fashion to be expected and, as I just now said, deserving of much leniency ? " "Yes, and of pity too," he said. "Then that we may not have to pity thus your thirty-year-old disciples, must you not take every precaution when you introduce them to the study of dialectics ? " "Yes, indeed," he said. "And is it not one chief safeguard not to suffer them to taste

cism or μισολογία of *Phaedo* 90 c-d. *Cf. What Plato Said*, p. 531, on *Phaedo* 89 d.
[d] For οἰκεία *cf. supra* 433 E, 443 D, and *Class. Phil.* xxiv. (1929) pp. 409-410.
[e] *Cf. Laws* 633 E and *supra* 442 A-B. Others render it, " than the life of the flatterers (parasites)." Why not both ?

225

PLATO

539 ὄντας αὐτῶν γεύεσθαι; οἶμαι γάρ σε οὐ λεληθέναι
ὅτι οἱ μειρακίσκοι, ὅταν τὸ πρῶτον λόγων γεύ-
ωνται, ὡς παιδιᾷ αὐτοῖς καταχρῶνται, ἀεὶ εἰς
ἀντιλογίαν χρώμενοι, καὶ μιμούμενοι τοὺς ἐξελέγ-
χοντας αὐτοὶ ἄλλους ἐλέγχουσι, χαίροντες ὥσπερ
σκυλάκια τῷ ἕλκειν τε καὶ σπαράττειν τῷ λόγῳ
τοὺς πλησίον ἀεί. Ὑπερφυῶς μὲν οὖν, ἔφη.
Οὐκοῦν ὅταν δὴ πολλοὺς μὲν αὐτοὶ ἐλέγξωσιν, ὑπὸ
C πολλῶν δὲ ἐλεγχθῶσι, σφόδρα καὶ ταχὺ ἐμπίπτουσιν
εἰς τὸ μηδὲν ἡγεῖσθαι ὧνπερ πρότερον· καὶ ἐκ
τούτων δὴ αὐτοί τε καὶ τὸ ὅλον φιλοσοφίας πέρι
εἰς τοὺς ἄλλους διαβέβληνται. Ἀληθέστατα, ἔφη.
Ὁ δὲ δὴ πρεσβύτερος, ἦν δ' ἐγώ, τῆς μὲν τοιαύτης μανίας οὐκ ἂν ἐθέλοι μετέχειν, τὸν δὲ
διαλέγεσθαι ἐθέλοντα καὶ σκοπεῖν τἀληθὲς μᾶλλον
μιμήσεται ἢ τὸν παιδιᾶς χάριν παίζοντα καὶ
D ἀντιλέγοντα, καὶ αὐτός τε μετριώτερος ἔσται καὶ
τὸ ἐπιτήδευμα τιμιώτερον ἀντὶ ἀτιμοτέρου ποιήσει.
Ὀρθῶς, ἔφη. Οὐκοῦν καὶ τὰ προειρημένα τούτου
ἐπ' εὐλαβείᾳ πάντα προείρηται, τὸ τὰς φύσεις
κοσμίους εἶναι καὶ στασίμους οἷς τις μεταδώσει

---

[a] See on 498 A–B. *Cf.* Richard of Bury, *Philobiblon*
(Morley, *A Miscellany*, pp. 49-50): "But the contemporaries
of our age negligently apply a few years of ardent youth,
burning by turns with the fire of vice; and when they have
attained the acumen of discerning a doubtful truth, they
immediately become involved in extraneous business, retire,
and say farewell to the schools of philosophy; they sip the
frothy must of juvenile wit over the difficulties of philosophy,
and pour out the purified old wine with economical care."

[b] *Cf. Apol.* 23 c, *Phileb.* 15 E, Xen. *Mem.* i. 2. 46, Isoc.
xii. 26 and x. 6; also Friedländer, *Platon*, ii. p. 568.

[c] But in another mood or from another angle this is the
bacchic madness of philosophy which all the company in the

of it while young ? [a] For I fancy you have not failed to observe that lads, when they first get a taste of disputation, misuse it as a form of sport, always employing it contentiously, and, imitating confuters, they themselves confute others.[b] They delight like puppies in pulling about and tearing with words all who approach them." " Exceedingly so," he said. " And when they have themselves confuted many and been confuted by many, they quickly fall into a violent distrust of all that they formerly held true ; and the outcome is that they themselves and the whole business of philosophy are discredited with other men." " Most true," he said. " But an older man will not share this craze,[c] " said I, " but will rather choose to imitate the one who consents to examine truth dialectically than the one who makes a jest [d] and a sport of mere contradiction, and so he will himself be more reasonable and moderate, and bring credit rather than discredit upon his pursuit." " Right," he said. " And were not all our preceding statements made with a view to this precaution— our requirement that those permitted to take part in such discussions must have orderly and stable natures,

Symposium have shared, 218 A-B. *Cf.* also *Phaedr.* 245 B-C, 249 C-E, *Sophist* 216 D, *Phileb.* 15 D-E, and *What Plato Said*, p. 493, on *Protag.* 317 D-E.

[d] *Cf. Gorg.* 500 B-C. Yet the prevailing seriousness of Plato's own thought does not exclude touches of humour and irony, and he vainly warns the modern reader to distinguish between jest and earnest in the drama of disputation in his dialogues. Many misinterpretations of Plato's thought are due to the failure to heed this warning. *Cf. e.g. Gorgias* 474 A (*What Plato Said*, p. 504), which Robin, *L'Année Philos.* xxi. p. 29, and others miss, *Rep.* 376 B, *Symp.* 196 C, *Protag.* 339 f., *Theaet.* 157 A-B, 160 B, 165 B, and *passim.* *Cf.* also on 536 C, p. 214, note *b*.

539 τῶν λόγων, καὶ μὴ ὡς νῦν ὁ τυχὼν καὶ οὐδὲν
προσήκων ἔρχεται ἐπ᾽ αὐτό; Πάνυ μὲν οὖν, ἔφη.

XVIII. Ἀρκεῖ δὴ ἐπὶ λόγων μεταλήψει μεῖναι
ἐνδελεχῶς καὶ ξυντόνως, μηδὲν ἄλλο πράττοντι,
ἀλλ᾽ ἀντιστρόφως γυμναζομένῳ τοῖς περὶ τὸ σῶμα
E γυμνασίοις, ἔτη διπλάσια ἢ τότε; Ἓξ, ἔφη, ἢ
τέτταρα λέγεις; Ἀμέλει, εἶπον, πέντε θές. μετὰ
γὰρ τοῦτο καταβιβαστέοι ἔσονταί σοι εἰς τὸ
σπήλαιον πάλιν ἐκεῖνο, καὶ ἀναγκαστέοι ἄρχειν
τά τε περὶ τὸν πόλεμον καὶ ὅσαι νέων ἀρχαί, ἵνα
μηδ᾽ ἐμπειρίᾳ ὑστερῶσι τῶν ἄλλων· καὶ ἔτι καὶ
ἐν τούτοις βασανιστέοι, εἰ ἐμμενοῦσιν ἑλκόμενοι
540 πανταχόσε ἤ τι καὶ παρακινήσουσιν. Χρόνον δέ,
ἦ δ᾽ ὅς, πόσον τοῦτον τίθης; Πεντεκαίδεκα ἔτη,
ἦν δ᾽ ἐγώ. γενομένων δὲ πεντηκοντουτῶν τοὺς
διασωθέντας καὶ ἀριστεύσαντας πάντα πάντῃ ἐν
ἔργοις τε καὶ ἐπιστήμαις πρὸς τέλος ἤδη ἀκτέον,
καὶ ἀναγκαστέον ἀνακλίναντας τὴν τῆς ψυχῆς
αὐγὴν εἰς αὐτὸ ἀποβλέψαι τὸ πᾶσι φῶς παρέχον,

---

[a] For the idiom μὴ ὡς νῦν etc. cf. supra on 410 B οὐχ
ὥσπερ; also 610 D, Gorg. 522 A, Symp. 179 E, 189 C, Epist.
vii. 333 A, Aristoph. Knights 784, Eurip. Bacchae 929, Il.
xix. 403, Od. xxiv. 199, xxi. 427, Dem. iv. 34, Aristot. De an.
414 a 22.

[b] It is very naïve of modern commentators to cavil at the
precise time allotted to dialectic, and still more so to infer
that there was not much to say about the ideas. Dialectic
was not exclusively or mainly concerned with the metaphysics of the ideas. It was the development of the reasoning powers by rational discussion.

[c] Cf. 519 c ff., pp. 139-145.

[d] Xen. Cyrop. i. 2. 13 seems to copy this. Cf. on 484 D.

instead of the present practice [a] of admitting to it any chance and unsuitable applicant?" "By all means," he said.

XVIII. "Is it enough, then, to devote to the continuous and strenuous study of dialectics undisturbed by anything else, as in the corresponding discipline in bodily exercises, twice as many years as were allotted to that?" "Do you mean six or four?" he said. "Well," I said, "set it down as five.[b] For after that you will have to send them down into the cave [c] again, and compel them to hold commands in war and the other offices suitable to youth, so that they may not fall short of the other type in experience [d] either. And in these offices, too, they are to be tested to see whether they will remain steadfast under diverse solicitations or whether they will flinch and swerve.[e]" "How much time do you allow for that?" he said. "Fifteen years," said I, "and at the age of fifty [f] those who have survived the tests and approved themselves altogether the best in every task and form of knowledge must be brought at last to the goal. We shall require them to turn upwards the vision of their souls [g] and fix their gaze on that which sheds light on all, and when they have thus beheld

Critics of Plato frequently overlook the fact that he insisted on practical experience in the training of his rulers. Newman, Aristot. *Pol.* i. p. 5, points out that this experience takes the place of special training in political science.

[e] *Cf.* ὑποκινήσαντ᾽, Aristoph. *Frogs* 643.

[f] An eminent scholar quaintly infers that Plato could not have written this page before he himself was fifty years old.

[g] Plato having made his practical meaning quite clear feels that he can safely permit himself the short cut of rhetoric and symbolism in summing it up. He reckoned without Neoplatonists ancient and modern. *Cf.* also on 519 B, p. 138, note *a*.

540 καὶ ἰδόντας τὸ ἀγαθὸν αὐτό, παραδείγματι χρωμένους ἐκείνῳ, καὶ πόλιν καὶ ἰδιώτας καὶ ἑαυτοὺς
B κοσμεῖν τὸν ἐπίλοιπον βίον ἐν μέρει ἕκαστους, τὸ
μὲν πολὺ πρὸς φιλοσοφίᾳ διατρίβοντας, ὅταν δὲ
τὸ μέρος ἥκῃ, πρὸς πολιτικοῖς ἐπιταλαιπωροῦντας
καὶ ἄρχοντας ἑκάστους τῆς πόλεως ἕνεκα, οὐχ ὡς
καλόν τι ἀλλ' ὡς ἀναγκαῖον πράττοντας, ἀντι-
οὕτως ἄλλους ἀεὶ παιδεύσαντας τοιούτους, ἀντι-
καταλιπόντας τῆς πόλεως φύλακας, εἰς μακάρων
νήσους ἀπιόντας οἰκεῖν· μνημεῖα δ' αὐτοῖς καὶ
C θυσίας τὴν πόλιν δημοσίᾳ ποιεῖν, ἐὰν καὶ ἡ Πυθία
ξυναναιρῇ, ὡς δαίμοσιν, εἰ δὲ μή, ὡς εὐδαίμοσί τε
καὶ θείοις. Παγκάλους, ἔφη, τοὺς ἄρχοντας, ὦ
Σώκρατες, ὥσπερ ἀνδριαντοποιὸς ἀπείργασαι. Καὶ
τὰς ἀρχούσας γε, ἦν δ' ἐγώ, ὦ Γλαύκων· μηδὲν
γάρ τι οἴου με περὶ ἀνδρῶν εἰρηκέναι μᾶλλον ἃ
εἴρηκα ἢ περὶ γυναικῶν, ὅσαι ἂν αὐτῶν ἱκαναὶ τὰς
φύσεις ἐγγίγνωνται. Ὀρθῶς, ἔφη, εἴπερ ἴσα γε
πάντα τοῖς ἀνδράσι κοινωνήσουσιν, ὡς διήλθομεν.
D Τί οὖν; ἔφην· ξυγχωρεῖτε περὶ τῆς πόλεώς τε καὶ
πολιτείας μὴ παντάπασιν ἡμᾶς εὐχὰς εἰρηκέναι,
ἀλλὰ χαλεπὰ μέν, δυνατὰ δέ πῃ, καὶ οὐκ ἄλλῃ ἢ

---

[a] Cf. supra 500 D-E. For παράδειγμα cf. 592 B and What
Plato Said, p. 458, on Euthyphro 6 E, and p. 599, on Polit.
277 D.
[b] Cf. 520 D.   [c] Cf. 347 C-D, 520 E.
[d] Plato's guardians, unlike Athenian statesmen, could
train their successors. Cf. Protag. 319 E-320 B, Meno 99 B.
Also ἄλλους ποιεῖν Meno 100 A, Gorg. 449 B, 455 C, Euthyph.
3 C, Phaedr. 266 C, 268 B, Symp. 196 E, Protag. 348 E, Isoc.
Demon. 3, Panath. 28, Soph. 13, Antid. 204, Xen. Oecon. 15.
10, and παιδεύειν ἀνθρώπους, generally used of the sophists,
Gorg. 519 E, Protag. 317 B, Euthyd. 306 E, Laches 186 D,
Rep. 600 c

the good itself they shall use it as a pattern *a* for the right ordering of the state and the citizens and themselves throughout the remainder of their lives, each in his turn,*b* devoting the greater part of their time to the study of philosophy, but when the turn comes for each, toiling in the service of the state and holding office for the city's sake, regarding the task not as a fine thing but a necessity *c* ; and so, when each generation has educated others *d* like themselves to take their place as guardians of the state, they shall depart to the Islands of the Blest *e* and there dwell. And the state shall establish public memorials *f* and sacrifices for them as to divinities if the Pythian oracle approves *g* or, if not, as to divine and godlike men.*h* "

"A most beautiful finish, Socrates, you have put upon your rulers, as if you were a statuary.*i* " " And on the women *j* too, Glaucon," said I ; " for you must not suppose that my words apply to the men more than to all women who arise among them endowed with the requisite qualities." " That is right," he said, " if they are to share equally in all things with the men as we laid it down." " Well, then," said I, " do you admit that our notion of the state and its polity is not altogether a day-dream,*k* but that though it is difficult,*l* it is in a way possible *m* and in no other way

---

e Cf. p. 139, note *d.* Plato checks himself in mid-flight and wistfully smiles at his own idealism. Cf. on 536 B-C, also 540 c and 509 c. Frutiger, *Mythes de Platon,* p. 170.

f Cf. *Symp.* 209 E.

g For this caution *cf.* 461 E and Vol. I. p. 344, note *c,* on 427 c.

h Plato plays on the words δαίμων and εὐδαίμων. *Cf.* also *Crat.* 398 B-C.   *i* Cf. 361 D.   *j* Lit. " female rulers."

k Cf. on 450 D and 499 c.   *l* Cf. 499 D.

m Cf. *What Plato Said,* p. 564 on *Rep.* 472 B-E, and *supra* p. 65, note *h,* on 499 D.

PLATO

540 εἴρηται, ὅταν οἱ ὡς ἀληθῶς φιλόσοφοι δυνάσται, ἢ πλείους ἢ εἷς, ἐν πόλει γενόμενοι τῶν μὲν νῦν τιμῶν καταφρονήσωσιν, ἡγησάμενοι ἀνελευθέρους εἶναι καὶ οὐδενὸς ἀξίας, τὸ δὲ ὀρθὸν περὶ πλείστου

E ποιησάμενοι καὶ τὰς ἀπὸ τούτου τιμάς, μέγιστον δὲ καὶ ἀναγκαιότατον τὸ δίκαιον, καὶ τούτῳ δὴ ὑπηρετοῦντές τε καὶ αὔξοντες αὐτὸ διασκευω-ρήσωνται τὴν ἑαυτῶν πόλιν; Πῶς; ἔφη. Ὅσοι μὲν ἄν, ἦν δ᾽ ἐγώ, πρεσβύτεροι τυγχάνωσι δεκετῶν

541 ἐν τῇ πόλει, πάντας ἐκπέμψωσιν εἰς τοὺς ἀγρούς, τοὺς δὲ παῖδας αὐτῶν παραλαβόντες ἐκτὸς τῶν νῦν ἠθῶν, ἃ καὶ οἱ γονῆς ἔχουσι, θρέψωνται ἐν τοῖς σφετέροις τρόποις καὶ νόμοις, οὖσιν οἵοις δι-εληλύθαμεν τότε· καὶ οὕτω τάχιστά τε καὶ ῥᾷστα πόλιν τε καὶ πολιτείαν, ἣν ἐλέγομεν, καταστᾶσαν αὐτήν τε εὐδαιμονήσειν καὶ τὸ ἔθνος ἐν ᾧ ἂν

B ἐγγένηται πλεῖστα ὀνήσειν; Πολύ γ᾽, ἔφη· καὶ ὡς ἂν γένοιτο, εἴπερ ποτὲ γίγνοιτο, δοκεῖς μοι, ὦ Σώκρατες, εὖ εἰρηκέναι. Οὐκοῦν ἅδην ἤδη, εἶπον ἐγώ, ἔχουσιν ἡμῖν οἱ λόγοι περί τε τῆς πόλεως ταύτης καὶ τοῦ ὁμοίου ταύτῃ ἀνδρός; δῆλος γάρ που καὶ οὗτος, οἷον φήσομεν δεῖν αὐτὸν εἶναι. Δῆλος, ἔφη· καὶ ὅπερ ἐρωτᾷς, δοκεῖ μοι τέλος ἔχειν.

Cf. 473 c-d, 499 b-c.
Cf. supra 521 b, 516 c-d.
τὸ ὀρθόν: cf. Theaet. 171 c, Meno 99 a.
This is another of the passages in which Plato seems to lend support to revolutionaries. Cf. supra p. 71, note g. It is what the soviets are said to be doing. Lowell points out that it is what actually happened in the New England of 1630-1660.
  Cf. Laws 752 c, where it is said that the children would accept the new laws if the parents would not. Cf. supra

than that described—when genuine philosophers,[a] many or one, becoming masters of the state scorn [b] the present honours, regarding them as illiberal and worthless, but prize the right [c] and the honours that come from that above all things, and regarding justice as the chief and the one indispensable thing, in the service and maintenance of that reorganize and administer their city?" "In what way?" he said. "All inhabitants above the age of ten," I said, "they will send out into the fields, and they will take over the children,[d] remove them from the manners and habits of their parents, and bring them up in their own customs and laws which will be such as we have described. This is the speediest and easiest way in which such a city and constitution as we have portrayed could be established and prosper and bring most benefit to the people among whom it arises." "Much the easiest," he said, "and I think you have well explained the manner of its realization if it should ever be realized." "Then," said I, "have we not now said enough [e] about this state and the corresponding type of man—for it is evident what our conception of him will be?" "It is evident," he said, "and, to answer your question, I think we have finished."

415 D, and also *What Plato Said*, p. 625, on *Laws* 644 A and p. 638, on 813 D.

There is some confusion in this passage between the inauguration and the normal conduct of the ideal state, and Wilamowitz, *Platon*, i. p. 439 calls the idea "ein hingeworfener Einfall." But Plato always held that the reformer must have or make a clean slate. *Cf.* 501 A, *Laws* 735 E. And he constantly emphasizes the supreme importance of education; *Rep.* 377 A-B, 423 E, 416 C, *Laws* 641 B, 644 A-B, 752 C, 765 E-766 A, 788 C, 804 D.

For παραλαβόντες cf. *Phaedo* 82 E παραλαβοῦσα.

[e] *Cf.* 535 A.

H

543   I. Εἶεν· ταῦτα μὲν δὴ ὡμολόγηται, ὦ Γλαύκων,
τῇ μελλούσῃ ἄκρως οἰκεῖν πόλει κοινὰς μὲν
γυναῖκας, κοινοὺς δὲ παῖδας εἶναι καὶ πᾶσαν
παιδείαν, ὡσαύτως δὲ τὰ ἐπιτηδεύματα κοινὰ ἐν
πολέμῳ τε καὶ εἰρήνῃ, βασιλέας δὲ αὐτῶν εἶναι
τοὺς ἐν φιλοσοφίᾳ τε καὶ πρὸς τὸν πόλεμον γεγονότας ἀρίστους. Ὡμολόγηται, ἔφη. Καὶ μὴν καὶ
B τάδε ξυνεχωρήσαμεν, ὡς, ὅταν δὴ καταστῶσιν οἱ
ἄρχοντες, ἄγοντες τοὺς στρατιώτας κατοικιοῦσιν
εἰς οἰκήσεις οἵας προείπομεν, ἴδιον μὲν οὐδὲν
οὐδενὶ ἐχούσας, κοινὰς δὲ πᾶσι· πρὸς δὲ ταῖς
τοιαύταις οἰκήσεσι καὶ τὰς κτήσεις, εἰ μνημονεύεις,
διωμολογησάμεθά που οἷαι ἔσονται αὐτοῖς. Ἀλλὰ
μνημονεύω, ἔφη, ὅτι γε οὐδὲν οὐδένα ᾠόμεθα δεῖν
κεκτῆσθαι ὧν νῦν οἱ ἄλλοι, ὥσπερ δὲ ἀθλητάς τε
C πολέμου καὶ φύλακας, μισθὸν τῆς φυλακῆς δεχο-
μένους εἰς ἐνιαυτὸν τὴν εἰς ταῦτα τροφὴν παρὰ τῶν
ἄλλων, αὑτῶν τε δεῖν καὶ τῆς ἄλλης πόλεως

---

[a] Strictly speaking, this applies only to the guardians,
but cf. Laws 739 c ff. Aristotle, Pol. 1261 a 6 and 1262 a
41, like many subsequent commentators, misses the point.
    [b] Cf. supra 445 D and What Plato Said, p. 539, on Menex.
238 c-D.
    [c] So Jowett. Adam ad loc. insists that the genitive is
partitive, "those of their number are to be kings."

BOOK VIII

I. "Very good. We are agreed then, Glaucon, that the state which is to achieve the height of good government must have community [a] of wives and children and all education, and also that the pursuits of men and women must be the same in peace and war, and that the rulers or kings [b] over them [c] are to be those who have approved themselves the best in both war and philosophy." "We are agreed," he said. "And we further granted this, that when the rulers are established in office they shall conduct these soldiers and settle them in habitations [d] such as we described, that have nothing private for anybody but are common for all, and in addition to such habitations we agreed, if you remember, what should be the nature of their possessions. [e]" "Why, yes, I remember," he said, "that we thought it right that none of them should have anything that ordinary men [f] now possess, but that, being as it were athletes [g] of war and guardians, they should receive from the others as pay [h] for their guardianship each year their yearly sustenance, and devote their entire attention to the

[d] Cf. 415 E.   [e] Cf. 416 c.
[f] Cf. 420 A.
[g] Cf. on 403 E and 521 D.   Polyb. i. 6. 6 ἀθληταὶ γεγονότες ἀληθινοὶ τῶν κατὰ τὸν πόλεμον ἔργων.
[h] Cf. 416 E.

235

543 ἐπιμελεῖσθαι. Ὀρθῶς, ἔφην, λέγεις. ἀλλ' ἄγε,
ἐπειδὴ τοῦτ' ἀπετελέσαμεν, ἀναμνησθῶμεν, πόθεν
δεῦρο ἐξετραπόμεθα, ἵνα πάλιν τὴν αὐτὴν ἴωμεν.
Οὐ χαλεπόν, ἔφη. σχεδὸν γάρ, καθάπερ νῦν, ὡς
διεληλυθὼς περὶ τῆς πόλεως τοὺς λόγους ἐποιοῦ
λέγων, ὡς ἀγαθὴν μὲν τὴν τοιαύτην, οἵαν τότε
D διῆλθες, τιθείης πόλιν, καὶ ἄνδρα τὸν ἐκείνῃ ὅμοιον,
καὶ ταῦτα, ὡς ἔοικας, καλλίω ἔτι ἔχων εἰπεῖν πόλιν
544 τε καὶ ἄνδρα· ἀλλ' οὖν δὴ τὰς ἄλλας ἡμαρτημένας
ἔλεγες, εἰ αὕτη ὀρθή. τῶν δὲ λοιπῶν πολιτειῶν
ἔφησθα, ὡς μνημονεύω, τέτταρα εἴδη εἶναι, ὧν καὶ
πέρι λόγον ἄξιον εἴη ἔχειν καὶ ἰδεῖν αὐτῶν τὰ
ἁμαρτήματα καὶ τοὺς ἐκείναις αὖ ὁμοίους, ἵνα
πάντας αὐτοὺς ἰδόντες καὶ ὁμολογησάμενοι τὸν
ἄριστον καὶ τὸν κάκιστον ἄνδρα ἐπισκεψαίμεθα, εἰ
ὁ ἄριστος εὐδαιμονέστατος καὶ ὁ κάκιστος ἀθλιώτατος ἢ ἄλλως ἔχοι· καὶ ἐμοῦ ἐρομένου, τίνας
B λέγοις τὰς τέτταρας πολιτείας, ἐν τούτῳ ὑπέλαβε
Πολέμαρχός τε καὶ Ἀδείμαντος, καὶ οὕτω δὴ σὺ

---

[a] Cf. Vol. I. p. 424, note c, and *What Plato Said*, p. 640,
on *Laws* 857 c.
[b] Cf. 449 λ-β.   [c] Cf. Aristot. *Pol.* 1275 b 1-2, 1289 b 9.
[d] Aristot. *Pol.* 1291-1292 censures the limitation to four.
But cf. *supra*, Introd. p. xlv. Cf. *Laws* 693 D, where only two
mother-forms of government are mentioned, monarchy and
democracy, with Aristot. *Pol.* 1301 b 40 δῆμος καὶ ὀλιγαρχία.
Cf. also *Eth. Nic.* 1160 a 31 ff. The *Politicus* mentions
seven (291 f., 301 f.). Isoc. *Panath.* 132-134 names three
kinds—oligarchy, democracy, and monarchy—adding that
others may say much more about them. See note *ad loc.* in
Loeb Isocrates and *Class. Phil.* vol. vii. p. 91. Cf. Hobbes,
Leviathan 19 "Yet he that shall consider the particular
commonwealths that have been and are in the world will not

care of themselves and the state." "That is right," I said. "But now that we have finished this topic let us recall the point at which we entered on the digression[a] that has brought us here, so that we may proceed on our way again by the same path." "That is easy," he said; "for at that time, almost exactly as now, on the supposition that you had finished the description of the city, you were going on to say[b] that you assumed such a city as you then described and the corresponding type of man to be good, and that too though, as it appears, you had a still finer city and type of man to tell of; but at any rate you were saying that the others are aberrations,[c] if this city is right. But regarding the other constitutions, my recollection is that you said there were four species[d] worth speaking of[e] and observing their defects[f] and the corresponding types of men, in order that when we had seen them all and come to an agreement about the best and the worst man, we might determine whether the best is the happiest and the worst most wretched or whether it is otherwise.[g] And when I was asking what were the four constitutions you had in mind, Polemarchus and Adeimantus thereupon broke in, and that was how you took up the discussion again and brought

perhaps easily reduce them to three . . . as, for example, elective kingdoms," etc.

[e] For ὧν καὶ πέρι λόγον ἄξιον εἴη *cf. Laws* 908 B ἃ καὶ διακρίσεως ἄξια, *Laches* 192 A οὗ καὶ πέρι ἄξιον λέγειν, *Tim.* 82 c ἐν γένος ἐνὸν ἄξιον ἐπωνυμίας. *Cf.* also *Euthydem.* 279 c, Aristot. *Pol.* 1272 b 32, 1302 a 13, *De part. an.* 654 a 13, Demosth. v. 16, Isoc. vi. 56, and Vol. I. p. 420, note *f*, on 445 c.
[f] For the relative followed by a demonstrative *cf.* also 357 B.
[g] Plato's main point again. *Cf.* 545 A, 484 A–B and Vol. I. p. xii, note *d*.

544 ἀναλαβὼν τὸν λόγον δεῦρ' ἀφῖξαι. Ὀρθότατα,
εἶπον, ἐμνημόνευσας. Πάλιν τοίνυν, ὥσπερ παλαι-
στής, τὴν αὐτὴν λαβὴν πάρεχε, καὶ τὸ αὐτὸ ἐμοῦ
ἐρομένου πειρῶ εἰπεῖν, ἅπερ τότε ἔμελλες λέγειν.
Ἐάνπερ, ἦν δ' ἐγώ, δύνωμαι. Καὶ μήν, ἦ δ' ὅς,
ἐπιθυμῶ καὶ αὐτὸς ἀκοῦσαι τίνας ἔλεγες τὰς
C τέτταρας πολιτείας. Οὐ χαλεπῶς, ἦν δ' ἐγώ,
ἀκούσει. εἰσὶ γὰρ ἃς λέγω, αἵπερ καὶ ὀνόματα
ἔχουσιν, ἥ τε ὑπὸ τῶν πολλῶν ἐπαινουμένη, ἡ Κρη-
τική τε καὶ Λακωνικὴ αὕτη· καὶ δευτέρα καὶ
δευτέρως ἐπαινουμένη, καλουμένη δ' ὀλιγαρχία,
συχνῶν γέμουσα κακῶν πολιτεία· ἥ τε ταύτῃ
διάφορος καὶ ἐφεξῆς γιγνομένη δημοκρατία, καὶ ἡ
γενναία δὴ τυραννὶς καὶ πασῶν τούτων δια-
φέρουσα, τέταρτόν τε καὶ ἔσχατον πόλεως νόσημα.
D ἢ τινα ἄλλην ἔχεις ἰδέαν πολιτείας, ἥτις καὶ ἐν
εἴδει διαφανεῖ τινι κεῖται; δυναστεῖαι γὰρ καὶ
ὠνηταὶ βασιλεῖαι καὶ τοιαῦταί τινες πολιτεῖαι
μεταξύ τι τούτων πού εἰσιν, εὕροι δ' ἄν τις αὐτὰς

---

[a] Cf. on 572 B, p. 339, note e.
[b] Cf. Phileb. 13 D εἰς τὰς ὁμοίας, Phaedr. 236 B, Laws 682 E,
Aristoph. Clouds 551 (Blaydes), Knights 841, Lysist. 672.
[c] Cf. What Plato Said, p. 596, on Sophist 267 D.
[d] Cf. Crito 52 E, Norlin on Isoc. Nicocles 24 (Loeb), Laws
712 D-E, Aristot. Pol. 1265 b 32, Xen. Mem. iii. 5. 15.
[e] ἢ . . . αὕτη, "ista." Cf. Midsummer Night's Dream, I. ii.
ad fin. and Gorg. 502 B, 452 E.
[f] Of course ironical. Cf. supra 454 A, and What Plato
Said, p. 592, on Soph. 231 B.
[g] Cf. 552 C, Protag. 322 D, Isoc. Hel. 34, Wilamowitz on

238

it to this point.[a] " " Your memory is most exact,"
I said. " A second time then, as in a wrestling-
match, offer me the same hold,[b] and when I repeat
my question try to tell me what you were then about
to say." " I will if I can," said I. " And indeed,"
said he, " I am eager myself to hear what four
forms of government you meant." " There will be
no difficulty about that," said I. " For those I mean
are precisely those that have names[c] in common
usage : that which the many praise,[d] your[e] Cretan
and Spartan constitution ; and the second in place
and in honour, that which is called oligarchy, a constitution teeming with many ills, and its sequent
counterpart and opponent, democracy ; and then the
noble[f] tyranny surpassing them all, the fourth and
final malady[g] of a state. Can you mention any other
type[h] of government, I mean any other that con-
stitutes a distinct species[i] ? For, no doubt, there are
hereditary principalities[j] and purchased[k] kingships,
and similar intermediate constitutions which one

Eurip. *Heracles* 542. For the effect of surprise *cf. Rep.*
334 A, 373 A, 555 A, *Theaet.* 146 A, *Phileb.* 46 A κακόν and
64 E συμφορά.

[h] ἰδέαν : *cf.* Introd. p. x.

[i] *Cf.* 445 c. For διαφανεῖ *cf. Tim.* 60 A, 67 A, *Laws* 634 c,
and *infra* on 548 c, p. 253, note *g*.

[j] δυναστεῖαι : *cf. Laws* 680 B, 681 D. But the word
usually has an invidious suggestion. See Newman on
Aristot. *Pol.* 1272 b 10. *Cf. ibid.* 1292 b 5-10, 1293 a 31,
1298 a 32 ; also Lysias ii. 18, where it is opposed to democracy, Isoc. *Panath.* 148, where it is used of the tyranny of
Peisistratus, *ibid.* 43 of Minos. *Cf. Panegyr.* 39 and Norlin
on *Panegyr.* 105 (Loeb). Isocrates also uses it frequently
of the power or sovereignty of Philip, *Phil.* 3, 6, 69, 133,
etc. *Cf.* also *Gorg.* 492 B, *Polit.* 291 D.

[k] Newman on Aristot. *Pol.* 1273 a 35 thinks that Plato
may have been thinking of Carthage. *Cf.* Polyb. vi. 56. 4.

PLATO

544 οὐκ ἐλάττους περὶ τοὺς βαρβάρους ἢ τοὺς Ἕλληνας. Πολλαὶ γοῦν καὶ ἄτοποι, ἔφη, λέγονται.

II. Οἶσθ' οὖν, ἦν δ' ἐγώ, ὅτι καὶ ἀνθρώπων εἴδη τοσαῦτα ἀνάγκη τρόπων εἶναι, ὅσαπερ καὶ πολιτειῶν; ἢ οἴει ἐκ δρυός ποθεν ἢ ἐκ πέτρας τὰς πολιτείας γίγνεσθαι, ἀλλ' οὐχὶ ἐκ τῶν ἠθῶν τῶν

E ἐν ταῖς πόλεσιν, ἃ ἂν ὥσπερ ῥέψαντα τἆλλα ἐφελκύσηται; Οὐδαμῶς ἔγωγ', ἔφη, ἄλλοθεν ἢ ἐντεῦθεν. Οὐκοῦν εἰ τὰ τῶν πόλεων πέντε, καὶ αἱ τῶν ἰδιωτῶν κατασκευαὶ τῆς ψυχῆς πέντε ἂν εἶεν. Τί μήν; Τὸν μὲν δὴ τῇ ἀριστοκρατίᾳ ὅμοιον δι- εληλύθαμεν ἤδη, ὃν ἀγαθόν τε καὶ δίκαιον ὀρθῶς

545 φαμὲν εἶναι. Διεληλύθαμεν. Ἆρ' οὖν τὸ μετὰ τοῦτο διτέον τοὺς χείρους, τὸν φιλόνικόν τε καὶ φιλότιμον, κατὰ τὴν Λακωνικὴν ἑστῶτα πολιτείαν, καὶ ὀλιγαρχικὸν αὖ καὶ δημοκρατικὸν καὶ τὸν τυραννικόν, ἵνα τὸν ἀδικώτατον ἰδόντες ἀντιθῶμεν τῷ δικαιοτάτῳ καὶ ἡμῖν τελέα ἡ σκέψις ᾖ, πῶς ποτὲ ἡ ἄκρατος δικαιοσύνη πρὸς ἀδικίαν τὴν ἄκρατον ἔχει εὐδαιμονίας τε πέρι τοῦ ἔχοντος καὶ

ᵃ Plato, as often, is impatient of details, for which he was rebuked by Aristotle. *Cf.* also *Tim.* 57 D, 67 C, and the frequent leaving of minor matters to future legislators in the *Republic* and *Laws*, Vol. I. p. 294, note *b*, on 412 B.

ᵇ For the correspondence of individual and state *cf.* also 435 E, 445 C-D, 579 c and on 591 E. *Cf. Laws* 829 A, Isoc. *Peace* 120.

ᶜ Or "stock or stone," *i.e.* inanimate, insensible things. For the quotation ἐκ δρυός ποθεν ἢ ἐκ πέτρας *cf. Odyssey* xix. 163, *Il.* xxii. 126 *aliter*, *Apol.* 34 D and Thompson on *Phaedrus* 275 B; also Stallbaum *ad loc.*

ᵈ The "mores," 435 E, 436 A. *Cf.* Bagehot, *Physics and Politics*, p. 206: "A lazy nation may be changed into an industrious, a rich into a poor, a religious into a profane,

240

could find in even greater numbers among the barbarians than among the Greeks.[a] " " Certainly many strange ones are reported," he said.

II. " Are you aware, then," said I, " that there must be as many types of character among men as there are forms of government [b]? Or do you suppose that constitutions spring from the proverbial oak or rock [c] and not from the characters [d] of the citizens, which, as it were, by their momentum and weight in the scales [e] draw other things after them ? " " They could not possibly come from any other source," he said. " Then if the forms of government are five, the patterns of individual souls must be five also." " Surely." " Now we have already described the man corresponding to aristocracy [f] or the government of the best, whom we aver to be the truly good and just man." " We have." " Must we not, then, next after this, survey the inferior types, the man who is contentious and covetous of honour,[g] corresponding to the Laconian constitution, and the oligarchical man in turn, and the democratic and the tyrant, in order that,[h] after observing the most unjust of all, we may oppose him to the most just, and complete our inquiry as to the relation of pure justice and pure injustice in respect of the happiness and unhappiness of the possessor, so that we may

as if by magic, if any single cause, though slight, or any combination of causes, however subtle, is strong enough to change the favourite and detested types of character."

[e] For the metaphor cf. also 550 E and on 556 E.
[f] ἀριστοκρατία is used by both Plato and Aristotle sometimes technically, sometimes etymologically as the government of the best, whoever they may be. Cf. 445 D, and Menex. 238 c-D (What Plato Said, p. 539).
[g] Cf. Phaedr. 256 c 1, supra 475 A, 347 B.
[h] Cf. on 544 A, p. 237, note g.

PLATO

545 ἀθλιότητος, ἵνα ἢ Θρασυμάχῳ πειθόμενοι διώ-
B κωμεν ἀδικίαν ἢ τῷ νῦν προφαινομένῳ λόγῳ
δικαιοσύνην; Παντάπασι μὲν οὖν, ἔφη, οὕτω
ποιητέον. Ἆρ' οὖν, ὥσπερ ἠρξάμεθα ἐν ταῖς
πολιτείαις πρότερον σκοπεῖν τὰ ἤθη ἢ ἐν τοῖς
ἰδιώταις, ὡς ἐναργέστερον ὄν, καὶ νῦν οὕτω πρῶτον μὲν τὴν φιλότιμον σκεπτέον πολιτείαν· ὄνομα
γὰρ οὐκ ἔχω λεγόμενον ἄλλο· ἢ τιμοκρατίαν ἢ
τιμαρχίαν αὐτὴν κλητέον· πρὸς δὲ ταύτην τὸν
C τοιοῦτον ἄνδρα σκεψόμεθα, ἔπειτα ὀλιγαρχίαν καὶ
ἄνδρα ὀλιγαρχικόν, αὖθις δὲ εἰς δημοκρατίαν
ἀποβλέψαντες θεασόμεθα ἄνδρα δημοκρατικόν, τὸ
δὲ τέταρτον εἰς τυραννουμένην πόλιν ἐλθόντες καὶ
ἰδόντες, πάλιν εἰς τυραννικὴν ψυχὴν βλέποντες,
πειρασόμεθα περὶ ὧν προυθέμεθα ἱκανοὶ κριταὶ
γενέσθαι; Κατὰ λόγον γέ τοι ἄν, ἔφη, οὕτω
γίγνοιτο ἥ τε θέα καὶ ἡ κρίσις.

---

[a] In considering the progress of degeneration portrayed in the following pages, it is too often forgotten that Plato is describing or satirizing divergences from an ideal rather than an historical process. *Cf.* Rehm, *Der Untergang Roms im abendländischen Denken*, p. 11: "Plato gibt eine zum Mythos gesteigerte Naturgeschichte des Staates, so wie Hesiod eine als Mythos zu verstehende Natur-, d.h. Entartungsgeschichte des Menschengeschlechts gibt." *Cf.* Sidney B. Fay, on Bury, *The Idea of Progress*, in "Methods of Social Science," edited by Stuart A. Rice, p. 289: ". . . there was a widely spread belief in an earlier 'golden age' of simplicity, which had been followed by a degeneration and decay of the human race. Plato's theory of degradation set forth a gradual deterioration through the successive stages of timocracy, oligarchy, democracy and despotism. The Greek theory of 'cycles,' with its endless, monotonous iteration, excluded the possibility of permanent advance or 'progress.'"

Kurt Singer, *Platon der Gründer*, p. 141, says that the timocratic state reminds one of late Sparta, the democratic

242

either follow the counsel of Thrasymachus and pursue injustice or the present argument and pursue justice ? " " Assuredly," he said, " that is what we have to do.ᵃ " " Shall we, then, as we began by ex- amining moral qualities in states before individuals, as being more manifest there, so now consider first the constitution based on the love of honour ? I do not know of any special name ᵇ for it in use. We must call it either timocracyᶜ or timarchy. And then in connexion with this we will consider the man of that type, and thereafter oligarchy and the oligarch, and again, fixing our eyes on democracy, we will con- template the democratic man ; and fourthly, after coming to the city ruled by a tyrant and observing it, we will in turn take a look into the tyrannical soul,ᵈ and so try to make ourselves competent judges ᵉ of the question before us." " That would be at least ᶠ a systematic and consistent way of conducting the observation and the decision," he said.

of Athens after Pericles, the oligarchic is related to Corinth, and the tyrannical has some Syracusan features. Cicero, *De div.* ii., uses this book of the *Republic* to console himself for the revolutions in the Roman state, and Polybius's theory of the natural succession of governments is derived from it, with modifications (Polyb. vi. 4. 6 ff. *Cf.* vi. 9. 10 αὕτη πολιτειῶν ἀνακύκλωσις). Aristotle objects that in a cycle the ideal state should follow the tyranny.

ᵇ *Cf.* on 544 c, p. 238, note *b*.

ᶜ In Aristot. *Eth. Nic.* 1160 a 33-34, the meaning is " the rule of those who possess a property qualification."

ᵈ *Cf.* 577 A-B.   ᵉ *Cf.* 582 A ff.

ᶠ For the qualified assent *cf. Hamlet* I. i. 19 " What? is Horatio there? A piece of him." It is very frequent in the *Republic*, usually with γοῦν. *Cf.* 442 D, 469 B, 476 c, 501 c, 537 c, 584 A, 555 B, 604 D, and Vol. I. p. 30, note *a*, on 334 A ; also 460 c and 398 B, where the interlocutor adds a con- dition, 392 B, 405 B, 556 E, 581 B, and 487 A, where he uses the corrective μὲν οὖν.

545 III. Φέρε τοίνυν, ἦν δ' ἐγώ, πειρώμεθα λέγειν,
τίνα τρόπον τιμοκρατία γένοιτ' ἂν ἐξ ἀριστο-
D κρατίας. ἢ τόδε μὲν ἁπλοῦν, ὅτι πᾶσα πολιτεία
μεταβάλλει ἐξ αὐτοῦ τοῦ ἔχοντος τὰς ἀρχάς, ὅταν
ἐν αὐτῷ τούτῳ στάσις ἐγγένηται· ὁμονοοῦντος δέ,
κἂν πάνυ ὀλίγον ᾖ, ἀδύνατον κινηθῆναι; Ἔστι
γὰρ οὕτως. Πῶς οὖν δή, εἶπον, ὦ Γλαύκων, ἡ
πόλις ἡμῖν κινηθήσεται, καὶ πῆ στασιάσουσιν οἱ
ἐπίκουροι καὶ οἱ ἄρχοντες πρὸς ἀλλήλους τε καὶ
πρὸς ἑαυτούς; ἢ βούλει, ὥσπερ Ὅμηρος, εὐχώ-
μεθα ταῖς Μούσαις εἰπεῖν ἡμῖν ὅπως δὴ πρῶτον
E στάσις ἔμπεσε, καὶ φῶμεν αὐτὰς τραγικῶς ὡς
πρὸς παῖδας ἡμᾶς παιζούσας καὶ ἐρεσχηλούσας,
ὡς δὴ σπουδῇ λεγούσας, ὑψηλολογουμένας λέγειν;
546 Πῶς; Ὧδέ πως· χαλεπὸν μὲν κινηθῆναι πόλιν
οὕτω ξυστᾶσαν· ἀλλ' ἐπεὶ γενομένῳ παντὶ φθορά
ἐστιν, οὐδ' ἡ τοιαύτη ξύστασις τὸν ἅπαντα μενεῖ
χρόνον, ἀλλὰ λυθήσεται· λύσις δὲ ἥδε. οὐ μόνον
φυτοῖς ἐγγείοις, ἀλλὰ καὶ ἐν ἐπιγείοις ζῴοις φορὰ
καὶ ἀφορία ψυχῆς τε καὶ σωμάτων γίγνονται, ὅταν
περιτροπαὶ ἑκάστοις κύκλων περιφορὰς ξυνάπτωσι,
βραχυβίοις μὲν βραχυπόρους, ἐναντίοις δὲ ἐναντίας·

---

a For the idea that the state is destroyed only by factions
in the ruling class cf. also *Laws* 683 E. *Cf.* 465 B, Lysias
xxv. 21, Aristot. *Pol.* 1305 b, 1306 a 10 ὁμονοοῦσα δὲ ὀλιγαρχία
οὐκ εὐδιάφθορος ἐξ αὑτῆς, 1302 a 10, Polybius, Teubner, vol. ii.
p. 298 (vi. 57). Newman, Aristot. *Pol.* i. p. 521, says that
Aristotle "does not remark on Plato's observation . . .
though he cannot have agreed with it." *Cf.* Halévy, *Notes
et souvenirs*, p. 153 " l'histoire est là pour démontrer claire-
ment que, depuis un siècle, nos gouvernements n'ont jamais
été renversés que par eux-mêmes"; Bergson, *Les Deux
Sources de la morale et de la religion*, p. 303: "Mais

THE REPUBLIC, BOOK VIII

III. " Come, then," said I, " let us try to tell in
what way a timocracy would arise out of an aristocracy. Or is this the simple and unvarying rule,
that in every form of government revolution takes
its start from the ruling class itself,[a] when dissension
arises in that, but so long as it is at one with itself,
however small it be, innovation is impossible ? "
" Yes, that is so." " How, then, Glaucon," I said,
" will disturbance arise in our city, and how will our
helpers and rulers fall out and be at odds with one
another and themselves ? Shall we, like Homer, in-
voke the Muses [b] to tell ' how faction first fell upon
them,' and say that these goddesses playing with us
and teasing us as if we were children address us in
lofty, mock-serious tragic [c] style ? " " How ? " " Somewhat in this fashion. Hard in truth [d] it is for a state
thus constituted to be shaken and disturbed ; but
since for everything that has come into being destruction is appointed,[e] not even such a fabric as this will
abide for all time, but it shall surely be dissolved, and
this is the manner of its dissolution. Not only for
plants that grow from the earth but also for animals
that live upon it there is a cycle of bearing and barren-
ness [f] for soul and body as often as the revolutions of
their orbs come full circle, in brief courses for the
short-lived and oppositely for the opposite ; but the

l'instinct résiste. Il ne commence à céder que lorsque la
classe supérieure elle-même l'y invite."
 [b] For the mock-heroic style of this invocation cf. Phaedr.
237 A, Laws 885 c.
 [c] Cf. 413 B, Meno 76 E, Aristot. Meteorol. 353 b 1,
Wilamowitz, Platon, ii. p. 146.
 [d] Cf. Alc. I. 104 E.
 [e] Cf. What Plato Said, p. 627 on Laws 677 A ; also Polyb.
vi. 57, Cic. De rep. ii. 25.
 [f] Cf. Pindar, Nem. vi. 10-12 for the thought.

546 γένους δὲ ὑμετέρου εὐγονίας τε καὶ ἀφορίας, καίπερ
B ὄντες σοφοί, οὓς ἡγεμόνας πόλεως ἐπαιδεύσασθε,
οὐδὲν μᾶλλον λογισμῷ μετ᾿ αἰσθήσεως τεύξονται,
ἀλλὰ πάρεισιν αὐτοὺς καὶ γεννήσουσι παῖδάς ποτε
οὐ δέον. ἔστι δὲ θείῳ μὲν γεννητῷ περίοδος, ἣν
ἀριθμὸς περιλαμβάνει τέλειος, ἀνθρωπείῳ δὲ ἐν
ᾧ πρώτῳ αὐξήσεις δυνάμεναί τε καὶ δυναστευό-
μεναι, τρεῖς ἀποστάσεις, τέτταρας δὲ ὅρους λα-
βοῦσαι ὁμοιούντων τε καὶ ἀνομοιούντων καὶ
αὐξόντων καὶ φθινόντων, πάντα προσήγορα καὶ
C ῥητὰ πρὸς ἄλληλα ἀπέφηναν· ὧν ἐπίτριτος πυθμὴν
πεμπάδι συζυγεὶς δύο ἁρμονίας παρέχεται τρὶς
αὐξηθείς, τὴν μὲν ἴσην ἰσάκις, ἑκατὸν τοσαυτάκις,
τὴν δὲ ἰσομήκη μὲν τῇ, προμήκη δέ, ἑκατὸν μὲν
ἀριθμῶν ἀπὸ διαμέτρων ῥητῶν πεμπάδος, δεομέ-
νων ἑνὸς ἑκάστων, ἀρρήτων δὲ δυοῖν, ἑκατὸν δὲ
κύβων τριάδος. ξύμπας δὲ οὗτος ἀριθμὸς γεωμετρικὸς τοιούτου κύριος, ἀμεινόνων τε καὶ χει-
D ρόνων γενέσεων, ἃς ὅταν ἀγνοήσαντες ὑμῖν οἱ
φύλακες συνοικίζωσι νύμφας νυμφίοις παρὰ καιρόν,
οὐκ εὐφυεῖς οὐδ᾿ εὐτυχεῖς παῖδες ἔσονται· ὧν
καταστήσουσι μὲν τοὺς ἀρίστους οἱ πρότεροι, ὅμως
δὲ ὄντες ἀνάξιοι, εἰς τὰς τῶν πατέρων αὖ δυνάμεις
ἐλθόντες, ἡμῶν πρῶτον ἄρξονται ἀμελεῖν φύλακες
ὄντες, παρ᾿ ἔλαττον τοῦ δέοντος ἡγησάμενοι τὰ
μουσικῆς, δεύτερον δὲ τὰ γυμναστικῆς· ὅθεν ἀ-

---

[a] Cf. *Tim.* 28 A δόξῃ μετ᾿ αἰσθήσεως.
[b] For its proverbial obscurity *cf.* Cic. *Ad Att.* vii. 13
"est enim numero Platonis obscurius," Censorinus, *De die
natali* xi.   See *supra*, Introd. p. xliv for literature on this
"number."   [c] προσήγορα: *cf. Theaet.* 146 A.
[d] *Cf.* 534 D; also *Theaet.* 202 B ῥητάς.
[e] *Cf.* 409 D.

laws of prosperous birth or infertility for your race, the men you have bred to be your rulers will not for all their wisdom ascertain by reasoning combined with sensation,[a] but they will escape them, and there will be a time when they will beget children out of season. Now for divine begettings there is a period comprehended by a perfect number,[b] and for mortal by the first in which augmentations dominating and dominated when they have attained to three distances and four limits of the assimilating and the dissimilating, the waxing and the waning, render all things conversable[c] and commensurable with one another, whereof a basal four-thirds wedded to the pempad yields two harmonies at the third augmentation, the one the product of equal factors taken one hundred times, the other of equal length one way but oblong,—one dimension of a hundred numbers determined by the rational diameters of the pempad lacking one in each case, or of the irrational[d] lacking two ; the other dimension of a hundred cubes of the triad. And this entire geometrical number is determinative of this thing, of better and inferior births. And when your guardians, missing this, bring together brides and bridegrooms unseasonably,[e] the offspring will not be well-born or fortunate. Of such offspring the previous generation will establish the best, to be sure, in office, but still these, being unworthy, and having entered in turn[f] into the powers of their fathers, will first as guardians begin to neglect us, paying too little heed to music[g] and then to gymnastics, so that

---

[f] αὖ : cf. my note in *Class. Phil.* xxiii. (1928) pp. 285-287.

[g] This does not indicate a change in Plato's attitude toward music, as has been alleged.

546 μουσότεροι γενήσονται ὑμῖν οἱ νέοι. ἐκ δὲ τούτων
Ε ἄρχοντες οὐ πάνυ φυλακικοὶ καταστήσονται πρὸς
547 τὸ δοκιμάζειν τὰ Ἡσιόδου τε καὶ τὰ παρ᾽
ὑμῖν γένη, χρυσοῦν τε καὶ ἀργυροῦν καὶ χαλκοῦν
καὶ σιδηροῦν· ὁμοῦ δὲ μιγέντος σιδηροῦ ἀργυρῷ
καὶ χαλκοῦ χρυσῷ ἀνομοιότης ἐγγενήσεται καὶ
ἀνωμαλία ἀνάρμοστος, ἃ γενόμενα, οὗ ἂν ἐγγένηται, ἀεὶ τίκτει πόλεμον καὶ ἔχθραν. ταύτης τοι
γενεᾶς χρὴ φάναι εἶναι στάσιν, ὅπου ἂν γίγνηται
ἀεί. Καὶ ὀρθῶς γ᾽, ἔφη, αὐτὰς ἀποκρίνεσθαι φήσομεν. Καὶ γάρ, ἦν δ᾽ ἐγώ, ἀνάγκη Μούσας γε
Β οὔσας. Τί οὖν, ἦ δ᾽ ὅς, τὸ μετὰ τοῦτο λέγουσιν αἱ
Μοῦσαι; Στάσεως, ἦν δ᾽ ἐγώ, γενομένης εἱλκέτην
ἄρα ἑκατέρω τὼ γένει, τὸ μὲν σιδηροῦν καὶ χαλκοῦν ἐπὶ χρηματισμὸν καὶ γῆς κτῆσιν καὶ οἰκίας
χρυσίου τε καὶ ἀργύρου, τὼ δ᾽ αὖ, τὸ χρυσοῦν τε
καὶ ἀργυροῦν, ἅτε οὐ πενομένω, ἀλλὰ φύσει ὄντε
πλουσίω, τὰς ψυχὰς ἐπὶ τὴν ἀρετὴν καὶ τὴν
ἀρχαίαν κατάστασιν ἡγέτην· βιαζομένων δὲ καὶ
ἀντιτεινόντων ἀλλήλοις, εἰς μέσον ὡμολόγησαν
γῆν μὲν καὶ οἰκίας κατανειμαμένους ἰδιώσασθαι,
C τοὺς δὲ πρὶν φυλαττομένους ὑπ᾽ αὐτῶν ὡς ἐλευθέρους φίλους τε καὶ τροφέας δουλωσάμενοι τότε
περιοίκους τε καὶ οἰκέτας ἔχοντες αὐτοὶ πολέμου
τε καὶ φυλακῆς αὐτῶν ἐπιμελεῖσθαι. Δοκεῖ μοι,
ἔφη, αὕτη ἡ μετάβασις ἐντεῦθεν γίγνεσθαι. Οὐκοῦν, ἦν δ᾽ ἐγώ, ἐν μέσῳ τις ἂν εἴη ἀριστοκρατίας

---

a Cf. supra 415 A-B.　　　b Cf. Theaet. 159 A.
c Cf. Homer, Il. vi. 211.
d γε vi termini. Cf. 379 A-B.
e Cf. supra 416 E-417 A, 521 A, Phaedrus 279 B-C.

248

our young men will deteriorate in their culture ; and the rulers selected from them will not approve themselves very efficient guardians for testing Hesiod's and our races of gold, silver, bronze and iron.[a] And this intermixture of the iron with the silver and the bronze with the gold will engender unlikeness[b] and an unharmonious unevenness, things that always beget war and enmity wherever they arise. ' Of this lineage,[c] look you,' we must aver the dissension to be, wherever it occurs and always." "'And rightly too,'" he said, "we shall affirm that the Muses answer." "They must needs," I said, " since they are[d] Muses." "Well, then," said he, "what do the Muses say next ? " "When strife arose," said I, " the two groups were pulling against each other, the iron and bronze towards money-making and the acquisition of land and houses and gold and silver, and the other two, the golden and silvern, not being poor, but by nature rich in their souls,[e] were trying to draw them back to virtue and their original consti- tution, and thus, striving and contending against one another, they compromised[f] on the plan of distributing and taking for themselves the land and the houses, enslaving and subjecting as *perioeci* and serfs[g] their former friends[h] and supporters, of whose freedom they had been the guardians, and occupying them- selves with war and keeping watch over these subjects." "I think," he said, " that this is the starting-point of the transformation." "Would not this polity, then," said I, " be in some sort inter-

[f] For εἰς μέσον cf. *Protag.* 338 A ; *infra* 572 D, 558 B.
[g] An allusion to Sparta. On slavery in Plato *cf.* Newman i. p. 143. *Cf.* 549 A, 578-579, *Laws* 776-777 ; Aristot. *Pol.* 1259 a 21 f., 1269 a 36 f., 1330 a 29.
[h] *Cf.* 417 A-B.

547 τε καὶ ὀλιγαρχίας αὕτη ἡ πολιτεία; Πάνυ μὲν οὖν.

IV. Μεταβήσεται μὲν δὴ οὕτω· μεταβᾶσα δὲ D πῶς οἰκήσει; ἢ φανερὸν ὅτι τὰ μὲν μιμήσεται τὴν προτέραν πολιτείαν, τὰ δὲ τὴν ὀλιγαρχίαν, ἅτ᾽ ἐν μέσῳ οὖσα, τὸ δέ τι καὶ αὑτῆς ἕξει ἴδιον; Οὕτως, ἔφη. Οὐκοῦν τῷ μὲν τιμᾶν τοὺς ἄρχοντας καὶ γεωργιῶν ἀπέχεσθαι τὸ προπολεμοῦν αὐτῆς καὶ χειροτεχνιῶν καὶ τοῦ ἄλλου χρηματισμοῦ, ξυσσίτια δὲ κατεσκευάσθαι καὶ γυμναστικῆς τε καὶ τῆς τοῦ πολέμου ἀγωνίας ἐπιμελεῖσθαι, πᾶσι τοῖς τοιούτοις τὴν προτέραν μιμήσεται; Ναί. Τῷ δέ E γε φοβεῖσθαι τοὺς σοφοὺς ἐπὶ τὰς ἀρχὰς ἄγειν, ἅτε οὐκέτι κεκτημένην ἁπλοῦς τε καὶ ἀτενεῖς τοὺς τοιούτους ἄνδρας ἀλλὰ μικτούς, ἐπὶ δὲ θυμοειδεῖς τε καὶ ἁπλουστέρους ἀποκλίνειν, τοὺς πρὸς πό- 548 λεμον μᾶλλον πεφυκότας ἢ πρὸς εἰρήνην, καὶ τοὺς περὶ ταῦτα δόλους τε καὶ μηχανὰς ἐντίμως ἔχειν, καὶ πολεμοῦσα τὸν ἀεὶ χρόνον διάγειν, αὐτὴ ἑαυτῆς αὖ τὰ πολλὰ τῶν τοιούτων ἴδια ἕξει; Ναί. Ἐπιθυμηταὶ δέ γε, ἦν δ᾽ ἐγώ, χρημάτων οἱ τοιοῦτοι ἔσονται, ὥσπερ οἱ ἐν ταῖς ὀλιγαρχίαις, καὶ τιμῶντες ἀγρίως ὑπὸ σκότου χρυσόν τε καὶ ἄργυρον, ἅτε κεκτημένοι ταμεῖα καὶ οἰκείους θησαυρούς, οἳ θέμενοι ἂν αὐτὰ κρύψειαν, καὶ αὖ περιβόλους οἰκήσεων, ἀτεχνῶς νεοττιὰς ἰδίας,

---

[a] Cf. Aristot. Pol. 1328 b 41 and Newman i. pp. 107-108.

[b] Cf. supra 416 E, 458 C, Laws 666 B, 762 C, 780 A-B, 781 C, 806 E, 839 C, Critias 112 C.

[c] Cf. 397 E, Isoc. ii. 46 ἁπλοῦς δ᾽ ἡγοῦνται τοὺς νοῦν οὐκ ἔχοντας. Cf. the psychology of Thucyd. iii. 83.

[d] This was said to be characteristic of Sparta. Cf. Newman on Aristot. Pol. 1270 a 13, Xen. Rep. Lac. 14. 2-3

mediate between aristocracy and oligarchy ? " " By all means."

IV. "By this change, then, it would arise. But after the change what will be its way of life ? Is it not obvious that in some things it will imitate the preceding polity, in some the oligarchy, since it is intermediate, and that it will also have some qualities peculiar to itself ? " " That is so," he said. " Then in honouring its rulers and in the abstention of its warrior class from farming *a* and handicraft and money-making in general, and in the provision of common public tables *b* and the devotion to physical training and expertness in the game and contest of war—in all these traits it will copy the preceding state ? " " Yes." " But in its fear to admit clever men to office, since the men it has of this kind are no longer simple *c* and strenuous but of mixed strain, and in its inclining rather to the more high-spirited and simple-minded type, who are better suited for war than for peace, and in honouring the stratagems and contrivances of war and occupying itself with war most of the time—in these respects for the most part its qualities will be peculiar to itself ? " " Yes." " Such men," said I, " will be avid of wealth, like those in an oligarchy, and will cherish a fierce secret lust for gold *d* and silver, owning storehouses *e* and private treasuries where they may hide them away, and also the enclosures *f* of their homes, literal private love-nests *g* in which they can lavish

and 7. 6, and the Chicago Dissertation of P. H. Epps, *The Place of Sparta in Greek History and Civilization*, pp. 180-184.

e Cf. 416 D.

f Cf. Laws 681 A, Theaet. 174 E.

g νεοττιάς suggests Horace's " tu nidum servas " (*Epist.* i. 10. 6). *Cf.* also Laws 776 A.

548 B ἐν αἷς ἀναλίσκοντες γύναιξί τε καὶ οἷς ἐθέλοιεν
ἄλλοις πολλὰ ἂν δαπανῷντο. Ἀληθέστατα, ἔφη.
Οὐκοῦν καὶ φειδωλοὶ χρημάτων, ἅτε τιμῶντες καὶ
οὐ φανερῶς κτώμενοι, φιλαναλωταὶ δὲ ἀλλοτρίων
δι' ἐπιθυμίαν, καὶ λάθρα τὰς ἡδονὰς καρπούμενοι,
ὥσπερ παῖδες πατέρα τὸν νόμον ἀποδιδράσκοντες,
οὐχ ὑπὸ πειθοῦς ἀλλ' ὑπὸ βίας πεπαιδευμένοι διὰ
τὸ τῆς ἀληθινῆς Μούσης τῆς μετὰ λόγων τε καὶ
C φιλοσοφίας ἠμεληκέναι καὶ πρεσβυτέρως γυμνα-
στικὴν μουσικῆς τετιμηκέναι. Παντάπασιν, ἔφη,
λέγεις μεμιγμένην πολιτείαν ἐκ κακοῦ τε καὶ
ἀγαθοῦ. Μέμικται γάρ, ἦν δ' ἐγώ· διαφανέστατον
δ' ἐν αὐτῇ ἐστιν ἕν τι μόνον ὑπὸ τοῦ θυμοειδοῦς
κρατοῦντος, φιλονικίαι καὶ φιλοτιμίαι. Σφόδρα
γε, ἦ δ' ὅς. Οὐκοῦν, ἦν δ' ἐγώ, αὕτη μὲν ἡ
πολιτεία οὕτω γεγονυῖα καὶ τοιαύτη ἄν τις εἴη, ὡς
D λόγῳ σχῆμα πολιτείας ὑπογράψαντα μὴ ἀκριβῶς
ἀπεργάσασθαι, διὰ τὸ ἐξαρκεῖν μὲν ἰδεῖν καὶ ἐκ
τῆς ὑπογραφῆς τόν τε δικαιότατον καὶ τὸν ἀδικώτατον, ἀμήχανον δὲ μήκει ἔργον εἶναι πάσας μὲν

---

[a] Cf. Laws 806 A-C, 637 B-C, Aristot. Pol. 1269 b 3, and
Newman ii. p. 318 on the Spartan women. Cf. Epps, op. cit.
pp. 322-346.

[b] φιλαναλωταί, though different, suggests Sallust's "alieni
appetens sui profusus" (Cat. 5). Cf. Cat. 52 "publice eges-
tatem, privatim opulentiam."

[c] Cf. 587 A, Laws 636 D, Symp. 187 E, Phaedr. 251 E.

[d] Cf. Aristot. Pol. 1270 b 34 with Newman's note; and
Euthyphro 2 c "tell his mother the state."

[e] Cf. Laws 720 D-E. This is not inconsistent with Polit.
293 A, where the context and the point of view are different.

[f] This is of course not the mixed government which Plato
approves Laws 691-692, 712 D-E, 759 B. Cf. What Plato
Said, p. 629.

[g] For διαφανέστατον cf. 544 D. The expression διαφανέστα-

THE REPUBLIC, BOOK VIII

their wealth on their women [a] and any others they please with great expenditure." "Most true," he said. "And will they not be stingy about money, since they prize it and are not allowed to possess it openly, prodigal of others' wealth [b] because of their appetites, enjoying [c] their pleasures stealthily, and running away from the law as boys from a father,[d] since they have not been educated by persuasion [e] but by force because of their neglect of the true Muse, the companion of discussion and philosophy, and because of their preference of gymnastics to music ? " " You perfectly describe," he said, " a polity that is a mixture [f] of good and evil." "Why, yes, the elements have been mixed," I said, " but the most conspicuous [g] feature in it is one thing only, due to the predominance of the high-spirited element, namely contentiousness and covetousness of honour.[h] " "Very much so," said he. " Such, then, would be the origin and nature of this polity if we may merely outline the figure of a constitution in words and not elaborate it precisely, since even the sketch will suffice to show us the most just and the most unjust type of man, and it would be an impracticable task to set forth all forms [i]

τον . . . ἔν τι μόνον, misunderstood and emended by Apelt, is coloured by an idea of Anaxagoras expressed by Lucretius i. 877-878 :

illud
apparere unum cuius sint plurima mixta.

Anaxag. fr. 12 *in fine*, Diels i.³ p. 405 ἀλλ' ὅτων πλεῖστα ἔνι, ταῦτα ἐνδηλότατα ἐν ἕκαστόν ἐστι καὶ ἦν. Cf. *Phaedr.* 238 A, *Cratyl.* 393 D, misunderstood by Dümmler and emended (ἐναργής for ἐγκρατής) with the approval of Wilamowitz, *Platon*, ii. p. 350.

[h] There is no contradiction between this and *Laws* 870 c if the passage is read carefully.

[i] *Cf.* on 544 D, p. 240, note *a*.

548 πολιτείας, πάντα δὲ ἤθη μηδὲν παραλιπόντα διελθεῖν. Καὶ ὀρθῶς, ἔφη.

V. Τίς οὖν ὁ κατὰ ταύτην τὴν πολιτείαν ἀνήρ; πῶς τε γενόμενος ποῖός τέ τις ὤν; Οἶμαι μέν, ἔφη ὁ Ἀδείμαντος, ἐγγύς τι αὐτὸν Γλαύκωνος

E τουτουὶ τείνειν ἕνεκά γε φιλονικίας.[a] Ἴσως, ἦν δ' ἐγώ, τοῦτό γε· ἀλλά μοι δοκεῖ τάδε οὐ κατὰ τοῦτον πεφυκέναι. Τὰ ποῖα; Αὐθαδέστερόν[b] τε δεῖ αὐτόν, ἦν δ' ἐγώ, εἶναι καὶ ὑποαμουσότερον, φιλόμουσον δὲ καὶ φιλήκοον μέν, ῥητορικὸν δ'

549 οὐδαμῶς. καὶ δούλοις μέν τις ἂν ἄγριος εἴη ὁ τοιοῦτος, οὐ καταφρονῶν δούλων, ὥσπερ ὁ ἱκανῶς πεπαιδευμένος,[c] ἐλευθέροις δὲ ἥμερος, ἀρχόντων δὲ σφόδρα ὑπήκοος, φίλαρχος δὲ καὶ φιλότιμος, οὐκ ἀπὸ τοῦ λέγειν ἀξιῶν ἄρχειν οὐδ' ἀπὸ τοιούτου οὐδενός, ἀλλ' ἀπὸ ἔργων τῶν τε πολεμικῶν καὶ τῶν περὶ τὰ πολεμικά,[d] φιλογυμναστής τέ τις ὢν καὶ φιλόθηρος. Ἔστι γάρ, ἔφη, τοῦτο τὸ ἦθος ἐκείνης τῆς πολιτείας. Οὐκοῦν καὶ χρημάτων,

B ἦν δ' ἐγώ, ὁ τοιοῦτος νέος μὲν ὢν καταφρονοῖ ἄν, ὅσῳ δὲ πρεσβύτερος γίγνοιτο, μᾶλλον ἀεὶ ἀσπάζοιτο ἂν τῷ τε μετέχειν τῆς τοῦ φιλοχρημάτου φύσεως καὶ μὴ εἶναι εἰλικρινὴς πρὸς ἀρετὴν διὰ

---

[a] Cf. *Phaedo* 65 A, Porphyry, *De abst.* i. 27, Teubner, p. 59 ἐγγὺς τείνειν ἀποσιτίας.

[b] αὐθαδέστερον. The fault of Prometheus (Aesch. *P. V.* 1034, 1037) and Medea must not be imputed to Glaucon.

[c] Cf. Arnold, *Culture and Anarchy,* who imitates or parodies Plato throughout, *e.g.* p. 83 "A little inaccessible to ideas and light," and pp. 54-55 "The peculiar serenity of aristocracies of Teutonic origin appears to come from their never having had any ideas to trouble them."

[d] Cf. 475 D, 535 D, *Lysis* 206 c.

[e] Cf. p. 249, note g, on 547 c, and Newman ii. p. 317. In

of government without omitting any, and all customs and qualities of men." "Quite right," he said.

V. "What, then, is the man that corresponds to this constitution? What is his origin and what his nature?" "I fancy," Adeimantus said, "that he comes rather close [a] to Glaucon here in point of contentiousness." "Perhaps," said I, "in that, but I do not think their natures are alike in the following respects." "In what?" "He will have to be somewhat self-willed [b] and lacking in culture, [c] yet a lover of music and fond of listening [d] to talk and speeches, though by no means himself a rhetorician; and to slaves such a one would be harsh, [e] not scorning them as the really educated do, but he would be gentle with the freeborn and very submissive to officials, a lover of office and of honour, [f] not basing his claim to office [g] on ability to speak or anything of that sort but on his exploits in war or preparation for war, and he would be a devotee of gymnastics and hunting. [h]" "Why, yes," he said, "that is the spirit of that polity. [i]" "And would not such a man be disdainful of wealth too in his youth, but the older he grew the more he would love it because of his participation in the covetous nature and because his virtue

i. p. 143, n. 3 he says that this implies slavery in the ideal state, in spite of 547 c.

[f] *Cf.* Lysias xix. 18. Lysias xxi. portrays a typical φιλό-τιμος. *Cf. Phaedr.* 256 c, Eurip. *I.A.* 527. He is a Xenophontic type. *Cf.* Xen. *Oecon.* 14. 10, *Hiero* 7. 3, *Agesil.* 10. 4. Isoc. *Antid.* 141 and 226 uses the word in a good sense. *Cf.* "But if it be a sin to covet honour," Shakes. *Henry V.* iv. iii. 28.

[g] *Cf.* the ἀξιώματα of *Laws* 690 A, Aristot. *Pol.* 1280 a 8 ff., 1282 b 26, 1283-1284.

[h] *Cf.* Arnold on the "barbarians" in *Culture and Anarchy*, pp. 78, 82, 84.

[i] For the ἦθος of a state *cf.* Isoc. *Nic.* 31.

549 τὸ ἀπολειφθῆναι τοῦ ἀρίστου φύλακος; Τίνος;
ἦ δ' ὃς ὁ Ἀδείμαντος. Λόγου, ἦν δ' ἐγώ, μουσικῇ
κεκραμένου· ὃς μόνος ἐγγενόμενος σωτὴρ ἀρετῆς
διὰ βίου ἐνοικεῖ τῷ ἔχοντι. Καλῶς, ἔφη, λέγεις.
Καὶ ἔστι μέν γ', ἦν δ' ἐγώ, τοιοῦτος ὁ τιμο-
κρατικὸς νεανίας, τῇ τοιαύτῃ πόλει ἐοικώς. Πάνυ
C μὲν οὖν. Γίγνεται δέ γ', εἶπον, οὗτος ὧδέ πως·
ἐνίοτε πατρὸς ἀγαθοῦ ὢν νέος ὑὸς ἐν πόλει
οἰκοῦντος οὐκ εὖ πολιτευομένῃ, φεύγοντος τάς τε
τιμὰς καὶ ἀρχὰς καὶ δίκας καὶ τὴν τοιαύτην πᾶσαν
φιλοπραγμοσύνην καὶ ἐθέλοντος ἐλαττοῦσθαι, ὥστε
πράγματα μὴ ἔχειν. Πῇ δή, ἔφη, γίγνεται; Ὅταν,
ἦν δ' ἐγώ, πρῶτον μὲν τῆς μητρὸς ἀκούῃ ἀχθομέ-
D νης, ὅτι οὐ τῶν ἀρχόντων αὐτῇ ὁ ἀνήρ ἐστι, καὶ
ἐλαττουμένης διὰ ταῦτα ἐν ταῖς ἄλλαις γυναιξίν,
ἔπειτα ὁρώσης μὴ σφόδρα περὶ χρήματα σπουδά-
ζοντα μηδὲ μαχόμενον καὶ λοιδορούμενον ἰδίᾳ τε
ἐν δικαστηρίοις καὶ δημοσίᾳ, ἀλλὰ ῥᾳθύμως πάντα
τὰ τοιαῦτα φέροντα, καὶ ἑαυτῷ μὲν τὸν νοῦν προσ-

ᵃ The Greek words λόγος and μουσική are untranslatable.
Cf. also 560 B. For μουσική *cf.* 546 D. Newman i. p. 414
fancies that this is a return to the position of Book IV.
from the disparagement of music in 522 A. *Cf. Unity of
Plato's Thought*, p. 4 on this supposed ABA development of
Plato's opinions.

ᵇ δέ γ' marks the transition from the description of the
type to its origin. *Cf.* 547 E, 553 B, 556 B, 557 B, 560 D,
561 E, 563 B, 566 E. Ritter, pp. 69-70, comments on its
frequency in this book, but does not note the reason. There
are no cases in the first five pages.

ᶜ *Cf.* Lysias xix. 18 ἐκείνῳ μὲν γὰρ ἦν τὰ ἑαυτοῦ πράττειν,
with the contrasted type ἀνήλωσεν ἐπιθυμῶν τιμᾶσθαι, Isoc.
Antid. 227 ἀπραγμονεστάτους μὲν ὄντας ἐν τῇ πόλει. *Cf.*
πολυπραγμοσύνη 444 B, 434 B, Isoc. *Antid.* 48, *Peace* 108, 30,

is not sincere and pure since it lacks the best guardian ? " " What guardian ? " said Adeimantus. " Reason," said I, " blended with culture,[a] which is the only indwelling preserver of virtue throughout life in the soul that possesses it." " Well said," he replied. " This is the character," I said, " of the timocratic youth, resembling the city that bears his name." " By all means." " His origin[b] is somewhat on this wise : Sometimes he is the young son of a good father who lives in a badly governed state and avoids honours and office and law-suits and all such meddlesomeness[c] and is willing to forbear something of his rights[d] in order to escape trouble.[e]" " How does he originate ? " he said. " Why, when, to begin with," I said, " he hears his mother complaining[f] that her husband is not one of the rulers and for that reason she is slighted among the other women, and when she sees that her husband is not much concerned about money and does not fight and brawl in private law-suits and in the public assembly, but takes all such matters lightly, and when she observes that he is self-

and 26, with Norlin's note (Loeb). *Cf.* also Aristoph. *Knights* 261.

[d] ἐλαττοῦσθαι: *cf.* Thuc. i. 77. 1, Aristot. *Eth. Nic.* 1198 b 26-32, *Pol.* 1319 a 3.

[e] For πράγματα ἔχειν *cf.* 370 A, *Gorg.* 467 D, *Alc. I.* 119 B, Aristoph. *Birds* 1026, *Wasps* 1392. *Cf.* πράγματα παρέχειν, *Rep.* 505 A, 531 B, *Theages* 121 D, Herod. i. 155, Aristoph. *Birds* 931, *Plutus* 20, 102.

[f] Wilamowitz, *Platon,* i. p. 434 with some exaggeration says that this is the only woman character in Plato and is probably his mother, Perictione. Pohlenz, *Gött. Gel. Anz.* 1921, p. 18, disagrees. For the complaints *cf.* Gerard, *Four Years in Germany,* p. 115 " Now if a lawyer gets to be about forty years old and is not some kind of a *Rat* his wife begins to nag him . . ."

549 ἔχοντα ἀεὶ αἰσθάνηται, ἑαυτὴν δὲ μήτε πάνυ
τιμῶντα μήτε ἀτιμάζοντα· ἐξ ἁπάντων τούτων
ἀχθομένης τε καὶ λεγούσης ὡς ἄνανδρός τε αὐτῷ
ὁ πατὴρ καὶ λίαν ἀνειμένος, καὶ ἄλλα δὴ ὅσα καὶ
Ε οἷα φιλοῦσιν αἱ γυναῖκες περὶ τῶν τοιούτων ὑμνεῖν.
Καὶ μάλ᾽, ἔφη ὁ Ἀδείμαντος, πολλά τε καὶ ὅμοια
ἑαυταῖς. Οἶσθα οὖν, ἦν δ᾽ ἐγώ, ὅτι καὶ οἱ οἰκέται
τῶν τοιούτων ἐνίοτε λάθρᾳ πρὸς τοὺς υἱεῖς τοιαῦτα
λέγουσιν, οἱ δοκοῦντες εὖνοι εἶναι, καὶ ἐάν τινα
ἴδωσιν ἢ ὀφείλοντα χρήματα, ᾧ μὴ ἐπεξέρχεται ὁ
πατήρ, ἤ τι ἄλλο ἀδικοῦντα, διακελεύονται ὅπως,
ἐπειδὰν ἀνὴρ γένηται, τιμωρήσεται πάντας τοὺς
550 τοιούτους καὶ ἀνὴρ μᾶλλον ἔσται τοῦ πατρός· καὶ
ἐξιὼν ἕτερα τοιαῦτα ἀκούει καὶ ὁρᾷ, τοὺς μὲν τὰ
αὑτῶν πράττοντας ἐν τῇ πόλει ἠλιθίους τε καλου-
μένους καὶ ἐν σμικρῷ λόγῳ ὄντας, τοὺς δὲ μὴ τὰ
αὑτῶν τιμωμένους τε καὶ ἐπαινουμένους. τότε δὴ
ὁ νέος πάντα τὰ τοιαῦτα ἀκούων τε καὶ ὁρῶν, καὶ
αὖ τοὺς τοῦ πατρὸς λόγους ἀκούων τε καὶ ὁρῶν
τὰ ἐπιτηδεύματα αὐτοῦ ἐγγύθεν παρὰ τὰ τῶν
ἄλλων, ἑλκόμενος ὑπ᾽ ἀμφοτέρων τούτων, τοῦ μὲν
Β πατρὸς αὐτοῦ τὸ λογιστικὸν ἐν τῇ ψυχῇ ἄρδοντός
τε καὶ αὔξοντος, τῶν δὲ ἄλλων τό τε ἐπιθυμητικὸν

---

[a] Cf. Symp. 174 D, Isoc. Antid. 227.

[b] Cf. the husband in Lysias i. 6.

[c] λίαν ἀνειμένος: one who has grown too slack or negligent.
Cf. Didot, Com. Fr. p. 728 τίς ὧδε μῶρος καὶ λίαν ἀνειμένος;
Porphyry, De abst. ii. 58.

[d] Cf. Phaedo 60 A. For Plato's attitude towards women
cf. What Plato Said, p. 632, on Laws 731 D.

[e] ὑμνεῖν. Cf. Euthydem. 297 D, Soph. Ajax 292. Commentators have been troubled by the looseness of Plato's
style in this sentence. Cf. Wilamowitz, Platon, ii. p. 385.

absorbed [a] in his thoughts and neither regards nor disregards her overmuch,[b] and in consequence of all this laments and tells the boy that his father is too slack [c] and no kind of a man, with all the other complaints with which women [d] nag [e] in such cases." "Many indeed," said Adeimantus, " and after their kind.[f] " " You are aware, then," said I, " that the very house-slaves of such men, if they are loyal and friendly, privately say the same sort of things to the sons, and if they observe a debtor or any other wrongdoer whom the father does not prosecute, they urge the boy to punish all such when he grows to manhood and prove himself more of a man than his father, and when the lad goes out he hears and sees the same sort of thing.[g] Men who mind their own affairs [h] in the city are spoken of as simpletons and are held in slight esteem, while meddlers who mind other people's affairs are honoured and praised. Then it is [i] that the youth, hearing and seeing such things, and on the other hand listening to the words of his father, and with a near view of his pursuits contrasted with those of other men, is solicited by both, his father watering and fostering the growth of the rational principle [j] in his soul and the others the appetitive and the passionate [k];

---

[f] Cf. Aristoph. Thesm. 167 ὅμοια γὰρ ποιεῖν ἀνάγκη τῇ φύσει.

[g] ἕτερα τοιαῦτα: cf. on 488 B; also Gorg. 481 E, 482 A, 514 D, Euthyd. 298 E, Protag. 326 A, Phaedo 58 D, 80 D, Symp. 201 E, etc.

[h] Cf. What Plato Said, p. 480, on Charm. 161 B.

[i] τότε δή: cf. 551 A, 566 C, 330 E, 573 A, Phaedo 85 A, 96 B and D, Polit. 272 E. Cf. also τότ᾽ ἤδη, on 565 C.

[j] Cf. on 439 D, Vol. I. p. 397, note d.

[k] For these three principles of the soul cf. on 435 A ff., 439 D-E ff., 441 A.

550 καὶ τὸ θυμοειδές, διὰ τὸ μὴ κακοῦ ἀνδρὸς εἶναι
τὴν φύσιν, ὁμιλίαις δὲ ταῖς τῶν ἄλλων κακαῖς
κεχρῆσθαι, εἰς τὸ μέσον ἑλκόμενος ὑπ' ἀμφοτέρων
τούτων ἦλθε, καὶ τὴν ἐν ἑαυτῷ ἀρχὴν παρέδωκε
τῷ μέσῳ τε καὶ φιλονίκῳ καὶ θυμοειδεῖ, καὶ
ἐγένετο ὑψηλόφρων τε καὶ φιλότιμος ἀνήρ. Κομιδῇ
μοι, ἔφη, δοκεῖς τὴν τούτου γένεσιν διεληλυθέναι.
C Ἔχομεν ἄρα, ἦν δ' ἐγώ, τήν τε δευτέραν πολιτείαν
καὶ τὸν δεύτερον ἄνδρα. Ἔχομεν, ἔφη.

VI. Οὐκοῦν μετὰ τοῦτο, τὸ τοῦ Αἰσχύλου, λέγωμεν ἄλλον ἄλλῃ πρὸς πόλει τεταγμένον, μᾶλλον
δὲ κατὰ τὴν ὑπόθεσιν προτέραν τὴν πόλιν; Πάνυ
μὲν οὖν, ἔφη. Εἴη δέ γ' ἄν, ὡς ἐγῷμαι, ὀλιγαρχία
ἡ μετὰ τὴν τοιαύτην πολιτείαν. Λέγεις δέ, ἦ δ'
ὅς, τὴν ποίαν κατάστασιν ὀλιγαρχίαν; Τὴν ἀπὸ
τιμημάτων, ἦν δ' ἐγώ, πολιτείαν, ἐν ᾗ οἱ μὲν
D πλούσιοι ἄρχουσι, πένητι δὲ οὐ μέτεστιν ἀρχῆς.
Μανθάνω, ἦ δ' ὅς. Οὐκοῦν ὡς μεταβαίνει πρῶτον
ἐκ τῆς τιμαρχίας εἰς τὴν ὀλιγαρχίαν, ῥητέον; Ναί.
Καὶ μήν, ἦν δ' ἐγώ, καὶ τυφλῷ γε δῆλον· ὡς
μεταβαίνει. Πῶς; Τὸ ταμιεῖον, ἦν δ' ἐγώ, ἐκεῖνο
ἑκάστῳ χρυσίου πληρούμενον ἀπόλλυσι τὴν τοιαύτην πολιτείαν. πρῶτον μὲν γὰρ δαπάνας αὑτοῖς
ἐξευρίσκουσι, καὶ τοὺς νόμους ἐπὶ τοῦτο παρ-
E άγουσιν, ἀπειθοῦντες αὐτοί τε καὶ γυναῖκες αὐτῶν.
Εἰκός, ἔφη. Ἔπειτά γε, οἶμαι, ἄλλος ἄλλον ὁρῶν

---

[a] Cf. the fragment of Menander, φθείρουσιν ἤθη χρήσθ'
ὁμιλίαι κακαί, quoted in 1 Cor. xv. 33 (Kock, C.A.F. iii.
No. 218). Cf. also Phaedr. 250 λ ὑπό τινων ὁμιλιῶν, Aesch.
Seven Against Thebes 599 ἔσθ' ὁμιλίας κακῆς κάκιον οὐδέν.

[b] Cf. p. 249, note f.

[c] Cf. infra 553 b-c, 608 b.

[d] ὑψηλόφρων is a poetical word. Cf. Eurip. I.A. 919.

and as he is not by nature of a bad disposition but has fallen into evil communications,[a] under these two solicitations he comes to a compromise[b] and turns over the government in his soul[c] to the intermediate principle of ambition and high spirit and becomes a man haughty of soul[d] and covetous of honour.[e] " " You have, I think, most exactly described his origin." " Then," said I, " we have our second polity and second type of man." " We have," he said.

VI. " Shall we then, as Aeschylus[f] would say, tell of another champion before another gate, or rather, in accordance with our plan,[g] the city first ? " " That, by all means," he said. " The next polity, I believe, would be oligarchy." " And what kind of a régime," said he, "do you understand by oligarchy ? " " That based on a property qualification,[h] " said I, " wherein the rich hold office and the poor man is excluded." " I understand," said he. " Then, is not the first thing to speak of how democracy passes over into this ? " " Yes." " And truly," said I, " the manner of the change is plain even to the proverbial blind man.[i] " " How so ? " " That treasure-house[j] which each possesses filled with gold destroys that polity ; for first they invent ways of expenditure for themselves and pervert the laws to this end, and neither they nor their wives obey them." " That is likely," he said. " And then, I take it, by observing

[e] Cf. p. 255, note f.

[f] *Seven Against Thebes* 451 λέγ' ἄλλον ἄλλαις ἐν πύλαις εἰληχότα.

[g] Cf. *Laws* 743 c, and *Class. Phil.* ix. (1914) p. 345.

[h] Cf. Aristot. *Eth. Nic.* 1160 a 33, Isoc. *Panath.* 131, *Laws* 698 b *aliter*.

[i] Cf. 465 D, *Soph.* 241 D.

[j] Cf. 548 A, 416 D.

550 καὶ εἰς ζῆλον ἰὼν τὸ πλῆθος τοιοῦτον αὑτῶν
ἀπειργάσαντο. Εἰκός. Τοὐντεῦθεν τοίνυν, εἶπον,
προϊόντες εἰς τὸ πρόσθεν[a] τοῦ χρηματίζεσθαι, ὅσῳ
ἂν τοῦτο τιμιώτερον ἡγῶνται, τοσούτῳ ἀρετὴν
ἀτιμοτέραν. ἢ οὐχ οὕτω πλούτου ἀρετὴ διέστηκεν,
ὥσπερ ἐν πλάστιγγι ζυγοῦ κειμένου ἑκατέρου ἀεὶ
τοὐναντίον ῥέποντε; Καὶ μάλ᾽, ἔφη. Τιμωμένου
551 δὴ πλούτου ἐν πόλει καὶ τῶν πλουσίων ἀτιμοτέρα
ἀρετή τε καὶ οἱ ἀγαθοί.[b] Δῆλον. Ἀσκεῖται[d] δὴ τὸ
ἀεὶ τιμώμενον, ἀμελεῖται δὲ τὸ ἀτιμαζόμενον.
Οὕτως. Ἀντὶ δὴ φιλονίκων καὶ φιλοτίμων ἀνδρῶν φιλοχρηματισταὶ καὶ φιλοχρήματοι τελευτῶντες ἐγένοντο, καὶ τὸν μὲν πλούσιον ἐπαινοῦσί τε
καὶ θαυμάζουσι καὶ εἰς τὰς ἀρχὰς ἄγουσι, τὸν δὲ
πένητα ἀτιμάζουσιν. Πάνυ γε. Οὐκοῦν τότε δὴ
B νόμον τίθενται ὅρον πολιτείας ὀλιγαρχικῆς ταξάμενοι πλῆθος χρημάτων, οὗ μὲν μᾶλλον ὀλιγαρχία,
πλέον, οὗ δ᾽ ἧττον, ἔλαττον, προειπόντες ἀρχῶν
μὴ μετέχειν, ᾧ ἂν μὴ ᾖ οὐσία εἰς τὸ ταχθὲν
τίμημα, ταῦτα δὲ ἢ βίᾳ μεθ᾽ ὅπλων διαπράττονται,
ἢ καὶ πρὸ τούτου φοβήσαντες κατεστήσαντο τὴν
τοιαύτην πολιτείαν. ἢ οὐχ οὕτως; Οὕτω μὲν

---

[a] εἰς τὸ πρόσθεν: cf. 437 A, 604 B, Prot. 339 D, Symp. 174 D,
Polit. 272 D, Soph. 258 C, 261 B, Alc. I. 132 B, Protag. 357 D
where ἧς is plainly wrong, Aristoph. Knights 751.

[b] Cf. 591 D, Laws 742 E, 705 B, 831 C ff., 836 A, 919 B
with Rep. 421 D; also Aristot. Pol. 1273 a 37-38.

[c] Cf. on 544 E, Demosth. v. 12.

[d] This sentence has been much quoted. Cf. Cic. Tusc. i.
2 " honos alit artes . . . iacentque ea semper, quae apud
quosque inprobantur." Themistius and Libanius worked it
into almost every oration. Cf. Mrs. W. C. Wright, The
Emperor Julian, p. 70, n. 3. Cf. also Stallbaum ad loc.
For ἀσκεῖται cf. Pindar, Ol. viii. 22.

and emulating one another they bring the majority of them to this way of thinking." "That is likely," he said. "And so, as time goes on, and they advance[a] in the pursuit of wealth, the more they hold that in honour the less they honour virtue. May not the opposition of wealth and virtue[b] be conceived as if each lay in the scale[c] of a balance inclining opposite ways?" "Yes, indeed," he said. "So, when wealth is honoured in a state, and the wealthy, virtue and the good are less honoured." "Obviously." "And that which men at any time honour they practise,[d] and what is not honoured is neglected." "It is so." "Thus, finally, from being lovers of victory and lovers of honour they become lovers of gain-getting and of money, and they commend and admire the rich man and put him in office but despise the man who is poor." "Quite so." "And is it not then that they pass a law defining the limits[e] of an oligarchical polity, prescribing[f] a sum of money, a larger sum where it is more[g] of an oligarchy, where it is less a smaller, and proclaiming that no man shall hold office whose property does not come up to the required valuation? And this law they either put through by force of arms, or without resorting to that they establish their government by terrorization.[h] Is not that the way of it?" "It is." "The

---

[e] ὅρον: cf. 551 c, *Laws* 714 c, 962 d, 739 d, 626 b, *Menex.* 238 d, *Polit.* 293 e, 296 e, 292 c, *Lysis* 209 c, Aristot. *Pol.* 1280 a 7, 1271 a 35, and Newman i. p. 220, *Eth. Nic.* 1138 b 23. *Cf.* also τέλος *Rhet.* 1366 a 3. For the true criterion of office-holding see *Laws* 715 c-d and Isoc. xii. 131. For wealth as the criterion *cf.* Aristot. *Pol.* 1273 a 37.

[f] For ταξάμενοι *cf.* Vol. I. p. 310, note c, on 416 e.

[g] *Cf.* Aristot. *Pol.* 1301 b 13-14.

[h] *Cf.* 557 a.

551 οὖν. Ἡ μὲν δὴ κατάστασις ὡς ἔπος εἰπεῖν αὕτη. Ναί, ἔφη· ἀλλὰ τίς δὴ ὁ τρόπος τῆς πολιτείας, καὶ ποῖά ἐστιν ἃ ἔφαμεν αὐτὴν ἁμαρτήματα
C ἔχειν;

VII. Πρῶτον μέν, ἔφην, τοῦτο αὐτό, ὅρος αὐτῆς οἷός ἐστιν. ἄθρει γάρ, εἰ νεῶν οὕτω τις ποιοῖτο κυβερνήτας ἀπὸ τιμημάτων, τῷ δὲ πένητι, εἰ καὶ κυβερνητικώτερος εἴη, μὴ ἐπιτρέποι. Πονηράν, ἦ δ' ὅς, τὴν ναυτιλίαν αὐτοὺς ναυτίλλεσθαι. Οὐκοῦν καὶ περὶ ἄλλου οὕτως ότουοῦν [ἤ τινος]¹ ἀρχῆς; Οἶμαι ἔγωγε. Πλὴν πόλεως, ἦν δ' ἐγώ, ἢ καὶ πόλεως πέρι; Πολύ γ', ἔφη, μάλιστα, ὅσῳ χαλεπωτάτη καὶ μεγίστη ἡ ἀρχή.
D Ἐν μὲν δὴ τοῦτο τοσοῦτον ὀλιγαρχία ἂν ἔχοι ἁμάρτημα. Φαίνεται. Τί δαί; τόδε ἆρά τι τούτου ἔλαττον; Τὸ ποῖον; Τὸ μὴ μίαν ἀλλὰ δύο ἀνάγκη εἶναι τὴν τοιαύτην πόλιν, τὴν μὲν πενήτων, τὴν δὲ πλουσίων, οἰκοῦντας ἐν τῷ αὐτῷ, ἀεὶ ἐπιβουλεύοντας ἀλλήλοις. Οὐδὲν μὰ Δί', ἔφη, ἔλαττον. Ἀλλὰ μὴν οὐδὲ τόδε καλόν, τὸ ἀδυνάτους εἶναι ἴσως πόλεμόν τινα πολεμεῖν διὰ τὸ ἀναγκάζεσθαι ἢ χρωμένους τῷ πλήθει ὡπλι
E σμένῳ δεδιέναι μᾶλλον ἢ τοὺς πολεμίους, ἢ μὴ

---

¹ ἤ τινος bracketed by Stallbaum, Burnet, and Hermann: ᾗστινος ci. Ast.

ᵃ Cf. supra 488, and Polit. 299 B-C, What Plato Said, p. 521, on Euthydem. 291 D.

ᵇ Stallbaum says that ἐπιτρέποι is used absolutely as in 575 D, Symp. 213 E, Lysis 210 B, etc. Similarly Latin permitto. Cf. Shorey on Jowett's translation of Meno 92 A-B, A.J.P. xiii. p. 367. See too Diog. L. i. 65.

ᶜ Men are the hardest creatures to govern. Cf. Polit. 292 D, and What Plato Said, p. 635, on Laws 766 A.

establishment then, one may say, is in this wise."
"Yes," he said; "but what is the character of this constitution, and what are the defects that we said it had?"

VII. "To begin with," said I, "consider the nature of its constitutive and defining principle. Suppose men should appoint the pilots [a] of ships in this way, by property qualification, and not allow [b] a poor man to navigate, even if he were a better pilot." "A sorry voyage they would make of it," he said. "And is not the same true of any other form of rule?" "I think so." "Except of a city," said I, "or does it hold for a city too?" "Most of all," he said, "by as much as that is the greatest and most difficult [c] rule of all." "Here, then, is one very great defect in oligarchy." "So it appears." "Well, and is this a smaller one?" "What?" "That such a city should of necessity be not one, [d] but two, a city of the rich and a city of the poor, dwelling together, and always plotting [e] against one another." "No, by Zeus," said he, "it is not a bit smaller." "Nor, further, can we approve of this—the likelihood that they will not be able to wage war, because of the necessity of either arming and employing the multitude, [f] and fearing them more than the enemy, or else, if they do not make use of them, of finding themselves

---

[d] For the idea that a city should be a unity cf. *Laws* 739 D and *supra* on 423 A-B. *Cf.* also 422 E with 417 A-B, Livy ii. 24 "adeo duas ex una civitate discordia fecerat." Aristot. *Pol.* 1316 b 7 comments ἄτοπον δὲ καὶ τὸ φάναι δύο πόλεις εἶναι τὴν ὀλιγαρχικήν, πλουσίων καὶ πενήτων . . . and tries to prove the point by his topical method.

[e] *Cf.* 417 B.

[f] For the idea that the rulers fear to arm the people *cf.* Thuc. iii. 27, Livy iii. 15 "consules et armare plebem et inermem pati timebant."

551 χρωμένους ὡς ἀληθῶς ὀλιγαρχικοὺς φανῆναι ἐν
αὐτῷ τῷ μάχεσθαι, καὶ ἅμα χρήματα μὴ ἐθέλειν
εἰσφέρειν, ἅτε φιλοχρημάτους. Οὐ καλόν. Τί δέ;
ὃ πάλαι ἐλοιδοροῦμεν, τὸ πολυπραγμονεῖν γεωρ-
552 γοῦντας καὶ χρηματιζομένους καὶ πολεμοῦντας
ἅμα τοὺς αὐτοὺς ἐν τῇ τοιαύτῃ πολιτείᾳ, ἦ δοκεῖ
ὀρθῶς ἔχειν; Οὐδ' ὁπωστιοῦν. Ὅρα δή, τούτων
πάντων τῶν κακῶν εἰ τόδε μέγιστον αὕτη πρώτη
παραδέχεται. Τὸ ποῖον; Τὸ ἐξεῖναι πάντα τὰ
αὑτοῦ ἀποδόσθαι καὶ ἄλλῳ κτήσασθαι τὰ τούτου,
καὶ ἀποδόμενον οἰκεῖν ἐν τῇ πόλει μηδὲν ὄντα τῶν
τῆς πόλεως μερῶν, μήτε χρηματιστὴν μήτε δημιουργὸν μήτε ἱππέα μήτε ὁπλίτην, ἀλλὰ πένητα καὶ
B ἄπορον κεκλημένον. Πρώτη, ἔφη. Οὔκουν δια-
κωλύεταί γε ἐν ταῖς ὀλιγαρχουμέναις τὸ τοιοῦτον·
οὐ γὰρ ἂν οἱ μὲν ὑπέρπλουτοι ἦσαν, οἱ δὲ παντάπασι πένητες. Ὀρθῶς. Τόδε δὲ ἄθρει· ἆρα
ὅτε πλούσιος ὢν ἀνήλισκεν ὁ τοιοῦτος, μᾶλλόν τι
τότ' ἦν ὄφελος τῇ πόλει εἰς ἃ νῦν δὴ ἐλέγομεν;
ἢ ἐδόκει μὲν τῶν ἀρχόντων εἶναι, τῇ δὲ ἀληθείᾳ
οὔτε ἄρχων οὔτε ὑπηρέτης ἦν αὐτῆς, ἀλλὰ τῶν
ἑτοίμων ἀναλωτής; Οὕτως, ἔφη· ἐδόκει, ἦν δὲ
C οὐδὲν ἄλλο ἢ ἀναλωτής. Βούλει οὖν, ἦν δ' ἐγώ,

---

[a] He plays on the word. In 565 c ὡς ἀληθῶς ὀλιγαρχικούς
is used in a different sense. *Cf. Symp.* 181 A ὡς ἀληθῶς
πάνδημος, *Phaedo* 80 D εἰς Ἅιδου ὡς ἀληθῶς.

[b] *Cf. supra* 374 B, 434 A, 443 D-E. For the specialty of
function *cf. What Plato Said*, p. 480, on *Charm.* 161 E.

[c] So in the *Laws* the householder may not sell his lot,
Laws 741 B-C, 744 D-E. *Cf.* 755 A, 857 A, Aristot. *Pol.*
1270 a 19, Newman i. p. 376.

on the field of battle, oligarchs indeed,[a] and rulers over a few. And to this must be added their reluctance to contribute money, because they are lovers of money." "No, indeed, that is not admirable." "And what of the trait we found fault with long ago [b] —the fact that in such a state the citizens are busybodies and jacks-of-all-trades, farmers, financiers and soldiers all in one ? Do you think that is right ? " "By no manner of means." "Consider now whether this polity is not the first that admits that which is the greatest of all such evils." "What ? " "The allowing a man to sell all his possessions,[c] which another is permitted to acquire, and after selling them to go on living in the city, but as no part of it,[d] neither a money-maker, nor a craftsman, nor a knight, nor a foot-soldier, but classified only as a pauper [e] and a dependent." "This is the first," he said. "There certainly is no prohibition of that sort of thing in oligarchical states. Otherwise some of their citizens would not be excessively rich, and others out and out paupers." "Right." "But observe this. When such a fellow was spending his wealth, was he then of any more use to the state in the matters of which we were speaking, or did he merely seem to belong to the ruling class, while in reality he was neither ruler nor helper in the state, but only a consumer of goods [f] ? " "It is so," he said ; " he only seemed, but was just a spendthrift." "Shall we, then, say of him that as

[a] *Cf.* Aristot. *Pol.* 1326 a 20, Newman i. pp. 98 and 109. *Cf.* Leslie Stephen, *Util.* ii. 111 "A vast populace has grown up outside of the old order."

[e] *Cf.* Aristot. *Pol.* 1266 b 13.

[f] ἑτοίμων : "things ready at hand." *Cf.* 573 A, Polyb. vi. (Teubner, vol. ii. p. 237) ; Horace *Epist.* i. 2. 27 "fruges consumere nati."

552 φῶμεν αὐτόν, ὡς ἐν κηρίῳ κηφὴν ἐγγίγνεται,
σμήνους νόσημα, οὕτω καὶ τὸν τοιοῦτον ἐν οἰκίᾳ
κηφῆνα ἐγγίγνεσθαι, νόσημα πόλεως; Πάνυ μὲν
οὖν, ἔφη, ὦ Σώκρατες. Οὐκοῦν, ὦ Ἀδείμαντε,
τοὺς μὲν πτηνοὺς κηφῆνας πάντας ἀκέντρους ὁ
θεὸς πεποίηκεν, τοὺς δὲ πεζοὺς τούτους ἐνίους μὲν
αὐτῶν ἀκέντρους, ἐνίους δὲ δεινὰ κέντρα ἔχοντας;
καὶ ἐκ μὲν τῶν ἀκέντρων πτωχοὶ πρὸς τὸ γῆρας
D τελευτῶσιν, ἐκ δὲ τῶν κεκεντρωμένων πάντες
ὅσοι κέκληνται κακοῦργοι; Ἀληθέστατα, ἔφη.
Δῆλον ἄρα, ἦν δ᾽ ἐγώ, ἐν πόλει, οὗ ἂν ἴδῃς πτω-
χούς, ὅτι εἰσί που ἐν τούτῳ τῷ τόπῳ ἀποκεκρυμ-
μένοι κλέπται τε καὶ βαλαντιατόμοι καὶ ἱερόσυλοι
καὶ πάντων τῶν τοιούτων κακῶν δημιουργοί.
Δῆλον, ἔφη. Τί οὖν; ἐν ταῖς ὀλιγαρχουμέναις πόλεσι πτωχοὺς οὐχ ὁρᾷς ἐνόντας; Ὀλίγου γ᾽, ἔφη,
πάντας τοὺς ἐκτὸς τῶν ἀρχόντων. Μὴ οὖν οἰό-
E μεθα, ἔφην ἐγώ, καὶ κακούργους πολλοὺς ἐν
αὐταῖς εἶναι κέντρα ἔχοντας, οὓς ἐπιμελείᾳ βίᾳ
κατέχουσιν αἱ ἀρχαί; Οἰόμεθα μὲν οὖν, ἔφη.
Ἆρ᾽ οὖν οὐ δι᾽ ἀπαιδευσίαν καὶ κακὴν τροφὴν καὶ
κατάστασιν τῆς πολιτείας φήσομεν τοὺς τοιούτους
αὐτόθι ἐγγίγνεσθαι; Φήσομεν. Ἀλλ᾽ οὖν δὴ
τοιαύτη γέ τις ἂν εἴη ἡ ὀλιγαρχουμένη πόλις καὶ
τοσαῦτα κακὰ ἔχουσα, ἴσως δὲ καὶ πλείω. Σχεδόν

---

[a] *Cf. Laws* 901 A, Hesiod, *Works and Days* 300 f., Aristoph.
Wasps 1071 ff., Eurip. *Suppl.* 242, Xen. *Oecon.* 17. 15, and
Virgil, *Georg.* iv. 168 "ignavum fucos pecus a praesepibus
arcent."
The sentence was much quoted. Stallbaum refers to
Ruhnken on *Tim.* 157 ff. for many illustrations, and to
Petavius *ad* Themist. *Orat.* xxiii. p. 285 D. *Cf.* Shelley,
Song to the Men of England:

the drone [a] springs up in the cell, a pest of the hive,
so such a man grows up in his home, a pest of the
state ? " " By all means, Socrates," he said. " And
has not God, Adeimantus, left the drones which have
wings and fly stingless one and all, while of the drones
here who travel afoot he has made some stingless but
has armed others with terrible stings ? And from the
stingless finally issue beggars in old age,[b] but from
those furnished with stings all that are denominated [c]
malefactors ? " " Most true," he said. " It is
plain, then," said I, " that wherever you see beggars
in a city, there are somewhere in the neighbourhood
concealed thieves and cutpurses and temple-robbers
and similar artists in crime." " Clearly," he said.
" Well, then, in oligarchical cities do you not see
beggars ? " " Nearly all are such," he said, " except
the ruling class." " Are we not to suppose, then, that
there are also many criminals in them furnished with
stings, whom the rulers by their surveillance forcibly [d]
restrain ? " " We must think so," he said. " And
shall we not say that the presence of such citizens is
the result of a defective culture and bad breeding
and a wrong constitution of the state ? " " We
shall." " Well, at any rate such would be the character of the oligarchical state, and these, or perhaps
even more than these, would be the evils that afflict

> Wherefore, Bees of England, forge
> Many a weapon, chain and scourge,
> That these stingless drones may spoil
> The forced produce of your toil ?

[b] *Cf.* 498 A, *Laws* 653 A; also the modern distinction between defectives and delinquents.

[c] κέκληνται : *cf.* 344 B-C.

[d] βίᾳ is so closely connected with κατέχουσιν that the double
dative is not felt to be awkward. But Adam takes ἐπιμελείᾳ
as an adverb.

553 τι, ἔφη. Ἀπειργάσθω δὴ ἡμῖν καὶ αὕτη, ἦν δ'
ἐγώ, ἡ πολιτεία, ἣν ὀλιγαρχίαν καλοῦσιν, ἐκ
τιμημάτων ἔχουσα τοὺς ἄρχοντας. τὸν δὲ ταύτῃ
ὅμοιον μετὰ ταῦτα σκοπῶμεν, ὥς τε γίγνεται οἷός
τε γενόμενος ἔστιν. Πάνυ μὲν οὖν, ἔφη.

VIII. Ἆρ' οὖν ὧδε μάλιστα εἰς ὀλιγαρχικὸν
ἐκ τοῦ τιμοκρατικοῦ ἐκείνου μεταβάλλει; Πῶς;
Ὅταν αὐτοῦ παῖς γενόμενος τὸ μὲν πρῶτον ζηλοῖ
τε τὸν πατέρα καὶ τὰ ἐκείνου ἴχνη διώκῃ, ἔπειτα
B αὐτὸν ἴδῃ ἐξαίφνης πταίσαντα ὥσπερ πρὸς ἕρματι
πρὸς τῇ πόλει, καὶ ἐκχέαντα τά τε αὐτοῦ καὶ
ἑαυτόν, ἢ στρατηγήσαντα ἤ τιν' ἄλλην μεγάλην
ἀρχὴν ἄρξαντα, εἶτα εἰς δικαστήριον ἐμπεσόντα,
βλαπτόμενον ὑπὸ συκοφαντῶν, ἢ ἀποθανόντα ἢ
ἐκπεσόντα ἢ ἀτιμωθέντα καὶ τὴν οὐσίαν ἅπασαν
ἀποβαλόντα. Εἰκός γ', ἔφη. Ἰδὼν δέ γε, ὦ
φίλε, ταῦτα καὶ παθὼν καὶ ἀπολέσας τὰ ὄντα
δείσας, οἶμαι, εὐθὺς ἐπὶ κεφαλὴν ὠθεῖ ἐκ τοῦ
C θρόνου τοῦ ἐν τῇ ἑαυτοῦ ψυχῇ φιλοτιμίαν τε καὶ
τὸ θυμοειδὲς ἐκεῖνο, καὶ ταπεινωθεὶς ὑπὸ πενίας
πρὸς χρηματισμὸν τραπόμενος γλίσχρως καὶ κατὰ
σμικρὸν φειδόμενος καὶ ἐργαζόμενος χρήματα

---

[a] Cf. on 550 c, p. 261, note h.
[b] Cf. 410 B, Homer, Od. xix. 436 ἴχνη ἐρευνῶντος, ii. 406,
iii. 30, v. 193, vii. 38 μετ' ἴχνια βαῖνε.
[c] For πταίσαντα cf. Aesch. Prom. 926, Ag. 1624 (Butl.
emend.).
[d] Cf. Aesch. Ag. 1007, Eumen. 564, Thuc. vii. 25. 7, and
Thompson on Phaedr. 255 D.
[e] Lit. "spilling." Cf. Lucian, Timon 23, Shakes. Merchant
of Venice, I. i. 31 ff.:

it." "Pretty nearly these," he said. "Then," I said, "let us regard as disposed of the constitution called oligarchy, whose rulers are determined by a property qualification.[a] And next we are to consider the man who resembles it—how he arises and what after that his character is." "Quite so," he said.

VIII. "Is not the transition from that timocratic youth to the oligarchical type mostly on this wise?" "How?" "When a son born to the timocratic man at first emulates his father, and follows in his footsteps[b]; and then sees him suddenly dashed,[c] as a ship on a reef,[d] against the state, and making complete wreckage[e] of both his possessions and himself—perhaps he has been a general, or has held some other important office, and has then been dragged into court by mischievous sycophants and put to death or banished[f] or outlawed and has lost all his property——" "It is likely," he said. "And the son, my friend, after seeing and suffering these things, and losing his property, grows timid, I fancy, and forthwith thrusts headlong[g] from his bosom's throne[h] that principle of love of honour and that high spirit, and being humbled by poverty turns to the getting of money, and greedily[i] and stingily and little by little by thrift and hard

> ... dangerous rocks
> Would scatter all her spices on the stream,
> Enrobe the roaring waters with my silks.

[f] For ἐκπεσόντα cf. 560 A, 566 A. In Xen. *An.* vii. 5. 13 it is used of shipwreck. Cf. ἐκβάλλοντες 488 c.

[g] Cf. Herod. vii. 136.

[h] Cf. Aesch. *Ag.* 983, Shakes. *Romeo and Juliet* v. i. 3:

> My bosom's lord sits lightly in his throne,

and *supra* 550 B.

[i] For γλίσχρως cf. on 488 A, *Class. Phil.* iv. p. 86 on Diog. L. iv. 59, Aelian, *Epist. Rust.* 18 γλίσχρως τε καὶ κατ᾽ ὀλίγον.

553 ξυλλέγεται. ἆρ' οὐκ οἴει τὸν τοιοῦτον τότε εἰς
μὲν τὸν θρόνον ἐκεῖνον τὸ ἐπιθυμητικόν τε καὶ
φιλοχρήματον ἐγκαθίζειν καὶ μέγαν βασιλέα ποιεῖν
ἐν ἑαυτῷ, τιάρας τε καὶ στρεπτοὺς καὶ ἀκινάκας
παραζωννύντα; Ἔγωγ', ἔφη. Τὸ δέ γε, οἶμαι,
D λογιστικόν τε καὶ θυμοειδὲς χαμαὶ ἔνθεν καὶ ἔνθεν
παρακαθίσας ὑπ' ἐκείνῳ καὶ καταδουλωσάμενος,
τὸ μὲν οὐδὲν ἄλλο ἐᾷ λογίζεσθαι οὐδὲ σκοπεῖν ἀλλ'
ἢ ὁπόθεν ἐξ ἐλαττόνων χρημάτων πλείω ἔσται, τὸ
δὲ αὖ θαυμάζειν καὶ τιμᾶν μηδὲν ἄλλο ἢ πλοῦτόν
τε καὶ πλουσίους, καὶ φιλοτιμεῖσθαι μηδ' ἐφ' ἑνὶ
ἄλλῳ ἢ ἐπὶ χρημάτων κτήσει καὶ ἐάν τι ἄλλο εἰς
τοῦτο φέρῃ. Οὐκ ἔστ' ἄλλη, ἔφη, μεταβολὴ οὕτω
ταχεῖά τε καὶ ἰσχυρὰ ἐκ φιλοτίμου νέου εἰς
E φιλοχρήματον. Ἆρ' οὖν οὗτος, ἦν δ' ἐγώ,
ὀλιγαρχικός ἐστιν; Ἡ γοῦν μεταβολὴ αὐτοῦ ἐξ
ὁμοίου ἀνδρός ἐστι τῇ πολιτείᾳ, ἐξ ἧς ἡ ὀλιγαρχία
554 μετέστη. Σκοπῶμεν δὴ εἰ ὅμοιος ἂν εἴη. Σκοπῶμεν.

IX. Οὐκοῦν πρῶτον μὲν τῷ χρήματα περὶ
πλείστου ποιεῖσθαι ὅμοιος ἂν εἴη; Πῶς δ' οὔ;
Καὶ μὴν τῷ γε φειδωλὸς εἶναι καὶ ἐργάτης, τὰς
ἀναγκαίους ἐπιθυμίας μόνον τῶν παρ' αὐτῷ
ἀποπιμπλάς, τὰ δὲ ἄλλα ἀναλώματα μὴ παρ-
εχόμενος, ἀλλὰ δουλούμενος τὰς ἄλλας ἐπιθυμίας
ὡς ματαίους. Πάνυ μὲν οὖν. Αὐχμηρός γέ τις, ἦν
δ' ἐγώ, ὢν καὶ ἀπὸ παντὸς περιουσίαν ποιούμενος,

ᵃ ἔνθεν καὶ ἔνθεν: cf. Protag. 315 B, Tim. 46 C, Critias
117 C, etc., Herod. iv. 175.

ᵇ Cf. 554 A, 556 C, Xen. Mem. ii. 6. 4 μηδὲ πρὸς ἓν ἄλλο
σχολὴν ποιεῖται ἢ ὁπόθεν αὐτός τι κερδανεῖ, and Aristot. Pol.
1257 b 4-7, and supra 330 C. See too Inge, Christian Ethics,
272

work collects property. Do you not suppose that such a one will then establish on that throne the principle of appetite and avarice, and set it up as the great king in his soul, adorned with tiaras and collars of gold, and girt with the Persian sword?" "I do," he said. "And under this domination he will force the rational and high-spirited principles to crouch lowly to right and left[a] as slaves, and will allow the one to calculate and consider nothing but the ways of making more money from a little,[b] and the other to admire and honour nothing but riches and rich men, and to take pride in nothing but the possession of wealth and whatever contributes to that?" "There is no other transformation so swift and sure of the ambitious youth into the avaricious type." "Is this, then, our oligarchical man?" said I. "He is developed, at any rate, out of a man resembling the constitution from which the oligarchy sprang." "Let us see, then, whether he will have a like character." "Let us see."

IX. "Would he not, in the first place, resemble it in prizing wealth above everything?" "Inevitably." "And also by being thrifty and laborious, satisfying only his own necessary[c] appetites and desires and not providing for expenditure on other things, but subduing his other appetites as vain and unprofitable?" "By all means." "He would be a squalid[d] fellow," said I, "looking for a surplus of

---

p. 220: "The *Times* obituary notice of Holloway (of the pills) will suffice. 'Money-making is an art by itself; it demands for success the devotion of the whole man,'" etc. For the phrase σκοπεῖν ὁπόθεν cf. Isoc. *Areop.* 83, *Panegyr.* 133-134 σκοπεῖν ἐξ ὧν.

[c] *Cf.* on 558 D, p. 291, note *i*.

[d] αὐχμηρός: cf. *Symp.* 203 D.

554 B θησαυροποιὸς ἀνήρ· οὓς δὴ καὶ ἐπαινεῖ τὸ πλῆθος·
ἢ οὐχ οὗτος ἂν εἴη ὁ τῇ τοιαύτῃ πολιτείᾳ ὅμοιος;
Ἐμοὶ γοῦν, ἔφη, δοκεῖ· χρήματα γοῦν μάλιστα
ἔντιμα τῇ τε πόλει καὶ παρὰ τῷ τοιούτῳ. Οὐ γάρ,
οἶμαι, ἦν δ’ ἐγώ, παιδείᾳ ὁ τοιοῦτος προσέσχηκεν.
Οὐ δοκῶ, ἔφη· οὐ γὰρ ἂν τυφλὸν ἡγεμόνα τοῦ
χοροῦ ἐστήσατο καὶ ἐτίμα μάλιστα.[1] Εὖ, ἦν δ’
ἐγώ. τόδε δὲ σκόπει· κηφηνώδεις ἐπιθυμίας ἐν
αὐτῷ διὰ τὴν ἀπαιδευσίαν μὴ φῶμεν ἐγγίγνεσθαι,
C τὰς μὲν πτωχικάς, τὰς δὲ κακούργους, κατεχο-
μένας βίᾳ ὑπὸ τῆς ἄλλης ἐπιμελείας; Καὶ μάλ’,
ἔφη. Οἶσθ’ οὖν, εἶπον, οἳ ἀποβλέψας κατόψει
αὐτῶν τὰς κακουργίας; Πῶς; ἔφη. Εἰς τὰς τῶν
ὀρφανῶν ἐπιτροπεύσεις καὶ εἴ πού τι αὐτοῖς
τοιοῦτον ξυμβαίνει, ὥστε πολλῆς ἐξουσίας λα-
βέσθαι τοῦ ἀδικεῖν. Ἀληθῆ. Ἆρ’ οὖν οὐ τούτῳ
δῆλον, ὅτι ἐν τοῖς ἄλλοις ξυμβολαίοις ὁ τοιοῦτος,
ἐν οἷς εὐδοκιμεῖ δοκῶν δίκαιος εἶναι, ἐπιεικεῖ τινι
D ἑαυτοῦ βίᾳ κατέχει ἄλλας κακὰς ἐπιθυμίας ἐνούσας,

---

[1] ἐτίμα μάλιστα Schneider. The ἔτι μάλιστα of the mss. is
impossible.

---

[a] For περιουσίαν cf. Blaydes on Aristoph. *Clouds* 50 and
Theaet. 154 E.
[b] Cf. *Phaedr.* 256 E, *Meno* 90 A-B by implication.
Numenius (ed. Mullach iii. 158) relates of Lacydes that he
was " a bit greedy (ὑπογλισχρότερος)—and after a fashion a
thrifty manager (οἰκονομικός)—as the expression is—the sort
approved by most people." Emerson, *The Young American*,
"They recommend conventional virtues, whatever will earn
and preserve property." But this is not always true in an envious democracy : cf. Isoc. xv. 159-160 and America to-day.

profit [a] in everything, and a hoarder, the type the multitude approves.[b] Would not this be the character of the man who corresponds to such a polity ? " " *I* certainly think so," he said. " Property, at any rate, is the thing most esteemed by that state and that kind of man." " That, I take it," said I, " is because he has never turned his thoughts to true culture." " I think not," he said, " else he would not have made the blind [c] one leader of his choir and first in honour.[d] " " Well said," I replied. " But consider this. Shall we not say that owing to this lack of culture the appetites of the drone spring up in him, some the beggarly, others the rascally, but that they are forcibly restrained by his general self-surveillance and self-control [e] ? " " We shall indeed," he said. " Do you know, then," said I, " to what you must look to discern the rascalities of such men ? " " To what ? " he said. " To guardianships of orphans,[f] and any such opportunities of doing injustice with impunity." " True." " And is it not apparent by this that in other dealings, where he enjoys the repute of a seeming just man, he by some better [g] element in himself forcibly keeps down other evil desires dwelling

[c] Plato distinctly refers to the blind god Wealth. *Cf.* Aristoph. *Plutus*, Eurip. fr. 773, *Laws* 631 c πλοῦτος οὐ τυφλός which was often quoted. *Cf. What Plato Said*, p. 624, Otto, p. 60.

[d] *Cf.* Herod. iii. 34, vii. 107.

[e] *Cf. supra* 552 E ἐπιμελείᾳ βίᾳ. For ἄλλης *cf.* 368 B ἐκ τοῦ ἄλλου τοῦ ὑμετέρου τρόπου.

[f] For the treatment of inferiors and weaker persons as a test of character *cf. Laws* 777 D-E, Hesiod, *Works and Days*, 330, and Murray, *Rise of the Greek Epic*, pp. 84-85, who, however, errs on the meaning of αἰδώς. For orphans *cf.* also *Laws* 926-928, 766 c, 877 c, 909 c-D.

[g] ἐπιεικεῖ is here used generally, and not in its special sense of " sweet reasonableness."

PLATO

554 οὐ πείθων, ὅτι οὐκ ἄμεινον, οὐδ' ἡμερῶν λόγῳ,
ἀλλ' ἀνάγκῃ καὶ φόβῳ, περὶ τῆς ἄλλης οὐσίας
τρέμων; Καὶ πάνυ γ', ἔφη. Καὶ νὴ Δία, ἦν δ'
ἐγώ, ὦ φίλε, τοῖς πολλοῖς γε αὐτῶν εὑρήσεις, ὅταν
δέῃ τἀλλότρια ἀναλίσκειν, τὰς τοῦ κηφῆνος ξυγγενεῖς ἐνούσας ἐπιθυμίας. Καὶ μάλα, ἦ δ' ὅς,
σφόδρα. Οὐκ ἄρ' ἂν εἴη ἀστασίαστος ὁ τοιοῦτος
ἐν ἑαυτῷ, οὐδὲ εἷς ἀλλὰ διπλοῦς τις, ἐπιθυμίας δὲ
E ἐπιθυμῶν ὡς τὸ πολὺ κρατούσας ἂν ἔχοι βελτίους
χειρόνων. Ἔστιν οὕτως. Διὰ ταῦτα δή, οἶμαι,
εὐσχημονέστερος ἂν πολλῶν ὁ τοιοῦτος εἴη·
ὁμονοητικῆς δὲ καὶ ἡρμοσμένης τῆς ψυχῆς
ἀληθὴς ἀρετὴ πόρρω ποι ἐκφεύγοι ἂν αὐτόν.
Δοκεῖ μοι. Καὶ μὴν ἀνταγωνιστής γε ἰδίᾳ ἐν
555 πόλει ὁ φειδωλὸς φαῦλος ἤ τινος νίκης ἢ ἄλλης
φιλοτιμίας τῶν καλῶν, χρήματά τε οὐκ ἐθέλων
εὐδοξίας ἕνεκα καὶ τῶν τοιούτων ἀγώνων ἀναλίσκειν, δεδιὼς τὰς ἐπιθυμίας τὰς ἀναλωτικὰς
ἐγείρειν καὶ ξυμπαρακαλεῖν ἐπὶ ξυμμαχίαν τε καὶ
φιλονικίαν, ὀλίγοις τισὶν ἑαυτοῦ πολεμῶν ὀλιγαρχικῶς τὰ πολλὰ ἡττᾶται καὶ πλουτεῖ. Καὶ μάλα,
ἔφη. Ἔτι οὖν, ἦν δ' ἐγώ, ἀπιστοῦμεν, μὴ κατὰ
τὴν ὀλιγαρχουμένην πόλιν ὁμοιότητι τὸν φειδωλόν
B τε καὶ χρηματιστὴν τετάχθαι; Οὐδαμῶς, ἔφη.

X. Δημοκρατίαν δή, ὡς ἔοικε, μετὰ τοῦτο

ᵃ For ἐνούσας cf. Phileb. 16 D, Symp. 187 E.
ᵇ Cf. 463 D. For the idea here cf. Phaedo 68-69, What
Plato Said, p. 527.
ᶜ For the idea " at war with himself," cf. supra 440 B and F
(στάσις), Phaedr. 237 D-E, and Aristot. Eth. Nic. 1099 a 12 f.
ᵈ Cf. 397 E.
ᵉ Cf. on 443 D-E, Vol. I. p. 414, note e; also Phaedo 61 A,
and What Plato Said, p. 485, on Laches 188 D.
ᶠ ὀλιγαρχικῶς keeps up the analogy between the man and

276

within,[a] not persuading them that it ' is better not '[b] nor taming them by reason, but by compulsion and fear, trembling for his possessions generally." " Quite so," he said. " Yes, by Zeus," said I, " my friend. In most of them, when there is occasion to spend the money of others, you will discover the existence of drone-like appetites." " Most emphatically." " Such a man, then, would not be free from internal dissension.[c] He would not be really one, but in some sort a double[d] man. Yet for the most part, his better desires would have the upper hand over the worse." " It is so." " And for this reason, I presume, such a man would be more seemly, more respectable, than many others; but the true virtue of a soul in unison and harmony[e] with itself would escape him and dwell afar." " I think so." " And again, the thrifty stingy man would be a feeble competitor personally in the city for any prize of victory or in any other honourable emulation. He is unwilling to spend money for fame and rivalries of that sort, and, fearing to awaken his prodigal desires and call them into alliance for the winning of the victory, he fights in true oligarchical[f] fashion with a small part of his resources and is defeated for the most part and—finds himself rich![g] " " Yes indeed," he said. " Have we any further doubt, then," I said, " as to the correspondence and resemblance[h] between the thrifty and money-making man and the oligarchical state?" " None," he said.

X. " We have next to consider, it seems, the origin of the state. *Cf.* my " Idea of Justice," *Ethical Record*, Jan. 1890, pp. 188, 191, 195.

[g] *i.e.* he saves the cost of a determined fight. For the effect of surprise *cf.* on 544 c, p. 239, note *f*.

[h] ὁμοιότητι: *cf.* 576 c.

555 σκεπτέον, τίνα τε γίγνεται τρόπον γενομένη τε
ποῖόν τινα ἔχει, ἵν' αὖ τὸν τοῦ τοιούτου ἀνδρὸς
τρόπον γνόντες παραστησώμεθ' αὐτὸν εἰς κρίσιν.
Ὁμοίως γοῦν ἄν, ἔφη, ἡμῖν αὐτοῖς πορευοίμεθα.
Οὐκοῦν, ἦν δ' ἐγώ, μεταβάλλει μὲν τρόπον τινὰ
τοιόνδε ἐξ ὀλιγαρχίας εἰς δημοκρατίαν, δι' ἀπληστίαν
τοῦ προκειμένου ἀγαθοῦ, τοῦ ὡς πλουσιώτατον
C δεῖν γίγνεσθαι; Πῶς δή; Ἅτε, οἶμαι, ἄρχοντες
ἐν αὐτῇ οἱ ἄρχοντες διὰ τὸ πολλὰ κεκτῆσθαι, οὐκ
ἐθέλουσιν εἴργειν νόμῳ τῶν νέων ὅσοι ἂν ἀκόλαστοι
γίγνωνται, μὴ ἐξεῖναι αὐτοῖς ἀναλίσκειν τε καὶ
ἀπολλύναι τὰ αὑτῶν, ἵνα ὠνούμενοι τὰ τῶν τοιούτων καὶ εἰσδανείζοντες ἔτι πλουσιώτεροι καὶ
ἐντιμότεροι γίγνωνται. Παντός γε μᾶλλον. Οὐκοῦν δῆλον ἤδη τοῦτο ἐν πόλει, ὅτι πλοῦτον τιμᾶν
καὶ σωφροσύνην ἅμα ἱκανῶς κτᾶσθαι ἐν τοῖς
D πολίταις ἀδύνατον, ἀλλ' ἀνάγκη ἢ τοῦ ἑτέρου
ἀμελεῖν ἢ τοῦ ἑτέρου; Ἐπιεικῶς, ἔφη, δῆλον.
Παραμελοῦντες δὴ ἐν ταῖς ὀλιγαρχίαις καὶ ἐφιέντες
ἀκολασταίνειν οὐκ ἀγεννεῖς ἐνίοτε ἀνθρώπους
πένητας ἠνάγκασαν γενέσθαι. Μάλα γε. Κάθ-
ηνται δή, οἶμαι, οὗτοι ἐν τῇ πόλει κεκεντρωμένοι
τε καὶ ἐξωπλισμένοι, οἱ μὲν ὀφείλοντες χρέα, οἱ
δὲ ἄτιμοι γεγονότες, οἱ δὲ ἀμφότερα, μισοῦντές τε
καὶ ἐπιβουλεύοντες τοῖς κτησαμένοις τὰ αὑτῶν
E καὶ τοῖς ἄλλοις, νεωτερισμοῦ ἐρῶντες. Ἔστι

---

a Cf. *Phileb.* 55 c εἰς τὴν κρίσιν, *Laws* 856 c, 943 c.
b The σκοπός or ὅρος. Cf. on 551 A, p. 263, note e, and
Aristot. *Eth. Nic.* 1094 a 2.

278

and nature of democracy, that we may next learn the character of that type of man and range him beside the others for our judgement.*a* " " That would at least be a consistent procedure." " Then," said I, " is not the transition from oligarchy to democracy effected in some such way as this—by the insatiate greed for that which it set before itself as the good,*b* the attainment of the greatest possible wealth ? " " In what way ? " " Why, since its rulers owe their offices to their wealth, they are not willing to prohibit by law the prodigals who arise among the youth from spending and wasting their substance. Their object is, by lending money on the property of such men, and buying it in, to become still richer and more esteemed." " By all means." " And is it not at once apparent in a state that this honouring of wealth is incompatible with a sober and temperate citizenship,*c* but that one or the other of these two ideals is inevitably neglected." " That is pretty clear," he said. " And such negligence and encouragement of licentiousness*d* in oligarchies not infrequently has reduced to poverty men of no ignoble quality.*e* " " It surely has." " And there they sit, I fancy, within the city, furnished with stings, that is, arms, some burdened with debt, others disfranchised, others both, hating and conspiring against the acquirers of their estates and the rest of the citizens, and eager for revolution.*f* " " 'Tis so."

---

c Ackermann, *Das Christliche bei Plato*, compares *Luke* xvi. 13 "Ye cannot serve God and Mammon." *Cf.* also *Laws* 742 D-E, 727 E f., 831 C.

d ἀκολασταίνειν : *cf. Gorg.* 478 A, *Phileb.* 12 D.

e *Cf. Laws* 832 A οὐκ ἀφυεῖς. For the men reduced to poverty swelling the number of drones *cf.* Eurip. *Herc. Fur.* 588-592, and Wilamowitz *ad loc.*

f *Cf.* Aristot. *Pol.* 1305 b 40-41, 1266 b 14.

555 ταῦτα. Οἱ δὲ δὴ χρηματισταὶ ἐγκύψαντες, οὐδὲ δοκοῦντες τούτους ὁρᾶν, τῶν λοιπῶν τὸν ἀεὶ ὑπείκοντα ἐνιέντες ἀργύριον τιτρώσκοντες, καὶ τοῦ πατρὸς ἐκγόνους τόκους πολλαπλασίους κομιζό-

556 μενοι, πολὺν τὸν κηφῆνα καὶ πτωχὸν ἐμποιοῦσι τῇ πόλει. Πῶς γάρ, ἔφη, οὐ πολύν; Οὔτε γ' ἐκείνη, ἦν δ' ἐγώ, τὸ τοιοῦτον κακὸν ἐκκαόμενον ἐθέλουσιν ἀποσβεννύναι, εἴργοντες τὰ αὑτοῦ ὅποι τις βούλεται τρέπειν, οὔτε τῇδε, ᾗ αὖ κατὰ ἕτερον νόμον τὰ τοιαῦτα λύεται. Κατὰ δὴ τίνα; Ὃς μετ' ἐκεῖνόν ἐστι δεύτερος καὶ ἀναγκάζων ἀρετῆς ἐπιμελεῖσθαι τοὺς πολίτας. ἐὰν γὰρ ἐπὶ τῷ αὑτοῦ κινδύνῳ τὰ πολλά τις τῶν ἑκουσίων ξυμβολαίων

B προστάττῃ ξυμβάλλειν, χρηματίζοιντο μὲν ἂν ἧττον ἀναιδῶς ἐν τῇ πόλει, ἐλάττω δ' ἐν αὐτῇ φύοιτο τῶν τοιούτων κακῶν, οἵων νῦν δὴ εἴπομεν. Καὶ πολύ γε, ἦ δ' ὅς. Νῦν δέ γ', ἔφην ἐγώ, διὰ πάντα τὰ τοιαῦτα τοὺς μὲν δὴ ἀρχομένους οὕτω διατιθέασιν ἐν τῇ πόλει οἱ ἄρχοντες· σφᾶς δὲ αὐτοὺς καὶ τοὺς αὑτῶν ἆρ' οὐ τρυφῶντας μὲν τοὺς νέους καὶ ἀπόνους καὶ πρὸς τὰ τοῦ σώματος καὶ πρὸς

C τὰ τῆς ψυχῆς, μαλακοὺς δὲ καρτερεῖν πρὸς ἡδονὰς

---

[a] Cf. Persius, Sat. ii. 61 "o curvae in terras animae, et caelestium inanes," Rossetti, Niniveh, in fine, "That set gaze never on the sky," Dante, Purg. xix. 71-73:

Vidi gente per esso che piangea,
Giacendo a terra tutta volta in giuso.
Adhaesit pavimento anima mea, etc.

Cf. infra 586 A κεκυφότες. Cf. also on 553 D for the general thought.

[b] Cf. Euthyph. 5 c, Polit. 287 A, Aristoph. Peace 1051, Plut. 837, Eurip. Hippol. 119, I.T. 956, Medea 67, Xen. Hell. iv. 5. 6.

[c] Or, as Ast, Stallbaum and others take it, "the poison of

" But these money-makers with down-bent heads,[a] pretending not even to see [b] them, but inserting the sting of their money [c] into any of the remainder who do not resist, and harvesting from them in interest as it were a manifold progeny of the parent sum, foster the drone and pauper element in the state." " They do indeed multiply it," he said. " And they are not willing to quench the evil as it bursts into flame either by way of a law prohibiting a man from doing as he likes with his own,[d] or in this way, by a second law that does away with such abuses." " What law?" " The law that is next best, and compels the citizens to pay heed to virtue.[e] For if a law commanded that most voluntary contracts [f] should be at the contractor's risk, the pursuit of wealth would be less shameless in the state and fewer of the evils of which we spoke just now would grow up there." " Much fewer," he said. " But as it is, and for all these reasons, this is the plight to which the rulers in the state reduce their subjects, and as for themselves and their offspring, do they not make the young spoiled [g] wantons averse to toil of body and mind, and too soft to stand

their money." τιτρώσκοντες suggests the poisonous sting, especially as Plato has been speaking of hives and drones. For ἐνιέντες cf. Eurip. Bacchae 851 ἐνείς . . . λύσσαν, " implanting madness." In the second half of the sentence the figure is changed, the poison becoming the parent, i.e. the principal, which breeds interest, cf. 507 A, p. 96.

[d] Cf. on 552 A, Laws 922 E-923 A.

[e] Cf. Protag. 327 D ἀναγκάζουσα ἀρετῆς ἐπιμελεῖσθαι, Symp. 185 B, and for ἐπιμελεῖσθαι cf. What Plato Said, p. 464, on Apol. 29 D-E.

[f] For refusing to enforce monetary contracts cf. Laws 742 C, 849 E, 915 E, and Newman ii. p. 254 on Aristot. Pol. 1263 b 21.

[g] Cf. What Plato Said, p. 483, on Laches 179 D, and Aristot. Pol. 1310 a 23.

556 τε καὶ λύπας καὶ ἀργούς; Τί μήν; Αὐτοὺς δὲ
πλὴν χρηματισμοῦ τῶν ἄλλων ἠμεληκότας, καὶ
οὐδὲν πλείω ἐπιμέλειαν πεποιημένους ἀρετῆς ἢ
τοὺς πένητας; Οὐ γὰρ οὖν. Οὕτω δὴ παρ-
εσκευασμένοι ὅταν παραβάλλωσιν ἀλλήλοις οἵ τε
ἄρχοντες καὶ οἱ ἀρχόμενοι ἢ ἐν ὁδῶν πορείαις ἢ ἐν
ἄλλαις τισὶ κοινωνίαις, ἢ κατὰ θεωρίας ἢ κατὰ
στρατείας, ἢ ξύμπλοι γιγνόμενοι ἢ συστρατιῶται,
D ἢ καὶ ἐν αὐτοῖς τοῖς κινδύνοις ἀλλήλους θεώμενοι,
μηδαμῇ ταύτῃ καταφρονῶνται οἱ πένητες ὑπὸ τῶν
πλουσίων, ἀλλὰ πολλάκις ἰσχνὸς ἀνὴρ πένης,
ἡλιωμένος, παραταχθεὶς ἐν μάχῃ πλουσίῳ ἐσκια-
τροφηκότι, πολλὰς ἔχοντι σάρκας ἀλλοτρίας, ἴδῃ
ἄσθματός τε καὶ ἀπορίας μεστόν, ἆρ᾽ οἴει αὐτὸν
οὐχ ἡγεῖσθαι κακίᾳ τῇ σφετέρᾳ πλουτεῖν τοὺς
τοιούτους, καὶ ἄλλον ἄλλῳ παραγγέλλειν, ὅταν
E ἰδίᾳ ξυγγίγνωνται, ὅτι ἄνδρες ἡμέτεροι εἰσὶ παρ᾽
οὐδέν[1]; Εὖ οἶδα μὲν οὖν, ἔφη, ἔγωγε, ὅτι οὕτω
ποιοῦσιν. Οὐκοῦν ὥσπερ σῶμα νοσῶδες μικρᾶς
ῥοπῆς ἔξωθεν δεῖται προσλαβέσθαι πρὸς τὸ
κάμνειν, ἐνίοτε δὲ καὶ ἄνευ τῶν ἔξω στασιάζει
αὐτὸ αὑτῷ, οὕτω δὴ καὶ ἡ κατὰ ταὐτὸ ἐκείνῳ
διακειμένη πόλις ἀπὸ σμικρᾶς προφάσεως, ἔξωθεν
ἐπαγομένων ἢ τῶν ἑτέρων ἐξ ὀλιγαρχουμένης

1 ἄνδρες ἡμέτεροι εἰσὶ παρ᾽ οὐδέν Baiter: γὰρ οὐδέν AFDM:
ἄνδρες ἡμέτεροι· Adam.

a Cf. 429 c-d, Laches 191 d-e, Laws 633 d.
b Cf. Tucker on Aesch. Suppl. 726.
c Cf. Soph. Ajax 758 περισσὰ κἀνόνητα σώματα.
d For a similar picture cf. Aristoph. Frogs 1086-1098.
Cf. also Gorg. 518 c, and for the whole passage Xen. Mem.
iii. 5. 15, Aristot. Pol. 1310 a 24-25.
e The poor, though stronger, are too cowardly to use force.
For κακίᾳ τῇ σφετέρᾳ cf. Lysias ii. 65 κακίᾳ τῇ αὑτῶν, Rhesus

up against pleasure and pain,[a] and mere idlers?"
"Surely." "And do they not fasten upon themselves the habit of neglect of everything except the
making of money, and as complete an indifference to
virtue as the paupers exhibit?" "Little they care."
"And when, thus conditioned, the rulers and the
ruled are brought together on the march, in wayfaring, or in some other common undertaking, either
a religious festival, or a campaign, or as shipmates or
fellow-soldiers or, for that matter, in actual battle, and
observe one another, then the poor are not in the least
scorned by the rich, but on the contrary, do you not
suppose it often happens that when a lean, sinewy,
sunburnt [b] pauper is stationed in battle beside a rich
man bred in the shade, and burdened with superfluous
flesh,[c] and sees him panting and helpless[d]—do you not
suppose he will think that such fellows keep their
wealth by the cowardice [e] of the poor, and that when
the latter are together in private, one will pass the
word to another ' our men are good for nothing '?"
"Nay, I know very well that they do," said he. "And
just as an unhealthy body requires but a slight impulse[f]
from outside to fall into sickness, and sometimes, even
without that, all the man is one internal war, in like
manner does not the corresponding type of state need
only a slight occasion,[g] the one party bringing in[h] allies

813-814 τῇ Φρυγῶν κακανδρίᾳ, *Phaedrus* 248 B, *Symp.* 182 D,
Crito 45 E, Eurip. *Androm.* 967, Aristoph. *Thesm.* 868 τῇ
κοράκων πονηρίᾳ.

[f] *Cf.* Soph. *O.T.* 961 σμικρὰ παλαιὰ σώματ' εὐνάζει ῥοπή,
"a slight impulse puts aged bodies to sleep," Demosth.
Olynth. ii. 9 and 21. *Cf.* 544 E.

[g] *Cf.* Polyb. vi. 57. Montaigne, *apud* Höffding, i. 30
"Like every other being each illness has its appointed time
of development and close—interference is futile," with *Tim.*
89 B. [h] *Cf.* Thuc. i. 3, ii. 68, iv. 64, Herod. ii. 108.

556 πόλεως ξυμμαχίαν ἢ τῶν ἑτέρων ἐκ δημοκρατου-
μένης, νοσεῖ τε καὶ αὐτὴ αὑτῇ μάχεται, ἐνίοτε δὲ
557 καὶ ἄνευ τῶν ἔξω στασιάζει; Καὶ σφόδρα γε.
Δημοκρατία δή, οἶμαι, γίγνεται, ὅταν οἱ πένητες
νικήσαντες τοὺς μὲν ἀποκτείνωσι τῶν ἑτέρων, τοὺς
δὲ ἐκβάλωσι, τοῖς δὲ λοιποῖς ἐξ ἴσου μεταδῶσι
πολιτείας τε καὶ ἀρχῶν καὶ ὡς τὸ πολὺ ἀπὸ
κλήρων αἱ ἀρχαὶ ἐν αὐτῇ γίγνονται. Ἔστι γάρ,
ἔφη, αὕτη ἡ κατάστασις δημοκρατίας, ἐάν τε καὶ
δι᾽ ὅπλων γένηται ἐάν τε καὶ διὰ φόβον ὑπεξ-
ελθόντων τῶν ἑτέρων.

XI. Τίνα δὴ οὖν, ἦν δ᾽ ἐγώ, οὗτοι τρόπον
B οἰκοῦσι; καὶ ποία τις ἡ τοιαύτη αὖ πολιτεία;
δῆλον γὰρ ὅτι ὁ τοιοῦτος ἀνὴρ δημοκρατικός τις
ἀναφανήσεται. Δῆλον, ἔφη. Οὐκοῦν πρῶτον μὲν
δὴ ἐλεύθεροι, καὶ ἐλευθερίας ἡ πόλις μεστὴ καὶ
παρρησίας γίγνεται, καὶ ἐξουσία ἐν αὐτῇ ποιεῖν
ὅ τί τις βούλεται; Λέγεταί γε δή, ἔφη. Ὅπου
δέ γε ἐξουσία, δῆλον ὅτι ἰδίαν ἕκαστος ἂν κατα-
σκευὴν τοῦ αὑτοῦ βίου κατασκευάζοιτο ἐν αὐτῇ,

---

a στασιάζει is applied here to disease of body. *Cf.* Herod.
v. 28 νοσήσασα ἐς τὰ μάλιστα στάσι, "grievously ill of faction."
Cf. supra on 554 D, p. 276, note c.

b *Cf.* 488 C, 560 A, *Gorg.* 466 C, 468 D, *Prot.* 325 B. Exile,
either formal or voluntary, was always regarded as the proper
thing for the defeated party in the Athenian democracy.
The custom even exists at the present time. Venizelos, for
instance, has frequently, when defeated at the polls, chosen
to go into voluntary exile. But that term, in modern as in
ancient Greece, must often be interpreted *cum grano salis*.

c ἐξ ἴσου: one of the watchwords of democracy. *Cf.* 561 B

from an oligarchical state, or the other from a democratic, to become diseased and wage war with itself, and sometimes even apart from any external impulse faction arises *a* ?" "Most emphatically." "And a democracy, I suppose, comes into being when the poor, winning the victory, put to death some of the other party, drive out *b* others, and grant the rest of the citizens an equal share *c* in both citizenship and offices—and for the most part these offices are assigned by lot.*d* " "Why, yes," he said, "that is the constitution of democracy alike whether it is established by force of arms or by terrorism *e* resulting in the withdrawal of one of the parties."

XI. "What, then," said I, "is the manner of their life and what is the quality of such a constitution ? For it is plain that the man of this quality will turn out to be a democratic sort of man." "It is plain," he said. "To begin with, are they not free ? and is not the city chock-full of liberty and freedom of speech ? and has not every man licence *f* to do as he likes ?" "So it is said," he replied. "And where there is such licence, it is obvious that everyone would arrange a plan *g* for leading his

and c, 599 B, 617 c, *Laws* 919 D, *Alc. I.* 115 D, *Crito* 50 E, Isoc. *Archid.* 96, *Peace* 3.

d But Isoc. *Areop.* 22-23 considers the lot undemocratic because it might result in the establishment in office of men with oligarchical sentiments. See Norlin *ad loc.* For the use of the lot in Plato *cf. Laws* 759 B, 757 E, 690 c, 741 B-C, 856 D, 946 B, *Rep.* 460 A, 461 E. *Cf.* Apelt, p. 520.

e *Cf.* 551 B.

f ἐξουσία: *cf.* Isoc. xii. 131 τὴν δ' ἐξουσίαν ὅ τι βούλεται τις ποιεῖν εὐδαιμονίαν. *Cf.* Arnold, *Culture and Anarchy*, chap. ii. Doing as One Likes.

g κατασκευή is a word of all work in Plato. *Cf.* 419 A, 449 A, 455 A, *Gorg.* 455 E, 477 B, etc.

557 ἥτις ἕκαστον ἀρέσκοι. Δῆλον. Παντοδαποὶ δὴ
C ἂν, οἶμαι, ἐν ταύτῃ τῇ πολιτείᾳ μάλιστ᾽ ἐγ-
γίγνοιντο ἄνθρωποι. Πῶς γὰρ οὔ; Κινδυνεύει,
ἦν δ᾽ ἐγώ, καλλίστη αὕτη τῶν πολιτειῶν εἶναι·
ὥσπερ ἱμάτιον ποικίλον πᾶσιν ἄνθεσι πεποικιλμένον, οὕτω καὶ αὕτη πᾶσιν ἤθεσι πεποικιλμένη
καλλίστη ἂν φαίνοιτο· καὶ ἴσως μέν, ἦν δ᾽ ἐγώ, καὶ
ταύτην, ὥσπερ οἱ παῖδές τε καὶ αἱ γυναῖκες τὰ
ποικίλα θεώμενοι, καλλίστην ἂν πολλοὶ κρίνειαν.
D Καὶ μάλ᾽, ἔφη. Καὶ ἔστι γε, ὦ μακάριε, ἦν δ᾽
ἐγώ, ἐπιτήδειον ζητεῖν ἐν αὐτῇ πολιτείαν. Τί δή;
Ὅτι πάντα γένη πολιτειῶν ἔχει διὰ τὴν ἐξουσίαν,
καὶ κινδυνεύει τῷ βουλομένῳ πόλιν κατασκευάζειν,
ὃ νῦν δὴ ἡμεῖς ἐποιοῦμεν, ἀναγκαῖον εἶναι εἰς
δημοκρατουμένην ἐλθόντι πόλιν, ὃς ἂν αὐτὸν
ἀρέσκῃ τρόπος, τοῦτον ἐκλέξασθαι, ὥσπερ εἰς
παντοπώλιον ἀφικομένῳ πολιτειῶν, καὶ ἐκλεξα-
μένῳ οὕτω κατοικίζειν. Ἴσως γοῦν, ἔφη, οὐκ
E ἂν ἀποροῖ παραδειγμάτων. Τὸ δὲ μηδεμίαν ἀνάγκην, εἶπον, εἶναι ἄρχειν ἐν ταύτῃ τῇ πόλει, μηδ᾽

---

[a] παντοδαπός usually has an unfavourable connotation in
Plato. *Cf.* 431 B-C, 561 D, 567 E, 559 D, *Symp.* 198 B,
Gorg. 489 C, *Laws* 788 B, etc. Isoc. iv. 45 uses it in a
favourable sense, but in iii. 16 more nearly as Plato does.
For the mixture of things in a democracy *cf.* Xen. *Rep.
Ath.* 2. 8 φωνῇ καὶ διαίτῃ καὶ σχήματι . . . Ἀθηναῖοι δὲ σε-
κραμένῃ ἐξ ἁπάντων τῶν Ἑλλήνων καὶ βαρβάρων ; and *Laws*
681 D. Libby, *Introduction to History of Science*, p. 273,
says " Arnold failed in his analysis of American civilization
to confirm Plato's judgement concerning the variety of
natures to be found in the democratic state." De Tocqueville
also, and many English observers, have commented on the
monotony and standardization of American life.

own life in the way that pleases him." "Obvious."
" All sorts *a* and conditions of men, then, would
arise in this polity more than in any other ? " " Of
course." " Possibly," said I, " this is the most
beautiful of polities ; as a garment of many colours,
embroidered with all kinds of hues, so this, decked
and diversified with every type of character, would
appear the most beautiful. And perhaps," I said,
" many would judge it to be the most beautiful, like
boys and women *b* when they see bright-coloured
things." " Yes indeed," he said. " Yes," said I, " and
it is the fit place, my good friend, in which to look for a
constitution." " Why so ? " " Because, owing to this
licence, it includes all kinds, and it seems likely that
anyone who wishes to organize a state, as we were just
now doing, must find his way to a democratic city and
select the model that pleases him, as if in a bazaar *c* of
constitutions, and after making his choice, establish
his own." " Perhaps at any rate," he said, " he
would not be at a loss for patterns." " And the
freedom from all compulsion to hold office in such a

b For the idea that women and children like many colours
cf. Sappho's admiration for Jason's mantle mingled with all
manner of colours (*Lyr. Graec.* i. 196). For the classing
together of women and boys *cf. Laws* 658 D, Shakes. *As
You Like It*, III. ii. 435 " As boys and women are for the
most part cattle of this colour," Faguet, *Nineteenth Century*
" Lamartine a été infiniment aimé des adolescents sérieux et
des femmes distinguées."

c Cf. Plutarch, *Dion* 53. Burke says " A republic, as
an ancient philosopher has observed, is no one species of
government, but a magazine of every species." *Cf. Laws*
789 B for an illustration of the point. Filmer, *Patriarcha*,
misquotes this, saying " The Athenians sold justice . . .,"
which made Plato call a popular estate a fair where everything is to be sold."

557 ἂν ᾖς ἱκανὸς ἄρχειν, μηδὲ αὖ ἄρχεσθαι, ἐὰν μὴ
βούλῃ, μηδὲ πολεμεῖν πολεμούντων, μηδὲ εἰρήνην
ἄγειν τῶν ἄλλων ἀγόντων, ἐὰν μὴ ἐπιθυμῇς
εἰρήνης, μηδ' αὖ, ἐάν τις ἄρχειν νόμος σε δια-
κωλύῃ ἢ δικάζειν, μηδὲν ἧττον καὶ ἄρχειν καὶ
558 δικάζειν, ἐὰν αὐτῷ σοι ἐπίῃ, ἆρ' οὐ θεσπεσία καὶ
ἡδεῖα ἡ τοιαύτη διαγωγὴ ἐν τῷ παραυτίκα; Ἴσως,
ἔφη, ἔν γε τούτῳ. Τί δαί; ἡ πρᾳότης ἐνίων τῶν
δικασθέντων οὐ κομψή; ἢ οὔπω εἶδες ἐν τοιαύτῃ
πολιτείᾳ, ἀνθρώπων καταψηφισθέντων θανάτου
ἢ φυγῆς, οὐδὲν ἧττον αὐτῶν μενόντων τε καὶ
ἀναστρεφομένων ἐν μέσῳ, καὶ ὡς οὔτε φροντίζοντος
οὔτε ὁρῶντος οὐδενὸς περινοστεῖ ὥσπερ ἥρως;
Καὶ πολλούς γ', ἔφη. Ἡ δὲ συγγνώμη καὶ οὐδ'
B ὁπωστιοῦν σμικρολογία αὐτῆς, ἀλλὰ καταφρόνησις
ὧν ἡμεῖς ἐλέγομεν σεμνύνοντες, ὅτε τὴν πόλιν
ᾠκίζομεν, ὡς εἰ μή τις ὑπερβεβλημένην φύσιν ἔχοι,
οὔποτ' ἂν γένοιτο ἀνὴρ ἀγαθός, εἰ μὴ παῖς ὢν
εὐθὺς παίζοι ἐν καλοῖς καὶ ἐπιτηδεύοι τὰ τοιαῦτα

---

[a] Cf. Aristot. Pol. 1271 a 12 δεῖ γὰρ καὶ βουλόμενον καὶ μὴ
βουλόμενον ἄρχειν τὸν ἄξιον τῆς ἀρχῆς. Cf. 347 B-C.

[b] Cf. Laws 955 B-C, where a penalty is pronounced for
making peace or war privately, and the parody in Aristoph.
Acharn. passim.

[c] διαγωγή: cf. 344 E, where it is used more seriously of the
whole conduct of life. Cf. also Theaet. 177 A, Polit. 274 D,
Tim. 71 D, Laws 806 E. Aristot. Met. 981 b 18 and 982 b 24
uses the word in virtual anaphora with pleasure. See too
Zeller, Aristot. ii. pp. 307-309, 266, n. 5.

[d] Cf. 562 D. For the mildness of the Athenian democracy cf. Aristot. Ath. Pol. 22. 19, Demosth. xxi. 184, xxii. 51,
xxiv. 51, Lysias vi. 34, Isoc. Antid. 20, Areopagit. 67-68,
Hel. 37; also Menex. 243 E and also Euthydem. 303 D δημοτικόν

city, even if you are qualified,[a] or again, to submit to
rule, unless you please, or to make war when the rest
are at war,[b] or to keep the peace when the others do
so, unless you desire peace ; and again, the liberty, in
defiance of any law that forbids you, to hold office and
sit on juries none the less, if it occurs to you to do so,
is not all that a heavenly and delicious entertainment[c]
for the time being ? " " Perhaps," he said, " for so
long." "And is not the placability[d] of some convicted
criminals exquisite[e] ? Or have you never seen in
such a state men condemned to death or exile who
none the less stay on, and go to and fro among
the people, and as if no one saw or heeded him, the
man slips in and out[f] like a *revenant*[g] ? " "Yes,
many," he said. "And the tolerance of democracy, its superiority[h] to all our meticulous requirements, its disdain for our solemn[i] pronouncements[j]
made when we were founding our city, that except
in the case of transcendent[k] natural gifts no one could
ever become a good man unless from childhood his
play and all his pursuits were concerned with things

τι καὶ πρᾷον ἐν τοῖς λόγοις. Here the word πρᾳότης is ironically
transferred to the criminal himself.

[e] κομψή: cf. 376 A, *Theaet.* 171 A.

[f] For περινοστεῖ cf. Lucian, *Bis Acc.* 6, Aristoph. *Plut.*
121, 494, *Peace* 762.

[g] His being unnoticed accords better with the rendering
"spirit," "one returned from the dead" (a perfectly
possible meaning for ἥρως). Wilamowitz, *Platon*, i. p. 435
translates "Geist") than with that of a hero returning from
the wars. *Cf.* Adam *ad loc.*

[h] For οὐδ' ὁπωστιοῦν σμικρολογία cf. on 532 B ἔτι ἀδυναμία.

[i] σεμνύνοντες here has an ironical or colloquial tone—
"high-brow," "top-lofty."

[j] *Cf.* 401 B-C, 374 C and on 467 A, *Laws* 643 B, Delacroix,
Psychologie de l'art, p. 46.

[k] For ὑπερβεβλημένη cf. *Laws* 719 D, Eurip. *Alcest.* 153.

558 πάντα, ὡς μεγαλοπρεπῶς καταπατήσασ᾽ ἅπαντα
ταῦτα οὐδὲν φροντίζει, ἐξ ὁποίων ἄν τις ἐπιτηδευμάτων ἐπὶ τὰ πολιτικὰ ἰὼν πράττῃ, ἀλλὰ τιμᾷ,
C ἐὰν φῇ μόνον εὔνους εἶναι τῷ πλήθει. Πάνυ γ᾽,
ἔφη, γενναία.¹ Ταῦτά τε δή, ἔφην, ἔχοι ἂν καὶ
τούτων ἄλλα ἀδελφὰ δημοκρατία, καὶ εἴη, ὡς
ἔοικεν, ἡδεῖα πολιτεία καὶ ἄναρχος καὶ ποικίλη,
ἰσότητά τινα ὁμοίως ἴσοις τε καὶ ἀνίσοις δια-
νέμουσα. Καὶ μάλ᾽, ἔφη, γνώριμα λέγεις.

XII. Ἄθρει δή, ἦν δ᾽ ἐγώ, τίς ὁ τοιοῦτος ἰδίᾳ.
ἢ πρῶτον σκεπτέον, ὥσπερ τὴν πολιτείαν ἐσκεψά-
μεθα, τίνα τρόπον γίγνεται; Ναί, ἔφη. Ἆρ᾽ οὖν
οὐχ ὧδε; τοῦ φειδωλοῦ ἐκείνου καὶ ὀλιγαρχικοῦ
D γένοιτ᾽ ἄν, οἶμαι, υἱὸς ὑπὸ τῷ πατρὶ τεθραμμένος
ἐν τοῖς ἐκείνου ἤθεσιν; Τί γὰρ οὔ; Βίᾳ δὴ καὶ
οὗτος ἄρχων τῶν ἐν αὑτῷ ἡδονῶν, ὅσαι ἀνα-
λωτικαὶ μέν, χρηματιστικαὶ δὲ μή, αἳ δὴ οὐκ
ἀναγκαῖαι κέκληνται. Δῆλον, ἔφη. Βούλει οὖν,
ἦν δ᾽ ἐγώ, ἵνα μὴ σκοτεινῶς διαλεγώμεθα, πρῶτον
ὁρισώμεθα τάς τε ἀναγκαίους ἐπιθυμίας καὶ τὰς
μή; Βούλομαι, ἦ δ᾽ ὅς. Οὐκοῦν ἅς τε οὐκ ἂν οἷοί

¹ γενναία M, γενναῖα AFD.

---

[a] μεγαλοπρεπῶς is often ironical in Plato. *Cf.* 362 c, *Symp.*
199 c, *Charm.* 175 c, *Theaet.* 161 c, *Meno* 94 B, *Polit.* 277 B,
Hipp. Maj. 291 E.

[b] In Aristoph. *Knights* 180 ff. Demosthenes tells the
sausage-seller that his low birth and ignorance and his trade
are the very things that fit him for political leadership.

[c] *Cf.* Aristoph. *Knights* 732 f., 741 and *passim.* Andoc. iv.
16 εὔνους τῷ δήμῳ. Émile Faguet, *Moralistes*, iii. p. 84, says of
Tocqueville, " Il est bien je crois le premier qui ait dit que la
démocratie abaisse le niveau intellectuel des gouvernements."
For the other side of the democratic shield see Thucyd. ii. 39.

[d] For the ironical use of γενναῖα *cf.* 544 c, *Soph.* 231 B,
Theaet. 209 E.

fair and good,—how superbly *a* it tramples under foot all such ideals, caring nothing from what practices *b* and way of life a man turns to politics, but honouring him if only he says that he loves the people ! *c* " " It is a noble *d* polity, indeed ! " he said. " These and qualities akin to these democracy would exhibit, and it would, it seems, be a delightful *e* form of government, anarchic and motley, assigning a kind of equality indiscriminately to equals and unequals alike ! *f* " " Yes," he said, " everybody knows that."

XII. " Observe, then, the corresponding private character. Or must we first, as in the case of the polity, consider the origin of the type ? " " Yes," he said. " Is not this, then, the way of it ? Our thrifty *g* oligarchical man would have a son bred in his father's ways." " Why not ? " " And he, too, would control by force all his appetites for pleasure that are wasters and not winners of wealth, those which are denominated unnecessary." " Obviously." " And in order not to argue in the dark, shall we first define *h* our distinction between necessary and unnecessary appetites *i* ? " " Let us do so." " Well,

---

e ἡδεῖα : *cf.* Isoc. vii. 70 of good government, τοῖς χρωμένοις ἡδίους.

f *Cf. What Plato Said*, p. 634, on *Laws* 744 B-C, and *ibid.* p. 508 on *Gorg.* 508 A, Aristot. *Eth. Nic.* 1131 a 23-24, Newman, i. p. 248, Xen. *Cyr.* ii. 2. 18.

g *Cf.* 572 c, Theogn. 915 f., *Anth. Pal.* x. 41, Democr. fr. 227 and 228, Diels ii.³ p. 106, and Epicharm. *fr.* 45, Diels i.³ p. 126.

h *Cf. What Plato Said*, p. 485, on *Laches* 190 B, and p. 551, on *Phaedr.* 237 E.

i *Cf.* 554 A, 571 B, *Phaedo* 64 D-E, *Phileb.* 62 E, Aristot. *Eth. Nic.* 1147 b 29. The Epicureans made much of this distinction. *Cf.* Cic. *De fin.* i. 13. 45, *Tusc.* v. 33, 93, Porphyry, *De abst.* i. 49. Ath. xii. 511 quotes this passage and says it anticipates the Epicureans.

558 τ' εἶμεν ἀποτρέψαι, δικαίως ἂν ἀναγκαῖαι καλοῖντο,
E καὶ ὅσαι ἀποτελούμεναι ὠφελοῦσιν ἡμᾶς; τούτων
γὰρ ἀμφοτέρων ἐφίεσθαι ἡμῶν τῇ φύσει ἀνάγκη·
559 ἢ οὔ; Καὶ μάλα. Δικαίως δὴ τοῦτο ἐπ' αὐταῖς
ἐροῦμεν, τὸ ἀναγκαῖον. Δικαίως. Τί δαί; ἅς γέ
τις ἀπαλλάξειεν ἄν, εἰ μελετῷ ἐκ νέου, καὶ πρὸς
οὐδὲν ἀγαθὸν ἐνοῦσαι δρῶσιν, αἱ δὲ καὶ τοὐναντίον,
πάσας ταύτας εἰ μὴ ἀναγκαίους φαῖμεν εἶναι, ἆρ'
οὐ καλῶς ἂν λέγοιμεν; Καλῶς μὲν οὖν. Προ-
ελώμεθα δή τι παράδειγμα ἑκατέρων, αἴ εἰσιν, ἵνα
τύπῳ λάβωμεν αὐτάς; Οὐκοῦν χρή. Ἆρ' οὖν
οὐχ ἡ τοῦ φαγεῖν μέχρι ὑγιείας τε καὶ εὐεξίας καὶ
B αὐτοῦ σίτου τε καὶ ὄψου ἀναγκαῖος ἂν εἴη; Οἶμαι.
Ἡ μέν γέ που τοῦ σίτου κατ' ἀμφότερα ἀναγκαία,
ᾗ τε ὠφέλιμος ᾗ τε παῦσαι ζῶντα οὐ δυνατή.[1]
Ναί. Ἡ δὲ ὄψου, εἴ πή τινα ὠφέλειαν πρὸς
εὐεξίαν παρέχεται. Πάνυ μὲν οὖν. Τί δέ; ἡ
πέρα τούτων καὶ ἀλλοίων ἐδεσμάτων ἢ τοιούτων
ἐπιθυμία, δυνατὴ δὲ κολαζομένη ἐκ νέων καὶ
παιδευομένη ἐκ τῶν πολλῶν ἀπαλλάττεσθαι, καὶ
βλαβερὰ μὲν σώματι, βλαβερὰ δὲ ψυχῇ πρός τε
C φρόνησιν καὶ τὸ σωφρονεῖν, ἆρα γε ὀρθῶς οὐκ
ἀναγκαία ἂν καλοῖτο; Ὀρθότατα μὲν οὖν. Οὐκοῦν καὶ ἀναλωτικὰς φῶμεν εἶναι ταύτας, ἐκείνας,
δὲ χρηματιστικὰς διὰ τὸ χρησίμους πρὸς τὰ ἔργα
εἶναι; Τί μήν; Οὕτω δὴ καὶ περὶ ἀφροδισίων
καὶ τῶν ἄλλων φήσομεν; Οὕτω. Ἆρ' οὖν καὶ

[1] παῦσαι ζῶντα οὐ δυνατή Hermann, παῦσαι ζῶντα οὐνατή
AFDM, μὴ παῦσαι ζῶντα δυνατή Mon., Burnet, παῦσαι πεινῶν-
τας Athenaeus, παύσασθαι ζῶντος ἀδυνατεῖ Wilamowitz (Platon,
ii. pp. 385-386).

then, desires that we cannot divert or suppress may be properly called necessary, and likewise those whose satisfaction is beneficial to us, may they not? For our nature compels us to seek their satisfaction. Is not that so?" "Most assuredly." "Then we shall rightly use the word 'necessary' of them?" "Rightly." "And what of the desires from which a man could free himself by discipline from youth up, and whose presence in the soul does no good and in some cases harm? Should we not fairly call all such unnecessary?" "Fairly indeed." "Let us select an example of either kind, so that we may apprehend the type.[a]" "Let us do so." "Would not the desire of eating to keep in health and condition and the appetite for mere bread and relishes[b] be necessary?" "I think so." "The appetite for bread is necessary in both respects, in that it is beneficial and in that if it fails we die." "Yes." "And the desire for relishes, so far as it conduces to fitness?" "By all means." "And should we not rightly pronounce unnecessary the appetite that exceeds these and seeks other varieties of food, and that by correction[c] and training from youth up can be got rid of in most cases and is harmful to the body and a hindrance to the soul's attainment of intelligence and sobriety?" "Nay, most rightly." "And may we not call the one group the spendthrift desires and the other the profitable,[d] because they help production?" "Surely." "And we shall say the same of sexual and other appetites?" "The same." "And were

---

[a] Or "grasp them in outline."
[b] For ὄψον cf. on 372 c, Vol. I. p. 158, note a.
[c] For κολαζομένη cf. 571 B, Gorg. 505 B. 491 E, 507 D. For the thought cf. also supra 519 A-B.
[d] Lit. "money-making." Cf. 558 D.

559 ὃν νῦν δὴ κηφῆνα ὠνομάζομεν, τοῦτον ἐλέγομεν
τὸν τῶν τοιούτων ἡδονῶν καὶ ἐπιθυμιῶν γέμοντα
καὶ ἀρχόμενον ὑπὸ τῶν μὴ ἀναγκαίων, τὸν δὲ
D ὑπὸ τῶν ἀναγκαίων φειδωλόν τε καὶ ὀλιγαρχικόν·
Ἀλλὰ τί μήν;

XIII. Πάλιν τοίνυν, ἦν δ᾽ ἐγώ, λέγωμεν, ὡς ἐξ
ὀλιγαρχικοῦ δημοκρατικὸς γίγνεται. φαίνεται δέ
μοι τά γε πολλὰ ὧδε γίγνεσθαι. Πῶς; Ὅταν
νέος τεθραμμένος ὡς νῦν δὴ ἐλέγομεν, ἀπαιδεύτως
τε καὶ φειδωλῶς, γεύσηται κηφήνων μέλιτος καὶ
ξυγγένηται αἴθωσι θηρσὶ καὶ δεινοῖς, παντοδαπὰς
ἡδονὰς καὶ ποικίλας καὶ παντοίως ἐχούσας δυνα-
μένοις σκευάζειν, ἐνταῦθά που οἴου εἶναι ἀρχὴν
E αὐτῷ μεταβολῆς ὀλιγαρχικῆς τῆς ἐν ἑαυτῷ εἰς
δημοκρατικήν.[1] Πολλὴ ἀνάγκη, ἔφη. Ἆρ᾽ οὖν,
ὥσπερ ἡ πόλις μετέβαλλε βοηθησάσης τῷ ἑτέρῳ
μέρει ξυμμαχίας ἔξωθεν ὁμοίας ὁμοίῳ, οὕτω καὶ
ὁ νεανίας μεταβάλλει βοηθοῦντος αὖ εἴδους
ἐπιθυμιῶν ἔξωθεν τῷ ἑτέρῳ τῶν παρ᾽ ἐκείνῳ
ξυγγενοῦς τε καὶ ὁμοίου; Παντάπασι μὲν οὖν.
Καὶ ἐὰν μέν, οἶμαι, ἀντιβοηθήσῃ τις τῷ ἐν ἑαυτῷ
ὀλιγαρχικῷ ξυμμαχία, ἢ ποθὲν παρὰ τοῦ πατρὸς
560 ἢ καὶ τῶν ἄλλων οἰκείων νουθετούντων τε καὶ
κακιζόντων, στάσις δὴ καὶ ἀντίστασις καὶ μάχη

---

[1] So mss.: μεταβολῆς . . . ὀλιγαρχικῆς Burnet, μεταβολῆς ὀλιγαρχίας . . . δημοκρατίαν, or insert πολιτείας after ἑαυτῷ Adam.
Jowett and Campbell suggest inserting ἐξ after μεταβολῆς.

[a] For γέμοντα cf. 577 D, 578 A, 603 D, 611 B, Gorg. 525 A,
522 E, etc.

[b] αἴθων occurs only here in Plato. It is common in Pindar
and tragedy. Ernst Maass, " Die Ironie. des Sokrates,"
Sokrates, 11, p. 94 " Platon hat an jener Stelle des Staats,
von der wir ausgingen, die schlimmen Erzieher gefährliche
Fuchsbestien genannt." (Cf. Pindar, Ol. xi. 20.)

we not saying that the man whom we nicknamed the drone is the man who teems [a] with such pleasures and appetites, and who is governed by his unnecessary desires, while the one who is ruled by his necessary appetites is the thrifty oligarchical man ? " " Why, surely."

XIII. " To return, then," said I, " we have to tell how the democratic man develops from the oligarchical type. I think it is usually in this way." " How ? " " When a youth, bred in the illiberal and niggardly fashion that we were describing, gets a taste of the honey of the drones and associates with fierce [b] and cunning creatures who know how to purvey pleasures of every kind and variety [c] and condition, there you must doubtless conceive is the beginning of the transformation of the oligarchy in his soul into democracy." " Quite inevitably," he said. " May we not say that just as the revolution in the city was brought about by the aid of an alliance from outside, coming to the support of the similar and corresponding party in the state, so the youth is revolutionized when a like and kindred [d] group of appetites from outside comes to the aid of one of the parties in his soul ? " " By all means," he said. " And if, I take it, a counter-alliance [e] comes to the rescue of the oligarchical part of his soul, either it may be from his father or from his other kin, who admonish and reproach him, then there arises faction [f] and counter-

---

[c] Cf. on 557 c, p. 286, note a.

[d] Cf. 554 D.

[e] For the metaphor cf. Xen. Mem. i. 2. 24 ἐδυνάσθην ἐκείνω χρωμένω συμμάχῳ τῶν μὴ καλῶν ἐπιθυμιῶν κρατεῖν, " they [Critias and Alcibiades] found in him [Socrates] an ally who gave them strength to conquer their evil passions." (Loeb tr.)

[f] Cf. supra on 554 D, p. 276, note c.

560 ἐν αὑτῷ πρὸς αὑτὸν τότε γίγνεται. Τί μήν; Καὶ ποτὲ μέν, οἶμαι, τὸ δημοκρατικὸν ὑπεχώρησε τῷ ὀλιγαρχικῷ, καί τινες τῶν ἐπιθυμιῶν αἱ μὲν διεφθάρησαν, αἱ δὲ καὶ ἐξέπεσον, αἰδοῦς τινος ἐγγενομένης ἐν τῇ τοῦ νέου ψυχῇ, καὶ κατεκοσμήθη πάλιν. Γίγνεται γὰρ ἐνίοτε, ἔφη. Αὖθις δέ, οἶμαι, τῶν ἐκπεσουσῶν ἐπιθυμιῶν ἄλλαι ὑπο-
B τρεφόμεναι ξυγγενεῖς δι' ἀνεπιστημοσύνην τροφῆς πατρὸς πολλαί τε καὶ ἰσχυραὶ ἐγένοντο. Φιλεῖ γοῦν, ἔφη, οὕτω γίγνεσθαι. Οὐκοῦν εἵλκυσάν τε πρὸς τὰς αὐτὰς ὁμιλίας, καὶ λάθρᾳ ξυγγιγνόμεναι πλῆθος ἐνέτεκον. Τί μήν; Τελευτῶσαι δή, οἶμαι, κατέλαβον τὴν τοῦ νέου τῆς ψυχῆς ἀκρόπολιν, αἰσθόμεναι κενὴν μαθημάτων τε καὶ ἐπιτηδευμάτων καλῶν καὶ λόγων ἀληθῶν, οἳ δὴ ἄριστοι φρουροί τε
C καὶ φύλακες ἐν ἀνδρῶν θεοφιλῶν εἰσὶ διανοίαις. Καὶ πολύ γ', ἔφη. Ψευδεῖς δὴ καὶ ἀλαζόνες, οἶμαι, λόγοι τε καὶ δόξαι ἀντ' ἐκείνων ἀναδραμόντες κατέσχον τὸν αὐτὸν τόπον τοῦ τοιούτου. Σφόδρα γ', ἔφη. Ἆρ' οὖν οὐ πάλιν τε εἰς ἐκείνους τοὺς λωτοφάγους ἐλθὼν φανερῶς κατοικεῖ, καὶ ἐὰν παρ' οἰκείων τις βοήθεια τῷ φειδωλῷ αὐτοῦ τῆς ψυχῆς ἀφικνῆται, κλῄσαντες οἱ ἀλαζόνες λόγοι ἐκεῖνοι τὰς τοῦ βασιλικοῦ τείχους ἐν αὑτῷ πύλας
D οὔτε αὐτὴν τὴν ξυμμαχίαν παριᾶσιν οὔτε πρέσβεις

ᵃ τινες . . . αἱ μὲν . . . αἱ δέ. For the partitive apposition cf. 566 E, 584 D, Gorg. 499 C. Cf. also Protag. 330 A, Gorg. 450 C, Laws 626 E, Eurip. Hec. 1185-1186.

ᵇ Cf. Tim. 90 A.

ᶜ For the idea of guardians of the soul cf. Laws 961 D, supra 549 B. Cf. also on Phaedo 113 D, What Plato said, p. 536.   ᵈ Cf. Phaedo 92 D.

ᵉ Plato, like Matthew Arnold, liked to use nicknames for

faction and internal strife in the man with himself."
"Surely." "And sometimes, I suppose, the democratic element retires before the oligarchical, some
of its appetites having been destroyed and others[a]
expelled, and a sense of awe and reverence grows
up in the young man's soul and order is restored."
"That sometimes happens," he said. "And sometimes, again, another brood of desires akin to those
expelled are stealthily nurtured to take their place,
owing to the father's ignorance of true education,
and wax numerous and strong." "Yes, that is wont
to be the way of it." "And they tug and pull back
to the same associations and in secret intercourse
engender a multitude." "Yes indeed." "And in
the end, I suppose, they seize the citadel[b] of the young
man's soul, finding it empty and unoccupied by
studies and honourable pursuits and true discourses,
which are the best watchmen and guardians[c] in the
minds of men who are dear to the gods." "Much
the best," he said. "And then false and braggart
words[d] and opinions charge up the height and take
their place and occupy that part of such a youth."
"They do indeed." "And then he returns, does he
not, to those Lotus-eaters[e] and without disguise lives
openly with them. And if any support[f] comes from
his kin to the thrifty element in his soul, those braggart discourses close the gates of the royal fortress
within him and refuse admission to the auxiliary
force itself, and will not grant audience as to envoys

classes of people; cf. Rep. 415 D γηγενεῖς, Theaet. 181 A
ῥέοντας, Soph. 248 A εἰδῶν φίλους, Phileb. 44 E τοῖς δυσχερέσιν.
So Arnold in Culture and Anarchy uses Populace, Philistines,
Barbarians, Friends of Culture, etc., Friends of Physical
Science, Lit. and Dogma, p. 3.
[f] βοήθεια: cf. Aristot. De an. 404 a 12.

PLATO

560 πρεσβυτέρων λόγους ἰδιωτῶν[1] εἰσδέχονται, αὐτοί τε
κρατοῦσι μαχόμενοι, καὶ τὴν μὲν αἰδῶ ἠλιθιότητα
ὀνομάζοντες ὠθοῦσιν ἔξω ἀτίμως φυγάδα, σωφροσύνην δὲ ἀνανδρίαν καλοῦντές τε καὶ προπηλακίζοντες
ἐκβάλλουσι, μετριότητα δὲ καὶ κοσμίαν δαπάνην
ὡς ἀγροικίαν καὶ ἀνελευθερίαν οὖσαν πείθοντες
ὑπερορίζουσι μετὰ πολλῶν καὶ ἀνωφελῶν ἐπιθυμιῶν. Σφόδρα γε. Τούτων δέ γέ που κενώ-
Ε σαντες καὶ καθήραντες τὴν τοῦ κατεχομένου τε
ὑπ' αὐτῶν καὶ τελουμένου ψυχὴν μεγάλοισι τέλεσι,
τὸ μετὰ τοῦτο ἤδη ὕβριν καὶ ἀναρχίαν καὶ ἀσωτίαν
καὶ ἀναίδειαν λαμπρὰς μετὰ πολλοῦ χοροῦ κατ-
άγουσιν ἐστεφανωμένας, ἐγκωμιάζοντες καὶ ὑπο-
κοριζόμενοι, ὕβριν μὲν εὐπαιδευσίαν καλοῦντες,
ἀναρχίαν δὲ ἐλευθερίαν, ἀσωτίαν δὲ μεγαλο-
561 πρέπειαν, ἀναίδειαν δὲ ἀνδρείαν. ἆρ' οὐχ οὕτω
πως, ἦν δ' ἐγώ, νέος ὢν μεταβάλλει ἐκ τοῦ ἐν
ἀναγκαίοις ἐπιθυμίαις τρεφομένου τὴν τῶν μὴ
ἀναγκαίων καὶ ἀνωφελῶν ἡδονῶν ἐλευθέρωσίν τε
καὶ ἄνεσιν; Καὶ μάλα γ', ἦ δ' ὅς, ἐναργῶς. Ζῇ

[1] Badham, followed by Apelt, reads δι' ὤτων. See Adam's
note and Appendix IV. to Book VIII.

[a] *Cf.* 474 D, Thucyd. iii. 82. Wilamowitz, *Platon*, i. 435-436
says that Plato had not used Thucydides. But *cf.* Gomperz
iii. 331, and *What Plato Said*, pp. 2-3, 6, 8. See Isoc. *Antid.*
284 σκώπτειν καὶ μιμεῖσθαι δυναμένους εὐφυεῖς καλοῦσι, etc.,
Areop. 20 and 49, Aristot. *Eth. Nic.* 1180 b 25, Quintil. iii.
7. 25 and viii. 6. 36, Sallust, *Cat.* c. 52 " iam pridem equidem
nos vera vocabula rerum amisimus," etc., Shakes., Sonnet
lxvi., " And simple truth miscalled simplicity . . .," Thomas
Wyatt, *Of the Courtier's Life*:

As drunkenness good fellowship to call ; . . .
Affirm that favel hath a goodly grace
In eloquence ; and cruelty to name
Zeal of justice and change in time and place, etc.

to the words of older friends in private life. And they themselves prevail in the conflict, and naming reverence and awe ' folly '[a] thrust it forth, a dishonoured fugitive. And temperance they call ' want of manhood ' and banish it with contumely, and they teach that moderation and orderly expenditure are ' rusticity ' and ' illiberality,' and they combine with a gang of unprofitable and harmful appetites to drive them over the border.[b] " " They do indeed." " And when they have emptied and purged[c] of all these the soul of the youth that they have thus possessed[d] and occupied, and whom they are initiating with these magnificent and costly rites,[e] they proceed to lead home from exile insolence and anarchy and prodigality and shamelessness, resplendent[f] in a great attendant choir and crowned with garlands, and in celebration of their praises they euphemistically denominate insolence ' good breeding,' licence ' liberty,' prodigality ' magnificence,' and shamelessness ' manly spirit.' And is it not in some such way as this," said I, " that in his youth the transformation takes place from the restriction to necessary desires in his education to the liberation and release of his unnecessary and harmful desires ? " " Yes, your description is most vivid," said he. " Then, in his subsequent life,

---

[b] ὑπερορίζουσι: cf. Laws 855 c ὑπερορίαν φυγάδα, 866 D.

[c] Cf. 567 c and 573 B, where the word is also used ironically, and Laws 735, Polit. 293 D, Soph. 226 D.

[d] κατέχομαι is used of divine " possession " or inspiration in Phaedr. 244 E, Ion 533 E, 536 B, etc., Xen. Symp. 1. 10.

[e] Plato frequently employs the language of the mysteries for literary effect. Cf. Gorg. 497 c, Symp. 210 A and 218 B, Theaet. 155 E-156 A, Laws 666 B, 870 D-E, Phaedr. 250 B-C, 249 C, Phaedo 81 A, 69 C, Rep. 378 A, etc., and Thompson on Meno 76 E.

[f] Cf. Eurip. fr. 628. 5 (Nauck), Soph. El. 1130.

PLATO

561 δή, οἶμαι, μετὰ ταῦτα ὁ τοιοῦτος οὐδὲν μᾶλλον εἰς
ἀναγκαίους ἢ μὴ ἀναγκαίους ἡδονὰς ἀναλίσκων καὶ
χρήματα καὶ πόνους καὶ διατριβάς· ἀλλ' ἐὰν
εὐτυχὴς ᾖ καὶ μὴ πέρα ἐκβακχευθῇ, ἀλλά τι καὶ
B πρεσβύτερος γενόμενος, τοῦ πολλοῦ θορύβου παρ-
ελθόντος, μέρη τε καταδέξηται τῶν ἐκπεσόντων καὶ
τοῖς ἐπεισελθοῦσι μὴ ὅλον ἑαυτὸν ἐνδῷ, εἰς ἴσον
δή τι καταστήσας τὰς ἡδονὰς διάγει, τῇ παρα-
πιπτούσῃ ἀεὶ ὥσπερ λαχούσῃ τὴν ἑαυτοῦ ἀρχὴν
παραδιδούς, ἕως ἂν πληρωθῇ, καὶ αὖθις ἄλλῃ,
οὐδεμίαν ἀτιμάζων, ἀλλ' ἐξ ἴσου τρέφων. Πάνυ
μὲν οὖν. Καὶ λόγον γ', ἦν δ' ἐγώ, ἀληθῆ οὐ
προσδεχόμενος οὐδὲ παριεὶς εἰς τὸ φρούριον, ἐάν
C τις λέγῃ ὡς αἱ μέν εἰσι τῶν καλῶν τε καὶ ἀγαθῶν
ἐπιθυμιῶν ἡδοναί, αἱ δὲ τῶν πονηρῶν, καὶ τὰς μὲν
χρὴ ἐπιτηδεύειν καὶ τιμᾶν, τὰς δὲ κολάζειν τε καὶ
δουλοῦσθαι· ἀλλ' ἐν πᾶσι τούτοις ἀνανεύει τε καὶ
ὁμοίας φησὶν ἁπάσας εἶναι καὶ τιμητέας ἐξ ἴσου.
Σφόδρα γάρ, ἔφη, οὕτω διακείμενος τοῦτο δρᾷ.
Οὐκοῦν, ἦν δ' ἐγώ, καὶ διαζῇ τὸ καθ' ἡμέραν οὕτω
χαριζόμενος τῇ προσπιπτούσῃ ἐπιθυμίᾳ, τοτὲ μὲν
μεθύων καὶ καταυλούμενος, αὖθις δὲ ὑδροποτῶν

---

[a] For the ironical δή cf. 562 D, 563 B, 563 D, 374 B, 420 E
and on 562 E, p. 307, note h.

[b] Cf. Phaedr. 241 A μεταβαλὼν ἄλλον ἄρχοντα ἐν αὑτῷ.
For this type of youth cf. Thackeray's Barnes Newcome.
For the lot cf. supra, p. 285, note d, on 557 A.

[c] Notice the frequency of the phrase ἐξ ἴσου in this passage.
Cf. 557 A.

[d] An obvious reference to the Gorgias. Cf. Gorg. 494 E,
Phileb. 13 B ff., Protag. 353 D ff., Laws 733.

[e] The Greek says " throws back his head "—the character-

I take it, such a one expends money and toil and time no more on his necessary than on his unnecessary pleasures. But if it is his good fortune that the period of storm and stress does not last too long, and as he grows older the fiercest tumult within him passes, and he receives back a part of the banished elements and does not abandon himself altogether to the invasion of the others, then he establishes and maintains all his pleasures on a footing of equality, forsooth,[a] and so lives turning over the guard-house[b] of his soul to each as it happens along until it is sated, as if it had drawn the lot for that office, and then in turn to another, disdaining none but fostering them all equally.[c]" "Quite so." "And he does not accept or admit into the guard-house the words of truth when anyone tells him that some pleasures arise from honourable and good desires, and others from those that are base,[d] and that we ought to practise and esteem the one and control and subdue the others; but he shakes his head[e] at all such admonitions and avers that they are all alike and to be equally esteemed." "Such is indeed his state of mind and his conduct." "And does he not," said I, "also live out his life in this fashion, day by day indulging the appetite of the day, now wine-bibbing and abandoning himself to the lascivious pleasing of the flute[f] and again drinking only water and dieting;

istic negative gesture among Greeks. In Aristoph. *Acharn.* 115 the supposed Persians give themselves away by nodding assent and dissent in Hellenic style, as Dicaeopolis says.

[f] For the word καταυλούμενος *cf.* 411 A, *Laws* 790 E, Lucian, *Bis acc.* 17, and for the passive Eur. *I.T.* 367. *Cf.* also Philetaerus, *Philaulus, fr.* 18, Kock ii. p. 235, Eur. *fr.* 187. 3 μολπαῖσι δ᾽ ἡσθεὶς τοῦτ᾽ ἀεὶ θηρεύεται. For the type *cf.* Theophrastus, *Char.* 11, Aristoph. *Wasps* 1475 ff.

561 D καὶ κατισχναινόμενος, τοτὲ δ' αὖ γυμναζόμενος,
ἔστι δ' ὅτε ἀργῶν καὶ πάντων ἀμελῶν, τοτὲ δ' ὡς
ἐν φιλοσοφίᾳ διατρίβων· πολλάκις δὲ πολιτεύεται,
καὶ ἀναπηδῶν ὅ τι ἂν τύχῃ λέγει τε καὶ πράττει·
κἂν ποτέ τινας πολεμικοὺς ζηλώσῃ, ταύτῃ φέρεται,
ἢ χρηματιστικούς, ἐπὶ τοῦτ' αὖ, καὶ οὔτε τις τάξις
οὔτε ἀνάγκη ἔπεστιν αὐτοῦ τῷ βίῳ, ἀλλ' ἡδύν τε
δὴ καὶ ἐλευθέριον καὶ μακάριον καλῶν τὸν βίον
E τοῦτον χρῆται αὐτῷ διὰ παντός. Παντάπασιν, ἦ
δ' ὅς, διελήλυθας βίον ἰσονομικοῦ τινὸς ἀνδρός.[a]
Οἶμαι δέ γε, ἦν δ' ἐγώ, καὶ παντοδαπόν τε καὶ
πλείστων ἠθῶν μεστόν, καὶ τὸν καλόν τε καὶ
ποικίλον,[c] ὥσπερ ἐκείνην τὴν πόλιν, τοῦτον τὸν
ἄνδρα εἶναι· ὃν πολλοὶ ἂν καὶ πολλαὶ ζηλώσειαν τοῦ
βίου, παραδείγματα πολιτειῶν τε καὶ τρόπων
πλεῖστα ἐν αὑτῷ ἔχοντα.[d] Οὕτω γάρ, ἔφη, ἔστιν.

562 Τί οὖν; τετάχθω ἡμῖν κατὰ δημοκρατίαν ὁ
τοιοῦτος ἀνήρ, ὡς δημοκρατικὸς ὀρθῶς ἂν προσ-
αγορευόμενος; Τετάχθω, ἔφη.

XIV. Ἡ καλλίστη δή,[e] ἦν δ' ἐγώ, πολιτεία τε
καὶ ὁ κάλλιστος ἀνὴρ λοιπὰ ἂν ἡμῖν εἴη διελθεῖν,
τυραννίς τε καὶ τύραννος. Κομιδῇ γ', ἔφη. Φέρε
δή, τίς τρόπος τυραννίδος, ὦ φίλε ἑταῖρε, γίγνεται;
ὅτι μὲν γὰρ ἐκ δημοκρατίας μεταβάλλει, σχεδὸν
δῆλον. Δῆλον. Ἆρ' οὖν τρόπον τινὰ τὸν αὐτὸν

---

[a] Cf. Protag. 319 D.

[b] For ὅ τι ἂν τύχῃ cf. on 536 A, p. 213, note f, ὅταν τύχῃ
Eurip. Hippol. 428, I.T. 722, Eurip. fr. 825 (Didot), ὅπου ἂν
τύχωσιν Xen. Oec. 20. 28, ὃν ἂν τύχῃς Eurip. Tro. 68.

[c] παντοδαπῶν: cf. on 557 C.

[d] Cf. 557 D.

[e] For the irony cf. 607 E τῶν καλῶν πολιτειῶν, supra 544 C
γενναία, 558 C ἡδεῖα.

and at one time exercising his body, and sometimes idling and neglecting all things, and at another time seeming to occupy himself with philosophy. And frequently he goes in for politics and bounces up [a] and says and does whatever enters his head.[b] And if military men excite his emulation, thither he rushes, and if moneyed men, to that he turns, and there is no order or compulsion in his existence, but he calls this life of his the life of pleasure and freedom and happiness and cleaves to it to the end." "That is a perfect description," he said, " of a devotee of equality." " I certainly think," said I, " that he is a manifold [c] man stuffed with most excellent differences, and that like that city [d] he is the fair and many-coloured one whom many a man and woman would count fortunate in his life, as containing within himself the greatest number of patterns of constitutions and qualities." " Yes, that is so," he said. " Shall we definitely assert, then, that such a man is to be ranged with democracy and would properly be designated as democratic ? " " Let that be his place," he said.

XIV. " And now," said I, " the fairest [e] polity and the fairest man remain for us to describe, the tyranny and the tyrant." " Certainly," he said. " Come then, tell me, dear friend, how tyranny arises.[f] That it is an outgrowth of democracy is fairly plain." " Yes, plain." " Is it, then, in a sense, in the same

---

[f] τίς τρόπος . . . γίγνεται is a mixture of two expressions that need not be pressed. Cf. Meno 96 D, Epist. vii. 324 B. A. G. Laird, in Class. Phil., 1918, pp. 89-90 thinks it means " What τρόπος (of the many τρόποι in a democracy) develops into a τρόπος of tyranny; for that tyranny is a transformation of democracy is fairly evident." That would be a recognition of what Aristotle says previous thinkers overlooked in their classification of polities.

562 ἔκ τε ὀλιγαρχίας δημοκρατία γίγνεται καὶ ἐκ
B δημοκρατίας τυραννίς; Πῶς; Ὃ προύθεντο, ἦν
δ' ἐγώ, ἀγαθόν, καὶ δι' οὗ ἡ ὀλιγαρχία καθ-
ίστατο—τοῦτο δ' ἦν πλοῦτος[1]· ἦ γάρ; Ναί. Ἡ
πλούτου τοίνυν ἀπληστία καὶ ἡ τῶν ἄλλων ἀμέλεια διὰ χρηματισμὸν αὐτὴν ἀπώλλυ. Ἀληθῆ,
ἔφη. Ἆρ' οὖν καὶ ὃ δημοκρατία ὁρίζεται ἀγαθόν,
ἡ τούτου ἀπληστία καὶ ταύτην καταλύει; Λέγεις
δ' αὐτὴν τί ὁρίζεσθαι; Τὴν ἐλευθερίαν, εἶπον.
τοῦτο γάρ που ἐν δημοκρατουμένῃ πόλει ἀκούσαις
C ἂν ὡς ἔχει τε κάλλιστον καὶ διὰ ταῦτα ἐν μόνῃ
ταύτῃ ἄξιον οἰκεῖν ὅστις φύσει ἐλεύθερος. Λέγεται γὰρ δή, ἔφη, καὶ πολὺ τοῦτο τὸ ῥῆμα. Ἆρ'
οὖν, ἦν δ' ἐγώ, ὅπερ ᾖα νῦν δὴ ἐρῶν, ἡ τοῦ τοιούτου ἀπληστία καὶ ἡ τῶν ἄλλων ἀμέλεια καὶ ταύτην τὴν πολιτείαν μεθίστησί τε καὶ παρασκευάζει
τυραννίδος δεηθῆναι; Πῶς; ἔφη. Ὅταν, οἶμαι,
δημοκρατουμένη πόλις ἐλευθερίας διψήσασα κακῶν
D οἰνοχόων προστατούντων τύχῃ, καὶ πορρωτέρω
τοῦ δέοντος ἀκράτου αὐτῆς μεθυσθῇ, τοὺς ἄρχοντας
δή, ἂν μὴ πάνυ πρᾷοι ὦσι καὶ πολλὴν παρέχωσι

---

[1] πλοῦτος F, ὑπέρπλουτος ADM, που πλοῦτος Campbell,
εἴπερ τι πλοῦτος Apelt, ὑπέρπλουτος πλοῦτος Stallbaum.

---

[a] Their idea of good. *Cf. supra* 555 B προκειμένου ἀγαθοῦ.
Cf. Laws 962 E with Aristot. *Pol.* 1293 b 14 ff. *Cf.* also
Aristot. *Pol.* 1304 b 20 αἱ μὲν οὖν δημοκρατίαι μάλιστα μετα-
βάλλουσι διὰ τὴν τῶν δημαγωγῶν ἀσέλγειαν. *Cf.* also p. 263,
note *e* on 551 B (ὅρος) and p. 139, note *c* on 519 C (σκοπός).

[b] *Cf.* 552 B, and for the disparagement of wealth p. 262,
note *b*, on 550 E.

[c] Zeller, *Aristot.* ii. p. 285, as usual credits Aristotle with
the Platonic thought that every form of government brings
ruin on itself by its own excess.

[d] *Cf.* Arnold, *Culture and Anarchy*, p. 43 "The central

way in which democracy arises out of oligarchy that
tyranny arises from democracy ? " " How is that ? "
" The good that they proposed to themselves [a] and that
was the cause of the establishment of oligarchy—it
was wealth,[b] was it not ? " " Yes." " Well, then, the
insatiate lust for wealth and the neglect of everything
else for the sake of money-making was the cause of
its undoing." " True," he said. " And is not the
avidity of democracy for that which is its definition and
criterion of good the thing which dissolves it [c] too ? "
" What do you say its criterion to be ? " " Liberty,[d] "
I replied ; " for you may hear it said that this is best
managed in a democratic city, and for this reason that
is the only city in which a man of free spirit will care
to live.[e] " " Why, yes," he replied, " you hear that
saying everywhere." " Then, as I was about to
observe,[f] is it not the excess and greed of this and the
neglect of all other things that revolutionizes this constitution too and prepares the way for the necessity of
a dictatorship ? " " How ? " he said. " Why, when a
democratic city athirst for liberty gets bad cupbearers
for its leaders [g] and is intoxicated by drinking too deep
of that unmixed wine,[h] and then, if its so-called
governors are not extremely mild and gentle with it

idea of English life and politics is the assertion of personal
liberty."

[e] Aristot. *Pol.* 1263 b 29 says life would be impossible in
Plato's *Republic*.

[f] ἦα . . . ἐρῶν : *cf.* 449 A, *Theaet.* 180 c.

[g] Or " protectors," " tribunes," προστατούντων. *Cf. infra*
on 565 c, p. 318, note *d*.

[h] *Cf.* Livy xxxix. 26 " velut ex diutina siti nimis avide
meram haurientes libertatem," Seneca, *De benefic.* i. 10
" male dispensata libertas," Taine, *Letter*, Jan. 2, 1867
" nous avons proclamé et appliqué l'égalité . . . C'est un
vin pur et généreux ; mais nous avons bu trop du nôtre."

562 τὴν ἐλευθερίαν, κολάζει αἰτιωμένη ὡς μιαρούς τε
καὶ ὀλιγαρχικούς. Δρῶσι γάρ, ἔφη, τοῦτο. Τοὺς
δέ γε, εἶπον, τῶν ἀρχόντων κατηκόους προ-
πηλακίζει ὡς ἐθελοδούλους τε καὶ οὐδὲν ὄντας,
τοὺς δὲ ἄρχοντας μὲν ἀρχομένοις, ἀρχομένους δὲ
ἄρχουσιν ὁμοίους ἰδίᾳ τε καὶ δημοσίᾳ ἐπαινεῖ τε
Ε καὶ τιμᾷ. ἆρ' οὐκ ἀνάγκη ἐν τοιαύτῃ πόλει ἐπὶ
πᾶν τὸ τῆς ἐλευθερίας ἰέναι; Πῶς γὰρ οὔ; Καὶ
καταδύεσθαί γε, ἦν δ' ἐγώ, ὦ φίλε, εἴς τε τὰς
ἰδίας οἰκίας καὶ τελευτᾶν μέχρι τῶν θηρίων τὴν
ἀναρχίαν ἐμφυομένην. Πῶς, ἦ δ' ὅς, τὸ τοιοῦτον
λέγομεν; Οἷον, ἔφην, πατέρα μὲν ἐθίζεσθαι παιδὶ
ὅμοιον γίγνεσθαι καὶ φοβεῖσθαι τοὺς υἱεῖς, υἱὸν δὲ
πατρί, καὶ μήτε αἰσχύνεσθαι μήτε δεδιέναι τοὺς
563 γονέας, ἵνα δὴ ἐλεύθερος ᾖ· μέτοικον δὲ ἀστῷ καὶ
ἀστὸν μετοίκῳ ἐξισοῦσθαι, καὶ ξένον ὡσαύτως.
Γίγνεται γὰρ οὕτως, ἔφη. Ταῦτά τε, ἦν δ' ἐγώ,
καὶ σμικρὰ τοιάδε ἄλλα γίγνεται· διδάσκαλός τε
ἐν τῷ τοιούτῳ φοιτητὰς φοβεῖται καὶ θωπεύει,

ᵃ μιαρούς is really stronger, "pestilential fellows." *Cf.*
Apol. 23 D, Soph. *Antig.* 746. It is frequent in Aristophanes.
ᵇ For the charge of oligarchical tendencies *cf.* Isoc. *Peace*
51 and 133, *Areop.* 57, *Antid.* 318, *Panath.* 148.
ᶜ *Cf. Symp.* 184 c, 183 A. *Cf.* the essay of Estienne de
la Boétie, *De la servitude volontaire.* Also Gray, *Ode for
Music*, 6 "Servitude that hugs her chain."
ᵈ For οὐδὲν ὄντας *cf.* 341 c, *Apol.* 41 E, *Symp.* 216 E, *Gorg.*
512 c, *Erastae* 134 c, Aristoph. *Eccles.* 144, Horace, *Sat.*
ii. 7. 102 "nil ego," Eurip. *I.A.* 371, Herod. ix. 58 οὐδένες
ἐόντες.
ᵉ *Cf. Laws* 699 E ἐπὶ πᾶσαν ἐλευθερίαν, Aristoph. *Lysistr.*
543 ἐπὶ πᾶν ἰέναι, Soph. *El.* 615 εἰς πᾶν ἔργον.
ᶠ *Cf.* 563 c, *Laws* 942 D.

and do not dispense the liberty unstintedly, it chastises them and accuses them of being accursed[a] oligarchs.[b]"
" Yes, that is what they do," he replied. " But those who obey the rulers," I said, " it reviles as willing slaves[c] and men of naught,[d] but it commends and honours in public and private rulers who resemble subjects and subjects who are like rulers. Is it not inevitable that in such a state the spirit of liberty should go to all lengths[e]?" " Of course." " And this anarchical temper," said I, " my friend, must penetrate into private homes and finally enter into the very animals.[f]" " Just what do we mean by that?" he said. " Why," I said, " the father habitually tries to resemble the child and is afraid of his sons, and the son likens himself to the father and feels no awe or fear of his parents,[g] so that he may be forsooth a free man.[h] And the resident alien feels himself equal to the citizen and the citizen to him, and the foreigner likewise." " Yes, these things do happen," he said. " They do," said I, " and such other trifles as these. The teacher in such case fears and fawns

<hr />

[g] A common conservative complaint. *Cf.* Isoc. *Areop.* 49, Aristoph. *Clouds*, 998, 1321 ff., Xen. *Rep. Ath.* 1. 10, *Mem.* iii. 5. 15; Newman i. pp. 174 and 339-340. *Cf.* also Renan, *Souvenirs*, xviii.-xx., on American vulgarity and liberty; Harold Lasswell, quoting Bryce, " Modern Democracies," in *Methods of Social Science*, ed. by Stuart A. Rice, p. 376: " The spirit of equality is alleged to have diminished the respect children owe to parents, and the young to the old. This was noted by Plato in Athens. But surely the family relations depend much more on the social, structural and religious ideas of a race than on forms of government"; Whitman, " Where the men and women think lightly of the laws . . . where children are taught to be laws to themselves . . . there the great city stands."

[h] For the ironical ἵνα δή *cf.* on 561 B. *Cf. Laws* 962 E ἐλεύθερον δή, *Meno* 86 D and Aristoph. *Clouds* 1414.

563 φοιτηταί τε διδασκάλων ὀλιγωροῦσιν, οὕτω δὲ καὶ
παιδαγωγῶν· καὶ ὅλως οἱ μὲν νέοι πρεσβυτέροις
ἀπεικάζονται καὶ διαμιλλῶνται καὶ ἐν λόγοις καὶ
ἐν ἔργοις, οἱ δὲ γέροντες ξυγκαθιέντες τοῖς νέοις
B εὐτραπελίας τε καὶ χαριεντισμοῦ ἐμπίπλανται,
μιμούμενοι τοὺς νέους, ἵνα δὴ μὴ δοκῶσιν ἀηδεῖς
εἶναι μηδὲ δεσποτικοί. Πάνυ μὲν οὖν, ἔφη. Τὸ
δέ γε, ἦν δ' ἐγώ, ἔσχατον, ὦ φίλε, τῆς ἐλευθερίας
τοῦ πλήθους, ὅσον γίγνεται ἐν τῇ τοιαύτῃ πόλει,
ὅταν δὴ οἱ ἐωνημένοι καὶ αἱ ἐωνημέναι μηδὲν
ἧττον ἐλεύθεροι ὦσι τῶν πριαμένων. ἐν γυναιξὶ
δὲ πρὸς ἄνδρας καὶ ἀνδράσι πρὸς γυναῖκας ὅση ἡ
ἰσονομία καὶ ἐλευθερία γίγνεται, ὀλίγου ἐπελαθό-
C μεθ' εἰπεῖν. Οὐκοῦν κατ' Αἰσχύλον, ἔφη, ἐροῦμεν ὅ τι νῦν ἦλθ' ἐπὶ στόμα; Πάνυ γε, εἶπον.
καὶ ἔγωγε οὕτω λέγω· τὸ μὲν γὰρ τῶν θηρίων
τῶν ὑπὸ τοῖς ἀνθρώποις ὅσῳ ἐλευθερώτερά ἐστιν
ἐνταῦθα ἢ ἐν ἄλλῃ, οὐκ ἄν τις πείθοιτο ἄπειρος.
ἀτεχνῶς γὰρ αἵ τε κύνες κατὰ τὴν παροιμίαν
οἷαίπερ αἱ δέσποιναι γίγνονταί τε δὴ καὶ ἵπποι καὶ
ὄνοι, πάνυ ἐλευθέρως καὶ σεμνῶς εἰθισμένοι πορεύεσθαι, κατὰ τὰς ὁδοὺς ἐμβάλλοντες τῷ ἀεὶ ἀπαν-
τῶντι, ἐὰν μὴ ἐξίστηται· καὶ τἆλλα πάντα οὕτω

---

[a] Cf. Protag. 336 A, Theaet. 174 A, 168 B.

[b] For εὐτραπελίας cf. Isoc. xv. 296, vii. 49, Aristotle, Eth.
Nic. 1108 a 24. In Rhet. 1389 b 11 he defines it as πεπαιδευ-
μένη ὕβρις. Arnold once addressed the Eton boys on the word.

[c] Cf. Xen. Rep. Ath. 1. 10 τῶν δούλων δ' αὖ καὶ τῶν μετοίκων
πλείστη ἐστὶν Ἀθήνησιν ἀκολασία, Aristoph. Clouds init., and
on slavery Laws 777 E, supra p. 249, note g on 547 c and
549 A.

[d] Nauck fr. 351. Cf. Plut. Amat. 763 B, Themist. Orat.
iv. p. 52 B; also Otto, p. 39, and Adam ad loc.

upon the pupils, and the pupils pay no heed to the teacher or to their overseers either. And in general the young ape their elders and vie with them in speech and action, while the old, accommodating [a] themselves to the young, are full of pleasantry [b] and graciousness, imitating the young for fear they may be thought disagreeable and authoritative." "By all means," he said. "And the climax of popular liberty, my friend," I said, "is attained in such a city when the purchased slaves, male and female, are no less free [c] than the owners who paid for them. And I almost forgot to mention the spirit of freedom and equal rights in the relation of men to women and women to men." "Shall we not, then," said he, "in Aeschylean phrase,[d] say 'whatever rises to our lips'?" "Certainly," I said, "so I will. Without experience of it no one would believe how much freer the very beasts [e] subject to men are in such a city than elsewhere. The dogs literally verify the adage [f] and 'like their mistresses become.' And likewise the horses and asses are wont to hold on their way with the utmost freedom and dignity, bumping into everyone who meets them and who does not step aside.[g] And so all things

---

[e] Cf. 562 E, Julian, *Misopogon*, 355 B . . . μέχρι τῶν ὄνων ἐστὶν ἐλευθερία παρ' αὐτοῖς καὶ τῶν καμήλων; ἄγουσί τοι καὶ ταύτας οἱ μισθωτοὶ διὰ τῶν στοῶν ὥσπερ τὰς νύμφας, " . . . what great independence exists among the citizens, even down to the very asses and camels? The men who hire them out lead even these animals through the porticoes as though they were brides." (Loeb tr.) *Cf.* Porphyry, *Vit. Pythag.* Teubner, p. 22, § 23 μέχρι καὶ τῶν ἀλόγων ζῴων διικνεῖτο αὐτοῦ ἡ νουθέτησις.

[f] Otto, p. 119. *Cf.* "Like mistress, like maid."

[g] Eurip. *Ion* 635-637 mentions being jostled off the street by a worse person as one of the indignities of Athenian city life.

563 D μεστὰ ἐλευθερίας γίγνεται. Τὸ ἐμόν γ᾽, ἔφη, ἐμοὶ
λέγεις ὄναρ· αὐτὸς γὰρ εἰς ἀγρὸν πορευόμενος
θαμὰ αὐτὸ πάσχω. Τὸ δὲ δὴ κεφάλαιον, ἦν δ᾽
ἐγώ, πάντων τούτων ξυνηθροισμένων ἐννοεῖς, ὡς
ἀπαλὴν τὴν ψυχὴν τῶν πολιτῶν ποιεῖ, ὥστε κἂν
ὁτιοῦν δουλείας τις προσφέρηται, ἀγανακτεῖν καὶ
μὴ ἀνέχεσθαι; τελευτῶντες γάρ που οἶσθ᾽ ὅτι
οὐδὲ τῶν νόμων φροντίζουσι γεγραμμένων ἢ
E ἀγράφων, ἵνα δὴ μηδαμῇ μηδεὶς αὐτοῖς ᾖ δεσπότης.
Καὶ μάλ᾽, ἔφη, οἶδα.

XV. Αὕτη μὲν τοίνυν, ἦν δ᾽ ἐγώ, ὦ φίλε, ἡ
ἀρχὴ οὑτωσὶ καλὴ καὶ νεανική, ὅθεν τυραννὶς
φύεται, ὡς ἐμοὶ δοκεῖ. Νεανικὴ δῆτα, ἔφη· ἀλλὰ
τί τὸ μετὰ τοῦτο; Ταὐτόν, ἦν δ᾽ ἐγώ, ὅπερ ἐν τῇ
ὀλιγαρχίᾳ νόσημα ἐγγενόμενον ἀπώλεσεν αὐτήν,
τοῦτο καὶ ἐν ταύτῃ πλέον τε καὶ ἰσχυρότερον ἐκ
τῆς ἐξουσίας ἐγγενόμενον καταδουλοῦται δημο-
κρατίαν· καὶ τῷ ὄντι τὸ ἄγαν τι ποιεῖν μεγάλην

ᵃ Cf. the reflections in Laws 698 f., 701 A-C, Epist. viii.
354 D, Gorg. 461 E; Isoc. Areop. 20, Panath. 131, Eurip.
Cyclops 120 ἀκούει δ᾽ οὐδὲν οὐδεὶς οὐδενός, Aristot. Pol.
1295 b 15 f.

Plato, by reaction against the excesses of the ultimate
democracy, always satirizes the shibboleth "liberty" in the
style of Arnold, Ruskin and Carlyle. He would agree with
Goethe (Eckermann i. 219, Jan. 18, 1827) "Nicht das macht
frei, das wir nichts über uns erkennen wollen, sondern eben,
dass wir etwas verehren, das über uns ist."

Libby, Introd. to Hist. of Science, p. 273, not understanding the irony of the passage, thinks much of it the unwilling
tribute of a hostile critic.

THE REPUBLIC, BOOK VIII

everywhere are just bursting with the spirit of liberty.[a]" "It is my own dream[b] you are telling me," he said; "for it often happens to me when I go to the country." "And do you note that the sum total of all these items when footed up is that they render the souls of the citizens so sensitive[c] that they chafe at the slightest suggestion of servitude[d] and will not endure it? For you are aware that they finally pay no heed even to the laws[e] written or unwritten,[f] so that forsooth they may have no master anywhere over them." "I know it very well," said he.

XV. "This, then, my friend," said I, "is the fine and vigorous root from which tyranny grows, in my opinion." "Vigorous indeed," he said; "but what next?" "The same malady," I said, "that, arising in oligarchy, destroyed it, this more widely diffused and more violent as a result of this licence, enslaves democracy. And in truth, any excess is wont to

In *Gorg.* 484 A Callicles sneers at equality from the point of view of the superman. *Cf.* also on 558 c, p. 291, note *f*; Hobbes, *Leviathan* xxi. and Theopompus's account of democracy in *Byzantium, fr.* 65. Similar phenomena may be observed in an American city street or Pullman club car.

[b] *Cf.* Callimachus, *Anth. Pal.* vi. 310, and xii. 148 μὴ λέγε . . . τοὐμὸν ὄνειρον ἐμοί, Cic. *Att.* vi. 9. 3, Lucian, *Somnium seu Gallus* 7 ὥσπερ γὰρ τοὐμὸν ἐνύπνιον ἰδών, Tennyson, "Lucretius": "That was mine, my dream, I knew it."

[c] This sensitiveness, on which Grote remarks with approval, is characteristic of present-day American democracy. *Cf.* also Arnold, *Culture and Anarchy*, p. 51 "And so if he is stopped from making Hyde Park a bear garden or the streets impassable he says he is being butchered by the aristocracy."

[d] *Cf. Gorg.* 491 E δουλεύων ὁτῳοῦν, *Laws* 890 A.

[e] *Cf. Laws* 701 B νόμων ζητεῖν μὴ ὑπηκόοις εἶναι.

[f] For unwritten law *cf. What Plato Said*, p. 637, on *Laws* 793 A.

563 φιλεῖ εἰς τοὐναντίον μεταβολὴν ἀνταποδιδόναι, ἐν
564 ὥραις τε καὶ ἐν φυτοῖς καὶ ἐν σώμασι, καὶ δὴ καὶ
ἐν πολιτείαις οὐχ ἥκιστα. Εἰκός, ἔφη. Ἡ γὰρ
ἄγαν ἐλευθερία· ἔοικεν οὐκ εἰς ἄλλο τι ἢ εἰς ἄγαν
δουλείαν μεταβάλλειν καὶ ἰδιώτῃ καὶ πόλει.
Εἰκὸς γάρ. Εἰκότως τοίνυν, εἶπον, οὐκ ἐξ ἄλλης
πολιτείας τυραννὶς καθίσταται ἢ ἐκ δημοκρατίας,
ἐξ οἶμαι τῆς ἀκροτάτης ἐλευθερίας δουλεία πλείστη
τε καὶ ἀγριωτάτη. Ἔχει γάρ, ἔφη, λόγον. Ἀλλ᾽
οὐ τοῦτ᾽, οἶμαι, ἦν δ᾽ ἐγώ, ἠρώτας, ἀλλὰ ποῖον
B νόσημα ἐν ὀλιγαρχίᾳ τε φυόμενον ταὐτὸν καὶ ἐν
δημοκρατίᾳ δουλοῦται αὐτήν. Ἀληθῆ, ἔφη, λέγεις.
Ἐκεῖνο τοίνυν, ἔφην, ἔλεγον, τὸ τῶν ἀργῶν τε καὶ
δαπανηρῶν ἀνδρῶν γένος, τὸ μὲν ἀνδρειότατον
ἡγούμενον αὐτῶν, τὸ δ᾽ ἀνανδρότερον ἑπόμενον·
οὓς δὴ ἀφωμοιοῦμεν κηφῆσι, τοὺς μὲν κέντρα
ἔχουσι, τοὺς δὲ ἀκέντροις. Καὶ ὀρθῶς γ᾽, ἔφη.
Τούτω τοίνυν, ἦν δ᾽ ἐγώ, ταράττετον ἐν πάσῃ
πολιτείᾳ ἐγγιγνομένω, οἷον περὶ σῶμα φλέγμα τε
C καὶ χολή· ᾧ δὴ καὶ δεῖ τὸν ἀγαθὸν ἰατρόν τε καὶ
νομοθέτην πόλεως μὴ ἧττον ἢ σοφὸν μελιττουργὸν

---

^a *Cf.* Lysias xxv. 27, Isoc. viii. 108, vii. 5, Cic. *De rep.* i. 44
"nam ut ex nimia potentia principum oritur interitus prin-
cipum, sic hunc nimis liberum . . ." etc. ; Emerson, *History*,
"A great licentiousness treads on the heels of a reformation."
Cf. too Macaulay on the comic dramatists of the Restoration ;
Arnold, *Lit. and Dogma*, p. 322 "After too much glorifica-
tion of art, science and culture, too little ; after Rabelais,
George Fox ; " Tennyson :

> He that roars for liberty
> Faster binds the tyrant's power.

See Coleridge's *Table Talk*, p. 149, on the moral law of

bring about a corresponding reaction[a] to the opposite in the seasons, in plants, in animal bodies,[b] and most especially in political societies." "Probably," he said. "And so the probable outcome of too much freedom is only too much slavery in the individual and the state." "Yes, that is probable." "Probably, then, tyranny develops out of no other constitution[c] than democracy—from the height of liberty, I take it, the fiercest extreme of servitude." "That is reasonable," he said. "That, however, I believe, was not your question,[d] but what identical[e] malady arising in democracy as well as in oligarchy enslaves it?" "You say truly," he replied. "That then," I said, "was what I had in mind, the class of idle and spendthrift men, the most enterprising and vigorous portion being leaders and the less manly spirits followers. We were likening them to drones,[f] some equipped with stings and others stingless." "And rightly too," he said. "These two kinds, then," I said, "when they arise in any state, create a disturbance like that produced in the body[g] by phlegm and gall. And so a good physician and lawgiver must be on his guard from afar

---

polarity. Émile Faguet says that this law of reaction is the only one in which he believes in literary criticism.

[b] For the generalization cf. *Symp.* 188 A-B.

[c] *Cf.* 565 D. The slight exaggeration of the expression is solemnly treated by Apelt as a case of logical false conversion in Plato.

[d] Plato keeps to the point. *Cf.* on 531 c, p. 193, note *i*.

[e] ταὐτόν implies the concept. *Cf. Parmen.* 130 D, *Phileb.* 34 E, 13 B, *Soph.* 253 D. *Cf.* also *Tim.* 83 c, *Meno* 72 c, *Rep.* 339 A.

[f] *Cf.* 555 D-E.

[g] *Cf.* the parallel of soul and body in 444 c f., *Soph.* 227 E, *Crito* 47 D f., *Gorg.* 504 B-C, 505 B, 518 A, 524 D.

For φλέγμα cf. *Tim.* 83 c, 85 A-B.

564 πόρρωθεν εὐλαβεῖσθαι, μάλιστα μὲν ὅπως μὴ
ἐγγενήσεσθον, ἂν δὲ ἐγγένησθον, ὅπως ὅ τι τάχιστα ξὺν αὐτοῖσι τοῖς κηρίοις ἐκτετμήσεσθον.
Ναὶ μὰ Δία, ἦ δ' ὅς, παντάπασί γε. ῟Ωδε τοίνυν,
ἦν δ' ἐγώ, λάβωμεν, ἵν' εὐκρινέστερον ἴδωμεν ὃ
βουλόμεθα. Πῶς; Τριχῇ διαστησώμεθα τῷ λόγῳ
δημοκρατουμένην πόλιν, ὥσπερ οὖν καὶ ἔχει. ἐν
D μὲν γάρ που τὸ τοιοῦτον γένος ἐν αὐτῇ ἐμφύεται
δι' ἐξουσίαν οὐκ ἔλαττον ἢ ἐν τῇ ὀλιγαρχουμένῃ.
῎Εστιν οὕτως. Πολὺ δέ γε δριμύτερον ἐν ταύτῃ ἢ
ἐν ἐκείνῃ. Πῶς; ᾿Εκεῖ μὲν διὰ τὸ μὴ ἔντιμον
εἶναι, ἀλλ' ἀπελαύνεσθαι τῶν ἀρχῶν, ἀγύμναστον
καὶ οὐκ ἐρρωμένον γίγνεται· ἐν δημοκρατίᾳ δὲ
τοῦτό που τὸ προεστὸς αὐτῆς, ἐκτὸς ὀλίγων,
καὶ τὸ μὲν δριμύτατον αὐτοῦ λέγει τε καὶ πράττει,
τὸ δ' ἄλλο περὶ τὰ βήματα προσίζον βομβεῖ τε καὶ
E οὐκ ἀνέχεται τοῦ ἄλλα λέγοντος, ὥστε πάντα ὑπὸ
τοῦ τοιούτου διοικεῖται ἐν τῇ τοιαύτῃ πολιτείᾳ
χωρίς τινων ὀλίγων. Μάλα γε, ἦ δ' ὅς. ῎Αλλο
τοίνυν τοιόνδε ἀεὶ ἀποκρίνεται ἐκ τοῦ πλήθους.
Τὸ ποῖον; Χρηματιζομένων που πάντων οἱ
κοσμιώτατοι φύσει ὡς τὸ πολὺ πλουσιώτατοι
γίγνονται. Εἰκός. Πλεῖστον δή, οἶμαι, τοῖς
κηφῆσι μέλι καὶ εὐπορώτατον ἐντεῦθεν βλίττεται.
Πῶς γὰρ ἄν, ἔφη, παρά γε τῶν σμικρὰ ἐχόντων

---

^a μάλιστα μὲν . . . ἂν δέ: cf. 378 A, 414 C, 461 C, 473 B,
Apol. 34 A, *Soph.* 246 D.
^b For εὐκρινέστερον cf. *Soph.* 242 C.
^c Cf. *Phileb.* 23 C, which Stenzel says argues an advance

against the two kinds, like a prudent apiarist, first and chiefly [a] to prevent their springing up, but if they do arise to have them as quickly as may be cut out, cells and all." "Yes, by Zeus," he said, "by all means." "Then let us take it in this way," I said, "so that we may contemplate our purpose more distinctly.[b]" "How?" "Let us in our theory make a tripartite [c] division of the democratic state, which is in fact its structure. One such class, as we have described, grows up in it because of the licence, no less than in the oligarchic state." "That is so." "But it is far fiercer in this state than in that." "How so?" "There, because it is not held in honour, but is kept out of office, it is not exercised and does not grow vigorous. But in a democracy this is the dominating class, with rare exceptions, and the fiercest part of it makes speeches and transacts business, and the remainder swarms and settles about the speaker's stand and keeps up a buzzing[d] and tolerates[e] no dissent, so that everything with slight exceptions is administered by that class in such a state." "Quite so," he said. "And so from time to time there emerges or is secreted from the multitude another group of this sort." "What sort?" he said. "When all are pursuing wealth the most orderly and thrifty natures for the most part become the richest." "It is likely." "Then they are the most abundant supply of honey for the drones, and it is the easiest to extract.[f]" "Why, yes," he said, "how could one squeeze it out of those who have

over the *Sophist*, because Plato is no longer limited to a bipartite division.   [d] Cf. 573 A.

[e] ἀνέχεται: cf. Isoc. viii. 14 ὅτι δημοκρατίας οὔσης οὐκ ἔστι παρρησία, etc. For the word cf. Aristoph. *Acharn.* 305 οὐκ ἀνασχήσομαι, *Wasps* 1337.

[f] For βλίττεται cf. Blaydes on Aristoph. *Knights* 794.

PLATO

564 τις βλίσειεν; Πλούσιοι δή, οἶμαι, οἱ τοιοῦτοι
καλοῦνται, κηφήνων βοτάνη. Σχεδόν τι, ἔφη.
565 XVI. Δῆμος δ᾽ ἂν εἴη τρίτον γένος, ὅσοι αὐτουργοί τε καὶ ἀπράγμονες, οὐ πάνυ πολλὰ κεκτη-
μένοι· ὃ δὴ πλεῖστόν τε καὶ κυριώτατον ἐν
δημοκρατίᾳ, ὅταν περ ἀθροισθῇ. Ἔστι γάρ, ἔφη·
ἀλλ᾽ οὐ θαμὰ ἐθέλει ποιεῖν τοῦτο, ἐὰν μὴ μέλιτός
τι μεταλαμβάνῃ. Οὐκοῦν μεταλαμβάνει, ἦν δ᾽
ἐγώ, ἀεί, καθ᾽ ὅσον δύνανται οἱ προεστῶτες, τοὺς
ἔχοντας τὴν οὐσίαν ἀφαιρούμενοι, διανέμοντες τῷ
δήμῳ τὸ πλεῖστον αὐτοὶ ἔχειν. Μεταλαμβάνει
B γὰρ οὖν, ἦ δ᾽ ὅς, οὕτως. Ἀναγκάζονται δή,
οἶμαι, ἀμύνεσθαι, λέγοντές τε ἐν τῷ δήμῳ καὶ
πράττοντες ὅπῃ δύνανται, οὗτοι ὧν ἀφαιροῦνται.
Πῶς γὰρ οὔ; Αἰτίαν δὴ ἔσχον ὑπὸ τῶν ἑτέρων,
κἂν μὴ ἐπιθυμῶσι νεωτερίζειν, ὡς ἐπιβουλεύουσι
τῷ δήμῳ καί εἰσιν ὀλιγαρχικοί. Τί μήν; Οὐκοῦν καὶ τελευτῶντες, ἐπειδὰν ὁρῶσι τὸν δῆμον

ᵃ That is the significance of πλούσιοι here, lit. "the rich."

ᵇ For the classification of the population cf. Vol. I. pp. 161-163, Eurip. Suppl. 238 ff., Aristot. Pol. 1328 b ff., 1289 b 33, 1290 b 40 ff., Newman i. p. 97.

ᶜ ἀπράγμονες: cf. 620 c, Aristoph. Knights 261, Aristot. Rhet. 1381 a 25, Isoc. Antid. 151, 227. But Pericles in Thuc. ii. 40 takes a different view. See my note in Class. Phil. xv. (1920) pp. 300-301.

ᵈ αὐτουργοί: cf. Soph. 223 D, Eurip. Or. 920, Shorey in Class. Phil. xxiii. (1928) pp. 346-347.

ᵉ Cf. Aristot. Pol. 1318 b 12.

ᶠ Cf. Isoc. viii. 13 τοὺς τὰ τῆς πόλεως διανεμομένους.

ᵍ For τοὺς ἔχοντας cf. Blaydes on Aristoph. Knights 1295. For the exploitation of the rich at Athens cf. Xen. Symp. 4. 30-32, Lysias xxi. 14, xix. 62, xviii. 20-21, Isoc. Areop. 32 ff.,

316

little?" "The capitalistic[a] class is, I take it, the name by which they are designated—the pasture of the drones." "Pretty much so," he said.

XVI. "And the third class,[b] composing the 'people,' would comprise all quiet[c] cultivators of their own farms[d] who possess little property. This is the largest and most potent group in a democracy when it meets in assembly." "Yes, it is," he said, "but it will not often do that,[e] unless it gets a share of the honey." "Well, does it not always share," I said, "to the extent that the men at the head find it possible, in distributing[f] to the people what they take from the well-to-do,[g] to keep the lion's share for themselves[h]?" "Why, yes," he said, "it shares in that sense." "And so, I suppose, those who are thus plundered are compelled to defend themselves by speeches in the assembly and any action in their power." "Of course." "And thereupon the charge is brought against them by the other party, though they may have no revolutionary designs, that they are plotting against the people, and it is said that they are oligarchs.[i]" "Surely." "And then finally, when they see the people, not of its own will[j] but through

Peace 131, Dem. *De cor.* 105 ff., on his triarchic law; and also Eurip. *Herc. Fur.* 588-592, Shakes. *Richard II.* i. iv. 49 f. :

> Whereto, when they shall know what men are rich.
> They shall subscribe them for large sums of gold.

Cf. Inge, *More Lay Thoughts of a Dean*, p. 13.

[h] *Cf.* Aristoph. *Knights* 717-718, 1219-1223, and Achilles in *Il.* ix. 363.

[i] *i.e.* reactionaries. *Cf. supra* on 562 D, p. 306, note *b*, Aeschines iii. 168, and 566 C μισόδημος. The whole passage perhaps illustrates the "disharmony" between Plato's upper-class sympathies and his liberal philosophy.

[j] So the Attic orators frequently say that a popular jury was deceived. *Cf.* also Aristoph. *Acharn.* 515-516.

PLATO

565 οὐχ ἑκόντα, ἀλλ' ἀγνοήσαντά τε καὶ ἐξαπατηθέντα
C ὑπὸ τῶν διαβαλλόντων, ἐπιχειροῦντα σφᾶς ἀδικεῖν,
τότ' ἤδη, εἴτε βούλονται εἴτε μή, ὡς ἀληθῶς
ὀλιγαρχικοὶ γίγνονται, οὐχ ἑκόντες, ἀλλὰ καὶ
τοῦτο τὸ κακὸν ἐκεῖνος ὁ κηφὴν ἐντίκτει κεντῶν
αὐτούς. Κομιδῇ μὲν οὖν. Εἰσαγγελίαι δὴ καὶ
κρίσεις καὶ ἀγῶνες περὶ ἀλλήλων γίγνονται. Καὶ
μάλα. Οὐκοῦν ἕνα τινὰ ἀεὶ δῆμος εἴωθε διαφερόντως προΐστασθαι ἑαυτοῦ, καὶ τοῦτον τρέφειν
τε καὶ αὔξειν μέγαν; Εἴωθε γάρ. Τοῦτο μὲν
D ἄρα, ἦν δ' ἐγώ, δῆλον, ὅτι, ὅταν περ φύηται
τύραννος, ἐκ προστατικῆς ῥίζης καὶ οὐκ ἄλλοθεν
ἐκβλαστάνει. Καὶ μάλα δῆλον. Τίς ἀρχὴ οὖν
μεταβολῆς ἐκ προστάτου ἐπὶ τύραννον; ἢ δῆλον
ὅτι ἐπειδὰν ταὐτὸν ἄρξηται δρᾶν ὁ προστάτης τῷ
ἐν τῷ μύθῳ, ὃς περὶ τὸ ἐν Ἀρκαδίᾳ τὸ τοῦ Διὸς
τοῦ Λυκαίου ἱερὸν λέγεται; Τίς, ἔφη. Ὡς ἄρα
ὁ γευσάμενος τοῦ ἀνθρωπίνου σπλάγχνου, ἐν
ἄλλοις ἄλλων ἱερείων ἑνὸς ἐγκατατετμημένου,
E ἀνάγκη δὴ τούτῳ λύκῳ γενέσθαι; ἢ οὐκ ἀκήκοας
τὸν λόγον; Ἔγωγε. Ἆρ' οὖν οὕτω καὶ ὃς ἂν
δήμου προεστώς, λαβὼν σφόδρα πειθόμενον ὄχλον,
μὴ ἀπόσχηται ἐμφυλίου αἵματος, ἀλλ' ἀδίκως

---

[a] Aristotle, *Eth. Nic.* 1110 a 1, in his discussion of voluntary and involuntary acts, says things done under compulsion or through misapprehension (δι' ἄγνοιαν) are involuntary.

[b] For τότ' ἤδη cf. 569 A, *Phaedo* 87 E, *Gorg.* 527 D, *Laches* 181 D, 184 A, and on 550 A, p. 259, note *i*.

[c] So Aristot. *Pol.* 1304 b 30 ἠναγκάσθησαν σύσταντες κατα-λῦσαι τὸν δῆμον, Isoc. xv. 318 ὀλιγαρχίαν ὀνειδίζοντες . . . ἠνάγ-κασαν ὁμοίους γενέσθαι ταῖς αἰτίαις.

[d] Cf. 562 D, Eurip. *Or.* 772 προστάτας, Aristoph. *Knights* 1128. The προστάτης τοῦ δήμου was the accepted leader of the democracy. *Cf.* Dittenberger, *S.I.G.* 2nd ed. 1900, no. 476.

misapprehension,[a] and being misled by the calumniators, attempting to wrong them, why then,[b] whether they wish it or not,[c] they become in very deed oligarchs, not willingly, but this evil too is engendered by those drones which sting them." "Precisely." "And then there ensue impeachments and judgements and lawsuits on either side." "Yes, indeed." "And is it not always the way of a demos to put forward one man as its special champion and protector[d] and cherish and magnify him?" "Yes, it is." "This, then, is plain," said I, "that when a tyrant arises he sprouts from a protectorate root[e] and from nothing else." "Very plain." "What, then, is the starting-point of the transformation of a protector into a tyrant? Is it not obviously when the protector's acts begin to reproduce the legend that is told of the shrine of Lycaean Zeus in Arcadia[f]?" "What is that?" he said. "The story goes that he who tastes of the one bit of human entrails minced up with those of other victims is inevitably transformed into a wolf. Have you not heard the tale?" "I have." "And is it not true that in like manner a leader of the people who, getting control of a docile mob,[g] does not withhold his hand from the shedding of

The implications of this passage contradict the theory that the oligarchy is nearer the ideal than the democracy. But Plato is thinking of Athens and not of his own scheme. *Cf. supra* Introd. pp. xlv-xlvi.

[e] *Cf.* Aristot. *Pol.* 1310 b 14 οἱ πλεῖστοι τῶν τυράννων γεγόνασιν ἐκ δημαγωγῶν, etc., *ibid.* 1304 b 20 ff.

[f] *Cf.* Frazer on Pausanias viii. 2 (vol. iv. p. 189) and Cook's *Zeus*, vol. i. p. 70. The archaic religious rhetoric of what follows testifies to the intensity of Plato's feeling. *Cf.* the language of the *Laws* on homicide, 865 ff.

[g] Note the difference of tone from 502 B. *Cf. Phaedr.* 260 c.

565 ἐπαιτιώμενος, οἷα δὴ φιλοῦσιν, εἰς δικαστήρια
ἄγων μιαιφονῇ, βίον ἀνδρὸς ἀφανίζων, γλώττῃ τε
καὶ στόματι ἀνοσίῳ γευόμενος φόνου ξυγγενοῦς,
566 καὶ ἀνδρηλατῇ καὶ ἀποκτιννύῃ καὶ ὑποσημαίνῃ
χρεῶν τε ἀποκοπὰς καὶ γῆς ἀναδασμόν, ἆρα τῷ
τοιούτῳ ἀνάγκη δὴ τὸ μετὰ τοῦτο καὶ εἵμαρται ἢ
ἀπολωλέναι ὑπὸ τῶν ἐχθρῶν ἢ τυραννεῖν καὶ λύκῳ
ἐξ ἀνθρώπου γενέσθαι; Πολλὴ ἀνάγκη, ἔφη.
Οὗτος δή, ἔφην, ὁ στασιάζων γίγνεται πρὸς τοὺς
ἔχοντας τὰς οὐσίας. Οὗτος. Ἆρ’ οὖν ἐκπεσὼν
μὲν καὶ κατελθὼν βίᾳ τῶν ἐχθρῶν τύραννος ἀπ-
ειργασμένος κατέρχεται; Δῆλον. Ἐὰν δὲ ἀδύ-
B νατοι ἐκβάλλειν αὐτὸν ὦσιν ἢ ἀποκτεῖναι διαβάλ-
λοντες τῇ πόλει, βιαίῳ δὴ θανάτῳ ἐπιβουλεύουσιν
ἀποκτιννύναι λάθρᾳ. Φιλεῖ γοῦν, ἦ δ’ ὅς, οὕτω
γίγνεσθαι. Τὸ δὴ τυραννικὸν αἴτημα τὸ πολυθρύλητον ἐπὶ τούτῳ πάντες οἱ εἰς τοῦτο προβεβηκότες
ἐξευρίσκουσιν, αἰτεῖν τὸν δῆμον φύλακάς τινας τοῦ
σώματος, ἵνα σῶς αὐτοῖς ᾖ ὁ τοῦ δήμου βοηθός.
C Καὶ μάλ’, ἔφη. Διδόασι δή, οἶμαι, δείσαντες μὲν
ὑπὲρ ἐκείνου,. θαρρήσαντες δὲ ὑπὲρ ἑαυτῶν. Καὶ
μάλα. Οὐκοῦν τοῦτο ὅταν ἴδῃ ἀνὴρ χρήματα ἔχων

ᵃ Cf. Pindar, *Pyth.* ii. 32 ; Lucan i. 331 :

> nullus semel ore receptus
> pollutas patitur sanguis mansuescere fauces.

ᵇ For ἀφανίζων cf. *Gorg.* 471 B.

ᶜ The apparent contradiction of the tone here with *Laws*
684 E could be regarded mistakenly as another "disharmony."
Grote iii. p. 107 says that there is no case of such radical
measures in Greek history. Schmidt, *Ethik der Griechen*,
ii. p. 374, says that the only case was that of Cleomenes at
Sparta in the third century. See Georges Mathieu, *Les Idées*

tribal blood,[a] but by the customary unjust accusations brings a citizen into court and assassinates him, blotting out [b] a human life, and with unhallowed tongue and lips that have tasted kindred blood, banishes and slays and hints at the abolition of debts and the partition of lands[c]—is it not the inevitable consequence and a decree of fate[d] that such a one be either slain by his enemies or become a tyrant and be transformed from a man into a wolf ? " " It is quite inevitable," he said. " He it is," I said, " who becomes the leader of faction against the possessors of property.[e] " "Yes, he." " May it not happen that he is driven into exile and, being restored in defiance of his enemies, returns a finished tyrant ? " " Obviously." " And if they are unable to expel him or bring about his death by calumniating him to the people, they plot to assassinate him by stealth." " That is certainly wont to happen," said he. " And thereupon those who have reached this stage devise that famous petition[f] of the tyrant—to ask from the people a bodyguard to make their city safe[g] for the friend of democracy." " They do indeed," he said. " And the people grant it, I suppose, fearing for him but unconcerned for themselves." " Yes, indeed." " And when he sees this, the man who has wealth and with his wealth

politiques d'Isocrate, p. 150, who refers to Andoc. *De myst.* 88, Plato, *Laws* 684, Demosth. *Against Timocr.* 149 (heliastic oath), Michel, *Recueil d'inscriptions grecques*, 1317, the oath at Itanos.

[d] *Cf.* 619 c. [e] *Cf.* 565 A.

[f] *Cf.* Herod. i. 59, Aristot. *Rhet.* 1357 b 30 ff. Aristotle, *Pol.* 1305 a 7-15, says that this sort of thing used to happen but does not now, and explains why. For πολυθρύλητον *cf. Phaedo* 100 B.

[g] For the ethical dative αὐτοῖς *cf.* on 343 A, Vol. I. p. 65, note c.

PLATO

566 καὶ μετὰ τῶν χρημάτων αἰτίαν μισόδημος εἶναι, τότε δὴ οὗτος, ὦ ἑταῖρε, κατὰ τὸν Κροίσῳ γενόμενον χρησμὸν

πολυψήφιδα παρ' Ἕρμον

φεύγει, οὐδὲ μένει, οὐδ' αἰδεῖται κακὸς εἶναι.

Οὐ γὰρ ἄν, ἔφη, δεύτερον αὖθις αἰδεσθείη. Ὁ δέ γε, οἶμαι, ἦν δ' ἐγώ, καταληφθεὶς θανάτῳ δίδοται. Ἀνάγκη. Ὁ δὲ δὴ προστάτης ἐκεῖνος αὐτὸς δῆλον δὴ ὅτι μέγας μεγαλωστί, οὐ κεῖται, ἀλλὰ
D καταβαλὼν ἄλλους πολλοὺς ἕστηκεν ἐν τῷ δίφρῳ τῆς πόλεως, τύραννος ἀντὶ προστάτου ἀποτετελεσμένος. Τί δ' οὐ μέλλει; ἔφη.

XVII. Διέλθωμεν δὴ τὴν εὐδαιμονίαν, ἦν δ' ἐγώ, τοῦ τε ἀνδρὸς καὶ τῆς πόλεως, ἐν ᾗ ἂν ὁ τοιοῦτος βροτὸς ἐγγένηται; Πάνυ μὲν οὖν, ἔφη, διέλθωμεν. Ἆρ' οὖν, εἶπον, οὐ ταῖς μὲν πρώταις ἡμέραις τε καὶ χρόνῳ προσγελᾷ τε καὶ ἀσπάζεται πάντας, ᾧ ἂν περιτυγχάνῃ, καὶ οὔτε τύραννός
E φησιν εἶναι, ὑπισχνεῖταί τε πολλὰ καὶ ἰδίᾳ καὶ δημοσίᾳ, χρεῶν τε ἠλευθέρωσε, καὶ γῆν διένειμε δήμῳ τε καὶ τοῖς περὶ ἑαυτόν, καὶ πᾶσιν ἵλεώς τε καὶ πρᾶος εἶναι προσποιεῖται; Ἀνάγκη, ἔφη. Ὅταν δέ γε, οἶμαι, πρὸς τοὺς ἔξω ἐχθροὺς τοῖς μὲν καταλλαγῇ, τοὺς δὲ καὶ διαφθείρῃ, καὶ ἡσυχία ἐκείνων γένηται, πρῶτον μὲν πολέμους τινὰς ἀεὶ κινεῖ, ἵν' ἐν χρείᾳ ἡγεμόνος ὁ δῆμος ᾖ. Εἰκός

---

[a] For μισόδημος cf. Aristoph. Wasps 474, Xen. Hell. ii. 3. 47, Andoc. iv. 16, and by contrast φιλόδημον, Aristoph. Knights 787, Clouds 1187. [b] Herod. i. 55.
[c] In Il. xvi. 776 Cebriones, Hector's charioteer, slain by Patroclus, κεῖτο μέγας μεγαλωστί, "mighty in his mightiness." (A. T. Murray, Loeb tr.)

322

the repute of hostility to 'democracy,[a] then in the words of the oracle [b] delivered to Croesus,

> By the pebble-strewn strand of the Hermos
> Swift is his flight, he stays not nor blushes to show the
> white feather."

" No, for he would never get a second chance to blush." " And he who is caught, methinks, is delivered to his death." " Inevitably." " And then obviously that protector does not lie prostrate, 'mighty with far-flung limbs,' in Homeric overthrow,[c] but overthrowing many others towers in the car of state[d] transformed from a protector into a perfect and finished tyrant." " What else is likely ? " he said.

XVII. " Shall we, then, portray the happiness," said I, " of the man and the state in which such a creature arises ? " " By all means let us describe it," he said. " Then at the start and in the first days does he not smile[e] upon all men and greet everybody he meets and deny that he is a tyrant, and promise many things in private and public, and having freed men from debts, and distributed lands to the people and his own associates, he affects a gracious and gentle manner to all?" " Necessarily," he said. " But when, I suppose, he has come to terms with some of his exiled enemies[f] and has got others destroyed and is no longer disturbed by them, in the first place he is always stirring up some war[g] so that the people may be in need of

---

[d] For the figure cf. Polit. 266 E. More common in Plato is the figure of the ship in this connexion. Cf. on 488.

[e] Cf. Eurip. I.A. 333 ff., Shakes. Henry IV. Part I. i. iii. 246 " This king of smiles, this Bolingbroke."

[f] Not " foreign enemies " as almost all render it. Cf. my note on this passage in Class. Rev. xix. (1905) pp. 438-439, 573 B ἔξω ὠθεῖ, Theognis 56, Thuc. iv. 66 and viii. 64.

[g] Cf. Polit. 308 A, and in modern times the case of Napoleon.

567 γε. Οὐκοῦν καὶ ἵνα χρήματα εἰσφέροντες πένητες
γιγνόμενοι πρὸς τῷ καθ' ἡμέραν ἀναγκάζωνται
εἶναι καὶ ἧττον αὐτῷ ἐπιβουλεύωσιν; Δῆλον.
Καὶ ἄν γέ τινας, οἶμαι, ὑποπτεύῃ ἐλεύθερα φρονή-
ματα ἔχοντας μὴ ἐπιτρέψειν αὐτῷ ἄρχειν, ὅπως
ἂν τούτους μετὰ προφάσεως ἀπολλύῃ, ἐνδοὺς τοῖς
πολεμίοις; τούτων πάντων ἕνεκα τυράννῳ ἀεὶ
ἀνάγκη πόλεμον ταράττειν[a]; Ἀνάγκη. Ταῦτα δὴ
B ποιοῦντα ἕτοιμον μᾶλλον ἀπεχθάνεσθαι τοῖς πολίταις; Πῶς γὰρ οὔ; Οὐκοῦν καί τινας τῶν
ξυγκαταστησάντων[b] καὶ ἐν δυνάμει ὄντων παρ-
ρησιάζεσθαι καὶ πρὸς αὐτὸν καὶ πρὸς ἀλλήλους,
ἐπιπλήττοντας τοῖς γιγνομένοις, οἳ ἂν τυγχάνω-
σιν ἀνδρικώτατοι ὄντες; Εἰκός γε. Ὑπεξαιρεῖν
δὴ[c] τούτους πάντας δεῖ τὸν τύραννον, εἰ μέλλει
ἄρξειν, ἕως ἂν μήτε φίλων μήτ' ἐχθρῶν λίπῃ
μηδένα, ὅτου τι ὄφελος. Δῆλον. Ὀξέως ἄρα δεῖ
C ὁρᾶν αὐτόν, τίς ἀνδρεῖος, τίς μεγαλόφρων, τίς
φρόνιμος, τίς πλούσιος· καὶ οὕτως εὐδαίμων ἐστίν,
ὥστε τούτοις ἅπασιν ἀνάγκη αὐτῷ, εἴτε βούλεται
εἴτε μή, πολεμίῳ εἶναι καὶ ἐπιβουλεύειν, ἕως ἂν
καθήρῃ τὴν πόλιν[d]. Καλόν γε, ἔφη, καθαρμόν.
Ναί, ἦν δ' ἐγώ, τὸν ἐναντίον ἢ οἱ ἰατροὶ τὰ σώματα·

---

[a] For ταράττειν in this sense cf. Dem. De cor. 151 ἐγκλήματα
καὶ πόλεμος . . . ἐταράχθη, Soph. Antig. 795 νεῖκος . . . ταράξας.
[b] ξυγκαταστησάντων is used in Aesch. Prom. 307 of those
who helped Zeus to establish his supremacy among the gods.
See also Xen. Ages. 2. 31, Isoc. Panegyr. 126.
[c] Cf. Thucyd. viii. 70, Herod. iii. 80. δή, as often in the
Timaeus, marks the logical progression of the thought. Cf.
Tim. 67 c, 69 A, 77 c, 82 B, and passim.
[d] Cf. on 560 D, p. 299, note c. Aristotle says that in a
democracy ostracism corresponds to this. Cf. Newman i.

a leader." "That is likely." "And also that being impoverished by war-taxes they may have to devote themselves to their daily business and be less likely to plot against him?" "Obviously." "And if, I presume, he suspects that there are free spirits who will not suffer his domination, his further object is to find pretexts for destroying them by exposing them to the enemy? From all these motives a tyrant is compelled to be always provoking wars [a]?" "Yes, he is compelled to do so." "And by such conduct will he not the more readily incur the hostility of the citizens?" "Of course." "And is it not likely that some of those who helped to establish [b] and now share in his power, voicing their disapproval of the course of events, will speak out frankly to him and to one another—such of them as happen to be the bravest?" "Yes, it is likely." "Then the tyrant must do away [c] with all such if he is to maintain his rule, until he has left no one of any worth, friend or foe." "Obviously." "He must look sharp to see, then, who is brave, who is great-souled, who is wise, who is rich; and such is his good fortune that, whether he wishes it or not, he must be their enemy and plot against them all until he purge the city.[d]" "A fine purgation," he said. "Yes," said I, "just the opposite of that which physicians practise on our bodies. For

---

p. 262. For the idea that the tyrant fears good or able and outstanding men *cf. Laws* 832 c, *Gorg.* 510 B-C, Xen. *Hiero* 5. 1, Isoc. viii. 112, Eurip. *Ion* 626-628, Milton, *Tenure of Kings*, etc., *init.*, Shakes., *Richard II.* III. iv. 33 ff. :

> Go thou, and like an executioner
> Cut off the heads of too fast growing sprays
> That look too lofty in our commonwealth.
> All must be even in our government.

But *cf.* Pindar, *Pyth.* iii. 71, of Hiero, οὐ φθονέων ἀγαθοῖς.

567 οἱ μὲν γὰρ τὸ χείριστον ἀφαιροῦντες λείπουσι τὸ βέλτιστον, ὁ δὲ τοὐναντίον. Ὡς ἔοικε γάρ, αὐτῷ, ἔφη, ἀνάγκη, εἴπερ ἄρξει.

XVIII. Ἐν μακαρίᾳ ἄρα, εἶπον ἐγώ, ἀνάγκῃ D δέδεται, ἢ προστάττει αὐτῷ ἢ μετὰ φαύλων τῶν πολλῶν οἰκεῖν καὶ ὑπὸ τούτων μισούμενον ἢ μὴ ζῆν. Ἐν τοιαύτῃ, ἦ δ' ὅς. Ἆρ' οὖν οὐχί, ὅσῳ ἂν μᾶλλον τοῖς πολίταις ἀπεχθάνηται ταῦτα δρῶν, τοσούτῳ πλειόνων καὶ πιστοτέρων δορυφόρων δεήσεται; Πῶς γὰρ οὔ; Τίνες οὖν οἱ πιστοί, καὶ πόθεν αὐτοὺς μεταπέμψεται; Αὐτόματοι, ἔφη, πολλοὶ ἥξουσι πετόμενοι, ἐὰν τὸν μισθὸν διδῷ. Κηφῆνας, ἦν δ' ἐγώ, νὴ τὸν κύνα, δοκεῖς αὖ τινάς E μοι λέγειν ξενικούς τε καὶ παντοδαπούς. Ἀληθῆ γάρ, ἔφη, δοκῶ σοι. Τί δέ; αὐτόθεν[1] ἆρ' οὐκ ἂν ἐθελήσειεν; Πῶς; Τοὺς δούλους ἀφελόμενος τοὺς πολίτας, ἐλευθερώσας, τῶν περὶ ἑαυτὸν δορυφόρων ποιήσασθαι. Σφόδρα γ', ἔφη· ἐπεί τοι καὶ πιστότατοι αὐτῷ οὗτοί εἰσιν. Ἦ μακάριον, ἦν δ' ἐγώ, λέγεις τυράννου χρῆμα, εἰ τοιούτοις φίλοις τε καὶ 568 πιστοῖς ἀνδράσι χρῆται, τοὺς προτέρους ἐκείνους ἀπολέσας. Ἀλλὰ μήν, ἔφη, τοιούτοις γε χρῆται. Καὶ θαυμάζουσι δή, εἶπον, οὗτοι οἱ ἑταῖροι αὐτὸν καὶ ξύνεισιν οἱ νέοι πολῖται, οἱ δ' ἐπιεικεῖς μισοῦσί

---

[1] τί δέ; αὐτόθεν Hermann, Adam : τίς δὲ αὐτόθεν; AFDM : τί δὲ αὐτόθεν Mon. (without punctuation): τοὺς δὲ αὐτόθεν Stephanus.

---

[a] Cf. *Laws* 952 E, *Rep.* 467 D.
[b] Cf. the Scottish guards of Louis XI. of France, the Swiss guards of the later French kings, the Hessians hired by George III. against the American colonies, and the Asiatics in the Soviet armies.

while they remove the worst and leave the best, he does the reverse." "Yes, for apparently he must," he said, "if he is to keep his power."

XVIII. "Blessed, then, is the necessity that binds him," said I, "which bids him dwell for the most part with base companions who hate him, or else forfeit his life." "Such it is," he said. "And would he not, the more he offends the citizens by such conduct, have the greater need of more and more trustworthy body-guards?" "Of course." "Whom, then, may he trust, and whence shall he fetch them?" "Unbidden," he said, "they will wing their way *a* to him in great numbers if he furnish their wage." "Drones, by the dog," I said, "I think you are talking of again, an alien *b* and motley crew.*c*" "You think rightly," he said. "But what of the home supply,*d* would he not choose to employ that?" "How?" "By taking their slaves from the citizens, emancipating them and enlisting them in his bodyguard." "Assuredly," he said, "since these are those whom he can most trust." "Truly," said I, "this tyrant business *e* is a blessed *f* thing on your showing, if such are the friends and 'trusties' he must employ after destroying his former associates." "But such are indeed those he does make use of," he said. "And these companions admire him," I said, "and these new citizens are his associates, while the better sort hate and avoid him."

---

c παντοδαπούς: cf. on 557 c.

d For αὐτόθεν cf. Herod. i. 64 τῶν μὲν αὐτόθεν, τῶν δὲ ἀπὸ Στρύμονος, Thuc. i. 11, Xen. Ages. 1. 28.

e For the idiomatic and colloquial χρῆμα cf. Herod. i. 36, Eurip. Androm. 181, Theaet. 209 ε, Aristoph. Clouds 1, Birds 826, Wasps 933, Lysistr. 83, 1085, Acharn. 150, Peace 1192, Knights 1219, Frogs 1278.

f For the wretched lot of the tyrant cf. p. 368, note a.

568 τε καὶ φεύγουσιν; Τί δ' οὐ μέλλουσιν; Οὐκ ἐτός,[a]
ἦν δ' ἐγώ, ἥ τε τραγῳδία ὅλως σοφὸν δοκεῖ εἶναι
καὶ ὁ Εὐριπίδης διαφέρων ἐν αὐτῇ. Τί δή; Ὅτι
καὶ τοῦτο πυκνῆς διανοίας ἐχόμενον ἐφθέγξατο,[c]
B ὡς ἄρα σοφοὶ τύραννοί εἰσι τῶν σοφῶν συνουσίᾳ.[b]
καὶ ἔλεγε δῆλον ὅτι τούτους εἶναι τοὺς σοφοὺς οἷς
ξύνεστιν. Καὶ ὡς ἰσόθεόν γ', ἔφη, τὴν τυραννίδα
ἐγκωμιάζει, καὶ ἕτερα πολλά, καὶ οὗτος καὶ οἱ
ἄλλοι ποιηταί. Τοιγάρτοι, ἔφην, ἅτε σοφοὶ ὄντες
οἱ τῆς τραγῳδίας ποιηταὶ ξυγγιγνώσκουσιν ἡμῖν
τε καὶ ἐκείνοις, ὅσοι ἡμῶν ἐγγὺς πολιτεύονται,
ὅτι αὐτοὺς εἰς τὴν πολιτείαν οὐ παραδεξόμεθα ἅτε
τυραννίδος ὑμνητάς. Οἶμαι ἔγωγ', ἔφη, ξυγγιγνώ-
C σκουσιν ὅσοιπέρ γε αὐτῶν κομψοί. Εἰς δέ γε,
οἶμαι, τὰς ἄλλας περιόντες πόλεις, ξυλλέγοντες
τοὺς ὄχλους, καλὰς φωνὰς καὶ μεγάλας καὶ πιθανὰς
μισθωσάμενοι εἰς τυραννίδας τε καὶ δημοκρατίας
ἕλκουσι τὰς πολιτείας. Μάλα γε. Οὐκοῦν καὶ
προσέτι τούτων μισθοὺς λαμβάνουσι καὶ τιμῶνται,
μάλιστα μέν, ὥσπερ τὸ εἰκός, ὑπὸ τυράννων,
δεύτερον δὲ ὑπὸ δημοκρατίας· ὅσῳ δ' ἂν ἀνωτέρω
ἴωσι πρὸς τὸ ἄναντες τῶν πολιτειῶν, μᾶλλον
D ἀπαγορεύει αὐτῶν ἡ τιμή, ὥσπερ ὑπὸ ἄσθματος
ἀδυνατοῦσα πορεύεσθαι. Πάνυ μὲν οὖν.

---

[a] For οὐκ ἐτός cf. 414 E. The idiom is frequent in Aristoph.
Cf. e.g. Acharn. 411, 413, Birds 915, Thesm. 921, Plut. 404,
1166, Eccl. 245.

[b] This is plainly ironical and cannot be used by the
admirers of Euripides.

[c] Cf. πυκιναὶ φρένες Iliad xiv. 294, πυκινὸς νόος xv. 41, etc.

[d] Cf. Theages 125 B f. The line is also attributed to
Sophocles. Cf. Stemplinger, Das Plagiat in der griechischen Literatur, p. 9; Gellius xiii. 18, F. Dümmler, Akademika, p. 16. Wilamowitz, Platon, i. p. 119 thinks this an

THE REPUBLIC, BOOK VIII

"Why should they not?" "Not for nothing,[a]" said
I, " is tragedy in general esteemed wise, and Euripides
beyond other tragedians.[b]" "Why, pray?" "Because among other utterances of pregnant thought[c]
he said, 'Tyrants are wise by converse with the wise.[d]'
He meant evidently that these associates of the
tyrant are the wise." "Yes, he and the other poets,"
he said, "call the tyrant's power 'likest God's'[e] and
praise it in many other ways." "Wherefore," said
I, " being wise as they are, the poets of tragedy will
pardon us and those whose politics resemble ours
for not admitting them[f] into our polity, since they
hymn the praises of tyranny." "I think," he said,
" that the subtle minds[g] among them will pardon us."
"But going about to other cities, I fancy, collecting
crowds and hiring fine, loud, persuasive voices,[h] they
draw the polities towards tyrannies or democracies."
"Yes, indeed." "And, further, they are paid and
honoured for this, chiefly, as is to be expected, by
tyrants, and secondly by democracy.[i] But the higher
they go, breasting constitution hill, the more their
honour fails, as it were from lack of breath[j] unable to
proceed." "Quite so."

allusion to Euripides and Agathon at the court of Archelaus
of Macedon.

Isocrates ix. 40, like the poets, praises the tyrants, but ii.
3-5 contrasts their education unfavourably with that of the
ordinary citizen. Throughout the passage he is plainly
thinking of Plato.

[e] *Cf.* Vol. I. p. 119, note *c*, Eurip. *Tro.* 1169, Isoc. ii. 5.
[f] *Cf. supra* 394 D, *What Plato Said*, p. 561, *infra* 598 ff.
[g] κομψοί is used playfully or ironically.
[h] *Cf. Gorg.* 502 B ff., *Laws* 817 C, and for the expression
Protag. 347 D.
[i] *Cf. Laches* 183 A-B.
[j] *Cf.* Shakes. *Ant.* and *Cleop.* III. x. 25 "Our fortune on
the sea is out of breath."

568 XIX. Ἀλλὰ δή, εἶπον, ἐνταῦθα μὲν ἐξέβημεν·
λέγωμεν δὲ πάλιν ἐκεῖνο τὸ τοῦ τυράννου στρατό-
πεδον τὸ καλόν τε καὶ πολὺ καὶ ποικίλον καὶ
οὐδέποτε ταὐτόν, πόθεν θρέψεται. Δῆλον, ἔφη,
ὅτι, ἐάν τε ἱερὰ χρήματα ᾖ ἐν τῇ πόλει, ταῦτα
ἀναλώσει ὅποι ποτὲ ἂν ἀεὶ ἐξαρκῇ, καὶ τὰ τῶν ἀπολομένων,[1] ἐλάττους εἰσφορὰς ἀναγκάζων τὸν δῆμον
Ε εἰσφέρειν. Τί δ' ὅταν δὴ ταῦτα ἐπιλείπῃ; Δῆλον,
ἔφη, ὅτι ἐκ τῶν πατρῴων θρέψεται αὐτός τε καὶ
οἱ συμπόται τε καὶ ἑταῖροι καὶ ἑταῖραι. Μανθάνω,
ἦν δ' ἐγώ· ὅτι ὁ δῆμος ὁ γεννήσας τὸν τύραννον
θρέψει αὐτόν τε καὶ ἑταίρους. Πολλὴ αὐτῷ, ἔφη,
ἀνάγκη. Πῶς δὲ λέγεις; εἶπον· ἐὰν δὲ ἀγανακτῇ
τε καὶ λέγῃ ὁ δῆμος, ὅτι οὔτε δίκαιον τρέφεσθαι
ὑπὸ πατρὸς υἱὸν ἡβῶντα, ἀλλὰ τοὐναντίον ὑπὸ
569 υἱέος πατέρα, οὔτε τούτου αὐτὸν ἕνεκα ἐγέννησέ
τε καὶ κατέστησεν, ἵνα, ἐπειδὴ μέγας γένοιτο,
τότε αὐτὸς δουλεύων τοῖς αὑτοῦ δούλοις τρέφοι
ἐκεῖνόν τε καὶ τοὺς δούλους μετὰ ξυγκλύδων
ἄλλων, ἀλλ' ἵνα ἀπὸ τῶν πλουσίων τε καὶ καλῶν
κἀγαθῶν λεγομένων ἐν τῇ πόλει ἐλευθερωθείη
ἐκείνου προστάντος, καὶ νῦν κελεύει ἀπιέναι ἐκ
τῆς πόλεως αὐτόν τε καὶ τοὺς ἑταίρους, ὥσπερ
πατὴρ υἱὸν ἐξ οἰκίας μετὰ ὀχληρῶν ξυμποτῶν
ἐξελαύνων; Γνώσεταί γε, νὴ Δία, ἦ δ' ὅς, τότ'
Β ἤδη ὁ δῆμος, οἷος οἷον θρέμμα γεννῶν ἠσπάζετο

---

[1] καὶ τὰ Baiter, τὰ mss.; ἀπολομένων A², ἀποδομένων AFDM,
πωλουμένων ci. Campbell.   See Adam, App. VI.

---

[a] Cf. on 572 B, p. 339, note e.
[b] Cf. 574 D, Diels¹ p. 578, Anon. Iambl. 3.
[c] Cf. Soph. O.T. 873 ὕβρις φυτεύει τύραννον.

XIX. " But this," said I, " is a digression.ᵃ Let us
return to that fair, multitudinous, diversified and
ever-changing bodyguard of the tyrant and tell how
it will be supported." " Obviously," he said, " if
there are sacred treasures in the city he will spend
these as long as they last and the property of those
he has destroyed, thus requiring smaller contribu-
tions from the populace." " But what when these
resources fail ᵇ ? " " Clearly," he said, " his father's
estate will have to support him and his wassailers, his
fellows and his she-fellows." " I understand," I said,
" that the people which begot the tyrant ᶜ will have
to feed him and his companions." " It cannot escape
from that," he said. " And what have you to say,"
I said, " in case the people protests and says that it
is not right that a grown-up son should be supported
by his father, but the reverse, and that it did not beget
and establish him in order that, when he had grown
great, it, in servitude to its own slaves, should feed
him and the slaves together with a nondescript rabble
of aliens, but in order that, with him for protector,
it might be liberated from the rule of the rich and
the so-called ' better classes,' ᵈ and that it now bids him
and his crew depart from the city as a father expels ᵉ
from his house a son together with troublesome
revellers ? " " The demos, by Zeus," he said, " will then
learn to its cost ᶠ what it is and what ᵍ a creature it

ᵈ For καλῶν κἀγαθῶν cf. Aristoph. *Knights* 185, and Blaydes
on 735. See also *supra* on 489 ᴇ, p. 27, note *d*.

ᵉ *Cf.* Blaydes on Aristoph. *Clouds* 123.

ᶠ For the threatening γνώσεται cf. 362 ᴀ, 466 ᴄ, *Il.* xviii.
270 and 125, Theocr. xxvi. 19 τάχα γνώσῃ, and Lucian,
Timon 33 εἴσεται.

ᵍ For the juxtaposition οἶος οἶον cf. *Symp.* 195 ᴀ, Sophocles
El. 751, *Ajax* 557, 923, *Trach.* 995, 1045.

569 τε καὶ ηὖξε, καὶ ὅτι ἀσθενέστερος ὢν ἰσχυροτέ-
ρους ἐξελαύνει. Πῶς, ἦν δ' ἐγώ, λέγεις; τολμήσει τὸν πατέρα βιάζεσθαι, κἂν μὴ πείθηται, τύπ-
τειν ὁ τύραννος; Ναί, ἔφη, ἀφελόμενός γε τὰ
ὅπλα. Πατραλοίαν, ἦν δ' ἐγώ, λέγεις τύραννον
καὶ χαλεπὸν γηροτρόφον, καὶ ὡς ἔοικε τοῦτο δὴ
ὁμολογουμένη ἂν ἤδη τυραννὶς εἴη, καὶ τὸ λεγόμενον ὁ δῆμος φεύγων ἂν καπνὸν δουλείας ἐλευθέ-
C ρων εἰς πῦρ δούλων δεσποτείας ἂν ἐμπεπτωκὼς
εἴη, ἀντὶ τῆς πολλῆς ἐκείνης καὶ ἀκαίρου ἐλευθερίας τὴν χαλεπωτάτην τε καὶ πικροτάτην δούλων
δουλείαν μεταμπισχόμενος. Καὶ μάλα, ἔφη, ταῦτα
οὕτω γίγνεται. Τί οὖν; εἶπον· οὐκ ἐμμελῶς
ἡμῖν εἰρήσεται, ἐὰν φῶμεν ἱκανῶς διεληλυθέναι,
ὡς μεταβαίνει τυραννὶς ἐκ δημοκρατίας, γενομένη
τε οἷά ἐστιν; Πάνυ μὲν οὖν ἱκανῶς, ἔφη.

---

[a] Cf. infra on 574 c, pp. 346-347, note e.
[b] As we say, "Out of the frying-pan into the fire." Cf.
Anth. Pal. ix. 17. 5 ἐκ πυρὸς ὡς αἶνος 'πεσες ἐς φλόγα, Theo-
doret, Therap. iii. p. 773 καὶ τὸν καπνὸν κατὰ τὴν παροιμίαν, ὡς
ἔοικε, φεύγοντες, εἰς αὐτὸ δὴ τὸ πῦρ ἐμπεπτώκαμεν. See Otto,
p. 137 ; also Solon 7 (17) (Anth. Lyr., Bergk-Hiller, 9 in
Edmonds, Greek Elegy and Iambus, i. p. 122, Loeb Classical

THE REPUBLIC, BOOK VIII

begot and cherished and bred to greatness, and that in its weakness it tries to expel the stronger." "What do you mean?" said I; "will the tyrant dare to use force against his father, and, if he does not yield, to strike him [a]?" "Yes," he said, "after he has once taken from him his arms." "A very parricide," said I, "you make the tyrant out to be, and a cruel nurse of old age, and, as it seems, this is at last tyranny open and avowed, and, as the saying goes, the demos trying to escape the smoke of submission to the free would have plunged into the fire [b] of enslavement to slaves, and in exchange for that excessive and unseasonable liberty [c] has clothed itself in the garb of the most cruel and bitter servile servitude. [d]" "Yes indeed," he said, "that is just what happens." "Well, then," said I, "shall we not be fairly justified in saying that we have sufficiently described the transformation of a democracy into a tyranny and the nature of the tyranny itself?" "Quite sufficiently," he said.

Library) εἰς δὲ μονάρχου δῆμος ἀιδρείῃ δουλοσύνην ἔπεσεν, Herod. iii. 81 τυράννου ὕβριν φεύγοντας ἄνδρας ἐς δήμου ἀκολάστου ὕβριν πεσεῖν, and for the idea *Epist.* viii. 354 D.

[c] *Cf. Epist.* viii. 354 D.

[d] For the rhetorical style *cf. Tim.* 41 A θεοὶ θεῶν, *Polit.* 303 C σοφιστῶν σοφιστάς, and the biblical expressions, God of Gods and Lord of Lords, *e.g. Deut.* x. 17, *Ps.* cxxxvi. 2-3, *Dan.* xi. 36, *Rev.* xix. 16. *Cf.* Jebb on Soph. *O.T.* 1063 τρίδουλος.

571 I. Αὐτὸς δὴ λοιπός, ἦν δ' ἐγώ, ὁ τυραννικὸς
ἀνὴρ σκέψασθαι, πῶς τε μεθίσταται ἐκ δημοκρα-
τικοῦ, γενόμενός τε ποῖός τίς ἐστι καὶ τίνα τρόπον
ζῇ, ἄθλιον ἢ μακάριον. Λοιπὸς γὰρ οὖν ἔτι οὗτος,
ἔφη. Οἶσθ' οὖν, ἦν δ' ἐγώ, ὃ ποθῶ ἔτι; Τὸ
ποῖον; Τὸ τῶν ἐπιθυμιῶν, οἷαί τε καὶ ὅσαι εἰσίν,
οὔ μοι δοκοῦμεν ἱκανῶς διῃρῆσθαι. τούτου δὴ
B ἐνδεῶς ἔχοντος, ἀσαφεστέρα ἔσται ἡ ζήτησις οὗ
ζητοῦμεν. Οὐκοῦν, ἦ δ' ὅς, ἔτ' ἐν καλῷ[1]; Πάνυ
μὲν οὖν· καὶ σκόπει γ' ὃ ἐν αὐταῖς βούλομαι ἰδεῖν.
ἔστι δὲ τόδε. τῶν μὴ ἀναγκαίων ἡδονῶν τε καὶ
ἐπιθυμιῶν δοκοῦσί τινές μοι εἶναι παράνομοι, αἳ
κινδυνεύουσι μὲν ἐγγίγνεσθαι παντί, κολαζόμεναι
δὲ ὑπό τε τῶν νόμων καὶ τῶν βελτιόνων ἐπιθυμιῶν
μετὰ λόγου ἐνίων μὲν ἀνθρώπων ἢ παντάπασιν
ἀπαλλάττεσθαι ἢ ὀλίγαι λείπεσθαι καὶ ἀσθενεῖς,
C τῶν δὲ ἰσχυρότεραι καὶ πλείους. Λέγεις δὲ καὶ
τίνας, ἔφη, ταύτας; Τὰς περὶ τὸν ὕπνον, ἦν δ'

[1] ἐν καλῷ M and almost all editions : ἐγκαλῶ AFD, defended
by Apelt, *Berl. Phil. Woch.* 1895, p. 965.

---

[a] For ἐν καλῷ cf. Soph. *El.* 348, Eurip. *Heracleid.* 971,
Aristoph. *Eccl.* 321, *Thesm.* 292.
[b] *Cf.* on 558 D.
[c] For κολαζόμεναι cf. on 559 B, p. 293, note *c*.
[d] *Cf.* Aristot. *Eth. Nic.* 1102 b 5 ff. ὁ δ' ἀγαθὸς καὶ κακὸς

334

BOOK IX

I. " There remains for consideration," said I, " the tyrannical man himself—the manner of his development out of the democratic type and his character and the quality of his life, whether wretched or happy." " Why, yes, he still remains," he said. " Do you know, then, what it is that I still miss ? " " What ? " " In the matter of our desires I do not think we sufficiently distinguished their nature and number. And so long as this is lacking our inquiry will lack clearness." " Well," said he, " will our consideration of them not still be opportune[a] ? " " By all means. And observe what it is about them that I wish to consider. It is this. Of our unnecessary pleasures[b] and appetites there are some lawless ones, I think, which probably are to be found in us all, but which, when controlled[c] by the laws and the better desires in alliance with reason, can in some men be altogether got rid of, or so nearly so that only a few weak ones remain, while in others the remnant is stronger and more numerous." " What desires do you mean ? " he said. " Those," said I, " that are awakened in sleep[d] when

ἥκιστα διάδηλοι καθ᾽ ὕπνον, etc.; also his *Problem.* 957 a 21 ff. Cic. *De divin.* i. 29 translates this passage. *Cf.* further Herod. vi. 107, Soph. *O.T.* 981-982.

Hazlitt writes " We are not hypocrites in our sleep," a modern novelist, " In sleep all barriers are down."

The Freudians have at last discovered Plato's anticipation

335

571 ἐγώ, ἐγειρομένας, ὅταν τὸ μὲν ἄλλο τῆς ψυχῆς
εὕδῃ, ὅσον λογιστικὸν καὶ ἥμερον καὶ ἄρχον
ἐκείνου, τὸ δὲ θηριῶδές τε καὶ ἄγριον, ἢ σίτων ἢ
μέθης πλησθέν, σκιρτᾷ τε καὶ ἀπωσάμενον τὸν
ὕπνον ζητῇ ἰέναι καὶ ἀποπιμπλάναι τὰ αὑτοῦ ἤθη·
οἶσθ' ὅτι πάντα ἐν τῷ τοιούτῳ τολμᾷ ποιεῖν, ὡς
ἀπὸ πάσης λελυμένον τε καὶ ἀπηλλαγμένον αἰσχύ-
νης καὶ φρονήσεως. μητρί τε γὰρ ἐπιχειρεῖν
D μίγνυσθαι, ὡς οἴεται, οὐδὲν ὀκνεῖ, ἄλλῳ τε ὁτῳοῦν
ἀνθρώπων καὶ θεῶν καὶ θηρίων, μιαιφονεῖν τε
ὁτιοῦν, βρώματός τε ἀπέχεσθαι μηδενός· καὶ ἑνὶ
λόγῳ οὔτε ἀνοίας οὐδὲν ἐλλείπει οὔτ' ἀναισχυντίας.
Ἀληθέστατα, ἔφη, λέγεις. Ὅταν δέ γε, οἶμαι,
ὑγιεινῶς τις ἔχῃ αὐτὸς αὑτοῦ καὶ σωφρόνως, καὶ
εἰς τὸν ὕπνον ἴῃ τὸ λογιστικὸν μὲν ἐγείρας ἑαυτοῦ
καὶ ἑστιάσας λόγων καλῶν καὶ σκέψεων, εἰς
σύννοιαν αὐτὸς αὑτῷ ἀφικόμενος, τὸ ἐπιθυμητικὸν
E δὲ μήτε ἐνδείᾳ δοὺς μήτε πλησμονῇ, ὅπως ἂν

---

of their main thesis. *Cf.* Trotter, *Instincts of the Herd in
Peace and War*, p. 74: " It has been perhaps Freud's most
remarkable thesis that dreams are manifestations of this
emergence of desires and memories from the unconscious
into the conscious field." " The barriers of the Freudian
unconscious are less tightly closed during sleep " senten-
tiously observes an eminent modern psychologist. *Cf.*
Valentine, *The New Psychology of the Unconscious*, p. xiii.
and *ibid.* p. 93: " Freud refers to Plato's view that the
virtuous man contents himself with dreaming that which the
wicked man does in actual life, but I believe he nowhere shows
a knowledge of the following passage in the *Republic*. . . ."
Cf. ibid. p. 95: " The germ of several aspects of the Freudian
view of dreams, including the characteristic doctrine of the
censor, was to be found in Plato. The Freudian view
becomes at once distinctly more respectable."

the rest of the soul, the rational, gentle and dominant part, slumbers, but the beastly and savage part, replete with food and wine, gambols and, repelling sleep, endeavours to sally forth and satisfy its own instincts.[a] You are aware that in such case there is nothing it will not venture to undertake as being released from all sense of shame and all reason. It does not shrink from attempting to lie with a mother in fancy or with anyone else, man, god or brute. It is ready for any foul deed of blood; it abstains from no food, and, in a word, falls short of no extreme of folly[b] and shamelessness." "Most true," he said. "But when, I suppose, a man's condition is healthy and sober, and he goes to sleep after arousing his rational part and entertaining it with fair words and thoughts, and attaining to clear self-consciousness, while he has neither starved nor indulged to repletion his appeti-

Many of the ancients, like some superstitious moderns, exalted the unconscious which reveals itself in dreams, and made it the source of prophecy. *Cf.* commentators on Aesch. *Eumen.* 104, Pindar, *fr.* 131 (96) Loeb, p. 589: εὕδει δὲ πρασσόντων μελέων, ἀτὰρ εὑδόντεσσιν ἐν πολλοῖς ὀνείροις δείκνυσι τέρπνων ἐφέρποισαν χαλεπῶν τε κρίσιν, "but it sleepeth while the limbs are active; yet to them that sleep, in many a dream it giveth presage of a decision of things delightful or doleful." (Sandys, Loeb tr.) *Cf.* Pausan. ix. 23, Cic. *De div.* i. 30, Sir Thomas Browne, *Religio Medici*, pp. 105-107 (ed. J. A. Symonds). Plato did not share these superstitions. *Cf.* the irony of *Tim.* 71 D-E, and my review of Stewart's "Myths of Plato," *Journal of Philos. Psychol. and Scientific Methods*, vol. iii., 1906, pp. 495-498.

[a] The Greeks had no good word for instinct, but there are passages in Plato where this translation is justified by the context for ἦθος, φύσις and such words.

[b] For the idiom οὐδὲν ἐλλείπει *cf.* Soph. *Trach.* 90, Demosth. liv. 34. *Cf.* also 602 D and on 533 A, p. 200, note *b*.

572 κοιμηθῇ καὶ μὴ παρέχῃ θόρυβον τῷ βελτίστῳ
χαῖρον ἢ λυπούμενον, ἀλλ' ἐᾷ αὐτὸ καθ' αὑτὸ
μόνον καθαρὸν σκοπεῖν καὶ ὀρέγεσθαί του καὶ
αἰσθάνεσθαι ὃ μὴ οἶδεν, ἤ τι τῶν γεγονότων ἢ
ὄντων ἢ καὶ μελλόντων, ὡσαύτως δὲ καὶ τὸ
θυμοειδὲς πραΰνας καὶ μή τισιν εἰς ὀργὰς ἐλθὼν
κεκινημένῳ τῷ θυμῷ καθεύδῃ, ἀλλ' ἡσυχάσας μὲν
τὼ δύο εἴδη, τὸ τρίτον δὲ κινήσας, ἐν ᾧ τὸ φρονεῖν
ἐγγίγνεται, οὕτως ἀναπαύηται, οἶσθ' ὅτι τῆς τ'
ἀληθείας ἐν τῷ τοιούτῳ μάλιστα ἅπτεται καὶ
B ἥκιστα παράνομοι τότε αἱ ὄψεις φαντάζονται τῶν
ἐνυπνίων. Παντελῶς μὲν οὖν, ἔφη, οἶμαι οὕτως.
Ταῦτα μὲν τοίνυν ἐπὶ πλέον ἐξήχθημεν εἰπεῖν· ὃ δὲ
βουλόμεθα γνῶναι, τόδ' ἐστίν, ὡς ἄρα δεινόν τι καὶ
ἄγριον καὶ ἄνομον ἐπιθυμιῶν εἶδος ἑκάστῳ ἔνεστι,
καὶ πάνυ δοκοῦσιν ἡμῶν ἐνίοις μετρίοις εἶναι·
τοῦτο δὲ ἄρα ἐν τοῖς ὕπνοις γίγνεται ἔνδηλον. εἰ
οὖν τὶ δοκῶ λέγειν καὶ ξυγχωρεῖς, ἄθρει. Ἀλλὰ
ξυγχωρῶ.

---

[a] Cf. Browning, *Bishop Blougram's Apology*, "And body gets its sop and holds its noise."

Plato was no ascetic, as some have inferred from passages in the *Republic, Laws, Gorgias,* and *Phaedo. Cf.* Herbert L. Stewart, "Was Plato an Ascetic?" *Philos. Rev.,* 1915, pp. 603-613; Dean Inge, *Christian Ethics,* p. 90: "The asceticism of the true Platonist has always been sane and moderate; the hallmark of Platonism is a combination of self-restraint and simplicity with humanism."

[b] Cf. *Ephesians* iv. 26 "Let not the sun go down upon your wrath."

[c] ἐν τῷ τοιούτῳ: cf. 382 B, 465 A, 470 C, 492 C, 590 A, *Lysis* 212 c, *Laws* 625 D.

[d] This sentence contains 129 words. George Moore says, "Pater's complaint that Plato's sentences are long may be regarded as Pater's single excursion into humour." But

tive part, so that it may be lulled to sleep [a] and not disturb the better part by its pleasure or pain, but may suffer that in isolated purity to examine and reach out towards and apprehend some of the things unknown to it, past, present or future ; and when he has in like manner tamed his passionate part, and does not after a quarrel fall asleep [b] with anger still awake within him, but if he has thus quieted the two elements in his soul and quickened the third, in which reason resides, and so goes to his rest, you are aware that in such case [c] he is most likely to apprehend truth, and the visions of his dreams are least likely to be lawless." [d]   "I certainly think so," he said. "This description has carried us too far,[e] but the point that we have to notice is this, that in fact there exists in every one of us, even in some reputed most respectable,[f] a terrible, fierce and lawless brood of desires, which it seems are revealed in our sleep. Consider, then, whether there is anything in what I say, and whether you admit it."   "Well, I do."

Pater is in fact justifying his own long sentences by Plato's example.   He calls this passage Plato's evening prayer.

[e] Plato always returns to the point after a digression. Cf. 543 c, 471 c, 544 B, 568 D, 588 B, Phaedo 78 B, Theaet. 177 c, Protag. 359 A, Crat. 438 A, Polit. 287 A-B, 263 c, 302 B, Laws 682 E, 697 c, 864 c, and many other passages. Cf. also Lysias ii. 61 ἀλλὰ ταῦτα μὲν ἐξήχθην, Demosth. De cor. 211, Aristot. De an. 403 b 16, also p. 193, note i, and Plato's carefulness in keeping to the point under discussion in 353 c, Theaet. 182 c, 206 c, Meno 93 A-B, Gorg. 479 D-E, 459 c-D, etc.

[f] For the irony of the expression cf. Laws 633 D, Aesch. Eumen. 373, and for the thought Othello III. iii. 138 :

> who has a breast so pure
> But some uncleanly apprehensions
> Keep leets and law-days, and in session sit
> With meditations lawful?

572 II. Τὸν τοίνυν δημοτικὸν ἀναμνήσθητι οἷον
C ἔφαμεν εἶναι. ἦν δέ που γεγονὼς ἐκ νέου ὑπὸ
φειδωλῷ πατρὶ τεθραμμένος, τὰς χρηματιστικὰς
ἐπιθυμίας τιμῶντι μόνας, τὰς δὲ μὴ ἀναγκαίους,
ἀλλὰ παιδιᾶς τε καὶ καλλωπισμοῦ ἕνεκα γιγνο-
μένας, ἀτιμάζοντι. ἦ γάρ; Ναί. Συγγενόμενος
δὲ κομψοτέροις ἀνδράσι καὶ μεστοῖς ὧν ἄρτι
διήλθομεν ἐπιθυμιῶν, ὁρμήσας εἰς ὕβριν τε πᾶσαν
καὶ τὸ ἐκείνων εἶδος μίσει τῆς τοῦ πατρὸς φειδω-
λίας, φύσιν δὲ τῶν διαφθειρόντων βελτίω ἔχων,
D ἀγόμενος ἀμφοτέρωσε κατέστη εἰς μέσον ἀμφοῖν
τοῖν τρόποιν, καὶ μετρίως δή, ὡς ᾤετο, ἑκάστων
ἀπολαύων οὔτε ἀνελεύθερον οὔτε παράνομον βίον
ζῇ, δημοτικὸς ἐξ ὀλιγαρχικοῦ γεγονώς. Ἦν γὰρ
ἔφη, καὶ ἔστιν αὕτη ἡ δόξα περὶ τὸν τοιοῦτον.
Θὲς τοίνυν, ἦν δ᾽ ἐγώ, πάλιν τοῦ τοιούτου ἤδη
πρεσβυτέρου γεγονότος νέον υἱὸν ἐν τοῖς τούτου
αὖ ἤθεσι τεθραμμένον. Τίθημι. Τίθει τοίνυν καὶ
τὰ αὐτὰ ἐκεῖνα περὶ αὐτὸν γιγνόμενα, ἅπερ καὶ
E περὶ τὸν πατέρα αὐτοῦ, ἀγόμενόν τε εἰς πᾶσαν
παρανομίαν, ὀνομαζομένην δ᾽ ὑπὸ τῶν ἀγόντων
ἐλευθερίαν ἅπασαν, βοηθοῦντά τε ταῖς ἐν μέσῳ
ταύταις ἐπιθυμίαις πατέρα τε καὶ τοὺς ἄλλους
οἰκείους, τοὺς δ᾽ αὖ παραβοηθοῦντας· ὅταν δ᾽
ἐλπίσωσιν οἱ δεινοὶ μάγοι τε καὶ τυραννοποιοὶ
οὗτοι μὴ ἄλλως τὸν νέον καθέξειν, ἔρωτά τινα
αὐτῷ μηχανωμένους ἐμποιῆσαι προστάτην τῶν

ᵃ Cf. 559 D f.

ᵇ εἰς μέσον : cf. p. 249, note f.

ᶜ Ironical δή. See p. 300, note a. Cf. modern satire on
" moderate " drinking and " moderate " preparedness.

ᵈ ὡς ᾤετο is another ironical formula like ἵνα δή, ὡς ἄρα, etc.

II. "Now recall [a] our characterization of the democratic man. His development was determined by his education from youth under a thrifty father who approved only the acquisitive appetites and disapproved the unnecessary ones whose object is entertainment and display. Is not that so?" "Yes." "And by association with more sophisticated men, teeming with the appetites we have just described, he is impelled towards every form of insolence and outrage, and to the adoption of their way of life by his hatred of his father's niggardliness. But since his nature is better than that of his corrupters, being drawn both ways he settles down in a compromise [b] between the two tendencies, and indulging and enjoying each in moderation, forsooth,[c] as he supposes,[d] he lives what he deems a life that is neither illiberal nor lawless, now transformed from an oligarch to a democrat." "That was and is our belief about this type." "Assume,[e] then, again," said I, "that such a man when he is older has a son bred in turn [f] in his ways of life." "I so assume." "And suppose the experience of his father to be repeated in his case. He is drawn toward utter lawlessness, which is called by his seducers complete freedom. His father and his other kin lend support to [g] these compromise appetites while the others lend theirs to the opposite group. And when these dread magi [h] and king-makers come to realize that they have no hope of controlling the youth in any other way, they contrive to engender in

---

[e] θές: cf. *Theaet.* 191 c, *Phileb.* 33 D.

[f] This is the αὖ of the succession of the generations. *Cf.* p. 247, note *f*.

[g] *Cf.* 559 E.

[h] An overlooked reference to the Magi who set up the false Smerdis. *Cf.* Herod. iii. 61 ff.

573 ἀργῶν καὶ τὰ ἕτοιμα διανεμομένων ἐπιθυμιῶν,
ὑπόπτερον καὶ μέγαν κηφῆνά τινα· ἢ τι[1] ἄλλο οἴει
εἶναι τὸν τῶν τοιούτων ἔρωτα; Οὐδὲν ἔγωγε, ἦ
δ᾽ ὅς, ἀλλ᾽ ἢ τοῦτο. Οὐκοῦν ὅταν περὶ αὐτὸν
βομβοῦσαι αἱ ἄλλαι ἐπιθυμίαι, θυμιαμάτων τε
γέμουσαι καὶ μύρων καὶ στεφάνων καὶ οἴνων καὶ
τῶν ἐν ταῖς τοιαύταις συνουσίαις ἡδονῶν ἀνει-
μένων, ἐπὶ τὸ ἔσχατον αὔξουσαί τε καὶ τρέφουσαι
πόθου κέντρον ἐμποιήσωσι τῷ κηφῆνι, τότε δὴ
B δορυφορεῖταί τε ὑπὸ μανίας καὶ οἰστρᾷ οὗτος ὁ
προστάτης τῆς ψυχῆς, καὶ ἐάν τινας ἐν αὐτῷ δόξας
ἢ ἐπιθυμίας λάβῃ ποιουμένας χρηστὰς καὶ ἔτι
ἐπαισχυνομένας, ἀποκτείνει τε καὶ ἔξω ὠθεῖ παρ᾽
αὐτοῦ, ἕως ἂν καθήρῃ σωφροσύνης, μανίας[2] δὲ
πληρώσῃ ἐπακτοῦ. Παντελῶς, ἔφη, τυραννικοῦ
ἀνδρὸς λέγεις γένεσιν. Ἆρ᾽ οὖν, ἦν δ᾽ ἐγώ, καὶ τὸ
πάλαι διὰ τὸ τοιοῦτον τύραννος ὁ Ἔρως λέγεται;
Κινδυνεύει, ἔφη. Οὐκοῦν, ὦ φίλε, εἶπον, καὶ
C μεθυσθεὶς ἀνὴρ τυραννικόν τι φρόνημα ἴσχει;
Ἴσχει γάρ. Καὶ μὴν ὅ γε μαινόμενος καὶ ὑπο-
κεκινηκὼς οὐ μόνον ἀνθρώπων ἀλλὰ καὶ θεῶν
ἐπιχειρεῖ τε καὶ ἐλπίζει δυνατὸς εἶναι ἄρχειν.
Καὶ μάλ᾽, ἔφη. Τυραννικὸς δέ, ἦν δ᾽ ἐγώ, ὦ

---

[1] ἤ τι A : ἢ τί FDM.   [2] μανίας FD : καὶ μανίας AM.

---

[a] Cf. Symp. 205 D.
[b] προστάτην: cf. 562 D and 565 C-D.
[c] For τὰ ἕτοιμα cf. 552 B, Symp. 200 D and E, and Horace, Odes i. 31. 17 "frui paratis."
[d] Cf. Alc. I. 135 E ἔρωτα ὑπόπτερον and the fragment of Eubulus (fr. 41, Kock ii. p. 178):

> τίς ἦν ὁ γράψας πρῶτος ἀνθρώπων ἄρα
> ἢ κηροπλαστήσας Ἔρωθ᾽ ὑπόπτερον;

his soul a ruling passion [a] to be the protector [b] of his idle and prodigal [c] appetites, a monstrous winged [d] drone. Or do you think the spirit of desire in such men is aught else?" "Nothing but that," he said. "And when the other appetites, buzzing [e] about it, replete with incense and myrrh and chaplets and wine, and the pleasures that are released in such revelries, magnifying and fostering it to the utmost, awaken in the drone the sting of unsatisfied yearnings,[f] why then this protector of the soul has madness for his bodyguard and runs amuck,[g] and if it finds in the man any opinions or appetites accounted [h] worthy and still capable of shame, it slays them and thrusts them forth until it purges [i] him of sobriety, and fills and infects him with frenzy brought in from outside.[j]" "A perfect description," he said, "of the generation of the tyrannical man." "And is not this analogy," said I, "the reason why Love has long since been called a tyrant [k]?" "That may well be," he said. "And does not a drunken man,[l] my friend," I said, "have something of this tyrannical temper?" "Yes, he has." "And again the madman, the deranged man, attempts and expects to rule over not only men but gods." "Yes indeed, he does," he said. "Then a man becomes

---

[e] Cf. 564 D.

[f] Cf. *Phaedrus* 253 E.

[g] For οἴστρῳ cf. *Phaedr.* 240 D.

[h] For ποιουμένας in this sense cf. 538 C, 498 A, 574 D.

[i] Cf. on 560 D, p. 299, note c.

[j] ἐπακτοῦ: cf. 405 B, Pindar, *Pyth.* vi. 10, Aesch. *Seven against Thebes* 583, Soph. *Trach.* 259.

[k] Cf. 573 D, Eurip. *Hippol.* 538, *Andromeda, fr.* 136 (Nauck) θεῶν τύραννε . . . Ἔρως, and *What Plato Said*, p. 546 on *Symp.* 197 B.

[l] For drunkenness as a tyrannical mood cf. *Laws* 649 B, 671 B, *Phaedr.* 238 B.

573 δαιμόνιε, ἀνὴρ ἀκριβῶς γίγνεται, ὅταν ἢ φύσει ἢ
ἐπιτηδεύμασιν ἢ ἀμφοτέροις μεθυστικός τε καὶ
ἐρωτικὸς καὶ μελαγχολικὸς γένηται. Παντελῶς
μὲν οὖν.

III. Γίγνεται μέν, ὡς ἔοικεν, οὕτω καὶ τοιοῦτος
ἀνήρ· ζῇ δὲ δὴ πῶς; Τὸ τῶν παιζόντων, ἔφη,
D τοῦτο σὺ καὶ ἐμοὶ ἐρεῖς. Λέγω δή, ἔφην. οἶμαι
γὰρ τὸ μετὰ τοῦτο ἑορταὶ γίγνονται παρ' αὐτοῖς
καὶ κῶμοι καὶ θάλειαι καὶ ἑταῖραι καὶ τὰ τοιαῦτα
πάντα, ὧν ἂν Ἔρως τύραννος ἔνδον οἰκῶν δια-
κυβερνᾷ τὰ τῆς ψυχῆς ἅπαντα. Ἀνάγκη, ἔφη.
Ἆρ' οὖν οὐ πολλαὶ καὶ δειναὶ παραβλαστάνουσιν
ἐπιθυμίαι ἡμέρας τε καὶ νυκτὸς ἑκάστης, πολλῶν
δεόμεναι; Πολλαὶ μέντοι. Ταχὺ ἄρα ἀναλίσκον-
ται, ἐάν τινες ὦσι πρόσοδοι. Πῶς δ' οὔ; Καὶ μετὰ
E τοῦτο δὴ δανεισμοὶ καὶ τῆς οὐσίας παραιρέσεις.
Τί μήν; Ὅταν δὲ δὴ πάντ' ἐπιλείπῃ, ἆρα οὐκ
ἀνάγκη μὲν τὰς ἐπιθυμίας βοᾶν πυκνάς τε καὶ
σφοδρὰς ἐννενεοττευμένας, τοὺς δ' ὥσπερ ὑπὸ
κέντρων ἐλαυνομένους τῶν τε ἄλλων ἐπιθυμιῶν
καὶ διαφερόντως ὑπ' αὐτοῦ τοῦ ἔρωτος, πάσαις ταῖς
ἄλλαις ὥσπερ δορυφόροις ἡγουμένου, οἰστρᾶν καὶ
σκοπεῖν, τίς τι ἔχει, ὃν δυνατὸν ἀφελέσθαι ἀπατή-
574 σαντα ἢ βιασάμενον; Σφόδρα γ', ἔφη. Ἀναγκαῖον
δὴ πανταχόθεν φέρειν, ἢ μεγάλαις ὠδῖσί τε καὶ

---

[a] Cf. Adam ad loc., who insists it means *his* origin as well
as that of others, and says his character is still to be
described. But it has been in c and before.
[b] Cf. Phileb. 25 B and perhaps Rep. 427 E with 449 D.
The slight jest is a commonplace to-day. Wilamowitz, *Platon*,
ii. p. 351, says it is a fragment of an elegy. He forgets the
Philebus.

tyrannical in the full sense of the word, my friend,"
I said, " when either by nature or by habits or by
both he has become even as the drunken, the erotic,
the maniacal." " Assuredly."

III. " Such, it seems, is his origin and character,[a]
but what is his manner of life ? " " As the wits say,
you shall tell *me*.[b] " " I do," I said ; " for, I take it,
next there are among them feasts and carousals and
revellings and courtesans [c] and all the doings of those
whose [d] souls are entirely swayed [e] by the indwelling
tyrant Eros." " Inevitably," he said. " And do not
many and dread appetites shoot up beside this master
passion every day and night in need of many things ? "
" Many indeed." " And so any revenues there may
be are quickly expended." " Of course." " And
after this there are borrowings and levyings [f] upon
the estate ? " " Of course." " And when all these
resources fail, must there not come a cry from the
frequent and fierce nestlings [g] of desire hatched in his
soul, and must not such men, urged, as it were by
goads, by the other desires, and especially by the
ruling passion itself as captain of their bodyguard—
to keep up the figure—must they not run wild and
look to see who has aught that can be taken from
him by deceit or violence ? " " Most certainly."
" And so he is compelled to sweep it in from every

---

[c] *Cf.* Vol. I. p. 160, note *a*, on 373 A. Emendations are
superfluous.

[d] ὧν ἄν: *cf.* 441 D-E ὅτου, etc., 583 A ἐν ᾧ, and my review
of Jowett and Campbell, *A.J.P.* xvi. p. 237.

[e] *Cf. Phaedr.* 238 B-C.

[f] For παραιρέσεις *cf.* Thuc. i. 122. 1, Aristot. *Pol.* 1311 a 12,
1315 a 38.

[g] ἐννενεοττευμένας: *cf. Alc.* I. 135 E, *Laws* 776 A, 949 c,
Aristoph. *Birds* 699, 1108.

574 ὀδύναις ξυνέχεσθαι. Ἀναγκαῖον. Ἆρ᾽ οὖν, ὥσπερ
αἱ ἐν αὐτῷ ἡδοναὶ ἐπιγιγνόμεναι τῶν ἀρχαίων
πλέον εἶχον καὶ τὰ ἐκείνων ἀφῃροῦντο, οὕτω καὶ
αὐτὸς ἀξιώσει νεώτερος ὢν πατρός τε καὶ μητρὸς
πλέον ἔχειν καὶ ἀφαιρεῖσθαι, ἐὰν τὸ αὑτοῦ μέρος
ἀναλώσῃ, ἀπονειμάμενος τῶν πατρῴων; Ἀλλὰ
τί μήν; ἔφη. Ἂν δὲ δὴ αὐτῷ μὴ ἐπιτρέπωσιν,
B ἆρ᾽ οὐ τὸ μὲν πρῶτον ἐπιχειροῖ ἂν κλέπτειν καὶ
ἀπατᾶν τοὺς γονέας; Πάντως. Ὁπότε δὲ μὴ
δύναιτο, ἁρπάζοι ἂν καὶ βιάζοιτο μετὰ τοῦτο;
Οἶμαι, ἔφη. Ἀντεχομένων δὴ καὶ μαχομένων, ὦ
θαυμάσιε, γέροντός τε καὶ γραός, ἆρ᾽ εὐλαβηθείη
ἂν καὶ φείσαιτο μή τι δρᾶσαι τῶν τυραννικῶν; Οὐ
πάνυ, ἦ δ᾽ ὅς, ἔγωγε θαρρῶ περὶ τῶν γονέων τοῦ
τοιούτου. Ἀλλ᾽, ὦ Ἀδείμαντε, πρὸς Διός, ἕνεκα
νεωστὶ φίλης καὶ οὐκ ἀναγκαίας ἑταίρας γεγονυίας
C τὴν πάλαι φίλην καὶ ἀναγκαίαν μητέρα, ἢ ἕνεκα
ὡραίου νεωστὶ φίλου γεγονότος οὐκ ἀναγκαίου τὸν
ἄωρόν τε καὶ ἀναγκαῖον πρεσβύτην πατέρα καὶ
τῶν φίλων ἀρχαιότατον δοκεῖ ἄν σοι ὁ τοιοῦτος
πληγαῖς τε δοῦναι καὶ καταδουλώσασθαι ἂν αὐτοὺς
ὑπ᾽ ἐκείνοις, εἰ εἰς τὴν αὐτὴν οἰκίαν ἀγάγοιτο;
Ναὶ μὰ Δί᾽, ἦ δ᾽ ὅς. Σφόδρα γε μακάριον, ἦν δ᾽
ἐγώ, ἔοικεν εἶναι τὸ τυραννικὸν υἱὸν τεκεῖν. Πάνυ
γ᾽, ἔφη. Τί δ᾽, ὅταν δὴ τὰ πατρὸς καὶ μητρὸς

---

[a] Cf. Aesch. Eumen. 554.
[b] Cf. Gorg. 494 A ἢ τὰς ἐσχάτας λυποῖτο λύπας.
[c] Cf. Vol. I. 349 B f.
[d] The word ἀναγκαίαν means both "necessary" and "akin." Cf. Eurip. Androm. 671 τοιαῦτα λάσκεις τοὺς ἀναγκαίους φίλους.
[e] For the idiom πληγαῖς ... δοῦναι cf. Phaedr. 254 E

source[a] or else be afflicted with great travail and pain.[b]" "He is." "And just as the new, upspringing pleasures in him got the better of the original passions of his soul and robbed them, so he himself, though younger, will claim the right to get the better[c] of his father and mother, and, after spending his own share, to seize and convert to his own use a portion of his father's estate." "Of course," he said, "what else?" "And if they resist him, would he not at first attempt to rob and steal from his parents and deceive them?" "Certainly." "And if he failed in that, would he not next seize it by force?" "I think so," he said. "And then, good sir, if the old man and the old woman clung to it and resisted him, would he be careful to refrain from the acts of a tyrant?" "I am not without my fears," he said, "for the parents of such a one." "Nay, Adeimantus, in heaven's name, do you suppose that, for the sake of a newly found *belle amie* bound to him by no necessary tie, such a one would strike the dear mother, his by necessity[d] and from his birth? Or for the sake of a blooming new-found *bel ami*, not necessary to his life, he would rain blows[e] upon the aged father past his prime, closest of his kin and oldest of his friends? And would he subject them to those new favourites if he brought them under the same roof?" "Yes, by Zeus," he said. "A most blessed lot it seems to be," said I, "to be the parent of a tyrant son." "It does indeed," he said. "And again, when the resources of his father and mother are exhausted[f] and

ὀδύναις ἔδωκεν with Thompson's note. *Cf. 566* c θανάτῳ δέδοται. For striking his father *cf. supra 569* B, *Laws* 880 E ff., Aristoph. *Clouds* 1375 ff., 1421 ff.
[f] For ἐπιλείπῃ *cf.* 568 E, 573 E.

574 D ἐπιλείπῃ τὸν τοιοῦτον, πολὺ δὲ ἤδη ξυνειλεγμένον
ἐν αὐτῷ ᾖ τὸ τῶν ἡδονῶν σμῆνος, οὗ πρῶτον μὲν
οἰκίας τινὸς ἐφάψεται τοίχου ἤ τινος ὀψὲ νύκτωρ
ἰόντος τοῦ ἱματίου, μετὰ δὲ ταῦτα ἱερόν τι νεωκορήσει; καὶ ἐν τούτοις δὴ πᾶσιν, ἃς πάλαι εἶχε
δόξας ἐκ παιδὸς περὶ καλῶν τε καὶ αἰσχρῶν, τὰς
δικαίας ποιουμένας, αἱ νεωστὶ ἐκ δουλείας λελυ-
μέναι, δορυφοροῦσαι τὸν ἔρωτα, κρατήσουσι μετ'
ἐκείνου, αἱ πρότερον μὲν ὄναρ ἐλύοντο ἐν ὕπνῳ,
E ὅτε ἦν αὐτὸς ἔτι ὑπὸ νόμοις τε καὶ πατρὶ δημοκρα-
τούμενος ἐν ἑαυτῷ· τυραννευθεὶς δὲ ὑπὸ ἔρωτος,
οἷος ὀλιγάκις ἐγίγνετο ὄναρ, ὕπαρ τοιοῦτος ἀεὶ
γενόμενος, οὔτε τινὸς φόνου δεινοῦ ἀφέξεται οὔτε
575 βρώματος οὔτ' ἔργου, ἀλλὰ τυραννικῶς ἐν αὐτῷ ὁ
ἔρως ἐν πάσῃ ἀναρχίᾳ καὶ ἀνομίᾳ ζῶν, ἅτε αὐτὸς
ὢν μόναρχος, τὸν ἔχοντά τε αὐτὸν ὥσπερ πόλιν
ἄξει ἐπὶ πᾶσαν τόλμαν, ὅθεν αὐτόν τε καὶ τὸν περὶ
αὐτὸν θόρυβον θρέψει, τὸν μὲν ἔξωθεν εἰσεληλυθότα
ἀπὸ κακῆς ὁμιλίας, τὸν δ' ἔνδοθεν ὑπὸ τῶν αὐτῶν
τρόπων καὶ ἑαυτοῦ ἀνεθέντα καὶ ἐλευθερωθέντα.
ἢ οὐχ οὗτος ὁ βίος τοῦ τοιούτου; Οὗτος μὲν οὖν,
ἔφη. Καὶ ἂν μέν γε, ἦν δ' ἐγώ, ὀλίγοι οἱ τοιοῦτοι
B ἐν πόλει ὦσι καὶ τὸ ἄλλο πλῆθος σωφρονῇ,

ᵃ Cf. Meno 72 ᴀ, Cratyl. 401 ᴇ, Blaydes on Aristoph.
Clouds 297.
ᵇ He becomes a τοιχωρύχος or a λωποδύτης (Aristoph.
Frogs 772-773, Birds 497, Clouds 1327). Cf. 575 ʙ, Laws
831 ᴇ.
ᶜ νεωκορήσει is an ironical litotes. So ἐφάψεται in the preceding line.
ᵈ For ποιουμένας cf. 573 ʙ. For the thought cf. 538 c.

fail such a one, and the swarm *a* of pleasures collected in his soul is grown great, will he not first lay hands on the wall *b* of someone's house or the cloak of someone who walks late at night, and thereafter he will make a clean sweep *c* of some temple, and in all these actions the beliefs which he held from boyhood about the honourable and the base, the opinions accounted just, *d* will be overmastered by the opinions newly emancipated *e* and released, which, serving as bodyguards of the ruling passion, will prevail in alliance with it—I mean the opinions that formerly were freed from restraint in sleep, when, being still under the control of his father and the laws, he maintained the democratic constitution in his soul. But now, when under the tyranny of his ruling passion, he is continuously and in waking hours what he rarely became in sleep, and he will refrain from no atrocity of murder nor from any food or deed, but the passion that dwells in him as a tyrant will live in utmost anarchy and lawlessness, and, since it is itself sole autocrat, will urge the polity, *f* so to speak, of him in whom it dwells *g* to dare anything and everything in order to find support for himself and the hubbub of his henchmen, *h* in part introduced from outside by evil associations, and in part released and liberated within by the same habits of life as his. Is not this the life of such a one ? " " It is this," he said. " And if," I said, " there are only a few of this kind in a city, and the others, the multitude as a whole, are sober-

---

e *Cf.* 567 E.

f *Cf.* on 591 E.

g τὸν ἔχοντα: *cf. Phaedr.* 239 C, *Laws* 837 B, Soph. *Antig.* 790 and also *Rep.* 610 C and E.

h For the tyrant's companions *cf.* Newman, i. p. 274, note 1.

575 ἐξελθόντες ἄλλον τινὰ δορυφοροῦσι τύραννον ἢ
μισθοῦ ἐπικουροῦσιν, ἐάν που πόλεμος ᾖ· ἐὰν δ'
ἐν εἰρήνῃ τε καὶ ἡσυχίᾳ γένωνται, αὐτοῦ δὴ ἐν τῇ
πόλει κακὰ δρῶσι σμικρὰ πολλά. Τὰ ποῖα δὴ
λέγεις; Οἷα κλέπτουσι, τοιχωρυχοῦσι, βαλαντιο-
τομοῦσι, λωποδυτοῦσιν, ἱεροσυλοῦσιν, ἀνδραπο-
δίζονται· ἔστι δ' ὅτε συκοφαντοῦσιν, ἐὰν δυνατοὶ
ὦσι λέγειν, καὶ ψευδομαρτυροῦσι καὶ δωροδο-
C κοῦσιν. Σμικρά γ', ἔφη, κακὰ λέγεις, ἐὰν ὀλίγοι
ὦσιν οἱ τοιοῦτοι. Τὰ γὰρ σμικρά, ἦν δ' ἐγώ, πρὸς
τὰ μεγάλα σμικρά ἐστι, καὶ ταῦτα δὴ πάντα πρὸς
τύραννον πονηρίᾳ τε καὶ ἀθλιότητι πόλεως, τὸ
λεγόμενον, οὐδ' ἴκταρ βάλλει. ὅταν γὰρ δὴ πολλοὶ
ἐν πόλει γένωνται οἱ τοιοῦτοι καὶ ἄλλοι οἱ ξυν-
επόμενοι αὐτοῖς, καὶ αἴσθωνται ἑαυτῶν τὸ πλῆθος,
τότε οὗτοί εἰσιν οἱ τὸν τύραννον γεννῶντες μετὰ
δήμου ἀνοίας ἐκεῖνον, ὃς ἂν αὐτῶν μάλιστα αὐτὸς
D ἐν αὑτῷ μέγιστον καὶ πλεῖστον ἐν τῇ ψυχῇ τύραννον ἔχῃ. Εἰκότως γ', ἔφη· τυραννικώτατος γὰρ
ἂν εἴη. Οὐκοῦν ἐὰν μὲν ἑκόντες ὑπείκωσιν· ἐὰν
δὲ μὴ ἐπιτρέπῃ ἡ πόλις, ὥσπερ τότε μητέρα καὶ
πατέρα ἐκόλαζεν, οὕτω πάλιν τὴν πατρίδα, ἐὰν
οἷός τ' ᾖ, κολάσεται ἐπεισαγόμενος νέους ἑταίρους,
καὶ ὑπὸ τούτοις δὴ δουλεύουσαν τὴν πάλαι φίλην

---

[a] Cf. the similar lists of crimes in Görg. 508 E, Xen. Mem.
i. 2. 62.
[b] So Shaw and other moderns argue in a somewhat
different tone that crimes of this sort are an unimportant
matter.

minded, the few go forth into exile and serve some tyrant elsewhere as bodyguard or become mercenaries in any war there may be. But if they spring up in time of peace and tranquillity they stay right there in the city and effect many small evils." "What kind of evils do you mean?" "Oh, they just steal, break into houses, cut purses, strip men of their garments, plunder temples, and kidnap,[a] and if they are fluent speakers they become sycophants and bear false witness and take bribes." "Yes, small evils indeed,[b]" he said, "if the men of this sort are few." "Why, yes," I said, "for small evils are relatively small compared with great, and in respect of the corruption and misery of a state all of them together, as the saying goes, don't come within hail [c] of the mischief done by a tyrant. For when men of this sort and their followers become numerous in a state and realize their numbers, then it is they who, in conjunction with the folly of the people, create a tyrant out of that one of them who has the greatest and mightiest tyrant in his own soul." "Naturally," he said, "for he would be the most tyrannical." "Then if the people yield willingly—'tis well,[d] but if the city resists him, then, just as in the previous case the man chastized his mother and his father, so now in turn will he chastize his fatherland if he can, bringing in new boon companions beneath whose sway he will hold and keep enslaved his once dear mother-

---

[c] οὐδ' ἴκταρ βάλλει was proverbial, "doesn't strike near," "doesn't come within range." Cf. Aelian, N.A. xv. 29. Cf. also οὐδ' ἐγγύς, Symp. 198 B, 221 D, Herod. ii. 121, Demosth. De cor. 97.

[d] In the Greek the apodosis is suppressed. Cf. Protag. 325 D. Adam refers to Herwerden, Mn. xix. pp. 338 f.

575 μητρίδα τε, Κρῆτές φασι, καὶ πατρίδα ἔξει τε καὶ
θρέψει· καὶ τοῦτο δὴ τὸ τέλος ἂν εἴη τῆς ἐπιθυμίας
Ε τοῦ τοιούτου ἀνδρός. Τοῦτο, ἦ δ' ὅς, παντάπασί
γε. Οὐκοῦν, ἦν δ' ἐγώ, οὗτοί γε τοιοίδε γίγνονται
ἰδίᾳ καὶ πρὶν ἄρχειν· πρῶτον μὲν οἷς ἂν ξυνῶσιν,
ἢ κόλαξιν ἑαυτῶν ξυνόντες καὶ πᾶν ἑτοίμοις
576 ὑπηρετεῖν, ἢ ἐάν τού τι δέωνται, αὐτοὶ ὑποπεσόντες, πάντα σχήματα τολμῶντες ποιεῖν ὡς οἰκεῖοι,
διαπραξάμενοι δὲ ἀλλότριοι; Καὶ σφόδρα γε.
Ἐν παντὶ ἄρα τῷ βίῳ ζῶσι φίλοι μὲν οὐδέποτε
οὐδενί, ἀεὶ δέ του δεσπόζοντες ἢ δουλεύοντες
ἄλλῳ, ἐλευθερίας δὲ καὶ φιλίας ἀληθοῦς τυραννικὴ
φύσις ἀεὶ ἄγευστος. Πάνυ μὲν οὖν. Ἆρ' οὖν
οὐκ ὀρθῶς ἂν τοὺς τοιούτους ἀπίστους καλοῖμεν;
Πῶς δ' οὔ; Καὶ μὴν ἀδίκους γε ὡς οἷόν τε
Β μάλιστα, εἴπερ ὀρθῶς ἐν τοῖς πρόσθεν ὡμολο-
γήσαμεν περὶ δικαιοσύνης, οἷόν ἐστιν. Ἀλλὰ μήν,
ἦ δ' ὅς, ὀρθῶς γε. Κεφαλαιωσώμεθα τοίνυν, ἦν δ'
ἐγώ, τὸν κάκιστον. ἔστι δέ που, οἷον ὄναρ διήλθομεν, ὃς ἂν ὕπαρ τοιοῦτος ᾖ. Πάνυ μὲν οὖν.
Οὐκοῦν οὗτος γίγνεται, ὃς ἂν τυραννικώτατος
φύσει ὢν μοναρχήσῃ, καὶ ὅσῳ ἂν πλείω χρόνον ἐν
τυραννίδι βιῷ, τοσούτῳ μᾶλλον τοιοῦτος. Ἀνάγκη, ἔφη διαδεξάμενος τὸν λόγον ὁ Γλαύκων.

---

[a] So also the Hindus of Bengal, *The Nation*, July 13, 1911,
p. 28. *Cf.* Isoc. iv. 25 πατρίδα καὶ μητέρα, Lysias ii. 18
μητέρα καὶ πατρίδα, Plut. 792 ε (*An seni resp.*) ἡ δὲ πατρὶς
καὶ μητρὶς ὡς Κρῆτες καλοῦσι. *Cf.* Vol. I. p. 303, note *e*, on
414 ε, *Menex.* 239 α.
[b] *Cf.* the accidental coincidence of Swinburne's refrain,
"This is the end of every man's desire" (*Ballad of Burdens*).
[c] ὑποπεσόντες: *cf.* on 494 c ὑποκείσονται.
[d] σχήματα was often used for the figures of dancing. *Cf.*

land *ᵃ*—as the Cretans name her—and fatherland. And this would be the end of such a man's desire.*ᵇ* " " Yes," he said, " this, just this." " Then," said I, " is not this the character of such men in private life and before they rule the state : to begin with they associate with flatterers, who are ready to do anything to serve them, or, if they themselves want something, they themselves fawn *ᶜ* and shrink from no contortion *ᵈ* or abasement in protest of their friendship, though, once the object gained, they sing another tune.*ᵉ* " " Yes indeed," he said. " Throughout their lives, then, they never know what it is to be the friends of anybody. They are always either masters or slaves, but the tyrannical nature never tastes freedom *ᶠ* or true friendship." " Quite so." " May we not rightly call such men faithless *ᵍ* ? " " Of course." " Yes, and unjust to the last degree, if we were right in our previous agreement about the nature of justice." " But surely," he said, " we were right." " Let us sum up,*ʰ* then," said I, " the most evil type of man. He is, I presume, the man who, in his waking hours, has the qualities we found in his dream state." " Quite so." " And he is developed from the man who, being by nature most of a tyrant, achieves sole power, and the longer he lives as an actual tyrant the stronger this quality becomes." " Inevitably," said Glaucon, taking up the argument.

Laws 669 D, Aristoph. *Peace* 323, Xen. *Symp.* 7. 5, Eurip. *Cyclops* 221. Isoc. *Antid.* 183 uses it of gymnastics.

ᵉ Cf. Phaedr. 241 A ἄλλος γεγονώς, Demosth. xxxiv. 13 ἕτερος ἤδη . . . καὶ οὐχ ὁ αὐτός.

ᶠ Cf. Lucian, *Nigrinus* 15 ἄγευστος μὲν ἐλευθερίας, ἀπείρατος δὲ παρρησίας, Aristot. *Eth. Nic.* 1176 b 19, 1179 b 15.

ᵍ Cf. Laws 730 c, 705 A.

ʰ Cf. Phaedr. 239 D ἐν κεφάλαιον.

576

IV. Ἆρ' οὖν, ἦν δ' ἐγώ, ὃς ἂν φαίνηται πονη-
C ρότατος, καὶ ἀθλιώτατος φανήσεται; καὶ ὃς ἂν
πλεῖστον χρόνον καὶ μάλιστα τυραννεύσῃ, μάλιστά
τε καὶ πλεῖστον χρόνον τοιοῦτος γεγονὼς τῇ ἀληθείᾳ; τοῖς δὲ πολλοῖς πολλὰ καὶ δοκεῖ. Ἀνάγκη,
ἔφη, ταῦτα γοῦν οὕτως ἔχειν. Ἄλλο τι οὖν, ἦν
δ' ἐγώ, ὅ γε τυραννικὸς κατὰ τὴν τυραννουμένην
πόλιν ἂν εἴη ὁμοιότητι, δημοτικὸς δὲ κατὰ δημοκρατουμένην, καὶ οἱ ἄλλοι οὕτως; Τί μήν; Οὐκοῦν, ὅ τι πόλις πρὸς πόλιν ἀρετῇ καὶ εὐδαιμονίᾳ,
D τοῦτο καὶ ἀνὴρ πρὸς ἄνδρα; Πῶς γὰρ οὔ; Τί
οὖν ἀρετῇ τυραννουμένη πόλις πρὸς βασιλευομένην,
οἵαν τὸ πρῶτον διήλθομεν; Πᾶν τοὐναντίον, ἔφη·
ἡ μὲν γὰρ ἀρίστη, ἡ δὲ κακίστη. Οὐκ ἐρήσομαι,
εἶπον, ὁποτέραν λέγεις· δῆλον γάρ· ἀλλ' εὐδαιμονίας τε αὖ καὶ ἀθλιότητος ὡσαύτως ἢ ἄλλως
κρίνεις; καὶ μὴ ἐκπληττώμεθα πρὸς τὸν τύραννον
ἕνα ὄντα βλέποντες, μηδ' εἴ τινες ὀλίγοι περὶ
ἐκεῖνον, ἀλλ' ὡς χρὴ ὅλην τὴν πόλιν εἰσελθόντας
E θεάσασθαι, καταδύντες εἰς ἅπασαν καὶ ἰδόντες
οὕτω δόξαν ἀποφαινώμεθα. Ἀλλ' ὀρθῶς, ἔφη,
προκαλεῖ· καὶ δῆλον παντί, ὅτι τυραννουμένης μὲν
οὐκ ἔστιν ἀθλιωτέρα, βασιλευομένης δὲ οὐκ

---

[a] Cf. Gorgias 473 c-e.
[b] Cf. the defiance of 473 a and 579 d κἂν εἰ μή τῳ δοκεῖ,
Phaedr. 277 e οὐδὲ ἂν ὁ πᾶς ὄχλος αὐτὸ ἐπαινέσῃ, and Phileb.
67 b, also Gorg. 473 e " you say what nobody else would
say," and perhaps 500 d διαβολὴ δ' ἐν πᾶσι πολλή. Cf.
Schopenhauer's "The public has a great many bees in its
bonnet."

IV. " And shall we find," said I, " that the man who is shown to be the most evil will also be the most miserable, and the man who is most of a tyrant for the longest time is most and longest miserable [a] in sober truth ? Yet the many have many opinions.[b] " " That much, certainly," he said, " must needs be true." " Does not the tyrannical man," said I, " correspond to the tyrannical state in similitude,[c] the democratic to the democratic and the others likewise ? " " Surely." " And may we not infer that the relation of state to state in respect of virtue and happiness is the same as that of the man to the man?" " Of course." " What is, then, in respect of virtue, the relation of a city ruled by a tyrant to a royal city as we first described it ? " " They are direct contraries," he said ; " the one is the best, the other the worst." " I'll not ask which is which," I said, " because that is obvious. But again in respect of happiness and wretchedness, is your estimate the same or different ? And let us not be dazzled [d] by fixing our eyes on that one man, the tyrant, or a few [e] of his court, but let us enter into and survey the entire city, as is right, and declare our opinion only after we have so dived to its uttermost recesses and contemplated its life as a whole." " That is a fair challenge," he said, " and it is clear to everybody that there is no city more wretched than that in which a tyrant rules, and none more happy than

---

[c] Cf. *Tim.* 75 D, *Rep.* 555 A, *Parmen.* 133 A. For the analogy of individual and state cf. on 591 E.

[d] Cf. 577 A, 591 D, 619 A ἀνέκπληκτος, *Crat.* 394 B, *Gorg.* 523 D, *Protag.* 355 B. Cf. also Epictet. iii. 22. 28 ὑπὸ τῆς φαντασίας περιλαμπομένοις, and Shelley, ". . . accursed thing to gaze on prosperous tyrants with a dazzled eye."

[e] εἴ τινες: cf. *Gorg.* 521 B ἐάν τι ἔχω.

PLATO

576 εὐδαιμονεστέρα. Ἆρ' οὖν, ἦν δ' ἐγώ, καὶ περὶ
577 τῶν ἀνδρῶν τὰ αὐτὰ ταῦτα προκαλούμενος ὀρθῶς
ἂν προκαλοίμην, ἀξιῶν κρίνειν περὶ αὐτῶν ἐκεῖνον,
ὃς δύναται τῇ διανοίᾳ εἰς ἀνδρὸς ἦθος ἐνδὺς διιδεῖν,
καὶ μὴ καθάπερ παῖς ἔξωθεν ὁρῶν ἐκπλήττεται
ὑπὸ τῆς τῶν τυραννικῶν προστάσεως, ἣν πρὸς
τοὺς ἔξω σχηματίζονται, ἀλλ' ἱκανῶς διορᾷ; εἰ
οὖν οἰοίμην δεῖν ἐκείνου πάντας ἡμᾶς ἀκούειν, τοῦ
δυνατοῦ μὲν κρῖναι, ξυνῳκηκότος δὲ ἐν τῷ αὐτῷ
καὶ παραγεγονότος ἔν τε ταῖς κατ' οἰκίαν πράξεσιν,
B ὥς πρὸς ἑκάστους τοὺς οἰκείους ἔχει, ἐν οἷς
μάλιστα γυμνὸς ἂν ὀφθείη τῆς τραγικῆς σκευῆς,
καὶ ἐν αὖ τοῖς δημοσίοις κινδύνοις, καὶ ταῦτα
πάντα ἰδόντα κελεύοιμεν ἐξαγγέλλειν, πῶς ἔχει
εὐδαιμονίας καὶ ἀθλιότητος ὁ τύραννος πρὸς τοὺς
ἄλλους; Ὀρθότατ' ἄν, ἔφη, καὶ ταῦτα προκαλοῖο.
Βούλει οὖν, ἦν δ' ἐγώ, προσποιησώμεθα ἡμεῖς
εἶναι τῶν δυνατῶν ἂν κρῖναι καὶ ἤδη ἐντυχόντων
τοιούτοις, ἵνα ἔχωμεν ὅστις ἀποκρινεῖται ἃ
ἐρωτῶμεν; Πάνυ γε.

C V. Ἴθι δή μοι, ἔφην, ὧδε σκόπει. τὴν ὁμοιό-

---

[a] For the contrast of tyranny and kingdom cf. 587 B,
Polit. 276 E. It became a commonplace in later orations
on the true king. Cf. Dümmler, Prolegomena, pp. 38-39.

[b] The word προστάσεως is frequent in Polybius. Cf. also
Boethius iv. chap. 2. Cf. 1 Maccabees xv. 32, "When he
saw the glory of Simon, and the cupboard of gold and silver
plate, and his great attendance [παράστασιν]." Cf. also Isoc.
ii. 32 ὄψιν, and Shakes. Measure for Measure II. ii. 59
"ceremony that to great ones 'longs," Henry V. IV. i. 280
"farced title running 'fore the king."

[c] For σχηματίζονται cf. Xen. Oecon. 2. 4 σὸν σχῆμα ὁ σὺ
περιβέβλησαι, Dio Cass. iii. fr. 13. 2 σχηματίσας . . ἑαυτόν
and σχηματισμός, Rep. 425 B, 494 D.

that governed by a true king.[a] " " And would it
not also be a fair challenge," said I, " to ask you to
accept as the only proper judge of the two men the
one who is able in thought to enter with understanding into the very soul and temper of a man, and who
is not like a child viewing him from outside, over-
awed by the tyrants' great attendance,[b] and the pomp
and circumstance which they assume[c] in the eyes
of the world, but is able to see through it all ?   And
what if I should assume, then, that the man to whom
we ought all to listen is he who has this capacity
of judgement and who has lived under the same roof
with a tyrant[d] and has witnessed his conduct in his
own home and observed in person his dealings with
his intimates in each instance where he would best
be seen stripped[e] of his vesture of tragedy,[f] and who
had likewise observed his behaviour in the hazards
of his public life—and if we should ask the man who
has seen all this to be the messenger to report on the
happiness or misery of the tyrant as compared with
other men ? "   " That also would be a most just
challenge," he said.   " Shall we, then, make believe,"
said I, " that we are of those who are thus able to
judge and who have ere now lived with tyrants, so
that we may have someone to answer our questions ? "
" By all means."

V.   " Come, then," said I, " examine it thus.   Re-

[d] It is an easy conjecture that Plato is thinking of himself
and Dionysius I.   Cf. *Laws* 711 A.

[e] Cf. Thackeray on Ludovicus and Ludovicus rex,
Hazlitt, " Strip it of its externals and what is it but a jest? "
also *Gorg.* 523 E, Xen. *Hiero* 2. 4, Lucian, *Somnium seu
Gallus* 24 ἦν δὲ ὑποκύψας ἴδῃς τὰ γ᾽ ἔνδον . . . , Boethius, *Cons.*
iii. chap. 8 (Loeb, p. 255), and for the thought Herod. i. 99.

[f] Cf. Longinus, *On the Sublime* 7 τὸ ἔξωθεν προστραγῳδού-
μενον, and Dümmler, *Akademika* p. 5.

577 γητα ἀναμιμνησκόμενος τῆς τε πόλεως καὶ· τοῦ
ἀνδρός, οὕτω καθ' ἕκαστον ἐν μέρει ἀθρῶν, τὰ
παθήματα ἑκατέρου λέγε. Τὰ ποῖα; ἔφη. Πρῶτον μέν, ἦν δ' ἐγώ, ὡς πόλιν εἰπεῖν, ἐλευθέραν ἢ
δούλην τὴν τυραννουμένην ἐρεῖς; Ὡς οἷόν τ', ἔφη,
μάλιστα δούλην. Καὶ μὴν ὁρᾷς γε ἐν αὐτῇ δεσπό-
τας καὶ ἐλευθέρους. Ὁρῶ, ἔφη, σμικρόν γέ τι
τοῦτο· τὸ δὲ ὅλον, ὡς ἔπος εἰπεῖν, ἐν αὐτῇ καὶ τὸ
ἐπιεικέστατον ἀτίμως τε καὶ ἀθλίως δοῦλον. Εἰ
D οὖν, εἶπον, ὅμοιος ἀνὴρ τῇ πόλει, οὐ καὶ ἐν ἐκείνῳ
ἀνάγκη τὴν αὐτὴν τάξιν ἐνεῖναι, καὶ πολλῆς μὲν
δουλείας τε καὶ ἀνελευθερίας γέμειν τὴν ψυχὴν
αὐτοῦ, καὶ ταῦτα αὐτῆς τὰ μέρη δουλεύειν, ἅπερ
ἦν ἐπιεικέστατα, σμικρὸν δὲ καὶ τὸ μοχθηρότατον
καὶ μανικώτατον δεσπόζειν; Ἀνάγκη, ἔφη. Τί
οὖν; δούλην ἢ ἐλευθέραν τὴν τοιαύτην φήσεις
εἶναι ψυχήν; Δούλην δή που ἔγωγε. Οὐκοῦν ἥ
γε αὖ δούλη καὶ τυραννουμένη πόλις ἥκιστα ποιεῖ
ἃ βούλεται; Πολύ γε. Καὶ ἡ τυραννουμένη ἄρα
E ψυχὴ ἥκιστα ποιήσει ἃ ἂν βουληθῇ, ὡς περὶ ὅλης
εἰπεῖν ψυχῆς· ὑπὸ δὲ οἴστρου ἀεὶ ἑλκομένη βίᾳ τα-
ραχῆς καὶ μεταμελείας μεστὴ ἔσται. Πῶς γὰρ
οὔ; Πλουσίαν δὲ ἢ πενομένην ἀνάγκη τὴν τυ-
578 ραννουμένην πόλιν εἶναι; Πενομένην. Καὶ ψυχὴν

ᵃ In *Menex.* 238 E Plato says that other states are composed of slaves and masters, but Athens of equals.
ᵇ For τάξιν· cf. 618 B ψυχῆς δὲ τάξιν.
ᶜ γέμειν: cf. 544 C, 559 C, *Gorg.* 522 E, 525 A.
ᵈ Cf. 445 B, *Gorg.* 467 B, where a verbal distinction is

call the general likeness between the city and the man, and then observe in turn what happens to each of them." " What things ?" he said. " In the first place," said I, " will you call the state governed by a tyrant free or enslaved, speaking of it as a state ? " " Utterly enslaved," he said. " And yet you see in it masters and freemen." " I see," he said, " a small portion of such, but the entirety, so to speak, and the best part of it, is shamefully and wretchedly enslaved.[a] " " If, then," I said, " the man resembles the state, must not the same proportion[b] obtain in him, and his soul teem[c] with boundless servility and illiberality, the best and most reasonable parts of it being enslaved, while a small part, the worst and the most frenzied, plays the despot ? " " Inevitably," he said. " Then will you say that such a soul is enslaved or free ? " " Enslaved, I should suppose." " Again, does not the enslaved and tyrannized city least of all do what it really wishes[d] ? " " Decidedly so." " Then the tyrannized soul—to speak of the soul as a whole[e]—also will least of all do what it wishes, but being always perforce driven and drawn by the gadfly of desire it will be full of confusion and repentance.[f] " " Of course." " And must the tyrannized city be rich or poor ? " " Poor." " Then the tyrant

drawn with which Plato does not trouble himself here. In *Laws* 661 B ἐπιθυμῇ is used. *Cf. ibid.* 688 B τἀναντία ταῖς βουλήσεσιν, and Herod. iii. 80.

[e] *Cf. Cratyl.* 392 C ὡς τὸ ὅλον εἰπεῖν γένος.

[f] *Cf.* Julian, *Or.* ii. 50 C. In the Stoic philosophy the *stultus* repents, and "omnis stultitia fastidio laborat sui." *Cf.* also Seneca, *De benef.* iv. 34 "non mutat sapiens consilium . . . ideo numquam illum poenitentia subit," Von Arnim, *Stoic. Vet. Frag.* iii. 147. 21, 149. 20 and 33, Stob. *Ec.* ii. 113. 5, 102. 22, and my emendation of *Eclogues* ii. 104. 6 W. in *Class. Phil.* xi. p. 338.

578 ἆρα τυραννικὴν πενιχρὰν καὶ ἄπληστον ἀνάγκη ἀεὶ
εἶναι. Οὕτως, ἦ δ' ὅς. Τί δέ; φόβου γέμειν ἆρ'
οὐκ ἀνάγκη τήν τε τοιαύτην πόλιν τόν τε τοιοῦτον
ἄνδρα; Πολλή γε. Ὀδυρμοὺς δὲ καὶ στεναγ-
μοὺς καὶ θρήνους καὶ ἀλγηδόνας οἴει ἔν τινι ἄλλῃ
πλείους εὑρήσειν; Οὐδαμῶς. Ἐν ἀνδρὶ δὲ ἡγεῖ
τὰ τοιαῦτα ἐν ἄλλῳ τινὶ πλείω εἶναι ἢ ἐν τῷ
μαινομένῳ ὑπὸ ἐπιθυμιῶν τε καὶ ἐρώτων τούτῳ
τῷ τυραννικῷ; Πῶς γὰρ ἄν; ἔφη. Εἰς πάντα
B δή, οἶμαι, ταῦτά τε καὶ ἄλλα τοιαῦτα ἀποβλέψας
τήν γε πόλιν τῶν πόλεων ἀθλιωτάτην ἔκρινας.
Οὐκοῦν ὀρθῶς; ἔφη. Καὶ μάλα, ἦν δ' ἐγώ.
ἀλλὰ περὶ τοῦ ἀνδρὸς αὖ τοῦ τυραννικοῦ τί λέγεις
εἰς ταὐτὰ ταῦτα ἀποβλέπων; Μακρῷ, ἔφη, ἀθλιώτατον εἶναι τῶν ἄλλων ἁπάντων. Τοῦτο, ἦν δ'
ἐγώ, οὐκέτ' ὀρθῶς λέγεις. Πῶς; ἦ δ' ὅς.
Οὔπω, ἔφην, οἶμαι, οὗτός ἐστιν ὁ τοιοῦτος μάλιστα.
Ἀλλὰ τίς μήν; Ὅδε ἴσως σοι ἔτι δόξει εἶναι
C τούτου ἀθλιώτερος. Ποῖος; Ὅς ἄν, ἦν δ' ἐγώ,
τυραννικὸς ὢν μὴ ἰδιώτην βίον καταβιῷ, ἀλλὰ
δυστυχὴς ᾖ καὶ αὐτῷ ὑπό τινος συμφορᾶς ἐκ-
πορισθῇ ὥστε τυράννῳ γενέσθαι. Τεκμαίρομαί σε,
ἔφη, ἐκ τῶν προειρημένων ἀληθῆ λέγειν. Ναί, ἦν
δ' ἐγώ· ἀλλ' οὐκ οἴεσθαι χρὴ τὰ τοιαῦτα, ἀλλ' εὖ

ᵃ Cf. *Laws* 832 A πεινῶσι τὴν ψυχήν, Xen. *Symp.* 4. 36
πεινῶσι χρημάτων, *Oecon.* xiii. 9 πεινῶσι γὰρ τοῦ ἐπαίνου,
Aristot. *Pol.* 1277 a 24 " Jason said he was hungry when he
was not a tyrant," Shakes. *Tempest* i. ii. 112 "so dry he
was for sway." Cf. Novotny, p. 192, on *Epist.* vii. 335 B,
also Max. Tyr. *Diss.* iv. 4 τί γὰρ ἂν εἴη πενέστερον ἀνδρὸς
ἐπιθυμοῦντος διηνεκῶς . . . ; Julian, *Or.* ii. 85 B, Teles (Hense),

soul also must of necessity always be needy[a] and suffer from unfulfilled desire." "So it is," he said. "And again, must not such a city, as well as such a man, be full of terrors and alarms?" "It must indeed." "And do you think you will find more lamentations and groans and wailing and anguish in any other city?" "By no means." "And so of man, do you think these things will more abound in any other than in this tyrant type, that is maddened by its desires and passions?" "How could it be so?" he said. "In view of all these and other like considerations, then, I take it, you judged that this city is the most miserable of cities." "And was I not right?" he said. "Yes, indeed," said I. "But of the tyrant man, what have you to say in view of these same things?" "That he is far and away the most miserable of all," he said. "I cannot admit," said I, "that you are right in that too." "How so?" said he. "This one," said I, "I take it, has not yet attained the acme of misery.[b]" "Then who has?" "Perhaps you will regard the one I am about to name as still more wretched." "What one?" "The one," said I, "who, being of tyrannical temper, does not live out[c] his life in private station[d] but is so unfortunate that by some unhappy chance he is enabled to become an actual tyrant." "I infer from what has already been said," he replied, "that you speak truly." "Yes," said I, "but it is not enough to suppose such things. We must examine them thoroughly by

pp. 32-33. For the thought see also *Gorg.* 493-494. *Cf.* also *supra* 521 A with 416 E, *Phaedr.* 279 c, and *Epist.* 355 c.

[b] *Cf. supra* on 508 E, p. 104, note *c*.

[c] *Cf. Protag.* 355 A, *Alc. I.* 104 E, 579 c.

[d] Stallbaum quotes Plut. *De virtut. et vit.* p. 101 D, Lucian, *Herm.* 67 ἰδιώτην βίον ζῆν, Philo, *Vit. Mos.* 3.

578 μάλα τῷ τοιούτῳ[1] λόγῳ σκοπεῖν. περὶ γάρ τοι
τοῦ μεγίστου ἡ σκέψις, ἀγαθοῦ τε βίου καὶ κακοῦ.
Ὀρθότατα, ἦ δ' ὅς. Σκόπει δή, εἰ ἄρα τὶ λέγω.
D δοκεῖ γάρ μοι δεῖν ἐννοῆσαι ἐκ τῶνδε περὶ αὐτοῦ
σκοποῦντας. Ἐκ τίνων; Ἐξ ἑνὸς ἑκάστου τῶν
ἰδιωτῶν, ὅσοι πλούσιοι ἐν πόλεσιν ἀνδράποδα
πολλὰ κέκτηνται. οὗτοι γὰρ τοῦτό γε προσόμοιον
ἔχουσι τοῖς τυράννοις, τὸ πολλῶν ἄρχειν· διαφέρει
δὲ τὸ ἐκείνου πλῆθος. Διαφέρει γάρ. Οἶσθ' οὖν
ὅτι οὗτοι ἀδεῶς ἔχουσι καὶ οὐ φοβοῦνται τοὺς
οἰκέτας; Τί γὰρ ἂν φοβοῖντο; Οὐδέν, εἶπον·
ἀλλὰ τὸ αἴτιον ἐννοεῖς; Ναί, ὅτι γε πᾶσα ἡ πόλις
E ἑνὶ ἑκάστῳ βοηθεῖ τῶν ἰδιωτῶν. Καλῶς, ἦν δ'
ἐγώ, λέγεις. τί δέ; εἴ τις θεῶν ἄνδρα ἕνα, ὅτῳ
ἔστιν ἀνδράποδα πεντήκοντα ἢ πλείω, ἄρας ἐκ τῆς
πόλεως αὐτόν τε καὶ γυναῖκα καὶ παῖδας θείη εἰς
ἐρημίαν μετὰ τῆς ἄλλης οὐσίας τε καὶ τῶν οἰκετῶν,
ὅπου αὐτῷ μηδεὶς τῶν ἐλευθέρων μέλλοι βοη-
θήσειν, ἐν ποίῳ ἄν τινι καὶ πόσῳ φόβῳ οἴει γενέσθαι αὐτὸν περί τε αὑτοῦ καὶ παίδων καὶ γυναικός,
μὴ ἀπόλοιντο ὑπὸ τῶν οἰκετῶν; Ἐν παντί, ἦ δ'
579 ὅς, ἔγωγε. Οὐκοῦν ἀναγκάζοιτο ἄν τινας ἤδη
θωπεύειν αὐτῶν τῶν δούλων, καὶ ὑπισχνεῖσθαι

---

[1] On τῷ τοιούτῳ, the reading of the MSS., see note a below.

---

[a] Adam ad loc. emends τῷ τοιούτῳ to τῶ τοιούτῳ, insisting
hat the MS. reading cannot be satisfactorily explained.
[b] Cf. supra Vol. I. p. 71, note f on 344 D-E and What
Plato Said, p. 484, on Laches 185 A.
[c] Cf. Polit. 259 B. But Plato is not concerned with the
question of size or numbers here.

reason and an argument such as this.[a] For our inquiry concerns the greatest of all things,[b] the good
life or the bad life." " Quite right," he replied.
" Consider, then, if there is anything in what I say.
For I think we must get a notion of the matter from
these examples." "From which?" "From individual
wealthy private citizens in our states who possess
many slaves. For these resemble the tyrant in being
rulers over many, only the tyrant's numbers are
greater.[c]" "Yes, they are." "You are aware,
then, that they are unafraid and do not fear their
slaves?" "What should they fear?" "Nothing,"
I said; " but do you perceive the reason why?"
" Yes, because the entire state is ready to defend each
citizen." "You are right," I said. " But now suppose some god should catch up a man who has fifty
or more slaves[d] and waft him with his wife and children
away from the city and set him down with his other
possessions and his slaves in a solitude where no freeman could come to his rescue. What and how great
would be his fear,[e] do you suppose, lest he and his
wife and children be destroyed by the slaves?"
" The greatest in the world,[f]" he said, "if you ask
me." "And would he not forthwith find it necessary to fawn upon some of the slaves and make them

[d] Plato's imaginary illustration is one of his many anticipations of later history, and suggests to an American many
analogies.

[e] Cf. Critias, fr. 37, Diels ii.³ p. 324, on Sparta's fear of
her slaves.

[f] For ἐν παντί cf. 579 B, Symp. 194 A ἐν παντὶ εἴης,
Euthyd. 301 A ἐν παντὶ ἐγενόμην ὑπὸ ἀπορίας, Xen. Hell.
v. 4. 29, Thucyd. vii. 55, Isoc. xiii. 20 ἐν πᾶσιν . . κακοῖς.
Cf. παντοῖος εἶναι (γίννεσθαι) Herod. ix. 109, vii. 10. 3,
iii. 124, Lucian, Pro lapsu 1.

579 πολλὰ καὶ ἐλευθεροῦν οὐδὲν δεόμενος, καὶ κόλαξ
αὐτὸς ἂν θεραπόντων ἀναφανείη; Πολλὴ ἀνάγκη,
ἔφη, αὐτῷ, ἢ ἀπολωλέναι. Τί δ', εἰ καὶ ἄλλους,
ἦν δ' ἐγώ, ὁ θεὸς κύκλῳ κατοικίσειε γείτονας
πολλοὺς αὐτῷ, οἳ μὴ ἀνέχοιντο, εἴ τις ἄλλος ἄλλου
δεσπόζειν ἀξιοῖ, ἀλλ' εἴ πού τινα τοιοῦτον λαμ-
βάνοιεν, ταῖς ἐσχάταις τιμωροῖντο τιμωρίαις; Ἔτι
B ἄν, ἔφη, οἶμαι, μᾶλλον ἐν παντὶ κακοῦ εἴη, κύκλῳ
φρουρούμενος ὑπὸ πάντων πολεμίων. Ἆρ' οὖν οὐκ
ἐν τοιούτῳ μὲν δεσμωτηρίῳ δέδεται ὁ τύραννος,
φύσει ὢν οἷον διεληλύθαμεν, πολλῶν καὶ παντοδαπῶν φόβων καὶ ἐρώτων μεστός· λίχνῳ δὲ
ὄντι αὐτῷ τὴν ψυχὴν μόνῳ τῶν ἐν τῇ πόλει οὔτε
ἀποδημῆσαι ἔξεστιν οὐδαμόσε οὔτε θεωρῆσαι ὅσων
δὴ καὶ οἱ ἄλλοι ἐλεύθεροι ἐπιθυμηταί εἰσι, κατα-
δεδυκὼς δὲ ἐν τῇ οἰκίᾳ τὰ πολλὰ ὡς γυνὴ ζῇ,
C φθονῶν καὶ τοῖς ἄλλοις πολίταις, ἐάν τις ἔξω
ἀποδημῇ καί τι ἀγαθὸν ὁρᾷ; Παντάπασι μὲν
οὖν, ἔφη.

VI. Οὐκοῦν τοῖς τοιούτοις κακοῖς πλείω καρ-
ποῦται ἀνήρ, ὃς ἂν κακῶς ἐν ἑαυτῷ πολιτευόμενος,
ὃν νῦν δὴ σὺ ἀθλιώτατον ἔκρινας, τὸν τυραννικόν,

---

[a] For the idiom οὐδὲν δεόμενος cf. 581 E, 367 A-B, 410 B,
405 C, *Prot.* 331 C, and Shorey in *Class. Journ.* ii. p. 171.
[b] For ancient denials of the justice of slavery cf. Newman,
Aristot. *Pol.* i. pp. 140 ff., Philemon, *fr.* 95 (Kock ii. p. 508)
κἂν δοῦλός ἐστι, σάρκα τὴν αὐτὴν ἔχει, φύσει γὰρ οὐδεὶς δοῦλος
ἐγενήθη ποτέ. ἡ δ' αὖ τύχη τὸ σῶμα κατεδουλώσατο, and *Anth.
Pal.* vii. 553 with Mackail's note, p. 415.
[c] *Cf.* p. 360, note a. For the tyrant's terrors cf. Menander,
'Ασπίς (*fr.* 74, Kock iii. p. 24), Tacitus, *Ann.* vi. 6, 579 E
and Xen. *Hiero* 6. 8. The tyrant sees enemies everywhere.

many promises and emancipate them, though nothing
would be further from his wish [a] ? And so he would
turn out to be the flatterer of his own servants."
" He would certainly have to," he said, " or else
perish." " But now suppose," said I, " that god
established round about him numerous neighbours
who would not tolerate the claim of one man to be
master of another,[b] but would inflict the utmost
penalties on any such person on whom they could
lay their hands." " I think," he said, " that his
plight would be still more desperate, encompassed
by nothing but enemies." " And is not that the
sort of prison-house in which the tyrant is pent, being
of a nature such as we have described and filled with
multitudinous and manifold terrors and appetites ?
Yet greedy [c] and avid of spirit as he is, he only of the
citizens may not travel abroad or view any of the
sacred festivals [d] that other freemen yearn to see,
but he must live for the most part cowering in the
recesses of his house like a woman,[e] envying among
the other citizens anyone who goes abroad and sees
any good thing." " Most certainly," he said.

VI. " And does not such a harvest of ills [f] measure
the difference between the man who is merely ill-
governed in his own soul, the man of tyrannical
temper, whom you just now judged to be most
miserable, and the man who, having this disposition,

---

[a] *Cf.* Xen. *Hiero* 1. 12 οἱ δὲ τύραννοι οὐ μάλα ἀμφὶ θεωρίας
ἔχουσιν· οὔτε γὰρ ἰέναι αὐτοῖς ἀσφαλές. *Cf. Crito* 52 B ἐπὶ
θεωρίαν.

[e] *Cf. Laws* 781 c, *Gorg.* 485 D.

[f] τοῖς τοιούτοις κακοῖς is the measure of the excess of the
unhappiness of the actual tyrant over that of the tyrannical
soul in private life. *Cf.* my review of Jowett, *A.J.P.* xiii.
p. 366.

579 μὴ ὡς ἰδιώτης καταβιῷ, ἀλλ' ἀναγκασθῇ ὑπό τινος
τύχης τυραννεῦσαι, καὶ ἑαυτοῦ ὢν ἀκράτωρ ἄλλων
ἐπιχειρήσῃ ἄρχειν, ὥσπερ εἴ τις κάμνοντι σώματι
καὶ ἀκράτορι ἑαυτοῦ μὴ ἰδιωτεύων ἀλλ' ἀγωνιζό-
D μενος πρὸς ἄλλα σώματα καὶ μαχόμενος ἀναγκάζοιτο διάγειν τὸν βίον. Παντάπασιν, ἔφη, ὁμοιό-
τατά τε καὶ ἀληθέστατα λέγεις, ὦ Σώκρατες.
Οὐκοῦν, ἦν δ' ἐγώ, ὦ φίλε Γλαύκων, παντελῶς τὸ
πάθος ἄθλιον, καὶ τοῦ ὑπὸ σοῦ κριθέντος χαλεπώ-
τατα ζῆν χαλεπώτερον ἔτι ζῇ ὁ τυραννῶν; Κομιδῇ
γ', ἔφη. Ἔστιν ἄρα τῇ ἀληθείᾳ, κἂν εἰ μή τῳ
δοκεῖ, ὁ τῷ ὄντι τύραννος τῷ ὄντι δοῦλος τὰς
E μεγίστας θωπείας καὶ δουλείας καὶ κόλαξ τῶν
πονηροτάτων· καὶ τὰς ἐπιθυμίας οὐδ' ὁπωστιοῦν
ἀποπιμπλάς, ἀλλὰ πλείστων ἐπιδεέστατος καὶ
πένης τῇ ἀληθείᾳ φαίνεται, ἐάν τις ὅλην ψυχὴν
ἐπίστηται θεάσασθαι, καὶ φόβου γέμων διὰ παντὸς
τοῦ βίου, σφαδασμῶν τε καὶ ὀδυνῶν πλήρης, εἴπερ
τῇ τῆς πόλεως διαθέσει ἧς ἄρχει ἔοικεν. ἔοικε δέ·
580 ἦ γάρ; Καὶ μάλα, ἔφη. Οὐκοῦν καὶ πρὸς τούτοις ἔτι ἀποδώσομεν τῷ ἀνδρὶ καὶ ἃ τὸ πρότερον
εἴπομεν, ὅτι ἀνάγκη καὶ εἶναι καὶ ἔτι μᾶλλον
γίγνεσθαι αὐτῷ ἢ πρότερον διὰ τὴν ἀρχὴν φθονερῷ, ἀπίστῳ, ἀδίκῳ, ἀφίλῳ, ἀνοσίῳ, καὶ πάσης
κακίας πανδοκεῖ τε καὶ τροφεῖ, καὶ ἐξ ἁπάντων

---

[a] Cf. infra 580 c and What Plato Said, p. 506, on Gorg.
491 D.

[b] For the analogy of soul and body cf. 591 B and on
564 B, p. 313, note g.

THE REPUBLIC, BOOK IX

does not live out his life in private station but is constrained by some ill hap to become an actual tyrant, and while unable to control himself[a] attempts to rule over others, as if a man with a sick and incontinent body[b] should not live the private life but should be compelled to pass his days in contention and strife with other persons?" "Your analogy is most apt and true,[c] Socrates," he said. "Is not that then, dear Glaucon," said I, "a most unhappy experience in every way? And is not the tyrant's life still worse than that which was judged by you to be the worst?" "Precisely so," he said. "Then it is the truth, though some may deny it,[d] that the real tyrant is really enslaved to cringings and servitudes beyond compare, a flatterer of the basest men, and that, so far from finding even the least satisfaction for his desires, he is in need of most things, and is a poor man in very truth, as is apparent if one knows how to observe a soul in its entirety; and throughout his life he teems with terrors and is full of convulsions and pains, if in fact he resembles the condition of the city which he rules; and he is like it, is he not?" "Yes, indeed," he said. "And in addition, shall we not further attribute to him all that we spoke of before, and say that he must needs be, and, by reason of his rule, come to be still more than he was,[e] envious, faithless, unjust, friendless, impious, a vessel and nurse[f] of all iniquity, and so in consequence be

[c] *Cf. Soph.* 252 c ὅμοιόν τε καὶ ἀληθές.
[d] *Cf.* on 576 c, p. 354, note b.
[e] *Cf.* 576 B-C.
[f] πανδοκεύς is a host or inn-keeper; *cf. Laws* 918 B. Here the word is used figuratively. *Cf.* Aristoph. *Wasps* 35 φάλαινα πανδοκεύτρια, "an all-receptive grampus" (Rogers).

580 τούτων μάλιστα μὲν αὐτῷ δυστυχεῖ εἶναι, ἔπειτα
δὲ καὶ τοὺς πλησίον αὐτῷ τοιούτους ἀπεργάζεσθαι.
Οὐδείς σοι, ἔφη, τῶν νοῦν ἐχόντων ἀντερεῖ. Ἴθι
B δή μοι, ἔφην ἐγώ, νῦν ἤδη, ὥσπερ ὁ διὰ πάντων
κριτὴς ἀποφαίνεται, καὶ σὺ οὕτω, τίς πρῶτος κατὰ
τὴν σὴν δόξαν εὐδαιμονίᾳ καὶ τίς δεύτερος, καὶ
τοὺς ἄλλους ἑξῆς πέντε ὄντας κρῖνε, βασιλικόν,
τιμοκρατικόν, ὀλιγαρχικόν, δημοκρατικόν, τυραννικόν. Ἀλλὰ ῥᾳδία, ἔφη, ἡ κρίσις. καθάπερ γὰρ
εἰσῆλθον, ἔγωγε ὥσπερ χοροὺς κρίνω ἀρετῇ καὶ
κακίᾳ καὶ εὐδαιμονίᾳ καὶ τῷ ἐναντίῳ. Μισθωσώ-
μεθα οὖν κήρυκα, ἦν δ' ἐγώ, ἢ αὐτὸς ἀνείπω, ὅτι
ὁ Ἀρίστωνος υἱὸς τὸν ἄριστόν τε καὶ δικαιότατον
C εὐδαιμονέστατον ἔκρινε, τοῦτον δ' εἶναι τὸν
βασιλικώτατον καὶ βασιλεύοντα αὑτοῦ, τὸν δὲ
κάκιστόν τε καὶ ἀδικώτατον ἀθλιώτατον, τοῦτον
δὲ αὖ τυγχάνειν ὄντα, ὃς ἂν τυραννικώτατος ὢν
ἑαυτοῦ τε ὅ τι μάλιστα τυραννῇ καὶ τῆς πόλεως;
Ἀνειρήσθω σοι, ἔφη. Ἦ οὖν προσαναγορεύω,
εἶπον, ἐάν τε λανθάνωσι τοιοῦτοι ὄντες ἐάν τε μὴ

---

a On the wretched lot of the tyrant cf. Xen. Hiero passim,
e.g. 4. 11, 6. 4, 8, 15. The Hiero is Xenophon's
rendering of the Socratico-Platonic conception of the
unhappy tyrant. Cf. 1. 2-3. See too Gerhard Heintzeler,
Das Bild des Tyrannen bei Platon, esp. pp. 43 ff. and 76 f.;
Cic. De amicit. 15, Isoc. Nic. 4-5, Peace 112, Hel.
32 ff. But in Euag. 40 Isocrates says all men would admit
that tyranny "is the greatest and noblest and most coveted
of all good things, both human and divine." In Epist. 6. 11 ff.
he agrees with Plato that the life of a private citizen is better
than the tyrant's. But in 2. 4 he treats this as a thesis which
many maintain. Cf. further Gorg. 473 E, Alc. I. 135 B,
Phaedr. 248 E, Symp. 182 C, Eurip. Ion 621 ff., Suppl. 429 ff.,
Medea 119 ff., I.A. 449-450, Herodotus iii. 80, Soph. Ajax
1350 "not easy for a tyrant to be pious"; also Dio Chrys.

himself most unhappy [a] and make all about him so?"
"No man of sense will gainsay that," he said.
"Come then," said I, "now at last, even as the judge
of last instance [b] pronounces, so do you declare who in
your opinion is first in happiness and who second, and
similarly judge the others, all five in succession, the
royal, the timocratic, the oligarchic, the democratic,
and the tyrannical man." "Nay," he said, "the
decision is easy. For as if they were choruses I judge
them in the order of their entrance, and so rank them
in respect of virtue and vice, happiness and its contrary." "Shall we hire a herald,[c] then," said I, "or
shall I myself make proclamation that the son of
Ariston pronounced the best man [d] and the most
righteous to be the happiest,[e] and that he is the one
who is the most kingly and a king over himself; [f] and
declared that the most evil and most unjust is the
most unhappy, who again is the man who, having
the most of the tyrannical temper in himself, becomes
most of a tyrant over himself and over the state?"
"Let it have been so proclaimed by you," he said.
"Shall I add the clause 'alike whether their character

Or. iii. 58 f., Anon. Iambl. *fr.* 7. 12, Diels ii.³ p. 333,
J. A. K. Thomson, *Greek and Barbarian*, pp. 111 ff.,
Dümmler, *Prolegomena*, p. 31, Baudrillart, *J. Bodin et son
temps*, pp. 292-293 "Bodin semble . . . se souvenir de
Platon flétrissant le tyran. . . ."

[b] Adam has an exhaustive technical note on this.

[c] Cf. *Phileb.* 66 A ὑπό τε ἀγγέλων πέμπων, etc., Eurip.
Alc. 737 κηρύκων ὕπο. Grote and other liberals are offended
by the intensity of Plato's moral conviction. See *What
Plato Said*, p. 364, *Laws* 662-663, *Unity of Plato's Thought*,
p. 25.

[d] Plato puns on the name Ariston. For other such puns
cf. *Gorg.* 463 E, 481 D, 513 B, *Rep.* 600 B, 614 B, *Symp.*
174 B, 185 C, 198 C.

[e] Cf. *Laws* 664 B-C.   [f] Cf. on 579 C, p. 367, note a.

580 πάντας ἀνθρώπους τε καὶ θεούς; Προσαναγόρευε, ἔφη.

VII. Εἶεν δή, εἶπον· αὕτη μὲν ἡμῖν ἡ ἀπόδειξις
D μία ἂν εἴη· δευτέραν δὲ ἰδὲ¹ τήνδε, ἐάν τι δόξῃ
εἶναι. Τίς αὕτη; Ἐπειδή, ὥσπερ πόλις, ἦν δ᾽
ἐγώ, διήρηται κατὰ τρία εἴδη, οὕτω καὶ ψυχὴ
ἑνὸς ἑκάστου τριχῇ, [τὸ λογιστικὸν]² δέξεται, ὡς
ἐμοὶ δοκεῖ, καὶ ἑτέραν ἀπόδειξιν. Τίνα ταύτην;
Τήνδε. τριῶν ὄντων τρατταὶ καὶ ἡδοναί μοι φαίνονται, ἑνὸς ἑκάστου μία ἰδία· ἐπιθυμίαι τε ὡσ-
αὔτως καὶ ἀρχαί. Πῶς λέγεις; ἔφη. Τὸ μέν,
φαμέν, ἦν ᾧ μανθάνει ἄνθρωπος, τὸ δὲ ᾧ θυμοῦται,
τὸ δὲ τρίτον διὰ πολυειδίαν ἑνὶ οὐκ ἔσχομεν ὀνό-
E ματι προσειπεῖν ἰδίῳ αὐτοῦ, ἀλλὰ ὃ μέγιστον καὶ
ἰσχυρότατον εἶχεν ἐν αὐτῷ, τούτῳ ἐπωνομάσαμεν·
ἐπιθυμητικὸν γὰρ αὐτὸ κεκλήκαμεν διὰ σφοδρό-
τητα τῶν περὶ τὴν ἐδωδὴν ἐπιθυμιῶν καὶ πόσιν
καὶ ἀφροδίσια καὶ ὅσα ἄλλα τούτοις ἀκόλουθα, καὶ
φιλοχρήματον δή, ὅτι διὰ χρημάτων μάλιστα
581 ἀποτελοῦνται αἱ τοιαῦται ἐπιθυμίαι. Καὶ ὀρθῶς
γ᾽, ἔφη. Ἆρ᾽ οὖν καὶ τὴν ἡδονὴν αὐτοῦ καὶ
φιλίαν εἰ φαῖμεν εἶναι τοῦ κέρδους, μάλιστ᾽ ἂν εἰς

¹ δὲ ἰδὲ Adam : δεῖ δὲ AFDM : δὲ δεῖ mss. recc.
² τὸ λογιστικὸν A, λογιστικὸν A²FDM, λογιστικὸν ἐπιθυμητικὸν θυμικὸν Par. 1642 : omitted by more recent mss.

ᵃ Cf. supra 367 E, 427 D, 445 A, infra 612 B.
ᵇ Cf. supra 435 B-C ff.
ᶜ Practically all editors reject τὸ λογιστικὸν. But Apelt,
p. 525, insists that δέξεται cannot be used without a subject
on the analogy of 453 D ἔοικεν, 497 C δηλώσει and δείξει,
hence we must retain λογιστικόν, in the sense of "ability to
reckon," and he compares Charm. 174 B and the double
sense of λογιστικόν in Rep. 525 B, 587 D, 602 E. He says it
is a mild mathematical joke, like Polit. 257 A.

is known to all men and gods or is not known '[a]?' "
" Add that to the proclamation," he said.

VII. " Very good," said I; " this, then, would
be one of our proofs, but examine this second one
and see if there is anything in it." " What is it?"
" Since," said I, " corresponding to the three types
in the city, the soul also is tripartite,[b] it will admit,[c]
I think, of another demonstration also." " What
is that?" " The following: The three parts have
also, it appears to me, three kinds of pleasure, one
peculiar to each, and similarly three appetites and
controls." " What do you mean?" he said. " One
part, we say, is that with which a man learns, one
is that with which he feels anger. But the third
part, owing to its manifold forms,[d] we could not
easily designate by any one distinctive name,[e] but
gave it the name of its chief and strongest element;
for we called it the appetitive part [f] because of the
intensity of its appetites concerned with food and
drink and love and their accompaniments, and likewise the money-loving part,[g] because money is the
chief instrument for the gratification of such desires."
" And rightly," he said. " And if we should also say
that its pleasure and its love were for gain or profit,

---

[d] Cf. *Phileb.* 26 c τὸ . . . πλῆθος. Cf. Friedländer, *Platon*,
ii. p. 492, n. 2.

[e] Here again the concept is implied (cf. *supra* on 564 B,
p. 313, note *e* and Introd. pp. x-xi). Cf. *Parmen.* 132 c,
135 B, *Phileb.* 16 D, 18 C-D, 23 E, 25 c, Aristot. *Eth. Nic.*
1130 b 2 ἑνὶ ὀνόματι περιλαβεῖν, and εἰς ἓν κεφάλαιον ἀπερειδοίμεθα,
581 A, Schleiermacher's interpretation of which, " so würden
wir uns in der Erklärung doch auf ein Hauptstück stützen,"
approved by Stallbaum, misses the point. For the point
that there is no one name for it cf. *What Plato Said*, p. 596,
on *Soph.* 267 D.

[f] Vol. I. 439 D.

[g] Cf. Vol. I. p. 380, note *b*.

581 ἓν κεφάλαιον ἀπερειδοίμεθα τῷ λόγῳ, ὥστε τι
ἡμῖν αὐτοῖς δηλοῦν, ὁπότε τοῦτο τῆς ψυχῆς τὸ
μέρος λέγοιμεν, καὶ καλοῦντες αὐτὸ φιλοχρήματον
καὶ φιλοκερδὲς ὀρθῶς ἂν καλοῖμεν; Ἐμοὶ γοῦν
δοκεῖ, ἔφη. Τί δέ; τὸ θυμοειδὲς οὐ πρὸς τὸ
κρατεῖν μέντοι φαμὲν καὶ νικᾶν καὶ εὐδοκιμεῖν
B ἀεὶ ὅλον ὡρμῆσθαι; Καὶ μάλα. Εἰ οὖν φιλόνικον
αὐτὸ καὶ φιλότιμον προσαγορεύοιμεν, ἦ ἐμμελῶς
ἂν ἔχοι; Ἐμμελέστατα μὲν οὖν. Ἀλλὰ μὴν ᾧ
γε μανθάνομεν, παντὶ δῆλον ὅτι πρὸς τὸ εἰδέναι τὴν
ἀλήθειαν ὅπῃ ἔχει πᾶν ἀεὶ τέταται, καὶ χρημάτων
τε καὶ δόξης ἥκιστα τούτων τούτῳ μέλει. Πολύ
γε. Φιλομαθὲς δὴ καὶ φιλόσοφον καλοῦντες αὐτὸ
κατὰ τρόπον ἂν καλοῖμεν; Πῶς γὰρ οὔ; Οὐκοῦν,
C ἦν δ' ἐγώ, καὶ ἄρχει ἐν ταῖς ψυχαῖς τῶν μὲν τοῦτο,
τῶν δὲ τὸ ἕτερον ἐκείνων, ὁπότερον ἂν τύχῃ; Οὕτως, ἔφη. Διὰ ταῦτα δὴ καὶ ἀνθρώπων λέγομεν
τὰ πρῶτα τριττὰ γένη εἶναι, φιλόσοφον, φιλόνικον,
φιλοκερδές; Κομιδῇ γε. Καὶ ἡδονῶν δὴ τρία
εἴδη, ὑποκείμενον[1] ἐν ἑκάστῳ τούτων; Πάνυ γε.

---

[1] ὑποκείμενον AFD, ὑποκείμενα A²M defended by Adam.

---

[a] Since there is no one specific name for the manifold
forms of this part (580 D-E), a makeshift term is to be used
for convenience' sake. See also p. 371, note e.

[b] Or "is bent on," τέταται. Cf. 499 A ζητεῖν . . . τὸ ἀληθὲς
συντεταμένως, Symp. 222 A and Bury ad loc., Symp. 186 B ἐπὶ
πᾶν ὁ θεὸς τείνει. For the thought cf. also Phileb. 58 D.

[c] Cf. Phaedo 67 B τοὺς ὀρθῶς φιλομαθεῖς.

[d] Cf. 338 D, 342 c.

[e] Cf. my review of Jowett in A.J.P. xiii. p. 366, which
Adam quotes and follows and Jowett and Campbell (Republic)
adopt. For the three types of men cf. also Phaedo 68 c, 82 c.
Stewart, Aristot. Eth. Nic. p. 60 (1095 b 17), says, "The

THE REPUBLIC, BOOK IX

should we not thus best bring it together under one
head [a] in our discourse so as to understand each other
when we speak of this part of the soul, and justify
our calling it the money-loving and gain-loving part?"
"I, at any rate, think so," he said. "And, again,
of the high-spirited element, do we not say that it
is wholly set on predominance and victory and good
repute?" "Yes, indeed." "And might we not
appropriately designate it as the ambitious part and
that which is covetous of honour?" "Most appropriately." "But surely it is obvious to everyone that
all the endeavour of the part by which we learn is ever
towards [b] knowledge of the truth of things, and that it
least of the three is concerned for wealth and reputation." "Much the least." "Lover of learning [c]
and lover of wisdom would be suitable designations
for that." "Quite so," he said. "Is it not also
true," I said, "that the ruling principle [d] of men's
souls is in some cases this faculty and in others one
of the other two, as it may happen?" "That is
so," he said. "And that is why we say that the
primary classes [e] of men also are three, the philosopher
or lover of wisdom, the lover of victory and the lover
of gain." "Precisely so." "And also that there are
three forms of pleasure, corresponding respectively

three lives mentioned by Aristotle here answer to the three
classes of men distinguished by Plato (*Rep.* 581). . . .
Michelet and Grant point out that this threefold division
occurs in a metaphor attributed to Pythagoras by Heracleides
Ponticus (*apud* Cic. *Tusc.* v. 3). . . ." *Cf.* Aristot. *Eth.
Nic.* 1097 a-b (i. 5. 1), also Diog. L. vii. 130 on Stoics,
Plutarch, *De liber. educ.* x. (8 A), Renan, *Avenir de la
science*, p. 8. Isoc. *Antid.* 217 characteristically recognizes
only the three motives, pleasure, gain, and honour. For the
entire argument *cf.* Aristot. *Eth. Nic.* 1176 a 31, 1177 a 10,
and *supra*, Introd. pp. liv-lv.

581 Οἶσθ' οὖν, ἦν δ' ἐγώ, ὅτι εἰ θέλοις τρεῖς τοιούτους ἀνθρώπους ἐν μέρει ἕκαστον ἀνερωτᾶν, τίς
τούτων τῶν βίων ἥδιστος, τὸν ἑαυτοῦ ἕκαστος
μάλιστα ἐγκωμιάσεται; ὅ γε¹ χρηματιστικὸς πρὸς
D τὸ κερδαίνειν τὴν τοῦ τιμᾶσθαι ἡδονὴν ἢ τὴν τοῦ
μανθάνειν οὐδενὸς ἀξίαν φήσει εἶναι, εἰ μὴ εἴ τι
αὐτῶν ἀργύριον ποιεῖ; Ἀληθῆ, ἔφη. Τί δὲ ὁ
φιλότιμος; ἦν δ' ἐγώ· οὐ τὴν μὲν ἀπὸ τῶν χρημάτων ἡδονὴν φορτικήν τινα ἡγεῖται, καὶ αὖ τὴν
ἀπὸ τοῦ μανθάνειν, ὅ τι μὴ μάθημα τιμὴν φέρει,
καπνὸν καὶ φλυαρίαν; Οὕτως, ἔφη, ἔχει. Τὸν δὲ
φιλόσοφον, ἦν δ' ἐγώ, τί οἰώμεθα τὰς ἄλλας
E ἡδονὰς νομίζειν πρὸς τὴν τοῦ εἰδέναι τἀληθὲς ὅπη
ἔχει καὶ ἐν τῷ τοιούτῳ τινὶ ἀεὶ εἶναι μανθάνοντα;
τῆς ἡδονῆς² οὐ πάνυ πόρρω, καὶ καλεῖν τῷ ὄντι

---

¹ ὅ γε Hermann, followed by Adam, ὅ τε MSS.
² τῆς ἡδονῆς punctis notata in A, secl. Baiter: . . . μανθάνοντα
τῆς ἡδονῆς; οὐ . . . Adam.

ᵃ For ἐν μέρει cf. 468 B, 520 c and D, 577 c, 615 A, Gorg.
496 B, Laws 876 B, 943 A, 947 c, Polit. 265 A; contrasted
with ἐν τῷ μέρει, Meno 92 E, Gorg. 462 A, 474 A.

The two expressions, similar in appearance, illustrate how
a slight change alters an idiom. So e.g. καινὸν οὐδέν (Gorg.
448 A) has nothing to do with the idiom οὐδὲν καινόν (Phaedo
100 B); τοῦ λόγου ἕνεκα (Rep. 612 c) is different from λόγου
ἕνεκα (Theaet. 191 c—dicis causa); πάντα τἀγαθά (Laws 631 B)
has no connexion with the idiomatic πάντ' ἀγαθά (Rep. 471 c,
cf. supra ad loc.); nor Pindar's πόλλ' ἄνω τὰ δ' αὖ κάτω (Ol.
xii. 6) with ἄνω κάτω as used in Phaedo 96 B, Gorg. 481 D,
etc. Cf. also ἐν τέχνῃ Prot. 319 c with ἐν τῇ τέχνῃ 317 c,
νῷ ἔχειν Rep. 490 A with ἐν νῷ ἔχειν 344 D, etc., τοῦ παντὸς
ἡμάρτηκεν Phaedr. 235 E with παντὸς ἁμαρτάνειν 237 c. The
same is true of words—to confuse καλλίχορος with καλλίχοιρος
would be unfortunate; and the medieval debates about
ὁμοουσία and ὁμοιουσία were perhaps not quite as ridiculous
as they are generally considered.

THE REPUBLIC, BOOK IX

to each?" "By all means." "Are you aware, then," said I, "that if you should choose to ask men of these three classes, each in turn,[a] which is the most pleasurable of these lives, each will chiefly commend his own[b]? The financier will affirm that in comparison with profit the pleasures of honour or of learning are of no value except in so far as they produce money." "True," he said. "And what of the lover of honour[c]?" said I; "does he not regard the pleasure that comes from money as vulgar[d] and low, and again that of learning, save in so far as the knowledge confers honour, mere fume[e] and moonshine?" "It is so," he said. "And what," said I, "are we to suppose the philosopher thinks of the other pleasures compared with the delight of knowing the truth[f] and the reality, and being always occupied with that while he learns? Will he not think them far removed from true pleasure,[g] and call[h] them literally[i]

---

[b] Cf. *Laws* 658 on judging different kinds of literature.

[c] Cf. p. 255, note f, on 549 A. Xenophon is the typical φιλότιμος. In *Mem.* iii. 3. 13 he says that the Athenians "excel all others . . . in love of honour, which is the strongest incentive to deeds of honour and renown" (Marchant, Loeb tr.). Cf. *Epist.* 320 A, *Symp.* 178 D, and also Xen. *Cyrop.* i. 2. 1, *Mem.* iii. i. 10.

[d] Cf. Aristot. *Eth. Nic.* 1095 b 16, and *supra* on 528 E.

[e] Cf. Blaydes on Aristoph. *Clouds* 320, and Turgeniev's novel, *Smoke*.   [f] Cf. *Phileb.* 58 c on dialectic.

[g] Cf. 598 B, *Epist.* iii. 315 c, Marc. Aurel. viii. 1 πόρρω φιλοσοφίας. Hermann's text or something like it is the only idiomatic one, and τῆς ἡδονῆς οὐ πάνυ πόρρω must express the philosopher's opinion of the pleasurableness of the lower pleasures as compared with the higher. Cf. *A.J.P.* xiii. p. 366.

[h] For the infinitive cf. 492 c καὶ φήσειν, 530 B καὶ ζητεῖν.

[i] τῷ ὄντι marks the etymological use of ἀναγκαίας. Cf. on 511 B and 551 E, p. 266, note a.

581 ἀναγκαίας, ὡς οὐδὲν τῶν ἄλλων δεόμενον, εἰ μὴ
ἀνάγκη ἦν; Εὖ, ἔφη, δεῖ εἰδέναι.

VIII. Ὅτε δὴ οὖν, εἶπον, ἀμφισβητοῦνται ἑκάστου τοῦ εἴδους αἱ ἡδοναὶ καὶ αὐτὸς ὁ βίος, μὴ ὅτι
πρὸς τὸ κάλλιον καὶ αἴσχιον ζῆν μηδὲ τὸ χεῖρον
καὶ ἄμεινον, ἀλλὰ πρὸς αὐτὸ τὸ ἥδιον καὶ ἀλυ-
582 πότερον, πῶς ἂν εἰδεῖμεν, τίς αὐτῶν ἀληθέστατα
λέγει; Οὐ πάνυ, ἔφη, ἔγωγε ἔχω εἰπεῖν. Ἀλλ᾽
ὧδε σκόπει. τίνι χρὴ κρίνεσθαι τὰ μέλλοντα
καλῶς κριθήσεσθαι; ἆρ᾽ οὐκ ἐμπειρίᾳ τε καὶ
φρονήσει καὶ λόγῳ; ἢ τούτων ἔχοι ἄν τις βέλτιον
κριτήριον; Καὶ πῶς ἄν; ἔφη. Σκόπει δή· τριῶν
ὄντων τῶν ἀνδρῶν τίς ἐμπειρότατος πασῶν ὧν
εἴπομεν ἡδονῶν; πότερον ὁ φιλοκερδής, μανθάνων
αὐτὴν τὴν ἀλήθειαν οἷόν ἐστι, ἐμπειρότερος δοκεῖ
B σοι εἶναι τῆς ἀπὸ τοῦ εἰδέναι ἡδονῆς, ἢ ὁ φιλόσοφος τῆς ἀπὸ τοῦ κερδαίνειν; Πολύ, ἔφη, διαφέρει. τῷ μὲν γὰρ ἀνάγκη γεύεσθαι τῶν ἑτέρων
ἐκ παιδὸς ἀρξαμένῳ· τῷ δὲ φιλοκερδεῖ, ὅπῃ πέ-
φυκε τὰ ὄντα μανθάνοντι, τῆς ἡδονῆς ταύτης, ὡς
γλυκεῖά ἐστιν, οὐκ ἀνάγκη γεύεσθαι οὐδ᾽ ἐμπείρῳ
γίγνεσθαι, μᾶλλον δὲ καὶ προθυμουμένῳ οὐ ῥᾴδιον.
Πολὺ ἄρα, ἦν δ᾽ ἐγώ, διαφέρει τοῦ γε φιλοκερδοῦς ὁ φιλόσοφος ἐμπειρίᾳ ἀμφοτέρων τῶν ἡδονῶν.
C Πολὺ μέντοι. Τί δὲ τοῦ φιλοτίμου; ἆρα μᾶλλον

---

[a] Cf. 558 D f.
[b] This anticipates Laws 663 A, 733 A-B, 734 A-B.
[c] i.e. what is the criterion? Cf. 582 D δι᾽ οὖ, Sext. Empir.
Bekker, p. 60 (Pyrrh. Hypotyp. ii. 13-14) and p. 197 (Adv.
Math. vii. 35). Cf. Diog. L. Prologue 21, and Laches
184 E. For the idea that the better soul is the better judge
cf. also Laws 663 C, Aristot. Eth. Nic. 1176 a 16-19.
[d] Cf. 582 D, On Virtue 373 D, Xen. Mem. iii. 3. 11.

the pleasures of necessity,[a] since he would have no use for them if necessity were not laid upon him ? " " We may be sure of that," he said.

VIII. " Since, then, there is contention between the several types of pleasure and the lives themselves, not merely as to which is the more honourable or the more base, or the worse or the better, but which is actually the more pleasurable [b] or free from pain, how could we determine which of them speaks most truly ? " " In faith, I cannot tell," he said. " Well, consider it thus : By what are things to be judged, if they are to be judged [c] rightly ? Is it not by experience, intelligence and discussion [d] ? Or could anyone name a better criterion than these ? " " How could he ? " he said. " Observe, then. Of our three types of men, which has had the most experience of all the pleasures we mentioned ? Do you think that the lover of gain by study of the very nature of truth has more experience of the pleasure that knowledge yields than the philosopher has of that which results from gain ? " " There is a vast difference," he said ; " for the one, the philosopher, must needs taste of the other two kinds of pleasure from childhood ; but the lover of gain is not only under no necessity of tasting or experiencing the sweetness of the pleasure of learning the true natures of things,[e] but he cannot easily do so even if he desires and is eager for it." " The lover of wisdom, then," said I, " far surpasses the lover of gain in experience of both kinds of pleasure." " Yes, far." " And how does he compare with the lover of honour ? Is he more un-

---

[e] The force of οὐ extends through the sentence. *Cf. Class. Phil.* vi. (1911) p. 218, and my note on *Tim.* 77 в in *A.J.P.* x. p. 74. *Cf. Il.* v. 408, xxii. 283, Pindar, *Nem.* iii. 15, *Hymn Dem.* 157.

582 ἄπειρός ἐστι τῆς ἀπὸ τοῦ τιμᾶσθαι ἡδονῆς ἢ ἐκεῖνος τῆς ἀπὸ τοῦ φρονεῖν; Ἀλλὰ τιμὴ μέν, ἔφη,
ἐάνπερ ἐξεργάζωνται ἐπὶ ὃ ἕκαστος ὥρμηκε,
πᾶσιν αὐτοῖς ἕπεται· καὶ γὰρ ὁ πλούσιος ὑπὸ
πολλῶν τιμᾶται καὶ ὁ ἀνδρεῖος καὶ ὁ σοφός, ὥστε
ἀπό γε τοῦ τιμᾶσθαι, οἷόν ἐστι, πάντες τῆς ἡδονῆς
ἔμπειροι· τῆς δὲ τοῦ ὄντος θέας, οἵαν ἡδονὴν ἔχει,
ἀδύνατον ἄλλῳ γεγεῦσθαι πλὴν τῷ φιλοσόφῳ.
D Ἐμπειρίας μὲν ἄρα, εἶπον, ἕνεκα κάλλιστα τῶν
ἀνδρῶν κρίνει οὗτος. Πολύ γε. Καὶ μὴν μετά
γε φρονήσεως μόνος ἔμπειρος γεγονὼς ἔσται. Τί
μήν; Ἀλλὰ μὴν καὶ δι' οὗ γε δεῖ ὀργάνου κρίνεσθαι, οὐ τοῦ φιλοκερδοῦς τοῦτο ὄργανον οὐδὲ τοῦ
φιλοτίμου, ἀλλὰ τοῦ φιλοσόφου. Τὸ ποῖον; Διὰ
λόγων που ἔφαμεν δεῖν κρίνεσθαι. ἦ γάρ; Ναί.
Λόγοι δὲ τούτου μάλιστα ὄργανον. Πῶς δ' οὔ;
Οὐκοῦν εἰ μὲν πλούτῳ καὶ κέρδει ἄριστα ἐκρίνετο
E τὰ κρινόμενα, ἃ ἐπῄνει ὁ φιλοκερδὴς καὶ ἔψεγεν,
ἀνάγκη ἂν ἦν ταῦτα ἀληθέστατα εἶναι. Πολλή γε.
Εἰ δὲ τιμῇ τε καὶ νίκῃ καὶ ἀνδρείᾳ, ἆρ' οὐχ ἃ
ὁ φιλότιμός τε καὶ ὁ φιλόνικος; Δῆλον. Ἐπειδὴ
δ' ἐμπειρίᾳ καὶ φρονήσει καὶ λόγῳ; Ἀνάγκη,
ἔφη, ἃ ὁ φιλόσοφός τε καὶ ὁ φιλόλογος ἐπαινεῖ,
583 ἀληθέστατα εἶναι. Τριῶν ἄρ' οὐσῶν τῶν ἡδονῶν
ἡ τούτου τοῦ μέρους τῆς ψυχῆς, ᾧ μανθάνομεν,
ἡδίστη ἂν εἴη, καὶ ἐν ᾧ ἡμῶν τοῦτο ἄρχει, ὁ

---

[a] For the periphrasis γεγονὼς ἔσται cf. *Charm.* 174 D
ἀπολελοιπὸς ἔσται.
[b] Cf. 508 B, 518 C, 527 D.
[c] Cf. on 582 A, p. 376, note d.

acquainted with the pleasure of being honoured than that other with that which comes from knowledge ? " " Nay, honour," he said, " if they achieve their several objects, attends them all; for the rich man is honoured by many and the brave man and the wise, so that all are acquainted with the kind of pleasure that honour brings ; but it is impossible for anyone except the lover of wisdom to have savoured the delight that the contemplation of true being and reality brings." " Then," said I, " so far as experience goes, he is the best judge of the three." " By far." " And again, he is the only one whose experience will have been accompanied[a] by intelligence." " Surely." " And yet again, that which is the instrument, or ὄργανον, of judgement[b] is the instrument, not of the lover of gain or of the lover of honour, but of the lover of wisdom." " What is that ? " " It was by means of words and discussion[c] that we said the judgement must be reached ; was it not ? " " Yes." " And they are the instrument mainly of the philosopher." " Of course." " Now if wealth and profit were the best criteria by which things are judged, the things praised and censured by the lover of gain would necessarily be truest and most real." " Quite necessarily." " And if honour, victory and courage, would it not be the things praised by the lover of honour and victory ? " " Obviously." " But since the tests are experience and wisdom and discussion, what follows ? " " Of necessity," he said, " that the things approved by the lover of wisdom and discussion are most valid and true." " There being, then, three kinds of pleasure, the pleasure of that part of the soul whereby we learn is the sweetest, and the life of the man in whom that part dominates is the most pleasur-

583 τούτου βίος ἥδιστος; Πῶς δ' οὐ μέλλει; ἔφη·
κύριος γοῦν ἐπαινέτης ὢν ἐπαινεῖ τὸν ἑαυτοῦ βίον
ὁ φρόνιμος. Τίνα δὲ δεύτερον, εἶπον, βίον καὶ
τίνα δευτέραν ἡδονήν φησιν ὁ κριτὴς εἶναι; Δῆλον
ὅτι τὴν τοῦ πολεμικοῦ τε καὶ φιλοτίμου· ἐγγυτέρω
γὰρ αὐτοῦ ἐστιν ἢ ἡ τοῦ χρηματιστοῦ. Ὑστάτην
δὴ τὴν τοῦ φιλοκερδοῦς, ὡς ἔοικεν. Τί μήν; ἦ
δ' ὅς.

B   IX. Ταῦτα μὲν τοίνυν οὕτω δὔ ἐφεξῆς ἂν εἴη
καὶ δὶς νενικηκὼς ὁ δίκαιος τὸν ἄδικον· τὸ δὲ
τρίτον Ὀλυμπικῶς τῷ σωτῆρί τε καὶ τῷ Ὀλυμ-
πίῳ Διί, ἄθρει ὅτι οὐδὲ παναληθής ἐστιν ἡ τῶν
ἄλλων ἡδονὴ πλὴν τῆς τοῦ φρονίμου οὐδὲ καθαρά,
ἀλλ' ἐσκιαγραφημένη τις, ὡς ἐγὼ δοκῶ μοι τῶν
σοφῶν τινος ἀκηκοέναι. καίτοι τοῦτ' ἂν εἴη μέγισ-
τόν τε καὶ κυριώτατον τῶν πτωμάτων. Πολύ
γε· ἀλλὰ πῶς λέγεις; Ὧδ', εἶπον, ἐξευρήσω,
C   σοῦ ἀποκρινομένου ζητῶν ἅμα. Ἐρώτα δή, ἔφη.
Λέγε δή, ἦν δ' ἐγώ· οὐκ ἐναντίον φαμὲν λύπην
ἡδονῇ; Καὶ μάλα. Οὐκοῦν καὶ τὸ μήτε χαίρειν
μήτε λυπεῖσθαι εἶναί τι; Εἶναι μέντοι. Με-

ᵃ The third cup of wine was always dedicated to Zeus the
Saviour, and τρίτος σωτήρ became proverbial. Cf. Charm.
167 A, Phileb. 66 D, Laws 692 A, 960 C, Epist. vii. 334 D,
340 A. Cf. Hesychius s.v. τρίτος κρατήρ. Brochard, La
Morale de Platon, missing the point, says, "Voici enfin un
troisième argument qui paraît à Platon le plus décisif
puisqu'il l'appelle une victoire vraiment olympique." For
the idea of a contest cf. Phileb. passim.

ᵇ Cf. Phileb. 36 c, 44 D ἡδοναὶ ἀληθεῖς. For the unreality
of the lower pleasures cf. Phileb. 36 A ff. and esp. 44 C-D,
Unity of Plato's Thought, pp. 23-25, What Plato Said,
pp. 322-323 and 609-610, supra Introd. pp. lvi-lix, Rodier,
Remarques sur le Philèbe, p. 281.

ᶜ Cf. Phileb. 52 c καθαρὰς ἡδονάς, and 53 c καθαρὰ λύπης.

able." "How could it be otherwise?" he said. "At any rate the man of intelligence speaks with authority when he commends his own life." "And to what life and to what pleasure," I said, "does the judge assign the second place?" "Obviously to that of the warrior and honour-loving type, for it is nearer to the first than is the life of the money-maker." "And so the last place belongs to the lover of gain, as it seems." "Surely," said he.

IX. "That, then, would be two points in succession and two victories for the just man over the unjust. And now for the third in the Olympian fashion to the saviour [a] and to Olympian Zeus—observe that other pleasure than that of the intelligence is not altogether even real [b] or pure,[c] but is a kind of scene-painting,[d] as I seem to have heard from some wise man [e]; and yet [f] this would be the greatest and most decisive over-throw.[g] " "Much the greatest. But what do you mean?" "I shall discover it," I said, "if you will answer my questions while I seek." "Ask, then," he said. "Tell me, then," said I, "do we not say that pain is the opposite of pleasure?" "We certainly do." "And is there not such a thing as a neutral state [h]?" "There is." "Is it not intermediate be-

---

[a] Cf. *Laws* 663 c, *Phaedo* 69 b, *supra* 365 c, 523 b, 602 d, 586 b, Wilamowitz, *Platon*, ii. p. 266.

[e] One of Plato's evasions. *Cf. What Plato Said*, p. 513, on *Meno* 81 a, *Phileb.* 44 b. Wilamowitz, *Platon*, ii. p. 266 misses the point and says that by the wise man Plato means himself.

[f] For this rhetorical καίτοι *cf.* 360 c, 376 b, 433 b, 440 d, *Gorg.* 452 e, *Laws* 663 e, 690 c.

[g] Cf. *Phileb.* 22 f, Aesch. *Prom.* 919, Soph. *Antig.* 1046.

[h] If any inference could be drawn from the fact that in the *Philebus* 42 d ff. and 32 e the reality of the neutral state has to be proved, it would be that the *Philebus* is earlier, which it is not.

583 ταξὺ τούτοιν ἀμφοῖν ἐν μέσῳ ὂν ἡσυχίαν τινὰ
περὶ ταῦτα τῆς ψυχῆς; ἢ οὐχ οὕτως αὐτὸ λέγεις;
Οὕτως, ἦ δ' ὅς. Ἆρ' οὐ μνημονεύεις, ἦν δ' ἐγώ,
τοὺς τῶν καμνόντων λόγους, οὓς λέγουσιν ὅταν
κάμνωσιν; Ποίους; Ὡς οὐδὲν ἄρα ἐστὶν ἥδιον
D τοῦ ὑγιαίνειν, ἀλλὰ σφᾶς ἐλελήθει, πρὶν κάμνειν,
ἥδιστον ὄν. Μέμνημαι, ἔφη. Οὐκοῦν καὶ τῶν
περιωδυνίᾳ τινὶ ἐχομένων ἀκούεις λεγόντων, ὡς
οὐδὲν ἥδιον τοῦ παύσασθαι ὀδυνώμενον; Ἀκούω.
Καὶ ἐν ἄλλοις γε, οἶμαι, πολλοῖς τοιούτοις αἰσθάνει
γιγνομένους τοὺς ἀνθρώπους, ἐν οἷς, ὅταν λυπῶν-
ται, τὸ μὴ λυπεῖσθαι καὶ τὴν ἡσυχίαν τοῦ τοιούτου ἐγκωμιάζουσιν ὡς ἥδιστον, οὐ τὸ χαίρειν.
Τοῦτο γάρ, ἔφη, τότε ἡδὺ ἴσως καὶ ἀγαπητὸν
E γίγνεται, ἡσυχία. Καὶ ὅταν παύσηται ἄρα, εἶπον,
χαίρων τις, ἡ τῆς ἡδονῆς ἡσυχία λυπηρὸν ἔσται.
Ἴσως, ἔφη. Ὃ μεταξὺ ἄρα νῦν δὴ ἀμφοτέρων
ἔφαμεν εἶναι, τὴν ἡσυχίαν, τοῦτό ποτε ἀμφότερα
ἔσται, λύπη τε καὶ ἡδονή. Ἔοικεν. Ἦ καὶ
δυνατὸν τὸ μηδέτερα ὂν ἀμφότερα γίγνεσθαι; Οὔ
μοι δοκεῖ. Καὶ μὴν τό γε ἡδὺ ἐν ψυχῇ γιγνόμενον καὶ τὸ λυπηρὸν κίνησίς τις ἀμφοτέρω ἐστόν·
584 ἢ οὔ; Ναί. Τὸ δὲ μήτε λυπηρὸν μήτε ἡδὺ οὐχὶ
ἡσυχία μέντοι καὶ ἐν μέσῳ τούτοιν ἐφάνη ἄρτι;
Ἐφάνη γάρ. Πῶς οὖν ὀρθῶς ἔστι τὸ μὴ ἀλγεῖν
ἡδὺ ἡγεῖσθαι ἢ τὸ μὴ χαίρειν ἀνιαρόν; Οὐδαμῶς.
Οὐκ ἔστιν ἄρα τοῦτο, ἀλλὰ φαίνεται, ἦν δ' ἐγώ,

---

[a] For ἐν μέσῳ cf. Phileb. 35 E.
[b] Cf. perhaps Phileb. 45 B, Aristot. Eth. Nic. 1095 a 24,
and Heracleit. fr. 111, Diels i.³ p. 99 νοῦσος ὑγιείην ἐποίησεν ἡδύ.
[c] Cf. Phileb. 43 E, Hipp. Maj. 300 B f.

tween them, and in the mean,[a] being a kind of quietude of the soul in these respects ? Or is not that your notion of it ? " " It is that," said he. " Do you not recall the things men say in sickness ? " " What sort of things ? " " Why, that after all there is nothing sweeter than to be well,[b] though they were not aware that it is the highest pleasure before they were ill." " I remember," he said. " And do you not hear men afflicted with severe pain saying that there is no greater pleasure than the cessation of this suffering ? " " I do." " And you perceive, I presume, many similar conditions in which men while suffering pain praise freedom from pain and relief from that as the highest pleasure, and not positive delight." " Yes," he said, " for this in such cases is perhaps what is felt as pleasurable and acceptable— peace." " And so," I said, " when a man's delight comes to an end, the cessation of pleasure will be painful." " It may be so," he said. " What, then, we just now described as the intermediate state between the two—this quietude—will sometimes be both pain and pleasure." " It seems so." " Is it really possible for that which is neither to become both[c] ? " " I think not." " And further, both pleasure and pain arising in the soul are a kind of motion,[d] are they not ? " " Yes." " And did we not just now see that to feel neither pain nor pleasure is a quietude of the soul and an intermediate state between the two ? " " Yes, we did." " How, then, can it be right to think the absence of pain pleasure, or the absence of joy painful ? " " In no way." " This is not a reality, then, but an illusion," said I ; " in such case the quietude

---

[d] Aristotle attacks this doctrine with captious dialectic in his *Topics* and *De anima*.

581 παρὰ τὸ ἀλγεινὸν ἡδὺ καὶ παρὰ τὸ ἡδὺ ἀλγεινὸν
τότε ἡ ἡσυχία, καὶ οὐδὲν ὑγιὲς τούτων τῶν φαν-
τασμάτων πρὸς ἡδονῆς ἀλήθειαν, ἀλλὰ γοητεία τις.
Ὡς γοῦν ὁ λόγος, ἔφη, σημαίνει. Ἰδὲ τοίνυν,
Β ἔφην ἐγώ, ἡδονάς, αἳ οὐκ ἐκ λυπῶν εἰσίν, ἵνα μὴ
πολλάκις οἰηθῇς ἐν τῷ παρόντι οὕτω τοῦτο πεφυκέναι, ἡδονὴν μὲν παῦλαν λύπης εἶναι, λύπην δὲ
ἡδονῆς. Ποῦ δή, ἔφη, καὶ ποίας λέγεις; Πολλαὶ μέν, εἶπον, καὶ ἄλλαι, μάλιστα δ᾽ εἰ θέλεις
ἐννοῆσαι τὰς περὶ τὰς ὀσμὰς ἡδονάς. αὗται γὰρ
οὐ προλυπηθέντι ἐξαίφνης ἀμήχανοι τὸ μέγεθος
γίγνονται, παυσάμεναί τε λύπην οὐδεμίαν κατα-
λείπουσιν. Ἀληθέστατα, ἔφη. Μὴ ἄρα πειθώ-
C μεθα καθαρὰν ἡδονὴν εἶναι τὴν λύπης ἀπαλλαγήν,
μηδὲ λύπην τὴν ἡδονῆς. Μὴ γάρ. Ἀλλὰ μέντοι,
εἶπον, αἵ γε διὰ τοῦ σώματος ἐπὶ τὴν ψυχὴν τείνου-
σαι καὶ λεγόμεναι ἡδοναὶ σχεδὸν αἱ πλεῖσταί τε καὶ
μέγισται τούτου τοῦ εἴδους εἰσί, λυπῶν τινὲς ἀπ-
αλλαγαί. Εἰσὶ γάρ. Οὐκοῦν καὶ αἱ πρὸ μελλόντων
τούτων ἐκ προσδοκίας γιγνόμεναι προησθήσεις τε
καὶ προλυπήσεις κατὰ ταὐτὰ ἔχουσιν; Κατὰ ταὐτά.
D   X. Οἶσθ᾽ οὖν, ἦν δ᾽ ἐγώ, οἷαί εἰσι καὶ ᾧ
μάλιστα ἐοίκασιν; Τῷ; ἔφη. Νομίζεις τι, εἶπον,
ἐν τῇ φύσει εἶναι τὸ μὲν ἄνω, τὸ δὲ κάτω, τὸ δὲ

---

  [a] Cf. 586 c, and Phileb. 42 B and 41 E.
  [b] For οὐδὲν ὑγιές in this sense cf. on 523 B.
  [c] Cf. Phileb. 44 C–D, Xen. Oecon. 1. 20 προσποιούμεναι
ἡδοναὶ εἶναι, etc.
  [d] For the idea that smells are not conditioned by pain
cf. Tim. 65 A, Phileb. 51 B and E, and Siebeck, Platon als
Kritiker Aristotelischer Ansichten, p. 161.
  [e] Cf. Gorg. 493–494, Phileb. 42 C ff., and Phaedr. 258 E,
which Wilamowitz, Platon, ii. p. 267 overlooks.

in juxtaposition [a] with the pain appears pleasure, and in juxtaposition with the pleasure pain. And these illusions have no real bearing [b] on the truth of pleasure, but are a kind of jugglery.[c] " " So at any rate our argument signifies," he said. " Take a look, then," said I, " at pleasures which do not follow on pain, so that you may not haply suppose for the present that it is the nature of pleasure to be a cessation from pain and pain from pleasure." " Where shall I look," he said, " and what pleasures do you mean ? " " There are many others," I said, " and especially, if you please to note them, the pleasures connected with smell.[d] For these with no antecedent pain [e] suddenly attain an indescribable intensity, and their cessation leaves no pain after them." " Most true," he said. " Let us not believe, then, that the riddance of pain is pure pleasure or that of pleasure pain." " No, we must not." " Yet, surely," said I, " the affections that find their way through the body [f] to the soul [g] and are called pleasures are, we may say, the most and the greatest of them, of this type, in some sort releases from pain.[h] " " Yes, they are." " And is not this also the character of the anticipatory pleasures and pains that precede them and arise from the expectation of them ? " " It is."

X. " Do you know, then, what their quality is and what they most resemble ? " " What ? " he said. " Do you think that there is such a thing in nature [i]

---

[f] Cf. *Phaedo* 65 A, *Phaedr.* 258 E, Vol. I. p. 8, note a, on 328 D, and *supra* p. 8, note b.

[g] Cf. *Tim.* 45 D (of sensations) μέχρι τῆς ψυχῆς, *Laws* 673 A, *Rep.* 462 C πρὸς τὴν ψυχὴν τεταμένη. Cf. also *Phileb.* 33 D-E, 34, 43 B-C, and *What Plato Said*, p. 608.

[h] Cf. *Phileb.* 44 B, 44 C λυπῶν . . . ἀποφυγάς, *Protag.* 354 B.

[i] For ἐν τῇ φύσει cf. *Parmen.* 132 D.

584 μέσον; Ἔγωγε. Οἴει οὖν ἄν τινα ἐκ τοῦ κάτω φερόμενον πρὸς μέσον ἄλλο τι οἴεσθαι ἢ ἄνω φέρεσθαι; καὶ ἐν μέσῳ στάντα, ἀφορῶντα ὅθεν ἐνήνεκται, ἀλλοθί που ἂν ἡγεῖσθαι εἶναι ἢ ἐν τῷ ἄνω, μὴ ἑωρακότα τὸ ἀληθῶς ἄνω; Μὰ Δί', οὐκ ἔγωγε, ἔφη, ἄλλως οἶμαι οἰηθῆναι ἂν τὸν τοιοῦτον.

Ε Ἀλλ' εἰ πάλιν γ', ἔφη, φέροιτο, κάτω τ' ἂν οἴοιτο φέρεσθαι καὶ ἀληθῆ οἴοιτο; Πῶς γὰρ οὔ; Οὐκοῦν ταῦτα πάσχοι ἂν πάντα διὰ τὸ μὴ ἔμπειρος εἶναι τοῦ ἀληθινῶς ἄνω τε ὄντος καὶ ἐν μέσῳ καὶ κάτω; Δῆλον δή. Θαυμάζοις ἂν οὖν, εἰ καὶ οἱ ἄπειροι ἀληθείας περὶ πολλῶν τε ἄλλων μὴ ὑγιεῖς δόξας ἔχουσι, πρός τε ἡδονὴν καὶ λύπην καὶ τὸ μεταξὺ τούτων οὕτω διάκεινται, ὥστε, ὅταν μὲν 585 ἐπὶ τὸ λυπηρὸν φέρωνται, ἀληθῆ τε οἴονται καὶ τῷ ὄντι λυποῦνται, ὅταν δὲ ἀπὸ λύπης ἐπὶ τὸ μεταξύ, σφόδρα μὲν οἴονται πρὸς πληρώσει τε καὶ ἡδονῇ γίγνεσθαι, ὥσπερ πρὸς μέλαν φαιὸν ἀποσκοποῦντες ἀπειρίᾳ λευκοῦ, καὶ πρὸς τὸ ἄλυπον οὕτω λύπην ἀφορῶντες ἀπειρίᾳ ἡδονῆς ἀπατῶνται; Μὰ Δία, ἦ δ' ὅς, οὐκ ἂν θαυμάσαιμι, ἀλλὰ πολὺ μᾶλλον, εἰ μὴ οὕτως ἔχει. Ὧδέ γ' οὖν, εἶπον, ἐννόει· οὐχὶ πεῖνα καὶ δίψα καὶ τὰ τοιαῦτα κενώσεις

---

[a] For the purposes of his illustration Plato takes the popular view of up and down, which is corrected in *Tim.* 62 c-d and perhaps by the ironical δή in *Phaedo* 112 c. *Cf.* Zeller, *Aristotle* (Eng.) i. p. 428.

[b] *Cf.* Aristot. *Met.* 1011 b 30-31 and *Eth. Nic.* 1154 a 30 διὰ τὸ παρὰ τὸ ἐναντίον φαίνεσθαι.

[c] The argument from the parallel of body and mind here belongs to what we have called confirmation. *Cf. What Plato Said*, p. 528, on *Phaedo* 78 B. The figurative use of repletion and nutrition is not to be pressed in proof of con-

as up and down and in the middle ? " " I do."
" Do you suppose, then, that anyone who is transported from below to the centre would have any
other opinion than that he was moving upward [a] ?
And if he took his stand at the centre and looked in
the direction from which he had been transported, do
you think he would suppose himself to be anywhere
but above, never having seen that which is really
above ? " " No, by Zeus," he said, " I do not think
that such a person would have any other notion."
" And if he were borne back," I said, " he would
both think himself to be moving downward and would
think truly." " Of course." " And would not all
this happen to him because of his non-acquaintance
with the true and real up and down and middle ? "
" Obviously." " Would it surprise you, then," said
I, " if similarly men without experience of truth and
reality hold unsound opinions about many other
matters, and are so disposed towards pleasure and
pain and the intermediate neutral condition that,
when they are moved in the direction of the painful,
they truly think themselves to be, and really are, in a
state of pain, but, when they move from pain to the
middle and neutral state, they intensely believe that
they are approaching fulfilment and pleasure, and just
as if, in ignorance of white, they were comparing
grey with black,[b] so, being inexperienced in true
pleasure, they are deceived by viewing painlessness
in its relation to pain ? " " No, by Zeus," he said,
" it would not surprise me, but far rather if it were
not so." " In *this* way, then, consider it.[c] Are not
hunger and thirst and similar states inanitions or

tradictions with the *Philebus* or *Gorgias*. *Cf. Matthew* v. 6
" Hunger and thirst after righteousness."

585 B τινές εἰσι τῆς περὶ τὸ σῶμα ἕξεως; Τί μήν;
Ἄγνοια δὲ καὶ ἀφροσύνη ἆρ᾽ οὐ κενότης ἐστὶ τῆς
περὶ ψυχὴν αὖ ἕξεως; Μάλα γε. Οὐκοῦν πληροῖτ᾽
ἂν ὅ τε τροφῆς μεταλαμβάνων καὶ ὁ νοῦν ἴσχων;
Πῶς δ᾽ οὔ; Πλήρωσις δὲ ἀληθεστέρα τοῦ ἧττον
ἢ τοῦ μᾶλλον ὄντος; Δῆλον, ὅτι τοῦ μᾶλλον.
Πότερα οὖν ἡγεῖ τὰ γένη μᾶλλον καθαρᾶς οὐσίας
μετέχειν, τὰ οἷον σίτου τε καὶ ποτοῦ καὶ ὄψου καὶ
ξυμπάσης τροφῆς, ἢ τὸ δόξης τε ἀληθοῦς εἶδος καὶ
C ἐπιστήμης καὶ νοῦ καὶ ξυλλήβδην αὖ πάσης
ἀρετῆς; ὧδε δὲ κρῖνε· τὸ τοῦ ἀεὶ ὁμοίου ἐχόμενον
καὶ ἀθανάτου καὶ ἀληθείας, καὶ αὐτὸ τοιοῦτον ὂν
καὶ ἐν τοιούτῳ γιγνόμενον, μᾶλλον εἶναί σοι δοκεῖ,
ἢ τὸ μηδέποτε ὁμοίου καὶ θνητοῦ, καὶ αὐτὸ
τοιοῦτο καὶ ἐν τοιούτῳ γιγνόμενον; Πολύ, ἔφη,
διαφέρει τὸ τοῦ ἀεὶ ὁμοίου. Ἡ οὖν ἀνομοίου[1]
οὐσία οὐσίας τι μᾶλλον ἢ ἐπιστήμης μετέχει;
Οὐδαμῶς. Τί δ᾽, ἀληθείας; Οὐδὲ τοῦτο. Εἰ δὲ
ἀληθείας ἧττον, οὐ καὶ οὐσίας; Ἀνάγκη. Οὐκ-
D οῦν ὅλως τὰ περὶ τὴν τοῦ σώματος θεραπείαν γένη
τῶν γενῶν αὖ τῶν περὶ τὴν τῆς ψυχῆς θεραπείαν

---

[1] ἀνομοίου Hermann : ἀεὶ ὁμοίου mss. followed by Ast and
Stallbaum. Adam reads ἀεὶ ἀνομοίου and inserts ἡ before
ἐπιστήμης. C. Ritter treats ἀεὶ ὁμοίου οὐσία as a marginal
note and reads ˙Η οὖν οὐσίας τι μᾶλλον ἢ ἐπιστήμης μετέχει
(*Philologus* 67, pp. 312-313). Apelt entirely recasts the
passage (*Woch. f. kl. Phil.*, 1903, pp. 348-350).

[a] For κενώσεις cf. *Phileb.* 35 B, 42 C-D, *Tim.* 65 A.
[b] For the figure of nourishment of the soul cf. *Protag.*
313 C, *Phaedr.* 248 B, and *Soph.* 223 E.
[c] Cf. *What Plato Said*, p. 517, on *Meno* 98 A-B.

emptinesses[a] of the bodily habit?" "Surely." "And is not ignorance and folly in turn a kind of emptiness of the habit of the soul?" "It is indeed." "And he who partakes of nourishment[b] and he who gets wisdom fills the void and is filled?" "Of course." "And which is the truer filling and fulfilment, that of the less or of the more real being?" "Evidently that of the more real." "And which of the two groups or kinds do you think has a greater part in pure essence, the class of foods, drinks, and relishes and nourishment generally, or the kind of true opinion,[c] knowledge and reason,[d] and, in sum, all the things that are more excellent[e]? Form your judgement thus. Which do you think more truly *is*, that which clings to what is ever like itself and immortal and to the truth, and that which is itself of such a nature and is born in a thing of that nature, or that which clings to what is mortal and never the same and is itself such and is born in such a thing?" "That which cleaves to what is ever the same far surpasses," he said. "Does the essence of that which never abides the same partake of real essence any more than of knowledge?" "By no means." "Or of truth and reality?" "Not of that, either." "And if a thing has less of truth has it not also less of real essence or existence?" "Necessarily." "And is it not generally true that the kinds concerned with the service of the body partake less of truth and reality than

---

[d] Different kinds of intelligence are treated as synonyms because for the present purpose their distinctions are irrelevant. *Cf.* 511 A, C, and D διάνοια. *Cf. Unity of Plato's Thought*, p. 43 and p. 47, n. 339. Plato does not distinguish synonyms nor virtual synonyms for their own sake as Prodicus did. *Cf. Protag.* 358 A-B.

[e] *Cf. Symp.* 209 A φρόνησίν τε καὶ τὴν ἄλλην ἀρετήν.

585 ἧττον ἀληθείας τε καὶ οὐσίας μετέχει; Πολύ γε.
Σῶμα δὲ αὐτὸ ψυχῆς οὐκ οἴει οὕτως; Ἔγωγε.
Οὐκοῦν τὸ τῶν μᾶλλον ὄντων πληρούμενον καὶ
αὐτὸ μᾶλλον ὂν ὄντως μᾶλλον πληροῦται ἢ τὸ τῶν
ἧττον ὄντων καὶ αὐτὸ ἧττον ὄν; Πῶς γὰρ οὔ;
Εἰ ἄρα τὸ πληροῦσθαι τῶν φύσει προσηκόντων
ἡδύ ἐστι, τὸ τῷ ὄντι καὶ τῶν ὄντων πληρούμενον
Ε μᾶλλον μᾶλλον ὄντως τε καὶ ἀληθεστέρως χαίρειν
ἂν ποιοῖ ἡδονῇ ἀληθεῖ, τὸ δὲ τῶν ἧττον ὄντων
μεταλαμβάνον ἧττόν τε ἂν ἀληθῶς καὶ βεβαίως
πληροῖτο καὶ ἀπιστοτέρας ἂν ἡδονῆς καὶ ἧττον
ἀληθοῦς μεταλαμβάνοι. Ἀναγκαιότατα, ἔφη. Οἱ
586 ἄρα φρονήσεως καὶ ἀρετῆς ἄπειροι, εὐωχίαις δὲ
καὶ τοῖς τοιούτοις ἀεὶ ξυνόντες, κάτω, ὡς ἔοικε,
καὶ μέχρι πάλιν πρὸς τὸ μεταξὺ φέρονταί τε καὶ
ταύτῃ πλανῶνται διὰ βίου, ὑπερβάντες δὲ τοῦτο
πρὸς τὸ ἀληθῶς ἄνω οὔτε ἀνέβλεψαν πώποτε οὔτε
ἠνέχθησαν, οὐδὲ τοῦ ὄντος τῷ ὄντι ἐπληρώθησαν,
οὐδὲ βεβαίου τε καὶ καθαρᾶς ἡδονῆς ἐγεύσαντο,
ἀλλὰ βοσκημάτων δίκην κάτω ἀεὶ βλέποντες καὶ
κεκυφότες εἰς γῆν καὶ εἰς τραπέζας βόσκονται
Β χορταζόμενοι καὶ ὀχεύοντες, καὶ ἕνεκα τῆς τούτων

---

[a] For ξυνόντες see Blaydes on Aristoph. *Clouds* 1404.

[b] *Cf. What Plato Said*, p. 528, on *Phaedo* 79 c for πλανάω of error in thought. This is rather the *errare* of Lucretius ii. 10 and the post-Aristotelian schools.

[c] *Cf.* on 576 A ἄγευστος, and for the thought of the whole sentence *cf.* Dio Chrys. *Or.* xiii., Teubner, vol. i. p. 240, and William Watson, " The things that are more excellent " :

> To dress, to call, to dine . . .
> How many a soul for these things lives
> With pious passion, grave intent . . .
> And never even in dreams hath seen
> The things that are more excellent.

those that serve the soul ? " " Much less." " And do you not think that the same holds of the body itself in comparison with the soul ? " " I do." " Then is not that which is fulfilled of what more truly is, and which itself more truly is, more truly filled and satisfied than that which being itself less real is filled with more unreal things ? " " Of course." " If, then, to be filled with what befits nature is pleasure, then that which is more really filled with real things would more really and truly cause us to enjoy a true pleasure, while that which partakes of the less truly existent would be less truly and surely filled and would partake of a less trustworthy and less true pleasure." " Most inevitably," he said. " Then those who have no experience of wisdom and virtue but are ever devoted to [a] feastings and that sort of thing are swept downward, it seems, and back again to the centre, and so sway and roam [b] to and fro throughout their lives, but they have never transcended all this and turned their eyes to the true upper region nor been wafted there, nor ever been really filled with real things, nor ever tasted [c] stable and pure pleasure, but with eyes ever bent upon the earth [d] and heads bowed down over their tables they feast like cattle, [e] grazing and copulating, ever greedy for more

---

[d] Cf. Milton, Comus, " Ne'er looks to heaven amid its gorgeous feast," Rossetti, " Nineveh," in fine, " That set gaze never on the sky," etc. Cf. S. O. Dickermann, De Argumentis quibusdam ap. Xenophontem, Platonem, Aristotelem obviis e structura hominis et animalium petitis, Halle, 1909, who lists Plato's Symp. 190 A, Rep. 586 A, Cratyl. 396 B, 409 C, Tim. 90 A, 91 E. and many other passages.

[e] Cf. Aristot. Eth. Nic. 1095 b 20 βοσκημάτων βίον. Cf. What Plato Said, p. 611, on Phileb., in fine.

586 πλεονεξίας λακτίζοντες καὶ κυρίττοντες ἀλλήλους
σιδηροῖς κέρασί τε καὶ ὁπλαῖς ἀποκτιννύασι δι᾽
ἀπληστίαν, ἅτε οὐχὶ τοῖς οὖσιν οὐδὲ τὸ ὂν οὐδὲ
τὸ στέγον ἑαυτῶν πιμπλάντες. Παντελῶς, ἔφη ὁ
Γλαύκων, τὸν τῶν πολλῶν, ὦ Σώκρατες, χρησμω-
δεῖς βίον. ῏Αρ᾽ οὖν οὐκ ἀνάγκη καὶ ἡδοναῖς ξυν-
εῖναι μεμιγμέναις λύπαις, εἰδώλοις τῆς ἀληθοῦς
ἡδονῆς καὶ ἐσκιαγραφημέναις, ὑπὸ τῆς παρ᾽
C ἀλλήλας θέσεως ἀποχραινομέναις, ὥστε σφοδροὺς
ἑκατέρας φαίνεσθαι καὶ ἔρωτας ἑαυτῶν λυττῶντας
τοῖς ἄφροσιν ἐντίκτειν καὶ περιμαχήτους εἶναι,
ὥσπερ τὸ τῆς Ἑλένης εἴδωλον ὑπὸ τῶν ἐν Τροίᾳ
Στησίχορός φησι γενέσθαι περιμάχητον ἀγνοίᾳ τοῦ
ἀληθοῦς; Πολλὴ ἀνάγκη, ἔφη, τοιοῦτόν τι αὐτὸ
εἶναι.

XI. Τί δέ; περὶ τὸ θυμοειδὲς οὐχ ἕτερα τοιαῦτα
ἀνάγκη γίγνεσθαι, ὃς ἂν αὐτὸ τοῦτο διαπράττηται
ἢ φθόνῳ διὰ φιλοτιμίαν ἢ βίᾳ διὰ φιλονικίαν ἢ
D θυμῷ διὰ δυσκολίαν, πλησμονὴν τιμῆς τε καὶ
νίκης καὶ θυμοῦ διώκων ἄνευ λογισμοῦ τε καὶ
νοῦ; Τοιαῦτα, ἦ δ᾽ ὅς, ἀνάγκη καὶ περὶ τοῦτο
εἶναι. Τί οὖν; ἦν δ᾽ ἐγώ· θαρροῦντες λέγωμεν,

---

[a] Cf. supra 373 E, Phaedo 66 c ff., Berkeley, Siris 330 "For these things men fight, cheat, and scramble."

[b] τὸ στέγον: cf. Gorg. 493 B, Laws 714 A.

[c] Plato laughs at himself. Cf. supra 509 c and 540 B-c. The picturesque, allegorical style of oracles was proverbial. For χρησμῳδεῖν cf. Crat. 396 D, Apol. 39 c, Laws 712 A.

[d] Cf. on 584 A, p. 384, note a.

[e] For περιμαχήτους cf. Aristot. Eth. Nic. 1168 b 19, Eth. Eud. 1248 b 27, and supra on 521 A, p. 145, note e.

[f] For the Stesichorean legend that the real Helen remained in Egypt while only her phantom went to Troy cf. Phaedr. 243 A-B, Eurip. Hel. 605 ff., Elect. 1282-1283, Isoc. Hel. 64,

of these delights; and in their greed [a] kicking and butting one another with horns and hooves of iron they slay one another in sateless avidity, because they are vainly striving to satisfy with things that are not real the unreal and incontinent part [b] of their souls." "You describe in quite oracular style, [c] Socrates," said Glaucon, "the life of the multitude." "And are not the pleasures with which they dwell inevitably commingled with pains, phantoms of true pleasure, illusions of scene-painting, so coloured by contrary juxtaposition [d] as to seem intense in either kind, and to beget mad loves of themselves in senseless souls, and to be fought for, [e] as Stesichorus says the wraith of Helen [f] was fought for at Troy through ignorance of the truth?" "It is quite inevitable," he said, "that it should be so."

XI. "So, again, must not the like hold of the high-spirited element, whenever a man succeeds in satisfying that part of his nature—his covetousness of honour by envy, his love of victory by violence, his ill-temper by indulgence in anger, pursuing these ends without regard to consideration and reason?" "The same sort of thing," he said, "must necessarily happen in this case too." "Then," said I, "may we

and *Philologus* 55, pp. 634 ff. Dümmler, *Akademika* p. 55, thinks this passage a criticism of Isoc. *Helena* 40. *Cf.* also Teichmüller, *Lit. Fehden*, i. pp. 113 ff. So Milton, *Reason of Church Government*, "A lawny resemblance of her like that air-born Helena in the fables." For the ethical symbolism *cf.* 520 c-d, Shelley, "Adonais" 39:

> 'Tis we who, lost in stormy visions, keep
> With phantoms an unprofitable strife.

Arnold, "Dover Beach," *in fine*:

> And we are here as on a darkling plain
> Swept with confused alarms of struggle and flight,
> Where ignorant armies clash by night.

586 ὅτι καὶ περὶ τὸ φιλοκερδὲς καὶ τὸ φιλόνικον ὅσαι
ἐπιθυμίαι εἰσίν, αἱ μὲν ἂν τῇ ἐπιστήμῃ καὶ λόγῳ
ἑπόμεναι καὶ μετὰ τούτων τὰς ἡδονὰς διώκουσαι,
ἃς ἂν τὸ φρόνιμον ἐξηγῆται, λαμβάνωσι, τὰς
ἀληθεστάτας τε λήψονται, ὡς οἷόν τε αὐταῖς
ἀληθεῖς λαβεῖν, ἅτε ἀληθείᾳ ἑπομένων, καὶ τὰς
E ἑαυτῶν οἰκείας, εἴπερ τὸ βέλτιστον ἑκάστῳ τοῦτο
καὶ οἰκειότατον; Ἀλλὰ μήν, ἔφη, οἰκειότατόν γε.
Τῷ φιλοσόφῳ ἄρα ἑπομένης ἁπάσης τῆς ψυχῆς
καὶ μὴ στασιαζούσης ἑκάστῳ τῷ μέρει ὑπάρχει εἴς
τε τἆλλα τὰ ἑαυτοῦ πράττειν καὶ δικαίῳ εἶναι, καὶ δὴ
καὶ τὰς ἡδονὰς τὰς ἑαυτοῦ ἕκαστον καὶ τὰς βελτίστας
587 καὶ εἰς τὸ δυνατὸν τὰς ἀληθεστάτας καρποῦσθαι.
Κομιδῇ μὲν οὖν. Ὅταν δὲ ἄρα τῶν ἑτέρων τι
κρατήσῃ, ὑπάρχει αὐτῷ μήτε τὴν ἑαυτοῦ ἡδονὴν
ἐξευρίσκειν, τά τε ἄλλ᾽ ἀναγκάζειν ἀλλοτρίαν καὶ
μὴ ἀληθῆ ἡδονὴν διώκειν. Οὕτως, ἔφη. Οὐκοῦν
ἃ πλεῖστον φιλοσοφίας τε καὶ λόγου ἀφέστηκε,
μάλιστ᾽ ἂν τοιαῦτα ἐξεργάζοιτο; Πολύ γε. Πλεῖστον δὲ λόγου ἀφίσταται οὐχ ὅπερ νόμου τε καὶ
τάξεως; Δῆλον δή. Ἐφάνησαν δὲ πλεῖστον ἀφεστῶ-
σαι οὐχ αἱ ἐρωτικαί τε καὶ τυραννικαὶ ἐπιθυμίαι;

---

[a] Cf. *Phaedo* 69 B, and *Theaet.* 176 B μετὰ φρονήσεως.

[b] ἐξηγῆται has a religious tone. See on ἐξηγητής 427 c.
Cf. 604 B.

[c] Cf. on 583 B, p. 380, note *b*.

[d] Cf. *What Plato Said*, p. 491, on *Lysis* 221 E.

[e] Cf. 352 A, 440 B and E, 442 D, 560 A, *Phaedr.* 237 E.

[f] Cf. *What Plato Said*, p. 480 on *Charm.* 161 B.

[g] For εἰς τὸ δυνατόν cf. 500 D, 381 c, *Laws* 795 D, 830 B,
862 B, 900 c.

[h] What follows (587 B-588 A) is not to be taken seriously. It illustrates the method of procedure by minute
links, the satisfaction of Plato's feelings by confirmations

not confidently declare that in both the gain-loving and the contentious part of our nature all the desires that wait upon knowledge and reason, and, pursuing their pleasures in conjunction with them,[a] take only those pleasures which reason approves,[b] will, since they follow truth, enjoy the truest[c] pleasures, so far as that is possible for them, and also the pleasures that are proper to them and their own, if for everything that which is best may be said to be most its 'own'[d]?"

"But indeed," he said, "it is most truly its very own." "Then when the entire soul accepts the guidance of the wisdom-loving part and is not filled with inner dissension,[e] the result for each part is that it in all other respects keeps to its own task[f] and is just, and likewise that each enjoys its own proper pleasures and the best pleasures and, so far as such a thing is possible,[g] the truest." "Precisely so." "And so when one of the other two gets the mastery the result for it is that it does not find its own proper pleasure and constrains the others to pursue an alien pleasure and not the true." "That is so," he said. "And would not that which is furthest removed from philosophy and reason be most likely to produce this effect[h]?" "Quite so," he said. "And is not that furthest removed from reason which is furthest from law and order?" "Obviously." "And was it not made plain that the furthest removed are the erotic and tyrannical appetites?" "Quite so." "And

and analogies, and his willingness to play with mathematical symbolism. *Cf.* 546 B f. and William Temple, *Plato and Christianity*, p. 55: "Finally the whole thing is a satire on the humbug of mystical number, but I need not add that the German commentators are seriously exercised. . . ." See however A. G. Laird in *Class. Phil.* xi. (1916) pp. 465-468.

587 B Πολύ γε. Ἐλάχιστον δὲ αἱ βασιλικαί τε καὶ
κόσμιαι; Ναί. Πλεῖστον δή, οἶμαι, ἀληθοῦς ἡδονῆς καὶ οἰκείας ὁ τύραννος ἀφεστήξει, ὁ δὲ ὀλί-
γιστον. Ἀνάγκη. Καὶ ἀηδέστατα ἄρα, εἶπον, ὁ
τύραννος βιώσεται, ὁ δὲ βασιλεὺς ἥδιστα. Πολλὴ
ἀνάγκη. Οἶσθ᾽ οὖν, ἦν δ᾽ ἐγώ, ὅσῳ ἀηδέστερον
ζῇ τύραννος βασιλέως; Ἄν εἴπῃς, ἔφη. Τριῶν
ἡδονῶν, ὡς ἔοικεν, οὐσῶν, μιᾶς μὲν γνησίας, δυοῖν
C δὲ νόθαιν, τῶν νόθων εἰς τὸ ἐπέκεινα ὑπερβὰς ὁ
τύραννος, φυγὼν νόμον τε καὶ λόγον, δούλαις τισὶ
δορυφόροις ἡδοναῖς ξυνοικεῖ, καὶ ὁπόσῳ ἐλαττοῦται
οὐδὲ πάνυ ῥᾴδιον εἰπεῖν, πλὴν ἴσως ὧδε. Πῶς;
ἔφη. Ἀπὸ τοῦ ὀλιγαρχικοῦ τρίτος που ὁ τύραννος
ἀφειστήκει· ἐν μέσῳ γὰρ αὐτῶν ὁ δημοτικὸς ἦν.
Ναί. Οὐκοῦν καὶ ἡδονῆς τρίτῳ εἰδώλῳ πρὸς
ἀλήθειαν ἀπ᾽ ἐκείνου ξυνοικοῖ ἄν, εἰ τὰ πρόσθεν
ἀληθῆ; Οὕτως. Ὁ δέ γε ὀλιγαρχικὸς ἀπὸ τοῦ
D βασιλικοῦ αὖ τρίτος, ἐὰν εἰς ταὐτὸν ἀριστο-
κρατικὸν καὶ βασιλικὸν τιθῶμεν. Τρίτος γάρ.
Τριπλασίου ἄρα, ἦν δ᾽ ἐγώ, τριπλάσιον ἀριθμῷ
ἀληθοῦς ἡδονῆς ἀφέστηκε τύραννος. Φαίνεται.
Ἐπίπεδον ἄρ᾽, ἔφην, ὡς ἔοικε, τὸ εἴδωλον κατὰ
τὸν τοῦ μήκους ἀριθμὸν ἡδονῆς τυραννικῆς ἂν εἴη.
Κομιδῇ γε. Κατὰ δὲ δύναμιν καὶ τρίτην αὔξην
δῆλον δὴ ἀπόστασιν ὅσην ἀφεστηκὼς γίγνεται.
Δῆλον, ἔφη, τῷ γε λογιστικῷ. Οὐκοῦν ἐάν τις
E μεταστρέψας ἀληθείᾳ ἡδονῆς τὸν βασιλέα τοῦ
τυράννου ἀφεστηκότα λέγῃ, ὅσον ἀφέστηκεν,

---

[a] Cf. Polit. 257 B ἀφεστᾶσιν.
[b] Cf. Vol. I. p. 282, note a, on 408 D and supra p. 344,
note b, on 573 D.
[c] For εἰς τὸ ἐπέκεινα cf. Phaedo 112 B and supra 509 B.
[d] Cf. Vol. I. p. 422, note b, on 445 D and Menex. 238 D.

least so the royal and orderly ? " " Yes." "Then the tyrant's place, I think, will be fixed at the furthest remove [a] from true and proper pleasure, and the king's at the least." " Necessarily." " Then the tyrant's life will be least pleasurable and the king's most." " There is every necessity of that." " Do you know, then," said I, " how much less pleasurably the tyrant lives than the king ? " " I'll know if you tell me,[b] " he said. " There being as it appears three pleasures, one genuine and two spurious, the tyrant in his flight from law and reason crosses the border beyond [c] the spurious, cohabits with certain slavish, mercenary pleasures, and the measure of his inferiority is not easy to express except perhaps thus." " How ? " he said. " The tyrant, I believe, we found at the third remove from the oligarch, for the democrat came between." " Yes." " And would he not also dwell with a phantom of pleasure in respect of reality three stages removed from that other, if all that we have said is true ? " " That is so." " And the oligarch in turn is at the third remove from the royal man if we assume the identity of the aristocrat and the king.[d] " " Yes, the third." " Three times three, then, by numerical measure is the interval that separates the tyrant from true pleasure." " Apparently." " The phantom [e] of the tyrant's pleasure is then by longitudinal mensuration a plane number." " Quite so." " But by squaring and cubing it is clear what the interval of this separation becomes." " It is clear," he said, " to a reckoner." " Then taking it the other way about, if one tries to express the extent of the interval between the king and the tyrant in respect of true

---

[e] *Cf. Phaedo* 66 c εἰδώλων, where Olympiodorus (Norvin, p. 36) takes it of the unreality of the lower pleasures.

PLATO

587 ἐννεακαιεικοσικαιεπτακοσιοπλασιάκις ἥδιον αὐτὸν
ζῶντα εὑρήσει τελειωθείσῃ τῇ πολλαπλασιώσει, τὸν
δὲ τύραννον ἀνιαρότερον τῇ αὐτῇ ταύτῃ ἀποστάσει.
Ἀμήχανον, ἔφη, λογισμὸν καταπεφόρηκας τῆς
διαφορότητος τοῖν ἀνδροῖν, τοῦ τε δικαίου καὶ
588 τοῦ ἀδίκου, πρὸς ἡδονήν τε καὶ λύπην. Καὶ
μέντοι καὶ ἀληθῆ καὶ προσήκοντά γε, ἦν δ᾽ ἐγώ,
βίοις ἀριθμόν, εἴπερ αὐτοῖς προσήκουσιν ἡμέραι
καὶ νύκτες καὶ μῆνες καὶ ἐνιαυτοί. Ἀλλὰ μήν,
ἔφη, προσήκουσιν. Οὐκοῦν εἰ τοσοῦτον ἡδονῇ
νικᾷ ὁ ἀγαθός τε καὶ δίκαιος τὸν κακόν τε καὶ
ἄδικον, ἀμηχάνῳ δὴ ὅσῳ πλεῖον νικήσει εὐ-
σχημοσύνῃ τε βίου καὶ κάλλει καὶ ἀρετῇ; Ἀμηχάνῳ μέντοι νὴ Δία, ἔφη.

XII. Εἶεν δή, εἶπον· ἐπειδὴ ἐνταῦθα λόγου
B γεγόναμεν, ἀναλάβωμεν τὰ πρῶτα λεχθέντα, δι᾽
ἃ δεῦρ᾽ ἥκομεν· ἦν δέ που λεγόμενον, λυσιτελεῖν
ἀδικεῖν τῷ τελέως μὲν ἀδίκῳ, δοξαζομένῳ δὲ
δικαίῳ. ἢ οὐχ οὕτως ἐλέχθη; Οὕτω μὲν οὖν.
Νῦν δή, ἔφην, αὐτῷ διαλεγώμεθα, ἐπειδὴ διωμολογησάμεθα τό τε ἀδικεῖν καὶ τὸ δίκαια πράττειν
ἣν ἑκάτερον ἔχει δύναμιν. Πῶς; ἔφη. Εἰκόνα
πλάσαντες τῆς ψυχῆς λόγῳ, ἵνα εἰδῇ ὁ ἐκεῖνα
C λέγων οἷα ἔλεγεν. Ποίαν τινά; ἦ δ᾽ ὅς. Τῶν
τοιούτων τινά, ἦν δ᾽ ἐγώ, οἷαι μυθολογοῦνται
παλαιαὶ γενέσθαι φύσεις, ἥ τε Χιμαίρας καὶ ἡ

---

[a] Cf. Spencer, *Data of Ethics*, p. 14 "Hence estimating
life by multiplying its length into its breadth." For the
mathematical jest cf. *Polit.* 257 A-B.

[b] Humorous as in 509 C ὑπερβολῆς.

[c] Cf. *Phileb.* 13 A, 14 A, *Parmen.* 141 C, *Theaet.* 209 A
and D.

pleasure he will find on completion of the multiplication that he lives 729 times as happily and that the tyrant's life is more painful by the same distance.[a] " An overwhelming[b] and baffling calculation," he said, " of the difference[c] between the just and the unjust man in respect of pleasure and pain ! " " And what is more, it is a true number and pertinent to the lives of men if days and nights and months and years pertain to them." " They certainly do," he said. " Then if in point of pleasure the victory of the good and just man over the bad and unjust is so great as this, he will surpass him inconceivably in decency and beauty of life and virtue." " Inconceivably indeed, by Zeus," he said.

XII. " Very good," said I. " And now that we have come to this point in the argument, let us take up again the statement with which we began and that has brought us to this pass.[d] It was, I believe, averred that injustice is profitable to the completely unjust[e] man who is reputed just. Was not that the proposition ? " " Yes, that." " Let us, then, reason with its proponent now that we have agreed on the essential nature of injustice and just conduct." " How ? " he said. " By fashioning in our discourse a symbolic image of the soul, that the maintainer of that proposition may see precisely what it is that he was saying." " What sort of an image ? " he said. " One of those natures that the ancient fables tell of," said I, " as that of the Chimaera[f] or Scylla[g] or Cerberus,[h] and

[d] Plato keeps to the point. Cf. 472 B, Phileb. 27 c, and p. 339, note e, on 572 B.   [e] Cf. 348 B, 361 A.
[f] Cf. Homer, Il. vi. 179-182, Phaedr. 229 D.
[g] Od. xii. 85 ff.
[h] Hesiod, Theog. 311-312.

588 Σκύλλης καὶ Κερβέρου, καὶ ἄλλαι τινὲς συχναὶ λέγονται ξυμπεφυκυῖαι ἰδέαι πολλαὶ εἰς ἓν γενέσθαι. Λέγονται γάρ, ἔφη. Πλάττε τοίνυν μίαν μὲν ἰδέαν θηρίου ποικίλου καὶ πολυκεφάλου, ἡμέρων δὲ θηρίων ἔχοντος κεφαλὰς κύκλῳ καὶ ἀγρίων, καὶ δυνατοῦ μεταβάλλειν καὶ φύειν ἐξ αὑτοῦ πάντα

D ταῦτα. Δεινοῦ πλάστου, ἔφη, τὸ ἔργον· ὅμως δέ, ἐπειδὴ εὐπλαστότερον κηροῦ καὶ τῶν τοιούτων λόγος, πεπλάσθω. Μίαν δὴ τοίνυν ἄλλην ἰδέαν λέοντος, μίαν δὲ ἀνθρώπου· πολὺ δὲ μέγιστον ἔστω τὸ πρῶτον καὶ δεύτερον τὸ δεύτερον. Ταῦτα, ἔφη, ῥᾴω καὶ πέπλασται. Σύναπτε τοίνυν αὐτὰ εἰς ἓν τρία ὄντα, ὥστε πῃ ξυμπεφυκέναι ἀλλήλοις. Συνῆπται, ἔφη. Περίπλασον δὴ αὐτοῖς ἔξωθεν ἑνὸς εἰκόνα, τὴν τοῦ ἀνθρώπου, ὥστε τῷ μὴ

E δυναμένῳ τὰ ἐντὸς ὁρᾶν, ἀλλὰ τὸ ἔξω μόνον ἔλυτρον ὁρῶντι, ἓν ζῷον φαίνεσθαι, ἄνθρωπον. Περιπέπλασται, ἔφη. Λέγωμεν δὴ τῷ λέγοντι,

---

ᵃ Stallbaum *ad loc.* gives a long list of writers who imitated this passage. Hesiod, *Theog.* 823 f., portrays a similar monster in Typhoeus, who had a hundred serpent-heads. For the animal in man *cf. Tim.* 70 ᴇ, *Charm.* 155 ᴅ-ᴇ, *Phaedr.* 230 ᴀ, 246 ᴀ ff., Boethius, *Cons.* iv. 2-3, Horace, *Epist.* i. 1. 76, Iamblichus, *Protrept.* chap. iii., Machiavelli, *Prince* xvii. (La Bestia), Emerson, *History*: " Every animal in the barnyard . . . has contrived to get a footing . . . in some one or other of these upright heaven-facing speakers. Ah, brother, hold fast to the man and awe the beast," etc. *Cf.* Tennyson, lines " By an Evolutionist ":

But I hear no yelp of the beast, and the Man is quiet at last.

the numerous other examples that are told of many forms grown together in one." "Yes, they do tell of them." "Mould, then, a single shape of a manifold and many-headed beast [a] that has a ring of heads of tame and wild beasts and can change them and cause to spring forth from itself all such growths." "It is the task of a cunning artist,[b]" he said, "but nevertheless, since speech is more plastic than wax [c] and other such media, assume that it has been so fashioned." "Then fashion one other form of a lion and one of a man and let the first be far the largest [d] and the second second in size." "That is easier," he said, "and is done." "Join the three in one, then, so as in some sort to grow together." "They are so united," he said. "Then mould about them outside the likeness of one, that of the man, so that to anyone who is unable to look within [e] but who can see only the external sheath it appears to be one living creature, the man." "The sheath is made fast about him," he said. "Let us,

"In Memoriam," cxviii. :

> Move upward, working out the beast,
> And let the ape and tiger die.

A modern scientific man solemnly writes: "The theory of evolution has prepared us to acknowledge the presence of something of the ape and tiger in us." For an example of modern nimiety or too-muchness cf. Sandburg's "There is a wolf in me. . . . There is a fox in me. . . . There is a hog in me . . . O, I got a zoo, I got a menagerie inside my ribs." Cf. Brunetière, *Questions actuelles*, p. 114.

[b] Cf. 596 c.

[c] Cf. Cic. *De or.* iii. 45 "sicut mollissimam ceram . . . fingimus." Otto, p. 80, says it is a proverb. For the development of this figure cf. Pliny, *Epist.* vii. 9 "ut laus est cerae, mollis cedensque sequatur." For the idea that word is more precise or easy than deed cf. *supra* 473 A, *Phaedo* 99 E, *Laws* 636 A, 736 B, *Tim.* 19 E.

[d] Cf. 442 A.

[e] Cf. 577 A.

588 ὡς λυσιτελεῖ τούτῳ ἀδικεῖν τῷ ἀνθρώπῳ, δίκαια
δὲ πράττειν οὐ ξυμφέρει, ὅτι οὐδὲν ἄλλο φησὶν ἢ
λυσιτελεῖν αὐτῷ τὸ παντοδαπὸν θηρίον εὐωχοῦντι
ποιεῖν ἰσχυρὸν καὶ τὸν λέοντα καὶ τὰ περὶ τὸν
589 λέοντα, τὸν δὲ ἄνθρωπον λιμοκτονεῖν καὶ ποιεῖν
ἀσθενῆ, ὥστε ἕλκεσθαι ὅπῃ ἂν ἐκείνων ὁπότερον
ἄγῃ, καὶ μηδὲν ἕτερον ἑτέρῳ ξυνεθίζειν μηδὲ φίλον
ποιεῖν, ἀλλ' ἐὰν αὐτὰ ἐν αὑτοῖς δάκνεσθαί τε καὶ
μαχόμενα ἐσθίειν ἄλληλα. Παντάπασι γάρ, ἔφη,
ταῦτ' ἂν λέγοι ὁ τὸ ἀδικεῖν ἐπαινῶν. Οὐκοῦν αὖ
ὁ τὰ δίκαια λέγων λυσιτελεῖν φαίη ἂν δεῖν ταῦτα
πράττειν καὶ ταῦτα λέγειν, ὅθεν τοῦ ἀνθρώπου ὁ
B ἐντὸς ἄνθρωπος ἔσται ἐγκρατέστατος, καὶ τοῦ
πολυκεφάλου θρέμματος ἐπιμελήσεται ὥσπερ γεωρ-
γός, τὰ μὲν ἥμερα τρέφων καὶ τιθασεύων, τὰ δὲ
ἄγρια ἀποκωλύων φύεσθαι, ξύμμαχον ποιησάμενος
τὴν τοῦ λέοντος φύσιν, καὶ κοινῇ πάντων κηδό-
μενος, φίλα ποιησάμενος ἀλλήλοις τε καὶ αὑτῷ,
οὕτω θρέψει; Κομιδῇ γὰρ αὖ λέγει ταῦτα ὁ τὸ
δίκαιον ἐπαινῶν. Κατὰ πάντα τρόπον δὴ ὁ μὲν
C τὰ δίκαια ἐγκωμιάζων ἀληθῆ ἂν λέγοι, ὁ δὲ τὰ
ἄδικα ψεύδοιτο. πρός τε γὰρ ἡδονὴν καὶ πρὸς
εὐδοξίαν καὶ ὠφέλειαν σκοπουμένῳ ὁ μὲν ἐπαινέτης
τοῦ δικαίου ἀληθεύει, ὁ δὲ ψέκτης οὐδὲν ὑγιὲς οὐδ'

---

[a] The whole passage illustrates the psychology of 440 B ff.
[b] Cf. Protag. 352 C περιελκομένης, with Aristot. Eth. Nic.
1145 b 24.
[c] Perhaps a latent allusion to Hesiod, Works and
Days 278.
[d] Cf. "the inward man," Romans vii. 22, 2 Cor. iv. 16,
Ephes. iii. 16.
[e] Cf. Arnold, Culture and Anarchy, p. 10 "Religion
says: 'The kingdom of God is within you'; and culture, in

then say to the speaker who avers that it pays this man to be unjust, and that to do justice is not for his advantage, that he is affirming nothing else than that it profits him to feast and make strong the multifarious beast and the lion and all that pertains to the lion, but to starve the man [a] and so enfeeble him that he can be pulled about [b] whithersoever either of the others drag him, and not to familiarize or reconcile with one another the two creatures but suffer them to bite and fight and devour one another.[c] " " Yes," he said, " that is precisely what the panegyrist of injustice will be found to say." " And on the other hand he who says that justice is the more profitable affirms that all our actions and words should tend to give the man within us [d] complete domination [e] over the entire man and make him take charge [f] of the many-headed beast—like a farmer [g] who cherishes and trains the cultivated plants but checks the growth of the wild—and he will make an ally [h] of the lion's nature, and caring for all the beasts alike will first make them friendly to one another and to himself, and so foster their growth." " Yes, that in turn is precisely the meaning of the man who commends justice." " From every point of view, then, the panegyrist of justice speaks truly and the panegyrist of injustice falsely. For whether we consider pleasure, reputation, or profit, he who commends justice speaks the truth, while there is no soundness or real know-

like manner, places human perfection in an *internal* condition, in the growth and predominance of our humanity proper, as distinguished from our animality."

[f] *Cf. Gorg.* 516 A-B.

[g] *Cf. Theaet.* 167 B-c, and *What Plato Said*, p. 456, on *Euthyphro* 2 D.

[h] *Cf.* 441 A.

PLATO

589 εἰδὼς ψέγει ὅ τι ψέγει. Οὔ μοι δοκεῖ, ἦ δ' ὅς,
οὐδαμῇ γε. Πείθωμεν τοίνυν αὐτὸν πρᾴως, οὐ
γὰρ ἑκὼν ἁμαρτάνει, ἐρωτῶντες· ὦ μακάριε, οὐ
καὶ τὰ καλὰ καὶ αἰσχρὰ νόμιμα διὰ τὰ τοιαῦτ' ἂν
D φαῖμεν γεγονέναι· τὰ μὲν καλὰ τὰ ὑπὸ τῷ ἀνθρώπῳ,
μᾶλλον δὲ ἴσως τὰ ὑπὸ τῷ θείῳ τὰ θηριώδη
ποιοῦντα τῆς φύσεως, αἰσχρὰ δὲ τὰ ὑπὸ τῷ ἀγρίῳ
τὸ ἥμερον δουλούμενα; ξυμφήσει ἢ πῶς; Ἐάν
μοι, ἔφη, πείθηται. Ἔστιν οὖν, εἶπον, ὅτῳ λυσιτελεῖ ἐκ τούτου τοῦ λόγου χρυσίον λαμβάνειν ἀ-
δίκως, εἴπερ τοιόνδε τι γίγνεται, λαμβάνων τὸ
χρυσίον ἅμα καταδουλοῦται τὸ βέλτιστον ἑαυτοῦ τῷ
E μοχθηροτάτῳ; ἢ εἰ μὲν λαβὼν χρυσίον υἱὸν ἢ
θυγατέρα ἐδουλοῦτο, καὶ ταῦτ' εἰς ἀγρίων τε καὶ
κακῶν ἀνδρῶν, οὐκ ἂν αὐτῷ ἐλυσιτέλει οὐδ' ἂν
πάμπολυ ἐπὶ τούτῳ λαμβάνειν, εἰ δὲ τὸ ἑαυτοῦ
θειότατον ὑπὸ τῷ ἀθεωτάτῳ τε καὶ μιαρωτάτῳ
δουλοῦται καὶ μηδὲν ἐλεεῖ, οὐκ ἄρα ἄθλιός ἐστι καὶ
590 πολὺ ἐπὶ δεινοτέρῳ ὀλέθρῳ χρυσὸν δωροδοκεῖ ἢ
Ἐριφύλη ἐπὶ τῇ τοῦ ἀνδρὸς ψυχῇ τὸν ὅρμον
δεξαμένη; Πολὺ μέντοι, ἦ δ' ὃς ὁ Γλαύκων· ἐγὼ
γάρ σοι ὑπὲρ ἐκείνου ἀποκρινοῦμαι.

XIII. Οὐκοῦν καὶ τὸ ἀκολασταίνειν οἴει διὰ
τοιαῦτα πάλαι ψέγεσθαι, ὅτι ἀνίεται ἐν τῷ τοιούτῳ

πρᾴως: cf. the use of ἠρέμα 476 E, 494 D.

Plato always maintains that wrong-doing is involuntary
and due to ignorance. Cf. What Plato Said, p. 640, on
Laws 860 D.

Cf. supra 501 B, Tennyson, "Locksley Hall Sixty Years
after," in fine. "The highest Human Nature is divine."

Cf. Matt. xvi. 26, Mark viii. 36, "What shall it profit
a man if he shall gain the whole world and lose his own
soul?" A typical argumentum ex contrario. Cf. 445 A-B and

ledge of what he censures in him who disparages it."
" None whatever, I think," said he. " Shall we, then,
try to persuade him gently,[a] for he does not willingly
err,[b] by questioning him thus : Dear friend, should
we not also say that the things which law and custom
deem fair or foul have been accounted so for a like
reason—the fair and honourable things being those
that subject the brutish part of our nature to that
which is human in us, or rather, it may be, to that
which is divine,[c] while the foul and base are the things
that enslave the gentle nature to the wild ? Will he
assent or not ? " " He will if he is counselled by me."
" Can it profit any man in the light of this thought to
accept gold unjustly if the result is to be that by the
acceptance he enslaves the best part of himself to the
worst ? Or is it conceivable that, while, if the taking
of the gold enslaved his son or daughter and that too to
fierce and evil men, it would not profit him,[d] no matter
how large the sum, yet that, if the result is to be the
ruthless enslavement of the divinest part of himself to
the most despicable and godless part, he is not to be
deemed wretched and is not taking the golden bribe
much more disastrously than Eriphyle[e] did when she
received the necklace as the price[f] of her husband's
life ? " " Far more," said Glaucon, " for I will
answer you in his behalf."

XIII. " And do you not think that the reason for
the old objection to licentiousness is similarly because

Vol. I. p. 40, note c.   On the supreme value of the soul cf.
Laws 726-728, 743 E, 697 B, 913 B, 959 A-B.   *Cf. supra* 585 D.
   [e] *Cf. Od.* xi. 326, Frazer on Apollodorus iii. 6. 2 (Loeb).
Stallbaum refers also to Pindar, *Nem.* ix. 37 ff., and Pausan.
x. 29. 7.
   [f] For ἐπί in this sense *cf.* Thompson on *Meno* 90 D.   *Cf.*
Apol. 41 A ἐπὶ πόσῳ, Demosth. xlv. 66.

590 τὸ δεινόν, τὸ μέγα ἐκεῖνο καὶ πολυειδὲς θρέμμα
πέρα τοῦ δέοντος; Δῆλον, ἔφη. Ἡ δ' αὐθάδεια
B καὶ δυσκολία ψέγεται οὐχ ὅταν τὸ λεοντῶδές τε
καὶ ὀφεῶδες αὔξηται καὶ συντείνηται ἀναρμόστως;
Πάνυ μὲν οὖν. Τρυφὴ δὲ καὶ μαλθακία οὐκ ἐπὶ
τῇ αὐτοῦ τούτου χαλάσει τε καὶ ἀνέσει ψέγεται,
ὅταν ἐν αὐτῷ δειλίαν ἐμποιῇ; Τί μήν; Κολακεία
δὲ καὶ ἀνελευθερία οὐχ ὅταν τις τὸ αὐτὸ τοῦτο, τὸ
θυμοειδές, ὑπὸ τῷ ὀχλώδει θηρίῳ ποιῇ, καὶ ἕνεκα
χρημάτων καὶ τῆς ἐκείνου ἀπληστίας προπηλα-
κιζόμενον ἐθίζῃ ἐκ νέου ἀντὶ λέοντος πίθηκον
C γίγνεσθαι; Καὶ μάλα, ἔφη. Βαναυσία δὲ καὶ
χειροτεχνία διὰ τί, οἴει, ὄνειδος φέρει; ἢ δι' ἄλλο
τι φήσομεν ἢ ὅταν τις ἀσθενὲς φύσει ἔχῃ τὸ τοῦ
βελτίστου εἶδος, ὥστε μὴ ἂν δύνασθαι ἄρχειν τῶν
ἐν αὐτῷ θρεμμάτων, ἀλλὰ θεραπεύειν ἐκεῖνα, καὶ
τὰ θωπεύματα αὐτῶν μόνον δύνηται μανθάνειν;
Ἔοικεν, ἔφη. Οὐκοῦν ἵνα καὶ ὁ τοιοῦτος ὑπὸ
ὁμοίου ἄρχηται οὗπερ ὁ βέλτιστος, δοῦλον αὐτόν
D φαμεν δεῖν εἶναι ἐκείνου τοῦ βελτίστου, ἔχοντος ἐν
αὐτῷ τὸ θεῖον ἄρχον, οὐκ ἐπὶ βλάβῃ τῇ τοῦ δούλου

---

[a] See Adam ad loc. on the asyndeton.
[b] αὐθάδεια: cf. supra 548 E.
[c] Not mentioned before, but, as Schleiermacher says,
might be included in τὰ περὶ τὸν λέοντα. Cf. Adam ad loc.
Or Plato may be thinking of the chimaera (Il. vi. 181).
[d] Cf. 620 c. [e] Cf. p. 49, note e.
[f] For the idea that it is better to be ruled by a better man
cf. Alc. I. 135 B-C, Polit. 296 B-C, Democr. fr. 75 (Diels ii.³
p. 77), Xen. Mem. i. 5. 5 δουλεύοντα δὲ ταῖς τοιαύταις ἡδοναῖς
ἱκετευτέον τοὺς θεοὺς δεσποτῶν ἀγαθῶν τυχεῖν, Xen. Cyr. viii.
1. 40 βελτίονας εἶναι. Cf. also Laws 713 D-714 A, 627 E,
Phaedo 62 D-E, and Laws 684 C. Cf. Ruskin, Queen of the
Air, p. 210 (Brantwood ed., 1891): "The first duty of every
man in the world is to find his true master, and, for his own

that sort of thing emancipates that dread,[a] that huge
and manifold beast overmuch ? ” “ Obviously,” he
said. “ And do we not censure self-will[b] and irasci-
bility when they foster and intensify disproportion-
ately the element of the lion and the snake[c] in us ? ”
“ By all means.” “ And do we not reprobate luxury
and effeminacy for their loosening and relaxation of
this same element when they engender cowardice in
it ? ” “ Surely.” “ And flattery and illiberality when
they reduce this same high-spirited element under
the rule of the mob-like beast and habituate it for
the sake of wealth and the unbridled lusts of the
beast to endure all manner of contumely from youth
up and become an ape[d] instead of a lion ? ” “ Yes,
indeed,” he said. “ And why do you suppose that
‘ base mechanic ’[e] handicraft is a term of reproach ?
Shall we not say that it is solely when the best part
is naturally weak in a man so that it cannot govern
and control the brood of beasts within him but can
only serve them and can learn nothing but the ways of
flattering them ? ” “ So it seems,” he said. “ Then
is it not in order that such an one may have a like
government with the best man that we say he ought
to be the slave of that best man[f] who has within

good, submit to him ; and to find his true inferior, and, for
that inferior's good, conquer him.” Inge, *Christian Ethics*,
p. 252 : “ It is ordained in the eternal constitution of things,
that men of intemperate minds cannot be free.” Carlyle
(*apud* M. Barton and O. Sitwell, *Victoriana*): “ Surely of
all the rights of man the right of the ignorant man to be
guided by the wiser, to be gently or forcibly held in the true
course by him, is the indisputablest.” Plato's idea is perhaps
a source of Aristotle's theory of slavery, though differently
expressed. *Cf.* Aristot. *Pol.* 1254 b 16 f., Newman i. pp.
109-110, 144 f., 378-379, ii. p. 107. *Cf.* also *Polit.* 309 A f.,
Epist. vii. 335 D, and Gomperz, *Greek Thinkers*, iii. p. 106.

PLATO

590 οἰόμενοι δεῖν ἄρχεσθαι αὐτόν, ὥσπερ Θρασύμαχος
ᾤετο τοὺς ἀρχομένους, ἀλλ' ὡς ἄμεινον ὂν παντὶ
ὑπὸ θείου καὶ φρονίμου ἄρχεσθαι, μάλιστα μὲν
οἰκεῖον ἔχοντος ἐν αὑτῷ, εἰ δὲ μή, ἔξωθεν ἐφ-
εστῶτος, ἵνα εἰς δύναμιν πάντες ὅμοιοι ὦμεν καὶ
φίλοι τῷ αὐτῷ κυβερνώμενοι; Καὶ ὀρθῶς γ', ἔφη.
E Δηλοῖ δέ γε, ἦν δ' ἐγώ, καὶ ὁ νόμος, ὅτι τοιοῦτον
βούλεται,[1] πᾶσι τοῖς ἐν τῇ πόλει ξύμμαχος ὤν·
καὶ ἡ τῶν παίδων ἀρχή, τὸ μὴ ἐᾶν ἐλευθέρους
εἶναι, ἕως ἂν ἐν αὐτοῖς ὥσπερ ἐν πόλει πολιτείαν
καταστήσωμεν, καὶ τὸ βέλτιστον θεραπεύσαντες
591 τῷ παρ' ἡμῖν τοιούτῳ ἀντικαταστήσωμεν φύλακα
ὅμοιον καὶ ἄρχοντα ἐν αὐτῷ, καὶ τότε δὴ ἐλεύθερον
ἀφίεμεν. Δηλοῖ γάρ, ἦ δ' ὅς. Πῇ δὴ οὖν φήσομεν, ὦ Γλαύκων, καὶ κατὰ τίνα λόγον λυσιτελεῖν
ἀδικεῖν ἢ ἀκολασταίνειν ἤ τι αἰσχρὸν ποιεῖν, ἐξ ὧν
πονηρότερος μὲν ἔσται, πλείω δὲ χρήματα ἢ ἄλλην
τινὰ δύναμιν κεκτήσεται; Οὐδαμῇ, ἦ δ' ὅς.
Πῇ δ' ἀδικοῦντα λανθάνειν καὶ μὴ διδόναι δίκην
B λυσιτελεῖν; ἢ οὐχὶ ὁ μὲν λανθάνων ἔτι πονηρότερος
γίγνεται, τοῦ δὲ μὴ λανθάνοντος καὶ κολαζομένου
τὸ μὲν θηριῶδες κοιμίζεται καὶ ἡμεροῦται, τὸ
δὲ ἥμερον ἐλευθεροῦται, καὶ ὅλη ἡ ψυχὴ εἰς
τὴν βελτίστην φύσιν καθισταμένη τιμιωτέραν ἕξιν

[1] βούλεται Iamblichus and Stobaeus: βουλεύεται ADM.
See Adam, *ad loc.*

---

[a] *Cf. supra* 343 B-C.
[b] *Cf. Lysis* 207 E f., *Laws* 808 D, Isoc. xv. 290, Antiphon, *fr.* 61 (Diels ii.[3] p. 303).
[c] *Cf.* on 591 E, p. 412, note *d.*
[d] *Cf.* on 501 D, p. 74, note *a.*
[e] The paradoxes of the *Gorgias* are here seriously re-affirmed. *Cf.* especially *Gorg.* 472 E ff., 480 A-B, 505 A-B,

himself the divine governing principle, not because we suppose, as Thrasymachus[a] did in the case of subjects, that the slave should be governed for his own harm, but on the ground that it is better for everyone to be governed by the divine and the intelligent, preferably indwelling and his own, but in default of that imposed from without, in order that we all so far as possible may be akin and friendly because our governance and guidance are the same?" "Yes, and rightly so," he said. "And it is plain," I said, "that this is the purpose of the law, which is the ally of all classes in the state, and this is the aim of our control of children,[b] our not leaving them free before we have established, so to speak, a constitutional government within them[c] and, by fostering the best element in them with the aid of the like in ourselves, have set up in its place a similar guardian and ruler in the child, and then, and then only, we leave it free." "Yes, that is plain," he said. "In what way,[d] then, Glaucon, and on what principle, shall we say that it profits a man to be unjust or licentious or do any shameful thing that will make him a worse man, but otherwise will bring him more wealth or power?" "In no way," he said. "And how that it pays him to escape detection in wrongdoing and not pay the penalty[e]? Or is it not true that he who evades detection becomes a still worse man, while in the one who is discovered and chastened the brutish part is lulled and tamed and the gentle part liberated, and the entire soul, returning to its nature at the best, attains to a much more precious condition in acquir-

---

509 A f. *Cf.* also Vol. I. p. 187, 380 B οἱ δὲ ὠνίναντο κολαζό-μενοι, and *Laws* 728 c; and for the purpose of punishment, *What Plato Said*, p. 495, on *Protag.* 324 A-B.

591 λαμβάνει, σωφροσύνην τε καὶ δικαιοσύνην μετὰ
φρονήσεως κτωμένη, ἢ σῶμα ἰσχύν τε καὶ κάλλος
μετὰ ὑγιείας λαμβάνον, τοσούτῳ ὅσῳπερ ψυχὴ
σώματος τιμιωτέρα; Παντάπασι μὲν οὖν, ἔφη.

C Οὐκοῦν ὅ γε νοῦν ἔχων πάντα τὰ αὑτοῦ εἰς τοῦτο
ξυντείνας βιώσεται, πρῶτον μὲν τὰ μαθήματα
τιμῶν, ἃ τοιαύτην αὐτοῦ τὴν ψυχὴν ἀπεργάσεται,
τὰ δὲ ἄλλ' ἀτιμάζων; Δῆλον, ἔφη. Ἔπειτά γ',
εἶπον, τὴν τοῦ σώματος ἕξιν καὶ τροφὴν οὐχ ὅπως
τῇ θηριώδει καὶ ἀλόγῳ ἡδονῇ ἐπιτρέψας ἐνταῦθα
τετραμμένος ζήσει, ἀλλ' οὐδὲ πρὸς ὑγίειαν βλέπων,
οὐδὲ τοῦτο πρεσβεύων, ὅπως ἰσχυρὸς ἢ ὑγιὴς ἢ
καλὸς ἔσται, ἐὰν μὴ καὶ σωφρονήσειν μέλλῃ ἀπ'

D αὐτῶν, ἀλλ' ἀεὶ τὴν ἐν τῷ σώματι ἁρμονίαν τῆς
ἐν τῇ ψυχῇ ἕνεκα ξυμφωνίας ἁρμοττόμενος φανεῖ-
ται.¹ Παντάπασι μὲν οὖν, ἔφη, ἐάνπερ μέλλῃ τῇ
ἀληθείᾳ μουσικὸς εἶναι. Οὐκοῦν, εἶπον, καὶ τὴν

---

¹ φανεῖται Iamblichus: φαίνηται ADM, φαίνεται pr. F.
Bracketed by Hermann.

ᵃ The a *fortiori* argument from health of body to health
of soul is one of the chief refutations of the immoralists.
Cf. supra 445 D-E f., *Gorg.* 479 B, *Crito* 47 D-E. For the
supreme importance of the soul *cf.* on 589 E.

ᵇ *Cf. Gorg.* 507 D, Isoc. *Epist.* vi. 9, Xen. *Ages.* 7. 1.

ᶜ Health in the familiar skolion (*cf. Gorg.* 451 E, *Laws*
631 c, 661 A, 728 D-E, *Euthydem.* 279 A-B, *Meno* 87 E, Soph.
frag. 356) is proverbially the highest of ordinary goods.
Cf. Gorg. 452 A-B, *Crito* 47 D, *Eryxias* 393 C. In fact, for
Plato as for modern "scientific" ethics, health in the higher
sense—the health of the soul—may be said to be the
ultimate sanction. *Cf.* Vol. I. Introd. pp. xvi and xxi,
Unity of Plato's Thought, p. 26, *Idea of Good in Plato's
Republic*, pp. 192-194 f. But an idealistic ethics sometimes
expresses itself in the paradox that "not even health,"

ing sobriety and righteousness together with wisdom, than the body *a* does when it gains strength and beauty conjoined with health, even as the soul is more precious than the body ? " " Most assuredly," he said. " Then the wise man will bend all his endeavours *b* to this end throughout his life ; he will, to begin with, prize the studies that will give this quality to his soul and disprize the others." " Clearly," he said. " And then," I said, " he not only will not abandon the habit and nurture of his body to the brutish and irrational pleasure and live with his face set in that direction, but he will not even make health his chief aim,*c* nor give the first place to the ways of becoming strong or healthy or beautiful unless these things are likely to bring with them soberness of spirit, but he will always be found attuning the harmonies of his body for the sake of the concord in his soul.*d* " " By all means," he replied, " if he is to be a true musician.*e* " " And will he not deal likewise

---

highest of earthly goods, is of any value compared with the true interests of the soul. *Cf. Laws* 661 c-e ff., 728 d-e, 744 a, 960 d, *Laches* 195 c; and Arnold, *Culture and Anarchy*, p. 17 "Bodily health and vigour . . . have a more real and essential value . . . but only as they are more intimately connected with a perfect spiritual condition than wealth and population are." This idea may be the source of the story from which the Christian Fathers and the Middle Ages derived much edification, that Plato intentionally chose an unhealthy site for the Academy in order to keep down the flesh. *Cf.* Aelian, *Var. Hist.* ix. 10, perhaps the first mention, Porphyry, *De abstinentia* i. 36, Zeller, *Phil. d. Gr.* ii. 1.⁴ 416, n. 2; Camden on Cambridge, Gosse, *Gossip in a Library*, p. 23, and Himerius, *Ecl.* iii. 18 (Diels ii.³ p. 18) ἐκὼν δὲ ἐνόσει σῶμα Δημόκριτος, ἵνα ὑγιαίνῃ τὰ κρείττονα.

d *Cf. What Plato Said*, p. 485, on *Laches* 188 d.

e *Cf. Phaedo* 61 a.

591 ἐν τῇ τῶν χρημάτων κτήσει ξύνταξίν τε καὶ
ξυμφωνίαν; καὶ τὸν ὄγκον τοῦ πλήθους οὐκ
ἐκπληττόμενος ὑπὸ τοῦ τῶν πολλῶν μακαρισμοῦ
ἄπειρον αὐξήσει, ἀπέραντα κακὰ ἔχων; Οὐκ
Ε οἶμαι, ἔφη. Ἀλλ' ἀποβλέπων γε, εἶπον, πρὸς
τὴν ἐν αὑτῷ πολιτείαν καὶ φυλάττων, μή τι
παρακινῇ αὐτοῦ τῶν ἐκεῖ διὰ πλῆθος οὐσίας ἢ δι'
ὀλιγότητα, οὕτως κυβερνῶν προσθήσει καὶ ἀναλώσει τῆς οὐσίας καθ' ὅσον ἂν οἶός τ' ᾖ. Κομιδῇ
μὲν οὖν, ἔφη. Ἀλλὰ μὴν καὶ τιμάς γε, εἰς
592 ταὐτὸν ἀποβλέπων, τῶν μὲν μεθέξει καὶ γεύσεται
ἑκών, ἃς ἂν ἡγῆται ἀμείνω αὐτὸν ποιήσειν, ἃς δ'
ἂν λύσειν τὴν ὑπάρχουσαν ἕξιν, φεύξεται ἰδίᾳ καὶ
δημοσίᾳ. Οὐκ ἄρα, ἔφη, τά γε πολιτικὰ ἐθελήσει
πράττειν, ἐάνπερ τούτου κήδηται. Νὴ τὸν κύνα,
ἦν δ' ἐγώ, ἔν γε τῇ ἑαυτοῦ πόλει καὶ μάλα, οὐ

ᵃ *Cf.* p. 355, note *d*, on 576 D.

ᵇ ὄγκον : *cf.* Horace's use of *acervus*, Shorey on *Odes* ii.
2. 24.

ᶜ *Cf.* Vol. I. p. 163, note *g*, Newman i. p. 136.　For the
evils of wealth *cf. Laws* 831 c ff., 870 B-C, *Rep.* 434 B,
550 D ff., etc.

ᵈ This analogy pervades the *Republic. Cf.* 579 c and
p. 240, note *b*, on 544 D-E, Introd. Vol. I. p. xxxv.　*Cf. ὥσπερ
ἐν πόλει* 590 E, 605 B.　For the subordination of everything
to the moral life *cf.* also 443 D and p. 509, note *d*, on 618 c.

ᵉ As in the state, extremes of wealth and poverty are to
be avoided.　*Cf. What Plato Said*, p. 645, on *Laws* 915 B.

ᶠ Almost Aristotle's use of ἕξις.

ᵍ *Cf.* pp. 52-55 on 496 D-E.　The later schools debated the
question whether the "sage" would take part in politics.
Cf. Seneca, *De otio*, xxx. 2 f. and Von Arnim, *Stoic. Vet.
Frag.* i. p. 62. 22 f.: "Zenon ait: accedet ad rempublicam
(sapiens), nisi si quid impedierit;" *ibid.* iii. p. 158. 31 ff.:
"consentaneum est huic naturae, ut sapiens velit gerere et
administrare rempublicam atque, ut e natura vivat, uxorem
adiungere et velle ex ea liberos;" *ibid.* p. 174. 32: "negant

with the ordering and harmonizing of his possessions ?
He will not let himself be dazzled [a] by the felicitations
of the multitude and pile up the mass [b] of his wealth
without measure,[c] involving himself in measureless
ills." " No, I think not," he said. " He will rather,"
I said, " keep his eyes fixed on the constitution in
his soul,[d] and taking care and watching lest he disturb
anything there either by excess or deficiency of wealth,[e]
will so steer his course and add to or detract from his
wealth on this principle, so far as may be." " Precisely
so," he said. " And in the matter of honours and office
too this will be his guiding principle : He will gladly
take part in and enjoy those which he thinks will make
him a better man, but in public and private life he
will shun those that may overthrow the established
habit [f] of his soul." " Then, if that is his chief concern," he said, " he will not willingly take part in
politics.[g] " " Yes, by the dog,[h] " said I, " in his own

nostri sapientem ad quamlibet rempublicam accessurum ; "
ibid. 37 ff. : " praeterea, cum sapienti rempublicam ipso
dignam dedimus, id est mundum, non est extra rempublicam,
etiamsi recesserit ; " *ibid.* iii. p. 157. 40 ff. ἑπόμενον δὲ τούτοις
ὑπάρχειν καὶ τὸ πολιτεύεσθαι τὸν σοφὸν καὶ μάλιστ᾽ ἐν ταῖς τοιαύταις πολιτείαις ταῖς ἐμφαινούσαις τινὰ προκοπὴν πρὸς τὰς τελείας
πολιτείας ; *ibid.* p. 172. 18 f. δεύτερον δὲ τὸν ἀπὸ τῆς πολιτείας,
πολιτεύεσθαι γὰρ κατὰ τὸν προηγούμενον λόγον . . . ; *ibid.* 173.
19 ff. ἔφαμεν δ᾽ ὅτι καὶ πολιτεύεσθαι κατὰ τὸν προηγούμενον λόγον
οἷόν ἐστι. μὴ πολιτεύεσθαι δὲ ἐάν τι ⟨κωλύῃ⟩ καὶ μάλιστ᾽ ⟨ἂν⟩
μηδὲν ὠφελεῖν μέλλῃ τὴν πατρίδα, κινδύνους δὲ παρακολουθεῖν
ὑπολαμβάνῃ μεγάλους καὶ χαλεποὺς ἐκ τῆς πολιτείας ; *ibid.*
p. 175. 3 f. πολιτεύεσθαι φασὶ τὸν σοφὸν ἂν μή τι κωλύῃ, ὥς
φησι Χρύσιππος ἐν πρώτῳ περὶ βίων ; *ibid.* 6 ff. Χρύσιππος δὲ
πάλιν ἐν τῷ Περὶ Ῥητορικῆς γράφων. οὕτω ῥητορεύσειν καὶ
πολιτεύεσθαι τὸν σοφόν, ὡς καὶ τοῦ πλούτου ὄντος ἀγαθοῦ, καὶ
τῆς δόξης καὶ τῆς ὑγείας.

[h] *Cf.* on 399 E, *Phaedr.* 228 B, *Gorg.* 466 C, 461 A, 482 B,
Phaedo 98 E, *supra* 567 E.

PLATO

592 μέντοι ἴσως ἔν γε τῇ πατρίδι, ἐὰν μὴ θεία τις
ξυμβῇ τύχη. Μανθάνω, ἔφη· ἐν ᾗ νῦν διήλθομεν
οἰκίζοντες πόλει λέγεις, τῇ ἐν λόγοις κειμένῃ,
B ἐπεὶ γῆς γε οὐδαμοῦ οἶμαι αὐτὴν εἶναι. Ἀλλ', ἦν

---

^a θεία . . . τύχη. So θεία μοῖρα is often used to account
for an exception, *e.g. supra* 493 A, *Laws* 875 c, 642 c, *Meno*
99 E, etc. *Cf.* θεῖον . . . ἐξαιρῶμεν λόγου 492 E.

^b Lit. "in words." This is one of the most famous
passages in Plato, and a source of the idea of the City of
God among both Stoics and Christians. *Cf.* Marc. Aurel.
ix. 29 μηδὲ τὴν Πλάτωνος πολιτείαν ἔλπιζε, Justin Martyr's
ἐπὶ γῆς διατρίβουσιν ἀλλ' ἐν οὐρανῷ πολιτεύονται, which recalls
Philippians iii. 20 ἡμῶν δὲ τὸ πολίτευμα ἐν οὐρανοῖς ὑπάρχει,
and also *Heb.* xii. 22, xi. 10 and 16, xiii. 14, *Eph.* ii. 19, *Gal.*
iv. 26, *Rev.* iii. 12 and xxi. 2 ff. Ackermann, *Das Christliche bei Platon*, p. 24, compares *Luke* xvii. 21 "the
kingdom of God is within you." *Cf.* also *John* xviii. 36.
Havet, *Le Christianisme et ses origines*, p. 207, says, "Platon
dit de sa République précisément ce qu'on a dit plus tard
du royaume de Dieu, qu'elle n'est pas de ce monde." *Cf.*
also Caird, *Evolution of Theology in Greek Philosophy*, ii.
p. 170, Harnack, *Hist. of Dogma* (tr. Buchanan), vol. i. p. 332,
ii. pp. 73-74 and 338, Proclus, *Comm.* § 352 (Kroll i. 16);
Pater, *Marius the Epicurean*, p. 212 "Marcus Aurelius
speaks often of that City on high, of which all other cities
are but single habitations . . .," p. 213 ". . . the vision
of a reasonable, a divine order, not in nature, but in the
condition of human affairs, that unseen Celestial City,
Uranopolis, Callipolis. . . "; *ibid.* p. 158 "thou hast
been a citizen in this wide city," and pp. 192-193. *Cf.*
further Inge, *Christian Ethics*, pp. 104-105, "let us fly
hence to our dear country, as the disciples of Plato have
repeated one after another. There are a few people who
are so well adjusted to their environment that they do
not feel, or rarely feel, this nostalgia for the infinite
. . ." Lamartine, in his poem, "Isolement" (*apud* Faguet,
Dix-Neuvième Siècle, p. 89) beautifully expresses this nostalgia for the home of the ideal:

414

city he certainly will, yet perhaps not in the city of
his birth, except in some providential conjuncture.[a] "
" I understand," he said ; " you mean the city whose
establishment we have described, the city whose
home is in the ideal ;[b] for I think that it can be
found nowhere on earth.[c] "   " Well," said I, " per-

> Là, je m'enivrerais à la source où j'aspire ;
> Là, je retrouverais et l'espoir et l'amour,
> Et ce bien idéal que toute âme désire,
> Et qui n'a pas de nom au terrestre séjour.

Likewise the lovely sonnet of Du Bellay which in an English
version might run as follows :

> If our brief life is to eternity
> But as a span ; if our ephemeral sun,
> Gilding the shadows that before it flee,
> Chases our days to darkness one by one,
> Why, O my soul, pent in this prison obscure,
> Wilt thou in these dim shadows take delight,
> When to soar upward to the eternal pure
> Luminous heavens thy wings are spread for flight?
> There is the good for which all hearts do burn.
> There is the peace for which all creatures yearn.
> There is the love supreme without a stain.
> There too is pleasure that is not bought with pain.
> There upon heaven's dome and outmost shore
> Thou'lt know the ideas and recognize once more
> The beauty whose image here thou must adore.

Somewhat different is the Stoic idea of a world state and
of the sage as citizen of the world, *e.g.* Marc. Aurel. iv. 4,
Sen. *De otio* 31, Cic. *Nat. deor.* ii. 62 (154).   *Cf.* Newman,
Aristot. Pol. i. p. 92 ; also *ibid.* pp. 87-88.   For the identification of the πόλις with philosophy *cf.* Diog. Laert. vi. 15
and vii. 40, Lucian, *Hermotim.* 22, *Sale of Lives* 17, *Ver.
Hist.* 17, Proclus i. 16 (Kroll).   Diogenes Laertius, ii. 7,
reports that, when Anaxagoras was reproached for not concerning himself with the affairs of his country, he replied,
" Indeed, I am greatly concerned with my country," and
pointed to heaven.

[c] *Cf.* 499 c-d.

592 δ' ἐγώ, ἐν οὐρανῷ ἴσως παράδειγμα ἀνάκειται τῷ
βουλομένῳ ὁρᾶν καὶ ὁρῶντι ἑαυτὸν κατοικίζειν·
διαφέρει δὲ οὐδέν, εἴτε που ἔστιν εἴτε ἔσται· τὰ
γὰρ ταύτης μόνης ἂν πράξειεν, ἄλλης δὲ οὐδεμιᾶς.
Εἰκός γ', ἔφη.

ᵃ Cf. Theaet. 176 E, which Wilamowitz, Platon, ii. p. 179
says must refer to the Republic, Laws 739 D-F, 746 B, and
What Plato Said, p. 458, on Euthyphro 6 E.

haps there is a pattern [a] of it laid up in heaven for him who wishes to contemplate it and so beholding to constitute himself its citizen.[b] But it makes no difference whether it exists now or ever will come into being.[c] The politics of this city only will be his and of none other." "That seems probable," he said.

[b] ἑαυτὸν κατοικίζειν: Adam "found a city in himself." See his note *ad loc.* Cf. Jebb on Soph. *Oed. Col.* 1004.
[c] Cf. 499 c-d, 472 b-e, and *What Plato Said*, p. 564.

I

595 I. Καὶ μήν, ἦν δ' ἐγώ, πολλὰ μὲν καὶ ἄλλα περὶ
αὐτῆς ἐννοῶ, ὡς παντὸς ἄρα μᾶλλον ὀρθῶς ᾠκίζομεν τὴν πόλιν, οὐχ ἥκιστα δὲ ἐνθυμηθεὶς περὶ
ποιήσεως λέγω. Τὸ ποῖον; ἔφη. Τὸ μηδαμῇ
παραδέχεσθαι αὐτῆς ὅση μιμητική· παντὸς γὰρ
μᾶλλον οὐ παραδεκτέα νῦν καὶ ἐναργέστερον, ὡς
B ἐμοὶ δοκεῖ, φαίνεται, ἐπειδὴ χωρὶς ἕκαστα δι-
ῄρηται τὰ τῆς ψυχῆς εἴδη. Πῶς λέγεις; Ὡς μὲν
πρὸς ὑμᾶς εἰρῆσθαι—οὐ γάρ μου κατερεῖτε πρὸς
τοὺς τῆς τραγῳδίας ποιητὰς καὶ τοὺς ἄλλους
ἅπαντας τοὺς μιμητικούς—λώβη ἔοικεν εἶναι
πάντα τὰ τοιαῦτα τῆς τῶν ἀκουόντων διανοίας, ὅσοι
μὴ ἔχουσι φάρμακον τὸ εἰδέναι αὐτὰ οἷα τυγχάνει
ὄντα. Πῇ δή, ἔφη, διανοούμενος λέγεις; Ῥητέον,
ἦν δ' ἐγώ, καίτοι φιλία γέ τίς με καὶ αἰδὼς ἐκ

---

a In Book III. On the whole question see Introd. pp. lxi-
lxiii. Max. Tyr. *Diss.* 23 Εἰ καλῶς Πλάτων Ὅμηρον τῆς Πολιτείας
παρῃτήσατο, and 32 Εἰ ἔστι καθ' Ὅμηρον αἵρεσις. Strabo i.
2 § 3. Athenaeus v. 12. 187 says that Plato himself in the
Symposium wrote worse things than the poets whom he
banishes. Friedländer, *Platon*, i. p. 138, thinks that the
return to the poets in Book X. is intended to justify the
poetry of Plato's dialogues. On the banishment of the

BOOK X

I. "And truly," I said, "many other considerations assure me that we were entirely right in our organization of the state, and especially, I think, in the matter of poetry.[a]" "What about it?" he said. "In refusing to admit[b] at all so much of it as is imitative[c]; for that it is certainly not to be received is, I think, still more plainly apparent now that we have distinguished the several parts[d] of the soul." "What do you mean?" "Why, between ourselves[e]—for you will not betray me to the tragic poets and all other imitators—that kind of art seems to be a corruption[f] of the mind of all listeners who do not possess as an antidote[g] a knowledge of its real nature." "What is your idea in saying this?" he said. "I must speak out," I said, "though a certain love and

poets and Homer *cf.* also Minucius Felix (Halm), pp. 32-33, Tertullian (Oehler), lib. ii. c. 7, Olympiodorus, Hermann vi. p. 367, Augustine, *De civ. Dei*, ii. xiv.

[b] *Supra* 394 D, 568 B, and on 398 A-B, *infra* 607 A.

[c] In the narrower sense. *Cf.* Vol. I. p. 224, note *c*, on 392 D, and *What Plato Said*, p. 561.

[d] Lit. "species." *Cf.* 435 B ff., 445 C, 580 D, 588 B ff., *Phaedr.* 271 D, *Unity of Plato's Thought*, p. 42.

[e] *Cf. Gorg.* 462 B, *Protag.* 309 A, 339 E.

[f] *Cf.* 605 C, *Meno* 91 C, *Laws* 890 B.

[g] φάρμακον: this passage is the source of Plutarch's view of literature in education; see *Quomodo adolescens poetas audire debeat* 15 C.

595 παιδὸς ἔχουσα περὶ Ὁμήρου ἀποκωλύει λέγειν.

C ἔοικε μὲν γὰρ τῶν καλῶν ἁπάντων τούτων τῶν τραγικῶν πρῶτος διδάσκαλός τε καὶ ἡγεμὼν γενέσθαι. ἀλλ' οὐ γὰρ πρό γε τῆς ἀληθείας τιμητέος ἀνήρ, ἀλλ', ὃ λέγω, ῥητέον. Πάνυ μὲν οὖν, ἔφη. Ἄκουε δή, μᾶλλον δὲ ἀποκρίνου. Ἐρώτα. Μίμησιν ὅλως ἔχοις ἄν μοι εἰπεῖν ὅ τί ποτ' ἐστίν; οὐδὲ γάρ τοι αὐτὸς πάνυ τι ξυννοῶ, τί βούλεται εἶναι. Ἦ που ἄρ', ἔφη, ἐγὼ συννοήσω. Οὐδέν γε, ἦν δ' ἐγώ, ἄτοπον, ἐπεὶ πολλά

596 τοι ὀξύτερον βλεπόντων ἀμβλύτερον ὁρῶντες πρότεροι εἶδον. Ἔστιν, ἔφη, οὕτως· ἀλλὰ σοῦ παρόντος οὐδ' ἂν προθυμηθῆναι οἷός τε εἴην εἰπεῖν, εἴ τί μοι καταφαίνεται· ἀλλ' αὐτὸς ὅρα. Βούλει οὖν ἐνθένδε ἀρξώμεθα ἐπισκοποῦντες, ἐκ τῆς εἰωθυίας μεθόδου; εἶδος γάρ πού τι ἓν ἕκαστον εἰώθαμεν τίθεσθαι περὶ ἕκαστα τὰ πολλά, οἷς

---

[a] Isoc. ii. 48-49 is perhaps imitating this. For Homer as a source of tragedy *cf.* also 598 D, 605 C-D, 607 A, 602 B, *Theaet.* 152 E, schol. Trendelenburg, pp. 75 ff.; Dryden, *Discourse on Epic Poetry*: " The origin of the stage was from the epic poem . . . those episodes of Homer which were proper for the state the poets amplified each into an action," etc. *Cf.* Aristot. *Poet.* 1448 b 35 f., Diog. Laert. iv. 20, and *supra* 393 A ff.

[b] *Cf. What Plato Said*, p. 532, on *Phaedo* 91 c, Aristot. *Eth. Nic.* 1096 a 16 ἀμφοῖν γὰρ ὄντοιν φίλοιν ὅσιον προτιμᾶν τὴν ἀλήθειαν, Henri-Pierre Cazac, *Polémique d'Aristote contre la théorie platonicienne des Idées*, p. 11, n. : " Platon lui-même, critiquant Homère, . . . fait une semblable réflexion, ' On doit plus d'égards à la vérité qu'à un homme.' Cousin croit, après Camérarius, que c'est là l'origine du mot célèbre d'Aristote." *Cf.* St. Augustine, *De civ. Dei* x. 30 " homini praeposuit veritatem."

[c] For ἦ του *cf. Phaedo* 84 D.

[d] Perhaps a slight failure in Attic courtesy. *Cf. Laws*

reverence for Homer [a] that has possessed me from a boy would stay me from speaking. For he appears to have been the first teacher and beginner of all these beauties of tragedy. Yet all the same we must not honour a man above truth,[b] but, as I say, speak our minds." "By all means," he said. "Listen, then, or rather, answer my question." "Ask it," he said. "Could you tell me in general what imitation is? For neither do I myself quite apprehend what it would be at." "It is likely, then,[c]" he said, "that I should apprehend!" "It would be nothing strange," said I, "since it often happens that the dimmer vision sees things in advance of the keener.[d]" "That is so," he said; "but in your presence I could not even be eager to try to state anything that appears to me, but do you yourself consider it." "Shall we, then, start the inquiry at this point by our customary procedure[e]? We are in the habit, I take it, of positing a single idea or form[f] in the case of the various multiplicities to

715 D-E, and for ὀξύτερον βλεπόντων 927 B, *Euthydem.* 281 D, *Rep.* 404 A, Themist. *Orat.* ii. p. 32 c. *Cf.* the saying πολλάκι καὶ κηπουρὸς ἀνὴρ μάλα καίριον εἶπεν.

[e] *Cf. Phaedo* 76 D, 100 B, *Phileb.* 16 D, *supra* 479 E, Thompson on *Meno* 72 D. See Zeller, *Phil. d. Gr.* ii. 1. p. 660. The intentional simplicity of Plato's positing of the concept here (*cf.* 597 A), and his transition from the concept to the "idea," has been mistaken for a primitive aspect of his thought by many interpreters. It is quite uncritical to use Aristot. *Met.* 991 b 6 ff. to prove that Plato's "later" theory of ideas did not recognize ideas of artefacts, and therefore that this passage represents an earlier phase of the theory. He deliberately expresses the theory as simply as possible, and a manufactured object suits his purpose here as it does in *Cratyl.* 389. See also *supra*, Introd. pp. xxii-xxiii.

[f] "Forms" with a capital letter is even more misleading than "ideas."

596 ταὐτὸν ὄνομα ἐπιφέρομεν. ἦ οὐ μανθάνεις; Μανθάνω. Θῶμεν δὴ καὶ νῦν ὅ τι βούλει τῶν πολλῶν.
B οἷον, εἰ θέλεις, πολλαί πού εἰσι κλῖναι καὶ τράπεζαι.
Πῶς δ' οὔ; Ἀλλὰ ἰδέαι γέ που περὶ ταῦτα τὰ
σκεύη δύο, μία μὲν κλίνης, μία δὲ τραπέζης. Ναί.
Οὐκοῦν καὶ εἰώθαμεν λέγειν, ὅτι ὁ δημιουργὸς
ἑκατέρου τοῦ σκεύους πρὸς τὴν ἰδέαν βλέπων
οὕτω ποιεῖ ὁ μὲν τὰς κλίνας, ὁ δὲ τὰς τραπέζας,
αἷς ἡμεῖς χρώμεθα, καὶ τἆλλα κατὰ ταὐτά; οὐ
γάρ που τήν γε ἰδέαν αὐτὴν δημιουργεῖ οὐδεὶς τῶν
δημιουργῶν· πῶς γάρ; Οὐδαμῶς. Ἀλλ' ὅρα δὴ
C καὶ τόνδε τίνα καλεῖς τὸν δημιουργόν. Τὸν ποῖον;
Ὃς πάντα ποιεῖ, ὅσαπερ εἷς ἕκαστος τῶν χειρο-
τεχνῶν. Δεινόν τινα λέγεις καὶ θαυμαστὸν ἄνδρα.
Οὔπω γε, ἀλλὰ τάχα μᾶλλον φήσεις. ὁ αὐτὸς γὰρ
οὗτος χειροτέχνης οὐ μόνον πάντα οἷός τε σκεύη
ποιῆσαι, ἀλλὰ καὶ τὰ ἐκ τῆς γῆς φυόμενα ἅπαντα
ποιεῖ καὶ ζῷα πάντα ἐργάζεται, τά τε ἄλλα καὶ
ἑαυτόν, καὶ πρὸς τούτοις γῆν καὶ οὐρανὸν καὶ
θεοὺς καὶ πάντα τὰ ἐν οὐρανῷ καὶ τὰ ἐν Ἅιδου
ὑπὸ γῆς ἅπαντα ἐργάζεται. Πάνυ θαυμαστόν,
D ἔφη, λέγεις σοφιστήν. Ἀπιστεῖς; ἦν δ' ἐγώ.
καί μοι εἰπέ· τὸ παράπαν οὐκ ἄν σοι δοκεῖ εἶναι

---

[a] Cf. *Cratyl.* 389 A-B. There is no contradiction, as
many say, with 472 D.

[b] Cf. Emerson, *The Poet*: " and therefore the rich poets—
as Homer, Chaucer, Shakespeare and Raphael—have no
limits to their riches except the limits of their lifetime, and
resemble a mirror carried through the streets ready to render
an image of every created thing." (*Cf.* 596 D-E κάτοπτρον
περιφέρειν and Julian, *Or.* v. 163 D.) Empedocles, *fr.* 23
(Diels i.³ pp. 234-235):

ὡς δ' ὁπόταν γραφέες . . .
δένδρεά τε κτίζοντε καὶ ἀνέρας ἠδὲ γυναῖκας . . .

which we give the same name. Do you not understand?" "I do." "In the present case, then, let us take any multiplicity you please; for example, there are many couches and tables." "Of course." "But these utensils imply, I suppose, only two ideas or forms, one of a couch and one of a table." "Yes." "And are we not also in the habit of saying that the craftsman who produces either of them fixes his eyes [a] on the idea or form, and so makes in the one case the couches and in the other the tables that we use, and similarly of other things? For surely no craftsman makes the idea itself. How could he?" "By no means." "But now consider what name you would give to this craftsman." "What one?" "Him who makes all the things [b] that all handicraftsmen severally produce." "A truly clever and wondrous man you tell of." "Ah, but wait,[c] and you will say so indeed, for this same handicraftsman is not only able to make all implements, but he produces all plants and animals, including himself,[d] and thereto earth and heaven and the gods and all things in heaven and in Hades under the earth." "A most marvellous sophist,[e]" he said. "Are you incredulous?" said I. "Tell me, do you deny altogether the possibility

[c] Climax beyond climax. *Cf.* on 508 E, p. 104, note *c*.

[d] It is a tempting error to refer this to God, as I once did, and as Wilamowitz, *Platon*, i. p. 604 does. So Cudworth, *True Intel. System of the Universe*, vol. ii. p. 70: "Lastly, he is called ὃς πάντα τά τε ἄλλα ἐργάζεται, καὶ ἑαυτόν, 'he that causeth or produceth both all other things, and even himself.'" But the producer of everything, including himself, is the imitator generalized and then exemplified by the painter and the poet. *Cf. Soph.* 234 A-B.

[e] Eurip. *Hippol.* 921 δεινὸν σοφιστὴν εἶπας.

596 τοιοῦτος δημιουργός, ἢ τινὶ μὲν τρόπῳ γενέσθαι
ἂν τούτων ἁπάντων ποιητής, τινὶ δὲ οὐκ ἄν; ἢ
οὐκ αἰσθάνει, ὅτι κἂν αὐτὸς οἷός τ᾽ εἴης πάντα
ταῦτα ποιῆσαι τρόπῳ γέ τινι; Καὶ τίς,ᵃ ἔφη, ὁ
τρόπος οὗτος; Οὐ χαλεπός, ἦν δ᾽ ἐγώ, ἀλλὰ
πολλαχῇ καὶ ταχὺ δημιουργούμενος· τάχιστα δέ
που, εἰ θέλεις λαβὼν κάτοπτρον περιφέρειν παν-
E ταχῇ· ταχὺ μὲν ἥλιον ποιήσεις καὶ τὰ ἐν τῷ
οὐρανῷ, ταχὺ δὲ γῆν, ταχὺ δὲ σαυτόν τε καὶ
τἆλλα ζῷα καὶ σκεύη καὶ φυτὰ καὶ πάντα ὅσα
νῦν δὴ ἐλέγετο. Ναί, ἔφη, φαινόμενα, οὐ μέντοι
ὄντα γέ που τῇ ἀληθείᾳ. Καλῶς, ἦν δ᾽ ἐγώ, καὶ
εἰς δέον ἔρχει τῷ λόγῳ. τῶν τοιούτων γάρ, οἶμαι,
δημιουργῶν καὶ ὁ ζωγράφοςᵇ ἐστίν. ἦ γάρ; Πῶς
γὰρ οὔ; Ἀλλὰ φήσεις οὐκ ἀληθῆ, οἶμαι, αὐτὸν
ποιεῖν ἃ ποιεῖ. καίτοι τρόπῳ γέ τινι καὶ ὁ ζω-

ᵃ καὶ τίς is sceptical as in Aristoph. *Acharn.* 86.
ᵇ Art is deception. Diels ii.³ p. 339, Dialex. 3 (10) ἐν
γὰρ τραγῳδοποιίᾳ καὶ ζωγραφίᾳ ὅστις ⟨κε⟩ πλεῖστα ἐξαπατῇ
ὅμοια τοῖς ἀληθινοῖς ποιέων, οὗτος ἄριστος, Xen. *Mem.* iii. 10. 1
γραφική ἐστιν εἰκασία τῶν ὁρωμένων. *Cf.* Plut. *Quomodo
adolescens* 17 F-18 A on painting and poetry. There are
many specious resemblances between Plato's ideas on art
and morality and those of the "lunatic fringe" of Platonism.
Cf. Jane Harrison, *Ancient Art and Ritual,* pp. 21-22,
Charles F. Andrews, *Mahatma Gandhi's Ideas,* p. 332.
Cf. further R. G. Collingwood, "Plato's Philosophy of Art,"
Mind, 34, pp. 154-172. Stewart, *Plato's Doctrine of Ideas,*
p. 60, fancifully says: "Between the lines of Plato's criticism
of bad art here, as copying the particular, we must read the
doctrine that true art copies or in some way sets forth the
idea." But the defenders of poetry have always taken this
line. *Cf.* Hartley Coleridge's sonnet:

The vale of Tempe had in vain been fair
. . . . if the sight inspired
Saw only what the visual organs show,
If heaven-born phantasy no more required

of such a craftsman, or do you admit that in a sense there could be such a creator of all these things, and in another sense not ? Or do you not perceive that you yourself would be able to make all these things in a way ? " " And in what way,ᵃ I ask you," he said. " There is no difficulty," said I, " but it is something that the craftsman can make everywhere and quickly. You could do it most quickly if you should choose to take a mirror and carry it about everywhere. You will speedily produce the sun and all the things in the sky, and speedily the earth and yourself and the other animals and implements and plants and all the objects of which we just now spoke." "Yes," he said, " the appearance of them, but not the reality and the truth." " Excellent," said I, " and you come to the aid of the argument opportunely. For I take it that the painter too belongs to this class of producers, does he not ? " " Of course." " But you will say, I suppose, that his creations are not real and true. And yet, after a fashion, the painter ᵇ too

> Than what within the sphere of sense may grow.
> The beauty to perceive of earthly things
> The mounting soul must heavenward prune her wings.

Mrs. Browning, " Aurora Leigh ":

> . . . Art's the nature of what is
> Behind this show. If this world's show were all,
> Then imitation would be all in art.

William Temple, *Plato and Christianity*, p. 89 : " In the tenth book of the *Republic* he says that, whereas the artificer in making any material object imitates the eternal idea, an artist only imitates the imitation (595 A-598 D); but in Book v. he said that we do not blame an artist who depicts a face more beautiful than any actual human face either is or ever could be (472 D)." But this does not affect Plato's main point here, that the artist imitates the " real" world, not the world of ideas. The artist's imitation may fall short of or better its model. But the model is not the (Platonic) idea.

PLATO

596 γράφος κλίνην ποιεῖ. ἢ οὔ; Ναί, ἔφη, φαινομένην
γε καὶ οὗτος.

597 II. Τί δὲ ὁ κλινοποιός; οὐκ ἄρτι μέντοι ἔλεγες,
ὅτι οὐ τὸ εἶδος ποιεῖ, ὃ δή φαμεν εἶναι ὃ ἔστι
κλίνη, ἀλλὰ κλίνην τινά; Ἔλεγον γάρ. Οὐκοῦν
εἰ μὴ ὃ ἔστι ποιεῖ, οὐκ ἂν τὸ ὂν ποιοῖ, ἀλλά τι
τοιοῦτον οἷον τὸ ὄν, ὂν δὲ οὔ· τελέως δὲ εἶναι ὂν
τὸ τοῦ κλινουργοῦ ἔργον ἢ ἄλλου τινὸς χειρο-
τέχνου εἴ τις φαίη, κινδυνεύει οὐκ ἂν ἀληθῆ λέγειν;
Οὔκουν, ἔφη, ὥς γ' ἂν δόξειε τοῖς περὶ τοὺς
τοιούσδε λόγους διατρίβουσιν. Μηδὲν ἄρα θαυμά-
ζωμεν, εἰ καὶ τοῦτο ἀμυδρόν τι τυγχάνει ὂν πρὸς
B ἀλήθειαν. Μὴ γάρ. Βούλει οὖν, ἔφην, ἐπ' αὐτῶν
τούτων ζητήσωμεν τὸν μιμητὴν τοῦτον, τίς ποτ'
ἐστίν; Εἰ βούλει, ἔφη. Οὐκοῦν τρυτταί τινες
κλῖναι αὗται γίγνονται· μία μὲν ἡ ἐν τῇ φύσει
οὖσα, ἣν φαῖμεν ἄν, ὡς ἐγῷμαι, θεὸν ἐργάσασθαι.
ἢ τίν' ἄλλον; Οὐδένα, οἶμαι. Μία δέ γε ἦν ὁ
τέκτων. Ναί, ἔφη. Μία δὲ ἦν ὁ ζωγράφος. ἢ
γάρ; Ἔστω. Ζωγράφος δή, κλινοποιός, θεός,
τρεῖς οὗτοι ἐπιστάται τρισὶν εἴδεσι κλινῶν. Ναὶ
C τρεῖς. Ὁ μὲν δὴ θεός, εἴτε οὐκ ἐβούλετο, εἴτε τις

---

[a] ὃ ἔστι belongs to the terminology of ideas. *Cf. Phaedo*
74 D, 75 B, 75 D, *Rep.* 507 B.

[b] τελέως . . . ὄν: *cf. supra* 477 A, and *Soph.* 248 E παντελῶς
ὄντι.

[c] An indirect reference to Plato and his school like the
" friends of ideas " in *Soph.* 248 A.

[d] *Cf.* 597 C, 598 A, 501 B φύσει, *Phaedo* 103 B, *Parmen.*
132 D.

426

makes a couch, does he not?" "Yes," he said, "the appearance of one, he too."

II. "What of the cabinet-maker? Were you not just now saying that he does not make the idea or form which we say is the real couch, the couch in itself,[a] but only some particular couch?" "Yes, I was." "Then if he does not make that which really is, he could not be said to make real being but something that resembles real being but is not that. But if anyone should say that being in the complete sense [b] belongs to the work of the cabinet-maker or to that of any other handicraftsman, it seems that he would say what is not true." "That would be the view," he said, "of those who are versed [c] in this kind of reasoning." "We must not be surprised, then, if this too is only a dim adumbration in comparison with reality." "No, we must not." "Shall we, then, use these very examples in our quest for the true nature of this imitator?" "If you please," he said. "We get, then, these three couches, one, that in nature,[d] which, I take it, we would say that God produces,[e] or who else?" "No one, I think." "And then there was one which the carpenter made." "Yes," he said. "And one which the painter. Is not that so?" "So be it." "The painter, then, the cabinet-maker, and God, there are these three presiding over three kinds of couches." "Yes, three." "Now God, whether because he so willed or because some compulsion was

---

[e] Proclus says that this is not seriously meant (*apud* Beckmann, *Num Plato artifactorum Ideas statuerit*, p. 12). *Cf.* Zeller, *Phil. d. Gr.* ii. 1, p. 666, who interprets the passage correctly; A. E. Taylor, in *Mind*, xii. p. 5 "Plato's meaning has been supposed to be adequately indicated by such half-jocular instances as that of the idea of a bed or table in *Republic* x.," etc.

PLATO

597 ἀνάγκη ἐπὴν μὴ πλέον ἢ μίαν ἐν τῇ φύσει ἀπεργάσασθαι αὐτὸν κλίνην, οὕτως ἐποίησε μίαν μόνον
αὐτὴν ἐκείνην ὃ ἔστι κλίνη· δύο δὲ τοιαῦται ἢ
πλείους οὔτε ἐφυτεύθησαν ὑπὸ τοῦ θεοῦ οὔτε μὴ
φύσωσιν. Πῶς δή; ἔφη. Ὅτι, ἦν δ' ἐγώ, εἰ
δύο μόνας ποιήσειε, πάλιν ἂν μία ἀναφανείη, ἧς
ἐκεῖναι ἂν αὖ ἀμφότεραι τὸ εἶδος ἔχοιεν, καὶ εἴη
ἂν ὃ ἔστι κλίνη ἐκείνη, ἀλλ' οὐχ αἱ δύο. Ὀρθῶς,
ἔφη. Ταῦτα δή, οἶμαι, εἰδὼς ὁ θεός, βουλόμενος
D εἶναι ὄντως κλίνης ποιητὴς ὄντως οὔσης, ἀλλὰ μὴ
κλίνης τινὸς μηδὲ κλινοποιός τις, μίαν φύσει
αὐτὴν ἔφυσεν. Ἔοικεν. Βούλει οὖν τοῦτον μὲν
φυτουργὸν τούτου προσαγορεύωμεν ἤ τι τοιοῦτον;
Δίκαιον γοῦν, ἔφη, ἐπειδήπερ φύσει γε καὶ τοῦτο
καὶ τἆλλα πάντα πεποίηκεν. Τί δὲ τὸν τέκτονα;
ἆρ' οὐ δημιουργὸν κλίνης; Ναί. Ἦ καὶ τὸν
ζωγράφον δημιουργὸν καὶ ποιητὴν τοῦ τοιούτου;
Οὐδαμῶς. Ἀλλὰ τί αὐτὸν κλίνης φήσεις εἶναι;
E Τοῦτο, ἦ δ' ὅς, ἔμοιγε δοκεῖ μετριώτατ' ἂν
προσαγορεύεσθαι, μιμητὴς οὗ ἐκεῖνοι δημιουργοί.
Εἶεν, ἦν δ' ἐγώ, τὸν τοῦ τρίτου ἄρα γεννήματος
ἀπὸ τῆς φύσεως μιμητὴν καλεῖς; Πάνυ μὲν οὖν,

ᵃ In *Tim.* 31 ᴀ the same argument is used for the creation
of one world ἵνα ... κατὰ τὴν μόνωσιν ὅμοιον ᾖ τῷ παντελεῖ ζώῳ.
See my *De Plat. Idearum doct.* p. 39.   *Cf.* Renan, *Dialogues
Phil.* p. 25: "Pour forger les premières tenailles, dit le
Talmud, il fallut des tenailles.   Dieu les créa."
    ᵇ The famous argument of the third man.   *Cf. What
Plato Said*, p. 585, on *Parmen.* 132 ᴀ and Introd. p. xxiii.
    ᶜ *Cf. Soph.* 265 ᴇ θήσω τὰ μὲν φύσει λεγόμενα ποιεῖσθαι θείᾳ
τέχνῃ, Hooker, *Eccles. Pol.* i. 3. 4 "those things which
Nature is said to do are by divine art performed, using
nature as an instrument," Browne, *apud* J. Texte, *Études
de littérature européenne*, p. 65 "la nature est l'art de

laid upon him [a] not to make more than one couch in nature, so wrought and created one only,[b] the couch which really and in itself is. But two or more such were never created by God and never will come into being." "How so?" he said. "Because," said I, "if he should make only two, there would again appear one of which they both would possess the form or idea, and that would be the couch that really is in and of itself, and not the other two." "Right," he said. "God, then, I take it, knowing this and wishing to be the real author of the couch that has real being and not of some particular couch, nor yet a particular cabinet-maker, produced it in nature unique." "So it seems." "Shall we, then, call him its true and natural begetter, or something of the kind?" "That would certainly be right," he said, "since it is by and in nature [c] that he has made this and all other things." "And what of the carpenter? Shall we not call him the creator of a couch?" "Yes." "Shall we also say that the painter is the creator and maker of that sort of thing?" "By no means." "What will you say he is in relation to the couch?" "This," said he, "seems to me the most reasonable designation for him, that he is the imitator of the thing which those others produce." "Very good," said I; "the producer of the product three removes [d] from nature you call the imitator?" "By all means," he said.

Dieu," Cic. *De nat. deor.* ii. 13 "deoque tribuenda, id est mundo," *De leg.* i. 7. 21, Seneca, *De benef.* iv. 7 "quid enim aliud est natura quam deus?" Höffding, *Hist. of Mod. Philos.* ii. 115 "Herder uses the word Nature in his book in order to avoid the frequent mention of the name of God."

[d] *Cf.* 587 c, *Phaedr.* 248 E, where the imitator is sixth in the scale.

597 ἔφη. Τοῦτ' ἄρα ἔσται καὶ ὁ τραγῳδοποιός,
εἴπερ μιμητής ἐστι, τρίτος τις ἀπὸ βασιλέως καὶ
τῆς ἀληθείας πεφυκώς, καὶ πάντες οἱ ἄλλοι μιμηταί.
Κινδυνεύει. Τὸν μὲν δὴ μιμητὴν ὡμολογήκαμεν·
598 εἰπὲ δέ μοι περὶ τοῦ ζωγράφου τόδε· πότερα ἐκεῖνο
αὐτὸ τὸ ἐν τῇ φύσει ἕκαστον δοκεῖ σοι ἐπιχειρεῖν
μιμεῖσθαι ἢ τὰ τῶν δημιουργῶν ἔργα; Τὰ τῶν
δημιουργῶν, ἔφη. Ἆρα οἷα ἔστιν ἢ οἷα φαίνεται;
τοῦτο γὰρ ἔτι διόρισον. Πῶς λέγεις; ἔφη. Ὧδε·
κλίνη, ἐάν τε ἐκ πλαγίου αὐτὴν θεᾷ ἐάν τε καταντικρὺ ἢ ὁπῃοῦν, μή τι διαφέρει αὐτὴ ἑαυτῆς,
ἢ διαφέρει μὲν οὐδέν, φαίνεται δὲ ἀλλοία; καὶ
τἆλλα ὡσαύτως; Οὕτως, ἔφη· φαίνεται, διαφέρει
B δ' οὐδέν. Τοῦτο δὴ αὐτὸ σκόπει· πρὸς πότερον ἡ
γραφικὴ πεποίηται περὶ ἕκαστον; πότερα πρὸς τὸ
ὄν, ὡς ἔχει, μιμήσασθαι, ἢ πρὸς τὸ φαινόμενον, ὡς
φαίνεται, φαντάσματος ἢ ἀληθείας οὖσα μίμησις;
Φαντάσματος, ἔφη. Πόρρω ἄρα που τοῦ ἀληθοῦς
ἡ μιμητική ἐστι καί, ὡς ἔοικε, διὰ τοῦτο πάντα
ἀπεργάζεται, ὅτι σμικρόν τι ἑκάστου ἐφάπτεται,
καὶ τοῦτο εἴδωλον. οἷον ὁ ζωγράφος, φαμέν,
ζωγραφήσει ἡμῖν σκυτοτόμον, τέκτονα, τοὺς ἄλ-
C λους δημιουργούς, περὶ οὐδενὸς τούτων ἐπαΐων
τῶν τεχνῶν· ἀλλ' ὅμως παῖδάς τε καὶ ἄφρονας
ἀνθρώπους, εἰ ἀγαθὸς εἴη ζωγράφος, γράψας ἂν
τέκτονα καὶ πόρρωθεν ἐπιδεικνὺς ἐξαπατῷ ἂν τῷ

---

[a] Cf. Gorg. 488 D, Soph. 222 C.
[b] Cf. Soph. 263 B, Cratyl. 385 B, Euthydem. 284 C.
[c] Cf. 599 A, Soph. 232 A, 234 E, 236 B, Prot. 356 D.
[d] Cf. 581 E.
[e] For εἴδωλον cf. p. 197, note e.

"This, then, will apply to the maker of tragedies also, if he is an imitator and is in his nature three removes from the king and the truth, as are all other imitators." "It would seem so." "We are in agreement, then, about the imitator. But tell me now this about the painter. Do you think that what he tries to imitate is in each case that thing itself in nature or the works of the craftsmen?" "The works of the craftsmen," he said. "Is it the reality of them or the appearance? Define that further point.ᵃ" "What do you mean?" he said. "This: Does a couch differ from itself according as you view it from the side or the front or in any other way? Or does it differ not at all in fact though it appears different, and so of other things?" "That is the way of it," he said; "it appears other but differs not at all." "Consider, then, this very point. To which is painting directed in every case, to the imitation of reality as it isᵇ or of appearance as it appears? Is it an imitation of a phantasm or of the truth?" "Of a phantasm,ᶜ" he said. "Then the mimetic art is far removedᵈ from truth, and this, it seems, is the reason why it can produce everything, because it touches or lays hold of only a small part of the object and that a phantomᵉ; as, for example, a painter, we say, will paint us a cobbler, a carpenter, and other craftsmen, though he himself has no expertness in any of these arts,ᶠ but nevertheless if he were a good painter, by exhibiting at a distance his picture of a carpenter he would deceive children and

---

ᶠ Commentators sometimes miss the illogical idiom. So Adam once proposed to emend τεχνῶν to τεχνίτων, but later withdrew this suggestion in his note on the passage. *Cf. supra* 373 c, *Critias* 111 ᴇ, and my paper in *T.A.P.A.* xlvii. (1916) pp. 205-234.

598 δοκεῖν ὡς ἀληθῶς τέκτονα εἶναι. Τί δ' οὔ;
'Αλλὰ γάρ, οἶμαι, ὦ φίλε, τόδε δεῖ περὶ πάντων
τῶν τοιούτων διανοεῖσθαι· ἐπειδάν τις ἡμῖν ἀπ-
αγγέλλῃ περί του, ὡς ἐνέτυχεν ἀνθρώπῳ πάσας
ἐπισταμένῳ τὰς δημιουργίας καὶ τἆλλα πάντα, ὅσα

D εἷς ἕκαστος οἶδεν, οὐδὲν ὅ τι οὐχὶ ἀκριβέστερον
ὁτουοῦν ἐπισταμένῳ, ὑπολαμβάνειν δεῖ τῷ τοιούτῳ,
ὅτι εὐήθης τις ἄνθρωπος, καί, ὡς ἔοικεν, ἐντυχὼν
γόητί τινι καὶ μιμητῇ ἐξηπατήθη, ὥστε ἔδοξεν
αὐτῷ πάσσοφος εἶναι, διὰ τὸ αὐτὸς μὴ οἷός τ'
εἶναι ἐπιστήμην καὶ ἀνεπιστημοσύνην καὶ μίμησιν
ἐξετάσαι. 'Αληθέστατα, ἔφη.

III. Οὐκοῦν, ἦν δ' ἐγώ, μετὰ τοῦτο ἐπισκεπτέον
τήν τε τραγῳδίαν καὶ τὸν ἡγεμόνα αὐτῆς Ὅμηρον,
ἐπειδή τινων ἀκούομεν, ὅτι οὗτοι πάσας μὲν τέχνας

E ἐπίστανται, πάντα δὲ τὰ ἀνθρώπεια τὰ πρὸς ἀρετὴν

---

[a] Cf. Soph. 234 B.

[b] So Dryden, *Essay on Satire*: "Shakespeare . . . Homer
. . . in either of whom we find all arts and sciences, all
moral and natural philosophy without knowing that they
ever studied them," and the beautiful rhapsody of Andrew
Lang, *Letters to Dead Authors*, p. 238: "They believe not
that one human soul has known every art, and all the
thoughts of women as of men," etc. Pope, pref. to his
translation of the *Iliad*: "If we reflect upon those innumer-
able knowledges, those secrets of nature and physical
philosophy which Homer is generally supposed to have
wrapped up in his allegories, what a new and ample scene
of wonder may this consideration afford us." Cf. Xen.
Symp. 4. 6. Brunetière, *Époques*, p. 105, says: "Corneille
. . . se piquait de connaître à fond l'art de la politique et
celui de la guerre." For the impossibility of universal knowledge cf. *Soph.* 233 A, *Charm.* 170 B, Friedländer, *Platon*, ii.
p. 146 on *Hipp. Min.* 366 c ff. Cf. also *Ion* 536 E, 541 B,
540 B, and *Tim.* 19 D. Tate, "Plato and Allegorical Inter-

foolish men,[a] and make them believe it to be a real carpenter." "Why not?" "But for all that, my friend, this, I take it, is what we ought to bear in mind in all such cases: When anyone reports to us of some-one, that he has met a man who knows all the crafts and everything else [b] that men severally know, and that there is nothing that he does not know [c] more exactly than anybody else, our tacit rejoinder must be that he is a simple fellow, who apparently has met some magician or sleight-of-hand man and imitator and has been deceived by him into the belief that he is all-wise,[d] because of his own inability to put to the proof and distinguish knowledge, ignorance [e] and imitation." "Most true," he said.

III. "Then," said I, "have we not next to scrutinize tragedy and its leader Homer,[f] since some people tell us that these poets know all the arts and all things human pertaining to virtue and vice, and all

---

pretation," *Class. Quarterly*, Jan. 1930, p. 2 says: "The true poet is for Plato philosopher as well as poet. He must know the truth." This ignores the ἄρα in 598 E. Plato there is not stating his own opinion but giving the arguments of those who claim omniscience for the poet. Wilamowitz, *Platon*, ii. p. 313 n. 1 completely misunderstands and misinterprets the passage. *Cf. Class. Phil.* xxvii. (1932) p. 85. E. E. Sikes, *The Greek View of Poetry*, p. 175, says Rymer held that "a poet is obliged to know all arts and sciences." Aristotle from a different point of view says we expect the wise man to know everything in the sense in which that is possible, *Met.* 982 a 8.

[c] *Cf.* οὐδενὸς ὅτου οὐχὶ *Charm.* 175 c, οὐδὲν ὅτι οὐ *Alc. I* 105 E, *Phil.* 54 B, *Phaedo* 110 E, *Euthyph.* 3 c, *Euthydem.* 294 D, Isoc. *Panegyr.* 14, Herod. v. 97.

[d] πάσσοφος is generally ironical in Plato. *Cf. What Plato Said*, p. 489, on *Lysis* 216 A.

[e] For ἀνεπιστημοσύνην *cf. Theaet.* 199 E f.

[f] For Homer as tragedian *cf.* on 595 B-c, p. 420, note a.

598 καὶ κακίαν, καὶ τά γε θεῖα· ἀνάγκη γὰρ τὸν ἀγαθὸν
ποιητήν, εἰ μέλλει περὶ ὧν ἂν ποιῇ καλῶς ποιήσειν, εἰδότα ἄρα ποιεῖν, ἢ μὴ οἷόν τε εἶναι ποιεῖν.
δεῖ δὴ ἐπισκέψασθαι, πότερον μιμηταῖς τούτοις
οὗτοι ἐντυχόντες ἐξηπάτηνται καὶ τὰ ἔργα αὐτῶν
599 ὁρῶντες οὐκ αἰσθάνονται τριττὰ ἀπέχοντα τοῦ
ὄντος καὶ ῥᾴδια ποιεῖν μὴ εἰδότι τὴν ἀλήθειαν·
φαντάσματα γάρ, ἀλλ' οὐκ ὄντα ποιοῦσιν· ἢ τὶ καὶ
λέγουσι καὶ τῷ ὄντι οἱ ἀγαθοὶ ποιηταὶ ἴσασι περὶ
ὧν δοκοῦσι τοῖς πολλοῖς εὖ λέγειν. Πάνυ μὲν
οὖν, ἔφη, ἐξεταστέον. Οἴει οὖν, εἴ τις ἀμφότερα
δύναιτο ποιεῖν, τό τε μιμηθησόμενον καὶ τὸ εἴδωλον, ἐπὶ τῇ τῶν εἰδώλων δημιουργίᾳ ἑαυτὸν
ἀφεῖναι ἂν σπουδάζειν καὶ τοῦτο προστήσασθαι
B τοῦ ἑαυτοῦ βίου ὡς βέλτιστον ἔχοντα; Οὐκ ἔγωγε.
'Αλλ' εἴπερ γε, οἶμαι, ἐπιστήμων εἴη τῇ ἀληθείᾳ
τούτων πέρι, ἅπερ καὶ μιμεῖται, πολὺ πρότερον ἐν
τοῖς ἔργοις ἂν σπουδάσειεν ἢ ἐπὶ τοῖς μιμήμασι,
καὶ πειρῷτο ἂν πολλὰ καὶ καλὰ ἔργα ἑαυτοῦ κατα-
λιπεῖν μνημεῖα, καὶ εἶναι προθυμοῖτ' ἂν μᾶλλον ὁ
ἐγκωμιαζόμενος ἢ ὁ ἐγκωμιάζων. Οἶμαι, ἔφη·
οὐ γὰρ ἐξ ἴσου ἥ τε τιμὴ καὶ ἡ ὠφέλεια. Τῶν μὲν
τοίνυν ἄλλων πέρι μὴ ἀπαιτῶμεν λόγον Ὅμηρον
C ἢ ἄλλον ὁντιναοῦν τῶν ποιητῶν ἐρωτῶντες, εἰ
ἰατρικὸς ἦν τις αὐτῶν ἀλλὰ μὴ μιμητὴς μόνον
ἰατρικῶν λόγων, τίνας ὑγιεῖς ποιητής τις τῶν
παλαιῶν ἢ τῶν νέων λέγεται πεποιηκέναι, ὥσπερ

---

[a] Cf. on 598 B.   [b] Cf. 598 B.
[c] Cf. Petit de Julleville, Hist. lit. française vii. p. 233,
on the poet Lamartine's desire to be a practical statesman,
and ibid. : " Quand on m'apprendrait que le divin Homère a
refusé les charges municipales de Smyrne ou de Colophon,

things divine ?   For the good poet, if he is to poetize things rightly, must, they argue, create with knowledge or else be unable to create. So we must consider whether these critics have not fallen in with such imitators and been deceived by them, so that looking upon their works they cannot perceive that these are three removes from reality, and easy to produce without knowledge of the truth.   For it is phantoms,[a] not realities, that they produce. Or is there something in their claim, and do good poets really know the things about which the multitude fancy they speak well ? " " We certainly must examine the matter," he said. " Do you suppose, then, that if a man were able to produce both the exemplar and the semblance, he would be eager to abandon himself to the fashioning of phantoms [b] and set this in the forefront of his life as the best thing he had ? " " I do not." " But, I take it, if he had genuine knowledge of the things he imitates he would far rather devote himself to real things [c] than to the imitation of them, and would endeavour to leave after him many noble deeds [d] and works as memorials of himself, and would be more eager to be the theme of praise than the praiser." " I think so," he said ; " for there is no parity in the honour and the gain."   " Let us not, then, demand a reckoning [e] from Homer or any other of the poets on other matters by asking them, if any one of them was a physician and not merely an imitator of a physician's talk, what men any poet, old or new, is reported to have restored to health as Asclepius

je ne croirais jamais qu'il eût pu mieux mériter de la Grèce en administrant son bourg natal qu'en composant l'*Iliade* et l'*Odyssée*."   [d] But *cf. Symp.* 209 D.

   [e] For the challenge to the poet to specify his knowledge *cf. Ion* 536 E f.

599 Ἀσκληπιός, ἤ τινας μαθητὰς ἰατρικῆς κατελίπετο, ὥσπερ ἐκεῖνος τοὺς ἐκγόνους, μηδ' αὖ περὶ τὰς ἄλλας τέχνας αὐτοὺς ἐρωτῶμεν, ἀλλ' ἐῶμεν· περὶ δὲ ὧν μεγίστων τε καὶ καλλίστων ἐπιχειρεῖ λέγειν Ὅμηρος, πολέμων τε πέρι καὶ στρατηγιῶν καὶ

D διοικήσεων πόλεων καὶ παιδείας πέρι ἀνθρώπου, δίκαιόν που ἐρωτᾶν αὐτὸν πυνθανομένους· ὦ φίλε Ὅμηρε, εἴπερ μὴ τρίτος ἀπὸ τῆς ἀληθείας εἶ ἀρετῆς πέρι, εἰδώλου δημιουργός, ὃν δὴ μιμητὴν ὡρισάμεθα, ἀλλὰ καὶ δεύτερος, καὶ οἷός τε ἦσθα γιγνώσκειν, ποῖα ἐπιτηδεύματα βελτίους ἤ χείρους ἀνθρώπους ποιεῖ ἰδίᾳ καὶ δημοσίᾳ, λέγε ἡμῖν τίς τῶν πόλεων διὰ σὲ βέλτιον ᾠκήσεν, ὥσπερ διὰ Λυκοῦργον Λακεδαίμων καὶ δι' ἄλλους πολλοὺς

E πολλαὶ μεγάλαι τε καὶ σμικραί· σὲ δὲ τίς αἰτιᾶται πόλις νομοθέτην ἀγαθὸν γεγονέναι καὶ σφᾶς ὠφεληκέναι; Χαρώνδαν μὲν γὰρ Ἰταλία καὶ Σικελία, καὶ ἡμεῖς Σόλωνα· σὲ δὲ τίς; ἕξει τινὰ εἰπεῖν; Οὐκ οἶμαι, ἔφη ὁ Γλαύκων· οὔκουν λέγεταί γε οὐδ' ὑπ' αὐτῶν Ὁμηριδῶν. Ἀλλὰ

600 δή τις πόλεμος ἐπὶ Ὁμήρου ὑπ' ἐκείνου ἄρχοντος ἤ ξυμβουλεύοντος εὖ πολεμηθεὶς μνημονεύεται; Οὐδείς. Ἀλλ' οἷα δὴ εἰς τὰ ἔργα σοφοῦ ἀνδρὸς πολλαὶ ἐπίνοιαι καὶ εὐμήχανοι εἰς τέχνας ἤ τινας ἄλλας πράξεις λέγονται, ὥσπερ αὖ Θάλεώ τε πέρι

---

[a] Cf. Ion 541 A f.
[b] Cf. Gorg. 515 B, Laches 186 B.
[c] Cf. Laws 630 D, 632 D, 858 E, Symp. 209 D, Phaedr. 258 B, Minos 318 C, Herod. i. 65-66, Xen. Rep. Lac. 1. 2 and passim, Plutarch, Life of Lycurgus.
[d] Cf. Symp. 209 D, Phaedr. 258 B, 278 C, Charm. 155 A,

did, or what disciples of the medical art he left after him as Asclepius did his descendants ; and let us dismiss the other arts and not question them about them; but concerning the greatest and finest things of which Homer undertakes to speak, wars and generalship [a] and the administration of cities and the education of men, it surely is fair to question him and ask, ' Friend Homer, if you are not at the third remove from truth and reality in human excellence, being merely that creator of phantoms whom we defined as the imitator, but if you are even in the second place and were capable of knowing what pursuits make men better or worse in private or public life, tell us what city was better governed owing to you,[b] even as Lacedaemon was because of Lycurgus,[c] and many other cities great and small because of other legislators. But what city credits you with having been a good legislator and having benefited them ? Italy and Sicily say this of Charondas and we of Solon.[d] But who says it of you?' Will he be able to name any ? " " I think not," said Glaucon ; " at any rate none is mentioned even by the Homerids themselves." " Well, then, is there any tradition of a war in Homer's time that was well conducted by his command or counsel ? " " None." " Well, then, as might be expected of a man wise in practical affairs, are many and ingenious inventions [e] for the arts and business of life reported of Homer as

157 E, *Prot.* 343 A, *Tim.* 20 E ff., Herod. i. 29 ff. and 86, ii. 177, v. 113, Aristot. *Ath. Pol.* v. ff., Diog. Laert. i. 45 ff., Plutarch, *Life of Solon*, Freeman, *The Work and Life of Solon*.

[e] On the literature of " inventions," εὑρήματα, see Newman ii. p. 382 on Aristot. *Pol.* 1274 b 4. *Cf.* Virgil, *Aen.* vi. 663 " inventas aut qui vitam excoluere per artes," and *Symp.* 209 A.

600 τοῦ Μιλησίου καὶ Ἀναχάρσιος τοῦ Σκύθου; Οὐδαμῶς τοιοῦτον οὐδέν. Ἀλλὰ δὴ εἰ μὴ δημοσίᾳ,
ἰδίᾳ τισὶν ἡγεμὼν παιδείας αὐτὸς ζῶν λέγεται
Ὅμηρος γενέσθαι, οἳ ἐκεῖνον ἠγάπων ἐπὶ συνουσίᾳ
B καὶ τοῖς ὑστέροις ὁδόν τινα παρέδοσαν βίου
Ὁμηρικήν, ὥσπερ Πυθαγόρας αὐτός τε διαφερόντως ἐπὶ τούτῳ ἠγαπήθη, καὶ οἱ ὕστεροι ἔτι καὶ
νῦν Πυθαγόρειον τρόπον ἐπονομάζοντες τοῦ βίου
διαφανεῖς πῃ δοκοῦσιν εἶναι ἐν τοῖς ἄλλοις; Οὐδ᾽
αὖ, ἔφη, τοιοῦτον οὐδὲν λέγεται. ὁ γὰρ Κρεώφυλος, ὦ Σώκρατες, ἴσως, ὁ τοῦ Ὁμήρου ἑταῖρος,
τοῦ ὀνόματος ἂν γελοιότερος ἔτι πρὸς παιδείαν
φανείη, εἰ τὰ λεγόμενα περὶ Ὁμήρου ἀληθῆ.
λέγεται γάρ, ὡς πολλή τις ἀμέλεια περὶ αὐτὸν ἦν
ὑπ᾽ αὐτοῦ[1] ἐκείνου, ὅτε ἔζη.

C IV. Λέγεται γὰρ οὖν, ἦν δ᾽ ἐγώ. ἀλλ᾽ οἴει, ὦ
Γλαύκων, εἰ τῷ ὄντι οἷός τ᾽ ἦν παιδεύειν ἀνθρώπους καὶ βελτίους ἀπεργάζεσθαι Ὅμηρος, ἅτε
περὶ τούτων οὐ μιμεῖσθαι ἀλλὰ γιγνώσκειν δυνά-
μενος, οὐκ ἄρ᾽ ἂν πολλοὺς ἑταίρους ἐποιήσατο καὶ
ἐτιμᾶτο καὶ ἠγαπᾶτο ὑπ᾽ αὐτῶν; ἀλλὰ Πρωτ-
αγόρας μὲν ἄρα ὁ Ἀβδηρίτης καὶ Πρόδικος ὁ
Κεῖος καὶ ἄλλοι πάμπολλοι δύνανται τοῖς ἐφ᾽
D ἑαυτῶν παριστάναι ἰδίᾳ ξυγγιγνόμενοι, ὡς οὔτε

---

[1] ὑπ᾽ αὐτοῦ Ast, Adam: ἐπ᾽ αὐτοῦ mss.

---

[a] Diog. Laert. i. 23-27.
[b] Diog. Laert. i. 105 says he was reported to be the
inventor of the anchor and the potter's wheel.
[c] In the (spurious?) seventh epistle, 328 A, Plato speaks
of the life and λόγος advocated by himself. *Cf.* Novotny,
Plato's Epistles, p. 168.
[d] Diels i.[3] pp. 27 f.
[e] *Cf.* ὀρφικοί . . . βίοι *Laws* 782 c.

they are of Thales [a] the Milesian and Anacharsis [b] the Scythian? " " Nothing whatever of the sort." " Well, then, if no public service is credited to him, is Homer reported while he lived to have been a guide in education to men who took pleasure in associating with him and transmitted to posterity a certain Homeric way of life [c] just as Pythagoras [d] was himself especially honoured for this, and his successors, even to this day, denominating a certain way of life the Pythagorean,[e] are distinguished among their contemporaries ? " " No, nothing of this sort either is reported ; for Creophylos,[f] Socrates, the friend of Homer, would perhaps be even more ridiculous than his name [g] as a representative of Homeric culture and education, if what is said about Homer is true. For the tradition is that Homer was completely neglected in his own lifetime by that friend of the flesh."

IV. " Why, yes, that is the tradition," said I ; " but do you suppose, Glaucon, that, if Homer had really been able to educate men [h] and make them better and had possessed not the art of imitation but real knowledge, he would not have acquired many companions and been honoured and loved by them ? But are we to believe that while Protagoras [i] of Abdera and Prodicus [j] of Ceos and many others are able by private teaching to impress upon their contemporaries the

---

[f] "Of the beef-clan." The scholiast says he was a Chian and an epic poet. See Callimachus's epigram *apud* Sext. Empir., Bekker, p. 609 (*Adv. Math.* i. 48), and Suidas *s.v.* κρεώφυλος.

[g] Modern Greeks also are often very sensitive to the etymology of proper names. *Cf.* also on 580 B, p. 369, note *d*.

[h] See on 540 B, p. 230, note *d*.

[i] *Cf. Prot.* 315 A-B, 316 C.

[j] See *What Plato Said*, p. 486, on *Laches* 197 D.

600 οἰκίαν οὔτε πόλιν τὴν αὑτῶν διοικεῖν οἷοί τ᾽
ἔσονται, ἐὰν μὴ σφεῖς αὐτῶν ἐπιστατήσωσι τῆς
παιδείας, καὶ ἐπὶ ταύτῃ τῇ σοφίᾳ οὕτω σφόδρα
φιλοῦνται, ὥστε μόνον οὐκ ἐπὶ ταῖς κεφαλαῖς
περιφέρουσιν αὐτοὺς οἱ ἑταῖροι· Ὅμηρον δ᾽ ἄρα
οἱ ἐπ᾽ ἐκείνου, εἴπερ οἷός τ᾽ ἦν πρὸς ἀρετὴν
ὀνινάναι ἀνθρώπους, ἢ Ἡσίοδον ῥαψῳδεῖν ἂν
περιόντας εἴων, καὶ οὐχὶ μᾶλλον ἂν αὐτῶν ἀντ-
είχοντο ἢ τοῦ χρυσοῦ καὶ ἠνάγκαζον παρὰ σφίσιν
E οἴκοι εἶναι, ἢ εἰ μὴ ἔπειθον, αὐτοὶ ἂν ἐπαιδ-
σγώγουν ὅπῃ ᾖσαν, ἕως ἱκανῶς παιδείας μετα-
λάβοιεν; Παντάπασιν, ἔφη, δοκεῖς μοι, ὦ Σώκρατες, ἀληθῆ λέγειν. Οὐκοῦν τιθῶμεν ἀπὸ Ὁμήρου
ἀρξαμένους πάντας τοὺς ποιητικοὺς μιμητὰς εἰδώλων ἀρετῆς εἶναι καὶ τῶν ἄλλων, περὶ ὧν ποιοῦσι,
τῆς δὲ ἀληθείας οὐχ ἅπτεσθαι; ἀλλ᾽ ὥσπερ νῦν
δὴ ἐλέγομεν, ὁ ζωγράφος σκυτοτόμον ποιήσει
601 δοκοῦντα εἶναι, αὐτός τε οὐκ ἐπαΐων περὶ σκυτοτομίας καὶ τοῖς μὴ ἐπαΐουσιν, ἐκ τῶν χρωμάτων
δὲ καὶ σχημάτων θεωροῦσιν; Πάνυ μὲν οὖν.
Οὕτω δή, οἶμαι, καὶ τὸν ποιητικὸν φήσομεν

---

[a] For διοικεῖν cf. Protag. 318 E.
[b] See Thompson on Meno 70 B.
[c] On μόνον οὐκ cf. Menex. 235 C, Ax. 365 B.
[d] Stallbaum refers to Themist. Orat. xxii. p. 254 A δν
ἡμεῖς διὰ ταύτην τὴν φαντασίαν μόνον οὐκ ἐπὶ ταῖς κεφαλαῖς
περιφέρομεν, Erasmus, Chiliad iv. Cent. 7 n. 98 p. 794, and
the German idiom "einen auf den Händen tragen."
[e] Cf. Protag. 328 B.

conviction that they will not be capable of governing their homes or the city *a* unless they put them in charge of their education, and make themselves so beloved for this wisdom *b* that their companions all but *c* carry them about on their shoulders,*d* yet, forsooth, that Homer's contemporaries, if he had been able to help men to achieve excellence,*e* would have suffered him or Hesiod to roam about rhapsodizing and would not have clung to them far rather than to their gold,*f* and constrained them to dwell with them *g* in their homes, or failing to persuade them, would themselves have escorted them wheresoever they went until they should have sufficiently imbibed their culture ? " " What you say seems to me to be altogether true, Socrates," he said. " Shall we, then, lay it down that all the poetic tribe, beginning with Homer,*h* are imitators of images of excellence and of the other things that they ' create,*i* ' and do not lay hold on truth ? but, as we were just now saying, the painter will fashion, himself knowing nothing of the cobbler's art, what appears to be a cobbler to him and likewise to those who know nothing but judge only by forms and colours *j* ? " " Certainly." " And similarly, I suppose, we shall say that the poet himself, knowing nothing

f The article perhaps gives the word a contemptuous significance. So *Meno* 89 B τὸ χρυσίον.

g οἴκοι εἶναι : J. J. Hartman, *Ad Platonis Remp.* 600 E, *Mnem.* 1916, p. 45, would change εἶναι to μεῖναι. But *cf.* Cic. *Att.* vii. 10 " erimus una."

h *Cf.* 366 E, *Gorg.* 471 C-D, *Symp.* 173 D.

i Or " about which they versify," playing with the double meaning of ποιεῖν.

j For the association of χρώματα and σχήματα *cf. Phileb.* 12 E, 47 A, 51 B, *Laws* 669 A, *Soph.* 251 A, *Meno* 75 A with Apelt's note, *Cratyl.* 431 C, *Gorg.* 465 B, *Phaedo* 100 D, Aristot. *Poet.* 1447 a 18-19.

601 χρώματ' ἄττα ἑκάστων τῶν τεχνῶν τοῖς ὀνόμασι
καὶ ῥήμασιν ἐπιχρωματίζειν αὐτὸν οὐκ ἐπαΐοντα
ἀλλ' ἢ μιμεῖσθαι, ὥστε ἑτέροις τοιούτοις ἐκ τῶν
B λόγων θεωροῦσι δοκεῖν, ἐάν τε περὶ σκυτοτομίας
τις λέγῃ ἐν μέτρῳ καὶ ῥυθμῷ καὶ ἁρμονίᾳ, πάνυ
εὖ δοκεῖν λέγεσθαι, ἐάν τε περὶ στρατηγίας ἐάν
τε περὶ ἄλλου ὁτουοῦν· οὕτω φύσει αὐτὰ ταῦτα
μεγάλην τινὰ κήλησιν ἔχειν. ἐπεὶ γυμνωθέντα γε
τῶν τῆς μουσικῆς χρωμάτων τὰ τῶν ποιητῶν,
αὐτὰ ἐφ' αὑτῶν λεγόμενα, οἶμαί σε εἰδέναι οἷα
φαίνεται. τεθέασαι γάρ που. Ἔγωγ', ἔφη. Οὐκοῦν, ἦν δ' ἐγώ, ἔοικε τοῖς τῶν ὡραίων προσώ-
ποις, καλῶν δὲ μή, οἷα γίγνεται ἰδεῖν, ὅταν αὐτὰ
τὸ ἄνθος προλίπῃ; Παντάπασιν, ἦ δ' ὅς. Ἴθι δή,
τόδε ἄθρει· ὁ τοῦ εἰδώλου ποιητής, ὁ μιμητής,
φαμέν, τοῦ μὲν ὄντος οὐδὲν ἐπαΐει, τοῦ δὲ φαινο-
C μένου· οὐχ οὕτως; Ναί. Μὴ τοίνυν ἡμίσεως

---

[a] Cf. Symp. 198 B, Apol. 17 C. The explicit discrimination of ὀνόματα as names of agents and ῥήματα as names of
actions is peculiar to Soph. 262. But cf. Cratyl. 431 B, 425 A,
Theaet. 206 D. And in Soph. 257 B ῥήματι is used generally.
See Unity of Plato's Thought, pp. 56-57. Cf. Euthydem.
304 E with Symp. 187 A, Phaedr. 228 D, 271 C and my note
in Class. Phil. xvii. (1922) p. 262.

[b] Cf. What Plato Said, p. 593 on Soph. 240 A.

[c] Cf. 607 C, Laws 840 C, Protag. 315 A-B.

[d] Cf. Gorg. 502 C εἴ τις περιέλοι τῆς ποιήσεως πάσης τό τε
μέλος καὶ τὸν ῥυθμόν, supra 392, Ion 530 B, Epicharmus apud
Diog. Laert. iii. 17 περιδύσας τὸ μέτρον ὃ νῦν ἔχει, Aeschines,
In Ctes. 136 περιελόντες τοῦ ποιητοῦ τὸ μέτρον, Isoc. Evag.
11 τὸ δὲ μέτρον διαλύσῃ with Horace, Sat. i. 4. 62 "invenias
etiam disiecti membra poetae," Aristot. Rhet. 1404 a 24 ἐπεὶ
δ' οἱ ποιηταὶ λέγοντες εὐήθη διὰ τὴν λέξιν ἐδόκουν πορίσασθαι τήνδε
τὴν δόξαν. Sext. Empir., Bekker, pp. 665-666 (Adv. Math.
ii. 288), says that the ideas of poets are inferior to those of
the ordinary layman. Cf. also Julian, Or. ii. 78 D, Coleridge,

but how to imitate, lays on with words and phrases [a] the colours of the several arts in such fashion that others equally ignorant, who see things only through words,[b] will deem his words most excellent, whether he speak in rhythm, metre and harmony about cobbling or generalship or anything whatever. So mighty is the spell [c] that these adornments naturally exercise ; though when they are stripped bare of their musical colouring and taken by themselves,[d] I think you know what sort of a showing these sayings of the poets make. For you, I believe, have observed them." " I have," he said. " Do they not," said I, " resemble the faces of adolescents, young but not really beautiful, when the bloom of youth abandons them ? [e] " " By all means," he said. " Come, then," said I, " consider this point : The creator of the phantom, the imitator, we say, knows nothing of the reality but only the appearance. Is not that so ? " " Yes." " Let us not, then, leave it half said but con-

---

Table Talk: "If you take from Virgil his diction and metre what do you leave him ? "

[e] Aristot. *Rhet.* 1406 b 36 f. refers to this. *Cf.* Tyrtaeus 8 (6). 28 ὄφρ' ἐρατῆς ἥβης ἀγλαὸν ἄνθος ἔχῃ, Mimnermus i. 4 ἥβης ἄνθη γίγνεται ἁρπαλέα, Theognis 1305 :

$$\text{παιδείας πολυηράτου ἄνθος}$$
$$\text{ὠκύτερον σταδίου,}$$

Xen. *Symp.* 8. 14 τὸ μὲν τῆς ὥρας ἄνθος ταχὺ δήπου παρακμάζει, Plato, *Symp.* 183 ε τῷ τοῦ σώματος ἄνθει λήγοντι, Spenser, "An Hymne in honour of Beautie" :

For that same goodly hew of white and red
    With which the cheekes are sprinckled shal decay,

Ségur's refrain : "Ah ! le Temps fait passer l'Amour," Emerson, *Beauty* : "The radiance of the human form . . . is only a burst of beauty for a few years or a few months, at the perfection of youth, and, in most, rapidly declines."

601 αὐτὸ καταλίπωμεν ῥηθέν, ἀλλ᾽ ἱκανῶς ἴδωμεν.
Λέγε, ἔφη. Ζωγράφος, φαμέν, ἡνίας τε γράψει
καὶ χαλινόν; Ναί. Ποιήσει δέ γε σκυτοτόμος
καὶ χαλκεύς; Πάνυ γε. Ἆρ᾽ οὖν ἐπαΐει οἵας δεῖ
τὰς ἡνίας εἶναι καὶ τὸν χαλινὸν ὁ γραφεύς; ἢ
οὐδ᾽ ὁ ποιήσας, ὅ τε χαλκεὺς καὶ ὁ σκυτεύς, ἀλλ᾽
ἐκεῖνος, ὅσπερ τούτοις ἐπίσταται χρῆσθαι, μόνος,
ὁ ἱππικός; Ἀληθέστατα. Ἆρ᾽ οὖν οὐ περὶ
D πάντα οὕτω φήσομεν ἔχειν; Πῶς; Περὶ ἕκαστον
ταύτας τινὰς τρεῖς τέχνας εἶναι, χρησομένην, ποιή-
σουσαν, μιμησομένην; Ναί. Οὐκοῦν ἀρετὴ καὶ
κάλλος καὶ ὀρθότης ἑκάστου σκεύους καὶ ζῴου καὶ
πράξεως οὐ πρὸς ἄλλο τι ἢ τὴν χρείαν ἐστί, πρὸς
ἣν ἂν ἕκαστον ᾖ πεποιημένον ἢ πεφυκός; Οὕτως.
Πολλὴ ἄρα ἀνάγκη τὸν χρώμενον ἑκάστῳ ἐμπειρό-
τατόν τε εἶναι, καὶ ἄγγελον γίγνεσθαι τῷ ποιητῇ,
οἷα ἀγαθὰ ἢ κακὰ ποιεῖ ἐν τῇ χρείᾳ ᾧ χρῆται·
E οἷον αὐλητής που αὐλοποιῷ ἐξαγγέλλει περὶ τῶν
αὐλῶν, οἳ ἂν ὑπηρετῶσιν ἐν τῷ αὐλεῖν, καὶ ἐπιτάξει
οἵους δεῖ ποιεῖν, ὁ δ᾽ ὑπηρετήσει. Πῶς δ᾽ οὔ;
Οὐκοῦν ὁ μὲν εἰδὼς ἐξαγγέλλει περὶ χρηστῶν καὶ
πονηρῶν αὐλῶν, ὁ δὲ πιστεύων ποιήσει; Ναί.
Τοῦ αὐτοῦ ἄρα σκεύους ὁ μὲν ποιητὴς πίστιν

---

[a] The δέ γε has almost the effect of a retort.

[b] Cf. Aristot. Eth. Nic. 1094 a 10-11 καθάπερ ὑπὸ τὴν
ἱππικὴν ἡ χαλινοποιικὴ . . .

[c] For the idea that the user knows best see Cratyl. 390 B,
Euthydem. 289 B, Phaedr. 274 E. Zeller, Aristotle (Eng.)
ii. p. 247, attributes this " pertinent observation " to Aristotle.
Cf. Aristot. Pol. 1277 b 30 αὐλητὴς ὁ χρώμενος. See
1282 a 21, 1289 a 17. Coleridge, Table Talk: " In general

sider it fully." " Speak on," he said. " The painter, we say, will paint both reins and a bit." " Yes." " But the maker *a* will be the cobbler and the smith." " Certainly." " Does the painter, then, know the proper quality of reins and bit ? Or does not even the maker, the cobbler and the smith, know that, but only the man who understands the use of these things, the horseman *b* ? " " Most true." " And shall we not say that the same holds true of everything ? " " What do you mean ? " " That there are some three arts concerned with everything, the user's art,*c* the maker's, and the imitator's." " Yes." " Now do not the excellence, the beauty, the rightness *d* of every implement, living thing, and action refer solely to the use *e* for which each is made or by nature adapted ? " " That is so." " It quite necessarily follows, then, that the user of anything is the one who knows most of it by experience, and that he reports to the maker the good or bad effects in use of the thing he uses. As, for example, the flute-player reports to the flute-maker which flutes respond and serve rightly in flute-playing, and will order the kind that must be made, and the other will obey and serve him." " Of course." " The one, then, possessing knowledge, reports about the goodness or the badness of the flutes, and the other, believing, will make them." " Yes." " Then in respect of the same implement the maker will have

those who do things for others know more about them than those for whom they are done. A groom knows more about horses than his master." But Hazlitt disagrees with Plato's view.

d So in *Laws* 669 A-B, Plato says that the competent judge of a work of art must know three things, first, what it is, second, that it is true and right, and third, that it is good.

e For the reference of beauty to use see *Hipp. Maj.* 295 c ff.

601 ὀρθὴν ἕξει περὶ κάλλους τε καὶ πονηρίας, ξυνὼν
τῷ εἰδότι καὶ ἀναγκαζόμενος ἀκούειν παρὰ τοῦ
602 εἰδότος· ὁ δὲ χρώμενος ἐπιστήμην. Πάνυ γε.
Ὁ δὲ μιμητὴς πότερον ἐκ τοῦ χρῆσθαι ἐπιστήμην
ἕξει ὧν ἂν γράφῃ, εἴτε καλὰ καὶ ὀρθὰ εἴτε μή,
ἢ δόξαν ὀρθὴν διὰ τὸ ἐξ ἀνάγκης συνεῖναι τῷ
εἰδότι καὶ ἐπιτάττεσθαι οἷα χρὴ γράφειν; Οὐδ-
έτερα. Οὔτε ἄρα εἴσεται οὔτε ὀρθὰ δοξάσει ὁ
μιμητὴς περὶ ὧν ἂν μιμῆται πρὸς κάλλος ἢ πονηρίαν. Οὐκ ἔοικεν. Χαρίεις ἂν εἴη ὁ ἐν τῇ ποιήσει
μιμητικὸς πρὸς σοφίαν περὶ ὧν ἂν ποιῇ. Οὐ πάνυ.
B Ἀλλ᾽ οὖν δὴ ὅμως γε μιμήσεται, οὐκ εἰδὼς περὶ
ἑκάστου, ὅπῃ πονηρὸν ἢ χρηστόν· ἀλλ᾽, ὡς ἔοικεν,
οἷον φαίνεται καλὸν εἶναι τοῖς πολλοῖς τε καὶ
μηδὲν εἰδόσι, τοῦτο μιμήσεται. Τί γὰρ ἄλλο;
Ταῦτα μὲν δή, ὥς γε φαίνεται, ἐπιεικῶς ἡμῖν
διωμολόγηται, τόν τε μιμητικὸν μηδὲν εἰδέναι
ἄξιον λόγου περὶ ὧν μιμεῖται, ἀλλ᾽ εἶναι παιδιάν
τινα καὶ οὐ σπουδὴν τὴν μίμησιν, τούς τε τῆς
τραγικῆς ποιήσεως ἁπτομένους ἐν ἰαμβείοις καὶ ἐν
ἔπεσι πάντας εἶναι μιμητικοὺς ὡς οἷόν τε μάλιστα.
Πάνυ μὲν οὖν.
C V. Πρὸς Διός, ἦν δ᾽ ἐγώ, τὸ δὲ δὴ μιμεῖσθαι
τοῦτο οὐ περὶ τρίτον μέν τί ἐστιν ἀπὸ τῆς ἀληθείας; ἢ γάρ; Ναί. Πρὸς δὲ δὴ ποῖόν τί ἐστι

---

[a] πίστιν ὀρθήν is used because of πιστεύων above. It is a
slightly derogatory synonym of δόξαν ὀρθήν below, 602 A.
Cf. 511 E.
[b] This does not contradict Book v. 477-478. For right
opinion and knowledge cf. 430 B and *What Plato Said*, p.
517, on *Meno* 98 A-B.
[c] χαρίεις is ironical like χαριέντως in 426 A and καλόν in
Theaet. 183 A, but Glaucon in his answer takes it seriously.

right belief[a] about its excellence and defects from association with the man who knows and being compelled to listen to him, but the user will have true knowledge." "Certainly." "And will the imitator from experience or use have knowledge whether the things he portrays are or are not beautiful and right, or will he, from compulsory association with the man who knows and taking orders from him for the right making of them, have right opinion[b]?" "Neither." "Then the imitator will neither know nor opine rightly concerning the beauty or the badness of his imitations." "It seems not." "Most charming,[c] then, would be the state of mind of the poetical imitator in respect of true wisdom about his creations." "Not at all." "Yet still he will none the less[d] imitate, though in every case he does not know in what way the thing is bad or good. But, as it seems, the thing he will imitate will be the thing that appears beautiful to the ignorant multitude." "Why, what else?" "On this, then, as it seems, we are fairly agreed, that the imitator knows nothing worth mentioning of the things he imitates, but that imitation is a form of play,[e] not to be taken seriously,[f] and that those who attempt tragic poetry, whether in iambics or heroic verse,[g] are all altogether imitators." "By all means."

V. "In heaven's name, then, this business of imitation is concerned with the third remove from truth, is it not?" "Yes." "And now again, to what

---

[a] Note the accumulation of particles in the Greek. Similarly in 619 B, *Phaedo* 59 D, 61 E, 62 B, 64 A, *Parmen.* 127 D, Demosth. xxiii. 101, *De cor.* 282, Pind. *Pyth.* iv. 64, Isoc. *Peace* 1, Aristot. *De gen. et corr.* 332 a 3, *Iliad* vii. 360.

[e] *Cf.* on 536 c, p. 214, note *b*.   [f] *Cf.* 608 A.
[g] For ἐν ἔπεσι *cf.* 607 A, 379 A, *Meno* 95 D.

602 τῶν τοῦ ἀνθρώπου ἔχον τὴν δύναμιν, ἣν ἔχει;
Τοῦ ποίου τινὸς πέρι λέγεις; Τοῦ τοιοῦδε.
ταὐτόν που ἡμῖν μέγεθος ἐγγύθεν τε καὶ πόρρωθεν
διὰ τῆς ὄψεως οὐκ ἴσον φαίνεται. Οὐ γάρ. Καὶ
ταὐτὰ καμπύλα τε καὶ εὐθέα ἐν ὕδατί τε θεω-
μένοις καὶ ἔξω, καὶ κοῖλά τε δὴ καὶ ἐξέχοντα διὰ
τὴν περὶ τὰ χρώματα αὖ πλάνην τῆς ὄψεως, καὶ
D πᾶσά τις ταραχὴ δήλη ἡμῖν ἐνοῦσα αὕτη ἐν τῇ
ψυχῇ· ᾧ δὴ ἡμῶν τῷ παθήματι τῆς φύσεως ἡ
σκιαγραφία ἐπιθεμένη γοητείας οὐδὲν ἀπολείπει
καὶ ἡ θαυματοποιία καὶ αἱ ἄλλαι πολλαὶ τοιαῦται
μηχαναί. Ἀληθῆ. Ἆρ᾽ οὖν οὐ τὸ μετρεῖν καὶ
ἀριθμεῖν καὶ ἱστάναι βοήθειαι χαριέσταται πρὸς
αὐτὰ ἐφάνησαν, ὥστε μὴ ἄρχειν ἐν ἡμῖν τὸ
φαινόμενον μεῖζον ἢ ἔλαττον ἢ πλέον ἢ βαρύτερον,
ἀλλὰ τὸ λογισάμενον καὶ μετρῆσαν ἢ καὶ στῆσαν;
E Πῶς γὰρ οὔ; Ἀλλὰ μὴν τοῦτό γε τοῦ λογιστικοῦ
ἂν εἴη τοῦ ἐν ψυχῇ ἔργον. Τούτου γὰρ οὖν.
Τούτῳ δὲ πολλάκις μετρήσαντι καὶ σημαίνοντι
μείζω ἄττα εἶναι ἢ ἐλάττω ἕτερα ἑτέρων ἢ ἴσα
τἀναντία φαίνεται ἅμα περὶ ταὐτά. Ναί. Οὐκοῦν
ἔφαμεν τῷ αὐτῷ ἅμα περὶ ταὐτὰ ἐναντία δοξάζειν
603 ἀδύνατον εἶναι; Καὶ ὀρθῶς γ᾽ ἔφαμεν. Τὸ παρὰ

---

^a The antithesis of περί and πρός marks the transition.
^b Cf. Protag. 356 c, supra 523 c.
^c Cf. Tennyson ("The Higher Pantheism") "For all we
have power to see is a straight staff bent in a pool." For the
illusions of sense, and measurement as a means of correcting
them cf. Phileb. 41 E-42 A f., 55 E, Protag. 356 C-D, Euthyphro 7 c.
^d ἐπιθεμένη helps to personify σκιαγραφία. Cf. Gorg. 464 c.
^e Adam's "leaves no magic art untried" is misleading.
ἀπολείπειν is here used as in 504 c. For the idiomatic οὐδὲν
ἀπολείπει see p. 200, note b, on 533 A.

448

element [a] in man is its function and potency related?"
"Of what are you speaking?" "Of this: The
same magnitude, I presume, viewed from near and
from far [b] does not appear equal." "Why, no."
"And the same things appear bent and straight [c] to
those who view them in water and out, or concave and
convex, owing to similar errors of vision about colours,
and there is obviously every confusion of this sort in
our souls. And so scene-painting in its exploitation [d]
of this weakness of our nature falls nothing short of
witchcraft, [e] and so do jugglery and many other such
contrivances." "True." "And have not measuring
and numbering and weighing [f] proved to be most
gracious aids to prevent the domination in our soul
of the apparently [g] greater or less or more or heavier,
and to give the control to that which has reckoned [h]
and numbered or even weighed?" "Certainly."
"But this surely would be the function [i] of the part
of the soul that reasons and calculates. [j]" "Why,
yes, of that." "And often when this has measured [k]
and declares that certain things are larger or that
some are smaller than the others or equal, there is at
the same time an appearance of the contrary." "Yes."
"And did we not say [l] that it is impossible for the same
thing at one time to hold contradictory opinions about
the same thing?" "And we were right in affirming
that." "The part of the soul, then, that opines in

[f] Cf. Xen. *Mem.* i. 1. 9.
[g] Cf. *Protag.* 356 D ἡ τοῦ φαινομένου δύναμις.
[h] λογισάμενον: cf. *Laws* 644 D, *Crito* 46 B.
[i] Cf. Vol. I. p. 36, note *a.* Of course some of the modern
connotations of "function" are unknown to Plato.
[j] For λογιστικοῦ cf. on 439 D.
[k] See p. 448, note *c*, and my *Platonism and the History of
Science*, p. 176.   [l] 436 B, Vol. I. p. 383.

603 τὰ μέτρα ἄρα δοξάζον τῆς ψυχῆς τῷ κατὰ τὰ
μέτρα οὐκ ἂν εἴη ταὐτόν. Οὐ γὰρ οὖν. Ἀλλὰ
μὴν τὸ μέτρῳ γε καὶ λογισμῷ πιστεῦον βέλτιστον
ἂν εἴη τῆς ψυχῆς. Τί μήν; Τὸ ἄρα τούτῳ
ἐναντιούμενον τῶν φαύλων ἄν τι εἴη ἐν ἡμῖν.
Ἀνάγκη. Τοῦτο τοίνυν διομολογήσασθαι βουλόμενος ἔλεγον, ὅτι ἡ γραφικὴ καὶ ὅλως ἡ μιμητικὴ
πόρρω μὲν τῆς ἀληθείας ὂν τὸ αὑτῆς ἔργον
ἀπεργάζεται, πόρρω δ᾽ αὖ φρονήσεως ὄντι τῷ ἐν
B ἡμῖν προσομιλεῖ τε καὶ ἑταίρα καὶ φίλη ἐστὶν ἐπ᾽
οὐδενὶ ὑγιεῖ οὐδ᾽ ἀληθεῖ. Παντάπασιν, ἦ δ᾽ ὅς.
Φαύλη ἄρα φαύλῳ ξυγγιγνομένη φαῦλα γεννᾷ ἡ
μιμητική. Ἔοικεν. Πότερον, ἦν δ᾽ ἐγώ, ἡ κατὰ
τὴν ὄψιν μόνον, ἢ καὶ κατὰ τὴν ἀκοήν, ἣν δὴ
ποίησιν ὀνομάζομεν; Εἰκός γ᾽, ἔφη, καὶ ταύτην.
Μὴ τοίνυν, ἦν δ᾽ ἐγώ, τῷ εἰκότι μόνον πιστεύ-
σωμεν ἐκ τῆς γραφικῆς, ἀλλὰ καὶ ἐπ᾽ αὐτὸ αὖ
C ἔλθωμεν τῆς διανοίας τοῦτο, ᾧ προσομιλεῖ ἡ τῆς
ποιήσεως μιμητική, καὶ ἴδωμεν, φαῦλον ἢ σπου-
δαῖόν ἐστιν. Ἀλλὰ χρή. Ὧδε δὴ προθώμεθα·
πράττοντας, φαμέν, ἀνθρώπους μιμεῖται ἡ μιμητικὴ
βιαίους ἢ ἑκουσίας πράξεις, καὶ ἐκ τοῦ πράττειν ἢ
εὖ οἰομένους ἢ κακῶς πεπραγέναι, καὶ ἐν τούτοις
δὴ πᾶσιν ἢ λυπουμένους ἢ χαίροντας. μή τι ἄλλο
ἦν[1] παρὰ ταῦτα; Οὐδέν. Ἆρ᾽ οὖν ἐν ἅπασι τούτοις
D ὁμονοητικῶς ἄνθρωπος διάκειται; ἢ ὥσπερ κατὰ

[1] ἦν Ast: ἢ AM, ἢ FD.

ᵃ Cf. 604 D, Phaedr. 253 D and E.
ᵇ Cf. Lysias ix. 4 ἐπὶ μηδενὶ ὑγιεῖ and for the idiom οὐδὲν
ὑγιὲς supra on 523 B, p. 153, note f.
ᶜ Cf. 496 A, and on 489 D, p. 26, note b.

contradiction of measurement could not be the same with that which conforms to it." "Why, no." "But, further, that which puts its trust in measurement and reckoning must be the best part of the soul." "Surely." "Then that which opposes it must belong to the inferior elements of the soul." "Necessarily." "This, then, was what I wished to have agreed upon when I said that poetry, and in general the mimetic art, produces a product that is far removed from truth in the accomplishment of its task, and associates with the part in us that is remote from intelligence, and is its companion and friend[a] for no sound and true purpose.[b]" "By all means," said he. "Mimetic art, then, is an inferior thing cohabiting with an inferior and engendering inferior offspring.[c]" "It seems so." "Does that," said I, "hold only for vision or does it apply also to hearing and to what we call poetry?" "Presumably," he said, "to that also." "Let us not, then, trust solely to the plausible analogy[d] from painting, but let us approach in turn that part of the mind to which mimetic poetry appeals and see whether it is the inferior or the nobly serious part." "So we must." "Let us, then, put the question thus: Mimetic poetry, we say, imitates human beings acting under compulsion or voluntarily,[e] and as a result of their actions supposing themselves to have fared well or ill and in all this feeling either grief or joy. Did we find anything else but this?" "Nothing." "Is a man, then, in all this of one mind with himself, or just as in the domain of sight there was faction

---

[d] Cf. *Phaedo* 92 D διὰ τῶν εἰκότων.

[e] Cf. *supra* 399 A-B, *Laws* 655 D, 814 E ff., Aristot. *Poet.* 1448 A 1-2 ἐπεὶ δὲ μιμοῦνται οἱ μιμούμενοι πράττοντας ἀνάγκη δὲ τούτους ἢ σπουδαίους ἢ φαύλους εἶναι, *ibid.* 1449 b 36-37 f.

603 τὴν ὄψιν ἐστασίαζε καὶ ἐναντίας εἶχεν ἐν ἑαυτῷ
δόξας ἅμα περὶ τῶν αὐτῶν, οὕτω καὶ ἐν ταῖς
πράξεσι στασιάζει τε καὶ μάχεται αὐτὸς αὑτῷ;
ἀναμιμνήσκομαι δέ, ὅτι τοῦτό γε νῦν οὐδὲν δεῖ
ἡμᾶς διομολογεῖσθαι· ἐν γὰρ τοῖς ἄνω λόγοις
ἱκανῶς πάντα ταῦτα διωμολογησάμεθα, ὅτι μυρίων
τοιούτων ἐναντιωμάτων ἅμα γιγνομένων ἡ ψυχὴ
γέμει ἡμῶν. Ὀρθῶς, ἔφη. Ὀρθῶς γάρ, ἦν δ'
ἐγώ· ἀλλ' ὃ τότε ἀπελίπομεν, νῦν μοι δοκεῖ ἀναγ-
E καῖον εἶναι διεξελθεῖν. Τὸ ποῖον; ἔφη. Ἀνήρ,
ἦν δ' ἐγώ, ἐπιεικὴς τοιᾶσδε τύχης μετασχών, υἱὸν
ἀπολέσας ἤ τι ἄλλο ὧν περὶ πλείστου ποιεῖται,
ἐλέγομέν που καὶ τότε ὅτι ῥᾷστα οἴσει τῶν ἄλλων.
Πάνυ γε. Νῦν δέ γε τόδε ἐπισκεψώμεθα· πότερον
οὐδὲν ἀχθέσεται, ἢ τοῦτο μὲν ἀδύνατον, μετριάσει
δέ πως πρὸς λύπην; Οὕτω μᾶλλον, ἔφη, τό γε
604 ἀληθές. Τόδε νῦν μοι περὶ αὐτοῦ εἰπέ· πότερον
μᾶλλον αὐτὸν οἴει τῇ λύπῃ μαχεῖσθαί τε καὶ
ἀντιτείνειν, ὅταν ὁρᾶται ὑπὸ τῶν ὁμοίων, ἢ ὅταν
ἐν ἐρημίᾳ μόνος αὐτὸς καθ' αὑτὸν γίγνηται; Πολύ
που, ἔφη, διοίσει, ὅταν ὁρᾶται. Μονωθεὶς δέ γε,
οἶμαι, πολλὰ μὲν τολμήσει φθέγξασθαι, ἃ εἴ τις
αὐτοῦ ἀκούοι αἰσχύνοιτ' ἄν, πολλὰ δὲ ποιήσει, ἃ
οὐκ ἂν δέξαιτό τινα ἰδεῖν δρῶντα. Οὕτως ἔχει,
ἔφη.

---

[a] See *What Plato Said*, p. 505, on *Gorg.* 482 A-B.

[b] *Cf.* 554 D, and p. 394, note e, on 586 E.

[c] 439 B ff.

[d] Plato sometimes pretends to remedy an omission or to
correct himself by an afterthought. So in Book v. 449 B-C
ff., and *Tim.* 65 c.

[e] 387 D-E.

[f] This suggests the doctrine of μετριοπάθεια as opposed

452

and strife and he held within himself contrary opinions at the same time about the same things,[a] so also in our actions there is division and strife [b] of the man with himself ? But I recall that there is no need now of our seeking agreement on this point, for in our former discussion [c] we were sufficiently agreed that our soul at any one moment teems with countless such self-contradictions." "Rightly," he said. "Yes, rightly," said I; "but what we then omitted[d] must now, I think, be set forth." "What is that ?" he said. "When a good and reasonable man," said I, "experiences such a stroke of fortune as the loss of a son or anything else that he holds most dear, we said, I believe, then too,[e] that he will bear it more easily than the other sort." "Assuredly." "But now let us consider this : Will he feel no pain, or, since that is impossible, shall we say that he will in some sort be moderate [f] in his grief ?" "That," he said, "is rather the truth." "Tell me now this about him : Do you think he will be more likely to resist and fight against his grief when he is observed by his equals or when he is in solitude alone by himself ?" "He will be much more restrained," he said, "when he is on view." "But when left alone, I fancy, he will permit himself many utterances which, if heard by another, would put him to shame, and will do many things which he would not consent to have another see him doing." "So it is," he said.

to the Stoic ἀπάθεια. Joel ii. p. 161 thinks the passage a polemic against Antisthenes. Seneca, *Epist*. xcix. 15 seems to agree with Plato rather than with the Stoics: "inhumanitas est ista non virtus." So Plutarch, *Cons. ad Apol*. 3 (102 c f.). See also *ibid*. 22 (112 E-F). *Cf*. Horace, *Odes* ii. 3. 1 "aequam memento rebus in arduis servare mentem," and also *Laws* 732 c, 960 A.

604   VI. Οὐκοῦν τὸ μὲν ἀντιτείνειν διακελευόμενον
B λόγος καὶ νόμος ἐστί, τὸ δὲ ἕλκον ἐπὶ τὰς λύπας
αὐτὸ τὸ πάθος; Ἀληθῆ. Ἐναντίας δὲ ἀγωγῆς
γιγνομένης ἐν τῷ ἀνθρώπῳ περὶ τὸ αὐτὸ ἅμα δύο
φαμὲν αὐτῷ ἀναγκαῖον εἶναι. Πῶς δ' οὔ; Οὐκοῦν
τὸ μὲν ἕτερον τῷ νόμῳ ἕτοιμον πείθεσθαι, ᾗ ὁ
νόμος ἐξηγεῖται; Πῶς; Λέγει που ὁ νόμος, ὅτι
κάλλιστον ὅ τι μάλιστα ἡσυχίαν ἄγειν ἐν ταῖς
ξυμφοραῖς καὶ μὴ ἀγανακτεῖν, ὡς οὔτε δήλου
ὄντος τοῦ ἀγαθοῦ τε καὶ κακοῦ τῶν τοιούτων, οὔτε
εἰς τὸ πρόσθεν οὐδὲν προβαῖνον τῷ χαλεπῶς
C φέροντι, οὔτε τι τῶν ἀνθρωπίνων ἄξιον ὂν μεγάλης
σπουδῆς, ὅ τε δεῖ ἐν αὐτοῖς ὅ τι τάχιστα παρα-
γίγνεσθαι ἡμῖν, τούτῳ ἐμποδὼν γιγνόμενον τὸ
λυπεῖσθαι. Τίνι, ἦ δ' ὅς, λέγεις; Τῷ βουλεύεσθαι,
ἦν δ' ἐγώ, περὶ τὸ γεγονὸς καὶ ὥσπερ ἐν πτώσει
κύβων πρὸς τὰ πεπτωκότα τίθεσθαι τὰ αὐτοῦ
πράγματα, ὅπῃ ὁ λόγος αἱρεῖ βέλτιστ' ἂν ἔχειν,
ἀλλὰ μὴ προσπταίσαντας καθάπερ παῖδας ἐχο-
μένους τοῦ πληγέντος ἐν τῷ βοᾶν διατρίβειν, ἀλλ'
D ἀεὶ ἐθίζειν τὴν ψυχὴν ὅ τι τάχιστα γίγνεσθαι πρὸς
τὸ ἰᾶσθαί τε καὶ ἐπανορθοῦν τὸ πεσόν τε καὶ

---

[a] Cf. Laws 645 A, Phaedr. 238 c, and for the conflict in
the soul also Rep. 439 B ff.

[b] The conflict proves that for practical purposes the soul
has parts.   Cf. 436 B ff.

[c] Cf. Apology, in fine.

[d] Cf. Laws 803 B and Class. Phil. ix. p. 353, n. 3, Friedländer, Platon, i. p. 143.

[e] Höffding, Outlines of Psychology, p. 99, refers to Saxo's
tale of the different effect which the news of the murder of
Regner Lodbrog produced on his sons: he in whom the
emotion was weakest had the greatest energy for action.

VI. " Now is it not reason and law that exhorts him to resist, while that which urges him to give way to his grief is the bare feeling itself ? " " True." " And where there are two opposite impulses *a* in a man at the same time about the same thing we say that there must needs be two things *b* in him." " Of course." " And is not the one prepared to follow the guidance of the law as the law leads and directs?" " How so ? " " The law, I suppose, declares that it is best to keep quiet as far as possible in calamity and not to chafe and repine, because we cannot know what is really good and evil in such things *c* and it advantages us nothing to take them hard, and nothing in mortal life is worthy of great concern,*d* and our grieving checks *e* the very thing we need to come to our aid as quickly as possible in such case." " What thing," he said, " do you mean ? " " To deliberate,*f* " I said, " about what has happened to us, and, as it were in the fall of the dice,*g* to determine the movements of our affairs with reference to the numbers that turn up, in the way that reason indicates *h* would be the best, and, instead of stumbling like children, clapping one's hands to the stricken spot *i* and wasting the time in wailing, ever to accustom the soul to devote itself at once to the curing of the hurt and the raising up of what

---

f Cf. Shakes. *Richard II.* iii. ii. 178 :

> My lord, wise men ne'er sit and wail their woes
> But presently prevent the ways to wail,

Herod. i. 20 πρὸς τὸ παρεὸν βουλεύηται.
  g Cf. Eurip. *Electra* 639 and *fr.* 175 πρὸς τὸ πῖπτον, *Iph. Aul.* 1343 and *Hippol.* 718 πρὸς τὰ νῦν πεπτωκότα, Epictet. ii. 5. 3. See also Stallbaum *ad loc.*
  h Cf. 440 B, 607 B, Herod. i. 132.
  i Cf. Demosthenes' description of how barbarians box iv. 40 (51), ἀεὶ τῆς πληγῆς ἔχεται.

604 νοσῆσαν, ἰατρικῇ θρηνῳδίαν ἀφανίζοντα. Ὀρθότατα γοῦν ἄν τις, ἔφη, πρὸς τὰς τύχας οὕτω
προσφέροιτο. Οὐκοῦν, φαμέν, τὸ μὲν βέλτιστον
τούτῳ τῷ λογισμῷ ἐθέλει ἕπεσθαι. Δῆλον δή.
Τὸ δὲ πρὸς τὰς ἀναμνήσεις τε τοῦ πάθους καὶ πρὸς
τοὺς ὀδυρμοὺς ἄγον καὶ ἀπλήστως ἔχον αὐτῶν
ἆρ᾽ οὐκ ἀλόγιστόν τε φήσομεν εἶναι καὶ ἀργὸν καὶ
δειλίας φίλον; Φήσομεν μὲν οὖν. Οὐκοῦν τὸ
E μὲν πολλὴν μίμησιν καὶ ποικίλην ἔχει, τὸ ἀγα-
νακτητικόν· τὸ δὲ φρόνιμόν τε καὶ ἡσύχιον ἦθος,
παραπλήσιον ὂν ἀεὶ αὐτὸ αὑτῷ, οὔτε ῥᾴδιον μιμήσασθαι οὔτε μιμούμενον εὐπετὲς καταμαθεῖν, ἄλλως
τε καὶ πανηγύρει καὶ παντοδαποῖς ἀνθρώποις εἰς
θέατρα ξυλλεγομένοις. ἀλλοτρίου γάρ που πάθους
605 ἡ μίμησις αὐτοῖς γίγνεται. Παντάπασι μὲν οὖν.
Ὁ δὴ μιμητικὸς ποιητὴς δῆλον ὅτι οὐ πρὸς τὸ
τοιοῦτον τῆς ψυχῆς πέφυκέ γε καὶ ἡ σοφία αὐτοῦ
τούτῳ ἀρέσκειν πέπηγεν, εἰ μέλλει εὐδοκιμήσειν
ἐν τοῖς πολλοῖς, ἀλλὰ πρὸς τὸ ἀγανακτητικόν τε
καὶ ποικίλον ἦθος διὰ τὸ εὐμίμητον εἶναι. Δῆλον.
Οὐκοῦν δικαίως ἂν αὐτοῦ ἤδη ἐπιλαμβανοίμεθα,
καὶ τιθεῖμεν ἀντίστροφον αὐτὸν τῷ ζωγράφῳ·
καὶ γὰρ τῷ φαῦλα ποιεῖν πρὸς ἀλήθειαν ἔοικεν
αὐτῷ, καὶ τῷ πρὸς ἕτερον τοιοῦτον ὁμιλεῖν τῆς
B ψυχῆς, ἀλλὰ μὴ πρὸς τὸ βέλτιστον, καὶ ταύτῃ
ὡμοίωται· καὶ οὕτως ἤδη ἂν ἐν δίκῃ οὐ παραδεχοί-

ᵃ Cf. Soph. Ajax 582 θρηνεῖν ἐπῳδὰς πρὸς τομῶντι πήματι
with Ovid, Met. i. 190:
                    sed immedicabile vulnus
          ense recidendum est.

has fallen, banishing threnody[a] by therapy." "That certainly," he said, "would be the best way to face misfortune and deal with it." "Then, we say, the best part of us is willing to conform to these precepts of reason." "Obviously." "And shall we not say that the part of us that leads us to dwell in memory on our suffering and impels us to lamentation, and cannot get enough of that sort of thing, is the irrational and idle part of us, the associate of cowardice[b]?" "Yes, we will say that." "And does not the fretful part of us present[c] many and varied occasions for imitation, while the intelligent and temperate disposition, always remaining approximately the same, is neither easy to imitate nor to be understood when imitated, especially by a nondescript mob assembled in the theatre? For the representation imitates a type that is alien to them." "By all means." "And is it not obvious that the nature of the mimetic poet is not related to this better part of the soul and his cunning is not framed[d] to please it, if he is to win favour with the multitude, but is devoted to the fretful and complicated type of character because it is easy to imitate?" "It is obvious." "This consideration, then, makes it right for us to proceed to lay hold of him and set him down as the counterpart[e] of the painter; for he resembles him in that his creations are inferior in respect of reality; and the fact that his appeal is to the inferior part of the soul and not to the best part is another point of resemblance. And so we may at last say that we should be

[b] *Cf.* on 603 в, p. 450, note *a*.
[c] ἔχει in the sense of "involves," "admits of," as frequently in Aristotle's *Metaphysics*.
[d] For πέπηγεν *cf.* 530 в.
[e] ἀντίστροφον is used as in Aristot. *Rhet.* 1354 a 1.

605 μεθα εἰς μέλλουσαν εὐνομεῖσθαι πόλιν, ὅτι τοῦτο
ἐγείρει τῆς ψυχῆς καὶ τρέφει καὶ ἰσχυρὸν ποιῶν
ἀπόλλυσι τὸ λογιστικόν, ὥσπερ ἐν πόλει ὅταν τις
μοχθηροὺς ἐγκρατεῖς ποιῶν παραδιδῷ τὴν πόλιν,
τοὺς δὲ χαριεστέρους φθείρῃ· ταὐτὸν καὶ τὸν
μιμητικὸν ποιητὴν φήσομεν κακὴν πολιτείαν ἰδίᾳ
ἑκάστου τῇ ψυχῇ ἐμποιεῖν, τῷ ἀνοήτῳ αὐτῆς
C χαριζόμενον καὶ οὔτε τὰ μείζω οὔτε τὰ ἐλάττω
διαγιγνώσκοντι, ἀλλὰ τὰ αὐτὰ τοτὲ μὲν μεγάλα
ἡγουμένῳ, τοτὲ δὲ σμικρά, εἴδωλα εἰδωλοποιοῦντα,
τοῦ δὲ ἀληθοῦς πόρρω πάνυ ἀφεστῶτα. Πάνυ
μὲν οὖν.

VII. Οὐ μέντοι πω τό γε μέγιστον κατηγο-
ρήκαμεν αὐτῆς. τὸ γὰρ καὶ τοὺς ἐπιεικεῖς ἱκανὴν
εἶναι λωβᾶσθαι, ἐκτὸς πάνυ τινῶν ὀλίγων, πάν-
δεινόν που. Τί δ᾽ οὐ μέλλει, εἴπερ γε δρᾷ αὐτό;
Ἀκούων σκόπει. οἱ γάρ που βέλτιστοι ἡμῶν
ἀκροώμενοι Ὁμήρου ἢ ἄλλου τινὸς τῶν τραγῳδο-
D ποιῶν μιμουμένου τινὰ τῶν ἡρώων ἐν πένθει
ὄντα καὶ μακρὰν ῥῆσιν ἀποτείνοντα ἐν τοῖς
ὀδυρμοῖς, ἢ καὶ ᾄδοντάς τε καὶ κοπτομένους, οἶσθ᾽
ὅτι χαίρομέν τε καὶ ἐνδόντες ἡμᾶς αὐτοὺς ἑπόμεθα
ξυμπάσχοντες καὶ σπουδάζοντες ἐπαινοῦμεν ὡς
ἀγαθὸν ποιητήν, ὃς ἂν ἡμᾶς ὅ τι μάλιστα οὕτω
διαθῇ. Οἶδα· πῶς δ᾽ οὔ; Ὅταν δὲ οἰκεῖόν τινι
ἡμῶν κῆδος γένηται, ἐννοεῖς αὖ ὅτι ἐπὶ τῷ ἐναντίῳ
καλλωπιζόμεθα, ἂν δυνώμεθα ἡσυχίαν ἄγειν καὶ
E καρτερεῖν, ὡς τοῦτο μὲν ἀνδρὸς ὄν, ἐκεῖνο δὲ

---

[a] Cf. p. 412, note d.   [b] Cf. p. 420, note a, on 595 B-C.
[c] For ἐν πένθει cf. Soph. El. 290, 846, Herod. i. 46.
[d] Cf. Phileb. 48 A.
[e] See the description in Ion 535 E, and Laws 800 D.

justified in not admitting him into a well-ordered state, because he stimulates and fosters this element in the soul, and by strengthening it tends to destroy the rational part, just as when in a state[a] one puts bad men in power and turns the city over to them and ruins the better sort. Precisely in the same manner we shall say that the mimetic poet sets up in each individual soul a vicious constitution by fashioning phantoms far removed from reality, and by currying favour with the senseless element that cannot distinguish the greater from the less, but calls the same thing now one, now the other." "By all means."

VII. "But we have not yet brought our chief accusation against it. Its power to corrupt, with rare exceptions, even the better sort is surely the chief cause for alarm." "How could it be otherwise, if it really does that?" "Listen and reflect. I think you know that the very best of us, when we hear Homer[b] or some other of the makers of tragedy imitating one of the heroes who is in grief,[c] and is delivering a long tirade in his lamentations or chanting and beating his breast, feel pleasure,[d] and abandon ourselves and accompany the representation with sympathy and eagerness,[e] and we praise as an excellent poet the one who most strongly affects us in this way." "I do know it, of course." "But when in our own lives some affliction comes to us, you are also aware that we plume ourselves upon the opposite, on our ability to remain calm and endure, in the belief that this is the conduct of a man, and what we were praising in the theatre that of a woman.[f]" "I do note that." "Do you think, then," said I, "that

---

[f] This is qualified in 387 E-388 A by οὐδὲ ταύταις σπουδαίαις. *Cf.* also 398 E.

605 γυναικός, ὃ τότε ἐπῃνοῦμεν. Ἐννοῶ, ἔφη. Ἡ
καλῶς οὖν, ἦν δ' ἐγώ, οὗτος ὁ ἔπαινος ἔχει, τὸ
ὁρῶντα τοιοῦτον ἄνδρα, οἷον ἑαυτόν τις μὴ ἀξιοῖ
εἶναι ἀλλ' αἰσχύνοιτο ἄν, μὴ βδελύττεσθαι ἀλλὰ
χαίρειν τε καὶ ἐπαινεῖν; Οὐ μὰ τὸν Δί', ἔφη, οὐκ
606 εὐλόγῳ ἔοικεν. Ναί, ἦν δ' ἐγώ, εἰ ἐκείνῃ γ' αὐτὸ
σκοποίης. Πῇ; Εἰ ἐνθυμοῖο, ὅτι τὸ βίᾳ κατ-
εχόμενον τότε ἐν ταῖς οἰκείαις ξυμφοραῖς καὶ πε-
πεινηκὸς τοῦ δακρῦσαί τε καὶ ἀποδύρασθαι ἱκανῶς
καὶ ἀποπλησθῆναι, φύσει ὂν τοιοῦτον οἷον τούτων
ἐπιθυμεῖν, τότ' ἐστὶ τοῦτο τὸ ὑπὸ τῶν ποιητῶν
πιμπλάμενον καὶ χαῖρον· τὸ δὲ φύσει βέλτιστον
ἡμῶν, ἅτε οὐχ ἱκανῶς πεπαιδευμένον λόγῳ οὐδὲ
ἔθει, ἀνίησι τὴν φυλακὴν τοῦ θρηνώδους τούτου,
B ἅτε ἀλλότρια πάθη θεωροῦν καὶ ἑαυτῷ οὐδὲν
αἰσχρὸν ὄν, εἰ ἄλλος ἀνὴρ ἀγαθὸς φάσκων εἶναι
ἀκαίρως πενθεῖ, τοῦτον ἐπαινεῖν καὶ ἐλεεῖν· ἀλλ'
ἐκεῖνο κερδαίνειν ἡγεῖται, τὴν ἡδονήν, καὶ οὐκ ἂν
δέξαιτο αὐτῆς στερηθῆναι καταφρονήσας ὅλου
τοῦ ποιήματος. λογίζεσθαι γάρ, οἶμαι, ὀλίγοις
τισὶ μέτεστιν, ὅτι ἀπολαύειν ἀνάγκη ἀπὸ τῶν
ἀλλοτρίων εἰς τὰ οἰκεῖα· θρέψαντα γὰρ ἐν ἐκείνοις
ἰσχυρὸν τὸ ἐλεεινὸν οὐ ῥᾴδιον ἐν τοῖς αὑτοῦ

---

[a] Cf. Vol. I. p. 509, note b, on 473 E.

[b] Cf. Isoc. Panegyr. 168 for a different application.

[c] This contains a hint of one possible meaning of the
Aristotelian doctrine of κάθαρσις, Poet. 1449 b 27-28. Cf.
κουφίζεσθαι μεθ' ἡδονῆς Pol. 1342 a 14, and my review of
Finsler, "Platon u. d. Aristot. Poetik," Class. Phil. iii. p. 462.
But the tone of the Platonic passage is more like that of
Ruskin, Sesame and Lilies: "And the human nature of us

this praise is rightfully bestowed when, contemplating a character that we would not accept but would be ashamed of in ourselves, we do not abominate it but take pleasure and approve?" "No, by Zeus," he said, "it does not seem reasonable." "Oh yes,[a]" said I, "if you would consider it in this way." "In what way?" "If you would reflect that the part of the soul that in the former case, in our own misfortunes,[b] was forcibly restrained, and that has hungered for tears and a good cry [c] and satisfaction, because it is its nature to desire these things, is the element in us that the poets satisfy and delight, and that the best element in our nature, since it has never been properly educated by reason or even by habit, then relaxes its guard [d] over the plaintive part, inasmuch as this is contemplating the woes of others and it is no shame to it to praise and pity another who, claiming to be a good man, abandons himself to excess in his grief; but it thinks this vicarious pleasure is so much clear gain,[e] and would not consent to forfeit it by disdaining the poem altogether. That is, I think, because few are capable of reflecting that what we enjoy in others will inevitably react upon ourselves.[f] For after feeding fat [g] the emotion of pity there, it is not easy to restrain it in our own sufferings." "Most

imperatively requiring awe and sorrow of some kind, for the noble grief we should have borne with our fellows, and the pure tears we should have wept with them, we gloat over the pathos of the police court and gather the night dew of the grave."

[d] This anticipates the idea of the "censor" in modern psychology.

[e] Cf. τῇ δ' ἀσφαλείᾳ κερδανεῖς Eurip. *Herc. Fur.* 604, which is frequently misinterpreted; Herod. viii. 60. 3.

[f] For the psychology cf. *Laws* 656 B and *supra* on 385 C-D.

[g] Cf. 442 A.

606 C πάθεσι κατέχειν. Ἀληθέστατα, ἔφη. Ἆρ᾽ οὐχ ὁ
αὐτὸς λόγος καὶ περὶ τοῦ γελοίου, ὅτι, ἂν αὐτὸς
αἰσχύνοιο γελωτοποιῶν, ἐν μιμήσει δὴ κωμῳδικῇ
ἢ καὶ ἰδίᾳ ἀκούων σφόδρα χαρῇς καὶ μὴ
μισῇς ὡς πονηρά, ταὐτὸν ποιεῖς ὅπερ ἐν τοῖς
ἐλέοις; ὃ γὰρ τῷ λόγῳ αὖ κατεῖχες ἐν σαυτῷ
βουλόμενον γελωτοποιεῖν, φοβούμενος δόξαν βωμο-
λοχίας, τότ᾽ αὖ ἀνίῃς καὶ ἐκεῖ νεανικὸν ποιήσας
ἔλαθες πολλάκις ἐν τοῖς οἰκείοις ἐξενεχθεὶς ὥστε
D κωμῳδοποιὸς γενέσθαι. Καὶ μάλα, ἔφη. Καὶ
περὶ ἀφροδισίων δὴ καὶ θυμοῦ καὶ περὶ πάντων
τῶν ἐπιθυμητικῶν τε καὶ λυπηρῶν καὶ ἡδέων ἐν
τῇ ψυχῇ, ἃ δή φαμεν πάσῃ πράξει ἡμῖν ἕπεσθαι,
ὅτι τοιαῦτα ἡμᾶς ἡ ποιητικὴ μίμησις ἐργάζεται;
τρέφει γὰρ ταῦτα ἄρδουσα, δέον αὐχμεῖν, καὶ
ἄρχοντα ἡμῖν καθίστησι, δέον ἄρχεσθαι αὐτά, ἵνα
βελτίους τε καὶ εὐδαιμονέστεροι ἀντὶ χειρόνων καὶ
ἀθλιωτέρων γιγνώμεθα. Οὐκ ἔχω ἄλλως φάναι,
E ἦ δ᾽ ὅς. Οὐκοῦν, εἶπον, ὦ Γλαύκων, ὅταν
Ὁμήρου ἐπαινέταις ἐντύχῃς λέγουσιν, ὡς τὴν
Ἑλλάδα πεπαίδευκεν οὗτος ὁ ποιητής, καὶ πρὸς
διοίκησίν τε καὶ παιδείαν τῶν ἀνθρωπίνων πραγ-
μάτων ἄξιος ἀναλαβόντι μανθάνειν τε καὶ κατὰ

ᵃ Cf. Vol. I. p. 211, note f, La Bruyère, Des Ouvrages de
l'esprit (Œuvres, ed. M. G. Servois, i. p. 137): "D'où vient
que l'on rit si librement au théâtre, et que l'on a honte d'y
pleurer?"

ᵇ In the Laws 816 D-E Plato says that the citizens must
witness such performances since the serious cannot be
learned without the laughable, nor anything without its
opposite; but they may not take part in them. That is left
to slaves and foreigners. Cf. also Vol. I. p. 239, note b, on
396 E.

ᶜ i.e. as opposed to public performances. Cf. Euthydem.

true," he said. " Does not the same principle apply to the laughable,[a] namely, that if in comic representations,[b] or for that matter in private talk,[c] you take intense pleasure in buffooneries that you would blush to practise yourself, and do not detest them as base, you are doing the same thing as in the case of the pathetic? For here again what your reason, for fear of the reputation of buffoonery, restrained in yourself when it fain would play the clown, you release in turn, and so, fostering its youthful impudence, let yourself go so far that often ere you are aware you become yourself a comedian in private." " Yes, indeed," he said. " And so in regard to the emotions of sex and anger, and all the appetites and pains and pleasures of the soul which we say accompany all our actions,[d] the effect of poetic imitation is the same. For it waters[e] and fosters these feelings when what we ought to do is to dry them up, and it establishes them as our rulers when they ought to be ruled, to the end that we may be better and happier men instead of worse and more miserable." " I cannot deny it," said he. "Then, Glaucon," said I, "when you meet encomiasts of Homer who tell us that this poet has been the educator of Hellas,[f] and that for the conduct and refinement [g] of human life he is worthy of our study

---

305 D ἐν δὲ τοῖς ἰδίοις λόγοις, *Theaet.* 177 B, *Soph.* 232 C ἔν γε ταῖς ἰδίαις συνουσίαις, and *Soph.* 222 C προσομιλητικήν with Quintil. iii. 4. 4. Wilamowitz, *Antigonos von Karystos*, p. 285, fantastically says that it means prose and refers to Sophron. He compares 366 E. But see *Laws* 935 B-C.

[d] *Cf. supra* 603 C. [e] *Cf.* 550 B.

[f] Isocrates, *Panegyr.* 159, says Homer was given a place in education because he celebrated those who fought against the barbarians. *Cf.* also Aristoph. *Frogs* 1034 ff.

[g] The same conjunction is implied in Protagoras's teaching, *Protag.* 318 E and 317 B.

606 τοῦτον τὸν ποιητὴν πάντα τὸν αὑτοῦ βίον κατα-
607 σκευασάμενον ζῆν, φιλεῖν μὲν χρὴ καὶ ἀσπάζεσθαι
ὡς ὄντας βελτίστους εἰς ὅσον δύνανται, καὶ
συγχωρεῖν Ὅμηρον ποιητικώτατον εἶναι καὶ πρῶτον τῶν τραγῳδοποιῶν, εἰδέναι δέ, ὅτι ὅσον μόνον
ὕμνους θεοῖς καὶ ἐγκώμια τοῖς ἀγαθοῖς ποιήσεως
παραδεκτέον εἰς πόλιν· εἰ δὲ τὴν ἡδυσμένην
Μοῦσαν παραδέξει ἐν μέλεσιν ἢ ἔπεσιν, ἡδονή σοι
καὶ λύπη ἐν τῇ πόλει βασιλεύσετον ἀντὶ νόμου τε
καὶ τοῦ κοινῇ ἀεὶ δόξαντος εἶναι βελτίστου λόγου.
Ἀληθέστατα, ἔφη.

B VIII. Ταῦτα δή, ἔφην, ἀπολελογήσθω ἡμῖν
ἀναμνησθεῖσι περὶ ποιήσεως, ὅτι εἰκότως ἄρα·
τότε αὐτὴν ἐκ τῆς πόλεως ἀπεστέλλομεν τοιαύτην
οὖσαν· ὁ γὰρ λόγος ἡμᾶς ᾕρει. προσείπωμεν δὲ
αὐτῇ, μὴ καί τινα σκληρότητα ἡμῶν καὶ ἀγροικίαν
καταγνῷ, ὅτι παλαιὰ μέν τις διαφορὰ φιλοσοφίᾳ
τε καὶ ποιητικῇ· καὶ γὰρ ἡ λακέρυζα πρὸς δε-
σπόταν κύων ἐκείνη κραυγάζουσα, καὶ μέγας ἐν

---

[a] For the μέν cf. Symp. 180 E, Herod. vii. 102.

[b] The condescending tone is that of Euthydem. 306 C-D.

[c] Aristotle, Poet. 1453 a 29, says that Euripides is τραγικώ-
τατος of poets.

[d] Cf. 605 C, 595 B-C.

[e] Cf. Laws 801 D-E, 829 C-D, supra 397 C-D, 459 E, 468 D,
Friedländer, Platon, i. p. 142, and my review of Pater, Plato
and Platonism, in The Dial, 14 (1893) p. 211.

[f] Cf. Laws 802 C τῆς γλυκείας Μούσης. See Finsler,
Platon u. d. aristot. Poetik, pp. 61-62.

[g] See on 604 C, p. 455, note h.

[h] For the quarrel between philosophy and poetry cf. Laws
967 C-D, Friedländer, Platon, ii. p. 136. It still goes on in
modern times. Cf. Keats, "Lamia":

and devotion, and that we should order our entire lives by the guidance of this poet, we must love [a] and salute them as doing the best they can,[b] and concede to them that Homer is the most poetic [c] of poets and the first of tragedians,[d] but we must know the truth, that we can admit no poetry into our city save only hymns to the gods and the praises of good men.[e] For if you grant admission to the honeyed muse [f] in lyric or epic, pleasure and pain will be lords of your city instead of law and that which shall from time to time have approved itself to the general reason as the best." "Most true," he said.

VIII. "Let us, then, conclude our return to the topic of poetry and our apology, and affirm that we really had good grounds then for dismissing her from our city, since such was her character. For reason constrained us.[g] And let us further say to her, lest she condemn us for harshness and rusticity, that there is from of old a quarrel [h] between philosophy and poetry. For such expressions as ' the yelping hound barking at her master and mighty in the idle babble of fools,' [i]

Do not all charms fly
At the mere touch of cold philosophy?

Wordsworth, "A Poet's Epitaph":

Philosopher! a fingering slave,
One that would peep and botanize
Upon his mother's grave.

But Anatole France thinks otherwise, "Les Torts de l'histoire," *Vie littéraire*, ii. p. 123: "J'ai remarqué que les philosophes vivaient généralement en bonne intelligence avec les poètes . . . Les philosophes savent que les poètes ne pensent pas; cela les désarme, les attendrit et les enchante."

[i] Wilamowitz, *Platon*, i. p. 252, conjectures that these quotations are from Sophron; *cf.* also *ibid.* ii. pp. 386-387.

607 C ἀφρόνων κεναγορίαισι, καὶ ὁ τῶν διασόφων ὄχλος
κρατῶν, καὶ οἱ λεπτῶς μεριμνῶντες ὅτι ἄρα
πένονται, καὶ ἄλλα μυρία σημεῖα παλαιᾶς ἐναντιώ-
σεως τούτων. ὅμως δὲ εἰρήσθω, ὅτι ἡμεῖς γε, εἴ
τινα ἔχοι λόγον εἰπεῖν ἡ πρὸς ἡδονὴν ποιητικὴ
καὶ ἡ μίμησις, ὡς χρὴ αὐτὴν εἶναι ἐν πόλει εὐ-
νομουμένῃ, ἄσμενοι ἂν καταδεχοίμεθα· ὡς ξύν-
ισμέν γε ἡμῖν αὐτοῖς κηλουμένοις ὑπ' αὐτῆς·
ἀλλὰ γὰρ τὸ δοκοῦν ἀληθὲς οὐχ ὅσιον προδιδόναι.

D ἦ γάρ, ὦ φίλε, οὐ κηλεῖ ὑπ' αὐτῆς καὶ σύ, καὶ
μάλιστα ὅταν δι' Ὁμήρου θεωρῇς αὐτήν; Πολύ
γε. Οὐκοῦν δικαία ἐστὶν οὕτω κατιέναι, ἀπολογησαμένη[1] ἐν μέλει ἤ τινι ἄλλῳ μέτρῳ; Πάνυ
μὲν οὖν. Δοῖμεν δέ γέ που ἂν καὶ τοῖς προστάταις
αὐτῆς, ὅσοι μὴ ποιητικοί, φιλοποιηταὶ δέ, ἄνευ
μέτρου λόγον ὑπὲρ αὐτῆς εἰπεῖν, ὡς οὐ μόνον
ἡδεῖα ἀλλὰ καὶ ὠφελίμη πρὸς τὰς πολιτείας καὶ
τὸν βίον τὸν ἀνθρώπινόν ἐστι· καὶ εὐμενῶς ἀκουσό-

E μεθα. κερδανοῦμεν γάρ που, ἐὰν μὴ μόνον ἡδεῖα
φανῇ ἀλλὰ καὶ ὠφελίμη. Πῶς δ' οὐ μέλλομεν,
ἔφη, κερδαίνειν; Εἰ δέ γε μή, ὦ φίλε ἑταῖρε,
ὥσπερ οἱ ποτέ του ἐρασθέντες, ἐὰν ἡγήσωνται μὴ
ὠφέλιμον εἶναι τὸν ἔρωτα, βίᾳ μέν, ὅμως δὲ ἀπ-
έχονται, καὶ ἡμεῖς οὕτως, διὰ τὸν ἐγγεγονότα μὲν

---

[1] ἀπολογησαμένη A, ἀπολογισαμένη FD, ἀπολογησομένη A²M.

a Cf. p. 420, note b, on 595 c.
b Cf. supra, Introd. p. lxiii.

and ' the mob that masters those who are too wise for their own good,' and the subtle thinkers who reason that after all they are poor, and countless others are tokens of this ancient enmity. But nevertheless let it be declared that, if the mimetic and dulcet poetry can show any reason for her existence in a well-governed state, we would gladly admit her, since we ourselves are very conscious of her spell. But all the same it would be impious to betray what we believe to be the truth.[a] Is not that so, friend ? Do not you yourself feel her magic [b] and especially when Homer [c] is her interpreter ? " " Greatly." " Then may she not justly return from this exile after she has pleaded her defence, whether in lyric or other measure ? " " By all means." " And we would allow her advo-cates who are not poets but lovers of poetry to plead her cause [d] in prose without metre, and show that she is not only delightful but beneficial to orderly govern-ment and all the life of man. And we shall listen benevolently, for it will be clear gain for us if it can be shown that she bestows not only pleasure but benefit." " How could we help being the gainers ? " said he. " But if not, my friend, even as men who have fallen in love, if they think that the love is not good for them, hard though it be,[e] nevertheless refrain, so we,

[c] In *Laws* 658 D Plato says that old men would prefer Homer and epic to any other literary entertainment.

[d] This challenge was taken up by Aristotle (*Poetics*), Plutarch (*Quomodo adolescens*), Sidney (*Defense of Poesie*), and many others.

[e] βίᾳ μέν, ὅμως δέ: cf. *Epist.* iii. 316 E, and vii. 325 A, and Raeder, *Rhein. Mus.* lxi. p. 470, Aristoph. *Clouds* 1363 μόλις μὲν ἀλλ' ὅμως, Eurip. *Phoen.* 1421 μόλις μέν, ἐξέτεινε δ', and also Soph. *Antig.* 1105, *O.T.* 998, Eurip. *Bacch.* 1027, *Hec.* 843, *Or.* 1023, *Phoen.* 1069, *I.A.* 688, 904.

607 ἔρωτα τῆς τοιαύτης ποιήσεως ὑπὸ τῆς τῶν καλῶν
608 πολιτειῶν τροφῆς, εὖνοι μὲν ἐσόμεθα φανῆναι
αὐτὴν ὡς βελτίστην καὶ ἀληθεστάτην, ἕως δ' ἂν
μὴ οἵα τ' ᾖ ἀπολογήσασθαι, ἀκροασόμεθ' αὐτῆς
ἐπάδοντες ἡμῖν αὐτοῖς τοῦτον τὸν λόγον, ὃν λέγομεν, καὶ ταύτην τὴν ἐπῳδήν, εὐλαβούμενοι
πάλιν ἐμπεσεῖν εἰς τὸν παιδικόν τε καὶ τὸν τῶν
πολλῶν ἔρωτα. αἰσθόμεθα[1] δ' οὖν, ὡς οὐ σπου-
δαστέον ἐπὶ τῇ τοιαύτῃ ποιήσει ὡς ἀληθείας τε
ἁπτομένῃ καὶ σπουδαίᾳ, ἀλλ' εὐλαβητέον αὐτὴν[2]

B τῷ ἀκροωμένῳ, περὶ τῆς ἐν αὑτῷ πολιτείας
δεδιότι, καὶ νομιστέα ἅπερ εἰρήκαμεν περὶ ποιήσεως. Παντάπασιν, ἦ δ' ὅς, ξύμφημι. Μέγας
γάρ, ἔφην, ὁ ἀγών, ὦ φίλε Γλαύκων, μέγας, οὐχ
ὅσος δοκεῖ, τὸ χρηστὸν ἢ κακὸν γενέσθαι, ὥστε
οὔτε τιμῇ ἐπαρθέντα οὔτε χρήμασιν οὔτε ἀρχῇ
οὐδεμιᾷ οὐδέ γε ποιητικῇ ἄξιον ἀμελῆσαι δικαιοσύνης τε καὶ τῆς ἄλλης ἀρετῆς. Ξύμφημί σοι,
ἔφη, ἐξ ὧν διεληλύθαμεν· οἶμαι δὲ καὶ ἄλλον
ὁντινοῦν.

C IX. Καὶ μήν, ἦν δ' ἐγώ, τά γε μέγιστα ἐπίχειρα
ἀρετῆς καὶ προκείμενα ἆθλα οὐ διεληλύθαμεν·
Ἀμήχανόν τι, ἔφη, λέγεις μέγεθος, εἰ τῶν εἰρημέ-

[1] αἰσθόμεθα AFDM, εἰσόμεθα scr. Mon., ᾀσόμεθα Madvig,
followed by Burnet.
[2] ADM have ὃν after αὐτήν, F ὅν. More recent mss.
omit it.

---

[a] Ironical, as καλλίστῃ in 562 A.

owing to the love of this kind of poetry inbred in us by our education in these fine [a] polities of ours, will gladly have the best possible case made out for her goodness and truth, but so long as she is unable to make good her defence we shall chant over to ourselves [b] as we listen the reasons that we have given as a counter-charm to her spell, to preserve us from slipping back into the childish loves of the multitude; for we have come to see that we must not take such poetry seriously as a serious thing [c] that lays hold on truth, but that he who lends an ear to it must be on his guard fearing for the polity in his soul [d] and must believe what we have said about poetry." "By all means," he said, "I concur." "Yes, for great is the struggle,[e] I said, "dear Glaucon, a far greater contest than we think it, that determines whether a man prove good or bad, so that not the lure of honour or wealth or any office, no, nor of poetry either, should incite us [f] to be careless of righteousness and all excellence." "I agree with you," he replied, "in view of what we have set forth, and I think that anyone else would do so too."

IX. "And yet," said I, "the greatest rewards of virtue and the prizes proposed for her we have not set forth." "You must have in mind an inconceivable [g] magnitude," he replied, "if there are other

[b] For ἐπᾴδοντες cf. Phaedo 114 D, 77 E.
[c] Cf. 602 B.
[d] Cf. on 591 E, p. 412, note d.
[e] Cf. Phaedo 114 C, 107 C, Phaedr. 247 B, Gorg. 526 E, Blaydes on Aristoph. Peace 276, and for the whole sentence Phaedo 83 B-C, supra 465 D, infra 618 B-C f. and p. 404, note d, on 589 E.
[f] ἐπαρθέντα: cf. 416 C.
[g] Cf. supra 494 C, 509 A, 548 D, 584 B, 588 A, Apol. 41 C, Charm. 155 D.

608 νων μείζω ἐστὶν ἄλλα. Τί δ' ἄν, ἦν δ' ἐγώ, ἔν γε
ὀλίγῳ χρόνῳ μέγα γένοιτο; πᾶς γὰρ οὗτός γε
ὁ ἐκ παιδὸς μέχρι πρεσβύτου χρόνος πρὸς πάντα
ὀλίγος πού τις ἂν εἴη. Οὐδὲν μὲν οὖν, ἔφη. Τί
οὖν; οἴει ἀθανάτῳ πράγματι ὑπὲρ τοσούτου δεῖν
D χρόνου ἐσπουδακέναι, ἀλλ' οὐχ ὑπὲρ τοῦ παντός;
Οἶμαι ἔγωγ', ἔφη· ἀλλὰ τί τοῦτο λέγεις; Οὐκ
ᾔσθησαι, ἦν δ' ἐγώ, ὅτι ἀθάνατος ἡμῶν ἡ ψυχὴ
καὶ οὐδέποτε ἀπόλλυται; καὶ ὃς ἐμβλέψας μοι
καὶ θαυμάσας εἶπε Μὰ Δί', οὐκ ἔγωγε· σὺ δὲ
τοῦτ' ἔχεις λέγειν; Εἰ μὴ ἀδικῶ γ', ἔφην· οἶμαι
δὲ καὶ σύ· οὐδὲν γὰρ χαλεπόν. Ἐμοιγ', ἔφη· σοῦ
δ' ἂν ἡδέως ἀκούσαιμι τὸ οὐ χαλεπὸν τοῦτο.
Ἀκούοις ἄν, ἦν δ' ἐγώ. Λέγε μόνον, ἔφη. Ἀγα-
E θόν τι, εἶπον, καὶ κακὸν καλεῖς; Ἔγωγε. Ἆρ'
οὖν ὥσπερ ἐγὼ περὶ αὐτῶν διανοεῖ; Τὸ ποῖον;
Τὸ μὲν ἀπολλύον καὶ διαφθεῖρον πᾶν τὸ κακὸν
εἶναι, τὸ δὲ σῷζον καὶ ὠφελοῦν τὸ ἀγαθόν. Ἔγωγ',

---

a Clement, *Strom.* iv. p. 496 в ὀθούνεκ' ἀρετὴ τῶν ἐν
ἀνθρώποις μόνη οὐκ ἐκ θυραίων τἀπίχειρα λαμβάνει, αὐτὴ δ' ἑαυτὴν
ἆθλα τῶν πόνων ἔχει. Tennyson, "Wages":

. . . if the wages of Virtue be dust,
  Would she have heart to endure for the life of the worm
    and the fly?
She desires no isles of the blest, no quiet seats of the just,
  To rest in a golden grove, or to bask in a summer sky:
Give her the wages of going on, and not to die.

b Tennyson, "Locksley Hall Sixty Years After":

Good, for Good is Good, he follow'd, yet he look'd beyond
    the grave . . .
Truth for truth, and good for good! The Good, the True,
    the Pure, the Just—
Take the charm "For ever" from them, and they crumble
    into dust.

things greater than those of which we have spoken.[a] "
" What great thing," said I, " could there be in a
little time[b]? For surely the whole time from the boy to
the old man would be small compared with all time.[c] "
" Nay, it is nothing," he said. " What then ? Do
you think that an immortal thing[d] ought to be seriously
concerned for such a little time, and not rather for all
time ? " " I think so," he said ; " but what is this
that you have in mind ? " " Have you never perceived," said I, " that our soul is immortal and never
perishes ? " And he, looking me full in the face[e] in
amazement,[f] said, "No, by Zeus, not I ; but are *you*
able to declare this ? " " I certainly ought to be,[g] " said
I, "and I think you too can, for it is nothing hard."
" It is for me," he said ; " and I would gladly hear
from you this thing that is not hard.[h] " " Listen,"
said I. " Just speak on," he replied. " You speak
of[i] good and evil, do you not ? " " I do." " Is your
notion of them the same as mine ? " " What is it ? "
" That which destroys and corrupts in every case is
the evil ; that which preserves and benefits is the

---

[a] Cf. on 486 A, p. 9, note f and 498 D.

[d] For the colourless use of πρᾶγμα see *What Plato Said*,
p. 497, on *Protag.* 330 C-D. Cf. Shakes. *Hamlet*, I. iv. 67
"being a thing immortal as itself."

[e] ἐμβλέψας: cf. *Charmides* 155 c.

[f] Glaucon is surprised in spite of 498 D. Many uncertain
inferences have been drawn from the fact that in spite of
the *Phaedo* and *Phaedrus* (245 c ff.) interlocutors in Plato
are always surprised at the idea of immortality. Cf. *supra*,
Introd. p. lxiv.

[g] For the idiomatic εἰ μὴ ἀδικῶ cf. 430 E, *Charm.* 156 A,
Menex. 236 B, *infra* 612 D.

[h] Cf. *Protag.* 341 A τὸ χαλεπὸν τοῦτο, which is a little
different, Herod. vii. 11 τὸ δεινὸν τὸ πείσομαι.

[i] See Vol. I. p. 90, note a and *What Plato Said*, p. 567, on
Cratyl. 385 B.

608 ἔφη. Τί δέ; κακὸν ἑκάστῳ τι καὶ ἀγαθὸν λέγεις;
609 οἷον ὀφθαλμοῖς ὀφθαλμίαν καὶ ξύμπαντι τῷ σώματι
νόσον, σίτῳ τε ἐρυσίβην, σηπεδόνα τε ξύλοις,
χαλκῷ δὲ καὶ σιδήρῳ ἰόν, καί, ὅπερ λέγω, σχεδὸν
πᾶσι ξύμφυτον ἑκάστῳ κακόν τε καὶ νόσημα;
Ἔγωγ’, ἔφη. Οὐκοῦν ὅταν τῷ τι τούτων προσ-
γένηται, πονηρόν τε ποιεῖ ᾧ προσεγένετο, καὶ τελευτῶν ὅλον διέλυσε καὶ ἀπώλεσεν; Πῶς γὰρ οὔ;
Τὸ ξύμφυτον ἄρα κακὸν ἑκάστου καὶ ἡ πονηρία
ἕκαστον ἀπόλλυσιν, ἢ εἰ μὴ τοῦτο ἀπολεῖ, οὐκ ἂν
B ἄλλο γε αὐτὸ ἔτι διαφθείρειεν. οὐ γὰρ τό γε
ἀγαθὸν μή ποτέ τι ἀπολέσῃ, οὐδὲ αὖ τὸ μήτε
κακὸν μήτε ἀγαθόν. Πῶς γὰρ ἄν; ἔφη. Ἐὰν
ἄρα τι εὑρίσκωμεν τῶν ὄντων, ᾧ ἔστι μὲν κακόν,
ὃ ποιεῖ αὐτὸ μοχθηρόν, τοῦτο μέντοι οὐχ οἷόν τε
αὐτὸ λύειν ἀπολλύον, οὐκ ἤδη εἰσόμεθα, ὅτι τοῦ
πεφυκότος οὕτως ὄλεθρος οὐκ ἦν; Οὕτως, ἔφη,
εἰκός. Τί οὖν; ἦν δ’ ἐγώ. ψυχῇ ἆρ’ οὐκ ἔστιν
ὃ ποιεῖ αὐτὴν κακήν; Καὶ μάλ’, ἔφη, ἃ νῦν δὴ
C διῆμεν πάντα, ἀδικία τε καὶ ἀκολασία καὶ δειλία
καὶ ἀμαθία. Ἦ οὖν τι τούτων αὐτὴν διαλύει τε
καὶ ἀπόλλυσι; καὶ ἐννόει, μὴ ἐξαπατηθῶμεν
οἰηθέντες τὸν ἄδικον ἄνθρωπον καὶ ἀνόητον, ὅταν
ληφθῇ ἀδικῶν, τότε ἀπολωλέναι ὑπὸ τῆς ἀδικίας,
πονηρίας οὔσης ψυχῆς· ἀλλ’ ὧδε ποιεῖ· ὥσπερ
σῶμα ἡ σώματος πονηρία νόσος οὖσα τήκει καὶ
διόλλυσι καὶ ἄγει εἰς τὸ μηδὲ σῶμα εἶναι, καὶ ἃ

---

a Ruskin, *Time and Tide* § 52 (Brantwood ed. p. 68):
"Every faculty of man's soul, and every instinct of it by
which he is meant to live, is exposed to its own special form
of corruption"; Boethius, *Cons.* iii. 11 (L.C.L. trans. p. 283),
things are destroyed by what is hostile; Aristot. *Top.*
124 a 28 εἰ γὰρ τὸ φθαρτικὸν διαλυτικόν.

good." "Yes, I think so," he said. "How about this: Do you say that there is for everything its special good and evil, as for example for the eyes ophthalmia, for the entire body disease, for grain mildew, rotting for wood, rust for bronze and iron, and, as I say, for practically everything its congenital evil and disease [a]?" "I do," he said. "Then when one of these evils comes to anything does it not make the thing to which it attaches itself bad, and finally disintegrate and destroy it?" "Of course." "Then the congenital evil of each thing and its own vice destroys it, or if that is not going to destroy it, nothing else remains that could; for obviously [b] the good will never destroy anything, nor yet again will that which is neutral and neither good nor evil [c]." "How could it?" he said. "If, then, we discover [d] anything that has an evil which vitiates it, yet is not able to dissolve and destroy it, shall we not thereupon know that of a thing so constituted there can be no destruction?" "That seems likely," he said. "Well, then," said I, "has not the soul something that makes it evil?" "Indeed it has," he said, "all the things that we were just now enumerating, injustice and licentiousness and cowardice and ignorance." "Does any one of these things dissolve and destroy it? And reflect, lest we be misled by supposing that when an unjust and foolish man is taken in his injustice he is then destroyed by the injustice, which is the vice of soul. But conceive it thus: Just as the vice of body which is disease wastes and destroys it so that it no longer is a body at all,[e] in like manner in all the

[b] γε vi termini. Cf. 379 A, Phaedo 106 D.
[c] See What Plato Said, p. 490, on Lysis 216 c.
[d] Cf. Vol. I. p. 529, note a, on 478 D.
[e] Cf. Aristot. Pol. 1309 b 28 μηδὲ ῥῖνα ποιήσει φαίνεσθαι.

609 νῦν δὴ ἐλέγομεν ἅπαντα ὑπὸ τῆς οἰκείας κακίας,
D τῷ προσκαθῆσθαι καὶ ἐνεῖναι διαφθειρούσης, εἰς τὸ
μὴ εἶναι ἀφικνεῖται—οὐχ οὕτως; Ναί. Ἴθι δή,
καὶ ψυχὴν κατὰ τὸν αὐτὸν τρόπον σκόπει, ἆρα
ἐνοῦσα ἐν αὐτῇ ἀδικία καὶ ἡ ἄλλη κακία τῷ ἐνεῖναι
καὶ προσκαθῆσθαι φθείρει αὐτὴν καὶ μαραίνει, ἕως
ἂν εἰς θάνατον ἀγαγοῦσα τοῦ σώματος χωρίσῃ;
Οὐδαμῶς, ἔφη, τοῦτό γε. Ἀλλὰ μέντοι ἐκεῖνό γε
ἄλογον, ἦν δ' ἐγώ, τὴν μὲν ἄλλου πονηρίαν ἀπολλύναι τι, τὴν δὲ αὐτοῦ μή. Ἄλογον. Ἐννόει
E γάρ, ἦν δ' ἐγώ, ὦ Γλαύκων, ὅτι οὐδ' ὑπὸ τῆς
τῶν σιτίων πονηρίας, ἣ ἂν ᾖ αὐτῶν ἐκείνων, εἴτε
παλαιότης εἴτε σαπρότης εἴτε ἡτισοῦν οὖσα, οὐκ
οἰόμεθα δεῖν σῶμα ἀπόλλυσθαι· ἀλλ' ἐὰν μὲν
ἐμποιῇ ἡ αὐτῶν πονηρία τῶν σιτίων τῷ σώματι
σώματος μοχθηρίαν, φήσομεν αὐτὸ δι' ἐκεῖνα ὑπὸ
τῆς αὐτοῦ κακίας νόσου οὔσης ἀπολωλέναι· ὑπὸ
610 δὲ σιτίων πονηρίας ἄλλων ὄντων ἄλλο ὂν τὸ σῶμα,
ὑπ' ἀλλοτρίου κακοῦ μὴ ἐμποιήσαντος τὸ ἔμφυτον
κακόν, οὐδέποτε ἀξιώσομεν διαφθείρεσθαι. Ὀρθότατα, ἔφη, λέγεις.[1]

X. Κατὰ τὸν αὐτὸν τοίνυν λόγον, ἦν δ' ἐγώ, ἐὰν
μὴ σώματος πονηρία ψυχῇ ψυχῆς πονηρίαν ἐμποιῇ,

---

[1] ὀρθότατα . . . λέγεις Adam: ὀρθότατ' ἂν . . . λέγεις
AFDM: ὀρθότατ' αὖ . . . λέγεις Stephanus: ὀρθότατ' ἂν . . .
λέγοις Hermann.

[a] The argument that follows is strictly speaking a fallacy
in that it confounds the soul with the physical principle of
life. Cf. on 335 c and on 352 ε, Gorg. 477 в-c, and supra,
Introd. p. lxvii. But Dean Inge, " Platonism and Human
Immortality "(Aristot. Soc., 1919, p. 288) says: "Plato's argument, in the tenth book of the Republic, for the immortality
of the soul, has found a place in scholastic theology, but is
supposed to have been discredited by Kant. I venture to

examples of which we spoke it is the specific evil which, by attaching itself to the thing and dwelling in it with power to corrupt, reduces it to nonentity. Is not that so?" "Yes." "Come, then, and consider the soul in the same way.[a] Do injustice and other wickedness dwelling in it, by their indwelling and attachment to it, corrupt and wither it till they bring it to death and separate it from the body?" "They certainly do not do that," he said. "But surely," said I, "it is unreasonable to suppose that the vice of something else destroys a thing while its own does not." "Yes, unreasonable." "For observe, Glaucon," said I, "that we do not think it proper to say of the body either that it is destroyed by the badness of foods themselves, whether it be staleness or rottenness or whatever it is;[b] but when the badness of the foods themselves engenders in the body the defect of body, then we shall say that it is destroyed *owing* to these foods, but *by*[c] its own vice, which is disease. But the body being one thing and the foods something else, we shall never expect the body to be destroyed by their badness, that is by an alien evil that has not produced in it the evil that belongs to it by nature." "You are entirely right," he replied.

X. "On the same principle," said I, "if the badness of the body does not produce in the soul the

think that his argument, that the soul can only be destroyed by an enemy (so to speak) *in pari materia*, is sound. Physical evils, including death, cannot touch the soul. And wickedness does not, in our experience, dissolve the soul, nor is wickedness specially apparent when the soul (if it perishes at death) would be approaching dissolution." *Cf.* 610 c. Someone might object that wickedness does destroy the soul, conceived as a spiritual principle.

[b] Plato generally disregards minor distinctions when they do not affect his point.

[c] *Cf.* 610 D.

610 μή ποτε ἀξιῶμεν ὑπ' ἀλλοτρίου κακοῦ ἄνευ τῆς
ἰδίας πονηρίας ψυχὴν ἀπόλλυσθαι, τῷ ἑτέρου κακῷ
ἕτερον. Ἔχει γάρ, ἔφη, λόγον. Ἤ τοίνυν ταῦτα
B ἐξελέγξωμεν ὅτι οὐ καλῶς λέγομεν, ἢ ἕως ἂν ᾖ
ἀνέλεγκτα, μή ποτε φῶμεν ὑπὸ πυρετοῦ μηδ' αὖ
ὑπ' ἄλλης νόσου μηδ' αὖ ὑπὸ σφαγῆς, μηδ' εἴ τις
ὅ τι σμικρότατα ὅλον τὸ σῶμα κατατέμοι, ἕνεκα
τούτων μηδὲν μᾶλλόν ποτε ψυχὴν ἀπόλλυσθαι,
πρὶν ἄν τις ἀποδείξῃ, ὡς διὰ ταῦτα τὰ παθήματα
τοῦ σώματος αὐτὴ ἐκείνη ἀδικωτέρα καὶ ἀνοσιω-
τέρα γίγνεται· ἀλλοτρίου δὲ κακοῦ ἐν ἄλλῳ
γιγνομένου, τοῦ δὲ ἰδίου ἑκάστῳ μὴ ἐγγιγνομένου,
C μήτε ψυχὴν μήτε ἄλλο μηδὲν ἐῶμεν φάναι τινὰ
ἀπόλλυσθαι. Ἀλλὰ μέντοι, ἔφη, τοῦτό γε οὐδεὶς
ποτε δείξει, ὡς τῶν ἀποθνησκόντων ἀδικώτεραι
αἱ ψυχαὶ διὰ τὸν θάνατον γίγνονται. Ἐὰν δέ γέ
τις, ἔφην ἐγώ, ὁμόσε τῷ λόγῳ τολμᾷ ἰέναι καὶ
λέγειν, ὡς πονηρότερος καὶ ἀδικώτερος γίγνεται
ὁ ἀποθνήσκων, ἵνα δὴ μὴ ἀναγκάζηται ἀθανάτους
τὰς ψυχὰς ὁμολογεῖν, ἀξιώσομέν που, εἰ ἀληθῆ
λέγει ὁ ταῦτα λέγων, τὴν ἀδικίαν εἶναι θανάσιμον
D τῷ ἔχοντι ὥσπερ νόσον, καὶ ὑπ' αὐτοῦ τούτου[1]
ἀποκτιννύντος τῇ ἑαυτοῦ φύσει ἀποθνήσκειν τοὺς
λαμβάνοντας αὐτό, τοὺς ·μὲν μάλιστα θᾶττον,
τοὺς δ' ἧττον σχολαίτερον, ἀλλὰ μὴ ὥσπερ νῦν

[1] τούτου scr. Mon. adopted by Hermann, Jowett and
Campbell, and Adam : τοῦ AFDM, followed by Burnet.

---

[a] For the challenge to refute or accept the argument *cf.*
Soph. 259 A, 257 A, *Gorg.* 467 B-C, 482 B, 508 A-B, *Phileb.*
60 D-E.

[b] Or " to take the bull by the horns." For ὁμόσε ἰέναι see

soul's badness we shall never expect the soul to be destroyed by an alien evil apart from its own defect—one thing, that is, by the evil of another." "That is reasonable," he said. "Either, then, we must refute this and show that we are mistaken, or,[a] so long as it remains unrefuted, we must never say that by fever or any other disease, or yet by the knife at the throat or the chopping to bits of the entire body, there is any more likelihood of the soul perishing because of these things, until it is proved that owing to these affections of the body the soul itself becomes more unjust and unholy. But when an evil of something else occurs in a different thing and the evil that belongs to the thing is not engendered in it, we must not suffer it to be said that the soul or anything else is in this way destroyed." "But you may be sure," he said, "that nobody will ever prove this, that the souls of the dying are made more unjust by death." "But if anyone," said I, "dares to come to grips with the argument[b] and say, in order to avoid being forced to admit the soul's immortality, that a dying man does become more wicked and unjust,[c] we will postulate that, if what he says is true, injustice must be fatal to its possessor as if it were a disease, and that those who catch it die because it kills them by its own inherent nature, those who have most of it quickest, and those who have less more slowly, and not, as now

---

What Plato Said, p. 457, on *Euthyph.* 3 c. *Cf.* ἐγγὺς ἰόντες *Phaedo* 95 B.

[c] Herbert Spencer nearly does this : " Death by starvation from inability to catch prey shows a falling short of conduct from its ideal." It recalls the argument with which Socrates catches Callicles in *Gorg.* 498 E, that if all pleasures are alike those who feel pleasure are good and those who feel pain are bad.

610 διὰ τοῦτο ὑπ᾽ ἄλλων δίκην ἐπιτιθέντων ἀποθνῄ-
σκουσιν οἱ ἄδικοι. Μὰ Δί᾽, ἦ δ᾽ ὅς, οὐκ ἄρα
πάνδεινον φανεῖται ἡ ἀδικία, εἰ θανάσιμον ἔσται
τῷ λαμβάνοντι· ἀπαλλαγὴ γὰρ ἂν εἴη κακῶν·
ἀλλὰ μᾶλλον οἶμαι αὐτὴν φανήσεσθαι πᾶν τοῦ-
E ναντίον τοὺς ἄλλους ἀποκτιννῦσαν, εἴπερ οἷόν τε,
τὸν δ᾽ ἔχοντα καὶ μάλα ζωτικὸν παρέχουσαν, καὶ
πρός γ᾽ ἔτι τῷ ζωτικῷ ἄγρυπνον· οὕτω πόρρω
που, ὡς ἔοικεν, ἐσκήνηται τοῦ θανάσιμος εἶναι.
Καλῶς, ἦν δ᾽ ἐγώ, λέγεις. ὁπότε γὰρ δὴ μὴ
ἱκανὴ ᾖ γε οἰκεία πονηρία καὶ τὸ οἰκεῖον κακὸν
ἀποκτεῖναι καὶ ἀπολέσαι ψυχήν, σχολῇ τό γε ἐπ᾽
ἄλλου ὀλέθρῳ τεταγμένον κακὸν ψυχὴν ἤ τι ἄλλο
ἀπολεῖ, πλὴν ἐφ᾽ ᾧ τέτακται. Σχολῇ γ᾽, ἔφη,
ὥς γε τὸ εἰκός. Οὐκοῦν ὁπότε μηδ᾽ ὑφ᾽ ἑνὸς
611 ἀπόλλυται κακοῦ, μήτε οἰκείου μήτε ἀλλοτρίου,
δῆλον ὅτι ἀνάγκη αὐτὸ ἀεὶ ὂν εἶναι, εἰ δ᾽ ἀεὶ ὄν,
ἀθάνατον. Ἀνάγκη, ἔφη.

XI. Τοῦτο μὲν τοίνυν, ἦν δ᾽ ἐγώ, οὕτως ἐχέτω·
εἰ δ᾽ ἔχει, ἐννοεῖς ὅτι ἀεὶ ἂν εἶεν αἱ αὐταί. οὔτε
γὰρ ἄν που ἐλάττους γένοιντο μηδεμιᾶς ἀπολλυ-
μένης, οὔτε αὖ πλείους· εἰ γὰρ ὁτιοῦν τῶν ἀθανά-
των πλέον γίγνοιτο, οἶσθ᾽ ὅτι ἐκ τοῦ θνητοῦ ἂν
γίγνοιτο καὶ πάντα ἂν εἴη τελευτῶντα ἀθάνατα.

ᵃ For the future indicative after εἰ, usually minatory or
monitory in tone, cf. Aristoph. *Birds* 759, *Phileb.* 25 D.

ᵇ Cf. *Phaedo* 107 c, 84 B, Blaydes on Aristoph. *Acharn.* 757.

ᶜ μάλα is humorous, as in 506 D, *Euthydem.* 298 D, *Symp.*
189 A.

ᵈ Cf. Horace, *Epist.* i. 2. 32 "ut iugulent hominem
surgunt de nocte latrones."

ᵉ For the metaphor cf. *Proverbs* viii. 12 σοφία κατεσκήνωσα
βουλήν. Plato personifies injustice, as he does justice in
612 D, σκιαγραφία in 602 D, bravery in *Laches* 194 A, κολα-

in fact happens, that the unjust die owing to this but by the action of others who inflict the penalty." "Nay, by Zeus," he said, "injustice will not appear a very terrible thing after all if it is going to be [a] fatal to its possessor, for that would be a release from all troubles.[b] But I rather think it will prove to be quite the contrary, something that kills others when it can, but renders its possessor very lively indeed,[c] and not only lively but wakeful,[d] so far, I ween, does it dwell[e] from deadliness." "You say well," I replied; "for when the natural vice and the evil proper to it cannot kill and destroy the soul, still less [f] will the evil appointed for the destruction of another thing destroy the soul or anything else, except that for which it is appointed."[g] "Still less indeed," he said, "in all probability." "Then since it is not destroyed by any evil whatever, either its own or alien, it is evident that it must necessarily exist always, and that if it always exists it is immortal." "Necessarily," he said.

XI. "Let this, then," I said, "be assumed to be so. But if it is so, you will observe that these souls must always be the same. For if none perishes they could not, I suppose, become fewer nor yet more numerous.[h] For if any class of immortal things increased you are aware that its increase would come from the mortal and all things would end by becoming immortal.[i]"

στική in *Soph.* 229 A, κολακευτική *Gorg.* 464 c, σμικρότης *Parmen.* 150 A, πονηρία *Apol.* 39 A-B, and many other abstract conceptions. See further *Phileb.* 63 A-B, 15 D, 24 A, *Rep.* 465 A-B, *Laws* 644 c, *Cratyl.* 438 D.

[f] σχολῇ: *cf.* 354 c, *Phaedo* 106 D.   [g] *Cf.* 345 D.

[h] *Cf.* Carveth Read, *Man and His Superstitions*, p. 104: "Plato thought that by a sort of law of psychic conservation there must always be the same number of souls in the world. There must therefore be reincarnation. . . ."

[i] *Cf. Phaedo* 72 c-D.

611 Ἀληθῆ λέγεις. Ἀλλ᾽, ἦν δ᾽ ἐγώ, μήτε τοῦτο
B οἰώμεθα, ὁ γὰρ λόγος οὐκ ἐάσει, μήτε γε αὖ τῇ
ἀληθεστάτῃ φύσει τοιοῦτον εἶναι ψυχήν, ὥστε
πολλῆς ποικιλίας καὶ ἀνομοιότητός τε καὶ δια-
φορᾶς γέμειν αὐτὸ πρὸς αὐτό. Πῶς λέγεις; ἔφη.
Οὐ ῥᾴδιον, ἦν δ᾽ ἐγώ, ἀΐδιον εἶναι σύνθετόν τε ἐκ
πολλῶν καὶ μὴ τῇ καλλίστῃ κεχρημένον συνθέσει,
ὡς νῦν ἡμῖν ἐφάνη ἡ ψυχή. Οὔκουν εἰκός γε.
Ὅτι μὲν τοίνυν ἀθάνατον ψυχή, καὶ ὁ ἄρτι λόγος
καὶ οἱ ἄλλοι ἀναγκάσειαν ἄν· οἷον δ᾽ ἐστὶ τῇ ἀλη-
C θείᾳ, οὐ λελωβημένον δεῖ αὐτὸ θεάσασθαι ὑπό τε
τῆς τοῦ σώματος κοινωνίας καὶ ἄλλων κακῶν,
ὥσπερ νῦν ἡμεῖς θεώμεθα, ἀλλ᾽ οἷόν ἐστι καθαρὸν
γιγνόμενον, τοιοῦτον ἱκανῶς λογισμῷ διαθεατέον,
καὶ πολὺ κάλλιον αὐτὸ εὑρήσει καὶ ἐναργέστερον
δικαιοσύνας τε καὶ ἀδικίας διόψεται καὶ πάντα ἃ
νῦν διήλθομεν. νῦν δὲ εἴπομεν μὲν ἀληθῆ περὶ
αὐτοῦ, οἷον ἐν τῷ παρόντι φαίνεται· τεθεάμεθα
D μέντοι διακείμενον αὐτό, ὥσπερ οἱ τὸν θαλάττιον
Γλαῦκον ὁρῶντες οὐκ ἂν ἔτι ῥᾳδίως αὐτοῦ ἴδοιεν
τὴν ἀρχαίαν φύσιν, ὑπὸ τοῦ τά τε παλαιὰ τοῦ

---

[a] The idea of self-contradiction is frequent in Plato. See
What Plato Said, p. 505, on *Gorg.* 482 B-C.

[b] σύνθετον: cf. *Phaedo* 78 c, Plotinus, *Enneades* i. 1. 12,
Berkeley, *Principles*, § 141 : "We have shown that the soul
is indivisible, incorporeal, unextended; and it is consequently incorruptible. . . . Changes, decay and dissolutions
. . . cannot possibly affect an active, simple, uncompounded
substance." See also Zeller, *Ph. d. Gr.* ii. 1, pp. 828-829.

[c] 603 D. See also Frutiger, *Mythes de Platon*, pp. 90 f.

[d] Such as are given in the *Phaedo*, *Phaedrus*, and perhaps
elsewhere.

[e] Cf. also *Phaedo* 82 E, 83 D-E, 81 C, and *Wisdom of
Solomon* ix. 14 φθαρτὸν γὰρ σῶμα βαρύνει ψυχήν, καὶ βρίθει τὸ

" You say truly." " But," said I, " we must not suppose this, for reason will not suffer it ; nor yet must we think that in its truest nature the soul is the kind of thing that teems with infinite diversity and unlikeness and contradiction in and with itself.[a] " " How am I to understand that ? " he said. " It is not easy," said I, " for a thing to be immortal that is composed of many elements [b] not put together in the best way, as now appeared to us [c] to be the case with the soul." " It is not likely." " Well, then, that the soul is immortal our recent argument and our other [d] proofs would constrain us to admit. But to know its true nature we must view it not marred by communion with the body [e] and other miseries as we now contemplate it, but consider adequately in the light of reason what it is when it is purified, and then you will find it to be a far more beautiful thing and will more clearly distinguish justice and injustice and all the matters that we have now discussed. But though we have stated the truth of its present appearance, its condition as we have now contemplated it resembles that of the sea-god Glaucus [f] whose first nature can hardly be made out by those who catch glimpses of him, because the original members of his

---

γεῶδες σκῆνος νοῦν πολυφρόντιδα, " for the corruptible body presseth down the soul, and the earthly tabernacle weigheth down the mind that museth upon many things."

[f] See schol. Hermann vi. 362, Eurip. Or. 364 f., Apollonius, Argon. 1310 ff., Athenaeus 296 B and D, Anth. Pal. vi. 164, Frazer on Pausanias ix. 22. 7, Gädecker, Glaukos der Meeresgott, Göttingen, 1860. Cf. Lionel Johnson's poem :

> Ah, Glaucus, soul of man !
> Encrusted by each tide
> That since the seas began
> Hath surged against thy side.

611 σώματος μέρη τὰ μὲν ἐκκεκλάσθαι, τὰ δὲ συντετρί-
φθαι καὶ πάντως λελωβῆσθαι ὑπὸ τῶν κυμάτων,
ἄλλα δὲ προσπεφυκέναι, ὄστρεά τε καὶ φυκία καὶ
πέτρας, ὥστε παντὶ μᾶλλον θηρίῳ ἐοικέναι ἢ οἷος
ἦν φύσει, οὕτω καὶ τὴν ψυχὴν ἡμεῖς θεώμεθα
διακειμένην ὑπὸ μυρίων κακῶν· ἀλλὰ δεῖ, ὦ Γλαύκων, ἐκεῖσε βλέπειν. Ποῖ; ἦ δ᾽ ὅς. Εἰς τὴν
E φιλοσοφίαν αὐτῆς, καὶ ἐννοεῖν ὧν ἅπτεται καὶ
οἵων ἐφίεται ὁμιλιῶν, ὡς ξυγγενὴς οὖσα τῷ τε
θείῳ καὶ ἀθανάτῳ καὶ τῷ ἀεὶ ὄντι, καὶ οἵα ἂν
γένοιτο τῷ τοιούτῳ πᾶσα ἐπισπομένη καὶ ὑπὸ
ταύτης τῆς ὁρμῆς ἐκκομισθεῖσα ἐκ τοῦ πόντου,
ἐν ᾧ νῦν ἐστί, καὶ περικρουσθεῖσα πέτρας τε καὶ
612 ὄστρεα, ἃ νῦν αὐτῇ ἅτε γῆν ἑστιωμένη γεηρὰ καὶ
πετρώδη πολλὰ καὶ ἄγρια περιπέφυκεν ὑπὸ τῶν
εὐδαιμόνων λεγομένων ἑστιάσεων. καὶ τότ᾽ ἄν τις
ἴδοι αὐτῆς τὴν ἀληθῆ φύσιν, εἴτε πολυειδὴς εἴτε
μονοειδὴς εἴτε ὅπη ἔχει καὶ ὅπως· νῦν δὲ τὰ ἐν
τῷ ἀνθρωπίνῳ βίῳ πάθη τε καὶ εἴδη, ὡς ἐγῷμαι,
ἐπιεικῶς αὐτῆς διεληλύθαμεν. Παντάπασι μὲν οὖν,
ἔφη.

XII. Οὐκοῦν, ἦν δ᾽ ἐγώ, τά τε ἄλλα ἀπελυσά-
B μεθα[1] ἐν τῷ λόγῳ, καὶ οὐ τοὺς μισθοὺς οὐδὲ τὰς
δόξας δικαιοσύνης ἐπηνέγκαμεν, ὥσπερ Ἡσίοδόν

---

[1] ἀπελυσάμεθα AFD Stobaeus: ἀπεδυσάμεθα M, defended
by Stallbaum.

---

[a] Cf. Tim. 42 c προσφύντα.
[b] Cf. Phaedr. 250 c ὀστρέου τρόπον δεδεσμευμένοι, Phaedo
110 A.
[c] Cf. Phaedo 79 D, Laws 899 D, and supra 494 D τὸ συγγενὲς
τῶν λόγων.
[d] Cf Phileb. 55 c περικρούωμεν, supra 519 A περιεκόπη.

body are broken off and mutilated and crushed and
in every way marred by the waves, and other parts
have attached themselves [a] to him, accretions of shells [b]
and sea-weed and rocks, so that he is more like any
wild creature than what he was by nature—even
such, I say, is our vision of the soul marred by countless evils. But we must look elsewhere, Glaucon."
" Where ? " said he. " To its love of wisdom. And
we must note the things of which it has apprehensions, and the associations for which it yearns, as
being itself akin to the divine [c] and the immortal and
to eternal being, and so consider what it might be
if it followed the gleam unreservedly and were raised
by this impulse out of the depths of this sea in
which it is now sunk, and were cleansed and scraped
free [d] of the rocks and barnacles which, because it now
feasts on earth, cling to it in wild profusion of earthy
and stony accretion by reason of these feastings that
are accounted happy. [e] And then one might see
whether in its real nature [f] it is manifold [g] or single in
its simplicity, or what is the truth about it and how. [h]
But for the present we have, I think, fairly well described its sufferings and the forms it assumes in this
human life of ours." " We certainly have," he said.

XII. "Then," said I, " we have met all the other
demands of the argument, and we have not invoked
the rewards and reputes of justice as you said Homer

---

[e] Cf. *Charm.* 158 A, *Laws* 695 A, 783 A. See λεγόμενα
ἀγαθά *supra* 491 c, 495 A, *Laws* 661 c.
[f] Cf. *Phaedo* 246 A. In *Tim.* 72 D Plato says that only
God knows the truth about the soul. See *Laws* 641 D, and
Unity of Plato's Thought, p. 42.
[g] Cf. *Phaedr.* 271 A.
[h] ὅπῃ καὶ ὅπως: cf. 621 B, *Phaedo* 100 D, *Tim.* 37 A-B,
Laws 652 A, 834 E, 899 A and B.

612 τε καὶ Ὅμηρον ὑμεῖς ἔφατε, ἀλλ' αὐτὸ δικαιοσύνην
αὐτῇ ψυχῇ ἄριστον εὕρομεν, καὶ ποιητέον εἶναι
αὐτῇ τὰ δίκαια, ἐάν τ' ἔχῃ τὸν Γύγου δακτύλιον,
ἐάν τε μή, καὶ πρὸς τοιούτῳ δακτυλίῳ τὴν Ἄϊδος
κυνῆν· Ἀληθέστατα, ἔφη, λέγεις. Ἆρ' οὖν, ἦν
δ' ἐγώ, ὦ Γλαύκων, νῦν ἤδη ἀνεπίφθονόν ἐστι
πρὸς ἐκείνοις καὶ τοὺς μισθοὺς τῇ δικαιοσύνῃ καὶ
C τῇ ἄλλῃ ἀρετῇ ἀποδοῦναι, ὅσους τε καὶ οἵους τῇ
ψυχῇ παρέχει παρ' ἀνθρώπων τε καὶ θεῶν, ζῶντός
τε ἔτι τοῦ ἀνθρώπου καὶ ἐπειδὰν τελευτήσῃ; Παντάπασι μὲν οὖν, ἦ δ' ὅς. Ἆρ' οὖν ἀποδώσετέ μοι
ἃ ἐδανείσασθε ἐν τῷ λόγῳ; Τί μάλιστα; Ἔδωκα
ὑμῖν τὸν δίκαιον δοκεῖν ἄδικον εἶναι καὶ τὸν ἄδικον
δίκαιον. ὑμεῖς γὰρ ἡγεῖσθε, κἂν εἰ μὴ δυνατὸν
εἴη ταῦτα λανθάνειν καὶ θεοὺς καὶ ἀνθρώπους,
ὅμως δοτέον εἶναι τοῦ λόγου ἕνεκα, ἵνα αὐτὴ
D δικαιοσύνη πρὸς ἀδικίαν αὐτὴν κριθείη. ἢ οὐ
μνημονεύεις; Ἀδικοίην μέντ' ἄν, ἔφη, εἰ μή.
Ἐπειδὴ τοίνυν κεκριμέναι εἰσίν, ἦν δ' ἐγώ, πάλιν
ἀπαιτῶ ὑπὲρ δικαιοσύνης, ὥσπερ ἔχει δόξης καὶ

---

[a] *Supra* 363 B-C.   [b] 359 D f.   [c] *Cf.* 367 E.
[d] *Iliad* v. 845, Blaydes on Aristoph. *Acharn.* 390.
[e] *Cf. Soph.* 243 A, *Laws* 801 E ἄνευ φθόνων, Eurip. *Hippol.*
497 οὐκ ἐπίφθονον, Aeschines, *De falsa legatione* 167 (49).
Friedländer, *Platon*, ii. p. 406 does object and finds the
passage inconsistent with the idealism of 592 and with *Laws*
899 D ff. and 905 B. *Cf.* Renan, *Averroes*, pp. 156-157,
Guyau, *Esquisse d'une morale*, pp. 140-141. See *Unity
of Plato's Thought*, p. 80 and n. 612, *Idea of Justice in
Plato's Republic*, pp. 197-198. Gomperz, ignoring this
passage and interpreting the *Republic* wholly from 367 E,
strangely argues that *Phaedo* 107 c proves that the *Phaedo*
must have been composed at a time when Plato was less
sure of the coincidence of justice and happiness.

and Hesiod [a] do, but we have proved that justice in itself is the best thing for the soul itself, and that the soul ought to do justice whether it possess the ring of Gyges [b] or not,[c] or the helmet of Hades [d] to boot." "Most true," he said. "Then," said I, "Glaucon, there can no longer be any objection,[e] can there, to our assigning to justice and virtue generally, in addition, all the various rewards and wages that they bring to the soul from men and gods, both while the man still lives and after his death?" "There certainly can be none," he said. "Will you, then, return to me what you borrowed[f] in the argument?" "What, pray?" "I granted to you that the just man should seem and be thought to be unjust and the unjust just; for you thought that, even if the concealment of these things from gods and men was an impossibility in fact, nevertheless it ought to be conceded for the sake of the argument,[g] in order that the decision might be made between absolute justice and absolute injustice. Or do you not remember?" "It would be unjust of me,[h]" he said, "if I did not." "Well, then, now that they have been compared and judged, I demand back from you in behalf of justice the repute

A religious thinker may in his theodicy justify the ways of God to man by arguing that worldly happiness is not the real happiness, and yet elsewhere remark that, as a rule, the righteous is not forsaken even in this world. *Cf. Psalm* xxxvii. 25 ff., *Prov.* x. 3 and *passim.* See Renan, *Hist. du Peuple d'Israel,* ii. p. 376: "Il en est de ces passages comme de tant de préceptes de l'Évangile, insensés si on en fait des articles de code, excellents si on n'y voit que l'expression hyperbolique de hauts sentiments moraux."

[f] *Cf. Polit.* 267 A.

[g] τοῦ λόγου ἕνεκα: not the same as λόγου ἕνεκα. See on 581 c, p. 374, note *a.*

[h] *Cf.* εἰ μὴ ἀδικῶ 608 D.

612 παρὰ θεῶν καὶ παρ' ἀνθρώπων, καὶ ἡμᾶς ὁμολογεῖν περὶ αὐτῆς δοκεῖσθαι οὕτως, ἵνα καὶ τὰ
νικητήρια κομίσηται, ἃ ἀπὸ τοῦ δοκεῖν κτωμένη
δίδωσι τοῖς ἔχουσιν αὐτήν, ἐπειδὴ καὶ τὰ ἀπὸ τοῦ
εἶναι ἀγαθὰ διδοῦσα ἐφάνη καὶ οὐκ ἐξαπατῶσα
τοὺς τῷ ὄντι λαμβάνοντας αὐτήν. Δίκαια, ἔφη,
Ε αἰτεῖ. Οὐκοῦν, ἦν δ' ἐγώ, πρῶτον μὲν τοῦτο
ἀποδώσετε, ὅτι θεούς γε οὐ λανθάνει ἑκάτερος
αὐτῶν οἷός ἐστιν; Ἀποδώσομεν, ἔφη. Εἰ δὲ μὴ
λανθάνετον, ὁ μὲν θεοφιλὴς ἂν εἴη, ὁ δὲ θεομισής,
ὥσπερ καὶ κατ' ἀρχὰς ὡμολογοῦμεν. Ἔστι ταῦτα.
Τῷ δὲ θεοφιλεῖ οὐχ ὁμολογήσομεν, ὅσα γε ἀπὸ
613 θεῶν γίγνεται, πάντα γίγνεσθαι ὡς οἷόν τε ἄριστα,
εἰ μή τι ἀναγκαῖον αὐτῷ κακὸν ἐκ προτέρας
ἁμαρτίας ὑπῆρχεν; Πάνυ μὲν οὖν. Οὕτως ἄρα
ὑποληπτέον περὶ τοῦ δικαίου ἀνδρός, ἐάν τ' ἐν
πενίᾳ γίγνηται ἐάν τ' ἐν νόσοις ἤ τινι ἄλλῳ τῶν
δοκούντων κακῶν, ὡς τούτῳ ταῦτα εἰς ἀγαθόν τι
τελευτήσει ζῶντι ἢ καὶ ἀποθανόντι. οὐ γὰρ δὴ
ὑπό γε θεῶν ποτε ἀμελεῖται, ὃς ἂν προθυμεῖσθαι
ἐθέλῃ δίκαιος γίγνεσθαι καὶ ἐπιτηδεύων ἀρετὴν εἰς
Β ὅσον δυνατὸν ἀνθρώπῳ ὁμοιοῦσθαι θεῷ. Εἰκός γ',
ἔφη, τὸν τοιοῦτον μὴ ἀμελεῖσθαι ὑπὸ τοῦ ὁμοίου.
Οὐκοῦν περὶ τοῦ ἀδίκου τἀναντία τούτων δεῖ
διανοεῖσθαι; Σφόδρα γε. Τὰ μὲν δὴ παρὰ θεῶν

---

[a] For the idiom ὥσπερ ἔχει δόξης cf. 365 A ὡς . . . ἔχουσι
τιμῆς, 389 C ὅπως . . . πράξεως ἔχει, Thucyd. i. 22 ὡς . . .
μνήμης ἔχοι. For the thought cf. Isoc. viii. 33.
[b] Cf. Phileb. 22 B and E.
[c] γε vi termini. Cf. 379 A and Class. Phil. x. p. 335.
[d] Cf. 365 D. [e] Cf. Phileb. 39 E. [f] Cf. 352 B.
[g] This recalls the faith of Socrates in Apol. 41 C-D and

that she in fact enjoys *a* from gods and men, and I ask that we admit that she is thus esteemed in order that she may gather in the prizes *b* which she wins from the seeming and bestows on her possessors, since she has been proved to bestow the blessings that come from the reality and not to deceive those who truly seek and win her." "That is a just demand," he said. "Then," said I, "will not the first of these restorations be that the gods certainly *c* are not unaware *d* of the true character of each of the two, the just and the unjust?" "We will restore that," he said. "And if they are not concealed, the one will be dear to the gods *e* and the other hateful to them, as we agreed in the beginning.*f*" "That is so." "And shall we not agree that all things that come from the gods work together for the best *g* for him that is dear to the gods, apart from the inevitable evil caused by sin in a former life *h*?" "By all means." "This, then, must be our conviction about the just man, that whether he fall into poverty or disease or any other supposed evil, for him all these things will finally prove good, both in life and in death. For by the gods assuredly that man will never be neglected who is willing and eager to be righteous, and by the practice of virtue to be likened unto god *i* so far as that is possible for man." "It is reasonable," he said, "that such a one should not be neglected by his like.*j*" "And must we not think the opposite of the unjust man?" "Most emphatically." "Such then are the prizes of victory

Phaedo 63 B-C, and anticipates the theodicy of *Laws* 899 D ff., 904 D-E ff.

h Besides obvious analogies with Buddhism, this recalls Empedocles *fr.* 115, Diels i.³ p. 267.

i Cf. ὁμοίωσις θεῷ *Theaet.* 176 B, and *What Plato Said*, p. 578, *supra* p. 72, note *d*.　　*j* Cf. *Laws* 716 C-D, 904 E.

613 τοιαῦτ' ἂν εἴη νικητήρια τῷ δικαίῳ. Κατὰ γοῦν
ἐμὴν δόξαν, ἔφη. Τί δέ, ἦν δ' ἐγώ, παρ' ἀνθρώπων; ἆρ' οὐχ ὧδε ἔχει, εἰ δεῖ τὸ ὂν τιθέναι; οὐχ
οἱ μὲν δεινοί τε καὶ ἄδικοι δρῶσιν ὅπερ οἱ δρομῆς
ὅσοι ἂν θέωσιν εὖ ἀπὸ τῶν κάτω, ἀπὸ δὲ τῶν
ἄνω μή; τὸ μὲν πρῶτον ὀξέως ἀποπηδῶσι, τελευ-
C τῶντες δὲ καταγέλαστοι γίγνονται, τὰ ὦτα ἐπὶ
τῶν ὤμων ἔχοντες καὶ ἀστεφάνωτοι ἀποτρέχοντες·
οἱ δὲ τῇ ἀληθείᾳ δρομικοὶ εἰς τέλος ἐλθόντες τά τε
ἆθλα λαμβάνουσι καὶ στεφανοῦνται. οὐχ οὕτω
καὶ περὶ τῶν δικαίων τὸ πολὺ ξυμβαίνει· πρὸς
τέλος ἑκάστης πράξεως καὶ ὁμιλίας καὶ τοῦ βίου
εὐδοκιμοῦσί τε καὶ τὰ ἆθλα παρὰ τῶν ἀνθρώπων
φέρονται; Καὶ μάλα. Ἀνέξει ἄρα λέγοντος ἐμοῦ
D περὶ τούτων, ἅπερ αὐτὸς ἔλεγες περὶ τῶν ἀδίκων;
ἐρῶ γὰρ δὴ ὅτι οἱ μὲν δίκαιοι, ἐπειδὰν πρεσβύτεροι γένωνται, ἐν τῇ αὑτῶν πόλει ἄρχουσί τε ἂν
βούλωνται τὰς ἀρχάς, γαμοῦσί τε ὁπόθεν ἂν βούλωνται, ἐκδιδόασί τε εἰς οὓς ἂν ἐθέλωσι, καὶ πάντα,
ἃ σὺ περὶ ἐκείνων, ἐγὼ νῦν λέγω περὶ τῶνδε· καὶ
αὖ καὶ περὶ τῶν ἀδίκων, ὅτι οἱ πολλοὶ αὐτῶν, καὶ
ἐὰν νέοι ὄντες λάθωσιν, ἐπὶ τέλους τοῦ δρόμου
αἱρεθέντες καταγέλαστοί εἰσι καὶ γέροντες γιγνόμενοι ἄθλιοι προπηλακίζονται ὑπὸ ξένων τε καὶ

---

[a] For the order cf. *Laws* 913 B λεγόμενον εὖ, Thucyd. i.
71. 7, Vahlen, *Op. Acad.* i. 495-496. For the figure of the
race cf. Eurip. *El.* 955, 1 *Corinthians* ix. 24 f., *Heb.* xii. 1,
Gal. ii. 2, v. 7, *Phil.* ii. 16.
[b] English idiom would say, "with their tails between
their legs." Cf. Horace, *Sat.* i. 9. 20 "dimitto auriculas."
For the idea cf. also *Laws* 730 C-D, Demosth. ii. 10, and for

which the gods bestow upon the just." " So I think, at any rate," he said. " But what," said I, " does he receive from men ? Is not this the case, if we are now to present the reality ? Do not your smart but wicked men fare as those racers do who run well [a] from the scratch but not back from the turn ? They bound nimbly away at the start, but in the end are laughed to scorn and run off the field uncrowned and with their ears on their shoulders.[b] But the true runners when they have come to the goal receive the prizes and bear away the crown. Is not this the usual outcome for the just also, that towards the end of every action and association and of life as a whole they have honour and bear away the prizes from men ? " " So it is indeed." " Will you, then, bear with me if I say of them all that you said [c] of the un-just ? For I am going to say that the just, when they become older, hold the offices in their own city if they choose, marry from what families they will, and give their children in marriage to what families they please, and everything that you said of the one I now repeat of the other ; and in turn I will say of the unjust that the most of them, even if they escape detection in youth, at the end of their course are caught and derided, and their old age [d] is made miser-able by the contumelies of strangers and townsfolk.

εἰς τέλος, *Laws* 899 ε πρὸς τέλος, Hesiod, *Works and Days* 216 ἐς τέλος ἐξελθοῦσα, Eurip. *Ion* 1621 εἰς τέλος γὰρ οἱ μὲν ἐσθλοὶ τυγχάνουσιν ἀξίων, "for the good at last shall overcome, at last attain their right." (Way, Loeb tr.)

[c] *Cf.* Vol. I. pp. 125-127, 362 B-C.
[d] *Cf. Macbeth* v. iii. 24 :

> And that which should accompany old age,
> As honour, love, obedience, troops of friends,
> I must not look to have.

PLATO

613 E ἀστῶν, μαστιγούμενοι καὶ ἃ ἄγροικα ἔφησθα σὺ
εἶναι, ἀληθῆ λέγων, [εἶτα στρεβλώσονται καὶ
ἐκκαυθήσονται·]¹ πάντα ἐκεῖνα οἴου καὶ ἐμοῦ ἀκηκοέναι ὡς πάσχουσιν. ἀλλ' ὃ λέγω, ὅρα εἰ ἀνέξει.
Καὶ πάνυ, ἔφη· δίκαια γὰρ λέγεις.

XIII. Ἃ μὲν τοίνυν, ἦν δ' ἐγώ, ζῶντι τῷ δικαίῳ
614 παρὰ θεῶν τε καὶ ἀνθρώπων ἆθλά τε καὶ μισθοὶ
καὶ δῶρα γίγνεται πρὸς ἐκείνοις τοῖς ἀγαθοῖς οἷς
αὐτὴ παρείχετο ἡ δικαιοσύνη, τοιαῦτ' ἂν εἴη. Καὶ
μάλ', ἔφη, καλά τε καὶ βέβαια. Ταῦτα τοίνυν, ἦν
δ' ἐγώ, οὐδέν ἐστι πλήθει οὐδὲ μεγέθει πρὸς ἐκεῖνα,
ἃ τελευτήσαντα ἑκάτερον περιμένει. χρὴ δ' αὐτὰ
ἀκοῦσαι, ἵνα τελέως ἑκάτερος αὐτῶν ἀπειλήφῃ τὰ
ὑπὸ τοῦ λόγου ὀφειλόμενα ἀκοῦσαι. Λέγοις ἄν,
B ἔφη, ὡς οὐ πολλὰ ἄλλ' ἥδιον ἀκούοντι. Ἀλλ' οὐ
μέντοι σοι, ἦν δ' ἐγώ, Ἀλκίνου γε ἀπόλογον ἐρῶ,
ἀλλ' ἀλκίμου μὲν ἀνδρός, Ἠρὸς τοῦ Ἀρμενίου, τὸ
γένος Παμφύλου· ὅς ποτε ἐν πολέμῳ τελευτήσας,
ἀναιρεθέντων δεκαταίων τῶν νεκρῶν ἤδη διεφθαρ-
μένων, ὑγιὴς μὲν ἀνῃρέθη, κομισθεὶς δ' οἴκαδε

---

¹ Ast, followed by Hermann and Stallbaum, omits εἶτα
στρεβλώσονται καὶ ἐκκαυθήσονται, "then they will be racked
and branded ": Jowett and Campbell and Burnet keep it.

ᵃ He turns the tables here as in *Gorg.* 527 A. The late
punishment of the wicked became an ethical commonplace.
Cf. Plutarch's *De sera numinis vindicta* 1, also *Job* and
Psalms passim.
ᵇ *Cf.* 361 ε ἀγροικοτέρως, and *Gorg.* 473 c.
ᶜ *i.e.* the just and unjust man.   ᵈ τελέως: *cf.* 361 A.
ᵉ See Proclus, *In Remp.*, Kroll ii. 96 ff., Macrob. in
Somnium Scip. i. 2. The Epicurean Colotes highly dis-

They are lashed and suffer all things ^a which you truly said are unfit for ears polite.^b Suppose yourself to have heard from me a repetition of all that they suffer. But, as I say, consider whether you will bear with me." " Assuredly," he said, " for what you say is just."

XIII. " Such then while he lives are the prizes, the wages, and the gifts that the just man receives from gods and men in addition to those blessings which justice herself bestowed." " And right fair and abiding rewards," he said. " Well, these," I said, " are nothing in number and magnitude compared with those that await both^c after death. And we must listen to the tale of them," said I, " in order that each may have received in full ^d what is due to be said of him by our argument." " Tell me," he said, " since there are not many things to which I would more gladly listen." " It is not, let me tell you," said I, " the tale ^e to Alcinous told ^f that I shall unfold, but the tale of a warrior bold,^g Er, the son of Armenius, by race a Pamphylian.^h He once upon a time was slain in battle, and when the corpses were taken up on the tenth day already decayed, was found intact,

approved of Plato's method of putting his beliefs in this form. See Chassang, *Histoire du roman*, p. 15. See also Dieterich, *Nekyia*, pp. 114 ff., and Adam *ad loc.*

^f *Odyssey* ix.-xii. The term also became proverbial for a lengthy tale. See K. Tümpel, 'Ἀλκίνου ἀπόλογος, *Philologus* 52. 523 ff.

^g Plato puns on the name Alcinous. For other puns on proper names see *supra* on 580 B. See Arthur Platt, " Plato's *Republic*, 614 B," *Class. Review*, 1911, pp. 13-14. For the ἀλλὰ μέν without a corresponding δέ he compares Aristoph. *Acharn.* 428 οὐ Βελλεροφόντης· ἀλλὰ κἀκεῖνος μὲν ἦ χωλός . . . (which Blaydes changed to ἀλλὰ μήν), *Odyssey* xv. 405 and *Eryxias* 398 B.

^h Perhaps we might say, " of the tribe of Everyman." For the question of his identity see Platt, *loc. cit.*

PLATO

614 μέλλων θάπτεσθαι δωδεκαταῖος ἐπὶ τῇ πυρᾷ κεί-
μενος ἀνεβίω, ἀναβιοὺς δ' ἔλεγεν ἃ ἐκεῖ ἴδοι. ἔφη
δέ, ἐπειδὴ οὗ ἐκβῆναι τὴν ψυχήν, πορεύεσθαι μετὰ
C πολλῶν, καὶ ἀφικνεῖσθαι σφᾶς εἰς τόπον τινὰ δαιμόνιον, ἐν ᾧ τῆς τε γῆς δύ' εἶναι χάσματα ἐχομένω
ἀλλήλοιν καὶ τοῦ οὐρανοῦ αὖ ἐν τῷ ἄνω ἄλλα
καταντικρύ· δικαστὰς δὲ μεταξὺ τούτων καθῆσθαι,
οὕς, ἐπειδὴ διαδικάσειαν, τοὺς μὲν δικαίους κελεύ-
ειν πορεύεσθαι τὴν εἰς δεξιάν τε καὶ ἄνω διὰ τοῦ
οὐρανοῦ, σημεῖα περιάψαντας τῶν δεδικασμένων
ἐν τῷ πρόσθεν, τοὺς δὲ ἀδίκους τὴν εἰς ἀριστεράν
τε καὶ κάτω, ἔχοντας καὶ τούτους ἐν τῷ ὄπισθεν
D σημεῖα πάντων ὧν ἔπραξαν. ἑαυτοῦ δὲ προσελθόν-

of the other world lies twelve days incorrupted, while his
soul was viewing the large stations of the dead." See also
Rohde, *Psyche* ii.⁶ pp. 92-93.

  ᵇ Stories of persons restored to life are fairly common in
ancient literature. There are Eurydice and Alcestis in
Greek mythology, in the Old Testament the son of the
widow revived by Elijah (1 *Kings* xvii. 17 ff. *Cf. 2 Kings*
iv. 34 ff. and xiii. 21), in the New Testament the daughter
of Jairus (*Matt.* ix. 23 f.), the son of the widow of Nain (*Luke*
vii. 11 ff.), and Lazarus (*John* xi.). But none of these recount
their adventures. *Cf.* Tennyson, "In Memoriam," xxxi.:

> Where wert thou, brother, those four days? . . .
> The rest remaineth unreveal'd;
> He told it not; or something seal'd
> The lips of that Evangelist.

Cf. also *Luke* xvi. 31 "If they hear not Moses and the
prophets neither will they be persuaded though one rose
from the dead." But in that very parable Lazarus is shown
in Abraham's bosom and the rich man in torment. See
further, Proclus, *In Remp.* ii. pp. 113-116, Rohde, *Psyche*
ii.⁶ p. 191.

  ᶜ For the indirect reflexive *cf.* p. 507, note *f*, on 617 ᴇ.

  ᵈ For the description of the place of judgement *cf.* also

492

and having been brought home, at the moment of his funeral, on the twelfth day [a] as he lay upon the pyre, revived,[b] and after coming to life related what, he said, he had seen in the world beyond. He said that when his soul [c] went forth from his body he journeyed with a great company and that they came to a mysterious region [d] where there were two openings side by side in the earth, and above and over against them in the heaven two others, and that judges were sitting [e] between these, and that after every judgement they bade the righteous journey to the right and upwards through the heaven with tokens attached [f] to them in front of the judgement passed upon them, and the unjust to take the road to the left [g] and downward, they too wearing behind signs of all that had befallen them, and that when he himself drew near they told

Gorg. 524 A. *Cf. Phaedo* 107 D, 113 D, where there is no description but simply the statement that the souls are brought to a place and judged. On the topography of the myth in general *cf.* Bréhier, *La Philos. de Plot.* pp. 28-29 : " Voyez, par exemple, la manière dont Numénius . . . interprète le mythe du Xe livre de la *République*, et comment il précise, avec la lourdeur d'un théologien, les traits que la poésie de Platon avait abandonnés à l'imagination du lecteur. Le lieu du jugement devient le centre du monde ; le ciel platonicien devient la sphère des fixes ; le ' lieu souterrain ' où sont punies les âmes, ce sont les planètes ; la ' bouche du ciel,' par laquelle les âmes descendront à la naissance, est le tropique du Cancer ; et c'est par le Capricorne qu'elles remontent."

[e] *Cf. Gorg.* 523 E f., 524 E-525 B, 526 B-C.

[f] *Cf. Gorg.* 526 B, Dante, *Inferno*, v. 9 f. :

> E quel conoscitor delle peccata
> vede qual luogo d' inferno è da essa ;
> cignesi con la coda tante volte
> quantunque gradi vuol che giù sia messa.

[g] *Cf. Gorg.* 525 A-B, 526 B. For "right" and "left" *cf.* the story of the last judgement, *Matt.* xxv. 33-34 and 41.

614 τος εἰπεῖν, ὅτι δέοι αὐτὸν ἄγγελον ἀνθρώποις
γενέσθαι τῶν ἐκεῖ καὶ διακελεύοιντό οἱ ἀκούειν τε
καὶ θεᾶσθαι πάντα τὰ ἐν τῷ τόπῳ. ὁρᾶν δὴ ταύτῃ
μὲν καθ᾽ ἑκάτερον τὸ χάσμα τοῦ οὐρανοῦ τε καὶ
τῆς γῆς ἀπιούσας τὰς ψυχάς, ἐπειδὴ αὐταῖς δικα-
σθείη, κατὰ δὲ τὼ ἑτέρω ἐκ μὲν τοῦ ἀνιέναι ἐκ
τῆς γῆς μεστὰς αὐχμοῦ τε καὶ κόνεως, ἐκ δὲ τοῦ
ἑτέρου καταβαίνειν ἑτέρας ἐκ τοῦ οὐρανοῦ καθαράς·
Ε καὶ τὰς ἀεὶ ἀφικνουμένας ὥσπερ ἐκ πολλῆς πορείας
φαίνεσθαι ἥκειν, καὶ ἀσμένας εἰς τὸν λειμῶνα
ἀπιούσας οἷον ἐν πανηγύρει κατασκηνᾶσθαι, καὶ
ἀσπάζεσθαί τε ἀλλήλας ὅσαι γνώριμαι, καὶ πυνθά-
νεσθαι τάς τε ἐκ τῆς γῆς ἡκούσας παρὰ τῶν ἑτέρων τὰ ἐκεῖ καὶ τὰς ἐκ τοῦ οὐρανοῦ τὰ παρ᾽
ἐκείναις· διηγεῖσθαι δὲ ἀλλήλαις τὰς μὲν ὀδυ-
615 ρομένας τε καὶ κλαιούσας, ἀναμιμνησκομένας ὅσα
τε καὶ οἷα πάθοιεν καὶ ἴδοιεν ἐν τῇ ὑπὸ γῆς πορείᾳ
—εἶναι δὲ τὴν πορείαν χιλιέτη—τὰς δ᾽ αὖ ἐκ
τοῦ οὐρανοῦ εὐπαθείας διηγεῖσθαι καὶ θέας ἀμηχά-
νους τὸ κάλλος. τὰ μὲν οὖν πολλά, ὦ Γλαύκων,
πολλοῦ χρόνου διηγήσασθαι· τὸ δ᾽ οὖν κεφάλαιον
ἔφη τόδε εἶναι, ὅσα πώποτέ τινα ἠδίκησαν καὶ
ὅσους ἕκαστοι, ὑπὲρ ἁπάντων δίκην δεδωκέναι ἐν
μέρει, ὑπὲρ ἑκάστου δεκάκις, τοῦτο δ᾽ εἶναι κατὰ
Β ἑκατονταετηρίδα ἑκάστην, ὡς βίου ὄντος τοσού-

---

[a] Cf. the rich man's request that a messenger be sent to
his brethren, *Luke* xvi. 27-31.

[b] ἐκεῖ: so in 330 D, 365 A, 498 C, *Phaedo* 61 E, 64 A,
67 B, 68 E, *Apol.* 40 E, 41 C, *Crito* 54 B, *Symp.* 192 E. In
500 D and *Phaedr.* 250 A it refers to the world of the ideas,
in 516 C and 520 C to the world of the cave.

[c] Cf. *Gorg.* 524 A.

him that he must be the messenger [a] to mankind to tell them of that other world,[b] and they charged him to give ear and to observe everything in the place. And so he said that here he saw, by each opening of heaven and earth, the souls departing after judgement had been passed upon them, while, by the other pair of openings, there came up from the one in the earth souls full of squalor and dust, and from the second there came down from heaven a second procession of souls clean and pure, and that those which arrived from time to time appeared to have come as it were from a long journey and gladly departed to the meadow [c] and encamped [d] there as at a festival,[e] and acquaintances greeted one another, and those which came from the earth questioned the others about conditions up yonder, and those from heaven asked how it fared with those others. And they told their stories to one another, the one lamenting and wailing as they recalled how many and how dreadful things they had suffered and seen in their journey beneath the earth [f]— it lasted a thousand years [g]—while those from heaven related their delights and visions of a beauty beyond words. To tell it all, Glaucon, would take all our time, but the sum, he said, was this. For all the wrongs they had ever done to anyone and all whom they had severally wronged they had paid the penalty [h] in turn tenfold for each, and the measure of this was by periods of a hundred years each,[i] so that on the assumption

---

[d] *Cf.* 621 A, 610 E, and *John* i. 14 ἐσκήνωσεν.
[e] *Cf.* 421 B.
[f] *Cf. Phaedr.* 256 D, *Epist.* vii. 335 B-C.
[g] *Phaedr.* 249 A, Virgil, *Aen.* vi. 748.
[h] *Cf. Phaedo* 113 D-E.
[i] The ideal Hindu length of life is said to be 100 years.

615 τοῦ τοῦ ἀνθρωπίνου, ἵνα δεκαπλάσιον τὸ ἔκτισμα
τοῦ ἀδικήματος ἐκτίνοιεν· καὶ οἷον εἴ τινες πολ-
λῶν¹ θανάτων ἦσαν αἴτιοι, ἢ πόλεις προδόντες ἢ
στρατόπεδα καὶ εἰς δουλείας ἐμβεβληκότες, ἢ
τινος ἄλλης κακουχίας μεταίτιοι, πάντων τούτων
δεκαπλασίας ἀλγηδόνας ὑπὲρ ἑκάστου κομίσαιντο,
καὶ αὖ εἴ τινας εὐεργεσίας εὐεργετηκότες καὶ
C δίκαιοι καὶ ὅσιοι γεγονότες εἶεν, κατὰ ταὐτὰ τὴν
ἀξίαν κομίζοιντο. τῶν δὲ εὐθὺς γενομένων καὶ
ὀλίγον χρόνον βιούντων πέρι ἄλλα ἔλεγεν οὐκ ἄξια
μνήμης· εἰς δὲ θεοὺς ἀσεβείας τε καὶ εὐσεβείας
καὶ γονέας καὶ αὐτόχειρος φόνου μείζους ἔτι τοὺς
μισθοὺς διηγεῖτο. ἔφη γὰρ δὴ παραγενέσθαι
ἐρωτωμένῳ ἑτέρῳ ὑπὸ ἑτέρου ὅπου εἴη Ἀρδιαῖος
ὁ μέγας. ὁ δὲ Ἀρδιαῖος οὗτος τῆς Παμφυλίας ἔν
τινι πόλει τύραννος ἐγεγόνει, ἤδη χιλιοστὸν ἔτος
εἰς ἐκεῖνον τὸν χρόνον, γέροντά τε πατέρα ἀπο-
D κτείνας καὶ πρεσβύτερον ἀδελφόν, καὶ ἄλλα δὴ
πολλά τε καὶ ἀνόσια εἰργασμένος, ὡς ἐλέγετο.
ἔφη οὖν τὸν ἐρωτώμενον εἰπεῖν, οὐχ ἥκει, φάναι,
οὐδ᾽ ἂν ἥξει δεῦρο.

XIV. Ἐθεασάμεθα γὰρ οὖν δὴ καὶ τοῦτο τῶν
δεινῶν θεαμάτων. ἐπειδὴ ἐγγὺς τοῦ στομίου ἦμεν
μέλλοντες ἀνιέναι καὶ τἆλλα πάντα πεπονθότες,

---

¹ πολλῶν scr. Ven. 184, Hermann and Adam: πολλοῖς
D Stobaeus: πολλοὶ AFM.

ᵃ For the words cf. *Tim.* 76 ε εὐθὺς γιγνομένοις. Plato
does not take up the problem of infant damnation!
Warburton says, "and I make no doubt but the things not
worthy to be remembered was the doctrine of infants in
purgatory, which appears to have given Plato much scandal,
who did not at that time at least reflect upon its original
and use." See also Mozley, *Augustinian Doctrine of Pre-*

that this was the length of human life the punishment might be ten times the crime ; as for example that if anyone had been the cause of many deaths or had betrayed cities and armies and reduced them to slavery, or had been participant in any other iniquity, they might receive in requital pains tenfold for each of these wrongs, and again if any had done deeds of kindness and been just and holy men they might receive their due reward in the same measure ; and other things not worthy of record he said of those who had just been born*a* and lived but a short time ; and he had still greater requitals to tell of piety and impiety towards the gods and parents *b* and of self-slaughter. For he said that he stood by when one was questioned by another ' Where is Ardiaeus*c* the Great ? ' Now this Ardiaeos had been tyrant in a certain city of Pamphylia just a thousand years before that time and had put to death his old father and his elder brother, and had done many other unholy deeds, as was the report. So he said that the one questioned replied, ' He has not come,' said he, ' nor will he be likely to come here.

XIV. " ' For indeed this was one of the dreadful sights we beheld ; when we were near the mouth and about to issue forth and all our other sufferings were

---

destination, p. 307, *apud* Seebohm, *The Oxford Reformers* (3rd ed.), p. 495 : " Augustine had laid down that the punishment of such children was the mildest of all punishment in hell. . . . Aquinas laid down the further hypothesis that this punishment was not pain of body or mind, but want of the Divine vision." *Cf.* Virgil, *Aen.* vi. 427, *Anth. Pal.* ix. 359. 10 θανεῖν αὐτίκα τικτόμενον. Stallbaum and Ast think ἀποθανόντων dropped out of the text after γενομένων.

b *Cf. Phaedo* 113 E-114 A, where there is a special penalty for murderers and parricides.

c *Cf.* Archelaus in *Gorg.* 471.

615 ἐκεῖνόν τε κατείδομεν ἐξαίφνης καὶ ἄλλους, σχεδόν
τι αὐτῶν τοὺς πλείστους τυράννους· ἦσαν δὲ καὶ
E ἰδιῶταί τινες τῶν μεγάλα ἡμαρτηκότων· οὓς
οἰομένους ἤδη ἀναβήσεσθαι οὐκ ἐδέχετο τὸ στόμιον,
ἀλλ' ἐμυκᾶτο, ὁπότε τις τῶν οὕτως ἀνιάτως
ἐχόντων εἰς πονηρίαν ἢ μὴ ἱκανῶς δεδωκὼς δίκην
ἐπιχειροῖ ἀνιέναι. ἐνταῦθα δὴ ἄνδρες, ἔφη, ἄγριοι,
διάπυροι ἰδεῖν, παρεστῶτες καὶ καταμανθάνοντες
τὸ φθέγμα τοὺς μὲν διαλαβόντες ἦγον, τὸν δὲ
616 Ἀρδιαῖον καὶ ἄλλους συμποδίσαντες χεῖράς τε καὶ
πόδας καὶ κεφαλήν, καταβαλόντες καὶ ἐκδεί-
ραντες, εἷλκον παρὰ τὴν ὁδὸν ἐκτὸς ἐπ' ἀσπαλάθων
κνάπτοντες καὶ τοῖς ἀεὶ παριοῦσι σημαίνοντες, ὧν
ἕνεκά τε καὶ ὅτι εἰς τὸν τάρταρον ἐμπεσούμενοι
ἄγοιντο. ἔνθα δὴ φόβων, ἔφη, πολλῶν καὶ παντοδαπῶν σφίσι γεγονότων, τοῦτον ὑπερβάλλειν, μὴ
γένοιτο ἑκάστῳ τὸ φθέγμα, ὅτε ἀναβαίνοι, καὶ
ἀσμενέστατα ἕκαστον σιγήσαντος ἀναβῆναι. καὶ
τὰς μὲν δὴ δίκας τε καὶ τιμωρίας τοιαύτας τινὰς
B εἶναι, καὶ αὖ τὰς εὐεργεσίας ταύταις ἀντιστρόφους·
ἐπειδὴ δὲ τοῖς ἐν τῷ λειμῶνι ἑκάστοις ἑπτὰ ἡμέραι
γένοιντο, ἀναστάντας ἐντεῦθεν δεῖν τῇ ὀγδόῃ πο-

---

[a] Cf. *Gorg.* 525 D-526 A, Dante, *Inferno* xii. 100 ff., Spenser, *F.Q.* i. v. 51 :

> But most of all which in that dungeon lay
> Fell from high Princes courtes or Ladies bowres.

Lang, " Helen of Troy " :

> Oh, Paris, what is power?   Tantalus
> And Sisyphus were kings long time ago,
> But now they lie in the Lake Dolorous;
> The halls of hell are noisy with their woe.

[b] Cf. *Gorg.* 525 c, and *What Plato Said*, p. 536, on *Phaedo*

ended, we suddenly caught sight of him and of others, the most of them, I may say, tyrants.[a] But there were some of private station, of those who had committed great crimes. And when these supposed that at last they were about to go up and out, the mouth would not receive them, but it bellowed when anyone of the incurably wicked [b] or of those who had not completed their punishment tried to come up. And thereupon,' he said, ' savage men of fiery aspect [c] who stood by and took note of the voice laid hold on them [d] and bore them away. But Ardiaeus and others they bound hand and foot and head and flung down and flayed them and dragged them by the wayside, carding them on thorns and signifying to those who from time to time passed by for what cause they were borne away, and that they were to be hurled into Tartarus.[e] ' And then, though many and manifold dread things had befallen them, this fear exceeded all —lest each one should hear the voice when he tried to go up, and each went up most gladly when it had kept silence. And the judgements and penalties were somewhat after this manner, and the blessings were their counterparts. But when seven days had elapsed for each group in the meadow, they were required to rise up on the eighth and journey on, and they came

113 E. Biggs, *Christian Platonists*, ii. p. 147 " At the first assize there will be found those who like Ardiaeus are incurable."

[c] This naturally suggests the devils of Dante (*Inferno* xxi. 25 ff.) and other mediaeval literature. See Dieterich, *Nekyia*, p. 4 and pp. 60 f.

[d] See Rogers on Aristoph. *Knights* 262. *Cf.* Herod. i. 92 ἐπὶ κνάφου ἕλκων διέφθειρε.

[e] *Il.* viii. 13 f., Hesiod, *Theog.* 682, 721, etc., Pind. *Pyth.* i. 15 f., Eurip. *Orest.* 265 μέσον μ' ὀχμάζεις ὡς βάλῃς εἰς Τάρταρον.

616 ῥεύεσθαι, καὶ ἀφικνεῖσθαι τεταρταίους ὅθεν καθορᾶν
ἄνωθεν διὰ παντὸς τοῦ οὐρανοῦ καὶ γῆς τεταμένον
φῶς εὐθύ, οἷον κίονα, μάλιστα τῇ ἴριδι προσφερῆ,
λαμπρότερον δὲ καὶ καθαρώτερον. εἰς ὃ ἀφικέσθαι
C προελθόντας ἡμερησίαν ὁδόν, καὶ ἰδεῖν αὐτόθι κατὰ
μέσον τὸ φῶς ἐκ τοῦ οὐρανοῦ τὰ ἄκρα αὐτοῦ τῶν
δεσμῶν τεταμένα· εἶναι γὰρ τοῦτο τὸ φῶς ξύνδεσμον τοῦ οὐρανοῦ, οἷον τὰ ὑποζώματα τῶν
τριήρων, οὕτω πᾶσαν ξυνέχον τὴν περιφοράν· ἐκ
δὲ τῶν ἄκρων τεταμένον Ἀνάγκης ἄτρακτον, δι᾽
οὗ πάσας ἐπιστρέφεσθαι τὰς περιφοράς· οὗ τὴν
μὲν ἠλακάτην τε καὶ τὸ ἄγκιστρον εἶναι ἐξ ἀδά-
μαντος, τὸν δὲ σφόνδυλον μικτὸν ἔκ τε τούτου καὶ
ἄλλων γενῶν. τὴν δὲ τοῦ σφονδύλου φύσιν εἶναι
D τοιάνδε· τὸ μὲν σχῆμα οἷαπερ ἡ τοῦ ἐνθάδε,
νοῆσαι δὲ δεῖ ἐξ ὧν ἔλεγε τοιόνδε αὐτὸν εἶναι,
ὥσπερ ἂν εἰ ἐν ἑνὶ μεγάλῳ σφονδύλῳ κοίλῳ καὶ
ἐξεγλυμμένῳ διαμπερὲς ἄλλος τοιοῦτος ἐλάττων
ἐγκέοιτο ἁρμόττων, καθάπερ οἱ κάδοι οἱ εἰς
ἀλλήλους ἁρμόττοντες· καὶ οὕτω δὴ τρίτον ἄλλον
καὶ τέταρτον καὶ ἄλλους τέτταρας. ὀκτὼ γὰρ
εἶναι τοὺς ξύμπαντας σφονδύλους, ἐν ἀλλήλοις

ᵃ *Cf.* Blaydes on Aristoph. *Knights* 279, Acts xxvii. 17.

ᵇ *Cf.* Plotinus, *Enn.* ii. 3 § 9, p. 35, vol. ii. Budé ed.
" Mais (dira-t-on) rappelons-nous ' le fuseau '; pour les
anciens, c'était un fuseau matériel que tournent en filant les
Moires; pour Platon, il représente le ciel des fixes; or les
Moires et la Nécessité, leur mère, en le faisant tourner, filent
le destin de chaque être à sa naissance; par elle, les êtres
engendrés arrivent à la naissance," etc. St. Paulinus Nolanus
calls it a *deliramentum.* Tannery, *Science hellène*, p. 238,
thinks it alludes to the system of Parmenides. " Le fuseau
central de la Nécessité l'indique suffisamment; si la présence

in four days to a spot whence they discerned, extended from above throughout the heaven and the earth, a straight light like a pillar, most nearly resembling the rainbow, but brighter and purer. To this they came after going forward a day's journey, and they saw there at the middle of the light the extremities of its fastenings stretched from heaven; for this light was the girdle of the heavens like the undergirders *a* of triremes, holding together in like manner the entire revolving vault. And from the extremities was stretched the spindle of Necessity,*b* through which all the orbits turned. Its staff and its hook were made of adamant, and the whorl of these and other kinds was commingled. And the nature of the whorl was this: Its shape was that of those in our world, but from his description we must conceive it to be as if in one great whorl, hollow and scooped out, there lay enclosed, right through, another like it but smaller, fitting into it as boxes that fit into one another,*c* and in like manner another, a third, and a fourth, and four others, for there were eight of the whorls in all, lying within one another, showing their

des sirènes est une marque de pythagorisme, elle peut seulement signifier soit les relations de Parménide avec l'école soit plutôt l'origine des déterminations particulières que donne Platon et qui évidemment ne remontent pas à l'Éléate." *Cf. ibid.* p. 246. For various details of the picture *cf.* Milton, the Genius's speech in "Arcades" (quoted and commented on in E. M. W. Tillyard, *Milton*, p. 376).

c Cf. Burnet, *Early Greek Philos.* pp. 216-217 "In Plato's Myth of Er, which is certainly Pythagorean in its general character, we do not hear of spheres but of the 'lips' of concentric whorls fitted into one another like a nest of boxes . . ." With 616-617 *cf. Laws* 822 A-B, *Tim.* 36 D, Dante, *Convivio,* ii. 3. 5 ff. The names of the planets occur first in *Epinomis* 987 B-C.

616 E ἐγκειμένους, κύκλους ἄνωθεν τὰ χείλη φαίνοντας,
νῶτον συνεχὲς ἑνὸς σφονδύλου ἀπεργαζομένους
περὶ τὴν ἠλακάτην· ἐκείνην δὲ διὰ μέσου τοῦ
ὀγδόου διαμπερὲς ἐληλάσθαι. τὸν μὲν οὖν πρῶτόν
τε καὶ ἐξωτάτω σφόνδυλον πλατύτατον τὸν τοῦ
χείλους κύκλον ἔχειν, τὸν δὲ τοῦ ἕκτου δεύτερον,
τρίτον δὲ τὸν τοῦ τετάρτου, τέταρτον δὲ τὸν τοῦ
ὀγδόου, πέμπτον δὲ τὸν τοῦ ἑβδόμου, ἕκτον δὲ τὸν
τοῦ πέμπτου, ἕβδομον δὲ τὸν τοῦ τρίτου, ὄγδοον δὲ
τὸν τοῦ δευτέρου. καὶ τὸν μὲν τοῦ μεγίστου
ποικίλον, τὸν δὲ τοῦ ἑβδόμου λαμπρότατον, τὸν δὲ
617 τοῦ ὀγδόου τὸ χρῶμα ἀπὸ τοῦ ἑβδόμου ἔχειν προσ-
λάμποντος, τὸν δὲ τοῦ δευτέρου καὶ πέμπτου παρα-
πλήσια ἀλλήλοις, ξανθότερα ἐκείνων, τρίτον δὲ
λευκότατον χρῶμα ἔχειν, τέταρτον δὲ ὑπέρυθρον,
δεύτερον δὲ λευκότητι τὸν ἕκτον. κυκλεῖσθαι δὲ
δὴ στρεφόμενον τὸν ἄτρακτον ὅλον μὲν τὴν αὐτὴν
φοράν, ἐν δὲ τῷ ὅλῳ περιφερομένῳ τοὺς μὲν ἐντὸς
ἑπτὰ κύκλους τὴν ἐναντίαν τῷ ὅλῳ ἠρέμα περι-
φέρεσθαι, αὐτῶν δὲ τούτων τάχιστα μὲν ἰέναι τὸν
B ὄγδοον, δευτέρους δὲ καὶ ἅμα ἀλλήλοις τόν τε
ἕβδομον καὶ ἕκτον καὶ πέμπτον· τρίτον[1] δὲ φορᾷ
ἰέναι, ὡς σφίσι φαίνεσθαι, ἐπανακυκλούμενον τὸν
τέταρτον· τέταρτον δὲ τὸν τρίτον καὶ πέμπτον
τὸν δεύτερον. στρέφεσθαι δὲ αὐτὸν ἐν τοῖς τῆς
Ἀνάγκης γόνασιν. ἐπὶ δὲ τῶν κύκλων αὐτοῦ
ἄνωθεν ἐφ᾽ ἑκάστου βεβηκέναι Σειρῆνα συμπερι-
φερομένην, φωνὴν μίαν ἱεῖσαν, ἕνα τόνον[2]· ἐκ πασῶν

---

[1] See note b, p. 503.

[2] ἕνα τόνον AM Proclus: ἀνὰ τόνον D: ἀνατόνον F: ἀνάτονον
mss. recc.

---

[a] Burnet, op. cit. p. 123, says: " This view that the planets

rims as circles from above and forming the continuous
back of a single whorl about the shaft, which was
driven home through the middle of the eighth. Now
the first and outmost whorl had the broadest circular
rim, that of the sixth was second, and third was that
of the fourth, and fourth was that of the eighth, fifth
that of the seventh, sixth that of the fifth, seventh
that of the third, eighth that of the second ; and that
of the greatest was spangled, that of the seventh
brightest, that of the eighth took its colour from the
seventh, which shone upon it. The colours of the
second and fifth were like one another and more yellow
than the two former. The third had the whitest colour,
and the fourth was of a slightly ruddy hue ; the sixth
was second in whiteness. The staff turned as a whole
in a circle with the same movement, but within the
whole as it revolved the seven inner circles revolved
gently in the opposite direction to the whole,[a] and of
these seven the eighth moved most swiftly, and next
and together with one another the seventh, sixth and
fifth ; and third [b] in swiftness, as it appeared to them,
moved the fourth with returns upon itself, and fourth
the third and fifth the second. And the spindle
turned on the knees of Necessity, and up above
on each of the rims of the circles a Siren stood,
borne around in its revolution and uttering one
sound, one note, and from all the eight there was

had an orbital motion from west to east is attributed by
Aetios ii. 16. 3 to Alkmaion (96), which certainly implies
that Pythagoras did not hold it. As we shall see (152) it is
far from clear that any of the Pythagoreans did. It seems
rather to be Plato's discovery." Cf. ibid. p. 352.

[b] The best mss. have τὸν before τρίτον. It is retained by
some editors, but Schleiermacher rejected it and Adam and
Burnet omit it.

617 δὲ ὀκτὼ οὐσῶν μίαν ἁρμονίαν ξυμφωνεῖν. ἄλλας
C δὲ καθημένας πέριξ δι' ἴσου τρεῖς, ἐν θρόνῳ
ἑκάστην, θυγατέρας τῆς Ἀνάγκης Μοίρας λευ-
χειμονούσας, στέμματά ἐπὶ τῶν κεφαλῶν ἐχούσας,
Λάχεσίν τε καὶ Κλωθὼ καὶ Ἄτροπον, ὑμνεῖν
πρὸς τὴν τῶν Σειρήνων ἁρμονίαν, Λάχεσιν μὲν
τὰ γεγονότα, Κλωθὼ δὲ τὰ ὄντα, Ἄτροπον δὲ τὰ
μέλλοντα. καὶ τὴν μὲν Κλωθὼ τῇ δεξιᾷ χειρὶ
ἐφαπτομένην συνεπιστρέφειν τοῦ ἀτράκτου τὴν ἔξω
περιφοράν, διαλείπουσαν χρόνον, τὴν δὲ Ἄτροπον
τῇ ἀριστερᾷ τὰς ἐντὸς αὖ ὡσαύτως· τὴν δὲ
D Λάχεσιν ἐν μέρει ἑκατέρας ἑκατέρᾳ τῇ χειρὶ
ἐφάπτεσθαι.

XV. Σφᾶς οὖν, ἐπειδὴ ἀφικέσθαι, εὐθὺς δεῖν
ἰέναι πρὸς τὴν Λάχεσιν. προφήτην οὖν τινα σφᾶς
πρῶτον μὲν ἐν τάξει διαστῆσαι, ἔπειτα λαβόντα ἐκ
τῶν τῆς Λαχέσεως γονάτων κλήρους τε καὶ βίων
παραδείγματα, ἀναβάντα ἐπί τι βῆμα ὑψηλὸν
εἰπεῖν· Ἀνάγκης θυγατρὸς κόρης Λαχέσεως λόγος.

---

a The music of the spheres. *Cf.* Cic. *De nat. deor.* iii.
9. 26, Mayor, vol. iii. p. 86, Macrob. on *Somn. Scip.* ii. 3,
Ritter-Preller (9th ed.), pp. 69-70 (§§ 81-82), K. Gronau, *Posei-
donios und die jüdisch-christliche Genesisexegese*, pp. 59-61.
Aristotle's comment, *De caelo* 290 b 12 ff., is that the notion
of a music of the spheres is pretty and ingenious, but not
true. He reports the (Pythagorean?) explanation that we
do not hear it because we have been accustomed to it from
birth. See Carl v. Jan, " Die Harmonie der Sphären,"
Philologus, lii. 13 ff. *Cf.* Shakes. *Merchant of Venice*, v. i. 60 :

There's not the smallest orb which thou behold'st
But in his motion like an angel sings,
Still quiring to the young ey'd cherubims . . .

Milton, " Arcades " (Tillyard, p. 60. *Ibid.* p. 375, he says that
Plato is referred to in Milton's academic exercise *De sphae-
rarum concentu*); Pope, *Essay on Man*, i. 201-202:

the concord of a single harmony.[a] And there were other three who sat round about at equal intervals, each one on her throne, the Fates,[b] daughters of Necessity, clad in white vestments with filleted heads, Lachesis, and Clotho, and Atropos, who sang in unison with the music of the Sirens, Lachesis singing the things that were, Clotho the things that are, and Atropos the things that are to be. And Clotho with the touch of her right hand helped to turn the outer circumference of the spindle, pausing from time to time. Atropos with her left hand in like manner helped to turn the inner circles, and Lachesis alternately with either hand lent a hand to each.

XV. " Now when they arrived they were straightway bidden to go before Lachesis, and then a certain prophet[c] first marshalled them in orderly intervals, and thereupon took from the lap of Lachesis lots and patterns of lives and went up to a lofty platform and spoke, ' This is the word of Lachesis, the maiden

> If Nature thundered in his opening ears
> And stunned him with the music of the spheres.

Complete Poems of Henry More, p. 77. Addison rationalizes the thought:

> The spacious firmament on high . . .
> What though in solemn silence all
> Move round the dark terrestrial ball;
> What though no real voice or sound
> Amidst their radiant orbs be found?
> In reason's ear they all rejoice
> And utter forth a glorious voice,
> For ever singing as they shine:
> The hand that made us is divine.

[b] Pictured in Michelangelo's *Le Parche*. *Cf.* Catullus 64. 306 ff.; Lowell, " Villa Franca ": " Spin, Clotho, spin, Lachesis twist and Atropos sever."

[c] See *What Plato Said*, p. 550, on *Phaedr.* 235 c.

617 ψυχαὶ ἐφήμεροι, ἀρχὴ ἄλλης περιόδου θνητοῦ
E γένους θανατηφόρου. οὐχ ὑμᾶς δαίμων λήξεται,
ἀλλ' ὑμεῖς δαίμονα αἱρήσεσθε. πρῶτος δ' ὁ
λαχὼν πρῶτος αἱρείσθω βίον, ᾧ συνέσται ἐξ
ἀνάγκης. ἀρετὴ δὲ ἀδέσποτον, ἣν τιμῶν καὶ
ἀτιμάζων πλέον καὶ ἔλαττον αὐτῆς ἕκαστος ἕξει.
αἰτία ἑλομένου· θεὸς ἀναίτιος. ταῦτα εἰπόντα
ῥῖψαι ἐπὶ πάντας τοὺς κλήρους, τὸν δὲ παρ' αὑτὸν
πεσόντα ἕκαστον ἀναιρεῖσθαι, πλὴν οὗ· ἓ δὲ οὐκ
ἐᾶν· τῷ δὲ ἀνελομένῳ δῆλον εἶναι, ὁπόστος εἰλήχει.
618 μετὰ δὲ τοῦτο αὖθις τὰ τῶν βίων παραδείγματα
εἰς τὸ πρόσθεν σφῶν θεῖναι ἐπὶ τὴν γῆν, πολὺ
πλείω τῶν παρόντων, εἶναι δὲ παντοδαπά· ζῴων
τε γὰρ πάντων βίους καὶ δὴ καὶ τοὺς ἀνθρωπίνους
ἅπαντας· τυραννίδας τε γὰρ ἐν αὐτοῖς εἶναι, τὰς
μὲν διατελεῖς, τὰς δὲ καὶ μεταξὺ διαφθειρομένας
καὶ εἰς πενίας τε καὶ φυγὰς καὶ εἰς πτωχείας

---

a Cf. Laws 923 A, Pindar, Pyth. viii. 95, Aesch. Prom.
83, 547, Aristot. Hist. an. 552 b 18 f., Cic. Tusc. i. 39. 94,
Plut. Cons. ad Apol. 6 (104 A) ἀνθρώπων . . . ἐφήμερα τὰ
σώματα, ibid. 27 (115 D) ἐφήμερον σπέρμα. See also Stallbaum
ad loc., and for the thought Soph. Ajax 125-126, Iliad vi.
146, Mimnermus ii. 1, Soph. fr. 12 and 859 (Nauck), Job
vii. 6, viii. 9, ix. 25, xiv. 2, xxi. 17, etc.

b Cf. Swinburne, " The Life of Man " (from Atalanta in
Calydon) :

Life the shadow of death.

ibid.

With life before and after
And death beneath and above,
For a day and a night and a morrow,
That his strength might endure for a span.

and " The Garden of Proserpine " : " Here life hath death for
neighbour."

daughter of Necessity, "Souls that live for a day,[a] now is the beginning of another cycle of mortal generation where birth is the beacon of death[b]. No divinity[c] shall cast lots for you, but you shall choose your own deity. Let him to whom falls the first lot first select a life to which he shall cleave of necessity. But virtue has no master over her,[d] and each shall have more or less of her as he honours her or does her despite. The blame is his who chooses: God is blameless.[e]" So saying, the prophet flung the lots out among them all, and each took up the lot that fell by his side, except himself; him they did not permit.[f] And whoever took up a lot saw plainly what number he had drawn. And after this again the prophet placed the patterns of lives before them on the ground, far more numerous than the assembly. They were of every variety, for there were lives of all kinds of animals and all sorts of human lives, for there were tyrannies among them, some uninterrupted till the end[g] and others destroyed midway and issuing in penuries and exiles and beg-

[c] Zeller-Nestle, p. 166, says that this looks like intentional correction of *Phaedo* 107 D. *Cf. Phaedo* 113 D and *Lysias* ii. 78 ὅ τε δαίμων ὁ τὴν ἡμετέραν μοῖραν εἰληχὼς ἀπαραίτητος. Arnobius, *Adversus gentes*, ii. 64, says that similarly Christ offers us redemption but does not force it upon us.

[d] *Cf.* Milton's "Love Virtue; she alone is free" (*Comus*).

[e] Justin Martyr, *Apol.* xliv. 8, quotes this. *Cf. Tim.* 42 D, Dieterich, *Nekyia*, p. 115, *Odyssey* i. 32 f., Bacchylides xiv. 51 f. (Jebb, p. 366) Ζεὺς . . . οὐκ αἴτιος θνατοῖς μεγάλων ἀχέων, etc., Manitius, *Gesch. d. lat. Lit. d. Mittelalters*, ii. p. 169. For the problem of evil in Plato see *What Plato Said*, p. 578 on *Theaet.* 176 A, and for the freedom of the will *ibid.* pp. 644-645 on *Laws* 904 c.

[f] *Cf. Symp.* 175 c, where the words are the same but the construction different. For the indirect reflexive *cf.* 614 B οὗ ἐκβῆναι, *Symp.* 176 D, *Symp.* 223 B ἒ δὲ ὕπνον λαβεῖν.

[g] For διατελεῖς *cf. Laws* 661 D τυραννίδα διὰ τέλους.

618 τελευτώσας· εἶναι δὲ καὶ δοκίμων ἀνδρῶν βίους,
τοὺς μὲν ἐπὶ εἴδεσι καὶ κατὰ κάλλη καὶ τὴν ἄλλην
B ἰσχύν τε καὶ ἀγωνίαν, τοὺς δ' ἐπὶ γένεσι καὶ
προγόνων ἀρεταῖς, καὶ ἀδοκίμων κατὰ ταὐτά,
ὡσαύτως δὲ καὶ γυναικῶν· ψυχῆς δὲ τάξιν οὐκ
ἐνεῖναι διὰ τὸ ἀναγκαίως ἔχειν ἄλλον ἑλομένην
βίον ἀλλοίαν γίγνεσθαι· τὰ δ' ἄλλα ἀλλήλοις τε καὶ
πλούτοις καὶ πενίαις, τὰ δὲ νόσοις, τὰ δὲ ὑγιείαις
μεμῖχθαι, τὰ δὲ καὶ μεσοῦν τούτων. ἔνθα δή, ὡς
ἔοικεν, ὦ φίλε Γλαύκων, ὁ πᾶς κίνδυνος ἀνθρώπῳ,
C καὶ διὰ ταῦτα μάλιστα ἐπιμελητέον ὅπως ἕκαστος
ἡμῶν τῶν ἄλλων μαθημάτων ἀμελήσας τούτου
τοῦ μαθήματος καὶ ζητητὴς καὶ μαθητὴς ἔσται,
ἐάν ποθεν οἷός τ' ᾖ μαθεῖν καὶ ἐξευρεῖν, τίς αὐτὸν
ποιήσει δυνατὸν καὶ ἐπιστήμονα, βίον καὶ χρηστὸν
καὶ πονηρὸν διαγιγνώσκοντα, τὸν βελτίω ἐκ τῶν
δυνατῶν ἀεὶ πανταχοῦ αἱρεῖσθαι, καὶ ἀναλογι-
ζόμενον πάντα τὰ νῦν δὴ ῥηθέντα, ξυντιθέμενα
ἀλλήλοις καὶ διαιρούμενα πρὸς ἀρετὴν βίου πῶς
ἔχει, εἰδέναι, τί κάλλος πενίᾳ ἢ πλούτῳ κραθὲν
D καὶ μετὰ ποίας τινὸς ψυχῆς ἕξεως κακὸν ἢ
ἀγαθὸν ἐργάζεται, καὶ τί εὐγένειαι καὶ δυσγένειαι
καὶ ἰδιωτεῖαι καὶ ἀρχαὶ καὶ ἰσχύες καὶ ἀσθένειαι
καὶ εὐμάθειαι καὶ δυσμάθειαι καὶ πάντα τὰ
τοιαῦτα τῶν φύσει περὶ ψυχὴν ὄντων καὶ τῶν

---

a For the idiom ἀναγκαίως ἔχειν cf. Phaedo 91 E, Laws
771 E, 928 E, Lysias vi. 35.
b μεσοῦν Phaedr. 241 D.
c Cf. Phaedo 107 C, 114 D, Gorg. 526 E, Eurip. Medea 235

garies; and there were lives of men of repute for their
forms and beauty and bodily strength otherwise and
prowess and the high birth and the virtues of their
ancestors, and others of ill repute in the same things,
and similarly of women. But there was no determination of the quality of soul, because the choice
of a different life inevitably[a] determined a different
character. But all other things were commingled
with one another and with wealth and poverty and
sickness and health and the intermediate[b] conditions.
—And there, dear Glaucon, it appears, is the supreme
hazard[c] for a man. And this is the chief reason why it
should be our main concern that each of us, neglecting
all other studies, should seek after and study this thing[d]
—if in any way he may be able to learn of and discover
the man who will give him the ability and the knowledge to distinguish the life that is good from that
which is bad, and always and everywhere to choose the
best that the conditions allow, and, taking into account
all the things of which we have spoken and estimating
the effect on the goodness of his life of their conjunction or their severance, to know how beauty commingled with poverty or wealth and combined with
what habit of soul operates for good or for evil, and
what are the effects of high and low birth and private
station and office and strength and weakness and
quickness of apprehension and dullness and all
similar natural and acquired habits of the soul, when

ἀγὼν μέγιστος, Thucyd. i. 32. 5 μέγας ὁ κίνδυνος, Aristoph.
Clouds 955 νῦν γὰρ ἅπας . . . κίνδυνος ἀνεῖται, *Frogs* 882
ἀγὼν . . . ὁ μέγας, Antiphon v. 43 ἐν ᾧ μοι ὁ πᾶς κίνδυνος ἦν.
For the expression *cf. Gorg.* 470 E ἐν τούτῳ ἡ πᾶσα εὐδαιμονία
ἐστίν.

[d] *Cf. supra* 443-444, 591 E-592 A, *Gorg.* 527 B f., *Laws*
662 B f., 904 A ff.

618 ἐπικτήτων τί ξυγκεραννύμενα πρὸς ἄλληλα ἐργάζεται, ὥστε ἐξ ἁπάντων αὐτῶν δυνατὸν εἶναι
συλλογισάμενον αἱρεῖσθαι, πρὸς τὴν τῆς ψυχῆς
φύσιν ἀποβλέποντα, τόν τε χείρω καὶ τὸν ἀμείνω
Ε βίον, χείρω μὲν καλοῦντα ὃς αὐτὴν ἐκεῖσε ἄξει, εἰς
τὸ ἀδικωτέραν γίγνεσθαι, ἀμείνω δὲ ὅστις εἰς τὸ
δικαιοτέραν, τὰ δὲ ἄλλα πάντα χαίρειν ἐάσει·
ἑωράκαμεν γάρ, ὅτι ζῶντί τε καὶ τελευτήσαντι
619 αὕτη κρατίστη αἵρεσις. ἀδαμαντίνως δὴ δεῖ ταύτην τὴν δόξαν ἔχοντα εἰς Ἅιδου ἰέναι, ὅπως ἂν ᾖ
καὶ ἐκεῖ ἀνέκπληκτος ὑπὸ πλούτων τε καὶ τῶν
τοιούτων κακῶν, καὶ μὴ ἐμπεσὼν εἰς τυραννίδας καὶ
ἄλλας τοιαύτας πράξεις πολλὰ μὲν ἐργάσηται καὶ
ἀνήκεστα κακά, ἔτι δὲ αὐτὸς μείζω πάθῃ, ἀλλὰ
γνῷ τὸν μέσον ἀεὶ τῶν τοιούτων βίον αἱρεῖσθαι καὶ
φεύγειν τὰ ὑπερβάλλοντα ἑκατέρωσε καὶ ἐν τῷδε
τῷ βίῳ κατὰ τὸ δυνατὸν καὶ ἐν παντὶ τῷ ἔπειτα
Β οὕτω γὰρ εὐδαιμονέστατος γίγνεται ἄνθρωπος.

XVI. Καὶ δὴ οὖν καὶ τότε ὁ ἐκεῖθεν ἄγγελος
ἤγγελλε τὸν μὲν προφήτην οὕτως εἰπεῖν· καὶ
τελευταίῳ ἐπιόντι, ξὺν νῷ ἑλομένῳ, συντόνως
ζῶντι κεῖται βίος ἀγαπητός, οὐ κακός. μήτε ὁ
ἄρχων αἱρέσεως ἀμελείτω μήτε ὁ τελευτῶν
ἀθυμείτω· εἰπόντος δὲ ταῦτα τὸν πρῶτον λαχόντα
ἔφη εὐθὺς ἐπιόντα τὴν μεγίστην τυραννίδα ἑλέσθαι,
καὶ ὑπὸ ἀφροσύνης τε καὶ λαιμαργίας οὐ πάντα
C ἱκανῶς ἀνασκεψάμενον ἑλέσθαι, ἀλλ᾽ αὐτὸν λαθεῖν

---

[a] The singular verb is used after plural subjects, because
the subjects are united in the writer's mind into one general
idea. Cf. Rep. 363 A, Laws 925 E, Symp. 188 B.

[b] See Unity of Plato's Thought, p. 25, Laws 661-662, and
for the word supra 360 B, Gorg. 509 A.

blended and combined with one another,[a] so that with consideration of all these things he will be able to make a reasoned choice between the better and the worse life, with his eyes fixed on the nature of his soul, naming the worse life that which will tend to make it more unjust and the better that which will make it more just. But all other considerations he will dismiss, for we have seen that this is the best choice, both for life and death. And a man must take with him to the house of death an adamantine [b] faith in this, that even there he may be undazzled [c] by riches and similar trumpery, and may not precipitate himself into tyrannies and similar doings and so work many evils past cure and suffer still greater himself, but may know how always to choose in such things the life that is seated in the mean [d] and shun the excess in either direction, both in this world so far as may be and in all the life to come ; for this is the greatest happiness for man.

XVI. " And at that time also the messenger from that other world reported that the prophet spoke thus : ' Even for him who comes forward last, if he make his choice wisely and live strenuously, there is reserved an acceptable life, no evil one. Let not the foremost in the choice be heedless nor the last be discouraged.' When the prophet had thus spoken he said that the drawer of the first lot at once sprang to seize the greatest tyranny,[e] and that in his folly and greed he chose it without sufficient examination, and failed to observe that it involved the fate of eating

[c] Cf. 576 D.

[d] An anticipation of the Aristotelian doctrine, *Eth. Nic.* 1106 b 6 f. Cf. *What Plato Said*, p. 629, on *Laws* 691 c.

[e] Cf. Isoc. *Epist.* vi. 12. Xen. *Hiero* 7. 2 ὅμως προπετῶς φέρεσθε εἰς αὐτήν.

619 ἐνοῦσαν εἱμαρμένην, παίδων αὐτοῦ βρώσεις καὶ
ἄλλα κακά· ἐπειδὴ δὲ κατὰ σχολὴν σκέψασθαι,
κόπτεσθαί τε καὶ ὀδύρεσθαι τὴν αἵρεσιν, οὐκ
ἐμμένοντα τοῖς προρρηθεῖσιν ὑπὸ τοῦ προφήτου·
οὐ γὰρ ἑαυτὸν αἰτιᾶσθαι τῶν κακῶν, ἀλλὰ τύχην
τε καὶ δαίμονας καὶ πάντα μᾶλλον ἀνθ' ἑαυτοῦ.
εἶναι δὲ αὐτὸν τῶν ἐκ τοῦ οὐρανοῦ ἡκόντων, ἐν
τεταγμένῃ πολιτείᾳ ἐν τῷ προτέρῳ βίῳ βεβιωκότα,
D ἔθει ἄνευ φιλοσοφίας ἀρετῆς μετειληφότα. ὡς δὲ
καὶ εἰπεῖν οὐκ ἐλάττους εἶναι ἐν τοῖς τοιούτοις
ἁλισκομένους τοὺς ἐκ τοῦ οὐρανοῦ ἥκοντας, ἅτε
πόνων ἀγυμνάστους· τῶν δ' ἐκ τῆς γῆς τοὺς πολλούς,
ἅτε αὐτούς τε πεπονηκότας ἄλλους τε ἑωρακότας,
οὐκ ἐξ ἐπιδρομῆς τὰς αἱρέσεις ποιεῖσθαι. διὸ δὴ
καὶ μεταβολὴν τῶν κακῶν καὶ τῶν ἀγαθῶν ταῖς
πολλαῖς τῶν ψυχῶν γίγνεσθαι, καὶ διὰ τὴν τοῦ
κλήρου τύχην. ἐπεὶ εἴ τις ἀεί, ὁπότε εἰς τὸν
E ἐνθάδε βίον ἀφικνοῖτο, ὑγιῶς φιλοσοφοῖ καὶ ὁ
κλῆρος αὐτῷ τῆς αἱρέσεως μὴ ἐν τελευταίοις
πίπτοι, κινδυνεύει ἐκ τῶν ἐκεῖθεν ἀπαγγελλομέ-
νων οὐ μόνον ἐνθάδε εὐδαιμονεῖν ἄν, ἀλλὰ καὶ τὴν
ἐνθένδε ἐκεῖσε καὶ δεῦρο πάλιν πορείαν οὐκ ἂν
χθονίαν καὶ τραχεῖαν πορεύεσθαι, ἀλλὰ λείαν τε
καὶ οὐρανίαν. ταύτην γὰρ δὴ ἔφη τὴν θέαν ἀξίαν
εἶναι ἰδεῖν, ὡς ἕκασται αἱ ψυχαὶ ᾑροῦντο τοὺς
620 βίους· ἐλεεινήν τε γὰρ ἰδεῖν εἶναι καὶ γελοίαν καὶ
θαυμασίαν· κατὰ συνήθειαν γὰρ τοῦ προτέρου βίου
τὰ πολλὰ αἱρεῖσθαι. ἰδεῖν μὲν γὰρ ψυχὴν ἔφη τήν
ποτε Ὀρφέως γενομένην κύκνου βίον αἱρουμένην,

---

[a] Cf. What Plato Said, p. 532, on Phaedo 90 D.
[b] Phaedo 82 B.

his own children, and other horrors, and that when he inspected it at leisure he beat his breast and bewailed his choice, not abiding by the forewarning of the prophet. For he did not blame himself [a] for his woes, but fortune and the gods and anything except himself. He was one of those who had come down from heaven, a man who had lived in a well-ordered polity in his former existence, participating in virtue by habit [b] and not by philosophy; and one may perhaps say that a majority of those who were thus caught were of the company that had come from heaven, inasmuch as they were unexercised in suffering. But the most of those who came up from the earth, since they had themselves suffered and seen the sufferings of others, did not make their choice precipitately. For which reason also there was an interchange of good and evil for most of the souls, as well as because of the chances of the lot. Yet if at each return to the life of this world a man loved wisdom sanely, and the lot of his choice did not fall out among the last, we may venture to affirm, from what was reported thence, that not only will he be happy here but that the path of his journey thither and the return to this world will not be underground and rough but smooth and through the heavens. For he said that it was a sight worth seeing to observe how the several souls selected their lives. He said it was a strange, pitiful, and ridiculous spectacle, as the choice was determined for the most part by the habits of their former lives.[c] He saw the soul that had been Orpheus', he said, selecting the life of a

---

[c] Cf. *Phaedo* 81 E ff., *Phaedr.* 248-249, *Tim.* 42 A-D, 91 D ff. For the idea of reincarnation in Plato see *What Plato Said*, p. 529, on *Phaedo* 81 E-82 B.

620 μισεῖ τοῦ γυναικείου γένους διὰ τὸν ὑπ᾽ ἐκείνων
θάνατον οὐκ ἐθέλουσαν ἐν γυναικὶ γεννηθεῖσαν
γενέσθαι· ἰδεῖν δὲ τὴν Θαμύρου ἀηδόνος ἑλομένην·
ἰδεῖν δὲ καὶ κύκνον μεταβάλλοντα εἰς ἀνθρωπίνου
βίου αἵρεσιν, καὶ ἄλλα ζῷα μουσικὰ ὡσαύτως.
B εἰκοστὴν δὲ λαχοῦσαν ψυχὴν ἑλέσθαι λέοντος βίον·
εἶναι δὲ τὴν Αἴαντος τοῦ Τελαμωνίου, φεύ-
γουσαν ἄνθρωπον γενέσθαι, μεμνημένην τῆς τῶν
ὅπλων κρίσεως· τὴν δ᾽ ἐπὶ τούτῳ Ἀγαμέμνονος·
ἔχθρα δὲ καὶ ταύτην τοῦ ἀνθρωπίνου γένους διὰ
τὰ πάθη ἀετοῦ διαλλάξαι βίον. ἐν μέσοις δὲ
λαχοῦσαν τὴν Ἀταλάντης ψυχήν, κατιδοῦσαν μεγάλας τιμὰς ἀθλητοῦ ἀνδρός, οὐ δύνασθαι παρελθεῖν,
C ἀλλὰ λαβεῖν. μετὰ δὲ ταύτην ἰδεῖν τὴν Ἐπειοῦ
τοῦ Πανοπέως εἰς τεχνικῆς γυναικὸς ἰοῦσαν φύσιν·
πόρρω δ᾽ ἐν ὑστάτοις ἰδεῖν τὴν τοῦ γελωτοποιοῦ
Θερσίτου πίθηκον ἐνδυομένην· κατὰ τύχην δὲ τὴν
Ὀδυσσέως, λαχοῦσαν πασῶν ὑστάτην, αἱρησο-
μένην ἰέναι· μνήμῃ δὲ τῶν προτέρων πόνων
φιλοτιμίας λελωφηκυῖαν ζητεῖν περιοῦσαν χρόνον
πολὺν βίον ἀνδρὸς ἰδιώτου ἀπράγμονος, καὶ μόγις
εὑρεῖν κείμενόν που καὶ παρημελημένον ὑπὸ τῶν

ᵃ Urwiek, *The Message of Plato*, p. 213, says: "If Plato
knew anything at all of Indian allegory, he must have
known that the swan (Hamsa) is in Hinduism the invariable
symbol of the immortal Spirit; and to say, as he does, that
Orpheus chose the life of a swan, refusing to be born again
of a woman, is just an allegorical way of saying that he
passed on into the spiritual life. . . ." One is tempted to
cap this with Donne:

Oh, do not die, for I shall hate
All women so when thou art gone
That thee I shall not celebrate
When I remember thou wert one.

swan,[a] because from hatred of the tribe of women, owing to his death at their hands, it was unwilling to be conceived and born of a woman. He saw the soul of Thamyras[b] choosing the life of a nightingale; and he saw a swan changing to the choice of the life of man, and similarly other musical animals. The soul that drew the twentieth lot chose the life of a lion; it was the soul of Ajax, the son of Telamon, which, because it remembered the adjudication of the arms of Achilles, was unwilling to become a man. The next, the soul of Agamemnon, likewise from hatred of the human race because of its sufferings, substituted the life of an eagle.[c] Drawing one of the middle lots the soul of Atalanta caught sight of the great honours attached to an athlete's life and could not pass them by but snatched at them. After her, he said, he saw the soul of Epeius,[d] the son of Panopeus, entering into the nature of an arts and crafts woman. Far off in the rear he saw the soul of the buffoon Thersites[e] clothing itself in the body of an ape. And it fell out that the soul of Odysseus drew the last lot of all and came to make its choice, and, from memory of its former toils having flung away ambition, went about for a long time in quest of the life of an ordinary citizen who minded his own business,[f] and with difficulty found it lying in some corner disregarded by the others, and upon seeing it said

---

[b] Like Orpheus a singer. He contended with the Muses in song and was in consequence deprived by them of sight and of the gift of song. *Cf.* also *Ion* 533 B-C, *Laws* 829 D-E, *Iliad* ii. 595.

[c] *Cf.* Aesch. *Ag.* 114 ff.

[d] Who built the Trojan horse. See Hesychius *s.v.*

[e] *Cf. Iliad* ii. 212 ff.

[f] For ἀπράγμονος *cf.* on 565 A, p. 316, note *b*.

620 D ἄλλων, καὶ εἰπεῖν ἰδοῦσαν, ὅτι τὰ αὐτὰ ἂν ἔπραξε
καὶ πρώτη λαχοῦσα, καὶ ἀσμένην ἑλέσθαι. καὶ ἐκ
τῶν ἄλλων δὴ θηρίων ὡσαύτως εἰς ἀνθρώπους
ἰέναι καὶ εἰς ἄλληλα, τὰ μὲν ἄδικα εἰς τὰ ἄγρια,
τὰ δὲ δίκαια εἰς τὰ ἥμερα μεταβάλλοντα, καὶ
πάσας μίξεις μίγνυσθαι. ἐπειδὴ δ᾽ οὖν πάσας τὰς
ψυχὰς τοὺς βίους ᾑρῆσθαι, ὥσπερ ἔλαχον, ἐν
τάξει προσιέναι πρὸς τὴν Λάχεσιν· ἐκείνην δ᾽
E ἑκάστῳ, ὃν εἵλετο δαίμονα, τοῦτον φύλακα ξυμπέμ-
πειν τοῦ βίου καὶ ἀποπληρωτὴν τῶν αἱρεθέντων.
ὃν πρῶτον μὲν ἄγειν αὐτὴν πρὸς τὴν Κλωθὼ ὑπὸ
τὴν ἐκείνης χεῖρά τε καὶ ἐπιστροφὴν τῆς τοῦ
ἀτράκτου δίνης, κυροῦντα ἣν λαχὼν εἵλετο μοῖραν·
ταύτης δ᾽ ἐφαψάμενον αὖθις ἐπὶ τὴν τῆς Ἀτρόπου
ἄγειν νῆσιν, ἀμετάστροφα τὰ ἐπικλωσθέντα ποιοῦν-
τα· ἐντεῦθεν δὲ δὴ ἀμεταστρεπτὶ ὑπὸ τὸν τῆς
621 Ἀνάγκης ἰέναι θρόνον, καὶ δι᾽ ἐκείνου διεξελθόντα,
ἐπειδὴ καὶ οἱ ἄλλοι διῆλθον, πορεύεσθαι ἅπαντας
εἰς τὸ τῆς Λήθης πεδίον διὰ καύματός τε καὶ
πνίγους δεινοῦ· καὶ γὰρ εἶναι αὐτὸ κενὸν δένδρων
τε καὶ ὅσα γῆ φύει· σκηνᾶσθαι οὖν σφᾶς ἤδη
ἑσπέρας γιγνομένης παρὰ τὸν Ἀμέλητα ποταμόν,

---

^a *Phaedr.* 249 specifies that only beasts who had once been
men could return to human form.
^b *Cf. supra* 617 E, and for daemons in Plato *What Plato
Said*, pp. 546-547, on *Symp.* 202 E, Dieterich, *Nekyia*, p. 59.
^c δίνης: *cf. Cratyl.* 439 c and *Phaedo* 99 B.
^d *Cf. Laws* 960 c.
^e τὰ ἐπικλωσθέντα: *cf. Laws* 957 E, *Theaet.* 169 c, and the
Platonic epigram on Dion, *Anth. Pal.* vii. 99 Μοῖραι ἐπέκλωσαν,

516

that it would have done the same had it drawn the first lot, and chose it gladly. And in like manner, of the other beasts some entered into men [a] and into one another, the unjust into wild creatures, the just transformed to tame, and there was every kind of mixture and combination. But when, to conclude, all the souls had chosen their lives in the order of their lots, they were marshalled and went before Lachesis. And she sent with each, as the guardian of his life and the fulfiller of his choice, the genius [b] that he had chosen, and this divinity led the soul first to Clotho, under her hand and her turning [c] of the spindle to ratify the destiny of his lot and choice; and after contact with her the genius again led the soul to the spinning of Atropos [d] to make the web of its destiny [e] irreversible, and then without a backward look it passed beneath the throne of Necessity. And after it had passed through that, when the others also had passed, they all journeyed to the Plain of Oblivion, [f] through a terrible and stifling heat, for it was bare of trees and all plants, and there they camped at eventide by the River of Forgetfulness, [g]

Od. i. 17, iii. 208, etc., Aesch. *Eumen.* 335, Callinus i. 9 Μοῖραι ἐπικλώσωσ'.

    [f] *Cf.* Aristoph. *Frogs* 186.

    [g] In later literature it is the river that is called Lethe. *Cf. Aeneid* vi. 714 f., Milton, *Par. L.* ii. :

> Lethe, the river of oblivion, rolls
> Her wat'ry labyrinth, whereof who drinks,
> Forthwith his former state and being forgets.

Keats, " Ode on Melancholy " : " No, no ! go not to Lethe," Tennyson, " The Two Voices " :

> As old mythologies relate,
> Some draught of Lethe might await
> The slipping thro' from state to state.

621 οὗ τὸ ὕδωρ ἀγγεῖον οὐδὲν στέγειν. μέτρον μὲν
οὖν τι τοῦ ὕδατος πᾶσιν ἀναγκαῖον εἶναι πιεῖν,
τοὺς δὲ φρονήσει μὴ σωζομένους πλέον πίνειν τοῦ
μέτρου· τὸν δὲ ἀεὶ πιόντα πάντων ἐπιλανθάνεσθαι.
B ἐπειδὴ δὲ κοιμηθῆναι καὶ μέσας νύκτας γενέσθαι,
βροντήν τε καὶ σεισμὸν γενέσθαι, καὶ ἐντεῦθεν
ἐξαπίνης ἄλλον ἄλλῃ φέρεσθαι ἄνω εἰς τὴν γένεσιν, ἄττοντας ὥσπερ ἀστέρας.[a] αὐτὸς δὲ τοῦ
μὲν ὕδατος κωλυθῆναι πιεῖν· ὅπῃ μέντοι καὶ ὅπως
εἰς τὸ σῶμα ἀφίκοιτο, οὐκ εἰδέναι, ἀλλ' ἐξαίφνης
ἀναβλέψας ἰδεῖν ἕωθεν αὐτὸν κείμενον ἐπὶ τῇ πυρᾷ.
καὶ οὕτως, ὦ Γλαύκων, μῦθος ἐσώθη καὶ οὐκ
C ἀπώλετο, καὶ ἡμᾶς ἂν σώσειεν, ἂν πειθώμεθα αὐτῷ,
καὶ τὸν τῆς Λήθης ποταμὸν εὖ διαβησόμεθα καὶ
τὴν ψυχὴν οὐ μιανθησόμεθα· ἀλλ' ἂν ἐμοὶ πειθώμεθα, νομίζοντες ἀθάνατον ψυχὴν καὶ δυνατὴν
πάντα μὲν κακὰ ἀνέχεσθαι, πάντα δὲ ἀγαθά, τῆς
ἄνω ὁδοῦ ἀεὶ ἑξόμεθα καὶ δικαιοσύνην μετὰ
φρονήσεως παντὶ τρόπῳ ἐπιτηδεύσομεν, ἵνα καὶ

---

[a] In *Tim.* 41 D-E each soul is given a star as its vehicle.
Cf. Aristoph. *Peace* 833 f. ὡς ἀστέρες γιγνόμεθ' ὅταν τις ἀποθάνῃ
. . with the Platonic epigram to Ἀστήρ : . . . νῦν δὲ θανὼν

whose waters no vessel can contain. They were all required to drink a measure of the water, and those who were not saved by their good sense drank more than the measure, and each one as he drank forgot all things. And after they had fallen asleep and it was the middle of the night, there was a sound of thunder and a quaking of the earth, and they were suddenly wafted thence, one this way, one that, upward to their birth like shooting stars.[a] Er himself, he said, was not allowed to drink of the water, yet how and in what way he returned to the body he said he did not know, but suddenly recovering his sight [b] he saw himself at dawn lying on the funeral pyre.—And so, Glaucon, the tale was saved,[c] as the saying is, and was not lost. And it will save us [d] if we believe it, and we shall safely cross the River of Lethe, and keep our soul unspotted from the world.[e] But if we are guided by me we shall believe that the soul is immortal and capable of enduring all extremes of good and evil, and so we shall hold ever to the upward way and pursue righteousness with wisdom always and ever,

λάμπεις Ἕσπερος ἐν φθιμένοις. There is an old superstition in European folklore to the effect that when a star falls a soul goes up to God. Cf. also Rohde, Psyche, ii.[6] p. 131.

[b] Cf Phaedrus 243 B ἀνέβλεψεν.

[c] Cf Phileb. 14 A, Laws 645 B, Theaet. 164 D.

[d] Cf. Phaedo 58 B ἔσωσε τε καὶ αὐτὸς ἐσώθη. σώζειν is here used in its higher sense, approaching the idea of salvation, not as in Gorg. 511 c f., 512 D-E, Laws 707 D, where Plato uses it contemptuously in the tone of " whosoever shall seek to save his life shall lose it."

[e] Cf. James i. 27, Phaedo 81 B, 2 Peter iii. 14, and the Emperor Julian's last speech "animum . . . immaculatum conservavi." Cf. Marius the Epicurean, pp. 15-16 : " A white bird, she told him once, looking at him gravely, a bird which he must carry in his bosom across a crowded public place— his own soul was like that."

621 ἡμῖν αὐτοῖς φίλοι ὦμεν καὶ τοῖς θεοῖς, αὐτοῦ τε
μένοντες ἐνθάδε, καὶ ἐπειδὰν τὰ ἆθλα αὐτῆς
D κομιζώμεθα, ὥσπερ οἱ νικηφόροι περιαγειρόμενοι,
καὶ ἐνθάδε καὶ ἐν τῇ χιλιέτει πορείᾳ, ἣν διεληλύθαμεν, εὖ πράττωμεν.

ᵃ Cf. Laws 693 B ἑαυτῇ φίλην, Rep. 589 B, Horace, Epist.
i. 3. 29 " si nobis vivere cari," Wordsworth :

> Hence lives he to his inner self endeared.

Jowett's "dear to one another" misses the point. Cf. my
review of Lemercier, Les Pensées de Marc-Aurèle, in Class.
Phil. vii. p. 115: " In iii. 4, in fine, the words οἵγε οὐδὲ αὐτοὶ
ἑαυτοῖς ἀρέσκονται are omitted because ' les gens que méprise
Marc-Aurèle sont loin de mépriser eux-mêmes.' This is to
forget that Seneca's ' omnis stultitia fastidio laborat sui '

that we may be dear to ourselves [a] and to the gods both during our sojourn here and when we receive our reward, as the victors in the games [b] go about to gather in theirs. And thus both here and in that journey of a thousand years, whereof I have told you, we shall fare well. [c] "

is good Stoic doctrine, and that the idea that only the wise and good man can be dear to himself is found in the last sentence of Plato's *Republic*." *Cf.* also Soph. *O.C.* 309 τίς γὰρ ἐσθλὸς οὐχ αὑτῷ φίλος ;

[b] *Cf.* Vol. I. p. 480, note *c*, on 465 D.

[c] For the thought *cf. Gorg.* 527 c εὐδαιμονήσεις καὶ ζῶν καὶ τελευτήσας. *Cf.* Vol. I. p. 104, note *b*, on 353 E. The quiet solemnity of εὖ πράττωμεν illustrates the same characteristic of style that makes Plato begin his *Laws* with the word θεός, and Dante close each of the three sections of the *Divine Comedy* with "stelle."

I. INDEX OF NAMES

(Mere references to an author in the notes are usually not listed here unless there is some definite statement or quotation. The references are to the Loeb Library pages.)

Achilles, I. 202, 203, 209, 218-219 f., II. 575
Adam, I. xlvi, lii, 23, 119, 142, 144, 165, 267, 326, 394, 412-413, 444, II. 162, 199, 344, 372
Addison, II. 505
Adeimantus, I. 145
Adrasteia, I. 431
Aelian, I. 341
Aeschylus, I. 123, 125, 187, 193, 197, 223, 469, II. 261, 309
Aesculapius, I. 273, 279, 281, II. 435-437
Agamemnon, II. 151, 515
Ajax, I. 491, II. 515
Alcibiades, II. 43
Alcinous, II. 491
Anacharsis, II. 438-439
Anaxagoras, II. 253, 415
Andocides, I. 347, 430
Antiphanes, I. 271, 400
Antiphon, I. 98, 516
Antisthenes, I. 12, II. 48, 50
Apelt, I. 505, II. 199, 212
Aphrodite, I. 219
Apollo, I. 197, 344
Arcadius, I. 509
Archilochus, I. 137, 329
Archytas, II. 189, 192
Ardiaeus, II. 497
Ares, I. 219
Aristippus, I. 110
Aristophanes, I. 65, 66, 118, 120, 133, 213, 271, 311, 340, 442, II. 282, 518. The problem of the *Ecclesiazusae*, I. 330, 453, 467

Aristophanes of Byzantium, I. viii
Aristotle, I. xxvi, xxxiii, xxxiv, 10, 14, 27, 28-29, 38, 48, 70, 74, 75, 77, 80, 98, 99, 100, 108, 110, 123, 146, 148, 150, 154, 156, 163, 182, 188-189, 191, 194, 207, 211, 217, 224, 225, 226, 258, 261, 266, 305, 308-309, 314, 326-327, 329, 331, 333, 348, 353, 354, 362, 370, 371, 373, 376, 377, 380-381, 382, 384, 385, 387, 392, 394, 395, 397, 398, 401, 402, 410, 415, 417, 420, 422, 426, 430, 433, 438, 454, 464, 471, 473, 476-477, 494, 508, 512, 514-515, 516, 526-527, 533, II. xii, xv, xliii, xlv, li, lviii, lxxi, 14, 15, 18, 55, 68, 70, 101, 111, 112, 119, 132, 136, 155, 158, 170, 171, 184, 187, 188-189, 201, 215, 219, 222, 234, 236, 243, 244, 265, 288, 303, 304, 305, 318, 319, 321, 336, 370, 372-373, 383, 407, 412, 420, 433, 442, 443, 444, 450, 460, 472, 504, 511
Arnold, I. xxxix, 10, 14, 48-49, 202, 210, 244, 357, 381, 431, II. xiii, xxx, xlvi, xlix, l, 25, 69, 91, 100, 143, 254, 255, 285, 286, 304, 312, 393, 402-403, 411
Ascham, Roger, I. 229, 289, II. 210
Asclepius, II. 435, 437
Atalanta, II. 515
Athanasius, I. 2-3
Athens, I. 187
Athens, I. xx, xxxviii, 340, 380, II. xlv-xlvi
Atropos, II. 505, 517

I. INDEX OF NAMES

Augustine, St., I. xliii, 180, II. 134, 420, 497
Autolycus, I. 30, 31

Bacon, I. 194, 508, II. 15, 119
Bagehot, I. 20, 398, II. 240-241
Bain, II. 197
Bendis, I. viii, 3
Bentham, I. 50
Bergson, II. 196, 244-245
Berkeley, I. 51, II. 119, 480
Bias, I. 37
Boethius, I. 508, II. 69, 124, 472
Bourguet, I. xiii
Brimley, II. 35
Brochard, II. 1, 71
Browne, Thomas, I. 16, 19, 354, II. 38-39, 107, 119, 492
Browning, II. lxii, 338
Browning, Mrs. I. 212, II. 425
Brunetière, I. 512
Buckle, I. 379
Bulwer-Lytton, I. 303
Burke, I. xxxix, 235, 284, II. xliv, 21, 287
Burnet, I. xv, II. 142
Burton, II. 31
Butcher, I. 165, 255
Butler, Samuel, I. 396
Byron, I. 176

Cadmus, I. 302
Callicles, I. 114-115
Callimachus, II. 311
Campbell, I. xlvi
Carlyle, I. 96, 157, II. 18, 35, 42, 407
Cephalus, I. 6 f.
Cerberus, II. 399
Chairemon, I. 210
Charondas, II. 437
Chaucer, I. 238-239, 275
Cheiron, I. 221
Chesterfield, Lord, I. 128, 211
Chesterton, G. K., I. xl-xli, 454, II. lxiii, 223
Chimaera, II. 399
Chryses, I. 227
Chrysippus, I. 98, 111
Cicero, I. 7, 8, 9, 13, 20, 22-23, 80, 124, 138-139, 210, 333, 397, 415, 435, 480, 495, 503, II. 1, 73, 101, 203, 243, 262, 312, 401, 429

Cleanthes, I. 184
Cleitophon, I. ix
Clement, II. 470
Clotho, II. 505, 517
Clough, A. H., II. 182
Coleridge, II. xxxvi, 202, 443, 444-445
Coleridge, Hartley, II. 424-425
Conrad, II. 18
Constantine, I. 509
Corneille, II. 432
Cornford, I. xxxvi, II. xiv
Cratinus, I. viii, 425
Creophylus, II. 438-439
Cretans, call country motherland, II. 352
Crete, constitution of, II. 238
Critias, II. 182
Croesus, oracle to, II. 322
Cronos, I. 179
Cudworth, II. 423

Daedalus, II. 185
Damascius, I. 375
Damon, I. 253, 333
Dante, I. 97, 366, II. 33, 69, 280, 493, 521
David, I. 395
Delphi, oracle of, I. 308, 344, II. 231
Demaistre, Xavier, I. xxx
Demetrius, I. 290
Democritus, I. 69, 80, 506
Demosthenes, I. xxxviii, 266, 322, 336, 364, 401, 507
De Quincey, I. 452-453
Descartes, I. 395
Dewey, II. 156
Diodorus Siculus, I. 144
Diogenes Laertius, I. viii, 211, 268, 298
Dryden, II. xlix, 420, 432
Du Bellay, II. 415
Dümmler, I. 172-173, 250, 338

Eddington, II. 119
Egyptians, I. 380
Eliot, George, I. 285, 446
Emerson, I. xxxiii, xliii, 122, 129, 160, 338, 371, 411, 421, 520, II. xliv, lxvii, lxix, 34-35, 61, 134, 274, 312, 400, 422, 443
Empedocles, II. 118, 422
Epaminondas, I. 15
Epeius, II. 515

524

I. INDEX OF NAMES

Epicharmus, I. 181, II. 442
Epictetus, I. 494
Epicurus, I. 531
Er, son of Arminius, II. 491
Erasmus, I. 508
Eriphyle, II. 405
Eros, II. 345
Eudoxus, II. 177, 192
Euripides, I. xxxix-xl, 12, 70, 71, 123, 177, 266, 323, 401, 435, 506, II. 182, 309. Supreme in tragedy, II. 328
Eurypylus, I. 272-273

Faguet, II. 287, 313
France, Anatole, II. 465
Francis, St., I. xliii, 164
Frederick the Great, I. 509
Freud, I. xxiv, II. 336-337

Glaucon, I. 145, II. 255
Glaucus, sea-god, II. 481
Goethe, I. xiii, 507, II. 101, 310
Gomperz, I. 431, II. xiii, xlviii, 192, 484
Grote, II. 369
Guyau, I. 415
Gyges, I. 117, II. 485

Hades, I. 130-131, 200 ff.   Helmet of, II. 484
Halévy, II. 244
Hardy, I. 365
Hazlitt, I. 228, II. 202
Hegel, I. 366
Helen, the wraith of, II. 392-393
Hephaestus, I. 181, 212-213, 219
Hera, I. 181, 217
Heracleitus, I. 168, 177, 396; the sun of, II. 59
Herodicus, I. 273
Herodotus, I. 117, 306, 325, 440
Herrick, I. 65
Hesiod, I. xliv, 8, 128-129, 133, 178-179, 304, 482-483, 490-491, II. 248-249, 441, 485
Hinduism, II. 514
Hippocrates, I. 379
Hirzel, I. 107
Hobbes, I. 508, II. 236-237
Hobhouse, I. 498-499
Holmes, I. 106
Homer, I. xiv, xlv, 7, 30-31, 128-129, 131, 184-135, 267, 291, 404-405, 490-491, 494, II. 245, 270, 323
    Banishment of, I. 242 f.
    Criticism of, I. 178 ff., 193, 196-197, 202 ff.
    His charm, II. lxiii, 467
    Knows all things, II. 432
    Most poetic of poets, II. 465
    No lawgiver or administrator, II. 437
    Not an educator, II. 439
    Not an inventor, II. 437
    Paraphrase of *Iliad*, I. 12 ff., 226 ff.
    Teacher of tragedy, II. 420, 433
    The educator of Hellas, II. 463
Homerids, II. 437
Hooker, I. 148-149, II. 428
Horace, I. 8, 128, 276, 312, II. 29, 36, 39, 192-193, 251, 267, 442, 453, 520
Howells, I. 239
Huxley, I. xxxi, 172, 304, 365, II. 18, 119, 140
Huxley, Aldous, II. 192
Hyperides, I. 9

Iamblichus, I. 397
Inge, Dean, II. 273, 407, 414, 474
Ismenias, I. 37
Isocrates, I. xxxviii, 72, 110, 287, 328, 334, 337, 338, 349, 409, 417, 441, 454, 496, 533, 535, II. xxxvii-xxxviii, 48, 166, 167, 214-215, 236, 239, 250, 255, 285, 298, 318, 329, 368, 373, 442
Italy, II. 437

James I., I. 509
Jeans, Sir James, II. 187
Jebb, I. 19, 182, 187, 214
Jesus, son of Sirach, I. 157, II. 49
Jevons, I. 88
Joel, I. 12
Jowett, I. xiii, xlvi, 87, 130, II. xiv, 194, 520
Judd, II. 197
Julian, I. 11, 508, II. 309, 519
Juvenal, I. 209, 520

Keats, II. 465

La Bruyère, II. 462
Lacedaemon, II. 437

I. INDEX OF NAMES

Lachesis, II. 505, 517
Lamartine, II. 414, 434
Landor, I. 202
Lang, A., II. 432, 498
La Rochefoucauld, I. 275, II. 33
Leibniz, I. 46
Leontius, I. 399
Lethe, II. 517, 519
Livy, II. 33, 265, 305
Locke, I. 97, 227
Lowell, I. 202, 421, II. 232, 505
Lucan, I. 464, 502, II. 320
Lucian, I. xxxiv, xliii, 55, 202, 217, 275, 434, 452, II. 48, 202, 311
Lucretius, I. 250, 512, II. 182, 253
Lycaean Zeus, II. 319
Lycurgus, II. 436-437
Lysias, I. ix, II. 255, 256

Macaulay, I. xxiv, 274, 276, 278, 279, II. xlii-xliii
Machaon, I. 272, 280
Macrobius, I. 342
Malebranche, II. 192
Mandeville, I. 159, 164
Manilius, II. xxix, 101
Marcus Aurelius, I. 354, 508, 509, II. 137, 138, 414, 415, 520
Maximus of Tyre, II. 54, 166, 360
Megara, battle of, I. 144
Menander, I. 284, II. 260
Menelaus, I. 281
Midas, I. 281
Mill, J. S., I. x, xx, xxxix, 81, 132-133, 347, 356, 879, 442-443, 470, II. xxxvi, xlvi, xlix, 61, 166
Milton, I. 9, 40, 109, 192, 246, 415, II. 58-59, 391, 393, 501, 505, 507, 517
Mimnermus, II. 443
Minucius Felix, I. 188, 292
Molière, I. 512
Mommsen, I. viii
Momus, II. 15
Montaigne, I. 234, 495, II. 91, 211, 283
Montesquieu, II. 163
More, Henry, II. 100, 101, 119, 142
More, Thomas, I. 508, II. 53
Morley, John, I. 134, 292, 450-451, II. xlix
Murray, Gilbert, I. xxxix
Musaeus, I. 129, 135
Muses, II. 245, 249

Napoleon, II. xlv, 196-197, 323
Napoleon III., I. 70
Natorp, II. xvi
Nemesis, I. 431
Neoplatonism, I. 180, 421, II. 106-107, 146, 197, 229
Newman, I. xxxiv, 314, 319, 497, II. 215, 229, 239, 364
Nietzsche, I. 447
Niobe, I. 187
Numenius, II. 274, 493

Odysseus, II. 515-517
Olympian Zeus, II. 381
Orpheus, I. 135, II. 513-515
Ovid, II. 138, 456

Palamedes, II. 151
Panathenaia, I. 181
Pandarus, I. 187
Pascal, I. 46
Pater, I. 58, 302, II. 338-339, 414, 519
Peiraeus, I. 2-3, 399, 516
Peirithous, I. 221
Peleus, I. 221
Perdiccas, I. 37
Periander, I. 37
Pericles, I. xxxvii-xxxviii, 208, 339
Persius, II. 280
Pherecydes, I. 275
Phocylides, I. 276-277
Phoenicians, I. 380
Pindar, I. 19, 135 f., 221, 249, 281, 332-333, 438, 452, II. lxv, 337
Pittacus, I. 37
Plato, historical background of, I. xxxvi-xxxvii
    Primitive?, II. xii, xiii, 154
    Indifferent to mere logical precision, II. 89
    Not dogmatic, I. 309, II. 220
    His apology for not entering politics, II. 52-53
    His fair-mindedness in stating the other side, I. x-xi, 316-317, 438-439
    A poet, II. lxiii
    Anti-scientific?, II. 180-181, 187-189, 190
    Not a mystic, II. xxviii, 200
    No ascetic, II. 338
    Radical or conservative?, II. 71, 76, 232-233

I. INDEX OF NAMES

Plato—
   His religious caution, I. 308
   His style, II. lxxiii
   Does not argue from a metaphor, I. xi-xii
Plautus, I. 72
Pliny, II. 401
Plotinus, I. 357, II. xxix, 101
Plutarch, I. 111, 267, 339, 458, 489, II. 62, 192, 453
Poe, I. xiii
Polemarchus, I. ix
Polybius, I. 288, 484, 504, 508, II. 235, 243
Polydamas, the pancratiast, I. 47
Pope, I. 234, 394, 514, II. 432, 505
Porphyry, II. 309
Priam, I. 209
Proclus, I. viii, xii, 96-97, 202, 212, 220
Prodicus, II. 439
Prometheus, II. 151, 254
Protagoras, I. 349, II. 439
Pythagoreans, I. xv, xxxiv, 177, 415, II. lxv, 189, 439, 501, 503

Quintilian, I. 121, 485

Rabelais, I. 17, 172, 470-471
Renan, I. 434, II. 43, 428, 485
Richard of Bury, II. 49, 226
Riley, Woodbridge, II. 187
Rome, I. 163
Rossetti, II., 280, 391
Rousseau, I. 55, 176, 193, 274, 451, 452, II. xxxiii, 180
Ruskin, I. xxxix, 41, 77, 180-181, 203, 247, 255, 258, 313, 347, II. xxxvii, 19, 406-407, 460-461, 472

Sallust, II. 252, 298
Sandburg, II. 401
Santayana, I. 512
Sappho, I. 398, 494, II. 287
Schiller, F. C. S., II. 188
Schleiermacher, II. 371
Schopenhauer, I. xxxiv, 11, 257, II. 354
Scott, I. 16
Scylla, II. 399
Selden, I. 339
Seneca, I. 274, II. 31, 305, 359, 429, 453, 520

Seriphus, I. 13
Shaftesbury, II. xlix
Shakespeare, I. 29, 65, 73, 87, 157, 235, 275, 290, 292, 305, 339, 361, 400, 414-415, 426, 442, 475, 512, II. 25, 39, 182, 270, 271, 287, 298, 317, 323, 325, 329, 339, 356, 360, 455, 489, 504
Shaw, I. xxxix-xl, 508, II. 350
Shelley, I. 176, 264-265, II. 143, 268-269, 355, 393
Sicily, II. 437
Sidgwick, I. 164
Sidney, I. 395, II. 39
Simonides, I. 20 ff., 136-137
Simplicius, I. 377
Sirens, II. 505
Smith, Adam, I. 151
Smith, Sidney, I. 440
Socrates, I. 50, II. 221
   Complaints of, I. 38
   References to his fate, II. 19, 129
Solon, I. 163, 314, II. 215, 436-437
Sophocles, I. 10-13, II. 283, 456, 521
Sophron, I. 433
Sparta, I. xx, 306, 307, 311, 326, II. 249, 250-251
   Constitution of, II. 238
   Spartan women, II. 252
Spencer, Herbert, I. xxxv, 51, 81, 96, 164, 169, 251, 272, 314, 379, 383, 387, II. xxviii-xxix, xxxix, 55, 156, 476-477
Spenser, I. 264, II. lxiv, 443, 498
Spercheius, I. 220-221
Spinoza, I. 470
Stenzel, II. x-xiii, xviii, 112, 164, 219, 314
Stephen, Leslie, I. xvi, xxi, 96, 315, 399, 443, II. xlviii, 1, lv, 267
Stesichorus, II. 392-393
Stewart, II. xvi, 142, 372-373, 424
Stoics, I. 108, 176, 207, 258, 279, 361, 397, 398, II. 412-413, 414-415, 453, 520
Strauss, I. 237
Swinburne, I. 5, 303, 502, II. 137, 352, 506

Tacitus, II. liv
Taine, II. lxxiii, 48, 305

I. INDEX OF NAMES

Tartarus, II. 499
Taylor, A. E., I. viii, xxv, II. x
Taylor, Bayard, II. 61
Teiresias, I. 203
Tennyson, I. 7, 10-11, 17, 138, 255, 291, 366, 394, II. 67, 73, 199, 312, 400, 404, 448, 470, 517
Terence, I. 180, 365
Tetzel, I. 132
Thales, II. 439
Thamyras, II. 515
Theages, II. 51
Themis, I. 187
Themistius, I. 508
Themistocles, I. 13, 68-69
Theognis, I. 459, II. 443
Theon, I. 11
Theophrastus, I. 4, 284, 435, 513, II. xlvi
Thersites, II. 515
Theseus, I. 221
Thetis, I. 193, 197
Thomas, St., I. 184
Thrasymachus, I. ix, 99
Thucydides, I. xxxvi, 13, 123, 242, 436-437, 486, 495, II. 250, 265
Thümser, I. 344

Tocqueville, II. 286, 290
Tyrtaeus, I. 280, II. 443

Uranus, I. 179

Verhaeren, I. 236-237
Virgil, I. 210, 261, II. 182, 268, 437

Wagner, I. 237
Waller, I. 16-17
Wells, H. G., I. 118, 303
Whitman, II. 181, 307
Whittier, I. 183
Wilamowitz, I. 220, 244, 379, 437, 496, 517, II. 13, 52, 60, 107, 113, 116, 233, 258, 344, 381, 415, 423, 433, 463, 465
Wordsworth, I. 253, 255, II. 465, 520

Xenophanes, I. 266
Xenophon, I. 36, 208, 326, 411, 447, 489, II. 144, 228, 255, 272, 295, 308, 364, 368, 375, 406, 443
Xerxes, I. 37

Zeller, I. xxv, 145, 314, 319, II. 35, 157, 221, 288, 304
Zeus, I. 186-187, 217, II. 319, 381

II. INDEX OF SUBJECTS

(Some important Greek words and idioms discussed or illustrated in the notes are here included.)

ABA style, II. 65
ABA in thought, II. 256
Abstract ideas, II. 159
  vs. mental images, II. 196-197
Academy, unhealthy, II. 411
Acoustics, II. 190 f.
"Admission" of interlocutor, II. 203
Adverb modifying noun, II. 198
Age, advantages and disadvantages of, I. 10-13
Age, more credulous of myths, I. 16-17
All time, contemplation of, II. 9
ἀλλ' εἴπερ, II. 58
Allegory, I. 182
ἀμηχάνως ὡς, II. 174
Animals, affected by excess of liberty, II. 309
  analogy from, I. 433
Animal in man, II. lxi, 400
Anticipation of objections, II. 14
The ἀνυπόθετον, II. xxxiii-xxxiv, 110 f.
(οὐδὲν) ἀπολείπειν, II. 200
Appetites, necessary and unnecessary, II. 291 ff.
ἀπράγμων, II. 316
Arcadia, legend of, II. 319
Arguments, the three, for justice, I. xx-xxi
Argumentum ex contrario, I. 40-41, II. 404-405
Aristocracy, II. 241
Arithmetic. See *s.v.* Mathematics
Art (τέχνη), II. 22-23, 135
  strives only for its own perfection, I. 58-61

(painting, poetry, etc.) is deception, II. 424-425
  See also *s.v.* Poetry and Mimetic Arts, analogy with, I. 24
  (τέχναι) are base and mechanical, II. 149
Artists, I. 260. See also *s.v.* Poets
Astronomy, practical uses of, II. 173
  does it turn the soul upward?, II. 180 f.
  to be studied abstractly, II. 186-189
Athletes, I. 266-267
Athletes of war (the guardians), I. 267, II. 148, 235
Attic courtesy, II. 55
αὐτὸ δηλώσει, II. 56
Autochthony of Athenians, I. 303
αὐτουργοί, II. 316
ἄξιος, double use of, II. 30
(καὶ) ἄξιον, II. 237

βαναυσία ("base mechanic"), II. 49, 407
Banishment of poets, I. 242-245, II. 465
Banter, II. 107
Barbarians, I. 496-497
Barbers, I. 163
Beast, the great, II. 38-39
Beast, the many-headed, II. 400 f.
Beauty, of mind and body, I. 261-263
  in the education of the young, I. 255 f.
  youthful bloom of brief, II. 443
Bees, II. 143

529

II. INDEX OF SUBJECTS

Beginning, good, makes good ending, I. 438
Being and not-being, I. 520 ff.
    Fallacy of not-being, I. 526
    Absolute being, I. 530
    Material objects and opinions intermediate between being and not-being, I. 532-533
Better man, best to be ruled by, II. 406-407
βία μέν, ὅμως δέ, II. 467
Body, beauty of, I. 261
    defects of, less important than of soul, I. 263
    dependent on soul, I. 264-265
    servant of mind, I. 446
    instrument of soul, I. 494
Bodyguards of the tyrant, II. 326-327
Bravery, I. 352 f.
    four kinds of, I. 356
Bridle of Theages, II. 51

Callipolis, II. 172
Cause, II. 106
Cave, image of the, II. xxx, 118-119 ff.
Challenge to refute argument, II. 476
Change, inevitable for all created things, II. xliii
Children, to be trained in the new customs, II. 232-233
    Control of, II. 408
    In a democracy, do not fear parents, II. 307
χρῆμα colloquial, II. 327
Christian Fathers, I. 2-3, 177
Christianity, I. xv, xxxiv, 124, 397, 433, II. 279, 387, 402, 404, 414, 492, 493, 506, 507, 519
Citizens, number of, to be kept the same, I. 462-463
City, the primitive, I. 158-159
    The luxurious, I. 160-163
City of God, I. xlii-xliii, II. lxi, 414-415
City-state, the Greek, I. 328
Civic or popular virtue, II. 71
Claims to rule, II. 255
Classes, the four, of men, I. 304-305
Classes of population, II. 316
Climate determines national character, I. 379-381

Climax after climax, I. xxi-xxii, 270, II. lxi, 104
Clubs, political, I. 137
Colour and form, association of, II. 441
Comedy, II. 462-463
Communism, purpose of, in Republic, I. xxxiv, 310-311
Community of wives, I. 330-331, 426 ff., 452-453, II. 234
Concept, II. ix-xi, 313, 371
    hypostatization of, II. ix, xiv-xvi
    not derived from problem of one and many, II. 160
Conceptual thought, II. xii-xiii
Confirmation, method of, II. 386-387
Contracts, monetary, not to be enforced, II. 281
Contradiction or inconsistency, alleged, I. 345, 422-423, II. 252, 253
Contradiction, law of, I. 382
Contrary and contradictory opposition, II. 32-33
Corruptio optimi pessima. II. 33
Counsel (εὐβουλία), I. 349
Craftsman, or artist as such, infallible, I. 54 ff.
Crimes, list of, II. 350
Criterion of judgement, II. 376
Cycles, II. 242-243

Daimonion, II. 52
Day-dreams, I. 454-455
δέ γε in transition, II. 256
Dead restored to life, II. 492
Dear to oneself, II. 520-521
Death, not to be feared, I. 200 ff., II. 10
Debts, abolition of, II. 320-321
Deeds preferable to poems, II. 434-435
Definition, Thrasymachus understands, I. 48
    terminology of, II. x
    first, I. 107
Definitions, in Plato, not absolute, I. 364
Delian problem, II. 176
Democracy, licence in, II. 285 ff.
    a mixture, II. 286-287
    mildness of, II. 288-289
    sensitiveness of, II. 311

II. INDEX OF SUBJECTS

Dependence of one conclusion on another, I. 385
Destruction appointed for all created things, II. 245
Details omitted, I. 294-295, 336-337, 456-457
Details, Plato impatient of, II. 240
Device for playing providence with the vulgar, I. 300-301
Devils, II. 499
διά, final use of, II. 158
διαγωγή, II. 288
Dialectic, II. xxxviii, 196-197, 200 ff., 207, 223
   unsettling effect of, II. xxxviii, 58-59, 220-221, 223 ff.
   constrains rather than persuades, II. 14-15
   seeks the truth, II. 63
   deals purely with concepts, II. 115, 219
   parties must be agreed on primary assumption, II. 175
   arguing for oneself or others, II. 175
   Platonic vs. Hegelian, II. 201
   the coping-stone of education, II. 209
   periphrasis for, II. 209
Dialectician vs. scientist, II. xxxiii-xxxiv, 110-111 ff., 168 f., 201 f., 206
Dialectician and sophist, II. 201, 206
διάνοια, II. 112, 115, 116-117, 137, 150
Dice, metaphor of, II. 455
Digressions, I. 424, II. 236-237
Diminutives, contemptuous, II. 49
Diomedean necessity, II. 41
Diseases, treatment of, I. 272-273, 278-281
"Disharmonies" in Plato, II. 317, 320
Dithyramb, I. 230-231
Divided line, symbol of, II. xxxxxxi, 108 ff.
Division of labour, II. 266
Dog, a philosopher, I. 172-173
   Socrates' oath by, II. 413
Doing as one likes, I. 37, II. 358-359
Draughts-players, metaphor of, II. 14
Dream state, I. 518-519
Dreams, II. 336-337
Drones in the state, II. 269, 281, 295, 313, 315

Drunkenness, a tyrannical mood, II. 343
δύναμις, I. 523
δυναστεῖαι, II. 239
Dyad, II. 159
Dyeing, process of, I. 354-355

"Economy of truth," II. li
Education, importance of, I. 330-331, II. 233
   not the insertion of knowledge, II. 134
   by play, II. 216-217
   of masses, I. 319
   of guardians, I. 174-175, II. xix, xxxvi-xlii. Purpose of, II. 146
εἰ ὅ τι μάλιστα, I. 429
εἶδος and ἰδέα, II. x, 104
εἰς τὸ πρόσθεν, II. 262
ἐκεῖ, II. 494
Elements (στοιχεῖα), I. 258-259
Ellipsis of verb, II. 65
Emotion, excessive, deprecated, I. 208 ff., 452 ff.
   poetry fosters, II. 457 ff.
ἐν παντί, II. 363
ἐν τῷ τοιούτῳ, II. 338
Enemies to be injured, friends benefited, I. 25
   treatment of, in war, I. 493 f.
ἐπαγγέλλομαι boastful, II. 133
Ephemeral nature of man, II. 506
Equality to unequals, II. 291
ἠρέμα, I. 520, II. 45
Eristic, I. 441
Erotic terminology, used of philosophy, II. 26, 28, 145
Eternal, the, contemplation of, II. 68-69
Ethical argument of the Republic, II. xlvi-lxi
Etymological meaning, recurrence to, II. 66-67
Eugenics, I. 459, II. xxxv
Euphemisms, II. 298-299
εὐτραπελία, II. 308
εὐχέρεια, I. 340-341, II. 212
Evil, everything destroyed by its own, II. 472
Evil, the problem of, II. 507
ἕξις vs. δύναμις, I. 28-29
   not technical in Plato, I. 371, 377, II. 105

II. INDEX OF SUBJECTS

Experience, does Plato neglect it?, II. 115, 200
    essential for the guardians, II. 5, 138-139, 229
Experts, II. 190
Explanation, dramatic, of expressions not clear, I. 47, 79, II. 153
Exposure of infants, I. 463
Eye of the mind, II. 138

"Faculties," I. 381
Faith (πίστις), II. 117, 205
Fallacy (double meaning of εὖ πράττειν), I. 101 f., 104-105
Falsehood, the essential, I. 194-195
    voluntary and involuntary, II. 213
Fates, the three, II. 505, 517
Fathers' admonitions (prudential morality), I. 126 ff.
Feast of reason, I. 99
Few chosen, II. 30, 50-51
Fighting against two, I. 322-323
Figures of speech, conscious use of, II. 23, 193
Fire-sticks, figure of, I. 375
Fish, I. 267
Flute-playing, II. 301
"Form," II. x-xi
Freedom, the true, I. 360-361
Function (ἔργον), I. 36, 100 ff.

Generalization of terms, I. 418
Generation and decay, II. 6
γενναῖος, II. 20
Geometry, II. 166 ff.
    for war, II. 166-168
    its true purpose, II. 168-171
    terminology of, II. 170-171
    gives pleasure, II. 177
    solid, II. 175 f.
        not yet sufficiently investigated, II. 176
γλίσχρως, II. 17
γνώσεται, threatening, II. 331
Goat-stags, II. 18
God, goodness of, I. 183, II. xxv
    not the author of evil, I. 184-185 ff., II. 507
    does not change, I. 188-189 f.
    does not lie, I. 194 ff.
    makes the ideas, II. 427 f.
    See also s.v. Idea of good

Gods, may be bribed, I. 132 ff., 138-139
    shameful deeds of, I. 178 ff.
    madden whom they would destroy, I. 186-187
Gold and silver, forbidden the guardians, I. 310-313
Good, several kinds of, I. 108-109
    the, everyone pursues, II. 90-91
    the, not definable, II. 95
Good in that which he knows, I. 90-91
Good life, the supreme thing, II. 509
Good men, unwilling to rule, I. 80-81, II. 144-145
    a few arise spontaneously, II. 141
Goods, the so-called, II. 32
    are sometimes harmful, II. 31
Gorgian figure, II. 62-63
Government, three forms of, I. 47
    four (five) types of, II. xlv-xlvi, 236-237 f.
    mixed, II. 252
Great-and-the-small, II. 159
Greatest happiness of greatest number, I. 50, 316-317, 320-321
Greeks, contrasted with Orientals and Romans, II. 162-163
Guardians, I. xliv, their life, I. 310-313
    must be kept disinterested, I. 309, 312-313
    Not happy?, I. 314-315
Gymnastics and music, training in, I. 174-175, 407, II. 148-149
Gymnastics, I. 266 f.
    should develop the spirited side of nature, I. 286-287
    too much, makes men brutal, I. 288 ff.
    for women, I. 434 ff.
    intensive, not compatible with study, II. 217

Happiness of any class not the aim of the law, I. 315, II. 140-141
Hard to accept and hard to reject, II. 199
Harm, the only, is making one less virtuous, I. 35
Harmonics, II. 190 f.

II. INDEX OF SUBJECTS

Harmony of the soul, I. 414-415, II. 276
Health, I. 111, II. 410-411
Hearing, requires no medium, II. 98
Heaven and hell, II. lxx
Heavens, the, II. 182 ff.
  contemplation, of, II. 68-69
Hedonism, II. lviii-lix
"Height of argument" (ἀνάβασις), I. 421
Hope, of the righteous, I. 18-19, II. 54
Hunger, of the soul, II. 360
Hunting, figure of, I. 365
Hydra's head, I. 342-343
Hypotheses, II. 114

Ideas, doctrine of, I. 260, 373, 420-421, 516-517, 529, 532-533, II. ix-xxiii, 68, 421 ff.
  terminology of, I. 364, 377, 388-389, II. x-xi, 4, 72, 97, 426
  as ideals, II. xix
  not thoughts of God, II. xx
  not merely thoughts in human mind, II. xxi
  and numbers, II. xx-xxi, 164, 165, 206
  mathematical, II. xxxi
  God makes, II. 427
ἰδέα, loose use of, II. 99
Idea of good, I. xl-xli, II. xxiii-xxxvi, 86 ff., 168
  and education, II. xxvi, xxvii-xxviii, xxxvi-xl, 82-83, 86 ff.
Idea of good and God, II. xxv-xxvii, xxix, xxxv, 102
  as the sanction, II. xxvii, xxix, xxx, 91
  as cause of world order, II. xxxv-xxxvi, 102
  not the basis of Plato's ethics, II. lvi, lix
  and truth, II. 103
Ideals, value of, I. 503 f.
Idiom, slight change alters, II. 374
If we find (method), I. 383, 529
ἱκανόν, II. 203, 206
  and ἀνυπόθετον, II. 114
Illogical idiom, II. 200-201, 430-431
  (sentence begins generally and ends specifically), II. 89
Illusions of sense, II. 448-449

Image (εἴδωλον), I. 412, 533, II. 197
Imitation, I. 224 ff., II. 419, 429 ff. (See also s.v. Mimetic)
Imitation becomes habit, I. 234-235
Immoralism, II. 222-223
  wide-spread in Plato's time, I. 112-113, II. xlvii
Immortality, II. lxiv-lxxi, 60-61, 470 ff.
  Plato's arguments for, II. lxvi, lxvii, 472 ff., 474-475
  not to be proved, II. lxiv-lxv
Importance of the subject under discussion. I. 71
Individual and state, I. xxxv, II. 240, 412
Infant damnation, II. 496-497
Injustice, the complete, I. 70-71. (See also s.v. Justice)
Instruction not to be compulsory, II. 215, 216-217
Intelligence, cannot be implanted by education, II. 135
Interest (τόκος), II. 96
Interlocutor is bewildered, I. 31
  misapprehends, II. 153
  is permitted to amend his statement, I. 54
Intoxication forbidden the guardians, I. 265
Inventions, II. 437-439
Islands of the Blest, II. 139

Jest and earnest, II. 214, 227
Judgement of the dead, II. 493 f.
Judges, should be inexperienced in evil when young, I. 282-285
Just and unjust man, contrast of, I. 122-127
Just man, dear to God, I. 98-99, II. 487
  wins in the end, II. 489
Justice, definition of, as rendering to each his due, I. 20-21
  is the advantage of the stronger, I. 46, 48-49
  is doing one's own business, I. 366 ff.
  is the other man's good, I. 67
  disadvantages of, I. 68-69
  the main theme of the Republic, II. 2
  honour among thieves, I. 96-97

II. INDEX OF SUBJECTS

Justice, only through fear of consequences, I. 116 ff.
Juxtaposition, antithetic, II. 53
of different forms of same word, II. 86, 331

κάθαρσις, II. lxiii, 460-461
καὶ μάλα, humorous, II. 94
καίτοι, rhetorical, II. 381
καλεῖς τι, I. 90
καλοκάγαθόν, II. 88
καλὸς κἀγαθός, II. 27
κατασκευή, II. 285
κατάστασις, II. 56
Keeping to the point, II. 193, 399
Returning to the point, II. 339
Kings, shepherds of the people, I. 64-65
Knowledge vs. opinion, I. 416, 522-523, 524-525, II. 93, 446
Knowledge, universal, is impossible, II. 432-433
κῶμος, figure of, II. 67

Labourers (wage-earners), I. 156-157
Laughs at himself, II. 107, 231
Laughter, violent, deprecated, I. 211
of others, no matter, I. 430
Law, unwritten, II. 311
Law-courts and judges, sign of degenerate state, II. 270-271
Laws, on insignificant things not obeyed, I. 335
without right principles useless, I. 338-339, 340-341
Laws, to be for the good of the whole state, II. 140-141
Legal metaphor, I. 432
Liberty, in a democracy, II. 306 ff.
Life after death, I. 16-17, 129-131. See also s.v. Immortality
Life, not a matter of great concern, II. 10
Light, essential to sight, II. 98-99
Like to like, I. 9
Likeness to God, the aim of the righteous, II. 487
Links, minute, in the argument, I. 48, 362, II. 389, 394 f.
Literary genres, I. 230-231
Logic, in the minor dialogues, II. xi
λόγον δοῦναι, II. 195
λόγος vs. λέξις, I. 224

Long vs. short speeches, I. 83, 93
Longer way, the, I. 378-379, II. 82-83
Lot, not to be sold, II. 266-267
Lots, use of in democracy, II. 285
for lives, II. 507 f.
Love, Platonic, I. 261-263
Love, a tyrant, II. 343
Lover, loves all varieties, I. 512-513

Magi, II. 341
μάλιστα μὲν . . . εἰ δέ, II. 314
Malthusianism, I. 462
Man, the hardest creature to govern, II. 264
Marriage, age for, I. 464-465
Materialism, II. xii, xv, xviii
Mathematical ideas, II. 116
Mathematics, ancient, II. 176-177
does not go back to metaphysical principles, II. 110 f.
value of, for guardians, II. 150 ff.
abstract and concrete, II. 152
practical application of, II. 162-163
effect of studying, II. 166, 172-173
and dialectic, II. 168-170, 202, 203; mathematicians are not dialecticians, II. 194-195
Matter and form, II. 70
Meals, common, II. 250
Mean, the, II. 511
Meaning, II. xiv
Measure, man the, II. 84
Measurement, II. 191, 448
Meat, only roast, eaten by Homeric heroes, I. 267-269
μεγαλοπρεπῶς, ironical, II. 290
Mental discipline, II. 166, 194
Merchants and shopkeepers, I. 156-157
Metaphysics separable, II. xvi-xix
Metempsychosis, II. 511 ff., sin in former life, II. 487
Mimetic art, appeals to inferior element of soul, II. 451
portrays fretful and emotional types, II. 457
fosters emotion, II. 459 ff. (See also s.v. Poetry and Imitation)

II. INDEX OF SUBJECTS

Misology, I. 292, II. 225

Misunderstanding, dramatic, I. 47

Moderation in grief, II. 452 ff.

Modulation of Plato's style, II. lxix

"Motherland," II. 352

Motion and rest, I. 383-385

Multitude, cannot be philosophers, II. 42-43

   not to be condemned. II. 66

   not to be feared, II. 173

Music, training in, I. 174-175 ff., 407, II. 148-149, 256

   Greek, I. 245 ff., II. 190 f.

   Indian, II. 192

   Plato and, II. 247

   too much, makes men's nature soft, I. 288 f.

   innovations in, forbidden, I. 330 ff.

   ethical power of, I. 332

   of virtuous life, I. 292-293

   of the spheres, II. 404-405

Mysteries, language of, II. 299

Myth of immortality, II. lxviii-lxxi, 491 ff.

Mythology, criticism of, I. 178 ff.

Names, not to be disputed about, II. 204-205

Nature and God, II. 428-429

Nature vs. custom, I. 116-117

Necessary vs. good, I. 80, II. 40

Necessity, the spindle of, II. 400-401

Neutral state (may seem pleasurable or painful), II. 382 f.

Nicknames, II. 297

νοητὸς τόπος, II. 130

Nourishment of soul, II. 28

Number, the nuptial, II. xliii-xlv, 246-247

Numbers and the good, II. 162, 168

Numbers, different kinds of, II. 164, 165. (See also s.v. Ideas) playing with, II. 395 ff.

Nurses for the children, I. 462-465

Oak or rock (proverb), II. 240

οἰκεία, II. 225

Olympic victors, I. 480-481, II. 521

One and many, II. 160, 161, 164-165

One city, I. 325-327

One man, one task (division of labour), I. 152-153, 232 ff., 242-243, 328-329

ὄνομα and ῥῆμα, II. 442

ὅπως ἄρξουσιν, II. 20

Orators' motif (How can they —?), II. 74

Origin of society due to individual's insufficiency, I. 148-149

ὅρος, II. 263

Orphans, II. 275

Orphism, II. 118, 142

"Other" (ἕτερον), II. 157

ὅ τι ἂν τύχωσι, II. 213, 302

οὐδὲν ὄντας, II. 306

οὐδὲν δέομαι, II. 364

οὐχ ὥσπερ, idiomatic, II. 228

παιδομαθία, I. 484-485

Pan-Hellenism, II. 492-493

πάντα ποιεῖν, II. 20

παντοδαπός, ironical, II. 286

Parables, II. 17

Paradox, to stimulate attention, I. 322

Particles, cumulative, II. 447

Partitive apposition, II. 296

Passion, deprecated, I. 216 ff. (See also s.v. Emotion)

Pattern, in the soul, II. 4

   (the good), II. 230

Peloponnesian War, I. xxxvi-xxxvii

Periact, II. 134-135

Periphrases, II. 105

Personal construction, II. 92

Personification, II. 213, 224, 478-479

Persuasion and compulsion, II. 140

Pessimism of Plato, I. 184-185, II. 454

φιλήκοος, I. 515

Philosopher, the true, loves all kinds of knowledge, I. 514-515

   a lover of true being, I. 534-535

   the only man who scorns office, II. 144-145

   the only true judge of pleasures, II. 377 f.

   in the courtroom, II. 128, 132

Philosophers must be kings, I. 508-509, II. 232

   popular view of, II. 15-17

Philosophical nature, qualities of, II. 11-13, 29, 211

   corruption of, II. 42-47

II. INDEX OF SUBJECTS

Philosophy, the shame of, II. 48, 211
   not for the young, II. 226
   madness of, II. 226-227
φιλότιμος, II. 255, 375
Phoenician tale, 302-303
φορτικῶς, II. 179
Physicians, need for, sign of poor training, I. 268-271
   should be well acquainted with diseases, I. 282-283
Physics, transcendental, II. xv-xvi
φύσιν (λόγον) ἔχει, II. 25
φύσις, and the theory of ideas, II. 72, 123
φύσις, μελέτη, ἐπιστήμη, I. 167, 324
πλανάω (of error), II. 89
Planets, II. 503. (See s.v. Stars)
πλάττειν (used of the lawgiver), II. 70
Play, children's, importance of, I. 333-335
Play on words, II. 231, 265
Play or jest (παίζειν), II. xxxii. (See also s.v. Jest and earnest)
Playful threat, I. 4
Playing with the dialogue, II. 57
Pleasure and pain, a kind of motion, II. 383
   is not cessation of pain, II. 385
Pleasure, as the good, II. 88-89
   three kinds of, II. liv-lv, 372 ff.
   extravagant, akin to madness, I. 262
Pleasures, harmless, I. 109
   good and bad, II. 90, 300
   of mind and body, I. 8, 408
   negativity of lower, II. lvi-lix, 380 ff., 390 ff.
πλεονεξία, I. 87 f.
Poetry, function of, II. lxiii
   is imitation, II. lxii, 419, 429 ff., 441
   stripped of its adornments, II. 442-443
   and philosophy, old quarrel between, II. 464-465
   challenge to defend, II. 467
Poets, inspired but not wise, I. 21
   cannot be questioned, I. 21
   make all things, II. 422-423
   know all things, II. 432-433
   banishment of, II. lxiii, 329, 418-419, 465-467

Political art, I. 349
   can it be taught?, II. 19
Politicians, fawning, I. 340-341
Politics vs. ethics, I. xxvi
   degeneracy of, II. 52-53
   will the sage take part in?, II. 412-413
πρᾶγμα, colourless use of, II. 471
πράγματα ἔχειν, II. 257
πραγματεία, II. 178
Prayer, begin with, I. 365
Prelude (preamble), II. 194
Pretence of accident, II. 147
Principles, knowledge of, helps practice, I. 261
Proclamation of the victor, II. 369
Prolixity, apology for, I. 428-429
Proportion, II. xxx-xxxi, xxxiii, 103, 108 f.
προσπίπτειν, II. 154-155
Protector (προστάτης), II. 318-319
Providence, II. 486-487
Psychological necessity, I. 341, 509, II. 43
Psychology (attraction and repulsion), I. 387
   freedom of will, II. 507
   perception and thought, II. 154, 156-157
   Freudian, II. 336-337
   emotions, the censor, II. 460-461
Public opinion, defiance of, II. 354
Punishment and reward, I. 129 ff. ; after death, II. 495-499
Punishment, remedial, I. 187, II. 408-409
   of the incurable, I. 286-287, II. 498-499
Puns, II. 108
   on names, II. 369
Puppet-shows, II. 121
Purgatory, II. lxx
Purpose, and idea of good, I. 104, 106

Qualification of sweeping statements, II. 41
Qualified assent, II. 243

Race, metaphor of, II. 488
Reaction, law of, II. 312-313
Realism in art deprecated, I. 236-237

II. INDEX OF SUBJECTS

Realism (*vs.* nominalism), II. xiv-xvi

Reason and emotion, conflict of, II. 454-455

Reincarnation, II. 513-517

Relative terms, I. 391 ff.

Relativity of good and bad, I. 19
of pleasures, II. lv
Plato's distaste for, II. 84-85

Release of the prisoners in the cave (λύσις), II. 123

Religion, ritual, etc., in the city, I. 344-345

Repentance, II. 359

Repetition, teasing or challenging, I. 49, II. 67

Republic, first edition of, I. xvi, xxv
date of, not to be inferred from treatment of ideas, II. xxii, or of pleasure, II. lvii
main subject of, ethical, I. xxvii, II. 237
modernity of, I. xxx-xxxi
realization of, I. xxxi-xxxii.
Difficult, but not impossible, II. 77, 231
solves problems of the minor dialogues, I. 26, 344-345, II. xxiii
unity of design of, I. xii-xiv, II. 237

Research, scientific, to be endowed by the state, II. 177

Residues, method of, I. 347

Returning a deposit, typical of justice, I. 22

Revolutions, due to discord of ruling classes, I. 478-479, II. xlv, 244

Rhetorical style, II. 333

Rich, exploitation of, II. 316-317

Rich men's doors, II. 25

Riddle, I. 530-531

Ridicule, no test of truth, I. 434

Ruler, the true, must be paid wages, I. 78-79
is unwilling to hold office, I. 81, II. 144-145, 231

Rulers, dissension among, the cause of revolutions. (See *s.v.* Revolutions)

Sanction, in ethics, II. xlvi. (See also *s.v.* Idea of Good)

Satire of socialistic millennium, I. 318-319

"Saving the phenomena," II. 185

Science, Plato and, I. xix, II. xxxviii-xxxix, xlii, 115, 180-181

Secret doctrine, II. 200

Seeming *vs.* being, I. 31, 136-137

Self, harmony with, I. 98
dear to, II. 520

Self-check, II. 214

Self-sufficiency (αὐτάρκεια), I. 207

Shell, turning of, in game, II. 146

Ship of state, I. 214, II. 18-19

σκοπός, II. 139

Slavery, I. 156-157, II. 249, 254-255, 308, 362-363 (to illustrate tyranny)
opinions against, in antiquity, II. 364

Sleep and waking, II. 208

Smell, pleasures of, II. 384

Social contract, I. 114-115

Social science, II. xxxix

Socratic *elenchus*, II. 124

Socratic ignorance, I. 50, 107

Soldiers, professional, I. 165 f.

Sophists, Plato's attitude towards, II. 34-35
are not the real corrupters of youth, II. 34-39

Soul, tripartite, I. 376 f., II. 82, 259, 370-371
and body, II. 313, 367, 386-387, 410
nourishment of, II. 388
supreme value of, II. 405, 410-411, 511
immortality of. (See *s.v.* Immortality)
not destroyed by wickedness, II. 475 ff.
true nature of, II. 480 ff.

Souls must always be the same in number, II. 479

σώζειν, II. 519

"Speak with the vulgar," II. 204

Specification, demand for, II. 88-89

Stars, II. 182 f.
movements of, II. 183-186
as gods, II. 100
and souls, II. 518-519

στάσις (faction) in the soul, I. 417, II. 276

State, Plato's, *vs.* the modern, I. xxviii

II. INDEX OF SUBJECTS

State—
derives its qualities from individual, I. 379
four types of, II. xlv
the individual perfected in, II. 55
should be a unity, II. 264-265
Statesman, the true, II. xxxiv-xxxv
must know better than other men, II. 92
Striking his father, II. 347
Sun, symbol of idea of good, II. xxviii-xxix, 100 ff.
Superstition, none in Plato, I. 339, II. 64
Supposititious son, parable of, II. 220 ff.
Surprise effect, II. 239, 277
Suspicious man not good judge, I. 284-285
(διὰ) συγχωρήσεων, II. 203
Synonyms, not distinguished, I. 386, II. 88, 137, 155, 388
Synoptic, II. 218-219
Syracusan table, I. 268-269
σωφροσύνη, I. 358-359 f.

Teleology and the idea of good, II. xxiii, xxv
Testing by pains, fears and pleasures, I. 298-299
Text of the *Republic*, I. xlv-liii, II. lxxi-lxxii
θεῖα μοῖρα, II. 414
Third man argument, II. xxiii, 428
Third person, used for politeness, I. 24
Thought portrayed as action, II. 24
Thought, a discussion of the soul with itself, II. 207
Three types of men, II. 372 f.
θυμός, I. 398 ff.
Time, infinite past, II. 64-65
Timocracy, II. 243
Torch-race, I. 5
Trade, ungentlemanly, II. 49
Tragedy, favourable to tyrants and democracies, II 328-329. (See also *s.v.* Poetry and Mimetic)
Train successors, II. 230
Transfer of argument, I. 20
τρίτος σωτήρ, II. 380

Truth and falsehood, I. 192 ff.
Truth, Plato's regard for, I. 194-197, II. 6-7, 27
to be honoured above man, II. 420
not concerned with size or seeming importance, I. 259
men unwillingly deprived of, I. 296-297
Two temperaments, I. 168-171, 288 ff.
Already blended in the guardians, I. 457
Not frequently combined, II. 80-81
Tyrannical man, II. lii-liii, his origin, II. 341 f., his manner of life, II. 344 ff.
Tyrant, II. liv. 350 ff.
origin of, II. 318 ff.
does not do what he wishes, II. 358-359
must destroy good men, II. 325
must provoke wars, II. 322-325
must be viewed without his external pomp, II. 357
misery of, II. 358 ff., 368
vs. true king, II. 356
"Noble tyranny," II. 238
Tyrants, compose most of the incurably wicked, II. 498

"Unction," II. 168, 174
Unity of feeling among the citizens essential, I. 470-471
Universal *vs.* particular, I. 226-227
"Up" and "down," II. 386
Urns, the two, of Zeus, I. 184-185
User knows best, II. 444-445
Utilitarianism of Plato, I. 50, 452
Utopias, I. xxvii, xxix

Valetudinarianism, I. 272-281
Vegetarianism, I. 46, 153
Virtue, can it be taught ?, II. 136
parts of, II. 212-213
unity of, I. 422
must be a good, I. 28
is health of soul, I. 418 ff.
of citizens, aim of true statesman, II. xxxv
and happiness, II. xlviii-xlix
importance of, II. 469

II. INDEX OF SUBJECTS

Virtue—
　rewards of, II. 484 ff.; after
　　death, II. 491 ff.
　without philosophy, unsafe,
　　II. 513
Virtues, the four cardinal, I. xv-
　xvi, 261, 346 ff., II. 212
　ethical and intellectual, II. 136
Visualizing *vs.* abstract thought,
　II. 196 197
Vulgar tests, for confirmation, I.,
　410-411

Wage-earning, I. 76-77
Wall, shelter of, II. 54
War, origin of, I. 164-165
　bravery in, rewarded, I. 488-491
　between Greeks, I. 492-501
Watch-dog, type of the guardian, I.
　168 ff.
Wealth, benefits of, I. 12-19
　is blind, II. 274-275
　inherited *vs.* acquired, I. 14-15
　the true, II. 144-145

and poverty, dangers of, I. 320-
　323, II. 412-413
Werewolf, legend of, II. 319
Wicked but clever men, II. 137,
　lose in the end, II. 489
Wicked, late punishment of, II. 490
Wisdom (σοφία), I. 348
Wise men, always tell the truth, I.
　21, 37
Wolf, seeing, deprives of speech, I.
　40
Women, inferior to men, I. 446-447,
　II. 459
　to share pursuits of men, I.
　　448-449, II. 231
　nagging, II. 257-259
　and boys, II. 287
Word *vs.* deed, II. 15, 209, 401
World state, II. 415
Worse element the larger, I. 360-
　361
Wrongdoing involuntary, II. 404

Young, labours belong to, II. 215

THE LOEB CLASSICAL LIBRARY

VOLUMES ALREADY PUBLISHED

Latin Authors

AMMIANUS MARCELLINUS. J. C. Rolfe. 3 Vols.

APULEIUS: THE GOLDEN ASS (METAMORPHOSES). W. Adlington (1566). Revised by S. Gaselee.

ST. AUGUSTINE: CITY OF GOD. 7 Vols. Vol. I. G. E. McCracken. Vols. II and VII. W. M. Green. Vol. III. D. Wiesen. Vol. IV. P. Levine. Vol. V. E. M. Sanford and W. M. Green. Vol. VI. W. C. Greene.

ST. AUGUSTINE, CONFESSIONS. W. Watts (1631). 2 Vols.

ST. AUGUSTINE, SELECT LETTERS. J. H. Baxter.

AUSONIUS. H. G. Evelyn White. 2 Vols.

BEDE. J. E. King. 2 Vols.

BOETHIUS: TRACTS and DE CONSOLATIONE PHILOSOPHIAE. Rev. H. F. Stewart and E. K. Rand. Revised by S. J. Tester.

CEASAR: ALEXANDRIAN, AFRICAN and SPANISH WARS. A. G. Way.

CEASAR: CIVIL WARS. A. G. Peskett.

CEASAR: GALLIC WAR. H. J. Edwards.

CATO: DE RE RUSTICA. VARRO: DE RE RUSTICA. H. B. Ash and W. D. Hooper.

CATULLUS. F. W. Cornish. TIBULLUS. J. B. Postgate. PERVIGILIUM VENERIS. J. W. Mackail. Revised by G. P. Goold.

CELSUS: DE MEDICINA. W. G. Spencer. 3 Vols.

CICERO: BRUTUS and ORATOR. G. L. Hendrickson and H. M. Hubbell.

[CICERO]: AD HERENNIUM. H. Caplan.

CICERO: DE ORATORE, etc. 2 Vols. Vol. I. DE ORATORE, Books I and II. E. W. Sutton and H. Rackham. Vol. II. DE ORATORE, Book III. DE FATO; PARADOXA STOICORUM; DE PARTITIONE ORATORIA. H. Rackham.

CICERO: DE FINIBUS. H. Rackham.

CICERO: DE INVENTIONE, etc. H. M. Hubbell.

CICERO: DE NATURA DEORUM and ACADEMICA. H. Rackham.

CICERO: DE OFFICIIS. Walter Miller.

CICERO: DE REPUBLICA and DE LEGIBUS. Clinton W. Keyes.

CICERO: DE SENECTUTE, DE AMICITIA, DE DIVINATIONE. W. A. Falconer.

CICERO: IN CATILINAM, PRO FLACCO, PRO MURENA, PRO SULLA. New version by C. Macdonald.

CICERO: LETTERS TO ATTICUS. E. O. Winstedt. 3 Vols.

CICERO: LETTERS TO HIS FRIENDS. W. Glynn Williams, M. Cary, M. Henderson. 4 Vols.

CICERO: PHILIPPICS. W. C. A. Ker.

CICERO: PRO ARCHIA, POST REDITUM, DE DOMO, DE HARUSPICUM RESPONSIS, PRO PLANCIO. N. H. Watts.

CICERO: PRO CAECINA, PRO LEGE MANILIA, PRO CLUENTIO, PRO RABIRIO. H. Grose Hodge.

CICERO: PRO CAELIO, DE PROVINCIIS CONSULARIBUS, PRO BALBO. R. Gardner.

CICERO: PRO MILONE, IN PISONEM, PRO SCAURO, PRO FONTEIO, PRO RABIRIO POSTUMO, PRO MARCELLO, PRO LIGARIO, PRO REGE DEIOTARO. N. H. Watts.

CICERO: PRO QUINCTIO, PRO ROSCIO AMERINO, PRO ROSCIO COMOEDO, CONTRA RULLUM. J. H. Freese.

CICERO: PRO SESTIO, IN VATINIUM. R. Gardner.

CICERO: TUSCULAN DISPUTATIONS. J. E. King.

CICERO: VERRINE ORATIONS. L. H. G. Greenwood. 2 Vols.

CLAUDIAN. M. Platnauer. 2 Vols..

COLUMELLA: DE RE RUSTICA. DE ARBORIBUS. H. B. Ash, E. S. Forster and E. Heffner. 3 Vols.

CURTIUS, Q.: HISTORY OF ALEXANDER. J. C. Rolfe. 2 Vols.

FLORUS. E. S. Forster.

FRONTINUS: STRATAGEMS and AQUEDUCTS. C. E. Bennett and M. B. McElwain.

FRONTO: CORRESPONDENCE. C. R. Haines. 2 Vols.

GELLIUS. J. C. Rolfe. 3 Vols.

HORACE: ODES and EPODES. C. E. Bennett.

HORACE: SATIRES, EPISTLES, ARS POETICA. H. R. Fairclough.

JEROME: SELECTED LETTERS. F. A. Wright.

JUVENAL and PERSIUS. G. G. Ramsay.

LIVY. B. O. Foster, F. G. Moore, Evan T. Sage, and A. C. Schlesinger and R. M. Geer (General Index). 14 Vols.

LUCAN. J. D. Duff.

LUCRETIUS. W. H. D. Rouse. Revised by M. F. Smith.

MANILIUS. G. P. Goold.

MARTIAL. W. C. A. Ker. 2 Vols. Revised by E. H. Warmington

MINOR LATIN POETS: from PUBLILIUS SYRUS to RUTILIUS NAMATIANUS, including GRATTIUS, CALPURNIUS SICULUS, NEMESIANUS, AVIANUS and others, with "Aetna" and the "Phoenix." J. Wight Duff and Arnold M. Duff. 2 Vols.

MINUCIUS FELIX. Cf. TERTULLIAN.

Nepos Cornelius. J. C. Rolfe.

Ovid: The Art of Love and Other Poems. J. H. Mozley. Revised by G. P. Goold.

Ovid: Fasti. Sir James G. Frazer. Revised by G. P. Goold.

Ovid: Heroides and Amores. Grant Showerman. Revised by G. P. Goold.

Ovid: Metamorphoses. F. J. Miller. 2 Vols. Revised by G. P. Goold.

Ovid: Tristia and Ex Ponto. A. L. Wheeler. Revised by G. P. Goold.

Persius. Cf. Juvenal.

Pervigilium Veneris. Cf. Catullus.

Petronius. M. Heseltine. Seneca: Apocolocyntosis. W. H. D. Rouse. Revised by E. H. Warmington.

Phaedrus and Babrius (Greek). B. E. Perry.

Plautus. Paul Nixon. 5 Vols.

Pliny: Letters, Panegyricus. Betty Radice. 2 Vols.

Pliny: Natural History. 10 Vols. Vols. I.–V. and IX. H. Rackham. VI.–VIII. W. H. S. Jones. X. D. E. Eichholz.

Propertius. H. E. Butler.

Prudentius. H. J. Thomson. 2 Vols.

Quintilian. H. E. Butler. 4 Vols.

Remains of Old Latin. E. H. Warmington. 4 Vols. Vol. I. (Ennius and Caecilius) Vol. II. (Livius, Naevius Pacuvius, Accius) Vol. III. (Lucilius and Laws of XII Tables) Vol. IV. (Archaic Inscriptions).

Res Gestae Divi Augusti. Cf. Velleius Paterculus.

Sallust. J. C. Rolfe.

Scriptores Historiae Augustae. D. Magie. 3 Vols.

Seneca, The Elder: Controversiae, Suasoriae. M. Winterbottom. 2 Vols.

Seneca: Apocolocyntosis. Cf. Petronius.

Seneca: Epistulae Morales. R. M. Gummere. 3 Vols.

Seneca: Moral Essays. J. W. Basore. 3 Vols.

Seneca: Tragedies. F. J. Miller. 2 Vols.

Seneca: Naturales Quaestiones. T. H. Corcoran. 2 Vols.

Sidonius: Poems and Letters. W. B. Anderson. 2 Vols.

Silius Italicus. J. D. Duff. 2 Vols.

Statius. J. H. Mozley. 2 Vols.

Suetonius. J. C. Rolfe. 2 Vols.

Tacitus: Dialogus. Sir Wm. Peterson. Agricola and Germania. Maurice Hutton. Revised by M. Winterbottom, R. M. Ogilvie, E. H. Warmington.

Tacitus: Histories and Annals. C. H. Moore and J. Jackson. 4 Vols.

Terence. John Sargeaunt. 2 Vols.

Tertullian: Apologia and De Spectaculis. T. R. Glover. Minucius Felix. G. H. Rendall.

Tibullus. Cf. Catullus.
Valerius Flaccus. J. H. Mozley.
Varro: De Lingua Latina. R. G. Kent. 2 Vols.
Velleius Paterculus and Res Gestae Divi Augusti. F. W. Shipley.
Virgil. H. R. Fairclough. 2 Vols.
Vitruvius: De Architectura. F. Granger. 2 Vols.

Greek Authors

Achilles Tatius. S. Gaselee.
Aelian: On the Nature of Animals. A. F. Scholfield. 3 Vols.
Aeneas Tacticus. Asclepiodotus and Onasander. The Illinois Greek Club.
Aeschines. C. D. Adams.
Aeschylus. H. Weir Smyth. 2 Vols.
Alciphron, Aelian, Philostratus: Letters. A. R. Benner and F. H. Fobes.
Andocides, Antiphon. Cf. Minor Attic Orators Vol. I.
Apollodorus. Sir James G. Frazer. 2 Vols.
Apollonius Rhodius. R. C. Seaton.
Apostolic Fathers. Kirsopp Lake. 2 Vols.
Appian: Roman History. Horace White. 4 Vols.
Aratus. Cf. Callimachus.
Aristides: Orations. C. A. Behr. Vol. 1.
Aristophanes. Benjamin Bickley Rogers. 3 Vols. Verse trans.
Aristotle: Art of Rhetoric. J. H. Freese.
Aristotle: Athenian Constitution, Eudemian Ethics, Vices and Virtues. H. Rackham.
Aristotle: Generation of Animals. A. L. Peck.
Aristotle: Historia Animalium. A. L. Peck. Vols. I.–II.
Aristotle: Metaphysics. H. Tredennick. 2 Vols.
Aristotle: Meteorologica. H. D. P. Lee.
Aristotle: Minor Works. W. S. Hett. On Colours, On Things Heard, On Physiognomies, On Plants, On Marvellous Things Heard, Mechanical Problems, On Indivisible Lines, On Situations and Names of Winds, On Melissus, Xenophanes, and Gorgias.
Aristotle: Nicomachean Ethics. H. Rackham.
Aristotle: Oeconomica and Magna Moralia. G. C. Armstrong (with Metaphysics, Vol. II).
Aristotle: On the Heavens. W. K. C. Guthrie.
Aristotle: On the Soul, Parva Naturalia, On Breath. W. S. Hett.
Aristotle: Categories, On Interpretation, Prior Analytics. H. P. Cooke and H. Tredennick.

4

ARISTOTLE: POSTERIOR ANALYTICS, TOPICS. H. Tredennick and E. S. Forster.

ARISTOTLE: ON SOPHISTICAL REFUTATIONS.
On Coming-to-be and Passing-Away, On the Cosmos. E. S. Forster and D. J. Furley.

ARISTOTLE: PARTS OF ANIMALS. A. L. Peck; MOTION AND PROGRESSION OF ANIMALS. E. S. Forster.

ARISTOTLE: PHYSICS. Rev. P. Wicksteed and F. M. Cornford. 2 Vols.

ARISTOTLE: POETICS and LONGINUS. W. Hamilton Fyfe; DEMETRIUS ON STYLE. W. Rhys Roberts.

ARISTOTLE: POLITICS. H. Rackham.

ARISTOTLE: PROBLEMS. W. S. Hett. 2 Vols.

ARISTOTLE: RHETORICA AD ALEXANDRUM (with PROBLEMS. Vol. II). H. Rackham.

ARRIAN: HISTORY OF ALEXANDER and INDICA. Rev. E. Iliffe Robson. 2 Vols. New version P. Brunt.

ATHENAEUS: DEIPNOSOPHISTAE. C. B. Gulick. 7 Vols.

BABRIUS AND PHAEDRUS (Latin). B. E. Perry.

ST. BASIL: LETTERS. R. J. Deferrari. 4 Vols.

CALLIMACHUS: FRAGMENTS. C. A. Trypanis. MUSAEUS: HERO AND LEANDER. T. Gelzer and C. Whitman.

CALLIMACHUS, Hymns and Epigrams and LYCOPHRON. A. W. Mair; ARATUS. G. R. Mair.

CLEMENT OF ALEXANDRIA. Rev. G. W. Butterworth.

COLLUTHUS. Cf. OPPIAN.

DAPHNIS AND CHLOE. Thornley's translation revised by J. M. Edmonds: and PARTHENIUS. S. Gaselee.

DEMOSTHENES I.: OLYNTHIACS, PHILIPPICS and MINOR ORATIONS I.–XVII. AND XX. J. H. Vince.

DEMOSTHENES II.: DE CORONA and DE FALSA LEGATIONE. C. A. Vince and J. H. Vince.

DEMOSTHENES III.: MEIDIAS, ANDROTION, ARISTOCRATES, TIMOCRATES and ARISTOGEITON I. and II. J. H. Vince.

DEMOSTHENES IV.–VI.: PRIVATE ORATIONS and IN NEAERAM. A. T. Murray.

DEMOSTHENES VII.: FUNERAL SPEECH, EROTIC ESSAY, EXORDIA and LETTERS. N. W. and N. J. DeWitt.

DIO CASSIUS: ROMAN HISTORY. E. Cary. 9 Vols.

DIO CHRYSOSTOM. J. W. Cohoon and H. Lamar Crosby. 5 Vols.

DIODORUS SICULUS. 12 Vols. Vols. I.–VI. C. H. Oldfather. Vol. VII. C. L. Sherman. Vol. VIII. C. B. Welles. Vols. IX. and X. R. M. Geer. Vol. XI. F. Walton. Vol. XII. F. Walton. General Index. R. M. Geer.

DIOGENES LAERTIUS. R. D. Hicks. 2 Vols. New Introduction by H. S. Long.

DIONYSIUS OF HALICARNASSUS: ROMAN ANTIQUITIES. Spelman's translation revised by E. Cary. 7 Vols.

DIONYSIUS OF HALICARNASSUS: CRITICAL ESSAYS. S. Usher. 2 Vols.
EPICTETUS. W. A. Oldfather. 2 Vols.
EURIPIDES. A. S. Way. 4 Vols. Verse trans.
EUSEBIUS: ECCLESIASTICAL HISTORY. Kirsopp Lake and J. E. L. Oulton. 2 Vols.
GALEN: ON THE NATURAL FACULTIES. A. J. Brock.
GREEK ANTHOLOGY. W. R. Paton. 5 Vols.
GREEK BUCOLIC POETS (THEOCRITUS, BION, MOSCHUS). J. M. Edmonds.
GREEK ELEGY AND IAMBUS with the ANACREONTEA. J. M. Edmonds. 2 Vols.
GREEK LYRIC. D. A. Campbell. 4 Vols. Vols. I. and II.
GREEK MATHEMATICAL WORKS. Ivor Thomas. 2 Vols.
HERODES. Cf. THEOPHRASTUS: CHARACTERS.
HERODIAN. C. R. Whittaker. 2 Vols.
HERODOTUS. A. D. Godley. 4 Vols.
HESIOD AND THE HOMERIC HYMNS. H. G. Evelyn White.
HIPPOCRATES and the FRAGMENTS OF HERACLEITUS. W. H. S. Jones and E. T. Withington. 5 Vols. Vols. I.–IV.
HOMER: ILIAD. A. T. Murray. 2 Vols.
HOMER: ODYSSEY. A. T. Murray. 2 Vols.
ISAEUS. E. W. Forster.
ISOCRATES. George Norlin and LaRue Van Hook. 3 Vols.
[ST. JOHN DAMASCENE]: BARLAAM AND IOASAPH. Rev. G. R. Woodward, Harold Mattingly and D. M. Lang.
JOSEPHUS. 10 Vols. Vols. I.–IV. H. Thackeray. Vol. V. H. Thackeray and R. Marcus. Vols. VI.–VII. R. Marcus. Vol. VIII. R. Marcus and Allen Wikgren. Vols. IX.–X. L. H. Feldman.
JULIAN. Wilmer Cave Wright. 3 Vols.
LIBANIUS. A. F. Norman. 2 Vols..
LUCIAN. 8 Vols. Vols. I.–V. A. M. Harmon. Vol. VI. K. Kilburn. Vols. VII.–VIII. M. D. Macleod.
LYCOPHRON. Cf. CALLIMACHUS.
LYRA GRAECA, III. J. M. Edmonds. (Vols. I.and II. have been replaced by GREEK LYRIC I. and II.)
LYSIAS. W. R. M. Lamb.
MANETHO. W. G. Waddell.
MARCUS AURELIUS. C. R. Haines.
MENANDER. W. G. Arnott. 3 Vols. Vol. I.
MINOR ATTIC ORATORS (ANTIPHON, ANDOCIDES, LYCURGUS, DEMADES, DINARCHUS, HYPERIDES). K. J. Maidment and J. O. Burtt. 2 Vols.
MUSAEUS: HERO AND LEANDER. Cf. CALLIMACHUS.
NONNOS: DIONYSIACA. W. H. D. Rouse. 3 Vols.
OPPIAN, COLLUTHUS, TRYPHIODORUS. A. W. Mair.
PAPYRI. NON-LITERARY SELECTIONS. A. S. Hunt and C. C. Edgar. 2 Vols. LITERARY SELECTIONS (Poetry). D. L. Page.

6

PARTHENIUS. Cf. DAPHNIS and CHLOE.
PAUSANIAS: DESCRIPTION OF GREECE. W. H. S. Jones. 4 Vols. and Companion Vol. arranged by R. E. Wycherley.
PHILO. 10 Vols. Vols. I.–V. F. H. Colson and Rev. G. H. Whitaker. Vols. VI.–IX. F. H. Colson. Vol. X. F. H. Colson and the Rev. J. W. Earp.
PHILO: two supplementary Vols. (*Translation only*.) Ralph Marcus.
PHILOSTRATUS: THE LIFE OF APOLLONIUS OF TYANA. F. C. Conybeare. 2 Vols.
PHILOSTRATUS: IMAGINES; CALLISTRATUS: DESCRIPTIONS. A. Fairbanks.
PHILOSTRATUS and EUNAPIUS: LIVES OF THE SOPHISTS. Wilmer Cave Wright.
PINDAR. Sir J. E. Sandys.
PLATO: CHARMIDES, ALCIBIADES, HIPPARCHUS, THE LOVERS, THEAGES, MINOS and EPINOMIS. W. R. M. Lamb.
PLATO: CRATYLUS, PARMENIDES, GREATER HIPPIAS, LESSER HIPPIAS. H. N. Fowler.
PLATO: EUTHYPHRO, APOLOGY, CRITO, PHAEDO, PHAEDRUS. H. N. Fowler.
PLATO: LACHES, PROTAGORAS, MENO, EUTHYDEMUS. W. R. M. Lamb.
PLATO: LAWS. Rev. R. G. Bury. 2 Vols.
PLATO: LYSIS, SYMPOSIUM, GORGIAS. W. R. M. Lamb.
PLATO: REPUBLIC. Paul Shorey. 2 Vols.
PLATO: STATESMAN, PHILEBUS. H. N. Fowler; ION. W. R. M. Lamb.
PLATO: THEAETETUS and SOPHIST. H. N. Fowler.
PLATO: TIMAEUS, CRITIAS, CLITOPHO, MENEXENUS, EPISTULAE. Rev. R. G. Bury.
PLOTINUS: A. H. Armstrong. 7 Vols.
PLUTARCH: MORALIA. 16 Vols. Vols. I.–V. F. C. Babbitt. Vol. VI. W. C. Helmbold. Vols. VII. and XIV. P. H. De Lacy and B. Einarson. Vol. VIII. P. A. Clement and H. B. Hoffleit. Vol. IX. E. L. Minar, Jr., F. H. Sandbach, W. C. Helmbold. Vol. X. H. N. Fowler. Vol. XI. L. Pearson and F. H. Sandbach. Vol. XII. H. Cherniss and W. C. Helmbold. Vol. XIII. 1–2. H. Cherniss. Vol. XV. F. H. Sandbach.
PLUTARCH: THE PARALLEL LIVES. B. Perrin. 11 Vols.
POLYBIUS. W. R. Paton. 6 Vols.
PROCOPIUS. H. B. Dewing. 7 Vols.
PTOLEMY: TETRABIBLOS. F. E. Robbins.
QUINTUS SMYRNAEUS. A. S. Way. Verse trans.
SEXTUS EMPIRICUS. Rev. R. G. Bury. 4 Vols.
SOPHOCLES. F. Storr. 2 Vols. Verse trans.
STRABO: GEOGRAPHY. Horace L. Jones. 8 Vols.
THEOCRITUS. Cf. GREEK BUCOLIC POETS.
THEOPHRASTUS: CHARACTERS. J. M. Edmonds. HERODES, etc. A. D. Knox.

THEOPHRASTUS: ENQUIRY INTO PLANTS. Sir Arthur Hort, Bart. 2 Vols.

THEOPHRASTUS: DE CAUSIS PLANTARUM. G. K. K. Link and B. Einarson. 3 Vols. Vol. I.

THUCYDIDES. C. F. Smith. 4 Vols.

TRYPHIODORUS. Cf. OPPIAN.

XENOPHON: CYROPAEDIA. Walter Miller. 2 Vols.

XENOPHON: HELLENICA. C. L. Brownson. 2 Vols.

XENOPHON: ANABASIS. C. L. Brownson.

XENOPHON: MEMORABILIA AND OECONOMICUS. E. C. Marchant. SYMPOSIUM AND APOLOGY. O. J. Todd.

XENOPHON: SCRIPTA MINORA. E. C. Marchant. CONSTITUTION OF THE ATHENIANS. G. W. Bowersock.

Continued from front flap

the nature of language. The great master-piece in ten books, the *Republic*, concerns righteousness (and involves education, equality of the sexes, socialism, communism, and even abolition of slavery). Of the six so called 'dialectical' dialogues *Euthydemus* deals with philosophy; metaphysical *Parmenides* about general concepts and absolute being; *Theaetetus* reasons about the theory of knowledge; of its sequels, *Sophist* deals with not-being; *Politicus* with good and bad statesmanship and governments, *Philebus* with what is good. The *Timaeus* seeks the origin of the visible universe out of abstract geometrical elements. The unfinished *Critias* treats of lost Atlantis. Unfinished also is Plato's last work of the twelve books of *Laws* (Socrates is absent from it), a critical discussion of principles of law which Plato thought the Greeks might accept. Of a dozen other extant dialogues and also some letters a few may be genuine. Six other extant dialogues have been rejected as spurious since ancient times.